REFERENCE

ED-R

Junior Worldmark Encyclopedia of World Cultures

Junior Worldmark Encyclopedia of

World Cultures

VOLUME 4

Germany to
Jamaica

AN IMPRINT OF GALE

DETROIT · LONDON

JUNIOR WORLDMARK ENCYCLOPEDIA OF WORLD CULTURES

U•X•L Staff

Jane Hoehner, *U•X•L Senior Editor*
Carol DeKane Nagel, *U•X•L Managing Editor*
Thomas L. Romig, *U•X•L Publisher*
Mary Beth Trimper, *Production Director*
Evi Seoud, *Assistant Production Manager*
Shanna Heilveil, *Production Associate*
Cynthia Baldwin, *Product Design Manager*
Barbara J. Yarrow, *Graphic Services Supervisor*
Pamela A. E. Galbreath, *Senior Art Director*
Margaret Chamberlain, *Permissions Specialist (Pictures)*

Library of Congress Cataloging-in-Publication Data
Junior worldmark encyclopedia of world cultures / Timothy L. Gall and
Susan Bevan Gall, editors.
p. cm.
Includes bibliographical references and index.
Summary: Arranges countries around the world alphabetically,
subdivides these countries into 250 culture groups, and provides
information about the ethnology and human geography of each group.
ISBN 0-7876-1756-X (set : alk. paper)
1. Ethnology--Encyclopedias, Juvenile. 2. Human geography-
-Encyclopedias, Juvenile. [1. Ethnology--Encyclopedias. 2. Human
geography--Encyclopedias.] I. Gall, Timothy L. II. Gall, Susan B.
GN307.J85 1999
306' .03--dc21   98-13810
                                                          CIP
                                                          AC

ISBN 0-7876-1756-X (set)
ISBN 0-7876-1757-1 (vol. 1)   ISBN 0-7876-1758-X (vol. 2)   ISBN 0-7876-1759-8 (vol. 3)
ISBN 0-7876-1760-1 (vol. 4)   ISBN 0-7876-1761-X (vol. 5)   ISBN 0-7876-1762-8 (vol. 6)
ISBN 0-7876-1763-6 (vol. 7)   ISBN 0-7876-1764-4 (vol. 8)   ISBN 0-7876-2761-5 (vol. 9)

Printed in the United States of America
10 9 8 7 6 5 4 3 2

Contents
Volume 4

Cumulative Contents

CUMULATIVE CONTENTS

CUMULATIVE CONTENTS

Volume 5

Volume 6

CUMULATIVE CONTENTS

Contributors

Editors: Timothy L. Gall and Susan Bevan Gall

Senior Editor: Daniel M. Lucas

Contributing Editors: Himanee Gupta, Jim Henry, Kira Silverbird, Elaine Trapp, Rosalie Wieder

Copy Editors: Deborah Baron, Janet Fenn, Jim Henry, Patricia M. Mote, Deborah Ring, Kathy Soltis

Typesetting and Graphics: Cheryl Montagna, Brian Rajewski

Cover Photographs: Cory Langley

Data Input: Janis K. Long, Cheryl Montagna, Melody Penfound

Proofreaders: Deborah Baron, Janet Fenn

Editorial Assistants: Katie Baron, Jennifer A. Spencer, Daniel K. Updegraft

Editorial Advisors

P. Boone, Sixth Grade Teacher, Oak Crest Middle School, San Antonio, Texas

Jean Campbell, Foothill Farms Middle School, Sacramento, California

Kathy Englehart, Librarian, Hathaway Brown School, Shaker Heights, Ohio

Catherine Harris, Librarian, Oak Crest Middle School, San Antonio, Texas

Karen James, Children's Services, Louisville Free Public Library, Louisville, Kentucky

Contributors to the Gale Edition

The articles presented in this encyclopedia are based on entries in the *Worldmark Encyclopedia of Cultures and Daily Life* published in 1997 by Gale. The following authors and reviewers contributed to the Gale edition.

ANDREW J. ABALAHIN. Doctoral candidate, Department of History, Cornell University.

JAMAL ABDULLAH. Doctoral candidate, Department of City and Regional Planning, Cornell University.

SANA ABED-KOTOB. Book Review Editor, Middle East Journal, Middle East Institute.

MAMOUD ABOUD. Charge d'Affaires, a.i., Embassy of the Federal and Islamic Republic of the Comoros.

JUDY ALLEN. Editor, Choctaw Nation of Oklahoma.

HIS EXCELLENCY DENIS G. ANTOINE. Ambassador to the United States, Embassy of Grenada.

LESLEY ANN ASHBAUGH. Instructor, Sociology, Seattle University.

HASHEM ATALLAH. Translator, Editor, Teacher; Fairfax, Virginia.

HECTOR AZEVES. Cultural Attaché, Embassy of Uruguay.

VICTORIA J. BAKER. Associate Professor of Anthropology, Anthropology (Collegium of Comparative Cultures), Eckerd College.

POLINE BALA. Doctoral candidate, Asian Studies, Cornell University.

MARJORIE MANDELSTAM BALZER. Research Professor; Coordinator, Social, Regional, and Ethnic Studies Sociology, and Center for Eurasian, Russian, and East European Studies.

JOSHUA BARKER. Doctoral candidate, Department of Anthropology, Cornell University.

IGOR BARSEGIAN. Department of Sociology, George Washington University.

IRAJ BASHIRI. Professor of Central Asian Studies, Department of Slavic and Central Asian Languages and Literatures, University of Minnesota.

DAN F. BAUER. Department of Anthropology, Lafayette College.

JOYCE BEAR. Historic Preservation Officer, Muscogee Nation of Oklahoma.

SVETLANA BELAIA. Byelorussian-American Cultural Center, Strongsville, Ohio.

HIS EXCELLENCY DR. COURTNEY BLACKMAN. Ambassador to the United States, Embassy of Barbados.

BETTY BLAIR. Executive Editor, Azerbaijan International.

ARVIDS BLODNIEKS. Director, Latvian Institute, American Latvian Association in the USA.

ARASH BORMANSHINOV. University of Maryland, College Park.

HARRIET I. BRADY. Cultural Anthropologist (Pyramid Lake Paiute Tribe), Native Studies Program, Pyramid Lake High School.

MARTIN BROKENLEG. Professor of Sociology, Department of Sociology, Augustana College.

REV. RAYMOND A. BUCKO, S.J. Assistant Professor of Anthropology, LeMoyne College.

JOHN W. BURTON. Department of Anthropology, Connecticut College.

DINEANE BUTTRAM. University of North Carolina-Chapel Hill.

RICARDO CABALLERO. Counselor, Embassy of Paraguay.

CHRISTINA CARPADIS. Researcher/Writer, Cleveland, Ohio.

SALVADOR GARCIA CASTANEDA. Department of Spanish and Portuguese, The Ohio State University.

SUSANA CAVALLO. Graduate Program Director and Professor of Spanish, Department of Modern Languages and Literatures, Loyola University, Chicago.

BRIAN P. CAZA. Doctoral candidate, Political Science, University of Chicago.

VAN CHRISTO. President and Executive Director, Frosina Foundation, Boston.

YURI A. CHUMAKOV. Graduate Student, Department of Sociology, University of Notre Dame.

J. COLARUSSO. Professor of Anthropology, McMaster University.

FRANCESCA COLECCHIA. Modern Language Department, Duquesne University.

DIANNE K. DAEG DE MOTT. Researcher/Writer, Tucson, Arizona.

MICHAEL DE JONGH. Professor, Department of Anthropology, University of South Africa.

GEORGI DERLUGUIAN. Senior Fellow, Ph.D., U. S. Institute of Peace.

CHRISTINE DRAKE. Department of Political Science and Geography, Old Dominion University.

ARTURO DUARTE. Guatemalan Mission to the OAS.

CALEB DUBE. Department of Anthropology, Northwestern University.

BRIAN DU TOIT. Professor, Department of Anthropology, University of Florida.

LEAH ERMARTH. Worldspace Foundation, Washington, DC.

NANCY J. FAIRLEY. Associate Professor of Anthropology, Department of Anthropology/Sociology, Davidson College.

GREGORY A. FINNEGAN, Ph.D. Tozzer Library, Harvard University.

ALLEN J. FRANK, Ph.D.

DAVID P. GAMBLE. Professor Emeritus, Department of Anthropology, San Francisco State University.

FREDERICK GAMST. Professor, Department of Anthropology, University of Massachusetts, Harbor Campus.

PAULA GARB. Associate Director of Global Peace and Conflict Studies and Adjunct Professor of Social Ecology, University of California, Irvine.

HAROLD GASKI. Associate Professor of Sami Literature, School of Languages and Literature, University of Tromsø.

STEPHEN J. GENDZIER.

FLORENCE GERDEL.

ANTHONY P. GLASCOCK. Professor of Anthropology; Department of Anthropology, Psychology, and Sociology; Drexel University.

LUIS GONZALEZ. Researcher/Writer, River Edge, New Jersey.

JENNIFER GRAHAM. Researcher/Writer, Sydney, Australia.

MARIE-CÉCILE GROELSEMA. Doctoral candidate, Comparative Literature, Indiana University.

ROBERT GROELSEMA. MPIA and doctoral candidate, Political Science, Indiana University.

MARIA GROSZ-NGATÉ. Visiting Assistant Professor, Department of Anthropology, Northwestern University.

ELLEN GRUENBAUM. Professor, School of Social Sciences, California State University, Fresno.

N. THOMAS HAKANSSON. University of Kentucky.

ROBERT HALASZ. Researcher/Writer, New York, New York.

MARC HANREZ. Professor, Department of French and Italian, University of Wisconsin-Madison.

ANWAR UL HAQ. Central Asian Studies Department, Indiana University.

LIAM HARTE. Department of Philosophy, Loyola University, Chicago.

FR. VASILE HATEGAN. Author, *Romanian Culture in America*.

BRUCE HEILMAN. Doctoral candidate, Department of Political Science, Indiana University.

JIM HENRY. Researcher/Writer, Cleveland, Ohio.

BARRY HEWLETT. Department of Anthropology, Washington State University.

SUSAN F. HIRSCH. Department of Anthropology, Wesleyan University.

MARIDA HOLLOS. Department of Anthropology, Brown University.

HALYNA HOLUBEC. Researcher/Writer, Cleveland, Ohio.

YVONNE HOOSAVA. Legal Researcher and Cultural Preservation Officer, Hopi Tribal Council.

HUIQIN HUANG, Ph.D. Center for East Asia Studies, University of Montreal.

ASAFA JALATA. Assistant Professor of Sociology and African and African American Studies, Department of Sociology, The University of Tennessee, Knoxville.

STEPHEN F. JONES. Russian Department, Mount Holyoke College.

THOMAS JOVANOVSKI, Ph.D. Lorain County Community College.

A. KEN JULES. Minister Plenipotentiary and Deputy Head of Mission, Embassy of St. Kitts and Nevis.

GENEROSA KAGARUKI-KAKOTI. Economist, Department of Urban and Rural Planning, College of Lands and Architectural Studies, Dar es Salaam, Tanzania.

EZEKIEL KALIPENI. Department of Geography, University of Illinois at Urbana-Champaign.

CONTRIBUTORS

DON KAVANAUGH. Program Director, Lake of the Woods Ojibwa Cultural Centre.

SUSAN M. KENYON. Associate Professor of Anthropology, Department of History and Anthropology, Butler University.

WELILE KHUZWAYO. Department of Anthropology, University of South Africa.

PHILIP L. KILBRIDE. Professor of Anthropology, Mary Hale Chase Chair in the Social Sciences, Department of Anthropology, Bryn Mawr College.

RICHARD O. KISIARA. Doctoral candidate, Department of Anthropology, Washington University in St. Louis.

KAREN KNOWLES. Permanent Mission of Antigua and Barbuda to the United Nations.

IGOR KRUPNIK. Research Anthropologist, Department of Anthropology, Smithsonian Institution.

LEELO LASS. Secretary, Embassy of Estonia.

ROBERT LAUNAY. Professor, Department of Anthropology, Northwestern University.

CHARLES LEBLANC. Professor and Director, Center for East Asia Studies, University of Montreal.

RONALD LEE. Author, *Goddam Gypsy, An Autobiographical Novel.*

PHILIP E. LEIS. Professor and Chair, Department of Anthropology, Brown University.

MARIA JUKIC LESKUR. Croatian Consulate, Cleveland, Ohio.

RICHARD A. LOBBAN, JR. Professor of Anthropology and African Studies, Department of Anthropology, Rhode Island College.

DERYCK O. LODRICK. Visiting Scholar, Center for South Asian Studies, University of California, Berkeley.

NEIL LURSSEN. Intro Communications Inc.

GREGORIO C. MARTIN. Modern Language Department, Duquesne University.

HOWARD J. MARTIN. Independent scholar.

HEITOR MARTINS. Professor, Department of Spanish and Portuguese, Indiana University.

ADELINE MASQUELIER. Assistant Professor, Department of Anthropology, Tulane University.

DOLINA MILLAR.

EDITH MIRANTE. Project Maje, Portland, Oregon.

ROBERT W. MONTGOMERY, Ph.D. Indiana University.

THOMAS D. MORIN. Associate Professor of Hispanic Studies, Department of Modern and Classical Literatures and Languages, University of Rhode Island.

CHARLES MORRILL. Doctoral candidate, Indiana University.

CAROL A. MORTLAND. Crate's Point, The Dalles, Oregon.

FRANCIS A. MOYER. Director, North Carolina Japan Center, North Carolina State University.

MARIE C. MOYER.

NYAGA MWANIKI. Assistant Professor, Department of Anthropology and Sociology, Western Carolina University.

KENNETH NILSON. Celtic Studies Department, Harvard University.

JANE E. ORMROD. Graduate Student, History, University of Chicago.

JUANITA PAHDOPONY. Carl Perkins Program Director, Comanche Tribe of Oklahoma.

TINO PALOTTA. Syracuse University.

ROHAYATI PASENG.

PATRICIA PITCHON. Researcher/Writer, London, England.

STEPHANIE PLATZ. Program Officer, Program on Peace and International Cooperation, The John D. and Catherine T. MacArthur Foundation.

MIHAELA POIATA. Graduate Student, School of Journalism and Mass Communication, University of North Carolina at Chapel Hill.

LEOPOLDINA PRUT-PREGELJ. Author, *Historical Dictionary of Slovenia.*

J. RACKAUSKAS. Director, Lithuanian Research and Studies Center, Chicago.

J. RAKOVICH. Byelorussian-American Cultural Center, Strongsville, Ohio.

HANTA V. RALAY. Promotions, Inc., Montgomery Village, Maryland.

SUSAN J. RASMUSSEN. Associate Professor, Department of Anthropology, University of Houston.

RONALD REMINICK. Department of Anthropology, Cleveland State University.

BRUCE D. ROBERTS. Assistant Professor of Anthropology, Department of Anthropology and Sociology, University of Southern Mississippi.

LAUREL L. ROSE. Philosophy Department, Carnegie-Mellon University.

ROBERT ROTENBERG. Professor of Anthropology, International Studies Program, DePaul University.

CAROLINE SAHLEY, Ph.D. Researcher/Writer, Cleveland, Ohio.

VERONICA SALLES-REESE. Associate Professor, Department of Spanish and Portuguese, Georgetown University.

MAIRA SARYBAEVA. Kazakh-American Studies Center, University of Kentucky.

DEBRA L. SCHINDLER. Institute of Arctic Studies, Dartmouth College.

KYOKO SELDEN, Ph.D. Researcher/Writer, Ithaca, New York.

ENAYATULLAH SHAHRANI. Central Asian Studies Department, Indiana University.

ROBERT SHANAFELT. Adjunct Lecturer, Department of Anthropology, The Florida State University.

TUULIKKI SINKS. Teaching Specialist for Finnish, Department of German, Scandinavian, and Dutch, University of Minnesota.

JAN SJÅVIK. Associate Professor, Scandinavian Studies, University of Washington.

MAGDA SOBALVARRO. Press and Cultural Affairs Director, Embassy of Nicaragua.

MICHAEL STAINTON. Researcher, Joint Center for Asia Pacific Studies, York University.

RIANA STEYN. Department of Anthropology, University of South Africa.

PAUL STOLLER. Professor, Department of Anthropology, West Chester University.

CRAIG STRASHOFER. Researcher/Writer, Cleveland, Ohio.

SANDRA B. STRAUBHAAR. Assistant Professor, Nordic Studies, Department of Germanic and Slavic Languages, Brigham Young University.

VUM SON SUANTAK. Author, *Zo History*.

MURAT TAISHIBAEV. Kazakh-American Studies Center, University of Kentucky.

CHRISTOPHER C. TAYLOR. Associate Professor, Anthropology Department, University of Alabama, Birmingham.

EDDIE TSO. Office of Language and Culture, Navajo Division of Education.

DAVID TYSON. Foreign Broadcast Information Service, Washington, D.C.

NICOLAAS G. W. UNLANDT. Assistant Professor of French, Department of French and Italian, Brigham Young University.

GORDON URQUHART. Professor, Department of Economics and Business, Cornell College.

CHRISTOPHER J. VAN VUUREN. Professor, Department of Anthropology, University of South Africa.

DALIA VENTURA-ALCALAY. Journalist, London, England.

CATHERINE VEREECKE. Assistant Director, Center for African Studies, University of Florida.

GREGORY T. WALKER. Associate Director, Office of International Affairs, Duquesne University.

GERHARD WEISS. Department of German, Scandinavian, and Dutch, University of Minnesota.

PATSY WEST. Director, The Seminole/Miccosukee Photographic Archive.

WALTER WHIPPLE. Associate Professor of Polish, Germanic and Slavic Languages, Brigham Young University.

ROSALIE WIEDER. Researcher/Writer, Cleveland, Ohio.

JEFFREY WILLIAMS. Professor, Department of Anthropology, Cleveland State University.

GUANG-HONG YU. Associate Research Fellow, Institute of Ethnology, Academia Sinica.

RUSSELL ZANCA. Department of Anthropology, College of Liberal Arts and Sciences, University of Illinois at Urbana-Champaign.

Reader's Guide

Junior Worldmark Encyclopedia of World Cultures contains articles exploring the ways of life of over 290 culture groups worldwide. Arranged alphabetically by country in nine volumes, this encyclopedia parallels the organization of its sister set, *Junior Worldmark Encyclopedia of the Nations*. Whereas the primary purpose of *Nations* is to provide information on the world's nations, this encyclopedia focuses on the traditions, living conditions, and personalities of many of the world's culture groups.

Defining groups for inclusion was not an easy task. Cultural identity is shaped by such factors as history, geography, nationality, ethnicity, race, language, and religion. Sometimes the distinctions are subtle, but important. Most chapters in this encyclopedia begin with an article on the people of the country as a nationality group. For example, the chapter on Kenya begins with an article entitled "Kenyans." This article explores the national character shared by all people living in Kenya. However, there are separate articles on the Gikuyu, Kalenjin, Luhya, and Luo—four of the largest ethnic groups living in the country. They are all Kenyans, but each group is distinct. Many profiled groups—like the Kazaks—inhabit lands that cross national boundaries. Although profiled in the chapter on Kazakstan, Kazaks are also important minorities in China, Uzbekistan, and Turkmenistan. In such cases, cross-references direct the student to the chapter where the group is profiled.

The photographs that illustrate the articles show a wonderfully diverse world. From the luxury liners docked in the harbor at Monaco to the dwellings made of grass sheltering the inhabitants of the rain forest, people share the struggles and joys of earning a living, bringing children into the world, teaching them to survive, and initiating them into adulthood. Although language, customs, and dress illustrate our differences, the faces of the people pictured in these volumes reinforce our similarities. Whether on the streets of Tokyo or the mountains of Tibet, a smile on the face of a child transcends the boundaries of nationality and cultural identity to reveal something common in us all. Photographer Cory Langley's images on pages 93 and 147 in Volume 6 serve to illustrate this point.

The picture of the world this encyclopedia paints today will certainly differ from the one painted in future editions. Indigenous people like the Jivaro in Ecuador (Volume 3, page 77) are being assimilated into modern society as forest lands are cleared for development and televisions and VCRs are brought to even the most remote villages. As the global economy expands, traditional diets are supplemented with Coke, Pepsi, and fast food; traditional storytellers are replaced by World Cup soccer matches and American television programs; and cultural heroes are overwhelmed by images of Michael Jordan and Michael Jackson. Photographer Cynthia Bassett was fortunate to be among a small group of travelers to visit a part of China only recently opened to Westerners. Her image of Miao dancers (Volume 2, page 161) shows a people far removed from Western culture . . . until one looks a little closer. Behind the dancers, in the upper corner of the photograph, is a basketball hoop and backboard. It turns out that Miao teenagers love basketball!

ORGANIZATION

Within each volume the chapters are arranged alphabetically by country. A cumulative table of contents for all volumes in the set follows the table of contents to each volume.

Each chapter covers a specific country. The contents of the chapter, listing the culture group articles, follows the chapter title. An overview of the composition of the population of the country appears after the contents list. The individual articles follow, and are organized according to a standard twenty-heading outline explained in more detail below. This structure allows for easy comparison between cultures and enhances the accessibility of the information.

Articles begin with the **pronunciation** of the group's name, a listing of **alternate names** by which the group is known, the group's **location** in the world, its **population**, the **languages** spoken, and the **religions** practiced. Articles are illustrated with maps showing the primary location of the group and photographs of the culture group being profiled. The twenty standard headings by which the articles are organized are presented below.

1 ● INTRODUCTION: A description of the group's historical origins provides a useful background for understanding its contemporary affairs. Information relating to migration helps explain how the group arrived at its present location. Political conditions and governmental structure(s) that affect members of the profiled ethnic group are also discussed.

2 ● LOCATION: The population size of the group is listed. This information may include official census data from various countries and/or estimates. Information on the size of a group's population located outside the traditional homeland may also be included, especially for those groups with large scattered populations. A description of the homeland includes information on location, topography, and climate.

3 ● LANGUAGE: Each article lists the name(s) of the primary language(s) spoken by members. Descriptions of linguistic origins, grammar, and similarities to other languages may also be included. Examples of common words, phrases, and proverbs are listed for many of the profiled groups, and some include examples of common personal names and greetings.

4 ● FOLKLORE: Common themes, settings, and characters in the profiled group's traditional oral and/or literary mythology are highlighted. Many entries include a short excerpt or synopsis of one of the group's noteworthy myths, fables, or legends. Some entries describe the accomplishments of famous heroes and heroines or other prominent historical figures.

5 ● RELIGION: The origins of traditional religious beliefs are profiled. Contemporary religious beliefs, customs, and practices are also discussed. Some groups may be closely associated with one particular faith (especially if religious and ethnic identification are interlinked), while others may have members of diverse faiths.

6 ● MAJOR HOLIDAYS: Celebrations and commemorations typically recognized by the group's members are described. These holidays commonly fall into two categories: secular and religious. Secular holidays often include an independence day and/or other days of observance recognizing important dates in history that affected the group as a whole. Religious holidays are typically the same as those honored by people of the same faith worldwide. Some secular and religious holidays are linked to the lunar cycle or to the change of seasons. Some articles describe customs practiced by members of the group on certain holidays.

7 ● RITES OF PASSAGE: Formal and informal events that mark an individual's procession through the stages of life are profiled. These events typically involve rituals, ceremonies, observances, and procedures associated with birth, childhood, the coming of age, milestones in education or religious training, adulthood, and death.

8 ● RELATIONSHIPS: Information on greetings, body language, gestures, visiting customs, and dating practices is included. The extent of formality to which members of a certain ethnic group treat others is also addressed, as some groups may adhere to customs governing interpersonal relationships more or less strictly than others.

9 ● LIVING CONDITIONS: General health conditions typical of the group's members are cited. Such information includes life expectancy, the prevalence of various diseases, and access to medical care. Information on urbanization, housing, and access to utilities is also included. Transportation methods typically utilized by the group's members are also discussed.

10 ● FAMILY LIFE: The size and composition of the family unit is profiled. Gender roles common to the group are also discussed, including the division of rights and responsibilities relegated to male and female group members. The roles that children, adults, and the elderly have within the group as a whole may also be addressed.

11 ● CLOTHING: Many entries include descriptive information (design, color, fabric, etc.) regarding traditional clothing (or national costume) for men and women, and indicate the frequency of its use in contemporary life. A description of typical clothing worn in modern daily life is also provided, especially if traditional clothing is no longer the usual form of dress. Distinctions between formal and work attire and descriptions of clothing preferences of young people are described for many groups as well.

12 ● FOOD: Descriptions of items commonly consumed by members of the group are listed. The frequency and occasion for meals is also described, as are any unique customs regarding eating and drinking, special utensils and furniture, and the role of food and beverages in ritual ceremonies. Many entries include a recipe for a favorite dish.

13 ● EDUCATION: The structure of formal education in the country or countries of residence is discussed, including information on primary, secondary, and higher education. For some groups, the role of informal education is also highlighted. Some articles include information regarding the relevance and importance of education among the group as a whole, along with parental expectations for children.

14 ● CULTURAL HERITAGE: Since many groups express their sense of identity through art, music, literature, and dance, a description of prominent styles is included. Some articles also cite the contributions of famous individual artists, writers, and musicians.

15 ● EMPLOYMENT: The type of labor that typically engages members of the profiled group is discussed. For some groups, the formal wage economy is the primary source of earnings, but for other groups, informal agriculture or trade may be the usual way to earn a living. Working conditions are also highlighted.

16 ● SPORTS: Popular sports that children and adults play are listed, as are typical spectator sports. Some articles include a description and/or rules to a sport or game.

17 ● RECREATION: Listed activities that people enjoy in their leisure time may include structured pastimes (such as public musical and dance performances) or informal get-togethers (such as meeting for conversation). The role of popular culture, movies, theater, and television in everyday life is also discussed where it applies.

18 ● CRAFTS AND HOBBIES: Entries describe arts and crafts commonly fabricated according to traditional methods, materials, and style. Such objects may often have a functional utility for everyday tasks.

19 ● SOCIAL PROBLEMS: Internal and external issues that confront members of the profiled group are described. Such concerns often deal with fundamental problems like war, famine, disease, and poverty. A lack of human rights, civil rights, and political freedom may also adversely affect a group as a whole. Other problems may include crime, unemployment, substance abuse, and domestic violence.

20 ● BIBLIOGRAPHY: References cited include works used to compile the article, benchmark publications often recognized as authoritative by scholars, and other reference sources accessible to middle school researchers. Website addresses are provided for researchers who wish to access the World Wide Web. The website citation includes the author and title of the website (if applicable). The address begins with characters that follow "http://" in the citation; the address ends with the character preceding the comma and date. For example, the citation for the website of the German embassy appears as follows:

German Embassy, Washington, D.C. [Online]
   Available http://www.germany-info.org/, 1998.

To access this site, researchers type:
   www.germany-info.org

A glossary and an index of groups profiled appears at the end of each volume.

ACKNOWLEDGMENTS

The editors express appreciation to the members of the U•X•L staff who were involved in a number of ways at various stages of development of the *Junior Worldmark Encyclopedia of World Cultures.*

SUGGESTIONS ARE WELCOME: We appreciate any suggestions that will enhance future editions. Please send comments to:

Editors
*Junior Worldmark Encyclopedia
of World Cultures*
U•X•L
27500 Drake Road
Farmington Hills, MI 48331-3535
(800) 877-4253

Germany

The people of Germany are known as Germans. Foreigners began immigrating to find work in Germany in the late 1950s. By the 1990s, there were approximately 6 million foreigners in Germany; 30 percent of these were Turks, 13 percent were Yugoslavs, 9 percent were Italians, 6 percent were Greeks, 5 percent were Poles, 3 percent were Austrians, and Spanish and Portuguese represented about 1 percent each.

Germans

PRONUNCIATION: JUR-mans
LOCATION: Germany
POPULATION: Over 81 million
LANGUAGE: Standard German (Hochdeutsch); Sorbian; Turkish
RELIGION: Protestantism; Catholicism; Methodist; Baptist; Mennonite; Society of Friends; small numbers of Jews and Muslims

1 ● INTRODUCTION

Germany is one of Europe's largest nations, with one of the largest populations. Although it has played a major part in European and world history, it has been a single, unified nation for less than 100 years. The area that now makes up Germany originally was a cluster of partially independent cities and states. In 1871 the Prussian chancellor Otto von Bismarck created a unified Germany. In this century, Germany fought in two world wars (World War I, 1914–1918, and World War II, 1939–1945), and lost both.

Following the defeat of Nazi Germany in World War II, the nation was divided by the countries that had defeated it: the United States, France, Great Britain, and the Soviet Union. The American, French, and British zones were combined in 1949 to create the Federal Republic of Germany (West Germany). That same year, the Soviet zone became the German Democratic Republic (East Germany). Germany was separated for four decades.

Both Germanys recovered from the damage of the war with impressive speed. However, progress was faster and more dramatic in the West than in the East. Because of this, nearly three million East Germans eventually fled to West Germany, seeking better lives. Finally, in 1961, the East Germans put up the Berlin Wall and sealed off the nation's borders.

In the late 1980s, however, Germany became caught up in the changes sweeping communist Eastern Europe. The destruction of the Berlin Wall in November 1989 became one of the most important symbols of the communist system's collapse. In March 1990, the East Germans held their first free elections. The two German nations were reunited on October 3, 1990.

2 ● LOCATION

Germany's main regions are the Bavarian Alps (which form the boundaries with Austria and Switzerland), the South German Hill Region, the Central Uplands, and the North German Plain. Major rivers include the Rhine in the west and the Danube, which flows from west to east.

Germany has the second largest population of any European country—over 81 million. More than 90 percent of the people are ethnic Germans, descended from Germanic tribes. Since the 1950s, significant numbers of foreign workers have come into Germany from countries including Turkey, Italy, Greece, and the former Yugoslavia. By the end of 1991, Germany had a foreign population of close to 6 million.

3 ● LANGUAGE

Standard (or High) German is the nation's official language, but many other dialects are spoken throughout the country. Low German is spoken along the North Sea and Baltic Sea coasts and on Germany's offshore islands. It has some features in common with Dutch and even English (examples: Standard German *Wasser,* Low German *Water;* Standard German *Apfel,* Low German *Appel*). Sorbian is a Slavic language spoken by approximately 60,000 people in eastern Germany. A number of different languages, including Turkish, are spoken by Germany's immigrant populations.

Germans must get government approval for the names of their children. Male children must have obviously male names, and female children must have obviously female names. Names must also be chosen from a pool of distinctly German names. These include Dieter and Helmut for boys and Katarina and Christa for girls.

NUMBERS

English	German
one	eins
two	zwei
three	drei
four	vier
five	fünf
six	sechs
seven	sieben
eight	acht
nine	neun
ten	zehn

DAYS OF THE WEEK

English	German
Sunday	Sonntag
Monday	Montag
Tuesday	Dienstag
Wednesday	Mittwoch
Thursday	Donnerstag
Friday	Freitag
Saturday	Samstag/Sonnabend

4 ● FOLKLORE

The most famous German folktale is the *Nibelungenlied* dating back to AD 1200. Its characters, including Siegfried, Brunhilde, and Hagen, have become famous around the world through the operas of Richard Wagner (1813–83).

Another important set of tales was collected by Jacob and Wilhelm Grimm in the nineteenth century. *Tales of the Brothers Grimm* is the second most frequently translated book after the Bible.

5 ● RELIGION

About 30 percent of Germans belong to the official Protestant church. An estimated 28 percent of the population is Catholic. The Protestants live mainly in the north, and the Catholics, in the south. Other Christian denominations include Methodists, Baptists, Mennonites, and the Society of Friends (Quakers).

Before the 1930s, Germany had a Jewish population of about 530,000. However, the great majority fled or were killed by the government during World War II (1939–45). Today, only about 40,000 Jews live in Germany. Most of these are recent refugees from Russia. Muslims (followers of Islam) now account for nearly 3 percent of the population. They are mostly guest workers from Turkey.

6 ● MAJOR HOLIDAYS

Germany's legal holidays include New Year's Day (January 1), Good Friday (late March or early April), Easter (late March or early April), Pentecost (in May), Labor Day (May 1), and Christmas (December 25). Many different local and regional festivals are celebrated as well. Even the observance of some religious holidays varies from one region to another. Catholic areas celebrate the Feast of Corpus Christi (eleven days after Pentecost) and All Saints' Day (November 1). Lutheran regions observe Reformation Day (October 31) and Repen-

tance and Prayer Day (the third Wednesday in November). In December, there are special Christmas markets *(Weihnachtsmarkte)* in many towns. They sell candles, Christmas trees, and other seasonal goods.

7 ● RITES OF PASSAGE

Germans live in a modern, industrialized Christian country. Many of the rites of passage that young people undergo are religious rituals, such as baptism, first communion, confirmation, and marriage. In addition, many familes mark a student's progress through the education system with graduation parties.

German young men between the ages of eighteen and twenty-five are subject to being drafted into the armed forces. As of the late 1990s, the length of service was one

Richard B. Levine, Levine & Roberts Stock Photography

*A group of German schoolboys at Steuben Day Parade. The four years of primary school (*Grundschule*) are followed by several different educational options.*

year. Duty is usually near a young man's home town. The German armed forces are an important part of the North Atlantic Treaty Organization (NATO) defense alliance. Conscientious objectors (people whose religious beliefs do not allow them to participate in warfare) can engage in substitute service in hospitals, nursing homes, and similar institutions. As of the late 1990s, conscientious objectors' service obligation was fifteen months.

8 ● RELATIONSHIPS

Germans are usually thought of as hardworking, efficient, and without a sense of humor. These are stereotypes, of course, but there is some truth to them. Regional differences make it hard to pin down a national character or set of traits. The division between north and south is older and deeper than that between the formerly divided East Germany and West Germany. The Rhinelanders of the north are said to be easygoing and good-natured, while the Bavarians of the south are thought of as lively and excitable. Frisians, who live between the North Sea and Baltic Sea, have a reputation for being quiet and unsophisticated.

On the whole, however, Germans tend to be more serious and aloof than Americans. In Germany, it is customary to shake hands when you greet another person.

The most common greetings (with regional differences) are *Guten Morgen* (good morning), *Guten Tag* (hello), *Guten Abend* (good evening), and *Gute Nacht* (good night). *Auf Wiedersehen* means "goodbye."

9 ● LIVING CONDITIONS

Germans take great pride in their homes; most spend about 10 percent of their income on home furnishings and decoration. Families live in small houses or apartments with a kitchen, a bathroom, a living room, and one or two bedrooms. Young children often share a bedroom.

Germans receive high-quality medical care, and the life expectancy (the average age a person can expect to live to) is seventy-two years for men and seventy-nine years for women. The German love of beer has taken its toll on the nation's health: alcoholism follows smoking as one of the nation's leading causes of death.

10 ● FAMILY LIFE

Most Germans have small families, and Germany today has one of the world's lowest birthrates.

German children are taught to be polite and respectful to their elders. An increasing number of unmarried couples are living together, either with or without children. In fact, a recent study found that 40 percent of German couples under the age of thirty-five are not married. About three out of every ten German marriages end in divorce.

Traditionally, Germans referred to the role of women in terms of "three K's": *Kinder* (children), *Kirche* (church), and *Küche* (kitchen). Today, however, German women have legal equality with men. Like others throughout the world, German women are challenging the restrictions that have been placed on them. Although women account for roughly a third of the labor force, men still are usually paid higher salaries.

11 ● CLOTHING

Germans wear modern Western-style clothing for everyday and formal occasions. However, at festivals such as the popular Oktoberfest in Munich, one may still see traditional clothes such as black feathered hats, white shirts, embroidered suspenders, and *Lederhosen* (leather shorts) for men. On such occassions, women will wear lacy white peasant blouses, black embroidered bodices, and white aprons.

Regional costumes are especially popular in southern Germany. The traditional outfit of the carpenters' guild (craft association), for example, may still be seen in some areas. It consists of a felt hat, a black corduroy suit with pearl buttons, bell-bottomed trousers, and a red kerchief worn around the neck.

12 ● FOOD

The traditional German diet is high in starch (noodles and dumplings in the south, potatoes in the north). *Würste* (sausages)—in hundreds of varieties—are a staple throughout the country. Bread is usually eaten at every meal. In addition, the Germans are famous for their love of beer.

Various regions have their own special foods. They include *Weisswurst* (light-colored sausage) and Black Forest cherry cake

Recipe

Spaetzle

Ingredients

4 cups flour
1 teaspoon salt
¼ teaspoon pepper
2 cups chicken broth (canned is fine)
4 eggs
¼ cup milk
2 Tablespoons butter
½ cup bread crumbs

Directions

1. Combine flour, salt, and pepper in a large bowl.
2. In a smaller bowl, blend broth, eggs, and milk.
3. Add liquid to flour mixture, beating vigorously for about 2 minutes.
4. Force dough through a large-holed colander.
5. Bring a large kettle of salted water to a boil. Gently add the dough bits, and simmer gently for about 5 minutes. Spaetzle will float to the surface when done.
6. Drain spaetzle and rinse with cold water.
7. Melt butter in a skillet, and add boiled spaetzle. Cook, shaking the pan, until the spaetzle are lightly browned. Sprinkle finished spaetzle with bread crumbs and serve.

in the south. *Labskaus* (stew), seafood dishes, and bean soup with bacon (*Bohnensuppe mit Speck*) are favorites in the north. Spaetzle, tiny dumplings, are enjoyed by all Germans. A recipe for spaetzle follows.

While it may be tasty, the traditional German diet, with its cold meats, starches, sugary desserts, and beer, is high in calories and cholesterol. Many Germans are trying to change their eating habits in order to improve their health.

Most Germans eat their main meal at noon and prefer a lighter, often cold, supper. Germans keep the knife and fork in their hands while eating and consider it bad manners to place a hand under the table, on one's lap.

13 ● EDUCATION

Education is free and required between the ages of six and eighteen. After four years of primary school (*Grundschule*), there are different roads students may take. They may spend two years in "orientation grades" and then six years in a *Realschule* in preparation for technical training. Or they may spend five years in a *Hauptschule*, followed by a three-year apprenticeship, a system in which a student learns a trade by working alongside a skilled worker.

The other option is a nine-year *gymnasium* program that prepares students for a university education. In addition, however, some states offer the comprehensive system (*Gesamtschulen*), in which all students attend a single school from the fifth year onward. This system was also used in the former East Germany. University attendance is free of charge.

14 ● CULTURAL HERITAGE

In music, Germany is famous for its great composers, including Johann Sebastian Bach (1685–1750), Ludwig van Beethoven (1770–1827), Felix Mendelssohn (1809–

47), Robert Schumann (1886–1963), Johannes Brahms (1833–97), and Richard Wagner (1813–83). Well-known twentieth-century composers include Paul Hindemith (1895–1963), Kurt Weill (1900–50), Karlheinz Stockhausen (1928–), Carl Orff (1895–1982), and Hans Werner Henze (1926–).

In literature, Germany's greatest names include Johann Wolfgang von Goethe (1749–1832), Friedrich von Schiller (1759–1805), Heinrich Heine (1797–1856), and Rainer Maria Rilke (1875–1926). Modern German writers include Bertolt Brecht (1898–1956), Nobel Prize winner Thomas Mann (1875–1955), Günter Grass (1927–), and Nobel Prize winner Heinrich Böll (1917–85).

A great early name in German visual arts is that of Albrecht Dürer, whose masterpieces include both paintings and woodcuts. In the twentieth century, German artists worked in the Expressionist movement. In 1919, German architect Walter Gropius founded the famous Bauhaus school of art and design. This school had a great influence on architecture around the world.

15 ● EMPLOYMENT

The total labor force of Germany numbers over 37 million people. Of these, nearly two million are foreign workers, including Turks, citizens of parts of the former Yugoslavia, and Italians.

The German workday begins early. Many people employed in factories start work at 7:00 AM, and most stores and offices are open by 8:00. Laborers in industry usually work a little more than thirty-five hours a week. Two of Germany's largest employers are auto manufacturers. DaimlerChrysler (producer of the Mercedes-Benz) employs over 320,000 people worldwide. Volkswagen has a total workforce throughout the world that is nearly as large. Nearly half of all German workers belong to labor unions.

The standard of living of the Germans is very high. It is higher, in fact, than in any previous generation. There is an extensive social security net and job security is very important. Wages are high, making the German labor force one of the best paid in the world. The German currency, the Deutsche Mark (German Mark), ranks among the strongest currencies in the world.

16 ● SPORTS

Football (the game that Americans call soccer) is Germany's most popular sport. Some German teams have an international reputation, and the national soccer association has over four million members. Germany has a tradition of world-class gymnasts. Other popular sports include shooting, handball, golf, horseback riding, and tennis. In tennis, Germany has produced two recent world masters: Steffi Graf and Boris Becker.

Recreational sports include hiking, bicycling, camping, sailing, and swimming, as well as both downhill skiing and cross-country skiing in the country's alpine regions.

17 ● RECREATION

Many Germans enjoy relaxing around the television set. Over 90 percent of the population owns a TV, and more than half of all Germans watch television daily. The use of television and radio is not free; people have to pay a small monthly fee. However, both television and radio are nearly free of commercials.

The German people enjoy the scenic forest, mountain, and lake regions of their country while engaging in hiking and jogging, and other outdoor activities. Cultural activities available in all major cities and many smaller ones include museums, concerts, exhibits, and historic sites.

Most Germans have as many as six weeks of paid vacation during the year. Vacation destinations include the mountains and the beaches of the North and Baltic seas. Since Germans love the sun, Italy, Greece, Spain, Egypt, and Florida have become favorite vacation spots for many families.

18 ● CRAFTS AND HOBBIES

In their homes or in small shops, German craftspeople still produce works of art and souvenirs, including the cuckoo clocks for which they are famous. The wood carvings produced in Bavaria are world-famous.

19 ● SOCIAL PROBLEMS

The high cost of the unification of East and West Germany, plus a worldwide recession, weakened the German economy in the early 1990s. Other challenges facing Germany include reducing pollution and providing enough housing at prices people can afford. As unemployment has increased, tensions between immigrants and Germans have led to discrimination and even violence.

The area that was East Germany still requires much social and economic rebuilding to make up for the lower living standards that took place there under the communist government.

20 ● BIBLIOGRAPHY

Germany in Pictures. Minneapolis: Lerner Publications, 1994.

Hargrove, Jim. *Germany. Enchantment of the World Series.* Chicago: Children's Press, 1991.

Lye, Keith. *Passport to Germany.* New York: Franklin Watts, 1992.

Porter, Darwin. *Frommer's Comprehensive Travel Guide (Germany '95).* New York: Prentice-Hall Travel, 1994.

WEBSITES

German Embassy, Washington, DC. [Online] Available http://www.germany-info.org/, 1998.

German Tourism Bureau. [Online] Available http://www.germany-tourism.de/, 1998.

Ghana

The people of Ghana are called Ghanaians. There are more than twenty-five different languages spoken by the different groups in Ghana. The people who speak Akan people make up more than 50 percent of the population. East of the Volta River, the country was formerly called Togoland and was controlled by the British.

Ghanaians

PRONUNCIATION: gah-NAY-uhns
LOCATION: Ghana
POPULATION: About 18 million
LANGUAGE: English; Akan; Hausa; more than twenty-five African languages
RELIGION: Islam; Christianity

1 ● INTRODUCTION

Modern Ghana was established in 1957, when colonial subjects of the Gold Coast ended more than seventy-five years of British rule. For the previous ten years, nationalists had conducted nonviolent boycotts, demonstrations, and mass strikes against the British. A leader of this anticolonial movement, Kwame Nkrumah, became the first elected head of the nation. As the first independent nation south of the Sahara Desert, the country was named for the ancient empire of Ghana.

In its forty years of independence, Ghana has experienced four military *coups d'état* (takeovers). The first was in 1966, and the most recent was in 1981. Ghana is now a constitutional democracy with several political parties. It is governed by a president, an executive branch composed of cabinet-level and regional ministers, and a two-hundred-member National Assembly.

2 ● LOCATION

Just under 18 million people live in Ghana. It is a small tropical country located just north of the equator. Consisting of 127,205 square miles (239,460 square kilometers), it is roughly the size of the state of Oregon.

The geographical features and climate zones of Ghana are varied. Its humid southern regions are marked by coastal plains and rain forest. The savanna lands (grassy plains) of the northern regions face *harmattan* (dust-laden) winds for four months each year. The country's central regions are marked by plateaus and escarpments (cliffs).

The nation's capital, Accra, is a busy international city with a population just under 2 million.

Other languages spoken by large numbers of Ghanaians include Ewe, Ga, Guan, and Gur. Most Ghanaians speak two or more African languages. Hausa, a Nigerian language introduced into Ghana nearly 200 years ago, has become a *lingua franca* (common language) throughout the country. Hausa is a second language for more Ghanaians, but can be used to communicate with people from other groups.

4 ● FOLKLORE

Before Ghana was a British colony, the history of most Ghanaians was preserved by oral historians. Today, the stories of many legendary leaders of Ghana's various ethnic groups are included in school history books. Storytelling is one of the most important recreational activities for Ghanaians, especially in rural villages.

Among the Akan-speaking and Guan-speaking peoples, folktale characters include the tortoise, hare, vulture, and crow. But Anansi the spider is the most popular animal character. Anansi defeats his larger opponents by using his intelligence, humor, and cunning, rather than through the use of physical force.

5 ● RELIGION

Islam was introduced into parts of Ghana as early as the fourteenth century. Christianity was introduced by missionaries in the nineteenth century. Today, about 40 percent of Ghanaians still practice traditional African religions. These religions include the concept of a supreme being and a belief in the power of ancestral spirits.

There are also some independent Christian sects. These were founded early in the

3 ● LANGUAGE

English is the official language of government and business. However, Ghanaians speak more than twenty-five distinct African languages belonging to the Niger-Congo language family. Akan is the first language of more than half of all Ghanaians.

Arriving at the international airport in Accra, travelers may observe colorful billboards with the word *Akwaba*, or "welcome" in Akan, written in bold letters. Here are typical Akan greetings one may hear in southern Ghana:

Eti sen	Hello!
Wo ho ti sen	How are you?
Me ho ye	I am fine.
Me ho wo ekyere	See you later!

century by African Christians who became dissatisfied with the churches controlled by white missionaries. The Harrist church, for example, includes African dance and song in its services. This church also gives women a greater role in religious matters than the white churches do.

Even those who identify themselves as Christian or Muslim (followers of Islam) do not totally abandon their traditional religions. They still take part in community festivals commemorating the ancestors.

6 ● MAJOR HOLIDAYS

Ghanaians celebrate Independence Day on March 6 and Republic Day on July 1. The government often sponsors major parades in the large cities on national holidays.

Their are two religious holidays, one Christian and one Muslim, recognized by all. These are Christmas and *Damba*, which marks the birth of the Islamic prophet Muhammad. At least one regional festival is held in some part of Ghana every month. For example, in August the Adkye-Ga people of Accra sponsor the Homowo Festival, a celebration of female adolescent rites.

7 ● RITES OF PASSAGE

Every part of the cycle of life from birth to death is marked by some type of celebration in Ghana. Throughout southern Ghana, ethnic groups carry out special naming ceremonies for newborn babies. Among the Adkye-Ga people for example, the mother or other female relatives of a newborn baby born will dress the infant in waist beads. This is believed to protect the baby from disease and evil spirits.

Many ethnic groups in Ghana sponsor events to mark adolescence. Among the Ashanti and other Akan groups, coming-of-age rites for girls include activities such as giftgiving, distribution of food on behalf of the girl, a hair-cutting ceremony, and the eating of a ritual meal.

8 ● RELATIONSHIPS

Among Ghana's varied groups, custom dictates how greetings should be given and received. Among the Akan peoples, one cannot initiate a conversation without first saying the proper greeting. Otherwise, one risks being labeled as rude and uncivilized.

9 ● LIVING CONDITIONS

Most city houses are one-story or two-story family units built of cement. Apartment buildings over ten stories high are rare in most cities. Wealthier suburbs have large two-story houses surrounded by walls and shaded by palm and fruit trees. The older areas in the center of the city are often made up of mud and cement houses with corrugated zinc roofs.

Traditional architectural styles are found in the rural communities, with variously shaped adobe houses with thatched roofs. Among the Gurensi of northern Ghana, women paint beautiful geometric designs in their circular adobe houses.

An average of five people live in each house in Ghana.

10 ● FAMILY LIFE

The usual family structure in Ghana is the extended family. Depending on the ethnic group, Ghanaians may trace their descent

© Corel Corporation

Ghanaians drying peanuts. Ghana's national dish is peanut stew, which may include chicken or beef.

wraparound skirt and matching blouse made from African cloth. It is considered as acceptable as a Western business suit. The *fugu is* a striped cotton shirt that men wear on ceremonial occasions. It was traditionally worn by men of the northern groups, and it is now worn by men all over the country.

All students attending elementary school, high shool, and college wear uniforms. But it is not unusual to see teenage boys in the cities dressed in fashionable blue jeans.

12 ● FOOD

Ghanaian cuisine is very savory, or strong-flavored. Cayenne, allspice, curry, ginger, garlic, and onions are used in most dishes. The national dish is groundnut (peanut) stew, which may include chicken or beef. Another common dish is *plava* sauce, a spinach stew which may be eaten with fish or chicken. *Jollof rice*, a spicy dish that includes tomato sauce and meat, is enjoyed by many Ghanaians. The main staple foods served with Ghanaian meals are rice, millet, corn, cassava, yams, and plantains. The recipe for *fufu*, served all over west Africa, that follows has been adapted for Western cooks. It is not authentic, but it approximates the finished product one would enjoy in Ghana. In Africa, fufu is made by boiling plantain, cassava, or rice, and then pounding it with a large wooden mortar and pestle.

Most rural people rarely eat Western food. For example, Fante villagers may eat fish and *bangu*, a fermented corn dish, for breakfast. Some of the fast foods sold by city street vendors include roasted plantains

through either their father (*patrilineal*) or their mother (*matrilineal*). The influence of descent groups is still very strong. They keep track of marriages and provide members with a system of mutual aid.

Most Ghanaians believe that marriage is a family matter, not just a contract between two individual persons. Marriage requires the approval of the family. It also involves a specific set of gifts from the potential groom to his fiancée's family.

11 ● CLOTHING

During the day, Ghanaians may choose to dress in either African or Western-style clothes. A popular African-style outfit for women is the *kaba and slit,* a long

Recipe

Fufu

Ingredients
2½ cups Bisquick
2½ cups instant mashed potato flakes

Directions

1. Measure 6 cups of water into a large saucepan. Heat to a rapid boil.
2. Combine the Bisquick and instant mashed potato flakes and add to the water.
3. Cook, stirring constantly for 10 to 15 minutes. This is best accomplished by two people working together: one to hold the pot while the other stirs vigorously with a strong wooden spoon. The mixture will become very thick and difficult to stir, but the cooks must keep stirring. Otherwise, the result will be lumpy mess.
4. Fill a medium-size bowl with water, thoroughly wetting the surface of the bowl. Empty the water out.
5. Gather a large mass of the mixture (about one cup) onto the spoon, and transfer it to the wet bowl. Shake the bowl vigorously until the dough forms into a smooth ball.

Serve on a large platter with soup or stew.

Adapted from Hultman, Tami. *The Africa News Cookbook.* Durham, N.C.: Africa News Service, 1985.

or peanuts, corn on the cob with pieces of coconut, and beef kebabs.

13 ● EDUCATION

After gaining independence, the Ghanaian government introduced free education. All educational expenses are paid from the time students enter primary school until they complete university. Primary education lasts six years and is compulsory (required). Secondary education lasts seven years. Competition to attend the nation's high schools and colleges is very intense. Entrance examinations, for high school and for the university weed out all but the very best students.

Ghana has public universities and professional and technical colleges that offer training in fields including nursing, teaching, fashion design, and computer programming.

14 ● CULTURAL HERITAGE

Traditional music and dance are performed at festivals and the funerals of high-ranking members of a community. A funeral ceremony among the Dagomba people may include musical performances by more than six groups, each playing in a different musical style.

The drum is the most important musical instrument among southern ethnic groups; the xylophone predominates in the music of northern groups. Other traditional instruments include various types of rattles such as the *shekere,* clapperless bells, and wind instruments such as the bamboo flute and single-note trumpet made from animal horns, ivory, or wood.

One of West Africa's most respected composers and experts in traditional music is the Ghanaian J. H. Kwabena Nketia. He bases his modern compositions on traditional elements of Ghanaian music. Since the time of independence, literature has flourished in Ghana, although Ghanaian

© Corel Corporation

A Ghanaian rural family compound. The dominant family structure in Ghana is the extended family, and the influence of descent groups is still very strong.

writers were severely censored during the nine years that Kwame Nkrumah served as head of state. Well-known authors include playwrights Efua Sutherland and Joe Graft and novelist Ayi Kwei Armah. *Halo,* oral poetry in the Ewe language, has been a major influence on the poetry of Kofi Awoonor.

15 ● EMPLOYMENT

Approximately two-thirds of Ghana's population is engaged in subsistence farming (growing just enough food for survival). In most groups, men carry out the heavy work of preparing the fields. Women and children plant, weed, and harvest most food crops.

Many women sell any surplus food crops to city traders in order to earn cash.

Fishing is an important economic activity, connecting communities from the farthest ends of the country. During the fishing season, small crews of men in brightly painted canoes cast their nets into the Atlantic Ocean. The fish they catch is processed and marketed by their wives or female relatives.

Manufacturing is growing at a slow pace. It includes wood processing, food processing, textiles, brewing, and distilling.

Women make up 40 percent of Ghana's non-farming workforce. Many work in retail sales as small traders. Professional women cluster in occupations such as nursing and teaching.

16 ● SPORTS

The most popular spectator sport in Ghana is soccer. Every major city supports at least one professional team and a stadium— Kotoko in Kumasi, the Vipers in Cape Coast, and the Hearts of Oak in Accra. Ghana's national team, the Black Stars, is made up of the best players from these teams. On any weekend, it is not unusual to find teenage boys or men competing in soccer matches.

Basketball and tennis are replacing cricket in popularity among the wealthy.

17 ● RECREATION

When they attend night clubs or house parties, Ghanaians dance to reggae or rhythm and blues music.

After World War II (1939–45), the concert party, a type of comic opera performed in the Akan language, became the most popular form of entertainment in the coastal towns. This folk theater is a combination of Akan performing arts, influenced by Western music and drama. Today, there are over fifty concert-party troupes that perform in both city and rural areas. The event opens at nine o'clock at night with a dance and live band playing popular tunes. Two hours later, the troupe performs a comic play which lasts until two or three o'clock in the morning.

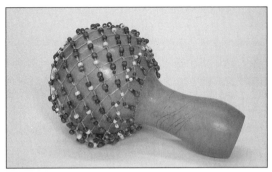

EPD Photos

Ghanaian music features various types of rattles. This one, the shekere, is made by attaching beads or small shells to a large dried gourd. Courtesy of the Center for the Study of World Musics, Kent State University.

18 ● CRAFTS AND HOBBIES

Ghana has maintained a rich tradition of arts and crafts. Certain crafts, such as *batik* (a method of dyeing or painting fabric), were introduced in the 1960s. However, others, such as pottery, have been practiced for thousands of years. The perfectly round clay pots produced by Shai women are known throughout southern and central Ghana. They are used for storage and cooking. Akan women are among the few female sculptors in Africa. Their clay figures are portraits of chiefs or important elders in their society. Women also produce the beads found in markets throughout Ghana. Asante smiths produce beautiful gold jewelry.

Traditional Ghanaian woven clothes, leather bags, bead necklaces, and beautifully carved masks and stools are sold in many large American cities. Many African Americans decorate their high school and college graduation robes with scarves of *kente* cloth produced by Asante weavers.

19 ● SOCIAL PROBLEMS

The minimum age to work is fifteen, but custom and a family's need for more income often force children to work at a younger age. The government has set up agencies to help protect children. Tensions between ethnic groups in the northern parts of Ghana have eased somewhat in the 1990s, but they have not completely disappeared.

20 ● BIBLIOGRAPHY

Brace, Steve. *Ghana, Economically Developing Countries*. New York: Thomson Learning, 1995.

Cole, Herbert M., and Doran H. Ross. *The Arts of Ghana*. Los Angeles: Museum of Cultural History, 1977.

Hultman, Tami. *The Africa News Cookbook: African Cooking for Western Kitchens.* Durham, N.C.: Africa News Service, 1985.

Myers, Robert A. *Ghana*. Santa Barbara, Calif.: Clio Press, 1991.

Priebe, Richard K., ed. *Ghanaian Literatures*. New York: Greenwood Press, 1988.

WEBSITES

Embassy of Ghana, Washington, D.C. [Online] Available http://www.ghana-embassy.org, 1998.

Garbrah, Steve. Ashanti Home Page [Online] Available http://www.ashanti.com.au/, 1997.

World Travel Guide. Ghana. [Online] Available http://www.wtgonline.com/country/gh/gen.html, 1998.

World Travel Guide. Ghana. [Online] Available http://www.wtgonline.com/country/gh/gen.html, 1998.

Greece

The people of Greece are called Greeks. Minority groups include Turks, Macedonian Slavs, Albanians, Armenians, Bulgarians, and Vlachs (a group of semi-nomads who live in the mountains of the north). See the chapters on Turkey in Volume 8, Macedonia in Volume 5, Albania and Armenia in Volume 1, and Bulgaria in Volume 2 for more information.

Greeks

PRONUNCIATION: GREECKS
LOCATION: Greece
POPULATION: 10 million
LANGUAGE: Greek
RELIGION: Eastern Orthodox Church of Christ

1 ● INTRODUCTION

There were two early societies in the area of present-day Greece. The Minoan civilization (c.2600–1200 BC) on the island of Crete was named after the legendary King Minos. The Mycenean civilization on the mainland (c.1600–1150 BC) was founded by people called the Hellenes. By the eighth century BC, the Greek city-state, or *polis*, had taken shape. By the sixth century BC, the city-states of Athens and Sparta were rivals for political control of Greece. The Classical "golden age" of Athens in the fifth century was marked by great achievements in government, philosophy, drama, sculpture, and architecture. The influence of Greek civilization expanded throughout much of Europe, northern Africa, the Middle East, and central Asia through the conquests of Alexander the Great. Greece was conquered by the Romans in 146 BC.

Greece fell under Turkish rule in AD 1453. After a long struggle for Greek independence, the Turks accepted Greek self-rule in 1831. This marked the beginning of modern Greece. Greece has been a parliamentary democracy since 1975. It is a full member of the North Atlantic Treaty Organization (NATO) and the European Community (EC).

2 ● LOCATION

Located at the southern end of the Balkan Peninsula, Greece includes over 1,500 islands in the Ionian and Aegean Seas. About 170 of these islands have people living on them. About 80 percent of the country is covered by mountains, which form part of the Alps. Mount Olympus, in east-central Greece, the legendary home of the gods, is the highest peak, rising to 9,573

GREEKS

feet. The nation's coastline—over 8,750 miles (14,000 kilometers) in length—is one of the longest in the world.

About 98 percent of Greece's ten million people are of ethnic Greek descent. Minority groups include Turks, Macedonian Slavs, Albanians, Armenians, and Vlachs—a group of semi-nomads (people who move from place to place, usually while herding livestock) who live in the mountains of the north.

The rapid population growth of the past century has been balanced by the large numbers of Greeks who have moved away to North America, northern Europe, Australia, and other places. In addition, many Greek men live abroad temporarily as guest workers in other countries.

3 ● LANGUAGE

About 98 percent of Greece's people speak Greek as their first language. There are two forms of modern Greek. The demotic form (*dimotiki*) is used in everyday conversation, and varies by region. It includes words from Slavic languages, Turkish, and Italian. The more formal version, *Katharevousa*, is used by the government and the press. It originated in the early nineteenth century in an attempt to revive ancient Greek, which is still really a dead language.

NUMBERS

English	Greek
one	éna
two	dío
three	tría
four	téssera
five	pénde
six	éxi
seven	eptá
eight	októ
nine	enéa
ten	déka

DAYS OF THE WEEK

English	Greek
Sunday	Kyriakí
Monday	Deftéra
Tuesday	Tríti
Wednesday	Tetárti
Thursday	Pémpti
Friday	Paraskeví
Saturday	Sávato

4 ● FOLKLORE

The ancient Greeks believed that gods and goddesses ruled their fate and could tell the future. Different gods and goddesses were considered responsible for the different aspects of life. They were believed to communicate with priests and priestesses at shrines called oracles. The most important oracle was at Delphi. People honored the gods publicly at great festivals (including the Olympics) and privately at altars in their homes, with offerings of food and wine.

5 ● RELIGION

The Eastern Orthodox Church plays a central role in Greek life. During the 400 years of Ottoman Turkish rule, the Orthodox Church was the main force uniting the Greek people. Greek history, art, literature, and music were preserved and passed down through the church. Over 97 percent of Greeks today belong to the Orthodox Church. Although freedom of religion is guaranteed to all Greeks, the Orthodox Church enjoys a special relationship with the government. It was recognized in the 1975 constitution as the "established religion" of Greece. The president of Greece must be a member and is sworn into office with church rites. Major religious holidays are also civil holidays. It is an unwritten rule that high-ranking military officers and judges are chosen from the Orthodox Church members.

Religion plays a more important role in the lives of village residents than those of city dwellers. In the city, only about 20 percent of the people regularly attend church services. Country life revolves around the local church and religious observances. It is common for rural Greeks to have religious statues and images in their homes, together with holy oil, holy water, and a special kind of lamp. Many Greeks pray to a particular saint or saints in times of trouble, and they make pilgrimages to shrines that are considered especially holy. Religious customs in some rural areas still contain elements from beliefs and superstitions of earlier times.

6 ● MAJOR HOLIDAYS

Many of the major Greek holidays are those of the Eastern Orthodox Church. The most important are Easter and the Holy Week before it, which occur on dates different from those of the Western calendar.

The New Year, which in Greece is a more joyous occasion than Christmas, is dedicated to St. Basil. It is celebrated with gift giving and parties. Children carry red and blue paper ships to symbolize the ship that brought St. Basil to Greece. One New Year's tradition is to hide a silver coin in the dough of a special bread spiced with cinnamon, nutmeg, and orange peel. Wealth is believed to come to whoever finds the coin.

Greeks celebrate their birthday on the day dedicated to the saint for whom they are named, rather than on the day of their birth.

7 ● RITES OF PASSAGE

Greece is a modern, industrialized Christian country. Many of the rites of passage that young people undergo are religious rituals, such as baptism, first communion, confirmation, and marriage. In addition, many families mark a student's progress through the education system with graduation parties.

8 ● RELATIONSHIPS

The Greeks are known for their lively, outgoing nature. Much of their leisure time is spent in *pareas*, or groups of friends. Gathering in coffee shops, waterfront taverns, and village squares, they drink, sing, dance, and discuss the events of the day. They generally gesture energetically while talking. It is acceptable for women or men to walk in public holding hands or arm in arm as a sign of companionship.

9 ● LIVING CONDITIONS

Rural Greeks—about half the population—live in flat-roofed houses of stone or brick, often without running water or with only wood stoves for heat. City dwellers live in government-subsidized housing or in small houses in suburban areas.

The sea has traditionally linked Greek cities and towns. Greece's transportation system has been greatly expanded since World War II (which ended in 1945). Most roads linking Athens to the main provincial centers are paved, and Athens itself has a subway system.

Health care is provided by the state-run National Health Service, which includes some private facilities. In spite of efforts to provide doctors to the most distant areas, medical care is still uneven. Care is much better and easier to obtain in the large cities. However, most towns do have hospitals or clinics.

Abortion is a major method of birth control. The number of abortions performed by both doctors and nondoctors may equal the number of live births. The Greek government legalized abortion on demand at state expense in 1986, and within three years the number of legal abortions per year had risen from 180 to 7,338.

Some members of the population, especially in rural areas, still use the services of folk healers, whose methods include spells and herbal remedies.

10 ● FAMILY LIFE

On the average, both men and women in Greece marry in their mid- to late twenties. Greece has a higher marriage rate and lower divorce rate than the countries of northern Europe. The basic family unit is the nuclear family—a husband, a wife, and their unmarried children. Among rural villagers, couples live with the husband's parents for a brief time. It is not unusual, in fact, for city couples to live with one spouse's family until they are ready to buy their own house. Aging parents often join a grown child's household when it becomes difficult for them to care for themselves.

In January 1983, the Greek parliament legislated changes in the family laws that made divorce easier, abolished the dowry as a legal requirement for marriage, and guaranteed legal equality between spouses.

11 ● CLOTHING

In everyday life, Western clothing is the norm. The traditional costume–tunic, vest, and tight pants bound at the knee for men–is seen only during festivals and in rural areas.

12 ● FOOD

Although Greece is part of Europe, the Greek diet has been influenced more by the countries of the Middle East. Lamb is the basic meat, and olive oil is used in many recipes. Other staples include rice, yogurt, figs, shish kebab, feta cheese (made from goat's or sheep's milk), and whole-grain bread.

A typical Greek dish consists of ground meat with spices, rice, and herbs, often wrapped in leaves or stuffed into vegetables.

Recipe

Avgolemono
(Greek Lemon Soup)

Ingredients

1 can of chicken with rice soup (condensed)
1 soup can filled with water
1 egg
2 Tablespoons fresh lemon juice
1 fresh lemon
Parsley for garnish (optional)

Directions:

1. Combine condensed soup and water in a double boiler. (A double boiler has one pot that nests inside another. The lower pot is filled with water.) Bring the water in the lower pot to a boil, and heat soup.

2. Beat egg well. Add lemon juice to the egg gradually, continuing to beat the mixture.

3. Gradually add one cup of the hot soup broth to the egg mixture.

4. Gradually add egg mixture to soup in double boiler. Keep the heat low so that the soup does not begin to boil.

5. Cook over low heat until egg, stirring until egg mixture is completely blended into soup.

6. Be careful not to overheat the soup, because it will curdle. Garnish with thin slices of lemon and parsley, if desired, and serve.

Adapted from *The International Cook,* Camden, N.J.: Campbell Soup Company, 1980.

Greek pastries are eaten not as desserts but as afternoon or late-night snacks. Many of them are extremely sweet and made from paper-thin dough called *filo.*

A popular Greek drink is *ouzo,* a strong alcoholic drink flavored with anise. Another popular beverage, *retsina,* is a white wine. The toast *"Yiassas"* (To your health) can often be heard, together with the clinking of glasses, wherever Greeks gather to enjoy food and drink. To the left is a simple recipe for Greek lemon soup, *avgolemono.*

13 ● EDUCATION

Greeks place great value on learning, and over 90 percent of the population can read and write. The literacy rate fell to less that 30 percent during and after World War II (1939–45).

Education is free and compulsory (required) for nine years until the age of fifteen. Three more years of free education, in college-preparatory or technical programs, are optional. At age eighteen, students may enter the government-run university system or other technical and vocational schools.

14 ● CULTURAL HERITAGE

Even before the great flowering of culture in Athens in the fifth century BC, Greece had already produced the *Iliad* and *Odyssey,* two epic poems by Homer. With the golden age of Athens came the philosophical teachings of Socrates, Plato, and Aristotle; the great tragedies of Aeschylus, Euripides, and Sophocles; and the comedies of Aristophanes. Greek sculptors perfected the art of natural representation of the human body. Greek architecture, which had already introduced the town plan based on a grid and organized around the temple, produced the Parthenon, the beautiful temple on the Acropolis, a hill in Athens.

In the twentieth century, there has been a renaissance of Greek literature that includes the writings of novelist Nikos Kazantzakis (author of *The Last Temptation of Christ* and *Zorba the Greek*) and the poetry of C. P. Cavafy, Nikos Gatsos, and the Nobel Prize winners George Seferis and Odysseus Elytis. Well-known composers include Mikis Theodorakis and Manos Hadjidakis, who wrote the film score for *Never on Sunday*. Modern composers often use the instruments and melodies of Greek folk music, especially the *bouzouki*, a mandolin-like string instrument, as well as the *santouri* (dulcimer), clarinet, lute, and drums.

15 ● WORK

The raising of cash crops, including grain, olives, cotton, tobacco, and fresh fruits, has replaced much of the farming of earlier times. Rural farms are mostly run without machines. Many of them are less than ten acres in size. Horse-drawn or donkey-drawn plows are used for tilling, and harvesting is done by hand and wagon.

Aside from farming, the other major occupations of Greek villagers are fishing and shepherding or goat-herding. Greece is one of the least industrialized nations of Europe. Most industries are concentrated in Athens and Thessaloniki. Many Greeks work in family-owned businesses. In 1990, 85 percent of Greek manufacturing companies had fewer than ten employees. Food, beverage, and tobacco processing are the main industries. Next in importance are textiles and clothing, metals, chemical manufacturing, and shipbuilding.

Cory Langley

Greek fisherman working his nets from the deck of his boat. Aside from farming, the other major occupations of Greek villagers are fishing and shepherding or goat-herding.

16 ● SPORTS

The first Olympic Games were held in Greece in ancient times. Today, football (the game called soccer in the United States) is the most popular sport. Other favorites include basketball, volleyball, tennis, swimming and waterskiing at the nation's many beaches, sailing, fishing, golf, and mountain climbing. Cricket is popular on the island of Corfu.

Cory Langley

The Greek coastline—over 8,750 miles (14,000 kilometers) in length—is one of the longest in the world.

17 ● RECREATION

In the country, coffee shops—usually in the village square—are popular gathering places. Men gather there after work to talk, drink dark coffee, and smoke cigarettes or hookahs (water pipes).

In cities and towns, Greeks enjoy television, movies, theater, and concerts. Forms of traditional entertainment include folk dances performed by dance troupes wearing colorful costumes, with accompaniment led by the bouzouki. Also popular is the *karagiozi*, a shadow-puppet show that is performed live. Karagiozi can be seen every week on television. Operas, concerts, ballets, and ancient Greek dramas are pre-sented at the Athens Festival each summer. Greek drama is also performed in the open-air theater at Epidaurus.

18 ● CRAFTS AND HOBBIES

Craftspeople throughout Greece practice weaving, knitting, embroidery, carving, metalworking, and pottery making. Village women are known for their colorful fabrics and carpets and elaborate wall hangings.

19 ● SOCIAL PROBLEMS

The proportion of drug users doubled in the 1980s, with the largest increase among women and poor people. Marijuana is the most frequently used drug. In the early

1990s, drug-related deaths numbered between sixty-six and seventy-nine per year. Aside from drug control, the other major problem in Greek society is illegal immigration of people from the Balkans and the Middle East.

20 ● BIBLIOGRAPHY

Bennett, A. Linda, ed. *Encyclopedia of World Cultures* (*Europe*). Boston: G. K. Hall, 1992.

Curtis, Glenn E., ed. *Greece: A Country Study.* U.S. Government Printing Office, 1994.

Fodor's Greece. Fodor's Travel Publications, 1995.

Gage, Nicholas. *Hellas: A Portrait of Greece.* New York: Villard Books, 1987.

Gall, Timothy, and Susan Gall, ed. *Junior Worldmark Encyclopedia of the Nations.* Detroit: UXL, 1996.

The International Cook. Camden, N.J.: Campbell Soup Company, 1980.

Moss, Joyce, and George Wilson. *Peoples of the World: Western Europeans.* Detroit: Gale Research, 1993.

Pettifer, James. *The Greeks: The Land and People Since the War.* New York: Viking, 1993.

Steinberg, Rolf, ed. *Continental Europe.* Insight Guides. Singapore: APA Publications, 1989.

Woodhouse, C. M. *Modern Greece: A Short History.* 4th ed. London: Faber & Faber, 1986.

WEBSITES

Embassy of Greece, Washington, DC. [Online] Available http://www.greekembassy.org, 1998.

Greek Tourism. [Online] Available http://www.compulink.gr/tourism/, 1998.

World Travel Guide. Greece. [Online] Available http://www.wtgonline.com/gr/gen.html, 1998.

Grenada

The people of Grenada are called Grenadians. Blacks, together with those of mixed black and white ancestry, make up over 90 percent of the population. The remainder consists of small groups of Asian (largely Indian) and European descent.

Grenadians

PRONUNCIATION: Gre-NAY-dee-uns
LOCATION: Grenada
POPULATION: 100,000
LANGUAGE: English; French-African-English dialect
RELIGION: Roman Catholicism; Protestantism; Hinduism; Christian-African sects

1 ● INTRODUCTION

Grenada was first sighted by Christopher Columbus in 1498, although he never landed there. The Caribs who inhabited the island drove off all settlers, both English and French, for more than one hundred and fifty years. In 1650 a French party succeeded in acquiring the island from the Caribs in exchange for knives, trinkets, and brandy. Having gained a foothold, they systematically killed most of the native population. Forty of the last Caribs on the island leaped to their death in a mass suicide at La Morne des Sauteurs, or "Leapers' Hill." Grenada became a British possession under the Treaty of Versailles in 1783. Independence was granted by Great Britain in 1974.

In 1979 the country's leader was overthrown. The new prime minister, Maurice Bishop, formed a Marxist government that established close ties with Cuba and other communist countries. In October 1983, a faction of the revolutionary government ousted Bishop, who was killed along with several of his associates. A week later, U.S. troops, together with forces from other Caribbean nations, subdued the military council that had seized power, imprisoning its leaders and removing the Cuban military presence from the island.

Since the 1983 invasion, Grenada has moved closer politically to the United States, which provided the nation with disaster relief and long-term economic aid and technical assistance. The international airport at Point Salines, begun under the Bishop government, was completed with U.S. aid, and much of the country's infrastructure was repaired and modernized.

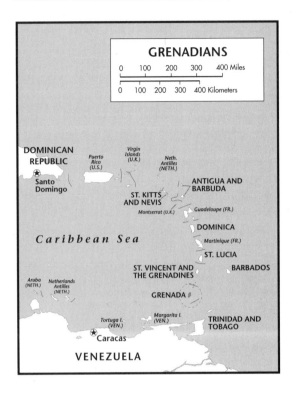

GRENADIANS

0   100   200   300   400 Miles

0   100   200   300   400 Kilometers

DOMINICAN REPUBLIC

Santo Domingo

Puerto Rico (U.S.)

Virgin Islands (U.K.)

Neth. Antilles (NETH.)

ANTIGUA AND BARBUDA

ST. KITTS AND NEVIS

Montserrat (U.K.)

Guadeloupe (FR.)

DOMINICA

Martinique (FR.)

Caribbean Sea

ST. LUCIA

ST. VINCENT AND THE GRENADINES

BARBADOS

Aruba (NETH.)

Netherlands Antilles (NETH.)

GRENADA

Tortuga I. (VEN.)

Margarita I. (VEN.)

TRINIDAD AND TOBAGO

Caracas

VENEZUELA

2 ● LOCATION

Grenada is the most southerly of the Windward Islands and is known for the beauty of its lush and fertile land. Its nickname is "the Isle of Spice" because of the nutmeg (one third of the world's supply), cloves, mace, and other spices grown there. In addition to its main island, the country has two dependencies—Petit Martinique and Carriacou—and a number of smaller islets. Grenada is one of the smallest independent nations in the Western Hemisphere. The three main islands have a total area of 133 square miles, a little less than twice the size of Washington, D.C.

The main island is green and hilly and has a mountain range that divides it in half. The interior also contains rain forests, waterfalls, crater lakes, and many rivers and streams. The coastal land has swamps, woodlands, and fertile plains.

Grenada's total population is estimated to be 100,000 people with about 90,000 living on the main island. The population is predominantly rural. About one-third live in urban areas. About 85 percent of Grenada's population is of African descent, while 11 percent have mixed black and white ancestry. The rest of the population is divided between Asians (mostly East Indians) and whites.

3 ● LANGUAGE

English is the official language of Grenada, but many Grenadians speak patois, a dialect that combines English words with elements of French and African languages.

4 ● FOLKLORE

Animals from the jungles of Africa play a prominent role in the popular *anancy* tales. In these stories, beasts frighten or trick their enemies, sometimes by taking on the shapes of human beings. One example is the story "King Cat," in which rats are invited to a party to celebrate the pretend death of a famous rat-catching cat, who suddenly pounces on them and eats them all except for a pregnant female who lives on to perpetuate the "rat race."

While belief in supernatural creatures is less common in Grenada today than in the past, the creatures live on in the region's Carnival figures and still appear as characters in bedtime stories. The name of one such creature—the zombie, or walking dead—has become a commonly used word in the United States. In African lore, zombies were dead people brought back to life to do the bidding of voodoo priests.

Popular folk remedies include drinking a tea made from lime bush leaves for an upset stomach, and a preparation made of mango leaves for treating rheumatism. Compresses made from the leaves of certain plants may be applied to the forehead to treat fevers.

5 ● RELIGION

About 65 percent of Grenadians are Roman Catholic. Most of the rest belong to Protestant denominations which include Anglican, Methodist, Seventh-Day Adventist, and Baptist. Most of Grenada's small Indian population is Hindu. Shango, a traditional African religion, is still practiced, generally in combination with Christian beliefs. African religious practices are especially prominent on the small island of Carriacou. The mingling of Christian and African traditions can be seen in the island's boat-christening ceremonies, which combine holy water, sacrificial goats, and African-derived Big Drum music.

6 ● MAJOR HOLIDAYS

Grenada's public holidays are New Year's Day (January 1), Independence Day (February 7), Good Friday and Easter Monday (March or April), Labor Day (May 1), Whit Monday (May or June), Corpus Christi (June), the August holidays on the first Monday and Tuesday of August, Carnival (mid-August), Thanksgiving (October 25), and Christmas (December 25 and 26).

The country's most important festival is Carnival. In Grenada, this celebration is held in August instead of the usual pre-Lenten time to avoid conflicting with the Grenadian Independence Day. Carnival begins with a Sunday night celebration leading into the Jouvert (*jour ouvert*–opening day) festivities at dawn on Monday, which feature *Djab Djab Molassi,* who represent devils (*Djab Djab* is derived from *diable,* the French word for "devil"). These merrymakers streak their faces and bodies with grease or molasses, which they delight in smearing on bystanders.

Another traditional festival is Fisherman's Birthday, celebrated on the feast day of Saints Peter and Paul at the end of June. It involves a ritual blessing of nets and boats, boat races, and food and dancing.

7 ● RITES OF PASSAGE

Major transitions in life, such as birth, marriage, and death, are noted with religious ceremonies appropriate to each Grenadian's particular faith community.

8 ● RELATIONSHIPS

Grenada's history of British colonization is shown in many of its customs, such as driving on the left side of the road and an occasional "tea party" which is usually a fundraising event.

9 ● LIVING CONDITIONS

While poverty does exist on Grenada, few people are hungry thanks to its fertile farmlands. Most Grenadians own land on which they can grow crops to feed their families. Whatever is left is sold at markets. Housing ranges from wooden shacks with tin or iron roofs among the poorer villages to the attractive, brightly painted bungalows of those who can afford them. Signs of urban poverty found in other developing countries, such as shantytowns (makeshift houses clustered in unsanitary villages around urban areas), are rarely seen. Average life expectancy in Grenada is seventy years.

The residents of Grenada depend upon narrow, winding roads, many of which are not paved, to get around. Most residents do not own cars and rely on bus transportation.

10 ● FAMILY LIFE

Many Grenadians live in extended-family households, which may include up to three generations. Grandparents commonly help raise children, although day-care facilities are available for working mothers. Older family members, when not actually part of the household, usually live only a short distance from their children. The elderly rely on their children to look after them.

It used to be common for a family to have as many as ten children. With more widespread use of birth control and more women working outside the home, the average number of children in a family dropped to four or five in the 1980s, and the country actually had a negative population growth rate between 1985 and 1992. Part of this negative growth rate was due to emigration.

11 ● CLOTHING

Grenadians wear modern Western-style clothing. Women often wear straw or cloth hats for protection from the sun.

12 ● FOOD

The cuisine of Grenada reflects a variety of influences: Amerindian, African, French, British, and East Indian. Foods commonly found at the market include yams, avocados,

Susan D. Rock

Grenadian women selling their wares to tourists on the beach in St. George.

callaloo greens (similar to spinach), oranges, papayas (called "paw-paws"), plantains, mangoes, and coconuts. Many fruits are available year-round.

About twenty different kinds of fish are caught off the coasts. Both fish and chicken dishes are served at many meals. Popular Caribbean staples include pigeon peas and rice, and "callaloo," a dish made from callaloo greens, okra, salted pork, crab, and fresh fish. The dish most closely identified with Grenada is "oildown," a mixture of salted pork and breadfruit steamed in coconut milk. Another favorite is "turtle toes," a combination of ground lobster, conch, and other seafood shaped into balls and deep fried.

Popular beverages include locally brewed beer; rum punch spiced with lime juice, syrup, and grated nutmeg; "mauby," a soft drink made from the bark of the maubi tree; and cocoa tea made from cocoa beans and spices steeped in hot milk.

13 ● EDUCATION

The adult literacy rate in Grenada is more than 90 percent. All children are required to attend school for twelve years. The average primary school has one teacher for every twenty-eight pupils, about the same as other developing nations. Higher education is offered at the T. A. Marryshow Community College and University Center which is a branch of the University of the West Indies. Recently, St. George's University began offering baccalaureate degree programs at its school of arts and sciences.

14 ● CULTURAL HERITAGE

Grenadian authors first came to public attention in the 1920s and 1930s. One of the nation's best-known contemporary writers is Wilfred Redhead, author of one-act plays and short stories. The visual arts reflect a high degree of African influence, and Grenada's artists are mostly self-taught. Canute Caliste, who lives on Carriacou, is one of the most prominent. His paintings show traditional life on the island, including Carnival bands, boat-launchings, dance festivals, and Big Drum performances. Many of his works include handprinted texts.

Another well-known artist is Elinus Cato, whose brightly painted renderings of town and rural life in Grenada have been exhibited in London and Washington, D.C. One of his paintings, *People at Work,* was presented to Queen Elizabeth II when she toured Grenada in 1985. The wooden frame for Cato's painting was crafted by renowned Grenadian woodcarver Stanley Coutain, one of the country's leading sculptors. Other recognized masters who transform the island's mahogany, teak, and cedar into works of art include Alexander Alexis and John Pivott.

15 ● EMPLOYMENT

Between 30 and 40 percent of Grenadians are employed by the government or work in a service industry job. About the same percentage work in agricultural jobs, often in the food processing industry. Typical food processing jobs include peeling nutmeg shells and sorting the seeds, and washing bananas and other produce.

The remainder of jobs in Grenada are mostly in construction and manufacturing. The country has a standard eight-hour work day. Grenada had a high rate of unemployment in the 1990s, with about one-fourth of the workforce unemployed.

16 ● SPORTS

Cricket is Grenada's most popular sport, and there is a large stadium at Queen's Park, outside the capital city of St. George's. Grenadians will start a game on any available flat area, even at the beach. Soccer, which they call football, is another favorite sport.

17 ● RECREATION

Calypso and steel drum music are both popular forms of entertainment in Grenada. The nation's television station, a division of Grenada Broadcasting Corporation (GBC), airs local news, sports, and covers local entertainment like Carnival, as well as broadcasting programs from the United States. There are also a number of privately owned and operated radio and televisions stations.

18 ● CRAFTS AND HOBBIES

The native music of Grenada is Big Drum music. Derived from the African call-and-response tradition, it consists of song, dance, and drumming. Although its roots are similar to those of calypso and reggae, it is more authenticly African. The Big Drum is actually a set of three drums, originally carved from trees and later made of rum kegs. The skin of male goats is used for the two side drums and the skin of a female goat for the middle one. The middle drum, which has pins threaded across its surface, produces the most complicated rhythms.

The singers are usually women, and the lead singer is called a "chantwell." The lyrics are usually satirical, making fun of governing figures or social customs. Dancing is performed inside a ring of people by dancers wearing full skirts and headdresses and who interact with the musicians. Big Drum music is performed on Carriacou at religious ceremonies including weddings and funerals.

Woven handicrafts include hats, purses, baskets, placemats, and other items made from straw, bamboo, and wicker. Salad bowls, kitchen utensils, furniture, and other items are made of mahogany and red cedar. Jewelry is made from black coral and turtle shells.

19 ● SOCIAL PROBLEMS

Poverty in Grenada increased in the 1980s due to the worldwide recession. Unemployment is high, and there was an increase in labor disputes in 1995.

20 ● BIBLIOGRAPHY

Cameron, Sarah, and Ben Box, ed. *Caribbean Islands Handbook.* Chicago: Passport Books, 1995.

Eisenberg, Joyce. *Grenada.* New York: Chelsea House, 1988.

Schoenhals, Kai P. *Grenada.* Santa Barbara, Calif.: Clio, 1990.

Sinclair, Norma. *Grenada: Isle of Spice.* New York: Macmillan, 1987.

U.S. Central Intelligence Agency. *World Fact Book.* Washington, D.C.: U.S. Government Printing Office, 1994.

Walton, Chelle Koster. *Caribbean Ways: A Cultural Guide.* Westwood, Mass.: Riverdale, 1993.

WEBSITES

World Away Travel. Grenada. [Online] Available http://www.worldaway.com/islands/grenada/home.html, 1998.

World Travel Guide. Grenada. [Online] Available http://www.wtgonline.com/country/gd/gen.html, 1998.

Guatemala

The people of Guatemala are called Guatemalans. The population has a larger proportion of Amerindians (native people) than any other country in Central America. Amerindians are estimated to be more than 50 percent of the total. Persons of mixed Amerindian and white ancestry, called *mestizos,* constitute about 42 percent. Blacks and *mulattoes* (mixed race) make up another 4 percent. The white population is estimated at about 1 percent.

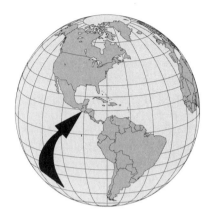

Guatemalans

PRONUNCIATION: gwah-teh-MAH-luhns
LOCATION: Guatemala
POPULATION: 10 million
LANGUAGE: Spanish; various Mayan languages; Carib
RELIGION: Roman Catholicism with ancient Mayan beliefs; Protestantism

1 ● INTRODUCTION

The Maya Indian civilization, thought to have evolved in about AD 100, established a number of city-states in what is now Guatemala. The largest of these, Tikal, covered ten square miles and included two hundred major stone structures, including high-rise temples and palaces. By AD 1000, however, the Mayan cities had been abandoned for reasons that are still not clear. The ancient Mayan civilization was very advanced and had a sophisticated knowledge of science, art, and astronomy.

After Spanish troops conquered Mexico in 1521, they moved south and controlled Guatemala. The area won its independence from Spain in 1821. Guatemala seceded from the resulting federation of the United Provinces of Central America in 1839.

During the 1800s, many of the native Indian people lost their land as it was developed into coffee and banana plantations.

In 1954 the government, considered to be pro-communist, was overthrown with help from the Central Intelligence Agency (CIA) of the United States. Leftist guerilla groups organized to oppose the military-dominated and U.S.-backed governments that subsequently ruled the country. Between 1960 and 1996, some one hundred thousand people lost their lives as a consequence of the fighting between the army and the guerrillas. Many other Guatemalans fled to Mexico and the United States.

2 ● LOCATION

Guatemala is slightly larger than Tennessee. It is bounded by Mexico to the north and west, by the Pacific Ocean to the south, and by Belize, Honduras, and El Salvador to the east. It had a population of about ten million people in 1994, making it the most populous country in Central America.

The southern half of the country is mountainous, with some thirty-three volcanic mountains. The northern third of the country consists of lowland rain forest.

The people are divided about evenly between Amerindians and *ladinos*. This word describes those who have adopted the Spanish language, dress, and lifestyle, regardless of race. Ladinos are usually *mestizos,* people of mixed Amerindian and European descent. About 1 percent of the population are of purely European ancestry. Blacks, along the Caribbean coast, make up another 1 percent of the population.

3 ● LANGUAGE

Spanish is the official language of Guatemala. There are twenty-one Mayan languages spoken in Guatemala, the principal ones being Quiché, Cakchiquel, Kekchí, and Mam. Carib is spoken along the Caribbean coast by the Garifunas, or Black Caribs, the descendants of fugitive slaves and Carib Indians.

4 ● FOLKLORE

Guatemala's folklore is based on Amerindian cultural beliefs as well as Spanish traditions. According to Quiché legend, for example, the first four humans were made of a corn paste into which the Heart of Heaven breathed life.

To assure good growing weather before spring planting, seeds are blessed at a special planting. The night before the planting, the men burn incense in the fields and sprinkle the ground with a brew made from fermented sugarcane. The women pray at home before lighted candles. In the morning the women go to the fields with food for the sowers and place their candles at points representing the four winds.

The shaman, or Mayan priest, is a man or woman who is able to bargain with the unknown forces that govern human destiny. Shamans are believed to be able to predict the future and cast spells. He or she is also a healer, *curandero,* who practices herbal medicine.

The Amerindians of Central America believe that every person has an animal counterpart called the *nagual* who shares his or her destiny.

Particular places serve as shrines for various gods. The people of Alta Verapaz, for example, are careful to leave kindling beside a hot spring for the god who boils the water. In return, it is hoped, the god will not cause fever by heating their blood.

5 ● RELIGION

About 67 to 80 percent of all Guatemalans are Roman Catholic. Within this faith, however, the Amerindians have preserved Mayan beliefs such as worshipping gods who control weather and crops. Jesus and Mary, for example, are identified with the Sun God and Moon Goddess. The cross is likened to the Four Winds of Heaven.

Cofradías (brotherhoods), rather than Catholic priests, lead a community's religious life. Fiestas are the major form of public worship and sometimes conform to the 260-day Mayan religious calendar. Routine attendance at church is difficult due to a shortage of priests

About 25 to 33 percent of the population are Protestant. Protestant missionaries have been active in Guatemala since the 1880s.

6 ● MAJOR HOLIDAYS

Pilgrims from all over Central America come to Esquipulas (January 15) to worship

Cory Langley

A vendor selling a multitude of fabrics.

at the shrine of the Black Christ. This icon is a sculpted balsam-wood image of Jesus. A temple housing the statue was completed in 1758. Also important is the pilgrimage on February second to the village church in Chiantla, famous for its silver image of the Virgin Mary.

The city of Antigua's Holy Week, in late March or early April, is the largest and most festive celebration in Latin America. It leads up to a Passion procession on the morning of Good Friday. *Chichicastenango* celebrates the day of St. Thomas (December 21) with a week-long fiesta that includes ritual dances of the Quiché people and the

Palo Volador in which costumed men dangle by ropes from a 60-foot-high (18-meter-high) maypole.

The Garifuna of the Caribbean celebrate their arrival in Guatemala with *Yuriman,* a simulation of the first farm plantings. The reenactment is held in Livingston each year from May 13 to 15. This festival is accompanied by singing, dancing, and hand-clapping. Like the other nations in Central America (except Panama) Independence day is celebrated on September 15, in honor of the region's declaration of independence from Spain in 1821.

7 ● RITES OF PASSAGE

In villages, both a midwife and a *brujo* (shaman or witch) attend a child's birth. The brujo prays for long life and good health and protection against the evil eye, which Guatemalans believe can be cast on children by a stranger or a blue-eyed person. A breech delivery or one with an umbilical cord around the neck is considered a sign of good fortune.

Baptism is the only church sacrament in which Amerindians normally partake. Amerindian babies are carried on their mother's back and are breast-fed. Children wear clothing identical to their parents and are put to work at an early age.

In conservative ladino society, boy-girl activities begin at about age fourteen, but real dating does not begin until later. A girl's fifteenth birthday marks her coming of age and calls for a special celebration. A boy's coming of age is recognized when he turns eighteen. A young man still asks a girl's father for her hand in marriage. Engagements of several years are common.

Among Indians, a youth's father may seek out a matchmaker to find a suitable bride for his son.

At Amerindian funerals a Mayan priest spins the coffin at the grave to fool the devil and point the deceased's spirit toward heaven. Yellow is the color of mourning, so yellow blossoms are hung in the form of a cross on the grave. Candles are lit. Food is placed at the head of the grave for the spirit of the departed.

8 ● RELATIONSHIPS

Both acquaintances and friends generally shake hands when meeting and parting. Men may pat each other on the back, and women often embrace and kiss each other on one or both cheeks. Family and friends often drop in on each other, especially on Sundays and holidays. These are brief, informal visits.

9 ● LIVING CONDITIONS

In 1990 it was estimated that the poorer half of the population was receiving only 60 percent of the daily minimum caloric requirements. The mortality rate for children up to age five is sixty-eight per one thousand children. Gastrointestinal and respiratory ailments take a heavy toll because of poor sanitation and poor nutrition. In rural areas, few people have access to drinkable water.

Because of rural overpopulation, the urban areas have swelled with migrants. Many of these people live in illegal squatter settlements, or shantytowns. Peasants mostly live in two-room, dirt-floor adobe structures. The roofs are made of palm leaves, straw, or tiles. Their small farm plots may be several hours' walk away.

10 ● FAMILY LIFE

Guatemala's families are very close. They are usually the only dependable source of support in a society where church and state are both weak. Among ladinos, the nuclear family of father, mother, and children is most common, but a moderately prosperous household often includes other relatives and servants or orphaned children. The extended family forms the basis of the Amerindian community. Amerindians rarely take mates

Cory Langley

Although Western-style dress is common, many Guatemalans prefer traditional clothing.

Traditional clothing is worn more frequently by women than men, and more often by poorer Guatemalans in general. Western-style dress is more frequent among people with a higher standing in their communities. Second-hand clothing from the United States, sold at bargain prices, has become popular. It is not uncommon to see traditional garments worn together with a college tee-shirt, for example.

12 ● FOOD

Guatemalan food is simple and not highly spiced. One exception is *pepian*, which is a thick, spicy soup made with tomatoes, onions, chiles, and ground pumpkin seeds. Corn tortillas, rice, beans, tamales, and plantains are the staples. Tortillas and black beans are served at every meal. A classic method of preparing meats is to cook them in water before adding sauce or seasonings. An essential seasoning of Mayan foods is squash seeds toasted and ground to a powder. Coffee is lighter and more watery than the brew Americans and Europeans are used to drinking.

13 ● EDUCATION

Education is free and compulsory between the ages of seven and thirteen. Enrollment is low in rural areas, however, and in 1991, one out of every five children was not enrolled in school. Many do not complete primary school because they must work to help their families. The adult literacy rate was fifty-five percent in 1990. Since school is taught in Spanish, Amerindians are at a disadvantage since Spanish is not their native language.

outside their own language group and village.

In spite of Guatemala's rapid population growth, children are greatly desired. In the late 1980s, six was the average number of children born by a woman.

11 ● CLOTHING

The clothing of many ladinos is similar to that of modern Westerners. Almost every Amerindian community, however, has its own style of dress. In fact, a person's village can be identified by the design of his or her clothes.

Six years of secondary school can lead either to university education or specialized training. There are six universities. The largest of these is the State University of San Carlos, in Guatemala City. The constitution guarantees it autonomy and 5 percent of the national budget. The university, which does not charge tuition, has more than fifty thousand students. Many students must work part-time while pursuing their studies.

14 ● CULTURAL HERITAGE

Native music developed from a blend of Spanish and Amerindian influences. Guatemala is better known for its traditional dances. These dances are really musical dramas that, through the use of costumes and masks, recall historical events. The dances are performed at fiestas in honor of the local saint. The Deer Dance symbolizes the struggle between humans and animals. The Dance of the Conquest recalls the victory of the Spanish over the Amerindians.

Tikal and other monumental sites are testimony to the architectural accomplishments of the Maya. The Spanish influence can be found in colonial-era churches, sculptures, and paintings. Guatemala's best-known twentieth-century painter is Carlos Mérida.

The Maya had the most advanced system of writing in the Americas. A Spanish priest, Francisco Ximénez, translated the rarest and most sacred book of the Quiché, the *Popol Vuh,* in 1680. This work is a treasure-trove of Mayan beliefs and practices.

Rafael Landival, a Jesuit, wrote the poem *Rusticatio Mexicana* while in exile in Italy. This was the outstanding Guatemalan work of the colonial era. The novelist and poet Miguel Ángel Asturias received the Nobel Prize for literature in 1967.

15 ● EMPLOYMENT

Although the country's constitution forbids employment of children under the age of fourteen, younger children are employed. Usually they work in family enterprises and in agriculture. Ladinos tend to become shopkeepers, government employees, or laborers in private industries. The *fincas,* or large plantations, employ both ladinos and Amerindians for seasonal labor during the harvest. A large part of the population continues to farm small plots. Many such farmers supplement their income with the sale of handicrafts and seasonal plantation work.

Many migrants to the cities are unable to find employment and so, take to street vending. It was estimated in 1992 that 46 percent of the labor force was unemployed or underemployed. The minimum wage was less than three dollars a day in 1994.

16 ● SPORTS

Football (called soccer in the United States) is a national passion, played even in the most traditional and remote villages. Guatemala City has the largest soccer stadium in Central America.

17 ● RECREATION

Fiestas continue to provide popular entertainment and to reflect much of the creative life of the people. They all include music and dance, eating and drinking, and fireworks. Movies are found only in the major cities and mostly show U.S. films that are dubbed or subtitled in Spanish. Television includes dubbed U.S. programs and variety shows and *telenovelas* (soap operas) imported from Mexico and Venezuela.

Guatemala is the heartland of marimba music. Almost every town has a marimba orchestra, which includes the accompaniment of a brass band. No wedding is complete without marimba music. Amerindians perform other music for their rites, and use pre-conquest drums and flutes.

18 ● CRAFTS AND HOBBIES

Guatemala's handspun and woven textiles are among the finest in the world. Made by highland Amerindians, they display brilliant colors and intricate designs, both in the form of raw cloth and finished garments. Cotton, wool, and silk are the traditional fibers for clothing, although acrylics have been introduced. Blankets and rugs are also made from these fibers. Hats, mats, hammocks, and baskets are made with different types of cane and reed as well as fibers from the maguey cactus.

Ceramics are produced by molding clay by hand and using natural clays and dyes, as was done before the European conquest. They are also made with the potter's wheel as well as glazes and enamels introduced from Spain. Jade jewelry dates from ancient times. Woodcrafted products include traditional masks, carved squash gourds, and colonial-style doors and furniture.

19 ● SOCIAL PROBLEMS

About 2 percent of the population owns about 70 percent of the useful land. About two-thirds of the original forest cover has been destroyed, and about 30 percent of the land is eroded or seriously damaged. Only one-third of the population has regular access to health services.

Domestic violence occurs but receives little attention. The labor code makes legal strikes difficult, and women, usually found in low-wage jobs, are paid significantly less than are men.

20 ● BIBLIOGRAPHY

Brill, M., and H. Targ. *Guatemala.* Chicago: Children's Press, 1993.

Gall, Timothy, and Susan Gall, eds. *Worldmark Encyclopedia of the Nations.* 8th ed. Detroit: Gale Research, 1995.

Glassman, Paul. *Guatemala Guide.* Moscow, Vt.: Passport Press, 1978.

Guatemala in Pictures. Minneapolis, Minn.: Lerner Publications Co., 1987.

Woodward, Ralph Lee. *Guatemala.* Santa Barbara, Calif.: Clio, 1992.

Wright, Ronald. *Time Among the Maya.* New York: Weidenfeld & Nicolson, 1989.

WEBSITES

Green Arrow Advertising. [Online] Available http://www.greenarrow.com/guatemal/guatemal.htm, 1998.

World Travel Guide. Guatemala. [Online] Available http://www.wtgonline.com/country/gt/gen.html, 1998.

Guinea

The people of Guinea are called Guineans. There are about twenty-four ethnic groups. The three largest are the Fulani (profiled here), the Malinké, and the Susu. For more information on the Malinké, see the chapter on Liberia in Volume 5.

Guineans

PRONUNCIATION: GHIN-ee-uhns

LOCATION: Guinea

POPULATION: 6–7 million, another 2 million living abroad

LANGUAGE: French; Pulaar (Fulfulde); Susu; thirty African languages

RELIGION: Islam; Christianity; traditional religions

1 ● INTRODUCTION

People have lived in the land now known as Guinea since the Stone Age. The Malinkes of Upper Guinea trace their ancestry to the founders of the great Mali Empire (AD 1200–1350).

Guinea's modern political boundaries were drawn by European colonists, especially the French, during the 1880s. In 1993, the first presidential elections in Guinea's history involving more than one party were held. However, the widespread evidence of cheating raised questions about the winner's right to rule.

2 ● LOCATION

Guinea is somewhat smaller than the state of Oregon. It shares borders with Guinea-Bissau and Senegal to the north, with Mali and Côte d'Ivoire to the east, and with Liberia and Sierra Leone to the south. Guinea's population is young—44 percent of its people are fourteen years old or younger—but it is growing more slowly than that of most African countries. Estimates place the total population between six and seven million. Another two million Guineans live outside the country. The population density is highest in the capital, Conakry.

To the east live the Fulani (also known as the Peul), who, with 36 percent of the total population, are considered the largest ethnic group in the country. The second largest group, the Malinke, live in eastern Guinea. The third largest group, the Susu, are con-

GUINEANS

centrated in the west and along the coast in the areas around Conakry.

3 ● LANGUAGE

The peoples of Guinea speak thirty languages, including the colonial language, French. French is used widely in government and is the language of instruction in high schools and universities. Other than French, the language in widest use is Pulaar (Fulfulde), which is spoken by the largest ethnic group, the Fulani. Susu is gaining speakers because it is the main language of the capital city.

4 ● FOLKLORE

Each ethnic group has its own myths, legends, and folktales.

5 ● RELIGION

The greatest number of Guineans (80 percent) are Muslims (followers of Islam). Christians, mainly Catholics, make up 10 percent of the population. Followers of traditional religions make up the rest. Many Guineans rely on their traditional spirit beliefs and rely on marabouts (dervishes believed to have supernatural powers) and fetishes (superstitious objects) in times of trouble. The region that is least Islamic is the Forest Region, where men continue to practice secret rituals in the "sacred forest." The coastal region has the largest number of Christians. Missionary work has been strongest in that region since the nineteenth century.

6 ● MAJOR HOLIDAYS

Besides the month-long Ramadan fast, one of the most important holidays in the country is the Muslim feast of *Tabaski*. It celebrates the story of God's sparing Abraham's son, Isaac. He was saved when God provided a lamb for sacrifice. At the time of this feast, trucks bring thousands of sheep and goats from the country to the capital city for sale. By Islamic custom, butchers must slaughter animals by cutting the throat.

On August 17, people mark the day in 1977 when women protested against the market police and the laws that forbade private business. The head of State Sékou Touré (1922–84) gave in to the demands and abolished the restrictions.

7 ● RITES OF PASSAGE

Most Guineans combine Islam with traditional beliefs in everyday life and ceremonies. For example, in both religions, circumcision is a necessary rite. In Islam, it symbolizes purification, while in traditional beliefs it has a supernatural connection.

Rites of passage remain important to Guineans of all ethnic groups and are times for family and community celebration. At baptism, the father whispers the baby's name into its ear so that the child alone knows its name.

Weddings, too, are occasions for celebration. After the ceremony at the mosque, a couple also has a civil ceremony at a government office.

Muslims bury their dead on the day after death and hold eulogy ceremonies forty days after death. At Malinke ceremonies, family and friends gather to pray and recite the Koran (sacred text of Islam). Mourners help the family pay expenses by giving offerings to the prayer leaders. They throw wadded-up paper money into the circle where the prayer reciters sit.

Consulate, Republic of Guinea

Several families share a common outdoor source of water.

8 ● RELATIONSHIPS

Greetings are an important part of everyday life. Guineans call this custom *salaam alekum*, meaning offering the "peace of God." In greetings, people ask each other questions about the well-being of their families. People touch their right hand to their heart to show respect, sincerity, and thanks to God. Men and women usually do not shake hands with the opposite sex. Friends who have not seen each other recently place their hands on the other's shoulders and embrace, touching cheeks three times.

In cities and towns, Western-style dating is common. In rural areas, a young man might visit a fiancée at her home. Friends go out together to parties in towns or meet at community gatherings in the villages. Visiting is usually unplanned and it is customary to offer a glass of water to a visitor.

9 ● LIVING CONDITIONS

Because health care is not well developed and sanitation (disposal of wastes) is poor, life expectancy at birth is forty-five years. Guinea's infant mortality rate (percentage of babies who die) is extremely high. In 1996, figures showed that about 13 percent

Houses are round or rectangular with thatched roofs.

of newborn babies would not live to reach their first birthday.

In rural areas, houses usually are made of mud brick in round or rectangular form with thatched roofs. People who can afford sturdier structures build with concrete and iron roofing. Indoor running water is not common, even in the cities. Several city families often share a common standpipe outdoors.

Toilets are usually in the form of a dry pit. In the 1990s, up to one-third of households in Conakry had no toilet facilities. Because garbage collection in the capital is not efficient, enormous trash piles litter the streets. Electricity is available irregularly in Conakry. When electricity is available, city neighborhoods receive it in six-hour shifts beginning at 6:00 PM.

10 ● FAMILY LIFE

Men may have up to four wives by Muslim law. Among the Peul, it is not unusual to find men aged sixty and over who have wives in their teens. Their wives may be younger than their children–and even their grandchildren. Such families often number well over twenty children, with ages varying by forty or more years. Wives of the same husband usually live in separate houses, apart from each other, or in separate huts within the same compound. Children refer to their "stepmothers" as co-mothers (*co-mères*).

11 ● CLOTHING

Guineans have made an art form of *boubous*, garments which they slip over their heads and wear over matching pants. The color and quality vary according to the owner's wealth. Women's outfits may be white or a single bright color. They are embroidered with thread in all colors.

Both men's and women's boubous are open at the side, both for style and to allow air circulation in hot and humid climates. Women usually wear matching turbans or head scarves, while men often wear Muslim skullcaps or stylish white or blue wool caps. Guineans usually reserve these for special occasions or Friday prayers, as the complete outfit costs a few hundred dollars.

European shirts and pants are popular with women, but it not common to see men in Western suits and ties.

12 ● FOOD

Local Guinean restaurants offer three types of dishes: greens, peanut dishes, and meat stews. White rice almost always accompanies the stew. Some coastal people enjoy palm nut stew, which is eaten like soup. Most Guineans eat these for the midday meal between 10:00 AM and 1:00 PM. At night, families eat leftovers or may have porridge, bread, and tea.

Ethnic groups usually have their own specialties. The Peul, for example, are fond of thick, sour milk served over fine grain called *fonio*. For supper, the Susu prepare *achecké*, finely grated manioc cooked briefly in oil and eaten with grilled fish or chicken.

People drink a beverage similar to coffee, which comes from a plentiful forest plant. Palm wine is also a favorite drink. Citrus fruits, pineapples, bananas, and mangoes are common. Guinea's variable climate allows for oranges year-round.

Some food taboos do exist. Certain coastal peoples do not eat meat from monkeys because they believe that monkeys are people who are being punished for not observing Muslim Friday prayers. Most Muslims do not eat pork.

13 ● EDUCATION

Literacy rates (the percentage of the people who can read and write) are improving, but in the 1990s as much as 80 percent of the population still was illiterate in French. Parents want their children to attend school. But because so many graduates are unemployed, people question the usefulness of schooling.

In the rural areas, parents often need extra help in the fields or with household chores. School fees are high for many families, and sometimes children must walk up to six miles to attend school.

14 ● CULTURAL HERITAGE

Guineans have a rich cultural heritage. Performances of music and dance mark special occasions and holidays. Peul musicians play

Some children walk as far as six miles to attend school. Here, students are eager to answer a question asked by their teacher.

handcrafted flutes, drums, and string instruments, and they use calabashes (gourds) to beat out rhythms. In Malinke traditional music, men drum and play *balafons* (xylophones made from wood and gourds). Women wearing elaborate boubous dance with graceful arm movements, suggesting butterflies.

Drumming is a major Guinean art form. Apprentices learn from masters over a period of years. During Sékou Touré's time, the government supported the arts. Guineans produced some of Africa's finest theater and folklore ballets in international competitions.

Guineans produce fine literature. Malinke and Peul traditional *griots*, or praise-singers, are poets who recite and pass on past traditions through story and song. Authors such as the Malinke Camara Laye have produced writings of international acclaim in French. His novel, *The African Child (L'Enfant Noir)*, tells of a child growing up in the Malinke homeland. The child's father is a goldsmith, and he learns about spirits and taboos from his parents. The novel is often used in French and literature classes at American universities.

15 ● EMPLOYMENT

Since economic reforms began in 1984, more than 50,000 Guineans have lost civil-service (government) jobs. Members of more than ten graduating classes from the university are looking for work. Guinea's economy depends on the mining and exporting of bauxite (aluminum ore) for 85 percent of its foreign earnings. But very little of the ore is processed in the country.

About 80 percent of the population works in subsistence or plantation farming, which accounts for only 24 percent of the gross domestic product.

16 ● SPORTS

Guineans are avid players of football (what Americans call soccer). During the 1970s, Guinea produced some of Africa's best teams. In the towns, children and young men play soccer wherever space allows. In Conakry, this means placing four large rocks as goal posts in the street. Since few people own cars, streets make convenient playing fields.

Basketball is also popular, and schools arrange competitions.

Girls play versions of hopscotch.

17 ● RECREATION

Few Guineans have television sets, and those who do must cope with failures of electric power. When the power is on, neighbors gather on the sidewalk to watch popular regional theater productions broadcast on Guinea's government TV station.

Guineans also go to the movies and to popular musical performances. The discos play a variety of Guinean, Cuban, Zairian, Senegalese, and American music.

Teenagers in rural areas are no longer shut off from international popular culture. It is becoming more common to find electri-cacal generators and satellite dishes in distant villages, where a night's entertainment can be had for a small admission fee.

18 ● CRAFTS AND HOBBIES

Besides modern art made for tourists, Guineans still produce significant folk art and crafts. Some ethnic groups specialize in painting pottery, masks, house walls, and tombs.

For five hundred years, the Kissi people have been making stone statuettes for ceremonial rituals and for communicating with ancestors.

The Baga people on the coast make wooden busts of females, the *Nimba*. These have become the national symbol of Guinean art.

19 ● SOCIAL PROBLEMS

After Guinea became an independent nation in 1958, a harsh military government took power. The country's first decades of independence have been characterized by government persecution, torture, and starvation of thousands of political prisoners. Changes in the political system are improving civil and human rights. Still, some abuses continue.

Cattle theft in the Fouta Djallon mountainous region and increased armed burglary in the capital are two types of social problems that disturb Guineans. Many people blame rising crime in the cities on Sierra Leonean and Liberian refugees. They accuse them of engaging in illegal trade in drugs and arms.

Guineans must also improve sanitation and health in the cities, ease overcrowding, and create jobs for unemployed people.

20 ● BIBLIOGRAPHY

Africa on File. New York: Facts on File, 1995.
Nelson, Harold D. et al, ed. *Area Handbook for Guinea.* Washington, D. C.: American University, 1975.

WEBSITES
World Travel Guide. Guinea. [Online] Available http://www.wtgonline.com/country/gn/gen.html, 1998.

Fulani

PRONUNCIATION: foo-LAH-nee
ALTERNATE NAMES: Fulbe; Peuls
LOCATION: From the western part of West Africa (Senegambia) to Chad in the east (some groups reaching as far as the Nile river in the countries of Sudan and Ethiopia); largest concentrations in Nigeria, Senegal, and Guinea
POPULATION: More than 6 million
LANGUAGE: Fulfulde; Arabic; French; English
RELIGION: Islam

1 ● INTRODUCTION

The Fulani peoples (also known as *Fulbe* or *Peuls*) live in West Africa. They are among the most widely dispersed and culturally diverse peoples in all of Africa. Many Fulani trace their beginnings back one thou-

sand years to the Senegambia area. By the eighteenth century some had migrated as far east as the Niger and Benue Rivers (now in Nigeria). In the eighteenth and nineteenth centuries, some Fulani populations adopted the Islamic religion and initiated *jihads* (holy wars) in several parts of West Africa.

Today, one finds both nomadic, pastoral Fulani *(mbororo'en)* and settled Fulani *(Fulbe wuro).* The pastoral Fulani (full-time cattle keepers) move about with their cattle for much of the year. In contrast, the settled Fulani live permanently in villages and cities. Although both groups share a common language and origin, they regard themselves as only distantly related.

2 ● LOCATION

The largest concentrations of Fulani are in the countries of Nigeria, Senegal, and Guinea. In these countries, Fulani became the ruling class and intermarried with the local populations. The total Fulani population numbers more than 6 million.

3 ● LANGUAGE

The language of the Fulani is known as Fulfulde (or Fula or Pulaar). There are at least five major dialects: Futa Toro, Futa Jallon, and Masina in the west and Central Nigeria; and Sokoto and Adamawa in the east. Although they have similarities in grammar and vocabulary, communication among Fulani from different regions is difficult. As Muslims, many Fulani can read and write Arabic.

An example of a saying in Fulfulde is *Tid'd'o yod'ad'd'o* (Work hard and succeed). An example of a Fulani proverb is:

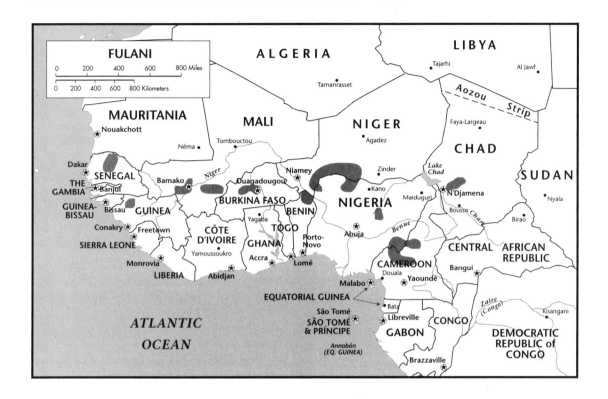

Hab'b'ere buri ginawol (Actions should be judged according to intention).

4 ● FOLKLORE

Despite the importance of Islam, some modern-day Fulani traditions recount the pre-Islamic origin of their people. These traditions state that cattle, as well as the first Fulani family, emerged from a river. They began migrating across Africa and gave birth to children who founded the various Fulani groups.

Folktales *(taali)* are popular among all Fulani. Children are told bedtime stories that usually have a moral. Among the nomadic Fulani, there are many stories pertaining to their cattle and migrations. All Fulani tell animal tales, recounting the adventures of squirrels, snakes, hyenas, and rabbits, some of which are extremely clever.

5 ● RELIGION

As Muslims, the Fulani observe the standard Islamic religious practices. They pray five times a day, learn to recite the holy scriptures *(Qur'an,* or Koran*)* by heart, and give alms to the needy. For one month each year (Ramadan) they fast in the daytime. And at least once in their lifetime, they make a pilgrimage *(hajj)* to the Islamic holy land in Mecca. The most important duty is to declare one's true faith in Islam and believe that Muhammad was a prophet sent by Allah (God).

6 ● MAJOR HOLIDAYS

All Fulani participate in Islamic holidays *(Id)*. The most important are the feast after the fasting period (Ramadan) and the feast celebrating the birth of the Prophet Muhammad. On these days, people pray in thanksgiving to Allah, visit their relatives, prepare special meals, and exchange gifts such as gowns or cloth.

7 ● RITES OF PASSAGE

Shortly after a child is born, a naming ceremony is held, following Islamic law and practice. Around the age of seven, boys are circumcised, followed by a small ceremony or gathering in their household. Shortly after this time, they begin performing herding or farming activities, sometimes on their own. At this age, girls help their mothers.

Girls are usually betrothed in marriage during their early to mid-teens. Boys remain *sukaa'be* (handsome young men) until around the age of twenty. At that time, they start a herd or obtain a farm, and marry. There are ceremonies to prepare the bride and groom for marriage. Afterward, their families sign a marriage contract under Islam. By middle age, a man may be known as a *ndottijo* (elder, old man) who has acquired wisdom over the years.

8 ● RELATIONSHIPS

All Fulani have an elaborate code for interacting among themselves and with other people. The code, known as *Pulaaku*, decrees *semteende* (modesty), *munyal* (patience), and *hakkiilo* (common sense). All of these virtues must be practiced in public, among one's in-laws, and with one's spouse. Islam, which also requires modesty and reserve, has tended to reinforce this code.

9 ● LIVING CONDITIONS

Among the nomadic Fulani, life can be extremely harsh. They often live in small, temporary camps. These can be quickly dismantled as they move in search of pasture and water for their herds. Because of the settlements' distance from towns, modern health care is not readily available.

Fulani have also settled in towns and cities. In the cities they usually reside in large family houses or compounds.

10 ● FAMILY LIFE

Among the Fulani, the family includes one's immediate kin and extended family, all of whom are all treated as close kin. In rural areas, these groups tend to live close together and join in work efforts. In the towns and cities, they tend to be more widely dispersed. Each kin group *(lenyol)* normally recognizes a common male ancestor who lived several generations ago and founded the family.

Male family members usually choose spouses for their children. Matches are generally made between relatives (particularly cousins) and social equals. This practice helps keep wealth (cattle and land) in the family. Polygyny (multiple wives) is not uncommon in Fulani society. A man's wives all help with domestic work and can bear him many children.

11 ● CLOTHING

Dress codes and styles vary greatly. In general, however, married men and women follow the Islamic dress code, which prescribes modesty. The men wear large gowns, trousers, and caps. Women wear wraps and blouses. Married Muslim women wear veils when they leave their household.

Nomadic Fulani also wear Islamic dress, but it is not as elaborate. The women do not wear veils. Younger men and women adorn themselves with jewelry and headdresses, and they braid their hair.

12 ● FOOD

The Fulani diet usually includes milk products such as yogurt, milk, and butter. Each morning they drink milk or gruel *(gari)* made with sorghum. Their main meals consist of a heavy porridge *(nyiiri)* made of flour from such grains as millet, sorghum, or corn. They eat it with soup *(takai, haako)* made from tomatoes, onions, spices, peppers, and other vegetables.

13 ● EDUCATION

All Fulani adults and older children help educate the younger children through scoldings, sayings and proverbs, and stories. Children also learn through imitation. In many communities, children from about the age of six attend Islamic *(Koranic)* school. Here they study, recite the scriptures, and learn about the practices, teachings, and morals of Islam. Nowadays, Fulani children in towns and cities attend primary and secondary schools. Some eventually enroll in universities.

[inset phto 1 from guinea book. Students in Guinea begin to attend school at around age six. Credit note: Consulate, Republic of Guinea]

It is more difficult for the children of nomadic families to attend school because they are often on the move.

14 ● CULTURE

Among the Fulani, music and art are part of daily life. Work music is sung and played on drums and flutes. Court music (drumming, horns, flutes) and praise-singing are popular in towns, especially during festivals. Praise-singers tell about a community's history and its leaders and other prominent individuals. Religious singers may cite Islamic scriptures.

Most commonly, decorative art occurs in the form of architecture, or in the form of personal adornments such as jewelry, hats, and clothing.

15 ● EMPLOYMENT

All Fulani communities have a strict division of labor according to age and sex. Men tend the cattle, work in the fields, or have formal employment in the city. Many men are either full- or part-time Islamic scholars or teachers. In the settled communities, Fulani men may work in government, education, business, or, to a lesser extent, as traders.

Women are responsible for managing the household (cooking, cleaning) and caring for the children. Even in the towns, most married women are housewives, but a few work as teachers, nurses, or secretaries.

16 ● SPORTS

Among the nomadic Fulani, young men participate in a kind of sport known as *sharro*. This is a test of bravery in which young men lash each other to the point of utmost endurance. This practice is most common as men enter manhood. However, some continue it until they become elders.

Among the settled Fulani, there is a variety of traditional local sports and games, including wrestling and boxing. Western sports such as soccer and track and field are now found in communities and schools.

17 ● RECREATION

Fulani children participate in various kinds of dances. Some are performed for their closest friends and kin, and some in the marketplace. Among the settled people, musicians and praise-singers perform at festivities such as weddings, naming ceremonies, and Islamic holidays. Today, most Fulani own radios and enjoy Western music. Among the settled Fulani, one commonly finds stereos, televisions, and VCRs.

18 ● CRAFTS AND HOBBIES

In their spare time, Fulani women make handicrafts including engraved gourds, weavings, knitting, and baskets. Fulani men are less involved in the production of crafts such as pottery, iron-working, and dyeing than some neighboring peoples. They believe these activities may violate their code of conduct (*Pulaaku*) and bring shame upon them.

19 ● SOCIAL PROBLEMS

The pastoral Fulani are currently facing many problems. Drought often reduces their water supply and pasture, and disease may also strike the herds. Increasingly, there is less land available for herding, and conflicts with settled people have increased. Present-day governments are also curtailing the Fulanis' movements or trying to force them to settle down.

20 ● BIBLIOGRAPHY

Hopen, C. E. *Pastoral Fulbe Family in Gwandu.* London: Oxford University Press, 1958.

Reisman, Paul. *Freedom in Fulani Social Life.* Chicago: University of Chicago Press, 1977.

Stenning, Derrick. *Savanna Nomads.* London: Oxford University Press, 1959.

WEBSITES

World Travel Guide. Guinea. [Online] Available http:/www.wtgonline.com/country/gn/gen.html, 1998.

Guyana

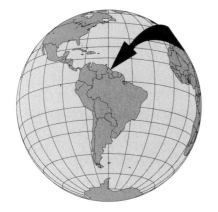

The people of Guyana are called Guyanans. A little more than half of the population is of Asian Indian descent. About 43 percent are Afro-Guyanans, of African descent. There are also Amerindians (native people), Chinese, Portuguese, and other Europeans.

Guyanans

PRONUNCIATION: ghuy-AHN-uhns
ALTERNATE NAMES: Guyanese
LOCATION: Guyana
POPULATION: 800,000
LANGUAGE: English (official); Creole patois; Hindi; Urdu
RELIGION: Hinduism; Christianity; Islam; native animism

1 ● INTRODUCTION

Guyana's official name is Cooperative Republic of Guyana. It is an independent republic and a member of the British Commonwealth. It is located in the northeast corner of South America, north of Brazil and east of Venezuela. Guyana's name comes from the Amerindian (native people) word *guiana,* "land of waters." During the sixteenth and seventeenth centuries, the great European colonial powers fought to claim the land for their sugarcane plantations. The region changed hands many times, mostly as a result of wars between the British and the French. After the 1815

Treaty of Vienna, it remained under British control.

Guyana became independent from Britain in 1966. Politically, the nation has moved on a steady course toward socialism since that time. Ties with the West have been strengthened since the death of its first prime minister, Forbes Burnham, in 1985.

2 ● LOCATION

Guyana covers 83,000 square miles (215,000 square kilometers) with a coastline that is 285 miles (459 kilometers) long. Most of the country's population of about 800,000 people live on the narrow coastal strip along the Atlantic coast. Much of this land has been reclaimed from the sea by a series of canals and dikes. Inland is a huge plateau that forms most of the country's center.

Guyana's people originally came from various parts of the British Empire. Asian Indians are the largest racial group, accounting for a little more than half of the population. They were originally brought to

GUYANANS

0   250   500   750 Miles

0   250   500   750 Kilometers

TRINIDAD AND TOBAGO

ATLANTIC OCEAN

Caracas

Orinoco •Ciudad Guayana

VENEZUELA

GUYANA ★Georgetown
              ★Paramaribo

SURINAME Cayenne
              French Guiana (FRANCE)

Negro   Macapá

Amazon   •Belém

Manaus   •Santarém

Amazon

Tocantins

Pôrto Velho   **BRAZIL**

Rio Branco

4 ● FOLKLORE

Much of Guyanan folklore springs from the religious and ethnic backgrounds of its diverse population. Hindus identify with their cultural heroes, such as Rama, Krishna, and Mahavira. In fact, many of them give their children names based on characters from the great epic stories of India.

Many Guyanan folktales are based on African traditions. They emphasize the unity between animals—including humans—and nature, and also the unity between the living and the dead.

5 ● RELIGION

About one-half of the population are Hindu, roughly one-fourth are Christian (Anglican or Roman Catholic), and a smaller number are Muslim. Many Guyanans of Indian descent accept baptism and membership in Christian churches but continue to participate in Hindu rituals. Traditional animistic (belief in spirits in nature) religions are still practiced by the Amerindian peoples. Some members of Christian groups also practice traditional African religions such as *winti,* literally meaning "wind." This traditional and secret religion of West African origin recognizes a multitude of gods and ghosts.

6 ● MAJOR HOLIDAYS

Holiday festivities—Hindu, Muslim, and Christian—are also recreational events in Guyana. Major holidays include Christmas (December 24), the end of Ramadan (the Muslim month of fasting), and the Hindu New Year known as Phagwah (early March). Phagwah is a joyous celebration involving the energetic throwing of perfume

Guyana as indentured workers (workers contracted to work for a specific length of time) in the 1800s. They replaced Afro-Guyanan slaves when slavery was abolished in 1804. A small number of Amerindians still live in the inland forest regions. The Afro-Guyanans, about 43 percent of the population, are descendants of the African slaves who were brought to work the sugarcane plantations. Portuguese, Chinese, Amerindians, and other Europeans make up the remainder of the population.

3 ● LANGUAGE

Guyana is the only South American country to have English as its official and principal language. But a Creole patois, a mixed-language dialect, is spoken in the country. Hindi and Urdu are also heard among older Asian Indians.

Juliette Adams

Guyanan women mark a special occasion.

and water. Easter Monday (March or April) is a traditional day for flying kites. On Republic Day (February 23), the president reports to the nation, and there is marching in the streets.

7 ● RITES OF PASSAGE

Baptism is common, even among Guyanans of Indian descent. Many attend Christian churches and still participate in Hindu rituals. In their homes, Hindus celebrate special occasions like birthdays and anniversaries with religious ceremonies called Pujas.

Christians as well as Hindus come from all over the country to participate in the seven-day festival, Ramayana Yajma. Brahmins, members of the Hindu religion, read and explain an epic poem called the *Ramayana*. This poem recounts the life of Rama, a Hindu heir who is exiled in the forest for fourteen years.

Many Afro-Guyanese couples consider themselves married without a civil license or church ceremony.

8 ● RELATIONSHIPS

Anyone paying a visit to a friend's home is expected to call on everyone else they know in that neighborhood. Not to do so is considered extremely rude. Hospitality is very

Recipe

Laoo Dal
(Red Lentils)

Ingredients

2 Tablespoons oil
1 onion, chopped
½ teaspoon ground turmeric
¼ teaspoon ground cumin
1 bay leaf
1 cup red lentils
½ teaspoon salt
1 teaspoon sugar
2 cups water
2 cups zucchini, cut into ¼-inch slices

Directions

1. Heat oil in a large saucepan.
2. Add onion, turmeric, cumin, and bay leaf and fry until onion begins to soften, about 3 minutes.
3. Add lentils, salt, sugar, and water. Bring mixture to a boil.
4. Reduce heat and cover. Simmer 15 minutes.
5. Add zucchini slices. Cover and continue simmering until all the liquid is absorbed and lentils and zucchini are soft. Stir every 2 or 3 minutes. Serve with rice.

Adapted from Schlabach, Joetta Handrich. *Extending the Table: a World Community Cookbook.* Scottdale, Penn.: Herald Press, 1991, p. 157.

special religious role in their Guyanan communities. Part of this special role is to interpret their sacred scriptures.

9 ● LIVING CONDITIONS

Guyana is one of the world's poorest countries. Food shortages have created widespread malnutrition. Diseases such as beriberi and malaria have become more common as problems with sanitation have increased.

About one-fourth of the people live in the capital of Georgetown. Most people live in small villages and towns along the coast. Their houses are built of wood with tin roofs, and are built on stilts that are eight or ten feet (about three meters) off the ground to avoid damage from floods.

10 ● FAMILY LIFE.

Family relationships differ among Guyana's different ethnic groups. The mother- and grandmother-dominated family is common among the Afro-Guyanans. The Asian Indian family is father-oriented. In the African community, bearing children out of wedlock is not viewed with disapproval. In African communities, households range from the nuclear family of parents and their children to a multigenerational extended family.

Many Asian Indian couples first live in an extended family with the husband's parents. The reason for this is a belief that it is the duty of the parents to help the young couple during the first years of marriage. After six or seven years, the son will set up his own household with his wife and children.

important in Guyana, and no visit is complete without the offer of a meal or snack.

Asian Indians in Guyana have not maintained the rigid caste (class) system that governs social relations in India. However, the Brahmins (a sacred caste) do retain a

11 ● CLOTHING

A skirt and blouse is the popular form of clothing for women. The sari, a traditional Indian garment, is increasing in popularity among Hindu women. Hindu men wear a type of shirt called a *kurta* and trousers called *dhoti*.

12 ● FOOD

A tasty Amerindian dish, called the pepper pot, is a spicy stew that is a typical Guyanese meal. The main ingredient is cassava. Farina, a coarse gravel-like flour made from cassava, is boiled with sun-dried beef to make a dish known as *tasso*. It is eaten by the ranchers who live in the interior of the country.

Dal, of Asian Indian origin, is also a popular meal throughout Guyana. It is a dish of lentil beans cooked in oil, often flavored with a mixture of spices such as cinnamon, pepper, and garlic.

Juliette Adams

A schoolgirl in the starters preschool program poses in her St. Margaret's School uniform.

13 ● EDUCATION

Children receive free, compulsory (required) education. There are also programs for preschool children. Due to economic problems, the school buildings have deteriorated, and books and supplies are limited. The literacy rate (proportion of the population able to read and write), however, is very high at 95 to 98 percent among adults. Educated Guyanans sometimes live outside of their own country, mostly in London or New York. The principal university is the University of Georgetown in the eastern part of the capital city.

14 ● CULTURAL HERITAGE

Guyana still bears the imprint of its colonial heritage in the continuing value placed on European culture. The nation's Amerindian heritage is also an important element in its cultural life. Amerindian artifacts are featured in museum displays, and their culture inspires local music and painting.

Amerindian groups include the Caribs, the Arawaks, and the Warraus. One of the mysterious aspects of Guyanese culture are the hieroglyphics known as the *timchri* which are scattered on the rocks in the interior of the country. They have not yet been deciphered but seem to be the artifacts of an advanced civilization.

The best-known work of literature is E. R. Braithwaite's novel, *To Sir With Love,* about a black teacher in an all-white London secondary school. It was made into a well-known movie.

15 ● EMPLOYMENT

The state-controlled sugar enterprise, Guysuco, employs more Guyanans than any other industry. Asian Indians and their families control most small businesses, such as small farms and shops. Africans dominate the government sector. Hindus are entering the legal and medical professions in increasing numbers. Wages are very low and many people depend on money sent by relatives overseas to survive. Many people also work at more than one job.

16 ● SPORTS

The Guyanans share a love of cricket as do other English-speaking Caribbean countries. Cricket in Guyana, however, is very different from the game played in England. Cricket in Guyana reflects the country's self-esteem and can be very emotional, like the bullfight is to Spain. Guyana hosts International Test Cricket Matches in Georgetown, competing against other countries in the British Commonwealth. In the villages outside Georgetown, street cricket is played with a sponge ball and the pitch (playing field) is a coconut mat laid out in a field.

17 ● RECREATION

Popular culture is as mixed as the various ethnic groups who live in Guyana. George-

town offers a wide mix of museums and art galleries. For the young people there are discos. One type of music popular throughout Guyana is "chutney," a hot, spicy mixture of traditional Hindu music and rock music. Movies play a large part in the lives of older people. Imported films from India reconnect the Hindus with their cultural roots.

18 ● CRAFTS AND HOBBIES

Many folk arts and crafts are connected with the various Guyanese religions, such as the kite-flying and bird-song competitions on Easter Sunday and Monday.

19 ● SOCIAL PROBLEMS

Racial tensions between Guyana's Asian Indian and Afro-Guyanan populations have been divisive. Street crime and violence are particularly notorious in Georgetown. Community police have now been introduced into the city by the government to recover control of the streets.

20 ● BIBLIOGRAPHY

Brill, M. *Guyana.* Chicago: Children's Press, 1994.

Chambers, Frances. *Guyana.* Santa Barbara, Calif.: Clio, 1989.

Gritzner, Charles F., ed. *Guyana in Pictures.* Minneapolis, Minn.: Lerner Publications Co., 1988.

Schlabach, Joetta Handrich. *Extending the Table: a World Community Cookbook.* Scottdale, Penn.: Herald Press, 1991.

WEBSITES

Tourism Association of Guyana. [Online] Available http://www.interknowledge.com/guyana/, 1998.

World Travel Guide. Guyana. [Online] Available http://www.wtgonline.com/country/gy/gen.html, 1998.

Haiti

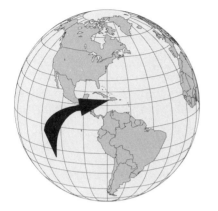

The people of Haiti are called Haitians. About 95 percent of the inhabitants are black, and 5 percent are mulatto (mixed black and white).

Haitians

PRONUNCIATION: HAY-shuns
LOCATION: Haiti
POPULATION: 6.6 million
LANGUAGE: Haitian Creole; French
RELIGION: Voudou (Voodoo); Roman Catholicism; Protestantism

1 ● INTRODUCTION

Sharing the Caribbean island of Hispaniola with the Dominican Republic, Haiti occupies a rich, lush land in a strategic location. Much of its history has been shaped by three foreign powers: Spain, France, and the United States.

When Christopher Columbus landed on the island of Hispaniola on December 6, 1492, he was greeted by the native people (Taino/Arawak Indians). By 1550, however, this native population had been almost entirely wiped out due to mistreatment, violent uprisings, and disease. The Spanish used the island as a shipping point to send riches to Europe.

The French began to settle on Tortuga, an island off the northwest coast of Hispaniola, in 1659. The first French residents, joined by runaway slaves from Hispaniola, survived by pirating Spanish ships, tanning hides, and curing meats. They were known as *buccaneers* from the Arawak word for smoking or curing meats. In 1697, the French took over the western part of the island, San Domingue, and turned it into one of its richest colonies. Coffee, sugar, cotton, and indigo (a blue dye) from Haiti accounted for nearly one-half of France's foreign trade.

In the mid-1700s, the number of runaway slaves, known as *maroons*, grew. From the mountains and forests, guerilla bands of maroons attacked the French colonists. When the mulattoes (persons of mixed African-European heritage) were denied the right to vote even though they owned land and paid taxes, they also began to revolt.

The Haitians won their independence early in the nineteenth century. The fight for independence began in 1791 when Tous-

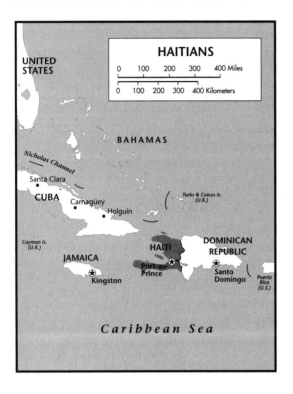

excluded from the formal political, educational, and economic structure.

From the middle of the nineteenth century to the beginning of the twentieth century, a series of dictators ruled Haiti. The American military occupied Haiti from 1915 until 1934. When the United States withdrew, they left behind a legacy of anti-American feeling and a well-trained national military.

After a very disorganized period, François Duvalier, known as "Papa Doc," was elected president in 1957. Using brutal tactics Duvalier created a rural militia to intimidate the population. In 1964 he declared himself president for life, and passed that office down to his nineteen-year-old son Jean-Claude, known as "Baby Doc," when he died in 1971.

Haitians angered by the poverty and suffering in their country began antigovernment protests. Jean-Claude Duvalier fled to exile in France in 1986. In 1990, a Roman Catholic priest, Jean-Bertrand Aristide, was elected president of Haiti. It was the country's first free democratic election, and Aristide was elected with almost 70 percent of the popular vote. In September 1991 the army under General Raoul Cédras, seized power and forced Aristide into exile. After Aristide's departure, some 50,000 Haitians fled by sea.

After refusing to honor his agreement to step down and allow Aristide to return to the presidency, Cédras was forced from power by the United States and the United Nations. On October 15, 1994, Aristide returned to power and began the difficult task of rebuilding Haiti. UN troops led by

saint L'Ouverture, an ex-slave, led a rebellion. On January 1, 1804, Haiti declared independence with Jean-Jacques Dessalines, a former slave, as the leader of the new nation. The only method of organization he knew was the military, so he used it to govern and began a tradition of military rule. Haiti was the second independent nation in the Americas (the first was the United States) and was the first free black republic in the world.

From its beginning as an independent nation, Haiti developed two distinct societies. The minority elite lived in towns and controlled the government, military, and trade. They imitated a European lifestyle and used the French language for government, commerce, and education. The peasants, the majority of the population, were

the United States were sent to Haiti as a peacekeeping force. In December 1995, former Prime Minister of Haiti, René G. Préval, was elected president. Haiti's first peaceful transfer of power between two civilian presidents took place on February 7, 1996.

2 ● LOCATION

The name "Haiti" comes from the native Taino/Arawak word *ayiti* or *hayti,* meaning "mountainous" or "high land." The Republic of Haiti occupies the western third of the island of Hispaniola in the Caribbean Sea. The Republic of Haiti includes several small islands and covers 10,714 square miles (17,239 square kilometers), making it slightly larger than the U.S. state of Maryland. Two mountain ranges cover fully two-thirds of the interior. The fertile plains that lie between the two ranges are used for agriculture. The coastline is irregular and the country is composed of two peninsulas. The climate is tropical, hot and humid. Due to deforestation and soil erosion, only 11 percent of Haiti's land is now arable (able to be farmed).

The population of Haiti was estimated to be more than 6.5 million in 1995. Over two-thirds of Haiti's inhabitants live in rural areas. Port-au-Prince, the capital, has a population of well over 1 million. Almost all Haitians are descendants of the 500,000 enslaved West Africans who won their freedom from France in 1804.

There are more than 800,000 Haitians living in the United States, with about 75 percent of them residing either in New York or Florida. Miami's "Little Haiti" is now an established community.

3 ● LANGUAGE

The two main languages of Haiti are Haitian Creole and French. All Haitians speak Haitian Creole, while only about 20 percent of the population speaks French. It was only in 1987 that the Constitution granted official status to Haitian Creole. Fluency in French carries high social status in Haiti, and those who cannot read, write, and speak French may have limited opportunity in business and government.

The Haitian Creole language evolved from a mixture of African dialect, the native Amerindian language, the Norman French spoken by pirates, and colonial French. Haitian Creole words show a variety of linguistic influences, including African (*houngan,* or Voudou priest and *zombi,* or ghost); Spanish (*ablado,* or talker); English (*bokit,* or bucket); and Caribbean (*kannari,* or earthen jar). Words borrowed from French (and their Creole meanings) include *kriye,* to weep; *boutik,* a family-operated store; and *kabare,* cafeteria tray.

Examples of Haitian Creole proverbs are:

Yon sel dwèt pa manje kalalou.
(You cannot eat okra with one finger)—we must all cooperate.

Gras a diri, ti wòch goute gres.
(Thanks to the rice, the pebble tastes of grease)—good things rub off.

4 ● FOLKLORE

Haitian culture reflects a profound reverence for one's ancestors. Ancestors' Day is a national holiday, celebrated on January second, the day after the celebration of Independence Day on January first. Folktales are popular in Haiti. Stories are introduced by an invitation to hear a story. For instance, the person wanting to tell the story shouts out: *"Krik!"* If people want to hear the tale, and they almost always do, they answer in chorus: *"Krak!"* The most popular folktales are about the smart but mischievous *Ti Malis* and his slow-witted friend *Bouki*. Here is one example:

> Ti Malis paid Bouki a visit one day. To his amazement, when he got to Bouki's *lakou* (yard), there was Bouki playing dominoes with his dog. "What a brilliant dog you have!" exclaimed Ti Malis. "He can play dominoes." "Ha!" said Bouki, "he's not as smart as you think. I've just won three out of five games!"

Another popular form of humor and amusement are riddles. (*See* 17-Recreation.)

5 ● RELIGION

Religion is an integral part of Haitian life and culture. The two main religions are Roman Catholicism and Voudou, or Voodoo, a mixture of African animism (belief in spirits and nature) and Christianity. Many Haitians practice both these religions at the same time. There are also Protestants of various denominations. The Haitian government does not impose any restrictions on religion or missionary activities.

Unlike the "black magic" reputation it has in books or movies, Voudou is in fact a religion based on ancestral spirits, tribal deities, and mythic figures such as the goddess of the sea. It keeps alive old African beliefs while borrowing freely from Christianity. At funerals, it is not uncommon for Voudou ceremonies and rituals to be performed for family members first, followed by a traditional Roman Catholic ceremony presided over by a priest.

6 ● MAJOR HOLIDAYS

Haitian holidays include Independence Day (January 1); the Anniversary of revolutionary hero Jean-Jacques Dessalines' death (October 17); the Anniversary of the Battle of Vertières (November 18); and the landing of Columbus on Hispaniola in 1492, commemorated on December 5. Other holidays include Ancestors' Day (January 2), Carnival (the three days before Ash Wednesday, in February), Pan American Day (April 14), Labor Day (May 1), Flag Day (May 18), and New Year's Eve (December 31).

Haitians also observe traditional Roman Catholic holidays, including Good Friday, Easter Sunday (in March or April), the Feast of the Assumption (August 15), All Saints' Day (November 1), All Souls' Day (November 2), Immaculate Conception (December 8), Christmas Eve (December 24), and Christmas Day (December 25).

7 ● RITES OF PASSAGE

Major life transitions, such as birth, marriage, and death, are marked by religious ceremonies, often including both Voudou and Christian rites.

8 ● RELATIONSHIPS

Many Haitian values are traditional and conservative. Manners are very important in Haitian society. Greetings are exchanged when entering a public place, such as an office or a store, or when boarding public transportation. When greeting friends, men generally shake hands. Women will exchange two kisses, the same as men do with female friends. Children are taught early to respect their elders and to formally greet visitors to their home.

Haitians at the inauguration of President Aristide in 1990.

It is not unusual for men to refer to each other by their last names. Individuals are often called nicknames, for example, the firstborn male in a family is often given the nickname *Fanfan*. A woman named Dominique may be called *Dodo* by her friends and family.

9 ● LIVING CONDITIONS

The poverty of Haiti, one of the thirty poorest countries in the world, is reflected in the health statistics of its population. The infant mortality rate is the highest in the Americas, and life expectancy, at approximately fifty-six years, is the lowest in the Caribbean. Malnutrition is widespread, especially among the young and the poor. About 70 percent of the population lives in rural areas, although this has been changing in recent years.

In 1984 less than 20 percent of the population had toilets. Poor sanitation and lack of medical services contribute to a number of infectious diseases that afflict Haitian people. These include tuberculosis, parasitic infections, and malaria.

10 ● FAMILY LIFE

In rural areas, the extended family has traditionally been the social unit. As peasants came to the cities in search of work, the nuclear family replaced the extended family. Men and women generally share household and financial responsibilities. Officially, there is no discrimination against women in Haiti, and a Ministry for Women's Affairs was established in 1995. In the coffee industry, those who transport coffee beans to markets are almost all female and are known as "Madam Saras."

Women do not have to share income from nonfarm activities with their husbands. These women can be economically independent.

The most common form of marriage among poorer Haitians is known as *plasaj,* a kind of common-law marriage. Although not recognized by the government as legitimate, plasaj is considered normal and proper among the poor. A man or woman may have a number of plasaj relationships in a lifetime. Children born to the same parent from different plasaj relationships regard each other as brothers and sisters, and often live in the same household. If parents separate, a child may take either the father or the mother's last name. Children are considered a gift from God. Haitians also make sure that each child receives an equal inheritance.

11 ● CLOTHING

Comfortable, lightweight Western-style clothes, often made of cotton and linen fabrics, are typically worn in Haiti. School children all wear uniforms. Men often wear a loose-fitting shirt called a *guayabera,* similar to other countries in the region and in Latin America. While it is acceptable for women to wear pants, most women, especially in rural areas, continue to wear skirts or dresses.

The traditional folk costume for men is a hand-embroidered shirt made of cotton, linen, or denim fabric. Women traditionally wear an embroidered short-sleeved blouse, a colorful skirt, and a scarf wrapped around their hair.

United Nations

Two Haitians working at a pottery wheel. Haitian handicrafts often make use of mahogany, sisal, and straw. Haitians are particularly skilled in woodcarving, weaving, and embroidery.

12 ● FOOD

Haitians grow corn, rice, bananas, mangoes, avocados, and other tropical fruits and vegetables. A typical meal usually includes one or two varieties of rice prepared with either red or black beans. Almost all meals feature plantains (very similar to bananas), which are usually parboiled, sliced, and deep fried. Those who can afford it eat deep-fried chicken. Other meats include goat, beef, and pork. Pork is often fried and barbecued (*grio*) and is very popular. Haitians especially favor seafoods, including barbecued lobster, shrimp, and many varieties of fish.

Vegetables include green beans, potatoes, squash, okra, cabbage, and eggplant. Salads are served with generous slices of avocado. Most Haitians love a spicy, very hot sauce called *pikles* to enhance their dishes. Desserts include cakes or tarts, often with a pineapple garnish.

13 ● EDUCATION

The first schools in Haiti were established shortly after 1805, but an accessible school system never developed. Despite education reforms in the 1970s and 1980s, dropout rates remain high: 50 percent in urban areas and 80 percent in rural ones. Education is highly valued, but the majority of Haitians do not have access to it. Technically, education is free in Haiti, but most cannot afford the supplemental fees, school supplies, and required uniforms.

The Haitian curriculum calls for many subjects to be learned in great detail, usually by memorizing. Grading and testing are very strict. It is much more difficult to achieve a grade of B in Haiti than it is in the United States. The teacher calls all students by their last names and has total authority over the class. A student speaks only when asked a question, and does not look the teacher in the eye but keeps his or her head down as a sign of respect. There are no parent-teacher organizations and if a parent is called to school it usually means that the student is in serious trouble.

Today the majority of Haitians receive no formal education. Only a small minority are educated beyond primary school.

14 ● CULTURAL HERITAGE

The uniqueness of Haiti is reflected in the originality of its paintings, music, and literature. Works by the better-known Haitian artists have been exhibited in galleries and museums in the United States and France.

Haitian music is an original blend of African drum rhythms and European dance music. Haitian *kompa* and the Voudou-influenced *rasin* are the most popular musical styles in Haiti today. Each year during Carnival, bands compete for the best song. Recent entries incorporate reggae and rap styles.

Haiti has produced writers, poets, and essayists of international reputation.

Recipe

Riz et Pois Rouges
(Rice and Red Beans)

Ingredients

1 onion, chopped
2 to 4 cloves of garlic, chopped
1 medium green pepper, chopped
2 Tablespoons cooking oil
1 cup white rice, uncooked
2 15-ounce cans of kidney beans, drained
¼ pound ham, chopped
½ teaspoon ground cumin
¼ teapoon dried oregano
¼ teaspoon crushed red pepper
2½ cups boiling water

Directions

1. Heat oil in a large saucepan. Add onion, garlic, and green pepper, and fry until onion and green pepper soften, about 3 minutes.
2. Combine with remaining ingredients in a 2-quart casserole.
3. Preheat oven to 350°F .
4. Cover casserole and bake until all the liquid is absorbed and rice is cooked, about 55 minutes.

Adapted from *Betty Crocker's International Cookbook.* New York: Random House, 1980, p. 217.

Attempts to write in Haitian Creole date to the eighteenth century, but because of its low status, Haitian literature has been written almost exclusively in French. With the recognition of Creole as an official language, more and more novels, poems, and plays are being written in Creole. In 1975, the first novel to be written entirely in Haitian Creole was published. It is titled *Dezafi* and was written by Franketienne. It describes a poetic picture of Haitian life.

15 ● EMPLOYMENT

About two-thirds of the labor force in Haiti still works in agriculture. The main cash crops are coffee and sugarcane. Deforestation, land erosion, and a declining economy have prompted many farm workers to migrate to the cities or abroad. A large number of Haitians work in the Dominican Republic as *braceros* (migrant workers) under grueling conditions. Migrant farm workers are hired temporarily, usually for a harvest. Harvesting sugarcane is still done by hand with a machete.

There are estimates that more than one hundred thousand children in Haiti are held in forced domestic labor, which is called *restevek* in Haitian Creole. Young children from rural families are "adopted" by wealthy city dwellers to work as unpaid domestics. These children often work long hours, and are underfed and mistreated.

16 ● SPORTS

Soccer is the national sport. During World Cup competition, held every four years, practically the entire country roots for the Brazilian national team. In rural areas cockfighting is also popular, but only as an informal weekend sport. For men, a typical social game is dominoes or cards. For the more affluent, tennis as a sport is increasing in popularity.

Children play hide-and-seek, hopscotch *(marelle)*, round dances, and marbles. Organized sports in school or local leagues include basketball for girls and soccer for boys.

17 ● RECREATION

Storytelling in Haiti is a performance art. The storyteller uses a different voice for each character in the story and may sing songs as part of the narrative. Telling stories, proverbs, riddles, and singing songs exemplify the rich spoken tradition of the Haitian people.

Perhaps the most popular form of humor and amusement is riddles. There is a definite form for the riddles. The person "throwing" the riddle or *tire pwen* says: *"Tim-tim,"* and those who want to hear it reply: *"Bwa sèch."* Then the riddle is given. If they get it, they announce it. If they give up, they say *"Bwa sèch,"* which means they eat dry wood, the penalty for not getting the riddle. The riddles themselves are very difficult. Here are several popular riddles:

RIDDLES
1. They serve it food, it stands on four feet, but it cannot eat.
2. I enter white, I come out mulatto.
3. Three very large men are standing under a single little umbrella, but not one of them gets wet. Why?
4. When I sit, I am taller than when I stand.
5. How many coconuts can you put into an empty sack?

ANSWERS
1. A table.
2. Bread.
3. It is not raining.
4. A dog.
5. Only one. After that the sack is not empty.

18 ● CRAFTS AND HOBBIES

Haitian craftspeople are particularly skilled in woodcarving, weaving, and embroidery. Wooden sculptures, plaques, and furniture (especially chairs with caned backs and seats) are popular crafts. So are embroidered women's dresses, skirts, and blouses, and men's shirts. Wrought iron items are also part of Haitian folk art, including candle holders, coffee tables, lamps, and animal figures.

Every year before Christmas, artisans use white cardboard and tissue paper to make elaborate works of art called *fanal,* in which lighted candles are carefully placed.

19 ● SOCIAL PROBLEMS

Haiti is the poorest country in the Western Hemisphere. A very small percentage of the population earns more than 60 percent of the national income. Unemployment is estimated to be as high as 70 percent. Peasants have traditionally depended on the extended family and cooperative labor to survive. Families living in urban slums do not have even these supports.

Wood as a fuel accounts for 75 percent of the country's energy consumption. Deforestation of Haiti's once green, tree-covered land is now critical. This destruction of trees has caused erosion of the soil, which in turn has made most of the land unsuitable for farming. Fluctuations in the price of coffee and sugar on the world market impact agricultural production and planning in Haiti.

20 ● BIBLIOGRAPHY

Portions of this article were adapted from *The Haitians: Their History and Culture.* Washington, D.C.: Center for Applied Linguistics, 1994.

Abbott, Elizabeth. *Haïti: The Duvaliers and Their Legacy.* New York: Touchstone, Simon and Schuster, 1991.

Betty Crocker's International Cookbook. New York: Random House, 1980.

Haggerty, Richard A. (ed.) *Dominican Republic and Haiti: Country Studies.* 2d ed. Washington, D.C.: Library of Congress, 1991.

Laguerre, Michel. *The Military and Society in Haïti.* Knoxville: University of Tennessee Press, 1993.

Leyburn, James G. *The Haitian People.* New Haven, Conn.: Yale University Press, 1966.

WEBSITES

Embassy of Haiti. Washington, D.C. [Online] Available http://www.haiti.org/embassy/, 1998.

World Travel Guide, Haiti. [Online] Available http://www.wtgonline.com/country/ht/gen.html, 1998.

Honduras

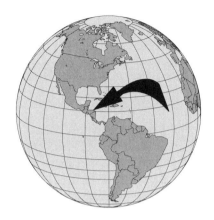

The people of Honduras are called Hondurans. The majority (more than 90 percent) are mestizo (mixture of white and Amerindian—native people). A little more than 5 percent of the population is Amerindian. There are also small numbers of Black Caribs (Garifuna—black and Amerindian) and Miskito (Amerindian, black, and white). Blacks are 2 percent, and about 1 percent are white (Spanish origin). For more information on the Garifuna, see the chapter on Belize in Volume 1; for the Miskito, see the chapter on Nicaragua in Volume 6.

Hondurans

PRONUNCIATION: hahn-DUR-uhns
LOCATION: Honduras
POPULATION: 5 million
LANGUAGE: Spanish; English; local dialects
RELIGION: Roman Catholicism (95 percent); Protestantism (Methodist, Church of God, Seventh-Day Adventist, Moravian, and Assembly of God churches); native religions combined with Christianity

1 ● INTRODUCTION

Honduras is the second-largest country in Central America, but one of the poorest. The magnificent Mayan ruins at Copán are the remains of a civilization that flourished there between the fourth and ninth centuries AD. Christopher Columbus landed in Honduras on his last voyage in 1502. In search of gold and silver, the Spanish conquered the land beginning in 1524. Within twenty years, the native population was reduced to only eight thousand by disease, mistreatment, and the export of slave to other countries.

Central America freed itself from Spanish rule in 1821. Honduras, however, did not become independent until 1838. Dictators ruled the country and there have been some three hundred internal rebellions, civil wars, and changes of government since then. A number of civilians have been elected president since the 1950s, but several of them have been overthrown by the military.

2 ● LOCATION

Honduras has a long Caribbean Sea coastline on the north and a small Pacific Ocean coastline on the south. Except for its coastal areas, Honduras is a mountainous country. Its numerous valleys are used for agriculture and raising livestock. Bananas, coffee, and cotton have been significant crops. Guatemala is the neighbor to the west, El

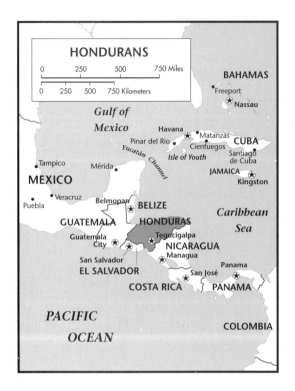

Salvador to the south and west, and Nicaragua to the south and east.

With just over 5 million people, Honduras is not a crowded country. About 90 percent of all Hondurans are mestizo, of mixed European and Amerindian ancestry.

3 ● LANGUAGE

Spanish is the national and official language. English is understood by many along the Caribbean coast. Black Caribs (Garifuna) are descendants of freed black slaves and Carib Indians, and speak a language related to Carib. Miskito, who are of mixed Indian, African, and European descent and live along the Caribbean coast, speak an Indian tongue with words from West African and European languages mixed in.

4 ● FOLKLORE

A folklore belief common throughout Central America is that a human being and a spirit, usually an animal, are so closely connected that they share the same soul. If one dies, so will the other. This belief is not as widespread in Honduras, however, as it is in neighboring Guatemala.

Honduran folktales are about a variety of spirits, many of whom live in wells or caves. One popular story is about *El Duende,* an imp with a big sombrero, red trousers and a blue jacket, who courts pretty young girls by tossing pebbles at them. *Curanderos* are faith healers who are believed to be able to cure nervous ailments and drive away the evil eye, the *vista fuerte.*

Lempira was a sixteenth-century Indian chieftain who fought the Spanish. He is much admired as a folk hero, and the national currency is named for him.

5 ● RELIGION

Nearly 95 percent of the population is Roman Catholic. However, there has been rapid growth among evangelical Protestant groups such as the Methodists, Church of God, Seventh-Day Adventists, and Assemblies of God.

Many Hondurans have combined traditional Amerindian religious practices, such as offerings to the sun, with Roman Catholicism. Each community has its own patron saint. Pilgrimages to saints' shrines are common. Most houses have an image or picture of a saint displayed on a wall.

Black Caribs combine many elements of African religion with Methodist religious

Cory Langley

Poorer Hondurans live in one-room dwellings with thatched roofs and dirt floors.

practices. Most Miskito now belong to the Moravian Church.

6 ● MAJOR HOLIDAYS

As in other Latin American countries, Christmas (December 25) and Holy Week leading up to Easter Sunday in late March or early April are the main religious holidays. A Christmastime tradition is the *posada*, a celebration held each night beginning on December 16.

Between December 25 and January 6, Garifuna men celebrate *Yancunú* with dancing, singing, and the wearing of masks to bring prosperity in the new year. On January 15 of each year, pilgrims from Honduras and other Central American countries attend a celebration in Esquipulas, Guatemala, home of a dark-skinned wooden sculpture of Jesus. The feast day of the Virgin of Suyapa, Honduras's patron saint, is on February 2. In the basilica in Suyapa there is a tiny wooden image of her that is believed to have miraculous powers.

Of the secular, or nonreligious, holidays, the most important are Independence Day on September 15, and the birthday of national leader Francisco Morazán on Octo-

Cory Langley

Many Hondurans supplement their income by working as street vendors.

ber 3. He was the last president of the United Provinces of Central America, a federation that only lasted from 1823 to 1842.

7 ● RITES OF PASSAGE

Most infants are baptized and the baptism is usually followed by a celebration. In the upper and middle classes, dating is restricted. A prospective suitor is checked out carefully by the girl's family and wedding engagements of several years are common. Perhaps half of all Honduran couples, however, live together without a marriage license or a religious ceremony. A novena, prayers said during nine consecutive days, is commonly held after a person's death and usually at home. A second novena may be held six months later.

8 ● RELATIONSHIPS

Friends express affection more openly than in the United States. Men often embrace on meeting and departing. Women often embrace and kiss one or both cheeks, or at least touch cheeks.

Since most Hondurans are named for a saint, they celebrate their saint's day as well as, or in place of, their own birthday. Friends and relatives are invited to the home for a celebration.

There has been less class conflict in Honduras than in the other Hispanic Central American countries.

9 ● LIVING CONDITIONS

At least two-thirds of the Honduran people live below the poverty line, about one-third have no access to health care, and about one-fifth of all young children are malnourished. The typical dwelling is a two-room adobe bungalow with a tiled roof. Poor peasants, however, live in one-room huts made of bamboo, sugarcane, and corn stalks, with dirt floors. Most poor peasants farm small, marginal plots of land, or they work for wages on larger farms. Migrants from the country to the city generally live in crowded slums.

The upper and middle classes generally have domestic servants and live in houses with thick adobe, brick, or concrete walls. Many have grillwork over the windows and balconies on the upper floors. These homes usually have an enclosed patio instead of a front yard.

10 ● FAMILY LIFE

Families are usually large—the average family has five children. In addition, grandparents, plus aunts and uncles and their children, may also live under the same roof. The various branches of a family share and cooperate. They find work for unemployed members, provide loans, and take in needy relatives. As in other Latin American countries, *compadres,* godparents, also provide support to family members.

11 ● CLOTHING

Most people dress casually. Men wear loose trousers and shirts. Women wear one-piece calico or cotton dresses, or loose blouses and skirts. Open sandals are a common form of footwear. Traditional costumes are worn only on special occasions. At such times, women may wear silk dresses, or cotton dresses embroidered with silk, using old Mayan patterns and designs.

One Amerindian group, the Tolupanes Indians, were the only distinctive dress in Honduras. The men wear a *balandrán,* a one-piece, sleeveless garment. Women wear brightly colored dresses and silver necklaces with brightly painted beads made of dried seeds and thorns.

12 ● FOOD

Tortillas, made of cornmeal rolled into thin pancakes, are the staple diet of Hondurans. Tortillas are supplemented by beans, the chief source of protein. The poor usually eat tortillas and beans for every meal. Although pigs and chickens are widely raised in the countryside, their meat is reserved for special occasions. Green vegetables are not common in the average diet.

Mondongo, a richly flavored tripe soup, is a popular Honduran dish. Other specialties include carrots stuffed with cheese, creamed beets and plantains, and corn dumplings in honey.

The Black Caribs (Garifuna) eat cassava, the roots of a tropical plant, in the form of big tortillas, and a mash made of ground plantains and bananas. Other dishes eaten by the Black Caribs include flour tortillas that are dipped in coconut soup with crab, and a soup made from coconut milk to which clams, crab, shrimp, fish heads, and plantains are added. They also make a beverage out of fermented corn and sugarcane.

13 ● EDUCATION

At least one-fourth of Hondurans cannot read or write. Education is free and mandatory between the ages of seven and fourteen, and the majority of all school-age children are in school. But fewer than half of those enrolled in public schools complete the primary level. The middle and upper classes generally send their children to private schools, which are often run by churches. The main institution of higher learning is the National Autonomous University of Honduras, located in the capital city, Tegucigalpa.

14 ● CULTURAL HERITAGE

In 1847, Father Jose Trinidad Reyes founded what later became the National University. Juan Ramon Molina was an important poet in the nineteenth century. Poet and historian Rafael Heliodoro Valle was the most respected Honduran literary figure of the twentieth century. Other twentieth-century Honduran writers include novelist Argentina Díaz Lozanto and poet Clementina Suarez.

Among twentieth-century Honduran painters are Arturo López Rodezno and Carlos Garay. The primitive landscape paintings of José Antonio Velásquez are much admired.

Drums and the flute were the musical instruments of the Indians before the Spanish conquest. The most popular musical instrument now is the marimba, which is similar to the xylophone.

15 ● EMPLOYMENT

More than half of the labor force is not formally employed. This includes subsistence farmers, small shopkeepers, and self-employed craftspeople. Women often seek jobs as domestic servants or, in urban areas, work as street vendors. Men supplement their income from tilling their small plots of land by working on plantations for part of the year. The small middle class consists of professionals, merchants, farmers, business employees, and civil servants.

16 ● SPORTS

As elsewhere in Central America, *fútbol* (soccer) is the most popular sport. The so-called Soccer War of 1969 followed matches between the national teams of Honduras and El Salvador. In that struggle, which lasted four days, more than one thousand Hondurans were killed. Honduras also has bullfights. Traditional sports still played at fiestas, or festivals, include greased-pole climbing and the *carrera de cintas,* a horse-back-riding race in which the rider, at full gallop, must run a stick through small rings.

17 ● RECREATION

Salsa, merengue, and Mexican *ranchero* music are popular, and social dances are held. Television is generally available only in the cities. Radio, however, reaches every part of the country. Fireworks are part of every celebration. There are more than twenty Honduran folk dances, reflecting Spanish, Amerindian, and African influences.

This young boy prepares plantains for cooking.

18 ● CRAFTS AND HOBBIES

Artisans carve objects (ranging from wall hangings to furniture) from mahogany and other tropical hardwoods. Baskets, mats, and hammocks are woven from plant fibers such as henequen. Ceramics include porcelain objects in the form of animals, especially roosters. In addition to pottery, other crafts are embroidery and the production of leather goods such as belts and purses.

19 ● SOCIAL PROBLEMS

Nearly two-thirds of the Honduran people live in poverty. Most of the people do not have access to running water and sanitation facilities. Diseases such as tuberculosis, influenza, malaria, typhoid, and pneumonia are serious health problems. Unemployment and underemployment are high. The country produces only two commodities to sell: bananas and coffee. The crime rate has risen in the 1990s, and domestic violence against women is widespread.

20 ● BIBLIOGRAPHY

Alvarado, Elvia. *Don't Be Afraid, Gringo: A Honduran Woman Speaks from the Heart.* San Francisco: Institute for Food and Development Policy, 1987.

Honduras in Pictures. Minneapolis, Minn.: Lerner Publications Co., 1987.

Howard-Reguindin, Pamela F. *Honduras.* Santa Barbara, Calif.: Clio, 1992.

Merrill, Tim L., ed. *Honduras: A Country Study.* 3rd ed. Washington, D.C.: U.S. Government Printing Office, 1995.

Meyer, Harvey Kessler. *Historical Dictionary of Honduras.* Metuchen, N.J.: Scarecrow, 1994.

Targ, H. and M. Brill. *Honduras.* Chicago: Children's Press, 1995.

WEBSITES

Green Arrow Advertising, Honduras. [Online] Available http://www.greenarrow.com/honduras/honduras.htm, 1998.

Ruiz-Garcia, Pedro, The Latino Connection. [Online] Available http://www.ascinsa.com/LATINOCONNECTION/honduras.html, 1998.

World Travel Guide, Honduras. [Online] Available http://www.wtgonline.com/country/hn/gen.html, 1998.

Hungary

The people of Hungary are called Hungarians. The majority of the population are of Hungarian, or Magyar, descent. Minority groups include Gypsies (a little more than 1 percent); Germans, Slovaks, Croats, and Romanians (all less than 1 percent). About 2 million Magyars live outside Hungary in Romania, Slovakia, the former Yugoslavia, and the Ukraine.

Hungarians

PRONUNCIATION: hun-GARE-ee-uns
ALTERNATE NAMES: Magyars (Ethnic Hungarians)
LOCATION: Hungary
POPULATION: 10 million
LANGUAGE: Hungarian (Magyar); German
RELIGION: Roman Catholicism; Reformed Calvinist; Lutheranism; Judaism; Eastern Orthodox Church; other Protestant sects

1 ● INTRODUCTION

Hungary is a landlocked nation in central Europe. The western portion of present-day Hungary was conquered by the Romans in 9 BC. The Magyars, who invaded the region in AD 896, were converted to Christianity at the beginning of the eleventh century by King Stephen, who remains a national hero. Turkish rule, beginning in the sixteenth century, was followed by union with the Austrian Hapsburg empire, which lasted until World War I (1914–18).

After over forty years behind the communist "Iron Curtain," Hungary held its first free elections in 1990 and began transforming its economy under Prime Minister Jozsef Antall. Hungary became an associate member of the European Union in 1994.

2 ● LOCATION

Although its neighbors' political boundaries were redrawn in the early 1990s, Hungary's territory remained unchanged. It consists of four major regions: the Danube River valley, the Great Plain, the Lake Balaton region, and the Northern Mountains. Ethnic Hungarians, or Magyars, make up the majority of Hungary's 10 million people.

3 ● LANGUAGE

The Hungarian, or Magyar, language is universally spoken in Hungary. It is a Finno-Ugric rather than an Indo-European language. Thus it has almost no resemblance to such Western languages as English, French, Spanish, or German. Instead, it is more like

Finnish, Estonian, and a few languages spoken in remote parts of Russia.

NUMBERS

English	Hungarian
one	egy
two	kettö
three	három
four	négy
five	öt
six	hat
seven	hét
eight	nyolc
nine	kilenc
ten	tíz

DAYS OF THE WEEK

English	Hungarian
Sunday	vasánarp
Monday	hétfö
Tuesday	kedd
Wednesday	szerda
Thursday	csütörtök
Friday	péntek
Saturday	szombat

4 ● FOLKLORE

For the most part, the traditional folklore of Hungary is dying out. One religious tradition revived in some rural areas is the Eastertime fertility ritual of *locsolkodas*. Boys and men sprinkle water or perfume on girls and receive a painted Easter egg in return.

5 ● RELIGION

About two-thirds of Hungarians are Roman Catholic. In general, the Hungarians are not a deeply religious people. The dominant religion of their country changed several times under different rulers. Thus the Hungarians are known for being more tolerant about religion than many of their neighbors.

6 ● MAJOR HOLIDAYS

New Year's (January 1), or *Farsang,* begins a season of formal dances and parties throughout the country that lasts until Ash Wednesday (sometime in February). On March 15, the 1848–49 Revolution is commemorated with speeches, flag-waving, and parades. Easter Monday (late March or early April) is the most important religious holiday in Hungary.

May Day (May 1) is celebrated as a workers' holiday. August 20, St. Stephen's Day, is Hungary's national day, celebrated with fireworks throughout the country. Proclamation of the Republic Day on October 23 commemorates the 1956 uprising against the Communist regime. It is marked by torch-lit processions. Christmas (December 25) and Boxing Day (December 26) are celebrated privately in family gatherings.

Instead of their own birthdays, Hungarians, like people in other primarily Catholic countries, tend to celebrate the feast day of the saint for whom they are named.

7 ● RITES OF PASSAGE

Many of the rites of passage that young people undergo in Hungary are Christian rituals such as baptism, first communion, confirmation, and marriage. In addition, many families mark a student's progress through the educational system with graduation parties.

Two special ceremonies mark students' graduation from high school. In February of their senior year, students take part in a ribbon-pinning ceremony called *szalagavato.* In May, just before final exams, comes the *ballagas,* or marching ritual. The seniors form a line and march through every classroom singing as the teachers and other students present them with flowers. In embroidered pouches, they carry salt, money, and a *pagacsa* or small roll, all of which are meant to symbolically support them as they embark on their adult lives.

8 ● RELATIONSHIPS

Social interactions in Hungary are formal and polite. Hungarians, especially older men, often greet young women by kissing their hands. Kissing a person's hand as a sign of respect is referred to in the traditional greeting of young people toward their elders (*Csókolom*— "I kiss it"). Even close friends shake hands when greeting each other.

Currently, young people like to use the English word "hello" as slang for "good-bye."

9 ● LIVING CONDITIONS

After World War II (1939–45), a severe housing shortage developed in Hungary as workers flocked to the cities from rural villages. Most existing apartments had only one room and a kitchen area. Many had been damaged in the war. Those who had to depend on government-funded housing were placed on long waiting lists. There is still a shortage of adequate housing in urban areas.

10 ● FAMILY LIFE

Traditionally, both nuclear and extended families were found in rural areas of Hungary. Today, the nuclear family is more common in the country, as well as in urban

areas. Hungarians generally marry between the ages of twenty and twenty-four.

Patterns of family life have shifted since World War II (1939–45). The most notable change is the increased number of women working outside the home. By 1987 about 75 percent of women had jobs. In recent decades the divorce rate has risen. About one in every three marriages ends in divorce.

11 ● CLOTHING

Hungarians generally wear modern Western-style clothing. Casual wear in the cities includes jeans, T-shirts, and sweatshirts. Pantsuits are popular with both men and women for casual and more formal occasions. In rural areas, one can still see more traditional clothing. Women may wear peas-

Recipe

Gulyás (Goulash)

Ingredients

3 slices of bacon

1½ pounds pork loin, cut into 1-inch cubes

1 medium onion, chopped

½ teaspoon caraway seeds

1 Tablespoon paprika (preferably Hungarian-style paprika)

1 can cream of chicken soup

¼ cup water

3 cups sauerkraut, rinsed and drained

½ green pepper, cut into small squares

1 tomato, chopped (½ cup chopped canned tomatoes may be substituted)

½ cup sour cream

2 Tablespoons flour

Parsley

Directions

1. Cook bacon until crisp. Cool on paper towels. Crumble bacon.
2. Add pork, onion, caraway seeds, and paprika to pan. Brown pork over medium heat.
3. Stir in soup, water, and sauerkraut. Cover pan and simmer over low heat for one hour, stirring occasionally.
4. Add green pepper and tomato and simmer 30 minutes more, stirring occasionally.
5. Combine sour cream and flour. Stir this combination into the pork mixture. Simmer over low heat, stirring constantly, until thickened.
6. Garnish with bacon and parsley.

Serve with rice, egg noodles, or boiled potatoes.

---

ant babushkas (scarves) on their heads, and men may wear hats with floppy brims.

The traditional costumes worn for festivals have fancy, brightly colored embroidery. Women wear white embroidered aprons with lace trim, while men wear plain or embroidered white shirts and dark vests.

12 ● FOOD

The Hungarian diet is heavily meat-based. Pork is the most commonly used ingredient. The most famous dish is probably goulash (*gulyás*). It is a soup or stew made with meat, onions, and potatoes, and seasoned with paprika. Often, other vegetables are added as well. Stews with sour cream are called *paprikash*. Fish soups (called *levesek* or *halászlé*) are also popular. Popular desserts include pancakes (*palacsinta*) with dessert fillings (a version of crèpes) and strudel.

13 ● EDUCATION

Schools provide eight years of primary and four years of secondary education, and education is required until the age of sixteen. About 40 percent of primary and secondary schools are now run by various religious groups. Institutions of higher learning include four comprehensive universities, fifteen specialized universities, and forty-two specialized colleges.

AP/Wide World Photos

Hungarians in national dress are moved to tears at the monument of their national hero, Sándor Petofi, in Budapest. Petofi wrote National Song, *the rallying cry in the 1848 War of Independence.*

14 ● CULTURAL HERITAGE

One distinctive feature of Hungarian culture is the merging of folk art and fine art. Two notable twentieth-century examples can be found in the compositions of Béla Bartók and the ceramic sculptures of Margit Kovács.

Notable painters include Mihály Munkácsy in the nineteenth century, and Szinyei Merse at the turn of the twentieth century. The famous nineteenth-century composer Franz Liszt was born in Hungary. Much Hungarian literature has been politically inspired. *National Song,* written by the nation's most celebrated poet, Sándor Petofi, became a rallying cry in the 1848 War of Independence. Famous twentieth-century poets include Endre Ady and Attila József.

15 ● EMPLOYMENT

In 1991 nearly one-third of Hungarians were employed in industry, and about one-fifth in agriculture. After the downfall of communism in 1990, unemployment rose from about 2 percent to over 13 percent by 1993. It is not uncommon for Hungarians to hold second and even third jobs. Women account for over 50 percent of the labor force.

16 ● SPORTS

Soccer and water polo are both very popular participant sports. Most cities and towns have both indoor and outdoor public pools. Besides soccer, other spectator sports include tennis, skiing, and horse racing.

17 ● RECREATION

Hungarians like to relax during their leisure hours by reading, watching television and videos, and playing sports. The most popular spectator sport is soccer (called "football"). Chess is also popular.

Vacation trips are extremely popular among Hungarians. Most go to the country in August. Many own or have access to summer cottages where they can spend time on weekends or during extended holidays.

18 ● CRAFTS AND HOBBIES

Many Hungarian homes are graced by traditional woodcarvings. The weavers of the Sárköz region produce a distinctive red and black fabric, and the Great Plain region is known for its pottery.

Hungarian folk music is known for its pentatonic scale (having five tones to the octave), adapted by such twentieth-century composers as Béla Bartók and Zoltán Kodály. The *csárdás* is a popular folk dance.

19 ● SOCIAL PROBLEMS

The transition from communism to a free-market economy since 1990 has caused much social disruption. Problems include inflation, rapidly growing unemployment, and the failure of many businesses. A severe housing shortage continues to be a fact of life in urban areas. There is widespread discrimination against the Gypsies in employment, housing, and other areas.

20 ● BIBLIOGRAPHY

Domjan, Joseph. *Hungarian Heroes and Legends.* Princeton, N.J.: Van Nostrand, 1963.

Handler, Andrew, and Susan V. Meschel (eds.). *Young People Speak: Surviving the Holocaust in Hungary.* New York: Franklin Watts, 1993.

Hill, Raymond. *Hungary, Nations in Transition.* New York: Facts on File, 1997.

Hungary: A Country Study. Washington, D.C.: U.S. Government Printing Office, 1990.

Jackson, Livia Bitton. *I Have Lived a Thousand Years: Growing Up in the Holocaust.* New York: Simon & Schuster Books for Young Readers, 1997.

Steins, Richard. *Hungary, Exploring Cultures of the World.* New York: Benchmark Books, 1998.

WEBSITES

Embassy of Hungary. Washington, D.C. [Online] Available http://www.hungaryemb.org/, 1998.

Hungarian National Tourist Office. [Online] Available http://www.hungarytourism.hu/, 1998.

World Travel Guide. Hungary. [Online] Available http://www.wtgonline.com/country/hu/gen.html, 1998.

Iceland

The population of Iceland is almost entirely descended from the original settlers from Norway in the late ninth and early tenth centuries.

Icelanders

PRONUNCIATION: ISE-lann-ders
LOCATION: Iceland
POPULATION: 262,000
LANGUAGE: Icelandic
RELIGION: Evangelical Lutheran Church; other Lutheran denominations; Roman Catholicism

1 ● INTRODUCTION

The Republic of Iceland (*Lýdveldidh Ísland*) is a country of dramatic contrasts and contradictions. It is located near the Arctic Circle but is considered part of Europe. It is one of the world's most volcanically active regions but also the site of Europe's largest ice-cap—hence its nickname, "the land of fire and ice."

Iceland was first settled, mostly by Norwegians, between AD 874 and 930. In 1380, the region—together with Norway—came under Danish rule, which lasted nearly 600 years. A strong nationalist movement late in the nineteenth century led to Denmark granting the Icelanders home rule in 1903 and independence in 1918. However, it was not until 1944 that Iceland fully broke its political ties with Denmark, becoming an independent republic on June 17, 1944.

2 ● LOCATION

Iceland is Europe's second-largest island and its westernmost nation. Its total area is 39,769 square miles (103,000 square kilometers), slightly smaller than the state of Kentucky. Iceland is made up of a main island and numerous smaller islands off its shores. The main island has a central plateau ringed with mountains. Iceland has many active volcanoes. On average, there is an eruption about once every five years.

The country's population is about 262,000, of which 90 percent is urban and 10 percent rural.

3 ● LANGUAGE

Icelandic is a Germanic language. It is most closely related to Faroese (the language spoken on the Faroe Islands). It is also related to Norwegian. The language has changed little since medieval times compared with other modern languages. Most Icelanders can still read thirteenth-century Icelandic sagas in their original versions. A special committee is charged with creating new Icelandic terms for words like "computer" (*tölva*, literally "word prophet").

COMMON WORDS AND PHRASES

English	Icelandic
men	karlar
women	konur
thank you	takk fyrir
today	í dag
tomorrow	á morgun
meat	kjöt
fish	fiskur
milk	mjólk
water	vatn

NUMBERS

English	Icelandic
zero	núll
one	einn
two	tveir
three	þrír
four	fjórir
five	fimm
six	sex
seven	sjö
eight	átta
nine	níu
ten	tíu

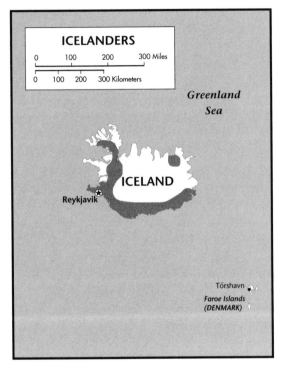

4 ● FOLKLORE

Common features of Icelandic folktales include ghosts, elves, mermaids, and sea monsters.

At Christmastime thirteen Santa Claus figures called Christmas Men (or Yuletide Lads) are said to visit every home in the land. They leave gifts but also cause mischief. The Door Slammer disturbs people's sleep by slamming doors. The Candle Beggar steals candles. The Meat Hooker lowers a hook down the chimney in order to make off with the Christmas roast.

5 ● RELIGION

Over 90 percent of Icelanders belong to the official state church, the Evangelical Lutheran Church. The entire country makes up a single diocese with 281 parishes. It is headed by a bishop based in the capital, Reykjavík. The Church is government-supported. However, people who do not want their taxes to go for its support may declare this on their returns. Their tax money is then used for other purposes.

6 ● MAJOR HOLIDAYS

Iceland's legal holidays include New Year's Day (January 1); Good Friday, Easter Sunday and Monday (late March or early

April); the First Day of Summer (celebrated on the third Thursday in April); Labor Day (May 1); Whitsunday and Whitmonday (sometime in May); National Day (June 17); Bank Holiday (first Monday in August); Independence Anniversary (December 1); and Christmas (celebrated December 24–26).

The traditional First Day of Summer is celebrated in April. It is based on a traditional calendar that divided the year into two seasons, summer and winter, each twenty-six weeks long. The occasion is still celebrated as a national holiday with parades and festivals.

7 ● RITES OF PASSAGE

Iceland is a modern, largely Christian country. Many of the rites of passage for young people are rituals within the church. These include baptism, first communion, confirmation, and marriage. In addition, a student's educational progress is often marked by graduation parties.

8 ● RELATIONSHIPS

Icelanders customarily shake hands when greeting and taking leave of each other. Common greetings include *gódan daginn* (good day), *gott kvöld* (good evening), and *bless* (goodbye). It is considered good manners to take off one's shoes before entering a dwelling.

Icelanders' last names are based on the first names of their parents, with *son* or *sson* added for males, and *dóttir* for females. Icelanders generally call each other by their first names, even in formal situations. They are listed in their country's telephone direc-

tories alphabetically by their first, rather than their last, names.

9 ● LIVING CONDITIONS

Icelanders enjoy a high standard of living. Traditionally, Icelanders in rural areas lived in dwellings built of stone and turf. Those in the cities had wooden houses. Today most Icelandic housing is built of reinforced concrete. This way it can withstand the country's harsh climatic conditions. Exteriors are generally painted in pastel colors. In Reykjavík, it is common to heat one's house with water from hot springs.

10 ● FAMILY LIFE

Icelanders tend to have a rather casual attitude toward marriage. Over 70 percent of firstborn children are born to unmarried couples. It is common for couples to have their own children present at their weddings, often as bridesmaids or pageboys. Married women often keep their original names. In Reykjavík, day care is readily available for the children of working couples. In smaller towns and in rural areas, parents are more likely to rely on family and friends to assist with child care.

The position of women is generally good in Iceland. Iceland is traditionally a matriarchal (led by women) society. Almost 90 percent of Icelandic women work outside the home. In 1980 Iceland became the first country in the world to elect a woman as president. President Vígdis Finnbogadóttir narrowly defeated three male opponents in the 1980 election. She was reelected in 1984, 1988, and 1992.

Group of young children in traditional Icelandic garb. Icelanders normally wear modern, Western-style clothing like that worn elsewhere in Europe and in developed countries in other parts of the world.

11 ● CLOTHING

Icelanders wear modern, Western-style clothing. The women's traditional costume is worn for festivals and other special occasions. It consists of a white blouse and ankle-length black skirt, with a black vest laced in front, long white apron, black shoes, and black cap.

12 ● FOOD

Fish, mutton, and lamb are staples of the Icelandic diet. Common varieties of fish—often eaten raw—include cod, salmon, trout, halibut, and redfish. Raw pickled salmon is a special favorite. *Hangikjöt* (smoked mutton) is a festive dish served at Christmas and New Year's, and at other times as well. Usually, it is accompanied by potatoes, white sauce, and peas. *Skyr* is a popular yogurtlike dairy food served either at breakfast or as a dessert, often with berries or other fresh fruit. .

13 ● EDUCATION

School is required between the ages of seven and fifteen, and all levels of education, including college, are free. Many five- and six-year-olds are enrolled in preprimary education. Primary school covers all subjects, including vocational guidance. Secondary schools offer either general

Recipe

Mondlukaka
(Almond Cake)

Ingredients

1 cup butter
1 cup sugar
4 eggs, separated
1 teaspoon vanilla
1 cup blanched almonds, ground
1 cup flour
½ teaspoon baking powder
½ cup strawberry jam
1 cup heavy cream, whipped
3 Tablespoons sugar

Directions

1. Beat butter until light and creamy. Gradually beat in 1 cup of sugar.
2. Add egg yolks, one at a time, beating well after each addition. Stir in vanilla and ground almonds.
3. Add flour and baking powder gradually, mixing well.
4. In a separate bowl, beat egg whites until stiff.
5. Stir beaten egg whites into batter carefully, using a spatula.
6. Preheat oven to 350°F. Grease three 8-inch round cake pans.
7. Divide batter among the three pans and bake 30 minutes until golden brown.
8. Cool in the pans for 5 minutes. Then remove from pans and cool completely.
9. Beat heavy cream with sugar. Spread strawberry jam between layers. Just before serving, spread top and sides with whipped cream.

Adapted from Hazelton, Nika Standen. *Classic Scandinavian Cooking.* New York: Scribner's Sons, 1987, p. 180.

education, vocational education, or university preparatory study. In 1991 Iceland had five universities and colleges, including the University of Iceland, located in Reykjavík.

14 ● CULTURAL HERITAGE

Iceland's most famous literary works are the Viking sagas, dating back to the tenth century AD. These family stories describe the important political and military events of their time and the daily lives of the early Icelandic settlers.

Traditional folk musical instruments have almost disappeared. A textbook was published in 1855 describing how to play the *langspil*, a long and narrow harp. The *fióla* is a stringed instrument that sits on a table and is played with a bow.

Iceland's best-known twentieth-century author is novelist Halldór Laxness, who won the Nobel Prize for literature in 1955. Other cultural resources include a national orchestra, an opera company, several theater companies, and the Icelandic Dance Company. Well-known names in the visual arts include those of sculptor Asmundur Sveinsson, and artists Jon Stefansson and Kristin Jonsdóttir.

15 ● EMPLOYMENT

Icelanders are hard workers. Their average work week of over forty-six hours is one of Europe's longest. Many Icelanders hold two or even three jobs. It is common for children to work during their school vacations. Many even have evening jobs during the school year. Fish processing and other industries employ nearly one-fifth of Iceland's work force. Government employs an equal share.

16 ● SPORTS

Not surprisingly, Icelanders, who live surrounded by water, are swimming enthusiasts. Soccer is another favorite activity, and Icelanders excel at sports requiring physical strength, such as weight lifting. Other popular sports include golf, basketball, badminton, horseback riding, hunting, fishing, and sailing. Icelanders have their own native form of wrestling called *glîma*.

17 ● RECREATION

Icelanders are avid readers. Their country is said to have more bookstores relative to its population size than any other in the world. Most families own good-sized book collections.

Chess is extremely popular in Iceland. The legendary 1972 world championship match between American Bobby Fischer and Russian Boris Spassky was held in Iceland's capital, Reykjavík. Bridge (a card game) is another favorite form of recreation in Iceland.

18 ● CRAFTS AND HOBBIES

Icelandic crafts include traditional hand-knitted woolen sweaters, ceramics, and jewelry.

19 ● SOCIAL PROBLEMS

Iceland has a very low crime rate. Crimes by Icelanders are related to the use of alcohol. With the exception of alcohol use, however, Iceland has fewer drug-related problems than most other European countries. Reykjavík is one of the world's safest capital cities.

20 ● BIBLIOGRAPHY

Hazelton, Nika Standen. *Classic Scandinavian Cooking.* New York: Scribner's Sons, 1987.

Leepthien, E. *Iceland.* Chicago: Children's Press, 1987.

Levanthes, Louise E. "Iceland: Life Under the Glaciers." *National Geographic* (February 1987): 184–215.

Roberts, David. *Iceland.* New York: H. N. Abrams, 1990.

Scherman, Katherine. *Daughter of Fire: A Portrait of Iceland.* Boston: Little, Brown, 1976.

WEBSITES

Embassy of Iceland, Washington, D.C. [Online] Available http://www.iceland.org/, 1998.

World Travel Guide. Iceland. [Online] Available http://www.wtgonline.com/country/is/gen.html, 1998

India

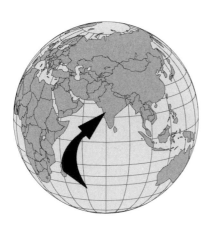

With a total population approaching 1 billion, India is the second most populous nation on earth after China. Collectively, the people of India are called Indians or Asian Indians. However, within its borders, there are dozens of ethnic and language groups with great diversity. These groups are mostly divided according to geographic region, making India seem more like a collection of countries than a single nation.

Among the largest of these groups are the (1) Andhras, a Hindu group in the southeast, (2) the Gonds, a large hill tribal group, (3) the Gujaratis, a Muslim group who inhabit western India, (4) the Marathas, a Hindu group that inhabit western India, (5) the Oriya, Hindus who inhabit eastern India, (6) Rajputs, Hindus who inhabit north and west India; and (7) the Tamils who practice Hinduism and Islam and inhabit southern India and Sri Lanka. This chapter has articles on all of these groups except the Tamils, who are profiled separately in the chapter on Sri Lanka in Volume 8. This chapter begins with an article on the people of India as a whole.

Indians

PRONUNCIATION: IN-dee-uhns

LOCATION: India

POPULATION: About 940 million

LANGUAGE: Fifteen official languages: Hindi;
Bengali; Telugu; Marathi; Tamil; Urdu;
Gujarat; Malayalam; Kannada; Oriya;
Punjab;Assames;Kashmiri; Sindhi; Sanskrit;
English widely spoken

RELIGION: Hinduism; Islam; Christianity;
Sikhism; Buddhism; Jainism; some Judaism,
Parsiism (Zoroastrianism), and animistic
tribal peoples

1 ● INTRODUCTION

India is the largest country in South Asia.
The word "Indian" comes from Sindhu, a
local name for the Indus River. Indians also
call their country "Bharat," the name of a
legendary emperor.

Indian history dates to the third millen-
nium BC when Harappan civilization flourished in the Indus Valley. Aryan-speaking
tribes from Central Asian began settling in
northwestern India around 1700 BC. These
groups eventually took over much of India.

At times, powerful kingdoms such as the
Mauryan (321–181 BC) and the Gupta (AD
319–c. 500) empires have ruled. But, over
the centuries, Persians, Greeks, Parthians,
Kushans, and White Huns invaded India.
Muslims entered India at the beginning of
the eleventh century AD and ruled much of
the subcontinent for eight hundred
years.The Mughal Dynasty conquered Delhi
and ruled from the sixteenth century until
the eighteenth century. Islam made important contributions to South Asian civilization and shaped a great deal of India's
cultural heritage.

Europeans reached South Asia in 1498
when Portuguese sailors landed on the
southwest coast of India. Over the next two
centuries, Portugal, Holland, Britain, and
France set up trading posts and factories. By
the middle of the eighteenth century, the
British East India Company controlled most
of the European trade in India, and Britain
ultimately ruled the entire region.

The inability of British, Hindu, and Muslim leaders to agree on a successor state to
the British Indian Empire resulted in the
partition of the subcontinent (by the United
Nations) into India and Pakistan in 1947.
This has caused three wars. India and Pakistan continue to be hostile toward each
other, particularly over the question of
which country should control the beautiful
mountain state of Kashmir.

2 ● LOCATION

Modern India has an area of about 3.2 million square kilometers (1.2 million square
miles), and a population of 940 million.

India stretches from Cape Comorin, 8°
north of the equator, to its border with the
disputed Kashmir region under Pakistani
control. Pakistan lies to the west, and to the
east, India shares borders with Bangladesh,
China, and Myanmar (Burma).

India has three geographic zones. In the
north lie the majestic Himalayas, which run
for more than 1,500 miles (2,400 kilometers) and contain many of the world's highest peaks. Below the mountains lie the Indo-
Gangetic plains. These lands run from the
Arabian Sea to the Bay of Bengal and along

the Indus and Ganges river valleys. The plains receive plenty of rain during the monsoon season and support much of India's agriculture. The Deccan Plateau forms the third geographical region. These are the uplands bordered by the Eastern and Western Ghats (mountains) that make up the interior of the Indian peninsula.

The seasonal rhythm of the monsoon sets a pattern of Indian life. Winters are bright and pleasant. In late February, temperatures start to rise until May and June, when daily maximums in the northwestern plains exceed 115°F (46°C). The hot season ends with the onset of rain. The monsoon reaches southwest India in late June and sweeps northward. Cherrapunji, in the northeast, is on record as the wettest place on earth, averaging nearly 453 inches (1,150 centimeters) of rain annually. For three months, water is plentiful and the land is green. At the end of September, the rains stop and winter approaches.

India has a wide range of ethnic and cultural diversity. It is less a nation and more a collection of countries. Throughout central and southern India there are tribal populations such as Mundas, Oraons and Santals, there are Dravidian groups in southern India such as Tamils and the Malayalam-speaking peoples in Kerala. In the north, Bengalis, Kashmiris, Punjabis, Gujaratis, Rajputs, and Marathas are among the prominent groups. India shares many of its cultural groups with Pakistan, Bangladesh, and Sri Lanka. Each region has its own mix of religion, caste (social class), language, and literary, cultural and historical traditions. These traditions existed long before modern nations were created, and many people identify

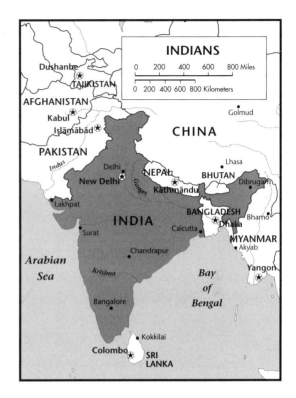

strongly with them. Thus, one can be a Punjabi and either a Pakistani or Indian, or a Bengali and either a Bangladeshi or Indian.

Large Indian communities are also found in Nepal, Malaysia, Sri Lanka, the Middle East, South Africa, Fiji, the West Indies, the United States, Canada, and the United Kingdom.

3 ● LANGUAGE

A Hindi proverb states: "Every two miles the water doth change, and every four the dialect." India has 1,653 dialects. There are about twenty-four languages that are spoken by more than a million people.

Indian languages belong to four major linguistic families (groups of languages with a common ancestor). Austro-Asiatic

Cynthia Bassett

Some buildings built by the Mughals in the eighteenth and nineteenth century are still standing in northern India.

languages (e.g., Munda, Ho, and Khasi) are spoken by tribal groups in central India and the northeastern hills. Bhotia and other languages in the mountain belt belong to the Sino-Tibetan linguistic family. Most Indian languages belong to the Indo-European or Dravidian families.

India today recognizes fourteen spoken languages as official: Hindi, Bengali, Telugu, Marathi, Tamil, Urdu, Gujarati, Malayalam, Kannada, Oriya, Punjabi, Assamese, Kashmiri, and Sindhi. Sanskrit, the classical language of northern India, is also an official language. English is widely used for national, political, and business purposes.

4 ● FOLKLORE

Hindus have a rich mythology and folklore associated with their deities and epic literature. Muslims revere Sufi mystics, and Sikhs have martyred Gurus. Tribal groups have distinct myths and legends. A few historical figures such as Shivaji, the seventeenth-century Maratha leader, are seen as national heroes.

Most of India's national heroes, however, come from the struggle against British imperialism in the early twentieth century. Jawaharlal Nehru (1889–1964), the first prime minister of India, and his daughter Indira Gandhi (1917–84) are among the most important Indian national leaders. The best known figure, however, is Mohandas Gandhi (1869–1948), known worldwide as Mahatma ("Great Soul"). Mohandas Gandhi led India's independence movement. (Independence from Great Britain was granted in 1947.)

5 ● RELIGION

About 80 percent of Indians are Hindus. India, however, prides itself on the freedom of religion guaranteed by its constitution. Religious minorities include Muslims (14 percent), Christians (2.4 percent), Sikhs (2 percent), Buddhists (0.7 percent), and Jains (0.5 percent). Other religious groups include Jews, Parsis (Zoroastrians), and animistic tribal peoples. The practices and beliefs associated with Hinduism vary by region, and from person to person. It is often said that Hinduism is not a religion but a way of life.

One major aspect of Hinduism that influences Indian society is the caste system. The Aryan-speaking peoples developed this system, which divides people into four categories: Brahmans (priests and scholars), Ksatriyas (warriors and rulers), Vaisyas (traders and farmers), and Sudras (servants and artisans). These categories are further divided by occupations, as well as by regional and cultural differences. However, most Indians fall outside the four categories and are referred to as Untouchables, the lowest caste. Although the system has its roots in Hinduism, most religious groups in this region of the world have adopted some aspect of the caste structure.

6 ● MAJOR HOLIDAYS

India officially celebrates the major holidays of its main religious communities. Hindu festivals include *Shivaratri* (dedicated to the god Shiva), *Holi* (the spring festival), *Janamashtami* (birthday of the god Krishna), *Dasahara* (the festival of the goddess Durga), and *Divali* (the Festival of Lights). The Muslim *Eid* festivals (*Eid al-Fitr* and *Bakr-Eid*) and Muharram are holidays. The Christian holy days of Good Friday and Christmas are also observed, as are the birthdays of the founders of Buddhism, Jainism, and Sikhism.

India also celebrates its Independence Day on August 15, the day in 1947 when British colonial rule ended. Republic Day, held on January 26, marks the inauguration of India as a Republic in 1950. Mahatma Gandhi's birthday, on October 2, 1869, also is a national holiday.

Cynthia Bassett

These children live in the very northern part of India, in the beautiful mountain region.

7 ● RITES OF PASSAGE

Most Hindu groups have some form of naming and head-shaving ceremonies. For Muslims, the circumcision of male children is the symbol of commitment to their religion, while for Christians it is baptism. Sikhs, Parsis, and tribal groups also mark the passage from childhood to adulthood. Marriage customs conform to the norms of each community, as do funeral rites. Hindus, Sikhs, and Buddhists cremate their dead, whereas Muslims and Christians bury them. Parsis and some Buddhist groups expose their corpses to vultures. Tribal funeral customs include both cremation and burial.

8 ● RELATIONSHIPS

A common greeting among Hindus is *Namaste,* which means "Greetings to you." It is said while joining one's own hands, palms together and held upright, in front of one's body. In parts of India, the word *Namaste* is replaced with *Namaskar.* *Salaam* or *Salaam alaikum* (Peace be with you) is a typical greeting among Muslims, and *Sat Sri Akal* (God is Truth) is used by Sikhs. Shaking hands, Western style, also is acceptable.

9 ● LIVING CONDITIONS

Medical advances, immunization, and public health programs have raised the average life expectancy in India to just over sixty years. Inadequate sewage disposal, contaminated drinking water, and poor nutrition still pose health problems. India has a high rate of population increase—almost 2 percent a year, which presents one of the country's greatest challenges. For many poor people, however, children provide valuable agricultural help and improve a family's income. People living in poverty are estimated to represent between 24 and 40 percent of the population of India.

India contains some of the largest cities in the world. Greater Bombay (or Mumbai) has about thirteen million people, Calcutta has twelve million, and Delhi has ten million. Yet almost three-fourths of India's people live in rural areas.

India has 1.3 million miles (2.2 million kilometers) of roads. Buses and trains are

Cory Langley

Women in India wear the sari, a six-yard (six-meter) length of cotton or silk cloth wrapped around the waist, with one end thrown over the right shoulder.

the most common means of long-distance travel. Several airlines also operate in India.

10 ● FAMILY LIFE

The joint family remains popular. In the north, families tend to be patriarchal. A household consists of two or three generations of males and their wives and children. In southern India, joint families often are matriarchal. It consists of one's grandmother and her brothers and sisters, one's mother and her brothers and sisters, and one's own brothers and sisters.

Marriages often are arranged, and caste plays an important role. In northern India, marriage partners are usually unrelated. In southern India, however, cross-cousin marriage often occurs, and it is preferred that a man marry his mother's brother's daughter.

11 ● CLOTHING

The common dress for Indian men is the *dhoti.* This is a long piece of white cotton wrapped around the waist and then drawn between the legs and tucked into the waist. In southern India, the chest is usually left bare, while in the north a shirt may be worn. Turbans or some form of headdress are common in northern India. Both men and women also wear a *kurta*, a long tunic-like shirt, and *pyjamas*, loose baggy trousers. People wear leather sandals or other shoes. Shoes usually are removed before entering a temple or an Indian home.

Women typically wear the *sari*, a length of cotton or silk cloth wrapped around the waist, with one end thrown over the right shoulder. The *choli,* a tight-fitting blouse that leaves the midriff bare, is worn under the sari. The sari is worn differently in different parts of India. In Maharashtra, for example, rural women draw one end of the sari through the legs and tuck it into the waist. In some rural areas, women do not wear the bodice; they use the end of the sari to cover their upper bodies

In urban areas, Western-style clothing has become the norm for males.

12 ● FOOD

A typical Indian meal consists of five or six dishes, served all on a *thali.* This is a round metal tray or plate that holds several little bowls (*katoris*). Each bowl holds a different dish. In some areas, food is served on banana leaves. Food is eaten with the hand, preferably the right hand.

The term "curry" was used by Europeans to describe the spicy dishes they found in India, but curries are not always hot. The "heat" in Indian food comes from chilies. Other spices include cumin, coriander, turmeric, black pepper, cardamom, and cloves. Curries are eaten with lentils (*dal*) and pickles and chutneys. In northern and western areas, meals are taken with flat breads (*roti*). These breads are replaced by rice (*chawal*) in the east and south. Yogurt (*dahi*) also may be eaten. Meals often end with a variety of sweets or *paan*, betel nut served with lime and wrapped in a betel leaf.

Mughal-style cooking is found in the north, while *dosas* (thin pancakes of rice-flour) and *idlis* (steamed rice-bread) are popular southern dishes. Madras is known for its fiery curries, while Bengal is famous for its fish dishes. Goan cooking shows Portuguese influences.

Many Hindus avoid eating beef. Muslims generally do not eat pork. Tribal groups avoid the flesh of animals that are their clan totems.

13 ● EDUCATION

It is estimated that over half of all Indians are literate (can read and write). However, this figure hides big differences between males and females, urban and rural populations, and among different social groups. Primary education is free but the quality of state-run schools tends to be poor. Still, education is important and many of India's universities have excellent reputations.

14 ● CULTURAL HERITAGE

Indian culture dates to the Indus Valley civilization, but every group that has entered the subcontinent has left an imprint.

Hindu literature includes sacred texts such as the Vedas, the great Mahabharata and Ramayana epics, and the works of the great Sanskrit playwright and poet, Kalidasa (fifth century AD). Bharata Natyam and Kathakali are forms of classical dance, while the Raga is a form of classical Indian music.

Famous Hindu temples include Mahabalipuram, Khajuraho, and the Sun Temple at Konarak in Orissa. Buddhists cave paintings at Ajanta offer an impressive monument to that faith. The temple city of Palitana in Gujarat and the white marble temples at Dilwara (Mount Abu) in Rajasthan are temple buildings of the Jainist religion. Islam's many contributions to Indian culture include miniature paintings and the Taj Mahal.

The most popular musical instrument in India is the sitar, an instrument similar to a guitar. It is played with a steel plucker called a *mazrab* worn on the right index finger, while the left index finger slides over the frets on the neck of the sitar. One sitar, the drone, provides the rhythm to support the melody.

Rabindranath Tagore (1861–1941), a Bengali poet and novelist was awarded the Nobel Prize for literature in 1913, and the films of Satyajit Ray (1921–92) have received worldwide praise.

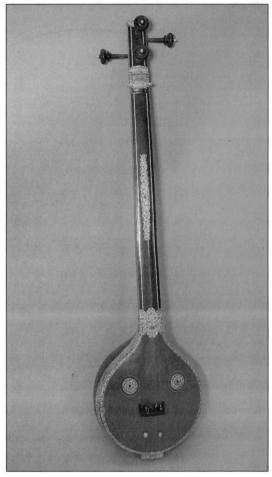

EPD Photos

Drone sitar, used to accompany the sitar soloist in performance. Courtesy of the Center for the Study of World Musics, Kent State University.

15 ● EMPLOYMENT

Over 60 percent of India's labor force works in agriculture. Despite this, India is highly industrialized. Its industries range from nuclear power production to garment making. Recent liberalization of the economy has seen faster growth and expanding trade, although many say these changes have not helped most of India's people.

16 ● SPORTS

Chess, dice, and card playing are old favorites. Traditional sports include cock fighting, camel racing, and wrestling. Hunting was a favorite sport and *kabaddi* (team wrestling) remains popular. Children's games include kite-flying, spinning tops, yo-yos, and hobbyhorses. Indians enthusiastically play or watch cricket and field hockey. Games such as soccer, tennis, badminton, squash, table tennis, and golf are also widely played.

17 ● RECREATION

India's film industry is enormous. Regional language films are produced in Calcutta and Madras, but the center of the industry is Bombay. "Bollywood," as it is known, produces love stories filled with action as well as singing and dancing. Film music is immensely popular. Film actors and actresses are pop idols and trendsetters, and their lives are followed with interest.

18 ● CRAFTS AND HOBBIES

Folk arts in India range from wall painting to puppetry to regional music and dance forms. India is known for textiles, rugs, metalwork, bronzes, copper- and brassware, stone carving, pottery, woodwork, and jewelry.

19 ● SOCIAL PROBLEMS

Despite efforts at population control, India soon will be the world's most populous nation. This might worsen existing problems such as poverty, high unemployment, illiteracy, and malnutrition. Another growing problem is AIDS. It is predicted that 1 million AIDS cases and 10 million HIV cases will have been reported in India by 2000.

Many groups in Assam, Kashmir, Punjab, Tamil Nadu, and other areas are demanding more freedom. Sometimes groups even express a desire to gain complete independence from India. Muslims fear that a rise of Hindu fundamentalism will threaten India's commitment to secularism (nonreligious government). India's Constitution recognizes three categories of disadvantaged groups that need special representation and assistance. This "reservations policy" is as controversial in India as affirmative action policies are now in the United States.

Despite these problems, India continues its fifty-year-old tradition as the world's largest democracy.

20 ● BIBLIOGRAPHY

Ardley, Bridget. *India.* Englewood Cliffs, N.J.: Silver Burdett Press, 1989.

Barker, Amanda. *India.* Crystal Lake, Ill.: Ribgy Interactive Library, 1996.

Cumming, David. *India.* New York: Bookwright, 1991.

Das, Prodeepta. *Inside India.* New York: F. Watts, 1990.

Dolcini, Donatella. *India in the Islamic Era and Southeast Asia (8th to 19th century).* Austin, Tex.: Raintree Steck-Vaughn, 1997.

Kalman, Bobbie. *India: The Culture.* Toronto: Crabtree Publishing Co., 1990.

Pandian, Jacob. *The Making of India and Indian Traditions.* Englewood Cliffs, N.J.: Prentice Hall, 1995.

Shalant, Phyllis. *Look What We've Brought You from India: Crafts, Games, Recipes, Stories, and Other Cultural Activities from Indian*

Americans. Parsippany, N.J.: Julian Messner, 1998.

WEBSITES

Consulate General of India in New York. [Online] Available http://www.indiaserver.com/cginyc/, 1998.

Embassy of India, Washington, D.C. [Online] Available http://www.indianembassy.org/, 1998.

Interknowledge Corporation. [Online] Available http://www.interknowledge.com/india/, 1998.

World Travel Guide. India. [Online] Available http://www.wtgonline.com/country/in/gen.html, 1998.

Andhras

PRONUNCIATION: AHN-druz
ALTERNATE NAMES: Telugu
LOCATION: India (Andhra Pradesh State)
POPULATION: 66 million
LANGUAGE: Telugu
RELIGION: Hinduism

1 ● INTRODUCTION

The Andhras are also known as Telugu. Their traditional home is the land between the Godavari and Kistna (Krishna) rivers in southeastern India. Today, Andhras are the dominant group in the state of Andhra Pradesh.

In the first century BC, the earliest Andhra dynasties emerged. When Europeans arrived in India (1498), the northern areas of Andhra country were in the Muslim state of Golkonda, while southern areas lay in Hindu Vijayanagara. The British administered the Andhra region as part of their Madras Presidency. Northwestern areas remained under the Muslim princely state of Hyderabad. The Nizam of Hyderabad—ruler of the largest Muslim princely state in India—refused to join India when it became an independent nation in 1947. The Indian army invaded Hyderabad and integrated it into the Indian Republic in 1949. Andhra pressure for a Telugu-speaking state resulted in the creation of Andhra Pradesh in 1956.

2 ● LOCATION

The population of Andhra Pradesh is over 66 million. Telegu-speaking peoples also live in surrounding states and in the state of Tamil Nadu. Telugu-speakers are also found in Africa, Asia, Europe, and the United States.

Andhra Pradesh has three geographic regions: the coastal plains, mountains, and interior plateaus. The coastal areas run for about 500 miles (800 kilometers) along the Bay of Bengal, and include the area formed by the deltas of the Godavari and Kistna rivers. This area receives a great deal of rainfall during the summer monsoon and is farmed heavily. The mountain region is formed by hills known as the Eastern Ghats. These mark the edge of the Deccan Plateau. They reach an elevation of 3,300 feet (1,000 meters) in the south and of 5,513 feet (1,680 meters) in the north. Numerous rivers break up the Eastern Ghats east to the ocean. The interior plateaus lie west of the Ghats. Most of this area is drier and supports only scrub vegetation. Summers in the coastal areas are hot, and temperatures exceed 104°F (40°C). Winters in the plateau region are mild, as temperatures fall only as low as 50°F (10°C).

3 ● LANGUAGE

Telugu, the official language of Andhra Pradesh, is a Dravidian language. Regional Telegu dialects include Andhra (spoken in the delta), Telingana (the dialect of the northwestern region), and Rayalasima (spoken in southern areas). Literary Telugu is quite distinct from spoken forms of the language. Telegu is one of the regional languages recognized by the Indian constitution.

4 ● FOLKLORE

Hero worship is important in Andhra culture. Andhra warriors who died on the battlefield or who sacrificed their lives for great or pious causes were worshiped as gods. Stone pillars called Viragallulu honor their bravery and are found all over Andhra country. The Katamaraju Kathala, one of the oldest ballads in Telugu, celebrates the twelfth-century warrior Katamaraju.

5 ● RELIGION

Andhras are mostly Hindus. The Brahman castes (priests and scholars) have the highest social status, and Brahmans serve as priests in temples. Andhras worship Shiva, Vishnu, Hanuman, and other Hindu gods. Andhras also worship *ammas* or village goddesses. Durgamma presides over the welfare of the village, Maisamma protects the village boundaries, and Balamma is a goddess of fertility. These deities are all forms of the Mother Goddess and play a big role in daily life. These deities often have priests drawn from the lower castes, and low castes may use their own priests rather than Brahmans.

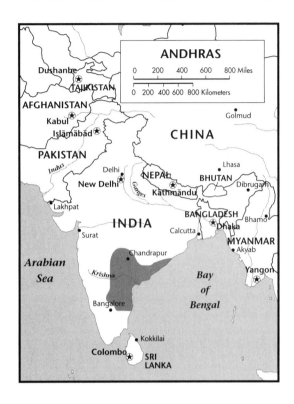

6 ● MAJOR HOLIDAYS

Important Andhra festivals include Ugadi (beginning of the new year), Shivaratri (honoring Shiva), Chauti (Ganesha's birthday), Holi (the end of the lunar year, in February or March), Dasahara (the festival of the goddess Durga), and Divali (the Festival of Lights). Preparations for Ugadi begin with a thorough washing of one's home, inside and out. On the actual day, everyone gets up before dawn to decorate the entrance to his or her home with fresh mango leaves. They also splash the ground outside the front door with water into which a little cow dung has been dissolved. This represents a wish that God bless the new year ahead. Ugadi food features raw mango.

On Holi, people throw colorful liquids at each other—from rooftops, or with squirt guns and balloons filled with colored water. Beautiful floral designs are drawn on the ground outside each person's house, and groups of people playfully cover each other with color while singing and dancing.

Different castes also have separate festivals. For example, Brahmans (priests and scholars) observe Rath Saptami, a worship of the Sun. In the northwestern Telingana region, the annual worship of Pochamma, the goddess of smallpox, is an important village festival. On the day before the festival, drummers go around the village, members of the potter caste clean shrines of village goddesses, and those of the washerman caste paint them white. Village youths build small sheds in front of the shrines, and women of the sweeper caste smear the ground with red earth. On the day of the festival, every household prepares rice in a pot called *bonam*. The drummers lead the village in procession to the Pochamma shrine, where a member of the potter caste acts as priest. Every family offers rice to the goddess. Goats, sheep, and fowl are offered too. Then, families return to their houses for a feast.

7 ● RITES OF PASSAGE

When a child is born, the mother and other family members are considered impure. Rituals are performed to remove this perceived impurity. The period of impurity lasts up to thirty days for the mother. A Brahman (member of the highest social class) may be consulted to cast the infant's horoscope. A name-giving ceremony is held within three to four weeks. As children grow up, they help their parents with daily tasks. Higher castes (social clases) often perform a special ceremony for males before puberty is reached. A girl's first menstruation is accompanied by elaborate rituals, including a period of seclusion, worship of household gods, and a gathering of village women for singing and dancing.

The higher Hindu castes usually cremate their dead. Children are normally buried. Burial also is common among low-caste and Untouchable groups (people who are not members of any of India's four castes). The corpse is bathed, dressed, and carried to the cremation ground or graveyard. On the third day after death, the house is cleaned, all the linens are washed and earthen pots used for cooking and for storing water are discarded. On the eleventh or thirteenth day, family members undergo other rites. The head and face are shaved if the deceased was one's father or mother. Food and water are offered to the soul of the deceased, and a feast is given. The higher castes collect bones and ashes from the funeral pyre and immerse them in a river.

8 ● RELATIONSHIPS

Andhras enjoy arguing and gossiping. They also are known for being generous.

9 ● LIVING CONDITIONS

In northern Andhra Pradesh, villages are usually built along a strip. Settlements in southern parts of the state are either built along a strip or are square-shaped, but they also may have adjoining villages. A typical house is square in shape and is built around a courtyard. The walls are made of stone, the floor is made of mud, and the roof is tiled. There are two or three rooms, used for living, sleeping, and housing livestock. One room is used for the family shrine and to keep valuables. The doors are often carved, and designs are painted on the walls. Most houses lack toilets, the inhabitants using the fields for their natural functions. There may be a backyard used for growing vegetables and keeping chickens. Furnishings consist of beds, wooden stools, and chairs. Kitchen utensils are usually of earthenware and are made by the village potters.

10 ● FAMILY LIFE

Andhras must marry within their caste or subcaste but outside their clan. Marriages are often arranged. Newlyweds usually move into the household of the groom's father. The extended family is regarded as ideal, although the nuclear family is also found.

Women are responsible for household chores and raising children. Among the cultivating castes, women also do farm work. Divorce and widow remarriage are permitted by lower castes. Property is divided among sons.

11 ● CLOTHING

Men typically wear the *dhoti* (loincloth) with a *kurta*. The dhoti is a long piece of white cotton wrapped around the waist and then drawn between the legs and tucked into the waist. The kurta is a tunic-like shirt that comes down to the knees. Women wear the *sari* (a length of fabric wrapped around the waist, with one end thrown over the right shoulder) and *choli* (tight-fitting, cropped blouse). Saris traditionally are dark blue, parrot green, red, or purple.

12 ● FOOD

The basic diet of Andhras consists of rice, millets, pulses (legumes), and vegetables. Nonvegetarians eat meat or fish. Brahmans (priests and scholars) and other high castes avoid meat, fish, and eggs. The well-to-do eat three meals a day. A typical meal would be rice or *khichri* (rice cooked with lentils and spices) or *paratha* (an unleavened bread made from wheat flour and fried in oil). This is taken with curried meat or vegetables (such as eggplant or okra), hot pickles, and tea. Coffee is a popular drink in coastal areas. Betel leaves, twisted into rolls and filled with nuts, are served after a meal. In a poor household, a meal might consist of millet bread, eaten with boiled vegetables, chili powder, and salt. Rice would be eaten, and meat would only rarely be consumed. Men dine first and the women eat after the men have finished. Children are served as soon as the food is ready.

13 ● EDUCATION

The literacy rate (percentage of the population who can read and write) for Andhra Pradesh is well under 50 percent. Even though this figure can be expected to rise, it compares unfavorably with many other Indian peoples. Still, the city of Hyderabad is an important center of learning, where several universities are located.

14 ● CULTURAL HERITAGE

The Andhra people have made major contributions to art, architecture, literature, music, and dance. The early Andhra rulers were great builders and patrons of religion and the arts. From the first century BC on, they developed a style of architecture that

EPD Photos

This pair of drums together is called tabla; the smaller drum is also called tabla, and the larger one is the baya. Courtesy of the Center for the Study of World Musics, Kent State University.

led to the creation of some of the greatest Buddhist monuments of central India. The *stupa* (a monument built to hold a relic of Buddha) at Sanchi is one of these. Some paintings in the famous Buddhist caves at Ajanta are ascribed to Andhra artists.

The Andhras perform *kuchipudi,* a dance-drama. The Andhra people also have contributed greatly to south Indian classical music. Tabla, the predecessor of the timapni or kettle drum, is a small drum. The drummer sits on the floor with a ring-shaped cloth pillow on the floor in front of him.

The tabla rests on the pillow, and is drummed with the fingers and palms.

South Indian compositions are mostly written in Telugu because of the smooth, rich, sound of the language. Telugu literature dates to the eleventh century AD.

15 ● EMPLOYMENT

Over three-quarters (77 percent) of Andhras make their living from agriculture. Rice is the dominant food grain. Sugarcane, tobacco, and cotton are grown as cash crops, in addition to chilies, oilseeds, and pulses (legumes). Today, Andhra Pradesh also is one of the most industrialized states in India. Industries such as aeronautics, light engineering, chemicals, and textiles are found in the Hyderabad and Guntur-Vijayawada areas. India's largest shipbuilding yard is in Andhra Pradesh.

16 ● SPORTS

Children play with dolls and enjoy ballgames, tag, and hide-and-seek. Playing with dice is common among men and women. Cockfighting and shadow plays are popular in rural areas. Modern sports such as cricket, soccer, and field hockey are played in schools.

17 ● RECREATION

Wandering entertainers put on puppet shows for villagers. Professional ballad singers recount the exploits of past heroes, or tell stories. Radio is used by many, and Andhra Pradesh has its own movie industry. Sometimes, film stars become political heroes. The late N. T. Rama Rao, for instance, starred in more than 300 Telugu films, then went on to serve as a chief minister of Andhra Pradesh.

18 ● CRAFTS AND HOBBIES

Andhras are known for their carvings of wooden birds, animals, human beings, and deities. Other crafts include lacquerware, handwoven carpets, handprinted textiles, and tie-dyed fabrics. Metalware, silverwork, embroidery, painting on ivory, basketry, and lace work are also products of the region. The making of leather puppets was developed in the sixteenth century.

19 ● SOCIAL PROBLEMS

Rural areas face problems of high population, poverty, illiteracy, and lack of social infrastructure. Drinking of arrack or country liquor has been such a problem that pressure from women in recent years has led to its prohibition. Economic problems are worsened by destructive cyclones that sweep in from the Bay of Bengal. Currently, Andhra Pradesh State is involved in a longstanding dispute with Karnataka over the use of the waters of the Kistna River. Through all of this, however, Andhras retain pride in their heritage.

20 ● BIBLIOGRAPHY

Ardley, Bridget. *India.* Englewood Cliffs, N.J.: Silver Burdett Press, 1989.

Barker, Amanda. *India.* Crystal Lake, Ill.: Ribgy Interactive Library, 1996.

Cumming, David. *India.* New York: Bookwright, 1991.

Das, Prodeepta. *Inside India.* New York: F. Watts, 1990.

Dolcini, Donatella. *India in the Islamic Era and Southeast Asia (8th to 19th century).* Austin, Tex.: Raintree Steck-Vaughn, 1997.

Furer-Haimendorf, Christoph von. *The Gonds of Andhra Pradesh: Tradition and Change in an Indian Tribe.* London, England: Allen & Unwin, 1979.

Kalman, Bobbie. *India: The Culture.* Toronto: Crabtree Publishing Co., 1990.

Pandian, Jacob. *The Making of India and Indian Traditions.* Englewood Cliffs, N.J.: Prentice Hall, 1995.

Shalant, Phyllis. *Look What We've Brought You from India: Crafts, Games, Recipes, Stories, and Other Cultural Activities from Indian Americans.* Parsippany, N.J.: Julian Messner, 1998.

WEBSITES

Consulate General of India in New York. [Online] Available http://www.indiaserver.com/cginyc/, 1998.

Embassy of India, Washington, D.C. [Online] Available http://www.indianembassy.org, 1998.

Interknowledge Corporation. [Online] Available http://www.interknowledge.com/india/, 1998.

World Travel Guide. India. [Online] Available http://www.wtgonline.com/country/in/gen.html, 1998.

Gonds

PRONUNCIATION: gAHNds
ALTERNATE NAMES: Koi; Koitur
LOCATION: India
POPULATION: Over 9 million
LANGUAGE: Gondi
RELIGION: Cult of the Persa Pen (clan deities); ancestor spirit worship

1 ● INTRODUCTION

The Gonds are among the largest tribal groups in South Asia and perhaps the world. The term Gond refers to tribal peoples who live all over India's Deccan Peninsula. Most describe themselves as Gonds (hill people) or as Koi or Koitur.

Scholars believe Gonds settled in Gondwana, now known as eastern Madhya Pradesh, between the ninth and thirteenth centuries AD. Muslim writers describe a rise of Gond states after the fourteenth century. Gond dynasties ruled in four kingdoms (Garha-Mandla, Deogarh, Chanda, and Kherla) in central India between the sixteenth and mid-eighteenth centuries.

Maratha power swept into Gond land in the 1740s. They overthrew Gond *rajas* (princes) and seized most of their territory.

Some Gond *zamindaris* (estates) survived until recently. However, Gonds are similar to many tribal groups today in that they face severe economic hardships. Although some Gond groups own a great deal of land, others are classified as Scheduled Tribes, which means they need special social and economic help.

2 ● LOCATION

Gonds live all over central India, and in the states of Maharashtra and Orissa. As "hill people," they traditionally have been associated with hills and uplands in the Deccan Peninsula. Many Gonds live around the Satpura Hills, Maikala Range and Son-Deogarh uplands, and on the Bastar plateau. Many Gond tribes also live in the Garhjat Hills of northern Orissa. The upland areas generally lie between 2,000 to 3,000 feet (600 to 900 meters), with isolated peaks occasionally exceeding approximately 4,000 feet (1,200 meters). The region is drained by the headwaters of many of India's major rivers (such as the Narmada, Tapti, Son, Mahanadi, and Godavari). Forest cover is dense in places, and communications are generally difficult. February sees the start of the hot season, with temperatures rising to over 40°C (104°F) in early June. The summer brings the monsoon rains, with precipitation amounts varying from 47 inches (120 centimeters) to over 63 inches (160 centimeters) in the more southeasterly locations. Late September marks the return of the cool, dry weather of winter.

3 ● LANGUAGE

Gondi belongs to the Dravidian family of languages and is related to Tamil and Kannada. The language offers a cultural connection between the many Gond groups. Many Gonds also speak Hindi, Marathi, or Telegu.

4 ● FOLKLORE

Hereditary bards and professional storytellers called Pardhans tell stories about Gond legends and myths. This makes for a rich oral tradition. In these stories, it is said that when Gond gods were born, their mother abandoned them. The goddess Parvati rescued them, but her consort Sri Shambhu Mahadeo (Shiva) kept them captive in a cave. Pahandi Kapar Lingal, a Gond hero, who received help from the goddess Jangu Bai, rescued them from the cave. They came out of the cave in four groups, thus laying the foundations of the basic fourfold division of Gond society. Lingal also is responsible for creating a Gond kinship system and establishing a group of great Gond gods.

5 ● RELIGION

Persa Pen is the most distinctive feature of Gond religion. Like many other tribes, Gonds worship a high god known as Baradeo, whose alternate names are Bhagavan, Sri Shambu Mahadeo, and Persa Pen. Baradeo oversees activities of lesser gods. He is respected but he does not receive fervent devotion, which is shown only to clan deities. Each Gond clan has its Persa Pen, who protects all clan members. The Persa Pen is essentially good but can be dangerous and violent. Many Gonds believe that when a Pardhan (bard) plays his fiddle, the deity's fierce powers can be controlled.

Each village has its Village-Guardian and Village-Mother who are worshipped

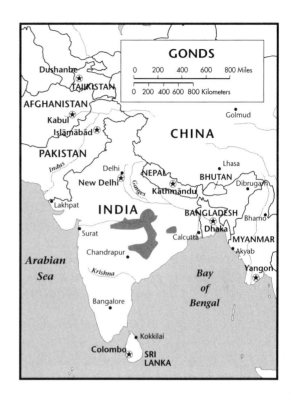

when villagers celebrate regular festivities. Gonds also worship family and household gods, gods of the field, and gods of cattle. Deities such as Shitala Mata, goddess of smallpox, help ward off disease. Spirits are also believed to inhabit hills, rivers, lakes and trees.

Village priests *(devari),* perform sacrifices and rituals for village festivals. The head of a household typically carries out family ceremonies. Clan priests *(katora)* tend the shrine and ritual objects of the clan's Persa Pen. These priests also guard the sacred spear point and organize annual festivals.

Most aspects of Gond life, from the greatest festivals to the building of a new cattle shed, are accompanied by sacrifice.

Certain deities, especially female ones, demand chickens, goats, and sometimes male buffaloes. Every nine or twelve years, Gonds sacrifice a pig to the god Narayan Deo in an important ceremony known as the *Laru Kaj* (Pig's Wedding). Other rituals also involve offerings of fruits, coconuts, flowers, colored powder, and strings.

Gonds believe evil spirits and the gods' displeasure cause most diseases and misfortunes. They ask soothsayers and diviners to find out the cause of problems and to suggest remedies. Sometimes, magicians and shamans (healers) can provide this advice. Magicians use special formulas to control the actions of a deity or spirit that is causing a particular affliction. Shamans fall into a trance and give voice to the demands of an offended god or spirit.

6 ● MAJOR HOLIDAYS

Many Gond festivals are connected to agriculture. Pola, a cattle festival, and Nagpanchami, the snake festival, are very popular.

Dasahara is an important Gond holiday. A Gond custom is stick dancing undertaken by young people. Bands of young people travel from village to village, dancing and singing. The dancing is a religious duty. It is also an occasion for fun.

7 ● RITES OF PASSAGE

Gonds protect pregnant women against spells and evil influences, and perform several rituals after a baby is born. A mother's brother generally names a baby boy, while the father's sister names a girl. Children grow up as part of a family, clan, and *phratry* (one of the four main divisions of Gond society), and gradually learn the ways of their people. Both boys and girls help guard family crops from birds and monkeys. Males undergo a ritual shaving of the beard, mustache, and eyebrows as a sign of adulthood. Girls are considered full-grown at their first menstruation.

Gonds cremate or bury their dead. Children, unmarried persons, and individuals dying an inauspicious death (for instance, in an epidemic) are buried without much ceremony. Gonds believe humans have a life force and a spirit. On death, the life force is reincarnated into another earthly existence, but the spirit remains in the other world. Gonds perform death rituals to help the spirit move into the other world and to ease its acceptance by other clan spirits. This rite, known as *karun*, must be done to fulfill an obligation to the deceased. Memorial pillars honor the dead. Gonds believe ancestral spirits watch over the living, punish offenders, and guard Gond communities.

8 ● RELATIONSHIPS

Gonds welcome visitors with dried tobacco leaves, fruits, or other small gifts. Many villages have guest huts.

9 ● LIVING CONDITIONS

Each Gond village has a headman (known by local names such as *mukhia, mahji,* or *patel*) and a village council (*panchayat*) chosen by the villagers. The council consists of the headman, priest, village watchman, and four or five elders. It helps keep the village running smoothly and upholds Gond customs. Villages also have service castes such as Ahir (cowherds), Agaria (blacksmiths), Dhulia (drummers), and Pardhan (bards and singers).

A typical Gond village has several hamlets. Each consists of homesteads that house extended families. Houses are usually built of mud and thatch. They consist of a living room, kitchen, veranda, a special room for women to use while menstruating, and a shrine for clan gods.

Gond houses contain cots and a few wooden stools; mats are used for sitting and sleeping.

10 ● FAMILY LIFE

Gond society is divided into four groups known as *phratries* or *sagas* in Gondi. Each saga traces its descent to one of the four groups of gods who emerged from the cave after their release by the hero Lingal. The saga is divided into several clans *(pari)*. A clan consists of a group of people who believe they share a common ancestor. Generally, it is good to marry outside the clan.

Kinship and marriage customs among Gonds reflect broader regional patterns. The norm is cross-cousin marriage (for example, marrying one's mother's brother's daughter), which is typical in southern India. Gond groups that have been influenced by northern peoples such as Marathas, however, follow northern customs in determining marriage partners. Similarly, northern Gonds allow widows to remarry a brother of the deceased husband.

Gonds typically choose their marriage mates, and a tribal council approves the matches. The father of a groom pays a bride price. Gond weddings include many significant ceremonies. The main part of the wedding occurs when the bride and groom walk seven times around a wedding post. Newly-weds live with the groom's family until it is possible for them to move into a house of their own.

Sometimes, Gond matches are made when a groom and bride elope. These marriages must be approved later by relatives and the village council. The council also can approve divorces.

11 ● CLOTHING

Gond men typically wear the *dhoti,* or loin-cloth. The dhoti is a long piece of white cotton cloth wrapped around the waist and then drawn between the legs and tucked into the waist. Women wear a cotton *sari* (a length of fabric wrapped around the waist, with one end thrown over the right shoulder) and *choli* (tight-fitting, cropped blouse).

12 ● FOOD

The staples of the Gond diet are two millets known as *kodo* and *kutki.* These are either boiled to a broth or cooked to a dry cereal. Broth is preferred for the first two meals of the day and the dry cereal is eaten at night, often with vegetables. Vegetables are either grown in gardens or collected from forests along with roots and tubers. Honey is also gathered from forests.

Rice is a luxury item that Gonds enjoy during feasts and festivals. Most Gonds like meat. Animals sacrificed at ceremonies are eagerly consumed, and animals hunted in the forest supplement the diet. Gonds must abstain from the flesh of animals that are their clan totems.

Gonds grow tobacco for smoking and for celebrations make liquor from the mahua tree.

13 ● EDUCATION

Literacy (percentage of the population who can read and write) among Gonds varies from just over 25 percent in Maharashtra to less than 15 percent in Madhya Pradesh. Among females in Madhya Pradesh, it drops to about 4 percent. Few children attend school regularly, and girls rarely continue past primary school.

14 ● CULTURAL HERITAGE

Gonds celebrate most festive occasions with song and dance. In some instances, such as with the Dandari dancers, dances retell events from Gond mythology. At other times, dances are performed simply for fun. Dhulia are a professional musician caste and Pardhans (bards) preserve legends, myths, and history, passing these traditions on from generation to generation. Gonds also enjoy assembling on full-moon nights to sing and dance. Cockfighting is a favorite pastime.

Both men and women enjoy wearing heavy silver ornaments. Women also like to wear colored glass bangles and marriage necklaces made of small black beads. They often tattoo their bodies.

15 ● EMPLOYMENT

Gonds today are mainly farmers. Although some Gond communities have risen to the status of landowners, many are landless laborers.

16 ● SPORTS

No sporting activities are associated with traditional Gond society.

17 ● RECREATION

Gonds enjoy singing and dancing. Some also enjoy cock-fighting (battle between two roosters, with spectators placing bets on the outcome).

18 ● CRAFTS AND HOBBIES

Gonds have a rich arts tradition that includes pottery, basket making, body tattooing, and floor painting. They paint designs in red and black on the walls of their houses. These drawings often celebrate festivals and depict animals, birds, human figures, hunting, and dancing. Gonds make musical instruments. They carve memorial pillars in wood and stone for their dead. They often decorate houses with carved doors and panels.

19 ● SOCIAL PROBLEMS

Gonds face problems typical of tribal peoples throughout South Asia and much of the world. They suffer exploitation and discrimination, and often are forced to live on less productive lands in remote areas. They are experiencing increasing pressure on their land, a rise in the number of landless laborers, and high levels of poverty. Lack of education and low levels of literacy further reduce economic opportunity.

20 ● BIBLIOGRAPHY

Ardley, Bridget. *India*. Englewood Cliffs, N.J.: Silver Burdett Press, 1989.

Barker, Amanda. *India*. Crystal Lake, Ill.: Ribgy Interactive Library, 1996.

Cumming, David. *India*. New York: Bookwright, 1991.

Das, Prodeepta. *Inside India*. New York: F. Watts, 1990.

Dolcini, Donatella. *India in the Islamic Era and Southeast Asia (8th to 19th century)*. Austin,

Tex.: Raintree Steck-Vaughn, 1997.

Kalman, Bobbie. *India: The Culture.* Toronto: Crabtree Publishing Co., 1990.

Pandian, Jacob. *The Making of India and Indian Traditions.* Englewood Cliffs, N.J.: Prentice Hall, 1995.

Shalant, Phyllis. *Look What We've Brought You from India: Crafts, Games, Recipes, Stories, and Other Cultural Activities from Indian Americans.* Parsippany, N.J.: Julian Messner, 1998.

WEBSITES

Consulate General of India in New York. [Online] Available http://www.indiaserver.com/cginyc/, 1998.

Embassy of India, Washington, D.C. [Online] Available http://www.indianembassy.org/, 1998.

Interknowledge Corporation. [Online] Available http://www.interknowledge.com/india/, 1998.

World Travel Guide. India. [Online] Available http://www.wtgonline.com/country/in/gen.html, 1998.

Gujaratis

PRONUNCIATION: goo-juh-RAH-teez
LOCATION: India (Gujarat state)
POPULATION: 48 million
LANGUAGE: Gujarati
RELIGION: Hindu; small populations of Muslims, Jains, Parsis

1 ● INTRODUCTION

Gujaratis live in Gujarat, one of the western states in India. The name comes from "Gujara," a branch of the White Huns. This group ruled the area during the eighth and ninth centuries. Gujara also is the name of a pastoral caste (social class).

Archaeological evidence shows the region had cities as early as 2000 BC. Muslims conquered Gujarat in the thirteenth century AD and ruled for the next 450 years. Control passed to the British East India Company in 1818. After India's independence in 1947, Gujarat was incorporated into Bombay state. In 1960, the Gujarati-speaking areas of Bombay were split off to form the present-day Gujarat.

2 ● LOCATION

Gujarat currently has a population of 48 million. There also is a sizable community of Gujaratis who live and work outside India.

Gujarat lies on India's west coast. Part of its western boundary lies at the edge of Pakistan. Its coastline runs from near the mouth of the Indus River, curves around the great peninsula of Saurashtra, and swings south to a point about 100 miles (160 kilometers) north of Bombay. Gujarat has three broad geographic divisions: mainland Gujarat, the Saurashtra Peninsula, and Kachch. Mainland Gujarat consists of coastal plains. These merge with lowlands around Ahmadabad and northern Gujarat. Fringing this area on the north and east are the uplands of the southern Aravallis, the western Vindhya and Satpura Ranges, and the Western Ghats. The southern areas are good for farming, even though most of the state is dry.

The Saurashtra (also known as Kathiawar) region consists of a peninsula bounded by the Gulf of Cambay, the Arabian Sea, and the Gulf of Kachch. Broad coastal plains surround low plateaus and

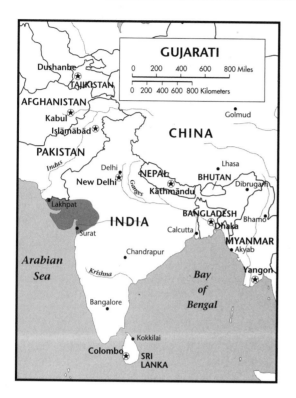

GUJARATI

hills. One of these, Gir Range (about 2,100 feet or 640 meters), is home to a wildlife sanctuary for the last Asian lion population in the world. The Rann, a vast expanse of tidal mud flats and salt marshes, take up much of Kachch.

3 ● LANGUAGE

The language, Gujarati, comes from Sanskrit—an ancient language. There are several dialects of Gujarati. These include Kachchi, Kathiawadi, and Surati. Bhili, a language similar to Gujarati, is spoken by tribal groups in northern and eastern Gujarat. Gujarati is written in a cursive script. Many Gujaratis can also understand and speak Hindi.

4 ● FOLKLORE

According to Hindu legend, the hero-god Krishna was forced to abandon his ancestral home of Mathura and moved his capital to Dvaraka (the modern Dwarka) at the western tip of the Saurashtra Peninsula. In one epic, Krishna's relatives began to quarrel and the entire city got involved in an uproar. Soon, many chiefs were dead. Krishna's son was killed, and his brother was mortally wounded. Disheartened, Krishna went to a nearby forest to think. A hunter saw him, thought he was a deer, and killed him. The city of Dvaraka was then swallowed by the sea.

5 ● RELIGION

About 90 percent of Gujaratis are Hindu. The Vallabhacharya sect of Krishna worshipers has a particularly strong following among the Gujarati bania (trading) castes. Dwarka is an important place of pilgrimage for this sect, and is considered one of India's seven sacred cities. Shiva also has his following among Gujaratis. The Somnath Temple, on Saurashtra's southern coast, is an important Shaivite shrine.

Muslims make up about 8 percent of Gujarati population. Jains, although comparatively few in number, have played a major role in shaping Gujarati culture. Girnar and Satrunjaya Hill, near Palitana, are major centers of Jain pilgrimage. There are small Parsi communities in the cities of Surat and Navsari.

6 ● MAJOR HOLIDAYS

Various Gujarati communities celebrate different religious festivals. *Navratri* is one holiday that is widely celebrated throughout the state. Navratri means "nine nights" and is celebrated on the nine nights leading up to Dasahara (the festival of the goddess Durga). It is a time of gaiety, when men and women gather in village squares and temple compounds to sing and dance. On Dasahara, artisans worship their tools, farmers their ploughs, and students their books. Gujaratis also pay special attention to the birthday of Indian national leader Mohandas "Mahatma" Gandhi. He was born in Porbandar in Saurashtra (Gujarat) on.October 2, 1869. (He was killed by a Hindu fanatic in 1948.)

7 ● RITES OF PASSAGE

Gujaratis follow the life-cycle rituals prescribed by their communities. Virtually all groups have some sort of period of seclusion followed by purification rites for girls at their first menstruation. Jain rituals in general follow Hindu patterns. Muslim practices include whispering the Call to Prayer *(azan)* in a newborn baby's ear, head shaving and naming ceremonies, and circumcision (sunnat) for males.

Most Gujarati Hindus cremate their dead, although some lower-caste groups bury them. Ashes and bone are collected from the funeral pyre to be scattered, if at all possible, in the sacred Ganges River. Jain funeral customs tend to follow the Hindu pattern, while Muslims bury their dead.

8 ● RELATIONSHIPS

Hindus greet each other by saying *Namaste* or *Namas* which means "Greetings to you." Muslims use *Salaam* or *Salaam alaikum* (Peace be with you) as a greeting.

9 ● LIVING CONDITIONS

A typical Gujarati village consists of a cluster of houses along a central street. A temple, a village square, a few shops, and a well are found in the village center. Agricultural and trading castes live in this central area, and artisan castes live farther out. In the past, mud walls surrounded villages for protection against robbers. Untouchables (people who are not members of any of India's four castes), such as Dheds (road sweepers) and Bhangis (cleaners), live outside the village boundaries. Houses are generally roomy, and built of mud or brick. Furniture consists of a couple of wooden boxes to hold valuables, wooden beds and coverings, and copper and earthenware cooking utensils. There is usually no stable for livestock, so cattle and goats are kept in the house.

10 ● FAMILY LIFE

In general, Gujaratis conform to northern Indian patterns of kinship, marriage practices, and family structure. The norm is to marry within one's caste, but outside one's clan. Newlyweds live with the father's family. Marriages are arranged. The joint family is typical among Gujaratis, with a household consisting of two or three generations of men and their dependents. Lower caste women are expected to work in the fields or otherwise contribute to the family income.

11 ● CLOTHING

Gujarati men wear the *dhoti* (loincloth consisting of a long piece of white cotton wrapped around the waist and then drawn between the legs and tucked into the waist), accompanied by a shirt and coat closed with strings. Women wear the *sari* (a length of

Cory Langley

Education in reading, writing, mathematics, and accounting begins early in life for members of the higher social classes, especially for boys.

fabric wrapped around the waist, with one end thrown over the right shoulder) and *choli* (tight-fitting, cropped blouse).

12 ● FOOD

Gujarati cuisine is mostly vegetarian, reflecting the strong influence of Jains and the Vaishnavas in the region. Wheat and the two kinds of millet *(jowar, bajri)* are the main staples. Flour is made into unleavened bread called *roti*. This is eaten with a variety of vegetable dishes. The villager takes a light breakfast of roti and milk or curds before setting out for the fields. Lunch is usually roti and buttermilk. The main meal

is eaten in the evening and consists of rice, split peas *(dal-bhat)*, and vegetables. Meals are served on a *thali*, a metal tray on which roti, rice, and small bowls are placed. The bowls may hold vegetables such as eggplant, potatoes, beans, *dal* (lentils), and *dahi* (curds). *Kadhi*, a savory curry of curds and fried cakes made from pulses (legumes), is a popular dish. No Gujarati would eat a meal without generous helpings of *ghee* (clarified butter). Milk-based desserts are common. *Srikhand* is a rich dessert made with curds and spiced with saffron, cardamom, nuts, and fruit. Gujarat is also known for its delicious ice cream.

13 ● EDUCATION

Among the Bania castes (higher social classes), education in reading, writing, mathematics, and accounting begins early in life. Literacy (percent of the population who can read and write) among these males approaches 100 percent. However, when tribal people and the lower castes are figured into the equation, literacy in Gujarat state drops to just over 60 percent (over 70 percent for males, but less than 50 percent for females).

14 ● CULTURAL HERITAGE

Gujaratis have a cultural heritage that can be traced back to a civilization that existed 3000 years ago. Signs of this include an ancient bead factory discovered at the archaeological site at Lothal. Gujarati literature dates to the twelfth century.

Many groups contribute to Gujarati culture. From the Vaishnavas come the legends and mythology of Krishna, to whom are ascribed the popular Ras and Garba folk dances. Jains influenced temple architecture and developed a distinctive style of painting. Muslim architecture in Gujarat combined Hindu elements with its own styles.

15 ● EMPLOYMENT

Bania castes (higher social classes) are quite numerous in Gujarat. They thrive as business people. Gujaratis also have traveled around the world in search of business opportunities. Gujarat is a leading industrial state and Ahmadabad is a major textile center. Cotton, sugarcane, oilseeds, and peanuts are major cash crops.

16 ● SPORTS

Gujarati girls play house, dress their dolls, and hold mock wedding ceremonies. Boys play marbles, spin tops, fly kites, and play such games as *kabaddi* (team wrestling). *Khokho,* a kind of team tag game, is another popular local pastime. Soccer, cricket, field hockey, and basketball are enjoyed throughout Gujarat.

17 ● RECREATION

In cities, Gujaratis have access to movies, radio, and television. In villages, however, traditional forms of entertainment remain part of community life. Traditional entertainment may be part of religious fairs and festivals or provided by traveling bands of professional entertainers. Castes who traditionally have been associated with music and theater perform a folk drama known as *Bhavai*. The Bhats and Charans are bards and genealogists who have preserved much of the region's folk culture and traditions.

18 ● CRAFTS AND HOBBIES

Gujarat is known for its beautiful handcrafts. Silk saris are made in Patan and block prints are produced in Ahmadabad. Surat is famous for its *zari,* embroidery using gold or silver thread. Jumnagar is a center of colorful tie-dyed work, while peasant women in Saurashtra and Kachch produce embroidery containing tiny mirrors as well as beadwork. Making jewelry and cutting precious stones also are traditional handicrafts in Gujarat. Artisans in Kachch are known for their silver work. Woodcarving is an ancient skill in Gujarat, as can be seen in the fine carvings found in houses and temples throughout the region. Wooden furniture is also produced in a distinctive Gujarati style.

19 ● SOCIAL PROBLEMS

Although Gujaratis have made great strides in improving their living conditions, poverty, malnutrition, and a lack of basic services such as drinking water and health facilities continue to be problems. The Gujarat government is deeply involved in the massive Sardar Sarovar Dam project on the Narmada River. Although it was planned to help provide irrigation and power to the state, a lack of resources and an anti-dam environmental movement have made the project controversial. As Mohandas Gandhi's home state, Gujarat has been identified with the nonviolence movement. However, violence between Hindus and Muslims erupts from time to time across the normally peaceful state.

20 ● BIBLIOGRAPHY

Ardley, Bridget. *India.* Englewood Cliffs, N.J.: Silver Burdett Press, 1989.

Barker, Amanda. *India.* Crystal Lake, Ill.: Ribgy Interactive Library, 1996.

Cumming, David. *India.* New York: Bookwright, 1991.

Das, Prodeepta. *Inside India.* New York: F. Watts, 1990.

Dolcini, Donatella. *India in the Islamic Era and Southeast Asia (8th to 19th century).* Austin, Tex.: Raintree Steck-Vaughn, 1997.

Kalman, Bobbie. *India: The Culture.* Toronto: Crabtree Publishing Co., 1990.

Pandian, Jacob. *The Making of India and Indian Traditions.* Englewood Cliffs, N.J.: Prentice Hall, 1995.

Shalant, Phyllis. *Look What We've Brought You from India: Crafts, Games, Recipes, Stories, and Other Cultural Activities from Indian Americans.* Parsippany, N.J.: Julian Messner, 1998.

WEBSITES
Consulate General of India in New York. [Online] Available http://www.indiaserver.com/cginyc/, 1998.

Embassy of India, Washington, D.C. [Online] Available http://www.indianembassy.org/, 1998.

Interknowledge Corporation. [Online] Available http://www.interknowledge.com/india/, 1998.

World Travel Guide. India. [Online] Available http://www.wtgonline.com/country/in/gen.html, 1998.

Marathas

PRONUNCIATION: muh-RAHT-uhz
ALTERNATE NAMES: Mahrattas; Mahrattis
LOCATION: India (Maharashtra state)
POPULATION: 78.7 million (total population; 50 percent are of the Maratha and Kunbi castes)
LANGUAGE: Marathi
RELIGION: Hinduism

1 ● INTRODUCTION

Marathas live in the Deccan Plateau area of western India. Outside the area, the term Maratha loosely identifies people who speak Marathi. Within the region, however, it refers to the dominant Maratha and Kunbis castes (social classes). Marathas typically trace their origins to chiefs and warriors. Kunbis are mainly farmers and Sudras (servants and artisans—the lowest of the four major caste groups).

Marathas first rose to prominence in the seventeenth-century. Their hero, Shivaji (1627–80) is known for uniting Marathas against Muslim rulers in India. Shivaji carved out a Maratha kingdom in the Konkan (the coastal and western areas of Maharashtra State). During the eighteenth century, a powerful Maratha Confederacy arose. Several groups extended Maratha territory as far as the Punjab in the north and Orissa in the east. Maratha power was greatly weakened by the Afghans at the Third Battle of Panipat in 1761. Nonetheless, marauding bands of Maratha horsemen continued to raid as far afield as the Punjab, Bengal, and southern areas of the Indian peninsula. A series of defeats by the British in the early years of the nineteenth century led to the final collapse of the Maratha Empire.

After India's independence, Marathas promoted the formation of states based on language. Popular sentiment led to the creation of Maharashtra state in 1960 to include the bulk of the Marathi-speaking peoples within its borders.

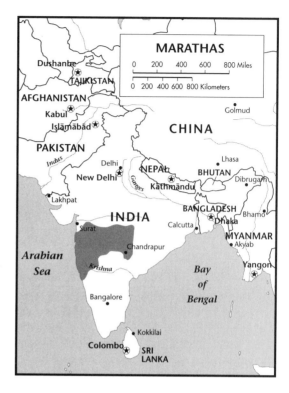

2 ● LOCATION

With 78.7 million people, Maharashtra is India's third largest state. About 50 percent of the population is either Maratha or Kunbis.

Maharashtra falls into three broad geographic divisions. The Konkan is the coastal lowland running from just north of Bombay (Mumbai) to Goa. Inland from this are the Western Ghats, a line of hills that parallels the west coast of India. They are 2,500 to 3,000 feet (760 to 915 meters) in elevation in Maharashtra and reach a height of 5,400 feet (1,646 meters) inland from Bombay. Many peaks in the Ghats are crowned by hill-forts that were once Maratha warrior strongholds. To the east of the Ghats lie the plateaus and uplands of the Deccan lava region, at elevations from 1,000 to 1,800 feet (300 to 550 meters). This region is drained by the eastward-flowing Godaveri River and tributaries of the Krishna. In the extreme north is Tapti River, which flows west to the Arabian Sea.

Average monthly temperatures in Bombay range from 75°F to 86°F (24°C to 30°C), with annual precipitation totaling 82 inches (208 centimeters). In the Ghats, some areas receive as much as 260 inches (660 centimeters) of rainfall during the monsoon. East of the Ghats, however, rainfall drops to between 20 and 40 inches (50 to 100 centimeters).

3 ● LANGUAGE

Marathi is derived from Maharashtri, a form of Prakit (a spoken version of the classical Sanskrit). Dialects of Marathi include Konkani, Varadhi, and Nagpuri. Marathi is written in a type of script known as Devanagari, or a cursive form of Devanagari called Modi.

4 ● FOLKLORE

The greatest Maratha hero is Shivaji (1627–80), who is known as a champion of Hindus. Shivaji challenged the might of the Islamic Mughal Empire and founded the last great Hindu empire in India. Many incidents in his life have entered local lore. Shivaji embraced the Mughal general and killed him with steel claws attached to his hands before the Muslim could stab him with a concealed dagger. On another occasion, Shivaji escaped from the Mughal emperor Aurangzeb by hiding in a fruit basket. Shivaji's men are reputed to have captured the hill-fort of Singadh from the Muslims by sending trained lizards up its walls. The lizards carried ropes for the attackers to climb.

5 ● RELIGION

Marathas and Kunbis are Hindu. Although most worship one or more gods as a "family deity," Shiva is of particular importance. In villages, Shiva is worshiped in several forms. Some of these forms include Khandoba, guardian of the Deccan; and Bhairav, protector of the village. Shiva's consort Parvati is worshiped in the forms local mother goddesses such as Bhavani and Janni Devi. Maruti is a kindly monkey god who protects villagers from evil spirits. Marathas believe in witchcraft, the evil eye, and in ghosts and evil spirits who can harm the living. Mashoba is the most widely feared of the evil spirits and when wronged is believed to bring sickness and ill fortune to a village.

Some Marathas worship Vishnu as well as Shiva.

6 ● MAJOR HOLIDAYS

Although Marathas observe major Hindu festivals, they also have their own regional celebrations. At Divali, for example, they sing hymns in praise of the Asura king Bali and worship cow-dung images of this demon-god. The birthday of elephant-headed Ganesha is a major event in Bombay. Images of Ganesha are worshiped for three days, then carried to the seashore to be immersed in the ocean. Nag Panchami, when snakes are worshiped, is celebrated widely in Maharashtra. Bendur or Pola, a festival at which bulls are decorated, worshiped, and taken in procession through the villages, is popular in the parts of Maharashtra. The folk hero Shivaji's birthday (Shivaji Jayanti) also is a public holiday.

7 ● RITES OF PASSAGE

A *jatakarma,* or birth ceremony, takes place a few days after a child is born. Marathas believe evil spirits may attack a newborn child in the fifth or sixth day after birth, so special rituals are performed. A purification ceremony takes place after ten days. A hair-cutting ceremony (*chaula karma*) is done on a child's first birthday.

Maratha death rites follow Hindu customs. They usually bathe a dead person and wrap the body in a white shroud. The body is then cremated, usually near a river or stream. After the body is burned, the ashes are placed in the water.

8 ● RELATIONSHIPS

Marathas typically greet each other by saying, *Namaste,* which means "Greetings to you." It is said while joining one's own hands, palms together and held upright, in front of one's body.

9 ● LIVING CONDITIONS

On the Deccan Plateau, villages are tight clusters of houses. Smaller houses are simply a rectangular block of four walls forming a single room. Larger houses are made of several such blocks arranged so they make a square, with a sun-court *(chowk)* in the middle. Rooms include living quarters, a kitchen, storerooms, and a *devgarh,* where images of the family gods are kept.

10 ● FAMILY LIFE

The basic kin unit for Marathas is the *kul,* which means "family." This is a lineage made up of extended families. Members of the kul worship a common totemic symbol called *devak.* The devak usually is a cobra, elephant, or blade of a sword. One cannot marry someone who worships the same devak. Other than that, Marathas have few marriage restrictions. They can marry within the village, cross-cousin marriage is allowed, and a man may have more than one wife. Marriages are arranged, and a bride price is paid to the girl's family. The actual marriage is elaborate, involving twenty-four separate ceremonies. The most important of these is installation of the devak.

11 ● CLOTHING

Maratha men wear a *dhoti* (loincloth made by wrapping a long piece of white cotton around the waist and then drawing the end between the legs and tucking it into the waist) or short trousers, known as *cholnas.* They also wear a tight-fitting coat. Sometimes they also wear a turban. Women wear the *sari* (a length of fabric wrapped around the waist, with one end thrown over the right shoulder) and *choli* (tight-fitting, cropped blouse).

12 ● FOOD

The standard diet of the Marathas consists of flat, unleavened bread *(roti)* with pulses (legumes) and vegetables. Among the poor, a typical meal consists of millet bread eaten with chopped chilies and lentils *(dal).* Among the more affluent, bread is made from wheat flour, while rice and more vegetables are served at meals. Marathas will eat fish, mutton, and chicken. For the poor, however, meat is a festival food.

13 ● EDUCATION

The literacy rate (percentage of the population who can read and write) in the state of Maharashtra is about 55 percent. Bombay, with the University of Bombay and the Indian Institute of Technology, is one of India's major educational centers.

14 ● CULTURAL HERITAGE

Marathi regional literature dates from around AD 1000. The devotional poetry and songs of Maharashtrian saints such as Namdev (1270–1350) and Ramdas (1608–81) are among its greatest achievements. The eighteenth century saw the rise of love lyrics and heroic ballads *(powada).* The nineteenth-century paintings of the Peshwa period were influenced by the earlier Rajasthani tradition. Maratha history in western

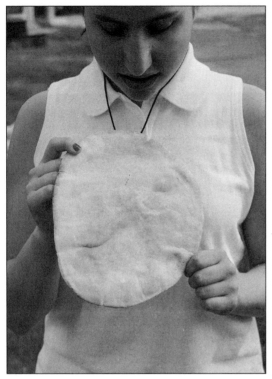

EPD Photos

The Maratha diet includes flat, unleavened bread called roti. Among the more affluent, the bread is made from wheat, rather than millet, flour.

India abounds with the military exploits of the great Maratha dynasties.

15 ● EMPLOYMENT

The Maratha cavalry was renowned throughout India in the seventeenth and eighteenth centuries. Many Marathas continue this tradition of service in the armed forces of modern India. Nevertheless, most Marathas and Kunbis are farmers. Still, Maharashtra is one of the most heavily urbanized Indian states. Its cities include Bombay, one of the world's major urban centers (with about thirteen million people), Pune, and Nagpur. Numerous Marathas now live in cities. They work in commerce and government, and as teachers, doctors and lawyers.

16 ● SPORTS

Maratha children enjoy role-playing. Boys pretend to be horse drivers or engine drivers, while girls play with dolls or at housekeeping. Organized games include various versions of tag, blind man's bluff, and hide-and-seek. Traditional Indian games such as *Gulli danda* (Indian cricket) and *Kabaddi* (team wrestling) are popular. Cricket is perhaps the most important spectator sport. Field hockey, soccer, tennis, and badminton are played in cities and towns. Popular indoor games include chess, cards, and *carrom* (a board game in which counters are used to knock one's opponent's counters into pockets).

17 ● RECREATION

Many Marathas go to local festivals and fairs, and enjoy traditional folk entertainment. The *Nandivala* is a traveling performer. He entertains village audiences with sound effects, tricks, soothsaying, and trained-animal shows. The *Bahrupi,* literally "one with many disguises," is an entertainer known for impersonating people. Bombay, India's equivalent of Hollywood, is the world's largest center of movie making and produces films in both Hindi and Marathi. Bombay is also one of India's major intellectual and cultural centers, with museums, modern and classical music, theater, and other cultural activities.

18 ● CRAFTS AND HOBBIES

Traditional crafts in Maharashtra include weaving and metalwork, as well as local specialties such as Kolhapuri leather sandals, and the Muslim himsa (weaving) and bidri (metal inlaid with silver) work of Aurangabad.

19 ● SOCIAL PROBLEMS

The dominant landowning and cultivating caste in their region, the Marathas and Kunbis are unified by a shared history and a common culture rooted in the Marathi language. This sense of identity often creates problems for others who live in Maharashtra, many of whom are peasants. Maratha nationalism has led to anti-foreigner sentiments, with calls for non-Marathas to be banished from the state. The recent renaming of Bombay as "Mumbai," the Marathi name for the city, is another expression of this sense of Maratha consciousness. The Shiv Sena, a conservative, Hindu, regional political party with strong Maratha support, has recently gained power in Maharashtra. It will no doubt continue to promote its policy of "Maharashtra for Maharashtrians."

20 ● BIBLIOGRAPHY

Ardley, Bridget. *India.* Englewood Cliffs, N.J.: Silver Burdett Press, 1989.

Barker, Amanda. *India.* Crystal Lake, Ill.: Ribgy Interactive Library, 1996.

Cumming, David. *India.* New York: Bookwright, 1991.

Das, Prodeepta. *Inside India.* New York: F. Watts, 1990.

Dolcini, Donatella. *India in the Islamic Era and Southeast Asia (8th to 19th century).* Austin, Tex.: Raintree Steck-Vaughn, 1997.

Kalman, Bobbie. *India: The Culture.* Toronto: Crabtree Publishing Co., 1990.

Pandian, Jacob. *The Making of India and Indian Traditions.* Englewood Cliffs, N.J.: Prentice Hall, 1995.

Shalant, Phyllis. *Look What We've Brought You from India: Crafts, Games, Recipes, Stories, and Other Cultural Activities from Indian Americans.* Parsippany, N.J.: Julian Messner, 1998.

WEBSITES

Consulate General of India in New York. [Online] Available http://www.indiaserver.com/cginyc/, 1998.

Embassy of India, Washington, D.C. [Online] Available http://www.indianembassy.org/, 1998.

Interknowledge Corporation. [Online] Available http://www.interknowledge.com/india/, 1998.

World Travel Guide. India. [Online] Available http://www.wtgonline.com/country/in/gen.html, 1998.

Oriya

PRONUNCIATION: aw-REE-yuh
ALTERNATE NAMES: Ksatriya caste
LOCATION: India (Orissa state)
POPULATION: 27.2 million
LANGUAGE: Oriya
RELIGION: Hinduism

1 ● INTRODUCTION

The Oriya are the dominant ethnic group in India's eastern state of Orissa. They share historical and cultural traditions that date to the sixth century BC. The Oriya are identified with the Odra (or Udra), a people mentioned in ancient Sanskrit texts. The lands to the north of the Mahanadi River, which flows into the Bay of Bengal, were known as Odradesha, or "country of the Odra."

The hilly nature of Orissa once helped many small kingdoms thrive. From the

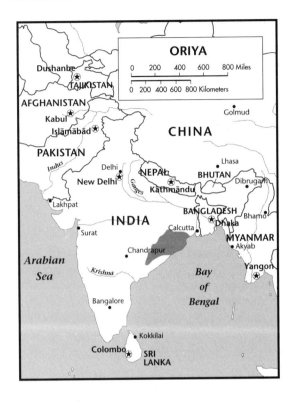

ORIYA

0   200   400   600   800 Miles

0   200 400 600 800 Kilometers

2 ● LOCATION

Oriyas make up about 75 percent of Orissa's population with the rest belonging to various tribal groups. Oriyas traditionally lived at the delta of the Mahanadi River and in coastal lowlands along the Bay of Bengal. The Garjat Hills and Eastern Ghats are hills on the edge of India's Deccan Plateau, and they lie inland within Oriya land. To the west of these hills are interior plateaus. These hills and plateaus are some of the most heavily forested regions in India. The Mahanadi River flows across the middle of the state. Orissa receives about 60 inches (150 centimeters) of rainfall during the monsoon season, which begins in July and ends in October. It has cool winters with temperatures of about 68°F (20°C). In mid-February, the thermometer begins to climb as the hot, humid summer weather approaches. In June, average temperatures approach 85°F (30°C).

3 ● LANGUAGE

Oriya is an Indo-Aryan language closely related to Bengali, Assamese, and other languages of eastern India. It has its own script and is one of official languages of India. Spoken Oriya varies throughout the region.

4 ● FOLKLORE

Puri, a coastal town located at the south end of the Mahanadi Delta, has a famous shrine to Krishna in his form of *Jagannath* (lord of the universe). As one story goes, a hunter saw Krishna in the forest, thought he was a deer and killed him. He left the deity's body under a tree, where a pious person found it, cremated it, and placed the ashes in a box. The god Vishnu then asked a king to make

fourth century BC on, however, major states such as Kalinga extended their control over much of the area. During the fourth and fifth centuries AD, a foreign people (possibly Greeks) rose to power in the region, followed by a series of local dynasties. The end of the eleventh century saw the rise of the Eastern Gangas, whose rule ushered in a golden era in Orissa's history. This dynasty remained a Hindu stronghold until Muslim rulers from Bengal conquered it in 1568. Orissa subsequently became part of the Mughal Empire, but its western areas later fell to the Marathas. The British acquired the coastal regions in 1757 and the Maratha-held lands in 1803. Orissa assumed its current form in 1947 when India gained its independence from Britain.

an image from these sacred relics. The king asked Vishvakarman, an artisan, to do the work. He said he would if he were allowed to do it without being disturbed. The king became impatient after fifteen days and disturbed the artisan. The artisan was so angry that he never finished the work. To this day, the image is only a stump without arms or legs. The god Brahma gave the image its eyes and a soul. The temple in Puri keeps this legend alive by representing Krishna as a block of wood.

5 ● RELIGION

Oriya are mostly Hindu. They worship Shiva, the Mother Goddess, the Sun God, and many other Hindu deities. The Vaishnava sect particularly reveres Krishna in his form as Jagannath.

Many local deities and spirits also influence Oriya life and activities. Often, they are believed to cause disease, and must either be appeased or handed over to shamans (kalisi)—healers who deal with them.

6 ● MAJOR HOLIDAYS

Oriya celebrate most Hindu festivals and several regional holidays. Their biggest regional holiday is the Chariot Procession (Ratha Yatra) of Jagannath in Puri. It takes place in June or July, and attracts visitors from all over India. Images of Jagannath and two lesser deities are taken from the Jagannath temple to a country house about 2 miles (3 kilometers) away. The images are placed in cars or chariots and pulled by pilgrims. The word "juggernaut" comes from "Jagannath" and refers to the god's massive chariot.

7 ● RITES OF PASSAGE

Most babies are born at home. Village women give birth by squatting, with a piece of cloth tied tightly around the abdomen. They grip a wooden pole to cope with labor pains. Male babies are greeted with special joy. After seven days, rites of purification are observed. The name-giving ceremony is held on the twenty-first day.

Children are the center of family life. They are spoiled and fussed over, but later they begin to share household tasks. Girls are usually segregated for seven days when they first menstruate. In some communities, they rub turmeric paste on their bodies and bathe before resuming their domestic and social activities.

The dead are cremated, although children and unmarried persons are usually buried. The corpse is anointed with turmeric, washed, and wrapped in a shroud. It is carried to the cremation ground by relatives, and placed on the funeral pyre with the head toward the north. Some groups place women facing up and men facing down. Relatives shave their own heads and don new clothes, and on the eleventh day they hold a feast.

8 ● RELATIOSHIPS

Caste (social class) plays an important role in daily relationships. People often greet newcomers by asking which caste they belong to.

9 ● LIVING CONDITIONS

Oriya mostly live in villages. Their villages usually have houses built along the sides of a single street and a small hamlet outside the central area where lower caste families live. Houses are usually rectangular and have mud walls and a gabled roof thatched with straw. Sometimes, richer families have a double roof, a small guest house, and a fence. Rooms in a typical Oriya home are used as cattle sheds, grain storage areas, bedrooms, and kitchens. Usually, part of the kitchen is set aside as an area where the family can pray. Furnishings include wooden beds, tables, and chairs. Oriya often decorate their walls with pictures of gods and goddesses, political leaders, and film stars.

10 ● FAMILY LIFE

Oriya prefer to marry within their caste or subcaste, and outside their clan. An Oriya proverb states that "marital relatives from distant places are beautiful, as distant hills are enchanting," and so people often seek a marital partner from outside their village. Marriages are arranged. The daughter-in-law usually lives with her husband's family. Divorce is uncommon.

11 ● CLOTHING

Men wear a *dhoti* (long piece of white cotton wrapped around the waist and drawn between the legs and tucked into the waist) and a *chaddar* (shawl draped over the shoulders). Women wear the *sari* (a length of fabric wrapped around the waist, with one end thrown over the right shoulder) and *choli* (tight-fitting, cropped blouse).

12 ● FOOD

Oriya generally eat rice at every meal. At breakfast, cold rice, puffed rice *(mudhi),* or various types of rice cake *(pitha)* are eaten

with molasses or salt, and tea. Thin rice pancakes are a specialty of Orissa. A typical meal consists of rice, *dal* (lentils), and vegetable curry using eggplant, spinach, and seasonal vegetables such as cauliflower, cabbages, or peas. Fish or goat meat also may be served. Food is cooked in mustard oil, except for offerings to the gods. Those offerings are prepared in clarified butter *(ghee).* A particular favorite in villages is a rice dish called *pakhala bata.* Rice is boiled in bulk, and whatever is not eaten is stored in cold water. When this rice becomes a little sour, it is served cold with fresh green chilies. This dish is popular in summer, when it is eaten with curds and green mangoes. Bananas, coconuts, and limes are the main fruits of the region. Oriya are fond of sweets such as sherbets, cookies, and drinks. Some Oriya drink a toddy (hot drink) made from fermented dates. Hashish (similar to marijuana) is combined with yogurt to make a drink called *bhang* and is drunk socially and at festivals.

Food plays an important role in Oriya ritual. At the feast for Shiva, for example, villagers prepare a huge, steamed rice cake made in the shape of a *lingam* (Shiva's phallic symbol) and stuffed with cheese, molasses, and coconut. It is dyed red and is worshiped before being eaten. More than fifty types of rice cake are cooked to be offered at the Jagannath Temple at Puri.

13 ● EDUCATION

Orissa has a literacy rate (percentage of the population who can read and write) of under 50 percent. More people tend to know how to read and write in cities than in villages. Girls rarely proceed beyond primary school.

Orissa has several government-run colleges and five universities. One of these, the Shri Jagannath Sanskrit University at Puri, is devoted to Sanskrit culture.

14 ● CULTURAL HERITAGE

Chronicles of the Jagannath Temple at Puri date from the twelfth century AD. Medieval *bhakti* (devotional) poets have left Oriya literature with a rich tradition. Orissa also is famous for its dance, music, and architecture. Odissi, for instance, is a classical dance that originated as a temple dance for the gods. The Chhau dance, performed by masked male dancers in honor of Shiva, is another feature of Oriya culture. Cuttack is a major center for dance and music.

Oriya culture also includes vivid dances and songs, folk opera *(jatra)*, puppet plays, and shadow plays (where the shadows of the characters are projected onto a screen using puppets).

Painting of icons (*patta* paintings), palm leaf painting, and woodcarving are important artistic traditions in Orissa. Orissan temples are decorated with carvings and sculptures and have a distinct style. The Sun Temple at Konarak is considered to be a particular Orissan masterpiece.

15 ● WORK

Most Oriya grow rice. The state of Orissa accounts for about 10 percent of India's total rice output. Farmers still use a great deal of animal power and traditional tools. Cash crops include oilseeds, pulses (legumes), sugarcane, jute, and coconuts. Fishing is important in coastal areas. Many families also make traditional handicrafts.

Since independence in 1947, some industrial development has occurred.

16 ● SPORTS

Children play ball, tag, and hide-and-seek. They also like to spin tops and fly kites. Traditional games for adults include cards and dice. Bodybuilding and wrestling are common sports for men, and *kabaddi* (team wrestling) is very popular. Cricket, soccer, and field hockey are played in schools.

17 ● RECREATION

Oriya enjoy folk dances and songs, puppet plays, and shadow plays. They also like a form of folk opera known as *jatra*.

18 ● CRAFTS AND HOBBIES

Orissa is known for its handicrafts, particularly its little carved wooden replicas of Jagannath. Painted masks and wooden animal toys for children also are popular. Local sculptors make soapstone copies of temple sculptures for pilgrims and tourists. Textiles include appliqué work, embroidery, tie-dyed fabrics, and various types of hand-loomed cloth. The artisans of Cuttack are skilled in filigree work and make gold and silver jewelry. Local artisans also produce brassware and items made from bell metal (an alloy of copper and tin). Orissa also is known for its tie-dyed saris. Village women often like to ornament their bodies with tattoos.

19 ● SOCIAL PROBLEMS

Orissa is one of the poorest states of India. Much of the region lacks a safe drinking-water supply, adequate schools, roads, and electricity. Alcoholism is such a problem that there is a popular movement to prohibit drinking.

20 ● BIBLIOGRAPHY

Ardley, Bridget. *India.* Englewood Cliffs, N.J.: Silver Burdett Press, 1989.

Barker, Amanda. *India.* Crystal Lake, Ill.: Ribgy Interactive Library, 1996.

Cumming, David. *India.* New York: Bookwright, 1991.

Das, Prodeepta. *Inside India.* New York: F. Watts, 1990.

Dolcini, Donatella. *India in the Islamic Era and Southeast Asia (8th to 19th century).* Austin, Tex.: Raintree Steck-Vaughn, 1997.

Kalman, Bobbie. *India: The Culture.* Toronto: Crabtree Publishing Co., 1990.

Pandian, Jacob. *The Making of India and Indian Traditions.* Englewood Cliffs, N.J.: Prentice Hall, 1995.

Shalant, Phyllis. *Look What We've Brought You from India: Crafts, Games, Recipes, Stories, and Other Cultural Activities from Indian Americans.* Parsippany, N.J.: Julian Messner, 1998.

WEBSITES

Consulate General of India in New York. [Online] Available http://www.indiaserver.com/cginyc/, 1998.

Embassy of India, Washington, D.C. [Online] Available http://www.indianembassy.org/, 1998.

Interknowledge Corporation. [Online] Available http://www.interknowledge.com/india/, 1998.

World Travel Guide. India. [Online] Available http://www.wtgonline.com/country/in/gen.html, 1998.

Rajputs

PRONUNCIATION: RAHJ-puts
ALTERNATE NAMES: Ksatriya caste
LOCATION: India (Rajasthan state)
POPULATION: 120 million
LANGUAGE: Language or dialect of their region
RELIGION: Hinduism

1 ● INTRODUCTION

"Rajput" identifies numerous *ksatriya* or warrior castes in northern and western India. The term "Rajput" comes from *rajaputra,* which means "son of kings." Rajputs are famed for their fighting abilities and once ruled numerous Indian princely states. The British grouped many of these states into the Rajputana Province. Today, it is the Indian state of Rajasthan.

Most believe Rajputs come from tribes in central Asia such as the Parthians, Kushans, Shakas, and Huns. These groups entered India as conquerors and became kings or rulers. They often married high-caste Hindu women or converted to Hinduism. By the ninth century, Rajputs controlled an empire that extended from Sind to the lower Ganges Valley, and from the Himalayan foothills to the Narmada River.

In 1192, Prithviraj Chauhan led the Rajputs against the Muslim Mughal ruler Muhammad Ghuri (d. 1206) who defeated them at the second battle of Tarain, near Delhi. This firmly established Muslim power and ended Rajput dominance. The only Rajput kingdoms that could challenge Mughal rule were those in the great Thar Desert.

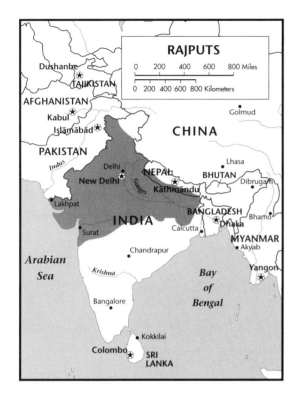

RAJPUTS

0 200 400 600 800 Miles

0 200 400 600 800 Kilometers

In the eighteenth century, many Rajput states came under control of Marathas and, by the early nineteenth century, the British. Many Rajput kings retained a status as rulers of princely states under the British. This ended when India gained its independence in 1947.

2 ● LOCATION

About 120 million people in India call themselves Rajputs. They live throughout northern India, although Rajasthan is considered their cultural homeland.

3 ● LANGUAGE

Rajputs speak the language or dialect of their region. In Rajasthan, Rajputs speak one of the dialects of Rajasthani, which

sounds a little like Hindi. Some Rajasthani dialects include Jaipuri, spoken in Jaipur, and Marwari, spoken in Marwar.

4 ● FOLKLORE

Many folktales describe Rajput exploits. In one story, a *ksatriya* (warrior) clan leader decided to kill all Brahman (priest and scholar) men after learning a Brahman had killed his father. This meant Brahman females had to marry ksatriya men and gave rise to various Rajput dynasties. In another story, gods created some ksatriya clans on Mount Abu in Rajasthan to help fight Buddhists and foreigners. These Rajputs were known as the *agnikula* ("fire-race") and were the ancestors of clans such as the Chauhan, Solanki, and Ponwar Rajputs. Other Rajput clans trace their ancestry to the Sun or Moon.

5 ● RELIGION

Most Rajputs are Hindu. They were known for protecting Hinduism against Buddhism and Islam. Today, in their religious practices, Rajputs differ little from other high-caste Hindus. They use Brahmans (priests and scholars) for ceremonial and ritual purposes. They worship all major Hindu deities. Most Rajputs are devotees of the god Shiva. Many also worship Surya (the Sun God), and Durga as Mother Goddess. In addition, nearly every Rajput clan has its own patron god to whom it turns for protection.

6 ● MAJOR HOLIDAYS

Rajputs celebrate all major Hindu holy days. Of particular importance is Dasahara, a festival dedicated to Durga (the Mother Goddess). It is customary for Rajputs to sacrifice a buffalo to the goddess, in commemoration of her victory over buffalo-demon Mahisha. The animal is beheaded with one stroke of a sword. The meat is usually distributed to servants or lower caste groups.

7 ● RITES OF PASSAGE

Rajputs celebrate major stages in life with twelve ceremonies called *karams*.

When a boy is born, a family Brahman (member of the highest social class) records details for the infant's horoscope. A family barber informs relatives and friends of the birth, and there is much celebration. The Brahman chooses a favorable day to name the infant. When the child is about two years old, a head-shaving ritual takes place. Many Rajputs regard the birth of a daughter as a misfortune and observe the day with little ceremony.

One important rite of passage for Rajput boys is tying of the *janeu* or sacred thread. As death approaches, a sick person is placed on a bed of sacred kusa grass on a spot that has been circled by cow dung. A sprig of tulsi plant, a piece of gold, or a few drops of Ganges River water are placed in the mouth to delay messengers of Yama, god of death. A cow is brought to the side of the dying person so that he or she can grasp its tail and be carried safely to the other world. After death, the corpse is washed and prepared for cremation. The body is placed on a funeral pyre, facing north. The eldest son lights the fire, and later cracks open the skull so the soul can leave the body.

8 ● RELATIONSHIPS

Rajput greeting practices vary by region.

9 ● LIVING CONDITIONS

Rajputs traditionally formed landowning classes. In the past, Rajput rulers of princely states such as Kashmir, Jaipur, and Jodhpur were known for their splendid courts. Rajput Maharajas (kings) often lived luxuriously in ornate palaces. After India's independence, however, the princes lost their titles and privileges.

In Rajput homes, men's quarters consist of a courtyard containing a platform about four to six feet (about one to two meters) high, reached by a series of steps and often shaded by trees. Men often gather on these platforms to chat and perhaps smoke the *hukka* (a pipe). At one end of the platform is a roofed porch. Men usually sleep behind this porch. Smaller side rooms are used for storage.

Women's quarters are enclosed by walls, with rooms facing an inner courtyard. A fireplace is built against one wall for cooking. Stairs provide access to the roof. The interconnecting roofs of the houses let Rajput women visit each other without being seen by men.

10 ● FAMILY LIFE

A distinctive feature of Rajput society is its clans. More than 103 clans have been identified in all. Among the more important ones are the Chauhans, whose former capital was Ajmer; the Gehlots of Mewar; the Rathors of Marwar; and the Kachhwaha of Jaipur.

Rajputs marry outside their clan. They also try to marry their daughters into clans of higher rank than their own, while accepting daughters-in-law from clans of lower rank.

The Rajput clans in Rajasthan have the highest standing, so families with sons in Rajasthan often are sought by those with daughters.

Rajput marriages are arranged. Marriages are occasions for great ceremony and feasting. The groom, accompanied by friends and relatives, rides in a *barat* (procession) to the bride's house. Mounted on a horse, he is dressed in colorful robes, with turban and sword. Sometimes, he rides a decorated elephant. Gifts and money are distributed to those who gather. A piece of cloth is tied to the edge of the bride's sari and groom's coat. The couple walks around a sacred fire while Brahmans (priests and scholars) chant prayers. This is known as *agni puja* (fire-worship ceremony). Several days of celebration follow.

In 1303, when the fort of Chitor in Rajasthan was about to fall to Muslims, the Rajput Rani and all the women in the fort burned themselves to death to avoid being taken prisoners. Women who practiced this act of *sati* were revered as saints and stone sati memorials exist in Rajasthan. Despite abundant folklore surrounding this tradition, it was never widely practiced.

11 ● CLOTHING

Rajput men wear the *dhoti* (loincloth consisting of a long piece of white cotton wrapped around the waist and then drawn between the legs and tucked into the waist), often with a cotton tunic. Rajput men may also wear a short jacket, or *angarhkha,* that fastens on the right side. Rajput men wear turbans that are tied to represent their particular clan. Rajput women wear either the *sari* (a length of fabric wrapped around the waist, with one end thrown over the right shoulder) or loose, baggy pants with a tunic. The *lengha* (long, flowing skirt) is also associated with the traditional dress of Rajasthan.

12 ● FOOD

Rajputs' dietary patterns vary by region. In drier parts of India, their staple diet consists of various unleavened breads *(roti)*, pulses (legumes), and vegetables. Rice *(chawal)* and milk products are also important. Rajputs are fond of hunting and enjoy eating venison and game birds such as goose, duck, partridge, and grouse.

13 ● EDUCATION

Formal education used to be of little significance among ruling and landowning Rajput clans. Boys were brought up in the traditions of Rajput culture, trained in martial arts and in a code of conduct based on valor and honor. The sons of Rajputs became huntsmen, polo players, horsemen, and swordsmen.

An educational institution of particular note is Mayo College in Ajmer, Rajasthan. The British founded the college in the early 1870s as a school for the sons of princes. Though many Rajputs still attend the school, it has become an exclusive private school for upper class Indian children.

14 ● CULTURAL HERITAGE

India's Rajput heritage is vibrant. Rajputs are seen as champions of Hindu *dharma* (faith). They have left a strong mark on India, particularly in Rajasthan. Members of the Bhat caste keep family records and can trace a Rajput genealogy to a clan's mythical ancestors. Member of the Charan caste record deeds and accomplishments of Rajput rulers. Rajput courts were centers of culture where literature, music, dance, painting, and sculpture flourished with support of the Rajput elite. A specific style of Rajput painting—often focusing on religious themes, portraiture, or miniatures—emerged at Rajput courts in the Himalayas (the Pahari school) and in the western desert (the Rajasthani school). Bardic literature such as *Prithviraj Raso* recounts deeds of Rajput heroes. Mira Bai, a poet born in the fifteenth century, was a Rajput princess who is known for her contributions to Hindu *bhakti* (devotional) literature.

Rajputs built irrigation canals, dams, and reservoirs. The beautiful temples at Khajuraho were built in the tenth and eleventh centuries, and some Rajput groups built many well-known temples in Gujarat and western Rajasthan. Many palaces and forts represent a pleasing blend of Hindu and Muslim architectural styles. Among the more notable are forts at Chitor, Gwalior, and Jodhpur, and the Palace of the Winds in Jaipur. Maharaja Jai Singh II of Jaipur constructed astronomical observatories in Jaipur and Delhi in the early eighteenth century.

15 ● EMPLOYMENT

Rajputs continue to be landowners and soldiers. Agriculture is the group's primary work today, but many Rajputs serve in the Rajput Rifles or other branches of the armed services. They also pursue careers as police officers.

16 ● SPORTS

Rajputs used to hunt tiger, panther, deer, and game birds. Also popular was pig-sticking, the dangerous sport of riding on horseback to hunt wild boar by sticking them with a lance. Polo sharpened riding skills.

17 ● RECREATION

Historically Rajputs have taken great pleasure in the elaborate rituals and ceremonies associated with their religion and community. Weddings and other festive occasions are observed with much enthusiasm and are often celebrated with feasting, and sometimes with *nautch* (dancing) girls.

18 ● CRAFTS AND HOBBIES

Rajput folk traditions include string puppet shows and ballads told by traveling storytellers known as *bhopas*. In one such ballad, Pabuji, a thirteenth-century chieftain, borrows a horse from a woman to ride to his wedding. Before he does so, he promises the woman he will protect her cows. Soon after the wedding ceremony has begun, Pabuji learns that the thieves are making off with the cows. He leaves his wedding to keep his word and recovers all but one calf. He risks another battle for the calf and is killed by the enemy. His bride then leaves her handprint on the gate of Pabuji's residence and commits *sati* (burns herself to death, a saintly act in Rajasthan).

19 ● SOCIAL PROBLEMS

As landowners, Rajputs do not face the social discrimination and problems of poverty that confront many others in India. While some may have fallen on hard times, Rajputs as a community are prosperous.

Cynthia Bassett

An early morning vegetable market in an area characterized by a maze of waterways.

One of the biggest challenges they face is adjusting to India's democratic environment. As former kings and members of the former ruling class, their power and prestige today is of less importance than in the past. Their economic resources have been threatened by government attempts to redistribute wealth. They have faced challenges from castes seeking economic and political independence from Rajput control. Rajputs lack the unity that would give them a powerful voice in modern Indian politics.

20 ● BIBLIOGRAPHY

Ardley, Bridget. *India.* Englewood Cliffs, N.J.: Silver Burdett Press, 1989.

Barker, Amanda. *India.* Crystal Lake, Ill.: Ribgy Interactive Library, 1996.

Cumming, David. *India.* New York: Bookwright, 1991.

Das, Prodeepta. *Inside India.* New York: F. Watts, 1990.

Dolcini, Donatella. *India in the Islamic Era and Southeast Asia (8th to 19th century).* Austin, Tex.: Raintree Steck-Vaughn, 1997.

Kalman, Bobbie. *India: The Culture.* Toronto: Crabtree Publishing Co., 1990.

Minturn, Leigh. *The Rajputs of Khalapur, India.* New York: Wiley, 1966.

Pandian, Jacob. *The Making of India and Indian Traditions.* Englewood Cliffs, N.J.: Prentice Hall, 1995.

Shalant, Phyllis. *Look What We've Brought You from India: Crafts, Games, Recipes, Stories, and Other Cultural Activities from Indian*

Americans. Parsippany, N.J.: Julian Messner, 1998.

WEBSITES

Embassy of India, Washington, D.C. [Online] Available http://www.indianembassy.org/, 1998.

Consulate General of India in New York. [Online] Available http://www.indiaserver.com/cginyc/, 1998.

Interknowledge Corporation. [Online] Available http://www.interknowledge.com/india/, 1998.

World Travel Guide. India. [Online] Available http://www.wtgonline.com/country/in/gen.html, 1998.

Indonesia

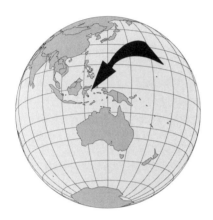

Indonesia, with over 195 million inhabitants, is the fourth-most-populous country in the world (after China, India, and the United States.) Collectively, the people of Indonesia are called Indonesians. However, by one estimate, there are more than 250 distinct cultural groups *(sukus)* in Indonesia, speaking as many as 700 languages. Among the largest are the Javanese, Balinese, and Sundanese, each of whom is profiled in this chapter. Also profiled in this chapter are the Asmat, an isolated group living on the island of New Guinea. To learn more about the Malays, another important group living in Indonesia, see the chapter on Malaysia in Volume 5.

Indonesians

PRONUNCIATION: in-do-NEE-zhuns
LOCATION: Indonesia
POPULATION: 195 million
LANGUAGE: Bahasa Indonesia (official language); various ethnic languages
RELIGION: Islam (87 percent); Protestantism (6 percent); Catholicism (3 percent); Hinduism (3 percent); Buddhism (1 percent)

1 ● INTRODUCTION

By one estimate, there are more than 250 distinct cultural groups *(sukus)* in Indonesia. They speak as many as 700 mutually unintelligible languages (the language spoken by any given group is not understood by the others), and represent a wide range of physical types. As one moves outward from the national capital, Jakarta, into the rural areas, ethnic group affiliation determines more and more of one's identity and way of life. The Indonesian republic strives to preserve each suku's distinctive heritage within a modern national culture. Its motto, *Bhinneka Tunggal Ika,* is an Old Javanese expression meaning "The Many Are One."

The Indonesian archipelago (chain of islands), crossed by major trade routes, has long been a prime source of spices. These

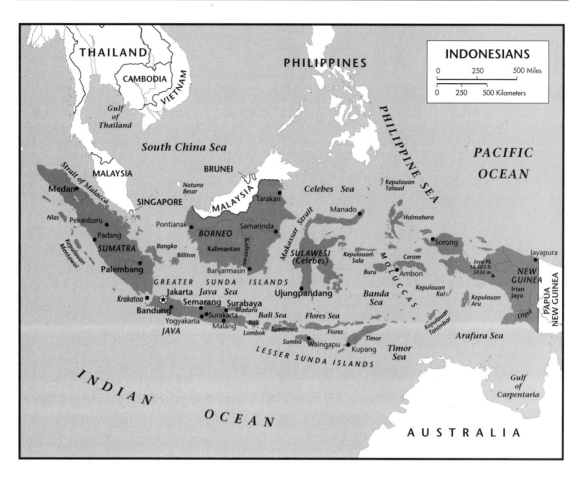

trade routes introduced Islam and Arabo-Persian culture to the region. From the late thirteenth century AD to the early seventeenth century, kingdom after kingdom converted to Islam. The modern state of Indonesia had its beginnings in outposts established by the Dutch East India Company in the early seventeenth century.

By the 1830s, the modern Dutch colonial state was founded. Over the next century, the power of this state expanded throughout the archipelago and penetrated deeply into the lives of those living inland. They lived within the framework of a common Dutch administration and European-style education. In the early years of the twentieth century, a small but rapidly growing group of native Indonesians began the struggle to free the "Indonesian nation." On August 17, 1945, Indonesian nationalist leaders Sukarno and Hatta proclaimed Indonesian independence. It would take years of bloody struggle before the Dutch formally recognized the Indonesian republic on December 17, 1949. Sukarno was president of Indonesia from 1949 to 1967 when he was removed from office after a coup d'état led by Suharto.

Under the thirty years of General's Suharto's "New Order," Indonesia became a favored destination for foreign investment and a major regional power. Political problems and unrest resulted in Suharto's resignation in May 1998. Transitional president B.J. Habibie assumed control and promised to hold elections within a year.

2 ● LOCATION

In the Indonesian national language, the usual expression for homeland, *Tanah Air Kita,* translates as "Our Land and Water." This phrase expresses the central fact of Indonesia's geography: the country consists of more than 17,000 islands. Of these, 6,000 are permanently inhabited (the total land area equals that of Mexico). The principal islands and island groups are Sumatra, Java, Bali, the Lesser Sundas, Irian Jaya (Indonesian New Guinea), the Moluccas, Sulawesi, and Kalimantan (Indonesian Borneo).

Much of the country's soil is extraordinarily fertile. Indonesia's islands straddle the equator in a broad belt longer than the continental United States. The overall climate varies little, remaining hot and humid year-round.

Indonesia, with over 195,000,000 inhabitants, is the fourth-most-populous country in the world. (It follows China, India, and the United States.)

3 ● LANGUAGE

Indonesians speak between 250 and 700 distinct languages. However, there is only one official language of government, commerce, education, and mass media. It is Bahasa Indonesia, a dialect of Malay. For the majority of Indonesians, Bahasa Indonesia is the language used in public. A regional language is used for private, family, and local community life. Bahasa Indonesia uses a Latin script (alphabet).

Several separate families of Papuan languages are spoken in Irian Jaya and some other eastern islands. Otherwise the tongues spoken in Indonesia belong to several branches of the Austronesian language family. This language family includes the closely related languages of Madagascar, Malaysia, and the Philippines.

The major ethnic groups in Indonesia are as follows:

Java: Javanese, Sandiness, and Madurese.

Sumatra: Iciness, Gaya, Toby Batak and Dairy Batak, Minangkabaus (in the west); Nias and Mentally (on islands off the west coast); Regan and Lumping (in southernmost Sumatra); and Malay (the dominant population of West Malaysia and present on the coasts of East Malaysia and in Brunei and Singapore).

Kalimantan: Banjarese (southeastern Kalimantan); and a great diversity of inland peoples generally known as "Adak."

Sulawesi: on the southwestern peninsula, Bugis, Makassares, and Mandar; in the central highlands, many diverse groups, of which the best known are the Sa'dan Toraja and Pamona; on the northern peninsula, the Tomini, Gorontalo, Bolaang Mongondow, and Minahasa; and in the east and on offshore islands, the Mori, Bungku, Muna, and Butonese.

The Lesser Sundas (better-known groups): Balinese; Sasak; Sumbawans; Bimanese; Sumbanese; Savunese; on Flores, the Manggarai, Ngada, Endenese, Sikanese; and on Timor, the Tetum, Atoni, Helong, and Rotinese.

The Moluccas: Non-Austronesian—Ternatans; Tidorese; and in northern Halmahera, the Tobelorese, Galelarese, and other small groups; Austronesian—in southern Halmahera, small language-groups such as Sawai; in the southern islands, the Tanimbarese, Aru, and Kei; the most important culture in the central islands is Ambonese.

Irian Jaya: Austronesian languages are spoken along the north and west coasts, while Papuan languages are spoken elsewhere (e.g., Asmat and Dani).

Chinese: numbering 4 million, they form the most important "nonindigenous" group (though most have resided in Indonesia for generations).

Naming practices vary from ethnic group to ethnic group as well as across class and religious lines. The most commonly encountered type of name is Arabic associated with Islam. Except for a few sukus (cultural groups), family names are not used.

In general, Indonesians are fond of nicknames, usually based on the last syllable of the full name. Thus, the male name "Hermawan" becomes "Wawan," or the female name "Hermawati" becomes "Titi." Etiquette requires that titles be used at all times to indicate respect. In Bahasa Indonesia, one addresses persons of greater age or status with the word "Bapak" for men and "Ibu" for women.

4 ● FOLKLORE

Indonesia has a long list of "national heroes," who are commemorated in monuments and in the names of streets, airports, universities, and other public institutions. A few of the best-known figures are Gajah Mada (d. 1364), a fourteenth-century Majapahit prime minister who furthered Indonesian nationalism; the Javanese prince Diponegoro (1785–1855) and the Minangkabau priest Imam Bonjol (1772–1864), who led an armed resistance to Dutch power; and Raden Ajeng Kartini (1879–1905), a Central Javanese noblewoman who advocated women's rights.

5 ● RELIGION

All Indonesians must register as followers of one of five recognized religions: Islam, Protestantism, Catholicism, Hinduism, or Buddhism. Atheism, associated with the banned communist movement, is not allowed. An elaborate bureaucracy oversees the operations of each of the five religious communities. Legislation discourages marriage between members of different religious communities: one of the prospective partners must officially convert to the religion of the other. Religious communities are forbidden to seek converts from each other's memberships.

The vast majority (87 percent) of the population adheres to Islam, making Indonesia the largest Muslim nation on earth. It has more Muslims than all of the Arab world put together. The degree of individual observance varies.

Six percent of the population is Protestant. Catholicism (3 percent of the population) was first introduced by the Portuguese in the sixteenth century. Hinduism (3 percent of the population) in Indonesia means almost exclusively the religion of Bali, which combines the Indian religion with native religious practices. Buddhism (no more than 1 percent of the population) claims mostly Chinese adherents. Their traditional practices combine Mahayana Buddhism with Taoism and Confucianism.

Embassy of the Republic of Indonesia

A busy street in Jakarta.

6 ● MAJOR HOLIDAYS

The Department of Religion authorizes a list of twelve public holidays (on which government offices and schools are closed). Two are purely secular: New Year's Day (January 1) and Independence Day (August 17). The others are feasts observed by the five recognized religions: Nyepi, the Hindu-Balinese New Year; Waisak, the birth of the Buddha; Christmas, Good Friday, and Ascension Thursday for Christians; and five Muslim holidays—the Islamic New Year; the Birth of Muhammad; the Night of the Ascent (Muhammad's visit to heaven); *Eid al-Fitr,* the end of the fasting month of *Ramadan;* and *Eid al-Adha,* recalling Abra-

ham's willingness to sacrifice his son at God's command.

On Independence Day, each village and city neighborhood is decorated with red and white national flags. Colorful paintings commemorate the Revolution. Parades, speeches, and performances of traditional music, dance, and theater also mark the day.

The end of the Muslim fast month of Ramadan is marked by a great celebration, called Eid al-Fitr, Lebaran, or Hari Raya. Throughout Indonesia, special feasts are prepared. These are heralded by the mass weaving of *ketupat,* small palm-leaf containers for cooked rice. Migrants return to their hometowns, and ancestral graves are cleaned and sprinkled with flower petals. Even non-Muslims visit family members, friends, neighbors, colleagues, and superiors to ask forgiveness for the offenses of the past year.

7 ● RITES OF PASSAGE

Rituals marking major life events differ greatly according to ethnic group, religion, and social class. For many, modernization has simplified the traditional rites of passage. However, many wealthy families display their status by holding elaborate traditional rituals. Celebrations are public affairs to which the extended family, friends, workmates, and local officials are invited. In fact, celebrations are generally open to the entire neighborhood or village—all of whom must be fed.

The most important celebrations accompany births, circumcisions (for Muslim boys), weddings, and funerals. Weddings usually consist of the legally required religious ceremony (usually Muslim or Christian) and rites following ethnic custom. These are followed by a large reception held in a family home, a hotel, or a rented hall.

Among the Muslim majority, funerals tend to be somewhat uniform among the different ethnic groups. They including the washing and enshrouding of the body, and burial within twenty-four hours. Mourners by the truckload accompany the body to the cemetery and, after collective prayer, each mourner tosses a handful of earth into the grave.

8 ● RELATIONSHIPS

In general, interpersonal relations throughout Indonesia are governed by a concern to preserve social harmony and personal honor. In their interactions with others, Indonesians take great care to show respect to those of higher status, whether due to age, nobler ancestry, superior educational attainment, or higher organizational rank.

Indonesian life tends to be group—rather than individual—oriented. Individuals have little personal space, rarely having even a bed to themselves, and privacy is largely an unknown concept. Putting the group's interests above one's own is a village value that has been carried into many aspects of modern urban life. Great care is taken to avoid overt disagreements within groups. Fear of bringing shame upon one's family and other groups to which one belongs has a powerful influence on personal decisions.

The Islamic greeting, *Wassalamu alaikum (warakhmatullahi wabarakatuh),* "Peace upon you (and God's blessings)," has become the standard greeting in public life, even for non-Muslims. It is often accompanied by the shaking of hands, concluded by bringing the right palm to one's chest. The most common informal greeting is *Dari mana,* "Where are you coming from?" Even in informal situations, great importance is placed on asking permission to depart (a common phrase is the Dutch-derived *Permisi?*).

While passing in front of older or higher-status people, it is customary to bow low, extend the right hand in front of oneself, and walk forward slowly. Especially in Java, the index finger is taboo. Pointing is done with the right thumb, and one beckons others to come with a downward, inward movement of the right palm. Folding one's arms over one's chest or holding them akimbo (hands on hips with elbows outward) while speaking appears aggressive.

Unannounced visits may be made in the late afternoon between nap time and dinnertime (4:00–6:00 PM). Visitors are served tea and snacks; one leaves a little food on the plate to show one wants no more. Indonesian attitudes toward punctuality are reflected in the expression *jam karet* (rubber time). Being late for appointments is the norm.

Although there is considerable variation, interaction between young men and women tends to be closely monitored by elders and peers. Dating and premarital sex are not condoned. Early marriage is the norm. Public displays of affection between the sexes (such as holding hands or kissing) are taboo (forbidden). However, physical contact between members of the same sex (such as walking arm in arm) is common and is not considered a sign of homosexuality.

9 ●LIVING CONDITIONS

Given the large average family size, Indonesian houses tend to be crowded. Some 30 percent of houses have walls of bamboo, the cheapest material. The rest have brick or wooden walls. Roofs are of tile, zinc, or thatch. The layout of a wealthy family's house is similar to that of Western houses, with separate rooms for receiving guests and eating dinner. Most bathrooms, however, have squat toilets and an open tank of water to be used for bathing and flushing. Many poorer Indonesian homes lack such facilities, forcing their owners to use public areas such as riversides. While nearly all houses in Jakarta have electricity, under half of all homes have electricity nationwide. Very few houses (mostly urban) have running water (not generally drinkable).

10 ●FAMILY LIFE

The family is the central institution of Indonesian society, and the model for other social relations. The family household includes not only parents and children but also grandparents, other unmarried relatives, and servants. Child-care responsibilities are shared among mothers, grandmothers, older daughters, and others. The father is often the ultimate authority figure, while the mother manages the family money. Remaining at home, children remain dependent on their parents until, and often well into, marriage. Children are dutybound to take care of their parents in old age. Older siblings likewise help younger ones, even going as far as financing their education.

Indonesian women play a more prominent public role than their counterparts in Middle Eastern Muslim societies. In Indonesian Islam, women are not segregated from men in the mosque. However, female illiteracy (percent who cannot read or write) is still higher than male illiteracy, and female attendance at educational institutions is lower than male attendance.

11 ●CLOTHING

Context and class determine the choice between modern and traditional clothes. For instance, a male office worker will wear a Western-style shirt and trousers to work, but

Susan D. Rock

A variety of crafts are practiced by individual Indonesian ethnic groups.

relax at home in some kind of sarong (a traditional skirtlike garment). Shorts are not worn by adults, except by low-status laborers. In their everyday clothing, members of the upper classes follow Western fashions closely (for example, young people commonly wear jeans and T-shirts). A number of Muslim women wear a head covering in public. This may be either a traditional scarf *(kudung)* or the current preference, a full veil *(jilbab)* exposing only the face.

A standard "national costume" has come into style for use on formal occasions. For men, a black felt *peci* cap is worn with a batik shirt (untucked) and trousers. Women wear a sarong and a *kebaya* (tight-sleeved, collarless shirt) and put their hair up into a bun (or tuck it under a wig of the required shape).

Elementary school students and civil servants all wear uniforms.

12 ● FOOD

"Indonesian cuisine" is the sum of the diverse food traditions of the country's numerous ethnic groups. These have been influenced by Indian, Middle Eastern, Chinese, Portuguese, and even Dutch cooking.

Throughout the country, rice is the primary staple. Many restaurants features *rijsttafel,* the Dutch word for "rice table." The definition of a full meal is cooked rice *(nasi)* with side dishes *(lauk-pauk).* Side dishes range from boiled vegetables with a piece of dried fish to fried and stewed dishes including meat curries. In most families, red meat is consumed only on special occasions. Chicken, seafood, and soybean products provide a cheaper protein. For special occasions, *nasi kuning* (yellow rice) is prepared. See accompanying recipe.

The traditional mode of eating is to scoop up food from flat dishes with the fingers of the right hand. Individual portions are not separated. Rather, everyone eats from common dishes laid out in the center of the table or dining mat.

Most Indonesians do not eat a distinct breakfast, other than leftovers from the previous evening's meal, if there are any. For lunch, office workers and students will either go to *warung* or *kedai* (small food stalls) or buy dishes like *bakso* (meatball soup) from mobile street vendors. For those who can afford them, afternoon snacks such

---

Recipe

Nasi Kuning
(Yellow Rice)

Ingredients

2 cups rice
2¼ cups coconut milk
2 teaspoons turmeric
1 blade lemon grass
Rice steamer

Procedure

1. Wash and drain rice.
2. Combine all ingredients in a saucepan and bring to a boil.
3. Lower heat to a simer, and continue to cook until all the coconut milk is absorbed.
4. Put rice into a steamer. (If a steamer is not available, use a vegetable steamer lined with cheesecloth set over boiling water.)
5. Steam until rice is tender.

---

as *rujak,* a fresh-fruit salad, are also common.

As unboiled water is usually unsafe, tea and coffee are drunk in great quantities, usually with sugar and sometimes milk. Soft drinks, including bottled tea and bottled water, are also popular.

13 ● EDUCATION

Six years of elementary school (ages seven to twelve) are required by law. Curriculum in primary and secondary schools is determined by the central government. Teaching methodology stresses rote memorization. For poorer families, sending a child to a public school is often a financial burden because of fees and other expenses such as textbooks and uniforms.

Few enroll in higher education, and only one in four applicants is admitted to state institutions. The requirement of a written thesis *(skripsi)* prevents most students from earning their degrees on time. Many must interrupt their study in order to work.

About 15 percent of the school-age population attends private (mostly Islamic) schools.

14 ● CULTURAL HERITAGE

No dance styles can be said to be truly national. However, three urban-based music genres have won nationwide popularity. Melancholy music for voice and strings, *kroncong,* is widely heard though considered old-fashioned. *Pop Indonesia* is modeled on American-European pop music. *Dangdut* features high-pitched vocals and an insistent beat and is derived from Indian film music. Holiday fairs will feature large tents where hundreds of young people crush together dancing to live *dangdut* singing.

Novels and poetry in the Bahasa Indonesia language have been written since the early years of the twentieth century. Internationally, Indonesia's most famous writer is Pramoedya Ananta Toer, a leftist author who was imprisoned for years. His novels, *This Earth of Mankind, Child of All Nations, Footsteps,* and *House of Glass,* explore the birth of Indonesian nationalism.

15 ● EMPLOYMENT

With more than 70 percent of the population living in rural areas, agriculture employs

Almost 25 percent of the work force labors at jobs requiring little skill or financial investment. Petty traders, including half of all nonfarming women, make up most of the 16 percent of the work force engaged in commerce. A further 13 percent are in service jobs. Industry employs 11 percent of all workers, including great numbers of young women in textile factories.

16 ● SPORTS

Part of the Dutch colonial heritage, the most popular modern sport is soccer. It is played in large open spaces in towns throughout the country. The other two most widely-played sports are basketball and badminton, which is often played in the middle of the street without a net.

Martial arts are also widely practiced, both the native *silat* and imported East Asian forms such as *kung fu* and *tae kwon do*. Many people can be seen jogging in streets and public squares and parks, especially on Sunday morning. Young people enjoy hiking in large groups through mountain areas.

17 ● RECREATION

Numerous radio stations broadcast programs in the national and regional languages and play regional, national, and foreign music (heavy metal, for instance, appeals to a wide teenage audience). Television programming includes government-produced news, comedies set in middle-class Jakarta homes, historical dramas, music concerts, and old movies. Dubbed or subtitled foreign imports consist of American TV series, Japanese cartoons and melodramas, and Latin American soap operas.

Cory Langley

Indonesian cuisine is influenced not only by the traditions of the country's numerous ethnic groups, but also by Indian, Middle Eastern, Chinese, Portuguese, and even Dutch cooking.

more than half of Indonesia's work force. Only a small percentage of cultivated land belongs to large plantations. The rest is divided among tens of millions of small farmers. Many peasants either do not own enough land to survive or they have none at all and are forced to work others' land.

Rice *(sawah)* grown in irrigated fields is by far the most important food crop, particularly in Java and Bali. Corn, cassava, taro, sago, soybeans, peanuts, and coconuts are also widely grown. Cattle, goats, chickens, and in non-Muslim areas, pigs are the main livestock. Fishing employs only a small part of the work force.

Many well-to-do households receive a wide selection of foreign channels through a satellite dish *(parabola)* and often allow neighbors to pay to tap in. In the countryside, families wealthy enough to purchase a television set permit fellow villagers to watch.

Upper-class audiences prefer to watch subtitled American movies and Hong Kong kung fu films. The masses watch Indonesian, Hong Kong, and Indian movies.

Other popular urban pastimes include window shopping in malls and department stores, browsing in all-night markets, and eating at evening-only food stalls.

18 ● CRAFTS AND HOBBIES

A variety of crafts are practiced by individual Indonesian ethnic groups, including woodcarving; weaving textiles, baskets, and mats; metalworking (gold, silver, copper, and iron); pottery and stonecarving; leatherworking; tie-dying and batiking; glasspainting; boat-building; and gardening.

19 ● SOCIAL PROBLEMS

Indonesia's large and growing population continues to strain national resources. Rapid development has not brought comparable benefits to all of Indonesia's people. Economic growth has widened the gap between the rich and the poor, especially the rural landless. Violations of human rights and widespread corruption have generated considerable discontent.

20 ● BIBLIOGRAPHY

Cribb, R. B. *Historical Dictionary of Indonesia.* Metuchen, N.J.: Scarecrow Press, 1992.

McNair, S. *Indonesia.* Chicago: Children's Press,1993.

Palmier, Leslie, ed. *Understanding Indonesia.* Brookfield, Vt.: Gower, 1985.

WEBSITES

Indonesian Embassy in Canada. [Online] Available http://www.prica.org/, 1998.

Interknowledge Corp. [Online] Available http://www.interknowledge.com/indonesia/, 1998.

World Travel Guide. Indonesia. [Online] Available http://www.wtgonline.com/country/id/gen.html, 1998.

Asmat

PRONUNCIATION: AWZ-mot
LOCATION: Indonesia (province of Irian Jaya on the island of New Guinea)
POPULATION: 65,000
LANGUAGE: Asmat-Kamoro language family; Bahasa Indonesia (national language of Indonesia)
RELIGION: Christianity; Asmat religion based on spirit worship

1 ● INTRODUCTION

The Asmat are a Melanesian people who live within the Indonesian province of Irian Jaya. They are widely known for the quality of their wood sculptures. They are also notorious for their traditional practices of headhunting and cannibalism. These Asmat practices have been linked to the unsolved 1961 disappearance of the twenty-three-year-old son of former New York governor Nelson Rockefeller, who was touring the region to collect native artwork.

The Asmat's first European contact was with the Dutch in 1623. For many years the group had few outside visitors due to their fearsome reputation. The Dutch began to settle the Asmat area in the 1920s, bringing in the first Catholic missionaries. Contact with the West has expanded steadily since the 1950s, and traditional Asmat warfare and cannibalistic practices have declined.

2 ● LOCATION

The Asmat are a coastal people occupying a low-lying swampy region. Their homeland covers approximately 9,652 square miles (25,000 square kilometers) in southwestern Irian Jaya. The swamps include sago palms, mangroves, and patches of tropical rain forest. The Asmat population is estimated at about 65,000 people, living in villages with populations of up to 2,000.

3 ● LANGUAGE

The Asmat languages belong to the Papuan language family known as Asmat-Kamoro, which has over 50,000 speakers. Due to missionary work in the region, the central Asmat now have a written form of their spoken language. A form of Bahasa Indonesia, the national language of the Republic of Indonesia, is spoken by many Asmat men.

4 ● FOLKLORE

Many Asmat myths are about their head-hunting tradition. According to one myth, two brothers were the original inhabitants of the Asmat region. The older brother convinced the younger brother to cut off the older brother's head. Then the decapitated head of the older brother instructed the younger one about headhunting, including how to use decapitated heads in initiation rituals for young males.

5 ● RELIGION

Before Christianity was introduced to their region, the Asmat practiced a native religion involving spirit worship and fear of the ghosts of the dead. It was believed that most deaths were deliberately caused by evil forces. The ancestral spirits were said to demand that wrongful deaths be avenged by killing and decapitating an enemy. The person's body was then offered to the community for cannibalistic consumption.

Missionary activity has introduced Christianity into the Asmat area.

6 ● MAJOR HOLIDAYS

In traditional Asmat societies, there were elaborate cycles of ceremonial feasting throughout the year. Feasts that celebrate deceased kinfolk are still very important celebrations. In the past, most feasting events were associated with raiding and headhunting.

Asmat who have embraced Christianity celebrate the major Christian holidays. Although Islam is the major religion of Indonesia, it not practiced among the Asmat population.

7 ● RITES OF PASSAGE

Male initiation, although still practiced, has lost much of the significance it held in pre-colonial Asmat society. Traditionally, each initiate was given a decapitated head so that he could absorb the power of the deceased warrior to whom the head had belonged. After being plunged into the sea by the older men, the initiates were symbolically reborn as warriors. Male initiation rites among the Asmat no longer involve decapitation.

When a death occurs, family and friends of the deceased roll in the mud of the riverbanks to hide their scent from the ghost of the deceased. Ceremonies ensure that the ghost passes to the land of the dead, referred to as "the other side." The skull of a person's mother is often used as a pillow.

8 ● RELATIONSHIPS

Little is known about everyday Asmat life. Currently Indonesia limits the amount of time researchers may spend in Asmat country. Missionary and government influence have effected social customs such as greetings and other forms of etiquette.

9 ● LIVING CONDITIONS

Asmat houses are elevated on stilts to prevent them from flooding during the rainy season. Ordinary Asmat dwellings do not have running water or electricity. Most houses have an outside porch area where people can gather to gossip, smoke, or just watch their neighbors.

10 ● FAMILY LIFE

Asmat society is divided into two halves called "moieties" by anthropologists. Within a given village, a person is supposed to marry someone who belongs to the opposite moiety. After the marriage, the bride moves in with her husband's family. Extended families occupy large houses built of bamboo, sago bark, and sago frond thatching. Men sleep apart from their wives in the men's longhouse (yew). Ceremonial activities that take place inside the men's house are prohibited to women.

Wife beating was an accepted practice in the past. Unmarried women and girls are still beaten by their fathers or brothers if their behavior is considered unacceptable. A woman's property is transferred to her husband at the time of marriage, and she loses control over it.

11 ● CLOTHING

The Asmat traditionally have worn little or no clothing. Footwear is not often owned. Due to missionaries and other outside influences, many Asmat today wear Western-style clothing. The most popular attire is rugby shorts for men and floral cotton dresses for women. Men may have their noses pierced and wear wild pig or boar tusks. Both men and women paint their bodies on ceremonial occasions.

12 ● FOOD

Fish and the sago palm are the staple foods of all Asmat groups. Canned meats and fish, as well as flour, tea, and sugar, have become important food items as well. A butterfly larva often found in rotting tree carcasses is an important ritual food considered a delicacy among the Asmat.

13 ● EDUCATION

Missionaries and colonial administrations have set up various schools in the Asmat region. Schoolhouses have been built in the coastal Asmat area.

14 ● CULTURAL HERITAGE

Asmat drums have an hourglass shape and a single, lizard-skin-covered head that is struck with the palm of the hand. The other hand is used to hold the drum by a carved

Cory Langley

Due to missionaries and other outside influences, many Asmat today wear Western-style clothing. However, men may have their noses pierced and wear wild pig or boar tusks.

handle. Although the Asmat regard drums as sacred objects, they do not define instrumental sounds as music. Only singing is classified as music in Asmat culture. Love songs and epic songs, which often take several days to perform, are still important forms of expression.

Traditionally, dance was an important part of Asmat ceremonial life. However, missionaries have discouraged it. The Asmat have a great deal of oral literature, but no written tradition.

The Asmat Museum of Culture and Progress is collecting artifacts from all areas of Asmat culture. It produces catalogues and other publications on Asmat culture, mythology, and history.

15 ● EMPLOYMENT

The Asmat are hunters and gatherers. They hunt crocodiles and other animals, and they gather and process the pulp of the sago palm. Some also grow vegetables or raise chickens. There is a traditional division of labor along gender lines. Women are responsible for net fishing, gathering, and other domestic tasks. Men are responsible for line and weir (enclosure) fishing, hunting, gardening, and the felling of trees. The sale of woodcarvings to outsiders represents an additional source of income.

16 ● SPORTS

Traditionally, male competition among the Asmat was intense. This competition centered on the demonstration of male prowess through success in headhunting, acquiring fishing grounds and sago palm stands, and gathering a number of feasting partners. Males still compete in these areas, except headhunting which is now prohibited.

17 ● RECREATION

The Asmat region of Irian Jaya is still very isolated. Western forms of entertainment and recreation are not available.

18 ● CRAFTS AND HOBBIES

Asmat art is highly valued by European and American art collectors. Much of the Asmat artistic tradition is tied to the practice of headhunting. Thus, since the prohibition of headhunting, the production of Asmat artifacts has declined.

The central and coastal Asmat traditionally produced decorated shields, spears, digging sticks, canoes, bows and arrows, and a wide range of elaborate carvings. The most famous ritual carving of these groups is the ancestor pole, or *bis*. These elaborate carved objects commemorate the deaths of those killed in battle or by sorcery. They were erected during the feasts that preceded headhunting raids to avenge those deaths.

19 ● SOCIAL PROBLEMS

The Asmat are fighting to retain their traditional ways of life in the face of pressure by Indonesian administrators. Many Asmat have converted to Christianity and are being educated in Western-run schools. However, they have been able to exercise some influence over government policy regarding the use of their land.

20 ● BIBLIOGRAPHY

Knauft, Bruce. *South Coast New Guinea Cultures.* New York: Cambridge University Press, 1993.

Muller, Kal. *New Guinea: Journey into the Stone Age.* Lincolnwood, Ill.: NTC Publishing Group, 1990.

Schneebaum, Tobias. *Asmat Images: From the Collection of the Asmat Museum of Culture and Progress.* Minneapolis, Minn.: Crosier Missions, 1985.

WEBSITES

Indonesian Embassy in Canada. [Online] Available http://www.prica.org/, 1998.

Interknowledge Corp. [Online] Available http://www.interknowledge.com/indonesia/, 1998.

University of Oregon. Asmat. [Online] Available http://darkwing.uoregon.edu/~st727/index.html, 1998.

World Travel Guide. Indonesia. [Online] Available http://www.wtgonline.com/country/id/gen.html, 1998.

Balinese

PRONUNCIATION: bahl-uh-NEEZ
LOCATION: Indonesia
POPULATION: 3 million
LANGUAGE: Balinese
RELIGION: Native version of Hinduism

1 ● INTRODUCTION

Much of the outside world's image of Indonesia is based on Bali, which is a prime tourist destination. However, Balinese culture is very different from the national mainstream, especially in its unique Hindu-animist religion. Inscriptions from the ninth and tenth centuries AD record the emergence of Balinese kingdoms that would later fall under Javanese domination. In the sixteenth century, King Batu Renggong of Gelgel unified Bali. The social and religious order that was established at that time continues to the present day.

Tourist money has made Bali one of Indonesia's wealthiest regions, both promoting and distorting traditional culture.

2 ● LOCATION

The island of Bali covers 2,243 square miles (5,808 square kilometers), an area slightly larger than the state of Delaware. Its population of three million is, however, three times as high as that of Delaware. The island has an unbroken east–west chain of volcanoes and a narrow plain along the north coast. A series of valleys stretches south to the Indian Ocean.

3 ● LANGUAGE

The Balinese speak an Austronesian language whose closest relative is Sasak, the language of Lombok. Although now they increasingly use Latin letters, their traditional script was a distinct version of the Javanese alphabet.

The Balinese language has a system of politeness levels. The High *(tinggi)* language is spoken only to Brahmana priests. The Middle *(madia)* or Refined *(halus)* level is used when addressing people of high social status, older people, or one's parents. The Low *(rendah)* or Ordinary

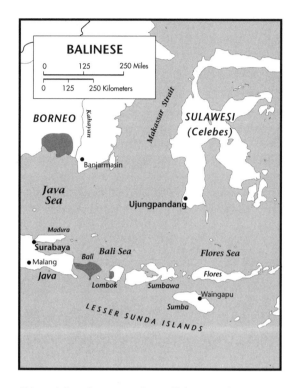

(biasa) level serves for talking to those one considers of equal or inferior status.

One common way of referring to adults is by a name that identifies them in relation to a child or grandchild, such as "Father *(Pan)* of," "Mother *(Men)* of," or "Grandfather *(Kak)* of." The Balinese also have a custom of assigning names according to birth order. For example, in Sudra families, the firstborn child will receive the name "Wayan"; the second, "Made"; the third, "Nyoman"; the fourth, "Ketut"; and the fifth, "Putu."

4 ● FOLKLORE

Leyak are witches who are ordinary people by day but who are believed to leave their bodies at night. They take many different shapes (a monkey, a bird, a disembodied head, a ghostly light). They can cause disease or crop failure, or poison food. Amulets (charms) or *mantra* (incantations) acquired from a priest or shaman can combat them.

5 ● RELIGION

Unlike the vast majority of Indonesians, the Balinese are not Muslim but Hindu (except for tiny Christian and Buddhist minorities). Their Hinduism combines the Indian model with elements of native religion. The object of their religious practices is to maintain a balance between good and evil forces. Thus, Balinese make offerings to both gods and demons. They recognize a wide range of supernatural beings, including demons, ancestral spirits, and divinities such as the sun god Surya and the rice goddess Dewi Sri.

6 ● MAJOR HOLIDAYS

Each of the thousands of temples on Bali celebrates its own *odalan* or festival, usually lasting three days.

Galungan is a ten-day festival celebrated throughout the island. The gods and deified ancestors are invited to descend from heaven. *Penjor*—tall, decorated bamboo poles—are raised in front of each house and temple to represent fertility.

Eka Dasa Rudra is a holiday that occurs only once every 100 years. (The last time was in 1979.) It entails several weeks of ceremonies at Bali's supreme temple, Besakih, on the slopes of Gunung Agung. The aim is to purify the entire universe by exorcising a chaotic element called *Rudra*.

7 ● RITES OF PASSAGE

Depending on a family's social status, as many as thirteen life-cycle rituals *(manusa yadnya)* may be performed. Events that are marked include the sixth month of pregnancy; birth; the falling off of the umbilical cord; the twelfth, forty-second, and one-hundred-fifth days after birth; the two-hundred-tenth day after birth, marking the child's first "touching of the earth"; the emergence of the first adult tooth; the loss of the last baby tooth; the onset of puberty (first menstruation for girls); tooth-filing; marriage; and purification for study.

When they are ready to become adults, tooth-filing is performed on teenagers. It is believed to purge them of their "animal nature," which is symbolized by the fang-like upper canine teeth.

Full adulthood, in the sense of full social responsibility, begins only with marriage. Weddings involve roughly three stages: (1) a ceremony in which the boy's family asks the girl's family for the hand of the girl; (2) the wedding ceremony itself; and (3) a formal visit by the new couple and the groom's family to the bride's family so that the bride may "ask leave" of her own ancestors.

Cremation is performed after death. However, a proper ceremony is extremely expensive. The family may take months or even years to accumulate the necessary funds. In the meantime they find a temporary storage or burial spot for the body. For the ceremony itself, the body is carried to the cremation field in a portable tower. The tower is rotated at each crossroads so that the deceased's spirit cannot find its way back home to haunt the living. The dead cannot become deified ancestors until they have been properly cremated.

8 ● RELATIONSHIPS

Balinese society is divided into four castes, or social classes: Brahmana, Satria, Wesia, and Sudra. When starting a conversation with a person of high social status, one bows. With children and people lower on the social ladder, one simply nods. One takes advice, instruction, or criticism by saying *nggih* (a respectful "yes") or with silence. Referring humbly to one's own person, property, or achievements is essential to polite conversation.

Between adolescents of opposite sexes, only chatting at food stalls in the presence of others is acceptable interaction.

9 ● LIVING CONDITIONS

The Balinese family lives in a walled compound *(uma)* inhabited by a group of brothers and their respective families. Within it, grouped around a central courtyard, are separate buildings for cooking, storing rice, keeping pigs, and sleeping. Each compound has a shrine *(sanggah)*. A thatched pavilion *(bale)* serves for meetings and ceremonies. A walled-in pavilion *(bale daja)* stores family heirlooms. Rivers serve for toilet and bathing functions.

10 ● FAMILY LIFE

Marriage between members of different castes is now common. Most newlywed couples remain in the groom's compound. Households include married sons and their families until they are able to establish their own households. At least one son must stay behind to care for the parents in their old age.

Although menstruating women are considered ritually impure and may not enter temples, discrimination against women is not pronounced. However, within the family there is a clear division of labor. Women buy and sell in the markets, cook, wash, care for the pigs, and prepare offerings. Men work for the *banjar* (community organization), prepare spices and meat for feasts, play in orchestras, attend cockfights, and drink together in the early evenings. Women join the caste of their husbands.

11 ● CLOTHING

In work outside the home, especially for office and store jobs, Balinese wear Western-style clothes. Around the house, men wear shorts and a tank top, or a sarong (a skirtlike garment). Men's traditional clothing includes a *kamben sarung* (a type of sarong) of *endek* (a locally made cloth) or batik cloth.

Women wear a *kamben lembaran* sarong, usually of mass-produced batik cloth. It is often worn with a sash *(selempot)* when outside the house. For temple ceremonies, women wear a *sabuk* belt wrapped around the body up to the armpits, with a *kebaya* jacket over it. Most women now wear their hair too short for traditional hairstyles, so they wear wigs to go with ritual dress.

12 ● FOOD

The Balinese eat their meals individually, quickly, and at no fixed times, snacking very frequently. Everyday food consists of rice and vegetable side dishes, sometimes with a bit of chicken, fish, tofu (bean curd),

A Balinese boy working in a rice field.

or tempeh (fermented bean curd), and seasoned with chili sauce *(sambel)* made fresh daily. Many dishes require *basa genep,* a standard spice mixture composed of sea salt, pepper, chili, garlic, shrimp paste, ginger, and other ingredients.

For ceremonial feasts, men prepare *ebat,* chopped pig or turtle meat mixed with spices, grated coconut, and slices of turtle cartilage or unripe mango. Other Balinese specialties are *babi guling* (stuffed pig turned over a fire), and *bebek betutu* (stuffed duck wrapped in banana leaves and cooked in ashes).

13 ● EDUCATION

See the article on "Indonesians" in this chapter.

14 ● CULTURAL HERITAGE

The traditional performing arts of the Balinese are an essential part of religious ceremonies, as well as entertainment. The numerous types of Balinese musical ensembles are variants of the *gamelan* orchestra, for which Indonesia is famous. It consists of drums, flutes, and bronze instruments (or substitutes of iron or bamboo). A vast array of dances are performed. The most famous include the *Baris* dance, depicting warriors; the *Legong* dance, depicting dueling princesses; and the *Barong,* in which a mythical lion, symbol of the good, combats an evil witch.

Several types of drama are practiced. These include the *wayang kulit* shadow play, and various forms of masked and unmasked theater *(topeng, wayang wong,* and *gambuh).*

Balinese literature has been preserved in *lontar,* palm-leaf books. It includes epics of gods and heroes, and tales of the old Balinese kingdoms.

15 ● EMPLOYMENT

Some 70 percent of the Balinese earn a living from agriculture. Wet-rice cultivation is practiced in areas where there is enough water. Elsewhere, nonirrigated crops such as dry rice, corn, cassava, and beans are raised. Sharecropping (working someone else's land in return for a share of the crop) has become common in the most densely populated areas.

Many Balinese are employed in cottage (small) and medium-scale industries. Since the 1970s, the garment industry has grown dramatically. There are also factories for printing, canning, and coffee and cigarette processing. Tourism provides work in hotels, travel bureaus, guide and taxi services, and craft shops.

16 ● SPORTS

Although officially banned in 1981 due to gambling, cockfights are still permitted as a necessary part of temple rituals. Cricket fighting continues as a milder substitute.

17 ● RECREATION

See the article on "Indonesians" in this chapter.

18 ● CRAFTS AND HOBBIES

The most popular crafts are painting, stone-carving, woodcarving, puppetmaking, weaving, and gold- and silverworking. The most popular locally made cloth is *endek.*

19 ● SOCIAL PROBLEMS

See the article on "Indonesians" in this chapter.

20 ● BIBLIOGRAPHY

Cribb, R. B. Historical Dictionary of Indonesia. Metuchen, N.J.: Scarecrow Press, 1992.

Lubis, Mochtar. *Indonesia: Land under the Rainbow.* New York: Oxford University Press, 1990.

Oey, Eric, ed. *Bali: Island of the Gods.* Berkeley: Periplus, 1990.

WEBSITES

Indonesian Embassy in Canada. [Online] Available http://www.prica.org/, 1998.

Interknowledge Corp. [Online] Available http://www.interknowledge.com/indonesia/, 1998.

World Travel Guide. Indonesia. [Online] Available http://www.wtgonline.com/country/id/gen.html, 1998.

Javanese

PRONUNCIATION: jav-uh-NEEZ
LOCATION: Indonesia (Central and East Java [minus the island of Madura], and the Special Region of Yogyakarta)
POPULATION: 60–80 million
LANGUAGE: Javanese
RELIGION: Islam; Christianity (Roman Catholicism); folk religion

1 ● INTRODUCTION

The Javanese are the dominant ethnic group of Indonesia. Non-Javanese Indonesians often complain of a Javanese "colonialism" having replaced the Dutch version. Although Javanese culture is just another regional culture, it has far greater power to influence national culture.

The Austronesian ancestors of the Javanese arrived perhaps as early as 3000 BC from the Kalimantan coast. Apparently the island's agricultural bounty was renowned from the earliest times: "Java" comes from the Sanskrit *Yavadvipa* ("island of barley").

Over the centuries, various native Javanese states emerged. Most were fragile coalitions of regional lords under central dynasties, often embroiled in bloody succession struggles. In the fifteenth century AD, Java's north coast ports fell under the influence of Muslim Malacca, and under the rule of the descendants of non-Javanese Muslim merchants. The Dutch government took control of Java in the 1830s. A population explosion turned three million Javanese in 1800 to twenty-eight million by 1900. The Javanese took the lead in the Islamic, communist, and nationalist movements that challenged colonialism from early in the twentieth century.

2 ● LOCATION

The island of Java is roughly the size of Britain. Some 63 percent of the island is cultivated; 25 percent of the surface is devoted to wet-rice paddies. The northern coastal plain faces the shallow and busy Java Sea. Along the southern shore, plateaus fall sharply to the Indian Ocean. The Javanese homeland consists of the provinces of Central Java and East Java (minus the island of Madura) and the Special Region of Yogyakarta. Javanese have also settled for centuries along the northern coast of West Java, particularly in the area of Cirebon and Banten.

Numbering between 60 million and 80 million people, the Javanese account for more than 40 percent of Indonesia's total population.

3 ● LANGUAGE

The Javanese language is Austronesian. It is most similar to neighboring Sandiness and Madurese. It divides into several regional dialects.

A speaker of Javanese must adjust his or her "speech level" according to the status of the person addressed. There are basically two "speech levels": *nikko* and *kromo*. *Nikko* is the language in which a person thinks. It is only appropriate to use nikko with people of equal status whom one knows intimately, and with social inferiors. *Kromo* is spoken to older people, people of higher status, and those whose status is not yet known by the speaker. Many of the most basic sentences differ markedly at the two

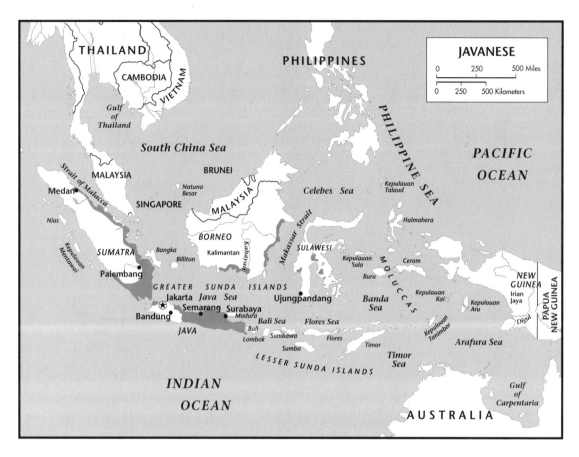

levels. In nikko, "Where [are you] coming from?" is *Soko ngendi*. In kromo, it is *Saking pundi*. Mastering kromo is an acquired skill.

Javanese do not use surnames. They go only by a single personal name. Two examples are the names of twentieth-century Indonesian leaders Sukarno and Suharto, both Javanese.

4 ● FOLKLORE

Javanese recognize several classes of supernatural beings. *Memedis* are frightening spirits. These include the *gendruwo,* which appear to people as familiar relatives in order to kidnap them, making them invisible. If the victim accepts food from the gendruwo, he or she will remain invisible forever.

The greatest spirit is Ratu Kidul, the Queen of the South Sea. She is believed to be the mystical bride of Java's rulers. Her favorite color is green. Young men avoid wearing green while at the Indian Ocean shore so that they will not be pulled down into Ratu Kidul's underwater realm.

Another set of legendary figures are the *wali songo*. These are the nine holy men who brought Islam to Java. They are credited with magical powers such as flying.

5 ● RELIGION

All but a fraction of Javanese are Muslim. However, only a portion regularly follow the "five pillars of Islam" and other practices of orthodox, Middle Eastern Islam. They have come to be called *santri* and are further divided into two subgroups. The "conservatives" keep to orthodox Islam as it has been practiced for centuries by the Javanese. The "modernists" reject local traditions and embrace a form of Islam supported by Western-style educational institutions.

Non-santri Javanese Muslims are popularly termed *abangan* or *Islam kejawen*. They do not perform the five daily prayers, fast during the month of Ramadan, or make the pilgrimage to Mecca. Their religious life focuses on ritual meals called *slametan*.

As much as 12 percent of the population of the island of Java adhere to religions other than Islam. There are several hundred thousand Christians. Among these, Roman Catholics are particularly numerous.

6 ● MAJOR HOLIDAYS

The first day (beginning at sunset) of the Islamic year *(1 Sura)* is regarded as a special day. On the eve of the holiday, people stay up all night. They watch processions such as the *kirab pusaka* (parading of the royal heirlooms) in the town of Solo. Many meditate on mountains or beaches. The birthday of Muhammad *(12 Mulud)* is celebrated in Yogya and Solo by holding the Sekaten fair the week preceding the date. Ancient *gamelans* (a type of orchestra) are played at the festival. On the holiday itself, there is a procession involving three or more

sticky-rice "mountains" (symbolizing male, female, and baby).

7 ● RITES OF PASSAGE

On the thirty-fifth day after birth, a ceremony is held with special food and much family celebrating.

Arranged marriages still occur in villages, but most Javanese choose their own partners. The process begins with the man formally asking the woman's father or male guardian *(wali)* for her hand. On the night before the wedding, the woman's kin visit the graves of ancestors to ask for their blessing. Kin, neighbors, and friends come for a *slametan* feast.

The wedding ceremony itself is the conclusion of the Islamic marriage contract between the groom and the bride's father or wali. The groom, with his party, proceeds to the bride's house. There is a festive meal with music and dancing. The groom can take the bride away after five days. The trend today is for wealthy families to display their status by reviving the more elaborate traditional ceremonies.

Javanese hold *slametan* (ceremonies) for the deceased on the third, seventh, fortieth, one-hundredth, and one-thousandth day after death. On Ramadan and certain other holidays, people put flowers on the graves of their departed loved ones.

8 ● RELATIONSHIPS

The Javanese avoid confrontation at all costs. They react even to disturbing news with a resigned smile and soft words. They never give a direct refusal to any request (however, they are very good at giving and taking hints). In addition to polite speech, proper respect requires appropriate body language: bowing and slow, graceful movements. Children who have not yet learned to behave in a dignified way are said to be *durung jawa,* "not yet Javanese."

9 ● LIVING CONDITIONS

In Javanese villages, individual houses and yards are enclosed by bamboo fences. Village houses sit on the ground and have earthen floors. They have a framework of bamboo, palm trunks, or teak. The walls are of plaited bamboo *(gedek),* wood planks, or bricks. The roofs are made of dried palm leaves *(blarak)* or tiles. Inside, rooms have movable gedek partitions. Traditional houses have no windows. Light and air enter through chinks in the walls or holes in the roof.

10 ● FAMILY LIFE

The nuclear family *(kuluwarga* or *somah)* is the basic unit of Javanese society. It includes a couple and their unmarried children. Sometimes a household also includes other relatives and married children and their families. A married couple prefers to set up a separate household if they can afford to. Otherwise, they usually move in with the wife's parents. Taking more than one wife is rare. The divorce rate is high among village folk and poorer city folk. After a divorce, the children stay with the mother. If she marries again, the children may go to live with other relatives.

Javanese mothers remain close to their children throughout their lives. Fathers, however, become more distant after children reach the age of four. Fathers are regarded as the heads of the house, but the mother exercises more real control. Parents are supposed to be constantly correcting and advising their children, however old the child is. Children, though, never criticize or correct their parents except in the most indirect ways.

Descendants of a common great-grandparent form a *golongan* or *sanak-sadulur.* Their members help each other hold major celebrations and gather on Islamic holidays. Larger still is the *alurwaris,* a kinship group directed toward the care of the graves of a common ancestor seven generations back.

11 ● CLOTHING

For everyday wear, Javanese follow the Indonesian style of dress. Men and women also commonly wear sarongs (a skirtlike garment) in public. Ceremonial clothing for men includes a sarong, high-collared shirt, jacket, and a *blangkon,* a head cloth wrapped to resemble a skullcap. Women wear the sarong, *kebaya* (long-sleeved blouse), and *selendang* (sash over the shoulder). The woman's hairstyle is called *sanggul* (long hair in a thick, flat bun at the back—now achieved with a wig addition). Handbags are always worn. Traditional dance costumes and wedding attire leave the chest bare for men and the shoulders bare for women.

12 ● FOOD

The most common meal ingredients are rice, stir-fried vegetables, dried salted fish, *tahu* (tofu), *tempeh* (a bar of fermented soybeans), *krupuk* (fish or shrimp crackers), and *sambel* (chili sauce). Favorite dishes include *gado-gado* (a salad of partially

Recipe

Nasi Tumpeng (Festive Rice Cone)

Ingredients

6 cups cooked white rice
6 scallions
1 hard-boiled egg
1 small shallot or pearl onion
1 small red chili
Bamboo skewer

Directions

1. With clean hands, mound the rice into a cone shape about four inches in diameter and about five inches high. Press firmly to form a cone that will hold its shape.

2. Carefully peel six or eight lengths of green scallion, and tie them together about one inch from their end. (A small rubber band could be used for this.)

3. Place the tied end on top of the rice cone. Drape the green ends evenly to form stripes down the side of the cone.

4. Thread the chili, pearl onion or shallot, and hard-boiled egg onto the skewer. Carefully insert the skewer into the rice cone to make a garnish top for the cone.

boiled vegetables eaten with a peanut sauce), *sayur lodeh* (a vegetable and coconut milk stew), *pergedel* (fat potato fritters), and *soto* (soup with chicken, noodles, and other ingredients). Dishes of Chinese origin are very popular, such as *bakso* (meatball soup), *bakmi* (fried noodles), and *cap cay* (stir-fried meat and vegetables). Common desserts are *gethuk* (a steamed cassava dish colored pink, green, or white) and various sticky-rice preparations *(jenang dodol, klepon,* and *wajik).*

Javanese often buy prepared food from peddlers making the rounds of neighborhoods. They enjoy *lesehan,* late-night dining on mats provided by sidewalk food vendors. For special occasions, the *tumpeng slematan,* a cone-shaped mound of steamed rice, is served ceremoniously. The guest of honor holds a knife in his right hand and a spoon in his left. First, he cuts off the top of the cone, usually featuring a hard-boiled egg and some chilies in a type of garnish, and places it on a serving plate. Then he cuts a horizontal slice from the top of the rice cone and serves it to the most-respected (usually the oldest) guest.

13 ● EDUCATION

See the article on "Indonesians" in this chapter.

14 ● CULTURAL HERITAGE

The full *gamelan* orchestra is an important part of traditional rituals, festivities, and theater. It consists of bronze gongs, keyed metallophones (like xylophones), drums, a flute, a *rebab* fiddle, and a *celempung* zither. It also includes male and female vocalists. The music (either loud or soft styles) includes hundreds of compositions *(gending)* in a variety of forms.

Traditional dance emphasizes precise control of the body, particularly in graceful hand movements. The most revered dances are the *bedoyo* and *srimpi,* in which young women symbolically enact combat. Male dancing includes the *tari topeng* in which solo performers portray folktale characters.

Javanese literature goes back to the eleventh century AD, beginning with adaptations of the Hindu epics *Ramayana* and *Mahabharata.* The earliest surviving literature in modern Javanese includes *babad,* poetical chronicles of Java's history. Novels and short stories are produced in Javanese but must compete with better-known works in Indonesian.

15 ● EMPLOYMENT

Some 60 percent of Javanese earn a living from agriculture. They grow wet rice and dry-field *(tegalan)* crops (cassava, corn, yams, peanuts, and soybeans). In mountain areas, many peasants engage in market gardening (vegetables and fruits).

Traditionally, Javanese look down on manual labor and commercial occupations. They prefer white-collar jobs and, most of all, aspire to bureaucratic service. However, most nonfarming Javanese work as artisans or as petty traders (many are women). With Indonesia's economic boom, more Javanese are taking factory or service jobs. Poverty has forced many Javanese into low-status jobs such as maid, street peddler, fare-collector, parking attendant, or *ngamen* (street musician who plays on sidewalks or on buses between stops).

16 ● SPORTS

See the article on "Indonesians" in this chapter.

17 ● RECREATION

On the whole, urban middle-class Javanese prefer pop culture to the traditional performing arts as a source of entertainment. However, the urban poor, peasants, and some members of the elite still enjoy the traditional performing arts.

Java's master art form is the *wayang kulit* shadow-puppet play. Flat puppets are manipulated against a screen lit by a lamp or electric bulb overhead. The plays are based on the Hindu epics *Mahabharata* and *Ramayana* and include intrigues, romance, comedy, and tragedy. Nowadays, wayang is broadcast on the radio, blaring from open-air eateries.

Today a popular form of theater is central-Javanese *ketoprak.* Based on stories from Javanese history, and Chinese and Arab tales, it emphasizes spoken comedy and melodrama rather than music and dance.

18 ● CRAFTS AND HOBBIES

Batik textiles are the best-known Javanese craft. The intricate designs are created in several dyeings. The space not to be dyed in a particular color is covered with wax. Batik styles differ radically. Some emphasize dense geometric patterns in brown, indigo, and white. Others feature delicate floral patterns in red and other bright colors.

Other noteworthy crafts are leatherwork (*wayang* puppets), woodcarving (dance masks, furniture, and screens), pottery, glass-painting, and ironsmithing (*kris* swords).

19 ● SOCIAL PROBLEMS

Javanese peasants must support themselves on smaller and smaller landholdings. Many lose their land and must become tenant farmers, sharecroppers, or wage-laborers for the better-off peasants who can afford fertilizers and some machinery. The military helps industrialists suppress labor unrest in the factories that are multiplying in Java's crowded cities.

20 ● BIBLIOGRAPHY

Keeler, Ward. *Javanese Shadow Plays, Javanese Selves.* Princeton, N.J.: Princeton University Press, 1987.

Oey, Eric, ed. *Java: Garden of the East.* Lincolnwood, Ill.: Passport Books, 1991.

WEBSITES

Indonesian Embassy in Canada. [Online] Available http://www.prica.org/, 1998.

Interknowledge Corp. [Online] Available http://www.interknowledge.com/indonesia/, 1998.

World Travel Guide. Indonesia. [Online] Available http://www.wtgonline.com/country/id/gen.html, 1998.

Sundanese

PRONUNCIATION: sun-duh-NEEZ
LOCATION: Indonesia (West Java)
POPULATION: 30 million
LANGUAGE: Sundanese; Indonesian
RELIGION: Orthodox Islam; Catholicism; Protestantism

1 ● INTRODUCTION

The Sundanese are the second-largest ethnic group in Indonesia. There is a complex history behind their rich cultural traditions. This history can be traced back to the fifth century AD and the Tarumanagara dynasty, which established trade links extending as far as China. A succession of Sundanese kingdoms was followed by 350 years of Dutch colonization. During this time Sundanese lands became an important source of spices, coffee, quinine, rubber, and tea for export.

In the twentieth century, the Sundanese joined in the struggle for an independent, united Indonesian nation, which was established on August 17, 1945. Even after independence, however, some Sundanese worked to establish a separate, autonomous (self-ruled) territory. These efforts were suppressed by Indonesia's first president, Sukarno (1901–70). By the late-1950s, "Sunda-land" had been fully integrated into Indonesia. Called West Java, it is one of the nation's richest provinces.

2 ● LOCATION

The Sundanese number more than thirty million people. The vast majority live on the island of Java. Java is a small island, but it is the administrative and economic center of the Indonesian archipelago (chain of islands). The larger Javanese ethnic group forms the majority in Java's central and eastern provinces. The Sundanese constitute a majority in West Java. West Java spreads over an area of 16,670 square miles (43,177 square kilometers), about half the size of greater metropolitan Los Angeles, California. The northern coast is flat, and the southern coast is hilly. The central area is mountainous and is marked by some spectacular volcanoes.

3 ● LANGUAGE

Like other Indonesians, most Sundanese are bilingual. They speak both their native tongue, Sundanese, and the Indonesian national language. Generally, Sundanese is the language of choice among family members and friends, while in the public sphere,

Indonesian is used. Both languages are part of the Austronesian language family.

Sundanese is extremely diverse, with various regional dialects. However, all are divided into different levels of formality depending on the social status of the person being addressed. Thus, the words one uses when talking to one's father differ from those used when talking to a friend or to one's younger sister. Most people use only two levels, or sometimes three. However, some older people make use of four.

Sundanese naming practices are extremely varied. Some people have only a single name, while others have a first name and a last name. Women do not legally change their names after marriage but are frequently called "Mrs. [name of husband]."

4 ● FOLKLORE

Myths and heroic stories are an extremely important part of Sundanese culture. Such stories are told through films, puppet shows, oral poetry, novels, and even comic books. Some are regional in character. They explain the history of a local kingdom, or the mythical origin of a lake or mountain. Others, like the *Ramayana,* are Hindu in origin.

One myth the Sundanese think of as distinctly their own is the legend of Nyi Loro Kidul, the Queen of the South Seas. As the story goes, in the fourteenth century there was a princess in the Pajajaran kingdom whose thirst for power was so great that her father placed a curse on her. The curse gave her more power than he himself had, but allowed her to wield it only over the South Seas. The princess was then reincarnated as the exquisitely beautiful Nyi Loro Kidul. Said to live off West Java's south coast to this day, she is more powerful than all the spirits. She is said to have received nighttime visits from Javanese kings and Muslim saints in her palace beneath the waves. Men who swim or fish off the south coast are warned not to wear green, for those who do are often spirited away by Nyi Loro Kidul and never return.

5 ● RELIGION

The overwhelming majority of Sundanese are orthodox Muslim, although some are Catholic or Protestant. Many Muslims pray five times a day, travel to Mecca at some point in their life, and fast during the holy month of Ramadan. In towns and cities, there is a mosque in every neighborhood. Each day the calls to prayer are broadcast over loudspeakers for everyone to hear. There are still many non-Islamic elements in Sundanese ceremonies and rituals, particularly those surrounding the growing of rice. They probably come from the Hindu religion that preceded the spread of Islam, or from pre-Hindu Sundanese culture.

6 ● MAJOR HOLIDAYS

The Sundanese have no special holidays of their own. They follow the calendar of Indonesian national holidays. It includes both secular holidays and those of the nation's official religions.

7 ● RITES OF PASSAGE

When a Sundanese child is born, a *paraji* (midwife) is usually present to provide advice. The paraji also prays to help the mother and the newborn get through the ordeal safely. Once the baby is born, its umbilical cord is cut with a special instrument called a *hanis*. The placenta is buried beneath a window at the rear of the house. A ritual party is held, attended by family and neighbors.

At the age of seven or eight years, boys undergo a circumcision ritual to usher them into adulthood. Before the circumcision takes place, the boy is bathed and dressed in a *sarung* (a skirtlike garment). The entire ceremony takes place at the boy's home. Frequently it is accompanied by a party.

Marriage is the most elaborate Sundanese rite of passage. Formally, it involves nine stages, from the initial visit between both sets of parents to the sharing of food and gifts on the day of the wedding. The groom's family brings gifts and money to the family of the bride. A few days before the wedding, the groom is "given" to the bride, along with clothing, jewelry, and money. On the day of the wedding, the groom is picked up at his home and taken to the bride's house, where he presents her with an agreed-upon amount of gold. The parents of the couple ceremonially feed them the last bites they will receive from their parents' hands. One week after the wedding, a gathering is held at the groom's house for his family and friends to meet the bride.

After a death, friends and relatives immediately gather at the house of the deceased. They bring gifts of money and rice for the family. Flowers are soaked in water, which is used for washing the body of the deceased. A religious leader *(kiai)* reads a prayer over the body before it is carried in a procession to the cemetery. The death is later marked by ritual gatherings on the third, seventh, fortieth, one-hundredth, and one-thousandth days after the person has passed away.

8 ● RELATIONSHIPS

The Sundanese place great value on showing people respect by following an unwritten code of behavior. Formal greetings are made by bowing the head and upper body. The hands are held together in front of the chest with fingers outstretched, and the fingertips touch the tips of the other person's fingers. In business settings, handshaking is acceptable. It is done with the right hand. When one lets go, the heart should be touched briefly with the same hand.

Social visits are governed by rules of etiquette for both guests and host. When the visitor is ready to go, she or he should always announce the intention to leave. The host will reply that the visitor is leaving too soon and has not even eaten yet (even if the visitor has been there for hours and the host had hoped to be doing something else).

A man must treat the woman he asks on a date with respect. This means he must pick her up at home, make small talk with her family, and pay for any food and entertainment. It would be considered humiliating for a woman to openly take the initiative in dating. However, Sundanese women have all sorts of tricks that allow them to do so while appearing to remain passive.

9 ● LIVING CONDITIONS

Living conditions in West Java are extremely diverse. Some people live in luxurious tropical mansions, while others live in squatter settlements with no running water or electricity. Most people live somewhere between these two extremes.

The growth of consumerism is apparent at all levels of society. The greatest objects of consumerism are cars, televisions, jewelry, and clothing.

10 ● FAMILY LIFE

Kinship among the Sundanese is bilateral, meaning that descent lines are traced through both the mother and the father. In principle, all the descendants of a seventh-generation ancestor are members of one extended family. The smallest kin group is the nuclear family of parents and their children. Members of a nuclear family usually live in their own house. However, it is not uncommon for relatives of either the husband or the wife to stay with them for a time.

Although marriages are sometimes arranged by parents in the traditional nine-step ritual, urbanization has made such matches increasingly rare. Couples often meet at school or in the workplace rather than at family or neighborhood gatherings. The parents of a woman often try to prevent her from seeing someone they do not approve of, in the hope that she will find someone more to their liking. The preferred marriage partner should come from the same neighborhood and be a descendant of a common ancestor. Such a marriage is called *perkawinan gulangkep*.

Sundanese society draws a clear line between male and female gender roles. In rural areas, women participate in subsistence agriculture and are thus quite powerful. But in cities, women are economically dependent on their husbands. To combat this dependence, many have taken on careers or part-time jobs to help earn additional cash.

11 ● CLOTHING

Traditional Sundanese clothing for women consists of a *kebaya* and a *sarung* (a skirt-like garment). The kebaya is a long-sleeved, fitted lace blouse that is worn over another layer of clothing. The sarung is a length of cloth that is wrapped around the waist and hangs down to the ankles. Men also wear a sarung, but instead of a kebaya, they wear a long-sleeved batik shirt or a fitted, embroidered jacket.

Increasingly, such traditional clothing is worn only on formal occasions such as weddings. Everyday dress follows either Western or Islamic styles.

12 ● FOOD

The Sundanese like to say, "If you have not eaten rice, then you have not eaten." Rice is prepared in hundreds of different ways. However, it is simple boiled rice that serves as the centerpiece of all meals. Side dishes of vegetables, fish, or meat are added to provide variety. These side dishes are spiced with any combination of garlic, *galingale* (a plant of the ginger family), turmeric, coriander, ginger, and lemon grass. Usually the food itself is not too spicy, but it is served with a very hot sauce made by grinding chili peppers and garlic together.

On the coast, saltwater fish are common; in the mountains, fish tend to be either pond-raised carp or goldfish. The Sundanese, being Muslim, do not eat pork. They eat the meat of goats, sheep, water buffalo, and cows. Preferred fowl include chickens, ducks, geese, and pigeons. A well-known Sundanese dish is *lalapan,* which consists only of raw vegetables, such as papaya leaves, cucumber, eggplant, and bitter melon. It is said to be the only Indonesian dish that features raw vegetables. Thus it often gives rise to jokes comparing Sundanese people to goats.

13 ● EDUCATION

The Sundanese follow Indonesia's national education system. Six years of compulsory primary school may be followed by three years of middle school, three years of high school, four years of college, and then studies toward a graduate degree.

West Java has been a center of education since colonial times. Education is valued very highly among the Sundanese. Parents will sacrifice a great deal to pay for their children's education. This is reflected in the fact that West Java has higher literacy rates than other areas of Indonesia.

14 ● CULTURAL HERITAGE

The Sundanese have an extremely rich cultural heritage. Many of Indonesia's most famous pop stars are Sundanese. Local music is sometimes set to the beat of "house music." One of the more traditional varieties is called *degung.* It is performed by a simplified *gamelan* orchestra blending soft-sounding percussion instruments with the melancholy sounds of a flute. Another type of orchestra is made up of an instrument called *angklung* (consisting of suspended bamboo tubes in different lengths that make a musical sound when shaken).

One of the oldest forms of Sundanese literature still in existence is the *pantun cerita.* It is a kind of traditional poetry, in which each verse consists of two couplets. It tells of Sundanese heroes from ancient times. More modern forms of literature, such as the novel, have also emerged among the Sundanese. Sundanese novels are strictly popular, rather than "high brow."

15 ● EMPLOYMENT

Unemployment is not as great a problem as is underemployment in West Java. Most people have some way of generating income, but they still have a hard time making ends meet. Even the new generation of college-educated youth is having a hard time finding work. When a job does open up, it is often for very low pay at one of the new factories that produce sneakers, televisions, clothing, or furniture. Such positions are usually filled by young women and uneducated men. Many jobs are filled by migrants from Central Java who are more willing to work long hours without vacations than are the family-oriented Sundanese.

16 ● SPORTS

The most popular sports in West Java are soccer, volleyball, badminton, and a martial art called *pencat silat.* Most neighborhoods have a small field in which children play volleyball and soccer. Badminton is played in neighborhood front yards or in courts at a community center. Soccer pulls in large crowds of local supporters. *Pencat silat* is a martial art that blurs the line between dance and self-defense. It is usually taught to groups of children at Islamic boarding schools *(pesantren).*

17 ● RECREATION

The central form of entertainment in West Java is called *sore,* or "evening." People go out to movies, take strolls, eat in open-air cafes, and watch public performances. It is a way to "see and be seen." People get a chance to put on their best clothes and show off their cars.

Cinemas in West Java show a mixture of Indonesian and foreign movies. Movie theaters in the city are air-conditioned and have plush seats. Poorer rural areas sometimes have open-air cinemas, which are like drive-ins without the cars. For those who prefer live performances, there is music and theater. One performance that always draws a crowd is *sinten,* in which magicians exhibit their powers. One can see, for example, people turned into birds, eggs cooked on someone's head, and people who are not hurt by the stab of a sword. Another is *wayang golek,* a type of puppet show, accompanied by singing and gamelan music.

At home, there is always television. Broadcasts include a peculiar blend of Indian movies, Latin American soap operas, American dramas, and Indonesian shows of all types. Television is sometimes considered a background entertainment like radio, with people going about their business while watching. It provides entertainment while people do their chores, and the soap operas provide a popular topic for discussion.

18 ● CRAFTS AND HOBBIES

Like the neighboring Javanese, the Sundanese are known for the art of batik. This is a technique that uses beeswax to create patterns on textiles. Originally, batik was made by painting the wax on by hand and then bathing the whole cloth in a dye. Using this process it could take up to six months to complete one *sarong.* Beginning in the mid-nineteenth century, however, an industrial technique of stamping the cloth with wax was developed. This allowed for mass production, and today batik can be found in American and European stores.

19 ● SOCIAL PROBLEMS

West Java has the usual problems of a society with a large gap between the rich and the poor. As in other urban environments, there is a certain amount of crime. The Indonesian government is known internationally for its high level of corruption and its infringements on human and civil rights. It is common for criminals who have money and influence to go free, while petty thieves are given sentences of six months or more for a first offense. While alcoholism is not a serious problem, drug use in all segments of the population appears to be on the rise.

20 ● BIBLIOGRAPHY

Cribb, R. B. *Historical Dictionary of Indonesia.* Metuchen, N.J.: Scarecrow Press, 1992.

McNair, S. *Indonesia.* Chicago: Children's Press, 1993.

Palmier, Leslie, ed. *Understanding Indonesia.* Brookfield, Vt.: Gower, 1985.

WEBSITES

Indonesian Embassy in Canada. [Online] Available http://www.prica.org/, 1998.

Interknowledge Corp. [Online] Available http://www.interknowledge.com/indonesia/, 1998.

World Travel Guide. Indonesia. [Online] Available http://www.wtgonline.com/country/id/gen.html, 1998.

Iran

The people of Iran are called Iranians. People who trace their descent to Iran, sometimes called Persians (a historical name for Iran), are nearly half the total population of Iran. Kurds make up about 9 percent. Groups of Azerbaijanis live in Iran, especially in major cities like the capital city, Tehran. Nomadic groups migrate in spring and fall between high mountain valleys and hot, lowland plains. The important nomadic groups include the Qashqai, Qajars, Bakhtiari, Baluchi, and Turkmens. For more information on the Baluchi, see the chapter on Pakistan in Volume 7; and on the Turkmens, the chapter on Turkey in Volume 9.

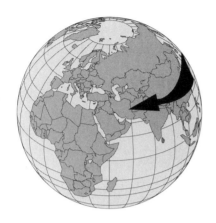

Iranians

PRONUNCIATION: i-RAHN-ee-uhns
LOCATION: Iran
POPULATION: 64 million
LANGUAGE: Farsi (Persian)
RELIGION: Islam (Shi'ah Muslim)

1 ● INTRODUCTION

Iran, known since ancient times as Persia, has had a long and turbulent history. Its location at the crossroads of Europe and Asia has resulted in many invasions and migrations. There is evidence that Iran played a role in the emergence of civilization as far back as 10,000 years ago.

In 553 BC, Cyrus the Great established the first Persian Empire, which extended to Egypt, Greece, and Russia. In 336–330 BC the Greeks, under Alexander the Great, overthrew the Persian Empire. They became the first of several groups to control the region over the following centuries.

During the seventh through the ninth centuries AD, the region was conquered by Muslims from Arabia whose goal was the spread of the Muslim religion. The Arab rulers were followed by various Turkish Muslim rulers and, in the thirteenth to fourteenth centuries, Mongol leader Genghis Khan (c.1162–1227). Between that time and the twentieth century, Persia was ruled by a succession of dynasties, some controlled by local groups and some by foreigners.

In 1921, Reza Khan, an Iranian army officer, established the Pahlavi dynasty. He became the emperor, or *shah,* with the name Reza Shah Pahlavi (1878–1944). In 1935, the Shah changed the country's name to Iran. This name was based on *Ariana,* which means "country of the Aryan people." Following World War II (1939–45), Shah Pahlavi, who had sided with Germany, was

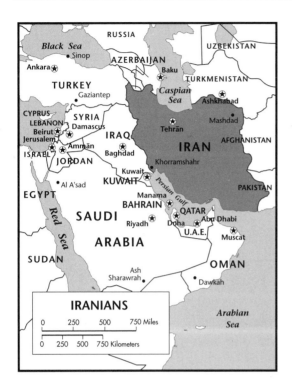

assassinated or arrested during Khomeini's ten-year reign.

From 1980 until 1988, Iran fought a severe and costly war with its neighbor, Iraq. More than 500,000 Iraqis and Iranians died, and neither side was really able to claim victory. The war ended in the summer of 1988, with Iran and Iraq signing a cease-fire agreement arranged by the United Nations.

In June 1989, spiritual leader and head of state Ayatollah Khomeini died. Some two million Iranians attended Khomeini's funeral in Tehran. Ali Khamenei replaced him as spiritual leader, and Ali Akbar Hashemi Rafsanjani became president.

2 ● LOCATION

Iran is located in southwest Asia. With an area of 635,932 square miles (1,647,063 square kilometers), Iran is slightly larger than the state of Alaska. A vast, dry plateau in the center of the country is encircled by a ring of snow-topped mountain ranges that cover about half of Iran's area. To the north and south are coastal lowlands. The Khorasan Mountains in the east have productive farmland and grasslands.

Iran has a total population of about 64 million people. Only Persians, the largest ethnic group, live in the developed farm areas and in the large cities of the northern and western plateau.

3 ● LANGUAGE

Iran's official language is Farsi, which is also known as Persian. Farsi is also spoken in parts of Turkey and Afghanistan. Many Iranians understand Arabic, the language of

forced from power by the Allies. His son, Muhammad Reza Shah Pahlavi, assumed rulership of the country. Under the Pahlavis, Western cultural influences grew, and Persia's oil industry was developed.

In 1978, Islamic and communist opposition to the Shah grew into what became known as the Islamic Revolution. It was organized by Ayatollah Ruhollah Khomeini (1900–89), a prominent religious leader who had returned from exile in Paris. On February 11, 1979, Khomeini and his supporters succeeded in replacing the secular government of the Shah with an Islamic republic. Religious standards became the guiding principles for the government and society, and religious leaders known as *mullahs* led Iran. Thousands of dissidents were

the Koran (the sacred text of Islam). The Azerbaijanis speak a Turkish dialect known as Azeri.

4 ● FOLKLORE

Many Muslims believe in *jinns,* spirits who can change shape and be either visible or invisible. Muslims sometimes wear amulets (charms) around their necks to protect themselves from jinns. Stories of jinns are often told at night, like ghost stories around a campfire.

5 ● RELIGION

The overwhelming majority of Iranians (about 98 percent) are Shi'ah Muslim. Shi'ah, one of the two schools of Islam, is the state religion.

The Islamic religion has five "pillars," or practices, that must be observed by all Muslims: (1) praying five times a day; (2) giving alms, or *zakat,* to the poor; (3) fasting during the month of Ramadan; (4) making the pilgrimage, or *hajj,* to Mecca; and (5) reciting the *shahada (ashhadu an la illah ila Allah wa ashhadu in Muhammadu rasul Allah)*, which means "I witness that there is no god but Allah and that Muhammad is the prophet of Allah."

6 ● MAJOR HOLIDAYS

The major secular holiday is Nawruz, the ancient Persian New Year. It takes place on March 21, which is also the first day of spring. In the cities, a gong is sounded or a cannon is fired to signal the beginning of the new year. Children are given money and gifts, and dancers perform at festivals. Other national holidays include Oil Nation-

alization Day (March 20), Islamic Republic Day (April 1), and Revolution Day (June 5).

One major Muslim holiday, *Eid al-Fitr,* comes at the end of Ramadan, the month of fasting. Another major Muslim holiday, *Eid al-Adha,* commemorates the willingness of the Prophet Abraham to sacrifice his son at God's command.

The Islamic month of *Muharram* is a month of mourning for the grandsons of the Prophet Muhammad. Some Iranians march in street processions in which they beat themselves. Those who can afford to do so give money, food, and goods to the poor. No weddings or parties can be held during the month of Muharram.

7 ● RITES OF PASSAGE

Marriage is the most important stage in a person's life, marking the official transition to adulthood. There are two ceremonies in the marital tradition: the *arusi* (the engagement ceremony) and the *agd* (the actual wedding ceremony).

Birthdays are particularly joyous occasions. Children have parties at which they eat and play traditional games. Elaborate gifts are usually given.

Loved ones gather at the home of a recently deceased person to sit and quietly pray or reflect. Mourning lasts for forty days, and special dark clothing is worn to show grief for the deceased.

8 ● RELATIONSHIPS

Most people in Iran employ an elaborate system of courtesy, known in Farsi as *taarof.* Polite and complimentary phrases are used to create an atmosphere of trust and mutual respect. For example, two people will insist that the other should proceed first through a door. There can be a long struggle before one person finally gives in.

Iranians, like many people of the Middle East, are very hospitable. A host will always offer a guest food or other refreshment, even on a brief visit. Hungry or not, a guest will most often take the offering in order to please the host.

Iranians are very demonstrative with their facial and hand gestures. The American "thumbs up" gesture, indicating something well done, is considered an aggressive gesture that can create ill feeling. When an Iranian finds he or she has had their back to someone, which is considered offensive body language, he or she will apologize. The other person will usually reply, "A flower has neither back nor front."

An Iranian is expected to rise to her or his feet when any person of equal or greater age or status enters the room.

9 ● LIVING CONDITIONS

Wooden houses are common along the Caspian coast. Square houses made of mud brick are found on the slopes in the mountain villages. Nomadic tribes in the Zagros Mountains live in round, black tents made of goat hair. The people of Baluchistan, in the southeast, are farmers who live in huts.

Larger cities have many high-rise apartments. Some have modern supermarket complexes that are several stories high.

Although Iran exports oil, fuel for use in homes is not always available. Appliances used for cooking include grill-like charcoal heaters, and coal stoves.

10 ● FAMILY LIFE

The average size of the nuclear family has been decreasing. Currently the average size is about six children per family. The father is the head of the Iranian household. However, there is an unspoken recognition of the mother's role and importance. Within the family there is a general respect for males, and for those older than oneself. The young show respect toward older siblings.

Aging parents are taken care of by their children until death. The elderly are honored for their wisdom, and for their place at the head of the family.

On Fridays, the Muslim day of rest and prayer, it is typical for families to go on outings, usually to a park. There they watch children play, talk about current events, and eat prepared food. Schools and government offices close early on Thursdays to honor this tradition.

11 ● CLOTHING

Western clothing for both men and women was popular until the Islamic Revolution of 1979. Since then, women have been forced to cover their hair and wear the Iranian *chador,* a long cloak, when in public. Iranian women wear very colorful chadors in some of the rural provinces.

Most men wear slacks, shirts, and jackets. Some men, especially religious leaders, wear floor-length, jacketlike garments, and cover their heads with turbans. Mountain-dwellers continue to wear their traditional clothing. For ethnic Kurdish men in Iran,

Recipe

Shereen Polo

Ingredients

½ cup dried orange peel slivers
2 Tablespoons corn oil
¼ cup blanched almond slivers
¼ cup pistachios, shelled
1 Tablespoon sugar
¼ teaspoon saffron, dissolved in ¼ cup hot
   water
2 cups raw rice, well rinsed
1 teaspoon salt
5 Tablespoons of cooking oil (any type is
   fine)
¼ teaspoon turmeric

Directions

1. Bring 1 cup of water to a boil. Add orange peel and simmer for 2 minutes. Drain and set aside.

2. Heat oil in skillet. Add almonds and pistachios, and stir over low heat until almond is light brown (3 minutes).

3. Add orange peel. Stir over low heat for 1 minute more.

4. Mix in sugar and saffron/water mixture. Cover and simmer for 3 more minutes. Remove from heat and set aside.

5. Prepare rice. Cover 2 cups of rinsed rice with cold water. Add 1 teaspoon salt. Allow to soak for 30 minutes.

6. Before draining the rice, pour ½ cup of the water into a measuring cup and save it.

7. Bring 4 cups of water to a boil. Add rice and the ½ cup of reserved soaking liquid. Cook 8 minutes.

8. Drain rice and rinse with cold water.

9. Pour 3 tablespoons of the oil and ¼ teaspoon turmeric in a large skillet. Shake the pan briskly to mix.

10. Add about one-half of the cooked rice. Cover with about one-half of the orange mixture. Repeat with two more layers, and form the combination into a pyramid-shaped mound. Cover and cook over low heat for 10 minutes.

11. Sprinkle the mounded rice mixture with 2 tablespoons oil and 2 tablespoons of water. Cover with a clean towel and the skillet cover. Cook over very low heat for 30 minutes to allow the rice to crisp. This is called *tadiq*.

12. Mix all the layers together and serve warm.

Adapted from Copeland Marks, *Sephardic Cooking,* New York: Donald I. Fine, 1982, p. 161.

this consists of a long-sleeved cotton shirt over baggy, tapered pants.

12 ●FOOD

Iranian food has been influenced by Turkey, Greece, India, and Arab countries. These influences can be seen in such dishes as shish kabob, stuffed grape leaves, spicy curry stews, and dishes made of lamb, dates, and figs.

Bread and rice are a must at an Iranian table. Breads come in a wide variety of shapes and sizes. Iranians make a popular skewered kabob known as *chelo kebab*. Boneless cubes of lamb are marinated in spicy yogurt and arranged with vegetables on metal skewers. These are then grilled over hot coals and served on a bed of rice.

One of Iran's most popular dishes is sweet orange-peel rice, *shereen polo*, also known as "wedding rice." The color and taste of the rice make it an appropriate dish to serve to wedding guests. The cook prepares a sauce made of orange peel, shelled almonds and pistachios. The sauce is cooked for about five minutes and then added to partially cooked (steamed) rice. The rice is then cooked for another thirty minutes. A recipe for a version of this dish can be found on the previous page.

Yogurt is a main part of the Iranian diet. Tea, the national beverage, is made in metal urns called *samovars*. It is served in glasses. When Iranians drink tea, they place a cube of sugar on the tongue and sip the tea through the sugar. Pork and alcoholic beverages are forbidden in Islam.

13 ● EDUCATION

Today, most Iranians complete elementary school. At this level, education is free, with pupils also receiving free textbooks. Students take a major examination to determine if they qualify to attend secondary school. (Secondary education is also free, except for small fees.) Secondary schools are academically demanding. Students take a major examination at the end of each school year. Failing one of the subjects could mean repeating the whole year. Universities are free.

14 ● CULTURAL HERITAGE

Iran is known for its magnificent mosques and other architecture, commissioned by rulers throughout history.

One of the most fascinating items of Iranian artwork is the "Peacock Throne," on which all of Iran's kings starting from the eighteenth century sat. The throne bears more than 20,000 precious gems.

The most famous of Iranian poets was Firdawsi (AD 940–1020), who wrote Iran's national epic, the *Shahnameh* (Book of Kings). Another internationally known Iranian poet was Omar Khayyam (eleventh century AD). He became famous when Edward Fitzgerald, a British writer, translated 101 of his poems in the book *The Rubaiyat of Omar Khayyam.*

15 ● EMPLOYMENT

Industry employs about one-third of Iran's work force. Occupations include mining, steel and cement production, and food processing. About 40 percent of the work force is employed in agriculture. This category includes farming, raising livestock, forestry, and fishing.

The typical urban workday in Iran is eight hours long, often starting at 7:00 AM. Workers commonly take a two-hour lunch break.

16 ● SPORTS

Iran's most popular sports are wrestling, weight lifting and horse racing. The *Zur Khaneh,* or House of Strength, is a physical training and wrestling center where young men undergo vigorous training with heavy clubs and perform in wrestling matches for spectators. Tennis and squash are popular, especially among urban Iranians. Camel and horse racing are popular in rural areas.

Cory Langley

A city street in Iran.

17 ● RECREATION

In rural areas, people are entertained by traveling groups of actors who recite poetry and perform plays. Generally, the plays tell stories about Iran's history. They dramatize important episodes and highlight the lives of famous Iranians.

In urban areas, men enjoy spending their leisure time in teahouses, socializing and smoking the *hookah,* or water pipe. Women enjoy entertaining family and friends in the home. They often spend time engaged in crafts.

Iranians enjoy the game of chess, and many argue that chess was invented in their country. Many Iranians attend the mosque every Friday, both for prayer and to socialize with friends.

18 ● CRAFTS AND HOBBIES

Persian carpets are sold in all parts of the world. Iran's handwoven carpets and rugs are made of either silk or wool, and use special knots dating from the Middle Ages. They come with many designs and patterns that vary from region to region. Geometric shapes are the most common.

The cities of Shiraz and Tabriz, known for their rugs, are also famous for their metalwork. Metals such as silver and copper are crafted into ornamental plates, cups, vases, trays, and jewelry. Picture frames and jewelry boxes are embellished with a form of

167

art known as *khatam*. This involves the use of ivory, bone, and pieces of wood to create geometric patterns.

Calligraphy (decorative lettering) is also a fine art in Iran, as it is in much of the Islamic world. Verses from the Koran (sacred text of Islam) are skillfully handwritten and painted in beautifully flowing lettering.

19 ● SOCIAL PROBLEMS

Some of the problems facing Iran include rapid population growth, unemployment, housing shortages, an inadequate educational system, and government corruption. On August 19, 1994, thousands of people in the city of Tabriz rioted, in addition to riots elsewhere.

A woman still does not have the right to divorce her husband unless there is proof that he has done something wrong. However, in the event of divorce, women have the right to be repaid for the years they were married. The role of women in the workplace has improved since the time of the Shah.

Unemployment is a severe problem, swelling the numbers of urban and rural poor.

Human rights abuses suffered by the press and by intellectuals in Iran are a source of concern for human-rights activists both within the country and abroad.

20 ● BIBLIOGRAPHY

Fox, Mary Virginia. *Iran*. Chicago, Ill.: Children's Press, 1991.

Iran: A Country Study. Washington, D.C.: Library of Congress, 1989.

Mackey, Sandra. *The Iranians: Persia, Islam and the Soul of a Nation*. New York: Penguin Books, 1996.

Marks, Copeland. *Sephardic Cooking*. New York: Donald I. Fine, 1982.

Nardo, Don. *The Persian Empire*. San Diego, Calif.: Lucent Books, 1998.

Rajendra, Vijeya, and Gisela Kaplan. *Cultures of the World: Iran*. New York: Times Books, 1993.

Spencer, William. *Iran: Land of the Peacock Throne*. New York: Benchmark Books, 1997.

WEBSITES

Iranian Cultural Information Center, Stanford University. [Online] Available http://www.persia.org/, 1998.

Iranian Embassy in Canada. [Online] Available http://www.salamiran.org/, 1998.

World Travel Guide. Iran. [Online] Available http://www.wtgonline.com/country/ir/gen.html, 1998.

Iraq

The people of Iraq are known as Iraqis. The Kurds, an Islamic non-Arab people, are the largest and most important minority group, constituting about 19 percent. Other minorities include Turkmens (about 2 percent), Yazidis, Assyrians, and Armenians. For more information on the Kurds and the Turkmens, see the chapters on Turkey and Turkmenistan, both in Volume 9; and on the Armenians, the chapter on Armenia in Volume 1.

Iraqis

PRONUNCIATION: i-RAH-keez
LOCATION: Iraq
POPULATION: 20 million
LANGUAGE: Arabic; Turkish; Aramaic (Syriac); Kurdish; Armenian; Persian
RELIGION: Islam (Shi'ah, 54 percent; Sunni, 41 percent); Christianity; Judaism

1 ● INTRODUCTION

Modern-day Iraq is located on the ancient land of Mesopotamia, or "the land between the rivers." The first human civilization is thought to have flourished here, on the fertile plain between the Tigris and Euphrates rivers. By the year 4000 BC, the Sumerians had established the earliest-known cities and government institutions. Writing, mathematics, and science also began in Sumer.

Eventually, a series of peoples invaded and conquered the region. These groups included the Babylonians, Assyrians, Chaldeans, Persians, Greeks, and Romans. During the Golden Age of Iraq (AD 750–1258), under the Abbasids, Baghdad became the capital and the center of political power and culture in the Middle East. Iraq was part of the Ottoman Empire from the sixteenth century until World War I (1914–18), when Britain invaded and conquered it in 1917–18. In 1920 an Iraqi Arab state under British mandate was created. Twelve years later, in October 1932, Iraq was recognized as an independent monarchy.

From 1980 until 1988, Iraq fought a severe and costly war with its neighbor, Iran. More than 500,000 Iraqis and Iranians died, and neither side was really able to claim victory. The war ended in the summer of 1988, with Iran and Iraq signing a cease-fire agreement arranged by the United Nations.

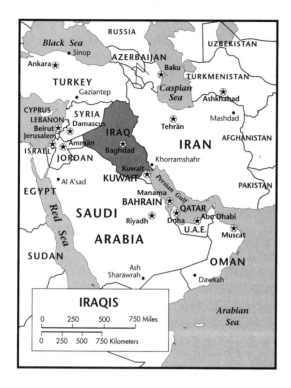

IRAQIS

| 0 | 250 | 500 | 750 Miles |

| 0 | 250 | 500 | 750 Kilometers |

square kilometers), a little larger than the state of California. Iraq has four distinct regions. The Delta region of the southeast is a broad alluvial (sand and clay) plain. West of the Delta are the Steppe-Desert Plains, part of the dry Syrian Desert, made up of sand and stony plains. The northern foothills between the Tigris and Euphrates rivers is a fertile area of grassy flatlands and rolling hills. In the Kurdish Country of the northeast, the land rises steeply into the Zagros Mountains.

The population of Iraq is about 20 million people. Baghdad, the capital and largest city, has a population of about 4 million people.

3 ●LANGUAGE

Arabic is Iran's official language and the first language of about three-fourths of the population. Other languages spoken in Iraq are Turkish, Aramaic, Kurdish, Armenian, and Persian. Arabic is written from right to left in a unique alphabet that has no distinction between capital and lowercase letters.

"Hello" in Arabic is *marhaba* or *ahlan,* to which one replies, *marhabtayn* or *ahlayn.* Other common greetings are *as-salam alaykum,* "peace be with you," with the reply of *walaykum as-salam,* "and to you peace." *Ma'assalama* means "goodbye." "Thank you" is *shukran* and "you're welcome" is *afwan;* "yes" is *na'am* and "no" is *la'a.* The numbers one to ten in Arabic are: *wahad, itnin, talata, arba'a, khamsa, sitta, saba'a, tamania, tisa'a,* and *ashara.*

Iraqi Arabs have very long names, consisting of their first name, their father's name, their paternal grandfather's name,

Internally, Iraq suffers from serious conflicts between the government and the Kurdish minority living in the mountains of the northeast, and between the ruling Sunni Muslim minority and the Shi'ah Muslim majority.

On August 2, 1990, Iraq's leadder, Saddam Hussein, led an invasion of the neighboring country of Kuwait. Other nations, including the United States, came to Kuwait's defense, sparking the Persian Gulf War. Iraq withdrew on February 26, 1991, and the war ended.

2 ●LOCATION

Iraq is located in southwestern Asia, in the heart of the Middle East. The total land area is about 170,000 square miles (400,300

and finally their family name. A woman does not take her husband's name when she marries. Instead, she maintains her family identity. Muslims use first names with Islamic religious significance, such as *Muhammad* and *Fatima*. Christians, however, often use Western names.

4 ●FOLKLORE

The most famous collection of Arab folk tales, *The Thousand and One Nights,* was probably put together in Iraq sometime around AD 1000–1500. Supposedly, a beautiful woman named Scheherazade marries a king who has killed all his previous wives. Every night she tells him a story that is a "cliffhanger," so that he must keep her alive to find out the ending. This goes on for one thousand and one nights. Finally the king decides to let her stay alive forever as his wife. Among the stories she tells are the well-known tales of "Ali Baba and the Forty Thieves," "Aladdin and the Magic Lamp," and "The Voyages of Sinbad the Sailor."

Another famous story originating in ancient Iraq (then known as Mesopotamia) is the *Epic of Gilgamesh.* The poem tells of Gilgamesh's struggles to achieve immortality.

Iraqi folklore includes some common superstitions. For example, it is considered good luck to have a stork build its nest on your roof. Women who have had no children and people with blue eyes are not allowed to attend birth celebrations to keep harm from coming to the baby.

5 ●RELIGION

The majority of Iraqis, about 95 percent, are Muslim. Of these, 54 percent are Shi'ah, and 41 percent are Sunni. The remainder of the population is Christian and other faiths, including a very small Jewish population. The difference between Sunni and Shi'ah Muslims has played an important part in Iraqi history.

The Islamic religion has five "pillars," or practices, that must be observed by all Muslims: (1) praying five times a day; (2) giving alms, or *zakat,* to the poor; (3) fasting during the month of *Ramadan;* (4) making the pilgrimage, or *hajj,* to Mecca; and (5) reciting the *shahada (ashhadu an la illah ila Allah wa ashhadu in Muhammadu rasul Allah),* which means "I witness that there is no god but Allah and that Muhammad is the prophet of Allah."

6 ●MAJOR HOLIDAYS

Muslim holidays are not official state holidays. However, since the overwhelming majority of Iraqis are Muslim, their holidays are similar to state holidays. Most businesses and services are closed on Fridays, the Islamic day of rest.

The following are the main Muslim holidays: Ramadan, the ninth month of the Muslim year, is celebrated by complete fasting from dawn until dusk. *Eid al-Fitr* is a three-day festival at the end of Ramadan. *Eid al-Adha* is a three-day feast at the end of the month of pilgrimage to Mecca (known as the *hajj*). Families who can afford it slaughter a lamb and share the meat with poorer Muslims. The First of *Muharram* is the Muslim New Year. *Mawoulid An-Nabawi* is the Prophet Muhammad's birthday. *Eid Al-Isra wa Al-Miraj* is a feast celebrating the nocturnal visit of Muhammad to heaven.

Ahura is commemorated only by Shi'ah Muslims. It marks the massacre of Muhammad's grandson, Husayn, and a small band of loyal followers. Iraq's leader, Saddam Hussein, who is a Sunni Muslim, has outlawed observance of this important Shi'ah holiday.

The main Christian holidays are Christmas (December 25) and Easter (late March or early April).

National secular holidays include Army Day (January 6), Saddam Hussein's birthday (April 28), Labor Day (May 1), Declaration of Republic (Ba'ath Party coup, July 14), and Independence from the British Mandate (October 13).

7 ● RITES OF PASSAGE

Aside from Islamic holy days, weddings are the most important festivals in Iraqi life. Relatives and friends hold parties for several days before a wedding. The actual wedding ceremony is modest and brief.

The birth of a child is another occasion for celebration, especially if the child is a boy. Three days after the birth, family members and friends visit and bring gifts for the child.

Sometime between the ages of nine and thirteen, children begin the *al'Khatma,* or the "reading of the Koran." A child studies for a year or more to prepare for this difficult task. Those who read without an error earn the title of *hafiz.* After a successful reading of the sacred text, the family holds a celebration in the child's honor. Relatives give the child gifts and money, and everyone wears colorful clothes.

8 ● RELATIONSHIPS

Iraqis are generous to their friends. If a friend asks for a favor, it is considered very rude to say no. While having a conversation, it is rude to turn one's foot out so that the sole is facing the other person. As in other Islamic cultures, the left hand is considered unclean so it is never used when eating. It is taboo to wish bad luck on someone because it might come true.

When talking, Iraqis touch each other more often and stand much closer together than Westerners do. People of the same sex will often hold hands while talking, even if they are practically strangers. (Members of the opposite sex, even married couples, never touch in public.)

The following are some common Iraqi gestures:

Gesture	Meaning
Eyebrows raised and head tilted back:	No
Clicking the tongue:	No
Waving forefinger right-to-left:	No
Right hand moving up and down with the palm facing down:	Be quiet!
Right hand moving away from the body with the palm down:	Go away!
Right hand out while opening and closing the hand:	Come here!
Right hand on heart after shaking hands:	Show of sincerity
Fist with thumb pointing upward:	Sign of victory

9 ● LIVING CONDITIONS

The middle and upper classes in Iraq enjoy much better living conditions than does the lower class. Members of the lower class, mostly rural dwellers, live in reed and mud huts, generally without electricity or running water. Doctors and nurses tend to cluster in larger cities, so there is a serious lack of health care available in rural areas.

Housing is comfortable for the urban middle and upper classes. Traditional Arab homes are very private. Older houses are behind high walls, totally sheltered from the street and passersby. Even in urban apartment buildings, family privacy is maintained. Inside the home, there is usually a formal outer parlor in which the men of the family can receive male visitors. Modern houses also have high-walled roofs (where it is cooler) for sleeping in the summer.

10 ● FAMILY LIFE

Technically, a family consists of all related kin and can include hundreds of people. Rural families live with or near each other. Urban families do not always live together. However, they are always willing to help each other out in times of need. It is considered a disgrace to speak badly about a family member or to tell family secrets.

The traditional household of a typical middle-aged couple consists of the husband and wife, their unmarried sons and daughters, their married sons with their wives and children, the man's mother if she is still alive, and frequently his unmarried sisters if he has any. Financial power is in the hands of the husband, although his wife is not completely without influence. Women have a great deal of power at home and over their children, including their grown sons. Sex roles are very clearly defined. The strict division of labor in rural areas causes the sexes to be almost completely segregated except when eating and sleeping.

Most marriages are still arranged by families. However, the couple must approve the match. Traditionally, first or second cousins are preferred as marriage partners. Divorce is fairly simple under Islamic law. Even so, it rarely occurs. Children belong to their father's family, and in the case of divorce the father is automatically awarded custody.

Iraqis believe that wisdom increases with age, so the elderly are deeply respected.

11 ● CLOTHING

Most urban Iraqis wear Western-style clothing, while most rural Iraqis wear traditional clothing. Women traditionally wear a veil (which they begin to wear after their first menstrual period) and a dark robe called an *abaaya*. The abaaya is an outer cloak that covers the body from head to ankle. Under the abaaya, they wear brightly colored dresses. Veils are only removed at home or in female-only groups. For men, traditional dress consists of a caftan and a head cloth. A caftan is an ankle-length robe with long sleeves. Light cotton caftans are worn in summer, and heavy woolen ones in winter. Rural men wrap their head cloths around their heads like a turban. Urban men drape theirs over their heads and hold them in place with a cord.

12 ● FOOD

Staple foods in Iraq are wheat, barley, rice, and dates. Iraqis cook almost every part of an animal, including the kidneys, liver, brain, feet, eyes, and ears. The meat is usually cut into strips and cooked with onions and garlic. It may also be minced for stew and served with rice. Sheep and goats are the most common meat animals. Islam forbids the eating of pork. Lamb and mutton are traditionally used for special feasts.

Iraqis usually drink their coffee with sugar and cream or milk. Coffee and tea are the favorite drinks, served before and after (not during) meals. Ice water is drunk frequently in the summer, and Western soft drinks are popular in the cities. Islam forbids the consumption of alcohol.

An Iraqi meal has several courses. It starts with appetizers, such as kebabs—cubes of marinated meat cooked on skewers. Next come soups (which are drunk from the bowl). They are followed by a simple main course (such as lamb with rice). The meal ends with a salad and *khubaz*—a flat wheat bread served buttered with fruit jelly spread on top. Iraqis love desserts, especially one called *ma'mounia,* dating from the ninth century AD. A recipe for ma'mounia follows.

13 ● EDUCATION

The quality of education in Iraq has improved dramatically in recent decades. Public education is free to all Iraqi citizens through the secondary level. Primary education lasts for six years, from ages six to eleven. Almost all Iraqi children complete primary school. Secondary education also lasts for six years, from ages twelve to seventeen. The first three years consist of training in math and science. Students can choose to spend the second three years either in a college preparatory program or in vocational training. Many rural families prefer to send their children to religious schools rather than the government-run public schools.

Recipe

Ma'mounia

Ingredients

3 cups water
2 cups sugar
1 teaspoon lemon juice
½ cup sweet (unsalted) butter
1 cup semolina flour (a type of wheat flour)
whipped cream
1 teaspoon ground cinnamon

Directions

1. Combine water and sugar in a large saucepan. Heat over low heat, stirring constantly until sugar dissolves.
2. Increase heat slowly, bringing the mixture (which will begin to look like syrup) to a boil. Add lemon juice.
3. Reduce heat and let simmer until syrup thickens slightly (about 10 minutes). Set aside.
4. In another saucepan, melt butter and add semolina flour. Stir until semolina is lightly browned.
5. Add the syrup from the other pan. Simmer the mixture another 10 minutes, stirring constantly.
6. Remove from heat and let cool 20 minutes.
7. Spoon ma'mounia into individual serving bowls, top with whipped cream, and sprinkle with cinnamon.

Makes 4 servings.

Adapted from Susan M. Hassig. *Cultures of the World: Iraq.* New York: Marshall Cavendish, 1993.

The number of women attending Iraq's colleges and universities has risen dramatically since the 1980s.

14 ● CULTURAL HERITAGE

Iraq has a rich cultural history dating back to the Sumerians, thought to be the first advanced civilization on Earth. The most famous literary works to emerge from this tradition are the *Epic of Gilgamesh* (an Akkadian hero tale) and *The Thousand and One Nights* (a collection of Arab folk tales). Modern Iraqi literature is becoming Westernized. It is turning from traditional poetry and narratives to short stories about everyday life and nonrhyming poetry on personal subjects.

Visual art in Iraq has been greatly influenced by the Islamic prohibition against depicting human or animal forms. Artists have focused on intricate geometric and floral patterns, as well as calligraphy (decorative lettering). The rich legacy of Islamic architecture can be seen particularly in Iraq's mosques. Iraq is also famous for its carpets, woven from fine threads in brilliant colors.

15 ● EMPLOYMENT

Iraq was once an agricultural nation. After oil was discovered, however, it quickly grew to become the principal industry. By 1986, only 30 percent of Iraqis were still farmers. Wheat, barley, tobacco, and dates are the major crops. Only 10 percent of the population work in small manufacturing. These industries include textiles, cement, paper products, food processing, and leather. When they grow up, rural children usually do the same type of work as their parents.

16 ● SPORTS

Soccer is the favorite sport in Iraq. There is also growing interest in boating, basketball, volleyball, weight lifting, and boxing.

17 ● RECREATION

Outdoor activities are popular in the mountains of the north. Swimming and fishing are favorite recreations in the Tigris and Euphrates rivers during the summer.

Iraqis are extremely social people. In rural areas, men hunt and fish with friends. Rural women visit with each other, talking, cooking, or making handicrafts. In the cities, people visit museums, haggle over prices in the bazaars (street markets), or shop in large shopping complexes with their families and friends. Men frequent teahouses, and everyone enjoys watching television.

18 ● CRAFTS AND HOBBIES

Handicrafts are very popular in Iraq. There are hundreds of arts and crafts fairs each year to sell all the handicrafts produced. Most crafts are in the form of jewelry, rugs, blankets, leather, and pottery. Several households may chip in together to buy a pottery wheel and share the use of it.

19 ● SOCIAL PROBLEMS

In the 1990s, the main social problems in Iraq stemmed from the aftermath of the Persian Gulf War (1990–91), including the economic embargo (other nations prohibiting trade with Iraq). The United Nations has estimated that 500,000 or more children in Iraq have died of malnutrition and diseases because of the embargo. There is continuing oppression of the Shi'ah majority by the

Iraqi government, as well as separation of the northern Kurdish population from the rest of Iraq.

20 ● BIBLIOGRAPHY

Foster, Leila Merrell. *Enchantment of the World: Iraq.* Chicago, IL: Children's Press, 1991.

Hassig, Susan M. *Cultures of the World: Iraq.* New York: Marshall Cavendish, 1993.

Iraq...in Pictures. Minneapolis, MN: Lerner Publications Co., 1990.

Simons, G. L. *Iraq: From Sumer to Saddam.* New York: St. Martin's Press, 1994.

WEBSITES

ArabNet. Iraq. [Online] Available http://www.arab.net/iraq/iraq_contents.html, 1998.

World Travel Guide. Iraq. [Online] Available http://www.wtgonline.com/country/iq/gen.html, 1998.

Ma'dan
(Marsh Arabs)

PRONUNCIATION: mah-DAHN
ALTERNATE NAMES: Marsh Arabs
LOCATION: Iraq (marshes at the junction of the Tigris and Euphrates rivers)
POPULATION: Unknown
LANGUAGE: Arabic
RELIGION: Islam (Shi'ah Muslim)

1 ● INTRODUCTION

The Ma'dan, or Marsh Arabs inhabit the marshy area at the junction of the Tigris and Euphrates rivers in Iraq. They are a seminomadic tribal people with their own distinct culture.

Ma'dan culture is based on the culture of the Bedu (Bedouin) nomads of the desert, adapted for life on the watery marshes. In general, the Ma'dan way of life has changed little in thousands of years. The pattern for simple reed canoes has been passed down from generation to generation. Their methods of hunting fish and the intricate designs for the woven walls of their houses have both existed for generations.

2 ● LOCATION

The marshes where the Ma'dan live are created by the annual flooding of the Tigris and Euphrates rivers. Covering about 6,000 square miles (15,540 square kilometers), they can be divided into three parts: the Eastern Marshes east of the Tigris, the Central Marshes west of the Tigris and north of the Euphrates, and the Southern Marshes south of the Euphrates and west of the Shatt al Arab river.

The marshes are covered with rushes and reeds. *Qasab*, a kind of giant grass that looks like bamboo, covers most of the permanent marsh lands. It can grow as tall as 25 feet (7.6 meters). Natural islands, some floating and some anchored, dot the waters of the marshes. These islands are called *tuhul*. Their ground looks solid but it is actually very soggy.

There is no current population count for the Ma'dan. The fighting in the marshes during the Iran-Iraq war (1980–88) drove many Ma'dan from their homes. Others have left the marshes to live in the cities and towns on the "mainland." The Ma'dan and their ancient way of life may soon disappear altogether.

3 ●LANGUAGE

The Ma'dan speak a form of Arabic. (Theirs is generally considered a "lower" form by other Arabic speakers).

"Hello" in Arabic is *marhaba* or *ahlan,* to which one replies *marhabtayn* or *ahlayn.* Other common greetings are *as-salam alay-kum,* "peace be with you," with the reply of *walaykum as-salam,* "and to you peace." *Ma'assalama* means "goodbye." "Thank you" is *hukran,* and "you're welcome" is `afwan; "yes" is *na'am* and "no" is *la'a.* The numbers one to ten in Arabic are *wahad, ithnayn, thalatha, arba'a, khamsa, sitta, saba'a, thamanya, tisa'a,* and *ashara.*

Arabs' names consist of their first name, their father's name, and their paternal grandfather's name. Women do not take their husband's name when they marry but rather keep their father's last name.

Many Ma'dan have unusual names, especially for Muslims. Often, they give unattractive names to children to ward off the evil eye, especially for sons whose brothers died in infancy. The names Chilaib ("little dog"), Bakur ("sow"), and Khanzir ("pig") are common (even though Muslims consider those animals unclean). Other names include Jahaish ("little donkey"), Jaraizi ("little rat"), Dhauba ("hyena"), and even Barur ("dung").

4 ●FOLKLORE

The Ma'dan believe in *jinn,* bad spirits who can take the form of humans or animals. Unique to Ma'dan folklore are two marsh monsters: the *anfish,* a giant serpent with hairy skin; and the *afa,* a giant serpent with legs. Both are said to live somewhere in the heart of the marshes, and both are considered to be deadly.

The Ma'dan also believe in a place called Hufaidh. It is an island paradise located in the southwest part of the marshes, although no one knows exactly where. The jinn can hide the island from human sight. On this island are palaces, palm trees, pomegranate orchards, and huge water buffalo. It is believed that anyone who sees Hufaidh is bewitched. Afterward, no one will be able to understand anything the person says.

5 ●RELIGION

The Ma'dan are Shi'ah Muslims. However, they are not strict about following Muslim practices, such as praying five times a day facing Mecca. Karbala and Najaf are the Ma'dan's holy cities.

6 ●MAJOR HOLIDAYS

Most Ma'dan observe Islamic holidays, such as Ramadan, *Eid al-Adha,* and *Eid al-Fitr.* Few Ma'dan make the traditional Islamic pilgrimage to Mecca. Instead, most wish to make a pilgrimage to the city of Meshed. The shrine of the holy man *(imam)* Ali ar Ridha is located in Meshed. Anyone who makes this pilgrimage is given the title of *zair.*

7 ●RITES OF PASSAGE

Ma'dan boys are traditionally circumcised at puberty. However, many boys refuse because of the frequent occurrence of infection afterward.

After a death, some Ma'dan dye their turbans dark blue to signify mourning. Others put mud on their heads and clothes.

8 ● RELATIONSHIPS

Ma'dan follow the traditional Arab code of honor, but with somewhat less dedication than other Arabs. The Ma'dan welcome all guests. They provide food and housing without expecting or accepting any payment. A host never helps to carry a guest's belongings out of the house because that would imply that the host wanted the guest to leave. Almost every village has a guest house, or a *mudhif*.

It is customary for a Ma'dan in a boat to offer the first greeting to a person on the shore. Similarly, a Ma'dan traveling downstream greets those traveling upstream.

9 ● LIVING CONDITIONS

The Ma'dan live in houses built of reeds, with reed mats for floors. There is no electricity, heat, or running water. All water is scooped out of the surrounding marshes. Ma'dan have few possessions, typically just a few water buffalo, a gun, some blankets and cooking utensils, and a reed canoe coated with bitumen (tar).

Houses are built on artificial islands created by enclosing a stretch of marsh with a fence of reeds about 20 feet (6 meters) high. Then reeds and rushes are packed inside the fence, becoming the foundation for the house. If the floor sinks or the water level rises, more reeds are added to the floor to bring it back up above water level. This type of house is called a *kibasha*.

A more permanent site is produced when mud from the floor of the marsh is used to cover the foundation. This type of house is called a *dibin*. If a family leaves a dibin unoccupied for more than a year, they lose their right to it and anyone may take possession of it.

Ma'dan homes have no indoor plumbing or toilets. In spite of this lack of sanitary conditions, the Ma'dan are a remarkably healthy people.

10 ● FAMILY LIFE

Each family group is headed by a sheik (leader). Marriages are arranged by parents, although a couple has some choice in the matter. Paternal first cousins have the first claim to a young woman for their bride. The father of an eligible paternal first cousin must grant permission in order for a young woman to marry anyone else. Polygyny is acceptable (up to four wives) but is rarely practiced.

Sex roles are clearly defined. Women do all the cooking and fetch the water. Men hunt and herd the water buffalo. Women never milk the buffalo. Men never pound or grind grain or make dung cakes for fuel. Ma'dan men and women do not eat together and are generally segregated in public life (although young children play together). Girls and women always sit behind boys and men in a canoe.

Children are called "chicks" by the Ma'dan.

11 ● CLOTHING

Men wear a long, thin shirtlike garment that reaches to their calves or ankles. In the winter, they sometimes wear a jacket over it. They also wear the traditional Arab head cloth, usually without a rope to hold it in place (they simply tie it around the head). All grown men have short mustaches.

Women wear dark robes that cover the entire body. Ma'dan women generally do not wear veils. However, they do cover their heads with long cloths or shawls. Only children wear colorful clothes; adults always wear plain light or dark clothes. Men usually wear white and women wear black.

12 ● FOOD

The staple foods are fish and curdled water-buffalo milk. Some Ma'dan also grow rice. Bread is cooked over a fire on round clay platters. Men and women eat separately, and meals are always eaten in silence. All talking is done before and after the meal, never during it.

13 ● EDUCATION

There are no schools in the marshes. Most Ma'dan parents want their children to have the advantages of a modern education. However, not all can afford to send them to the schools in the surrounding cities and towns. Their experience at these schools causes some young people to become unhappy with their lives and they leave the marshes.

14 ● CULTURAL HERITAGE

Ma'dan culture is largely inherited from the Bedu (or Bedouin, a nomadic Arab group). They love to recite poetry, sing, and dance. Men do a war dance called the *hausa*. They dance in a circle holding their rifles over their heads and firing them.

15 ● EMPLOYMENT

Most Ma'dan support themselves by fishing and by hunting wild boars and birds. They also keep small herds of water buffalo,

which they use for milk. Some Ma'dan also grow rice. Fish are traditionally caught with a five-pronged spear thrown from the bow of a canoe. A more modern method is to stun them with poisoned bait tossed onto the surface of the water. Only professional fishers, referred to as *berbera,* use nets.

Collecting the grass used as fodder for the water buffalo is a constant chore, usually assigned to young boys. Weaving reed mats for sale in the surrounding towns is a common source of extra income for the Ma'dan.

16 ● SPORTS

Hunting is both a necessity for survival and a favorite sport among the Ma'dan.

17 ● RECREATION

Singing and dancing are popular forms of entertainment among the Ma'dan. They also play a popular Arab game called *mahaibis,* or "hunt the ring." The players divide into two teams. One team gets the ring. Its members sit in a row with their hands under a cloak. One member of the other team stands in front of them and tries to guess who has the ring and in which hand.

18 ● CRAFTS AND HOBBIES

The most common crafts among the Ma'dan are building and repairing canoes, weaving reed mats, and blacksmithing. Ma'dan blacksmiths make fishing spears, reed splitters, sickles (curved cutting tools), and nails for the canoes. Some Ma'dan weave woolen cloth that both men and women use for cloaks.

19 ● SOCIAL PROBLEMS

During the Iran-Iraq war (1980–88), many Ma'dan were driven out of their homes. Their few possessions were stolen, and their water buffalo were slaughtered for food by the armies.

Dams on the Tigris and Euphrates rivers are reducing the flow of water to the marshes. This threatens the Ma'dan's territory and way of life. Since 1992, the Iraqi government has begun extensive irrigation projects that have included plans to drain the marshes. Young Ma'dan are leaving the marshes to live in the towns and cities. For all these reasons, the Ma'dan's numbers are decreasing rapidly.

20 ● BIBLIOGRAPHY

Fulanain [pseud.]. *The Marsh Arab, Haji Rikkan.* Philadelphia, PA: J. B. Lippincott Co., 1928.

Hassig, Susan M. *Cultures of the World: Iraq.* New York: Marshall Cavendish Corp., 1993.

Thesiger, Wilfred. *The Marsh Arabs.* New York: E. P. Dutton & Co., 1964.

WEBSITES

ArabNet. Iraq. [Online] Available http://www.arab.net/iraq/iraq_contents.html, 1998.

World Travel Guide. Iraq. [Online] Available http://www.wtgonline.com/country/iq/gen.html, 1998.

Ireland

The people of Ireland are called Irish. Throughout history, Ireland has been inhabited by Celts, Norsemen, French Normans, and English, and these groups have been so intermingled that no purely ethnic divisions remain.

Irish

PRONUNCIATION: EYE-rish
LOCATION: Ireland
POPULATION: 3.6 million
LANGUAGE: Irish Gaelic (official); English (primary)
RELIGION: Roman Catholicism; Protestantism; Judaism

1 ● INTRODUCTION

The Republic of Ireland, which consists of twenty-six counties, covers five-sixths of the island of Ireland. The remaining portion is occupied by the six counties of Northern Ireland, which is part of the United Kingdom. The division of the island into two political entities is the legacy of a long period of British rule. It dates back as far as 1171, when England's King Henry II declared himself king of Ireland. Eventually the English controlled most of the island. With the Protestant Reformation of the sixteenth century, the division between the conquering and conquered peoples took on a religious dimension. The Protestant English began to try to eliminate native Irish Catholicism, further increasing hostility between the two. When the Republic of Ireland won its independence in 1922, Northern Ireland became a separate political entity, remaining part of the United Kingdom. In recent decades it has been the site of violent conflict between Catholic nationalists and Protestant extremist groups. The Republic of Ireland became a member of the European Community in 1973.

2 ● LOCATION

Ireland occupies an area smaller than the state of Maine. It is bounded by the Atlantic Ocean on the south, west, and northwest, and by the Irish Sea on the east. The country's two main topographic regions are a fertile central lowland and the mountain ranges that surround it. Most of the country is less than 500 feet (150 meters) above sea level. The Irish trace their ethnic origins to the various groups who inhabited and ruled their land over the course of history. These include the Celts, Norsemen, French Nor-

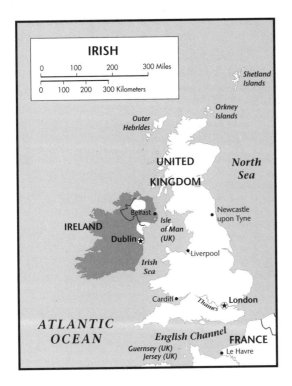

IRISH

Irish people speak English with an accent known as a brogue.

COMMON GAELIC WORDS

English	Gaelic	Pronunciation
man	fear	fahr
woman	bean	bahn
yes	sea	shah
no	ní-hea	nee hah
hand	lámh	awv
leg	cos	kuss
good night	codladh sámh	kull-uh sawv

DAYS OF THE WEEK

English	Gaelic	Pronunciation
Monday	Luan	loo-un
Tuesday	Máirt	mawrt
Wednesday	Céadaoin	kay-deen
Thursday	Déardaoin	dayr-deen
Friday	Aoine	een-uh
Saturday	Satharn	sahurn
Sunday	Domhnach	doh-nukh

NUMBERS

English	Gaelic	Pronunciation
one	aon	een
two	dó	doh
three	trí	tree
four	ceathair	kay-hir
five	cúig	koo-ig
six	sé	shay
seven	seacht	shakht
eight	ocht	ukht
nine	naoi	nee
ten	deich	deh

mans, and English. The people living east of the Shannon River generally have a higher standard of living, with a more advanced level of industrialization and richer farmland. The *Gaeltacht* along the western coast is the nation's Gaelic-speaking region.

3 ● LANGUAGE

Irish Gaelic is the official language of the Republic of Ireland. However, English is actually more widely used. Only about 30 percent of the population know Gaelic well enough to use it in daily conversation. Gaelic is a required subject in school. Signs throughout Ireland are written in both English and Gaelic. Irish Gaelic is a Celtic language closely related to Scottish Gaelic.

4 ● FOLKLORE

The Irish are master storytellers. Their tales and legends date back to Druid priests and early Celtic poets who preserved the stories of Ireland's pre-Christian heroes and heroines. Many tales recall the exploits of Cuchulainn, who defended Ulster (Ireland's northern counties) single-handedly. Other tales come from the era of Cormac Mac Art, Ireland's first king. They include the love story of Diarmid and Grania and the exploits of Finn MacCool. Modern authors have helped keep these folk traditions alive. The poet William Butler Yeats wrote five plays based on the legendary adventures of Cuchulainn. James Joyce's final novel, *Finnegans Wake*—whose main character is identified with the mythic figure of Finn MacCool—is filled with Irish legends and mythology. Irish children today still learn tales about these legendary heroes, including MacCool and Saint Finnabar, who is said to have slain Ireland's last dragon.

5 ● RELIGION

Ireland is a staunchly Catholic country. Roman Catholics account for about 95 percent of Ireland's population, and nearly 90 percent of the Irish people attend Mass every week. Pilgrimages to shrines and holy places at home and abroad attract tens of thousands of people each year. Catholicism is deeply intertwined with Irish nationalism (patriotism). Before Irish independence, the British attempted to eliminate Catholicism from Ireland. This caused the Irish to cling even more fiercely to their faith. The non-Catholic minority is mostly Episcopalian, Methodist, Presbyterian, or Jewish.

The patron saint of Ireland, St. Patrick, is honored by people (not only those of Irish descent) worldwide on March 17 each year. Patrick, according to legend, dreamed that he received a call from the Irish people to help them. Ireland was overrun with snakes and reptiles in such large numbers that it was considered a plague. Patrick went a high mountain, carrying a staff to show that he was a priest. He charmed the snakes with prayers, and gathered them all together. When every last snake had responded,

Patrick drove them all into the sea, freeing Ireland from the reptile plague. The Irish people gathered around him to thank him, and he began to preach Christianity to them. The peasant people could not grasp the meaning of Christianity's holy trinity—Father, Son, and Holy Ghost. When Patrick spotted the three-leafed shamrock, he picked it and used it to help explain how three gods, represented by the three leaves, could be one. This is the legend explaining how St. Patrick eliminated snakes from Ireland, led the Irish people to Christianity, and became their patron saint. It also explains why the shamrock is the national symbol of Ireland.

6 ● MAJOR HOLIDAYS

Ireland's legal holidays are New Year's Day (January 1), St. Patrick's Day (March 17), Good Friday, Easter Sunday and Easter Monday, bank holidays (days when banks, schools, etc., are closed) on the first Mondays of June and August, Christmas (December 25), and St. Stephen's Day (December 26). St. Stephen's Day is referred to as "Wren Day," reflecting the ancient druid belief that the wren was sacred. On this day, young men ("Wren Boys") dress in outrageous costumes and paint their faces. They go from house to house in a silly parade "hunting the wren," and people may throw them a few coins. In addition to these holidays, a variety of customs and celebrations are associated with various saints' days. St. John's Day (June 24), for example, is traditionally the time to dig up and eat the first new potatoes. On the night before, bonfires are lit on hilltops throughout the west of Ireland. A dish called *colcannon,* made from cabbage, pota-

Irish Tourist Board

A jogger on the Irish countryside.

toes, and milk, was traditionally served on Halloween with a ring, coin, thimble, and button inserted into it. Whoever found the ring was supposed to be married within a year. The coin symbolized wealth; the button, bachelorhood (a man who never marries); and the thimble, spinsterhood (a woman who never marries). Sometimes, the colcannon is left out on Halloween as a snack for the fairies.

7 ● RITES OF PASSAGE

As in most West European countries, most births occur in hospitals. In Roman Catholic families, the child is baptized within a week or so of birth. First communion and confirmation are important events for Catholic children. Marriage generally takes place in church. Weddings are festive events. In the west they may still be attended by "straw-boys," uninvited guests dressed in straw disguises who crash the wedding and play about in good-humored fashion.

Death is a solemn occasion. Although the Irish were once known for their wild wakes (a time for people to view the body before burial), these are quickly becoming a thing of the past.

8 ● RELATIONSHIPS

The Irish are famous for their hospitality, which dates back to olden times. It was believed that turning away a stranger would bring bad luck and a bad name to the household. (According to one Christian belief, a stranger might be Christ in disguise coming to test the members of the household.) The front doors of houses were commonly left open at meal times. Anyone who passed by would feel free to enter and join in the meal. While many of the old superstitions are a thing of the past, Irish warmth and hospitality toward strangers remains. Hospitality is practiced not only at home, but also at the neighborhood pub (bar). Anyone joining a group of drinkers immediately buys a round of drinks for everyone at the table. (Similarly, no one smokes a cigarette without first offering the pack to everyone present.)

9 ● LIVING CONDITIONS

The traditional rural home was narrow and rectangular. It was built from a combination of stones and mortar (made from mud, lime, or whatever material was locally available). The roof was often thatched. Rural homes and those in some urban areas are commonly heated by fireplaces that burn peat (called "turf" in Ireland) instead of wood. (Peat is soil from marshy or damp regions, composed of partially decayed vegetable matter. It is cut and dried for use as fuel.) Modern homes are replacing traditional dwellings both in the country and the city. Families generally live in brick or concrete houses or apartment buildings. Large numbers of people have emigrated to Ireland's cities since the 1950s. Consequently, a great demand for new housing has been created, and developments have gone up around most large towns and cities.

10 ● FAMILY LIFE

The Irish have an extremely strong loyalty to the family. The nuclear family is the primary family unit. However, an ailing elderly relative and an unmarried aunt or uncle may also be included. Young people have traditionally lived at home with their parents until they marry, often after the age of twenty-five or even thirty. Bonds between siblings are unusually strong, especially in the western part of the country. Unmarried siblings often live together, sometimes joined by a widowed sibling later in life. While women are playing an increasingly active role in the work force, traditional gender roles are still common at home. Women perform most of the household chores and child-rearing, and the men fill the traditional role of breadwinner (the one who earns money to support the family, or "buy the bread").

11 ● CLOTHING

People in Ireland wear modern Western-style clothing. Durability, comfort, and protection from Ireland's often wet weather are of primary concern. The Irish have been known for their fine cotton lace-making since the early 1800s. Handknitted sweaters are another famous Irish product, especially those made on the Aran Islands. Tweed—a thick cloth of woven wool used for pants, skirts, jackets, and hats—is another type of textile for which the Irish are known. The Irish have decorated (and fastened) their clothing with bronze and silver brooches since the third century AD, Traditional designs have included detailed engravings, animal designs, and enamel inlays.

Recipe

Irish Soda Bread

Ingredients

4 cups flour
¼ cup sugar
1 teaspoon salt
1 teaspoon baking soda
1 teaspoon baking powder
3 Tablespoons caraway seeds
½ cup raisins
¼ cup butter, softened
1½ cups buttermilk

Directions

1. Place raisins in a small saucepan and cover with water. Heat over medium heat until the water boils. Lower heat, cover pan, and simmer about 5 minutes. Drain well.

2. Stir together flour, sugar, salt, baking power, and baking soda. Add caraway seeds and well-drained raisins and mix well.

3. Add butter and mix with very clean hands until butter and dry indredients are combined well.

4. Add buttermilk and mix with a fork.

5. Grease well a round baking pan or cast iron frying pan about 8 or 9 inches in diameter.

6. Pat dough into greased pan and bake at 325°F about 75 minutes until lightly browned. The soda bread is done if a fork poked into the bread comes out clean.

7. Remove from pan and cool before cutting.

Serve by cutting into pie-shaped wedges. May be served with butter or preserves.

12 ●FOOD

The Irish have hearty appetites. Potatoes are the main staple and, together with cabbage, the most popular vegetable in Ireland. Dairy products are a favorite, and a great deal of milk and butter are consumed. Irish stew, one of the most common traditional dishes, consists of lamb or mutton, potatoes, onions, herbs, and stock. The main meals of the day are breakfast and lunch. The traditional Irish breakfast includes sausages, bacon, eggs, tomatoes, pudding (hot cereal), other meat dishes (such as liver or lamb chops), and bread, all washed down with plenty of tea. (Many have abandoned this menu in favor of lighter fare.) A typical lunch might include a hearty soup, a serving of chicken or beef, and vegetables. Supper usually consists of sandwiches, cold meats, or fish. Soda bread, made with baking soda and buttermilk, accompanies many meals. Popular desserts (called "sweets") include scones, tarts, and cakes.

13 ● EDUCATION

Adult literacy is nearly universal in Ireland. All children must attend school between the ages of six and fifteen. Most go to single-sex rather than coeducational (girls and boys together) schools. Both English and Gaelic are taught in primary school (called National School). Secondary school students receive an Intermediate Certificate at the age of fifteen or sixteen. Following an optional two more years of study, they receive a Leaving Certificate, which is required for admission to one of Ireland's three universities. Ireland's oldest university is Trinity College, also known as the University of Dublin.

14 ● CULTURAL HERITAGE

The Irish place great value on the arts. Ireland's writers, composers, painters, and sculptors do not have to pay income taxes as long as their work is recognized as having "artistic or cultural merit." Ireland's greatest contribution has been in the field of literature. Its great writers include Jonathan Swift, author of *Gulliver's Travels;* the playwrights Oliver Goldsmith and Oscar Wilde; and such giants of twentieth-century literature as playwright George Bernard Shaw, poet William Butler Yeats, and novelist James Joyce. Yeats won the Nobel Prize for literature in 1923, as did his fellow Irishman, playwright Samuel Beckett in 1969. Contemporary Irish writers include poets Seamus Deane and Seamus Heaney. Heaney won the Nobel Prize for literature in 1995. There is also a considerable amount of modern literature written in Irish Gaelic, including poets Nuala Ní Dhomhnaill and Máirtín Ó Direáin.

15 ● EMPLOYMENT

In 1992, 59 percent of Ireland's labor force was employed in service sector jobs, 28 percent worked in industry, and 13 percent were in agriculture, forestry, and fishing. Primary industries include meat, dairy, and grain processing; electronics, machinery, beer, shoe, and glassware production. Farming takes place on both small subsistence farms where families raise just enough to support themselves, and on large sophisticated commercial farms that produce food for export. Tourism is a mainstay of the service sector. It provides restaurant, hotel, and retail jobs and it expands the range of government employment.

16 ● SPORTS

Ireland's most popular sports are hurling and Gaelic football. Hurling, similar to field hockey, is played by two teams of fifteen players who, with long sticks called *hurleys* or *camans,* attempt to knock a leather ball through their opponents' goalposts. The All-Ireland Hurling Championship is the Irish equivalent of the World Series in the United States. It is held in Dublin every September. The women's version of hurling is called *camogie.* Gaelic football combines elements of soccer and rugby, and also culminates in an All-Ireland match in the nation's capital. Another popular traditional Irish sport is road bowling (played mostly in County Cork). Its object is to advance a metal ball, called a "bullet," over a two- or three-mile (three-to-five-kilometer) course in as few throws as possible. Other widely played sports include soccer, rugby, cricket, boxing, and track and field. Horse racing is a favorite national pastime, and Ireland's famous races include the Irish Derby and the Grand National (the race featured in the movie *National Velvet*).

17 ● RECREATION

Irish men spend many of their hours in pubs (bars), drinking beer or ale, playing darts, and socializing with their friends. In recent years, it has become increasingly acceptable for women to frequent pubs, although the neighborhood pub still remains primarily male territory. Pubs are also the scene of traditional music sessions, which are associated with *craic* (pronounced "crack"). This is an all-around term for having a good time that can include playing and/or listening to music, joking, getting drunk, or flirting with members of the opposite sex. "The craic was mighty" means that someone had a good time. Other popular leisure-time pursuits include chess, bingo, and bridge (a card game).

18 ● CRAFTS AND HOBBIES

Traditional crafts include tweed and linen weaving, wool knitting, glass blowing, and woodcarving. Belleek china and Waterford crystal are especially famous. Rathborne, which has been producing candles for over 450 years, is Europe's oldest candle maker. The women of the Aran Islands are known for their distinctive woolen sweaters. (At one time, every family on the islands had its own sweater pattern, which aided in identifying drowned sailors.) Ireland has a rich folk music tradition, and ancient jigs and reels can be heard at local festivals and during informal performances at neighborhood pubs. Since the 1960s, groups like the Chieftains and Planxty have revived national interest in traditional tunes and instruments. They have also gained an inter-

national audience for Irish music, both live and recorded. Traditional instruments include the fiddle, flute, Celtic harp, accordion, bodhran (a hand-held drum), and uilleann pipes (a bagpipe-like instrument powered by bellows).

19 ● SOCIAL PROBLEMS

Ever since the great potato famine of 1845, Ireland has lost a large percentage of its population to emigration. People regularly leave in search of better opportunities abroad. In addition to inflation, high unemployment, and the highest taxes in Europe, the nation must deal with one of the largest per capita (per person) foreign debts in the world. Terrorist attacks among competing Protestant and Catholic factions have killed more than 3,200 people in Northern Ireland since 1969.

20 ● BIBLIOGRAPHY

Fairclough, Chris. *We Live in Ireland.* New York: Bookwright Press, 1986.

Gall, Timothy, and Susan Gall, eds. *Junior Worldmark Encyclopedia of the Nations.* Detroit: UXL, 1996.

Ireland in Pictures. Minneapolis: Lerner Publications, 1993.

Pomeray, J.K. *Ireland.* New York: Chelsea House, 1988.

WEBSITES

Lecturer at Trinity College. [Online] Available http://www.bess.tcd.ie/ireland.htm, 1998.

Mystical Ireland. [Online] Available http://1adventure.com/Ireland/default.htm, 1998.

Interknowledge Corporation and Northern Ireland Tourist Board. Northern Ireland. [Online] Available http://www.interknowledge.com/northern-ireland/, 1998.

World Travel Guide. Ireland. [Online] Available http://www.wtgonline.com/country/ie/gen.html, 1998.

Israel

Of Israel's estimated population of 5.2 million, about 82 percent are Jews and 18 percent are non-Jews. Of the non-Jews, 76 percent are Muslims, 15 percent are Arab Christians, and 9 percent are Druzes or members of other ethnic groups. The state of Israel, however, also occupies by force large portions of a disputed territory known as Palestine. This territory is claimed by the Arab Palestinians as their homeland. There are 4.5 million Palestinians in the world. Although not counted in Israel's population, about 2 million live in Israel and the occupied territories.

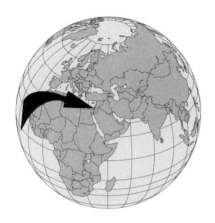

Israelis

PRONUNCIATION: iz-RAY-leez
LOCATION: Israel
POPULATION: 5 million
LANGUAGE: Hebrew; Arabic; English
RELIGION: Judaism; Islam; Christianity; Druze

1 ● INTRODUCTION

The modern state of Israel was established in 1948 as a homeland for the Jewish people, who had been living in exile for two thousand years. Jews from all over the world have immigrated to Israel. This has resulted in a very diverse society. The population of Israel more than doubled in the first four years of its existence (1948–52). Jews from Eastern and Western Europe flocked there to finally be safe from persecution. From 1989 to 1992, some five hun-dred thousand new immigrants arrived. They were mostly from the former Soviet Union, plus almost the entire population of Ethiopian Jews.

Israel also has a sizable population of non-Jews to integrate into its society. Most are Arabs—Muslim, Druze, and Christian. The world center for the Baha'i faith is in Israel. There is also a small but significant population of Bedouin Arabs (former nomadic herders who are now trying to make the transition to a settled life).

Israel and its Arab neighbors have been at war for many, many years. Muslim and Christian Arabs feel that they also have claims to the land of Israel. It is the historical and spiritual center of their religions as well, and they continue to struggle for their perceived land rights. This puts Israeli Arabs in a difficult and confusing position

2 ● LOCATION

Israel is a small, narrow country (with continually disputed borders). Its size is comparable to the state of Maryland. Israel has an amazing diversity of landscape, including mountains, desert, and a fertile river valley. The lowest point on Earth is in Israel; the Dead Sea is 1,300 feet (400 meters) below sea level. Israel has a tremendous variety of plants and animals for its small size. The rainy season does not provide enough moisture to last through the dry season, so lack of water is always a problem. Sophisticated irrigation and water-transportation and -conservation techniques have been developed. Israel has managed to create enough arable (able to be farmed) land to grow almost all the food needed by its people.

More than 90 percent of Israelis live in cities. The other 10 percent live in *kibbutzim* and *moshavim* (communal farms) or in small villages. There are about 110,000 Bedouin Arabs scattered throughout the Negev desert. Israel's largest cities are Jerusalem, Tel Aviv–Yafo, and Haifa.

3 ● LANGUAGE

The official languages of Israel are Hebrew, Arabic, and English. Hebrew is the language of the majority. Most Israelis also speak English. Modern Hebrew is a very young language, born only about one hundred years ago. After the exile of the Jews from ancient Israel, Hebrew was used only for religious writings and services for two thousand years. For everyday use, Jews learned to speak the language of whatever country they ended up in. In the late nineteenth century, Eliezer Ben Yehuda (1858–1922) moved to the Holy Land with his

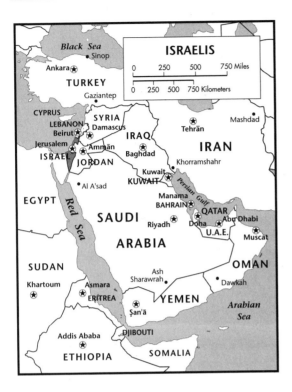

and creates tremendous tensions within Israeli society. Many programs are in place to try to reduce these tensions by breaking down stereotypes, encouraging cooperation among different elements of the Israeli population, and improving conditions for disadvantaged minorities.

Perhaps the most interesting factor in Israeli society at present is that, for the first time in two thousand years, a generation of Jews is growing up as the majority in their homeland. Known as Sabras (native-born Israelis), this new generation is developing a very unique self-image. Unlike their parents or grandparents, they have no experience of being a persecuted minority in the country where they live.

Cory Langley

A sign written in Hebrew, Arabic, and English.

family and decided that they would never-again speak a word in any language but Hebrew. This forced them to create many new words, and modern Hebrew was born.

Hebrew uses a unique alphabet with no vowels. It is read from right to left, except for numerals, which are read from left to right. Some common words in Hebrew are *toda* (thank you), *ken*, (yes), and *lo* (no). The numbers from one to ten in Hebrew are: *ehad, shtayim, shalosh, arba', hamesh, shesh, sheva', shmoney, taysha'*, and *esser*. Common male names are *Menahem, Avraham, Moshe, Benyamin*, and *Shlomo*. Common female names are *Esther, Hannah, Sareh, Rachel*, and *Galit*.

4 ● FOLKLORE

Most of Israeli folklore reflects their history of exile in other lands, their return to the land of their ancestors, and the modern-day battles over establishing and maintaining statehood. For example, the story of Passover, or *Pesach*, is a reference to the deliverance of the children of Israel from over two centuries of bondage in Egypt. It refers to the Jewish exodus (mass departure) from Egypt more than three thousand years ago. The *Torah* (the holiest Jewish scriptures) calls Passover the "season of our freedom." It is the time when the plague that struck Egypt passed over the Israelites without destroying them.

Another important event in the history of Judaism is the *zman matan Torateinu*, "the season of the giving of our Torah." This commemorates the Revelation of the Ten Commandments, seven weeks after the Israelites escaped from Egypt, as they camped at the foot of Mount Sinai.

Some modern-day Israeli heroes include Theodor Herzl (1860–1904), who convened the first Zionist Congress, held in Basel, Switzerland, in 1897, and is the author of *The Jewish State*; Chaim Weizmann (1874–1952), Israel's first president; and David Ben-Gurion (1886–1973), Israel's first prime minister, who announced the independence of Israel in 1948.

5 ● RELIGION

The modern state of Israel was established in 1948 as a homeland for Jews. It is therefore not surprising that 82 percent of the population is Jewish. Of the 18 percent who are non-Jews, most are Muslim Arabs. There are also small numbers of Christians and Druze. The Baha'i world center is also located in Israel, in the Mediterranean coastal city of Haifa. The Baha'i religion developed out of the mystical Islamic movement around AD 1850.

Religious freedom is guaranteed by the state. However, there is little separation between "church and state." The Jewish faith and rabbinical law are intricately entwined with the political and public spheres.

6 ● MAJOR HOLIDAYS

Because the majority of the Israeli population is Jewish, Jewish holidays are, in effect, state holidays. During the Jewish *shabbat,* or *Sabbath* (from sunset Friday to sunset Saturday each week), almost all public and commercial enterprise stops. On *Yom Kippur,* the Day of Atonement (ten days after *Rosh Hashana,* the Jewish New Year), the whole country comes to a standstill while observant Jews complete twenty-five hours of total fasting and prayer. No Jewish hotels or restaurants will serve bread or fermented foods during the week of *Pesach,* or Passover. This holiday commemorates the exodus of the Jews from Egypt during Biblical times.

At *kibbutzim* and *moshavim* (communal farms), a distinctive cultural life has developed. Celebrations are based on traditional Jewish holidays combined with ancient earth-cycle customs, such as first-fruits and harvest feasts.

Independence Day is observed on May 15, as the founding of the state of Israel was first declared on May 15, 1948.

7 ● RITES OF PASSAGE

Circumcision *(brit milah)* of boys is both a Jewish and Muslim ritual. The Jewish circumcision is performed eight days after birth. It involves prayers and expresses the intent of bringing the son into the covenant with God. The son is named at circumcision. (A newborn daughter is given her name in the synagogue the week following her birth.) Muslim circumcisions take place either at birth or during the boy's youth. They are followed by a feast in celebration.

On his thirteenth birthday, a Jewish boy goes through the *Bar Mitzvah* ceremony. The ritual signifies a boy's attainment of maturity when he assumes responsibility for the observance of Jewish laws. During the service, the boy reads from the Torah and speaks from memory on a Biblical theme. A feast and dancing are part of the celebration. A girl assumes the same responsibility for the observance of Jewish laws at her twelfth birthday, during the *Bat Mitzvah*. There has never been a traditional ceremony to commemorate this threshold for girls, but some modern families and religious schools do hold some type of celebration.

8 ● RELATIONSHIPS

Given the extremely diverse population of Israel, it is difficult to define any standard Israeli ways of relating to one another. Native-born Israelis (known as Sabras), however, tend to be very straightforward, plain-talking people, even to the point of rudeness. They detest sentimentality of any kind and love a good argument. They are fierce and articulate, friendly and hospitable, self-confident, ambitious, and proud. Because Sabras love to argue and drink coffee so much, it is considered perfectly acceptable to sit at a streetside cafe (cafes are the center of Israeli social life) and talk for hours over a cup of coffee and a piece of cake.

Modern high-rise apartment buildings in Tel Aviv.

The common greeting is *Shalom,* which means both "hello" and "goodbye" as well as "peace" and "good health." For the Arabs of Israel, *Salam* also means "peace and good health," and *as-salamu 'alaykum* means "peace be with you," also used as a common greeting. *Toda* means "thanks" in Hebrew to which the reply is usually *"bev-akasha* (please) or *alo davar* (it's nothing). *Lehitra'ot* is "See you!"

9 ● LIVING CONDITIONS

More than 90 percent of Israelis are urban dwellers. They live in housing built mostly of stone, concrete block, or stucco. About 3 percent of the population live in some 270 *kibbutzim.* These are communes where property is commonly owned, decisions are made by all members, meals are prepared and served communally, and children live, eat, and study together in a "children's community." Kibbutzim were traditionally the backbone of Israeli agriculture. They are now branching out into light industry as well.

Another rural communal arrangement are the *moshavim,* where about 60 individually owned family farms cooperate in purchasing, marketing, and community services. There are some 450 moshavim in Israel. These supply much of Israel's farm produce.

Small villages in Israel are mostly inhabited by Arabs. In northern Israel, there are a few villages of Druze. Bedouin Arabs live in tent communities in the Negev desert, cooking over open fires and tending sheep and goats.

10 ● FAMILY LIFE

Israeli children are generally well cared for, even pampered. Most Jewish families have three children. The Arab average was eight or nine children in 1968 and has fallen continuously since then. The equality of women is protected under law in Israel. However, religious and cultural traditions often overrule the law.

Traditional Arab families have been exposed to huge changes since the establishment of the Israeli state in 1948. New laws contradict age-old Arab cultural practices. These laws include the protection of women's rights, prohibitions against polygamy (multiple spouses) and child marriage, as well as laws making education compulsory. New participation in economics and politics, and a shift away from an agricultural way of life, have also upset the former balance of Arab families. The new generation is growing up very different from the old. This puts tremendous pressure on the Arab family.

11 ● CLOTHING

Daily wear in Israel is generally informal and Western-style. Ultra-Orthodox Jews wear traditional clothing every day. Some Orthodox males wear their hair in sidelocks called *payes*. Married Orthodox women often wear a wig called a *shietel,* and a scarf tied to the back. Orthodox men wear long black or gray coats over a shirt and pants, and a black hat on their heads.

Muslim men and women dress similarly to Palestinians. The *kaffiyyeh* (scarflike headdress) is worn by many of the more traditional and elderly men. Most Muslim women in Israel no longer wear the traditional *thob* (long black peasant dress) of the Palestinians, choosing Western attire instead.

12 ● FOOD

Because of the great diversity in the Israeli population, there is really no such thing as Israeli cuisine. By far the most popular food in Israel, however, is *felafel*—deep-fried balls of ground chickpeas. All along city streets, one finds felafel stands (not unlike hot dog stands in the United States) where a large variety of things to put with felafel in pita (pocket) bread are available. Eggplant is another popular food item.

Israelis love to eat and do it often. They start the day with a huge breakfast and continue to eat frequently throughout the day. Due to kosher restrictions, Jewish Israelis tend to eat a main "meat" meal at midday and a lighter "dairy" meal in the evening, since meat and dairy cannot be eaten together or from the same utensils. Camels, pigs, and rabbits are forbidden in the Jewish diet, as are lobsters, oysters, shrimp, clams, and crabs. Animals that have cloven hoofs and chew cud are permitted, such as sheep, cattle, and deer. Only fish with both fins and scales are permitted. The dietary restrictions of Judaism, known as *kashrut* (right or fit), are considered a personal matter in modern Israel.

An Jewish man and his son hurry to worship.

13 ● EDUCATION

Israel is a land of the educated. Schooling is highly valued, and Israeli students are high achievers. Even Arabs, who did not traditionally send their children to school, now have a relatively high attendance rate. Schooling is free and required for children ages five to sixteen. It continues to be free (although not required) until age eighteen. Programs are available for both gifted and disabled students. From fourth grade through high school, special attention is given to the Arab–Israeli conflict. Many programs are designed to eliminate stereotypes and promote cooperation, mutual respect, and tolerance.

Most Israelis are over twenty-one when they begin college because of the compulsory military service that begins after high school. Women must serve for two years and men for three.

14 ● CULTURAL HERITAGE

Israel has become one of the most active music centers in the world. Both folk music and folk dance are dynamic blends of the diverse backgrounds of Israel's various immigrant groups. Classical "art" dance was introduced in Israel in the 1920s when Moscow-trained ballerina Rina Nikova moved there. Classical music, now extremely popular, arrived with European immigrants fleeing Nazism in the 1930s.

Visual art and cinema both struggle to define an Israeli style. Poetry and literature, on the other hand, are vibrant and vital expressions of the Israeli spirit. In 1966, Shmuel Yosef Agnon (1888–1970) was the first author writing in modern Hebrew to win the Nobel Prize for Literature. Amos Oz and other Hebrew writers have become known worldwide. A number of Arab Israeli authors have also achieved success.

15 ● EMPLOYMENT

Working conditions have minimum requirements established by law. These include a forty-seven-hour maximum work week, minimum wages, overtime compensation, severance pay, and paid vacation and work leave. Laws also exist to protect working women, particularly those with children or who are expecting. Women are legally entitled to equal pay as men. However, in practice it does not always work out that way. Israel's largest employers are the government and the Histadrut, a federation of trade unions.

16 ● SPORTS

Soccer and basketball are Israel's most popular sports. Mass sporting events, such as the Jerusalem March, the swim across Lake Kinneret (Sea of Galilee), and various marathons are also very popular. Jewish athletes from around the world compete in the Maccabiah Games, also known as the Jewish Olympics. These have been held in what is now Israel every four years since 1932.

17 ● RECREATION

Many of Israel's urban centers, most notably Tel Aviv, are home to dozens of art galleries, theatrical companies, movie theaters, and concert halls. Classical music is a favorite in Israel. Israelis take pride in their native musicians, such as violinists Yitzhak Perlman and Pinchas Zukerman. Hebrew pop music is also popular. It is a mixture of the many Israeli ethnic backgrounds, including Arabic, Latin, and North American.

One of the favorite Israeli pastimes is eating out. Outdoor vendors and sit-down restaurants offer a wide range of food choices, from Middle Eastern felafel to pizza and McDonald's. Israelis also enjoy going to the beach for recreation.

18 ● CRAFTS AND HOBBIES

Not surprisingly, Israel is the world center for the production of Judaica—crafts relating to Jewish religious life. There are no design restrictions in Jewish law on these objects, so artists can exercise their own creativity. Items include Hanukkah lamps; wine cups, candlesticks, and spice boxes for the Sabbath and other holidays; and cases for *mezuzot* (parchment scrolls hung on every Jewish doorpost).

The national hobby is archaeology. The tiny country of Israel has more than 3,500 archeological sites, so there is plenty of opportunity for amateur and professional archaeologists. Archaeological finds date back as far as 150,000 BC.

19 ● SOCIAL PROBLEMS

Israel's social problems stem primarily from the newness of the state (less than fifty years old) and the tremendous diversity of its population (most are newcomers). The huge, ongoing arrival of immigrants creates overcrowding, unemployment, and cultural confusion. Schools are constantly having to accommodate more students who speak different languages and come from different backgrounds. Some of the immigrant groups come from very poor rural commu-

nities and have a difficult time adapting to a fast-paced technological society.

The other major problem in Israel is the Arab–Israeli conflict. Arab–Jewish tensions continue because of the long-standing war with Israel's Arab neighbors; the differences in language, religion, and customs; and the self-segregation practiced by both groups. Government, public, and private organizations now sponsor Jewish–Arab encounters. The Ministry of Education has programs in place in the schools to overcome prejudice and prevent conflicts.

20 ● BIBLIOGRAPHY

Facts about Israel. Jerusalem: Israel Information Center, 1993.

Ganor, Avi, and Ron Maiberg. *Taste of Israel: A Mediterranean Feast.* New York: Rizzoli International, 1990.

Israel Today. Jerusalem: Ahva Press, 1993.

Willard, Jed, ed. *Let's Go: The Budget Guide to Israel and Egypt, 1996.* New York: St. Martin's Press, 1996.

WEBSITES

Embassy of Israel, Washington, D.C. [Online] Available http://www.israelemb.org/, 1998.

World Travel Guide. [Online] Available http://www.wtgonline.com/country/il/gen.html, 1998.

Palestinians

PRONUNCIATION: pal-uh-STIN-ee-uhns
LOCATION: Israel and the Occupied Territories
(West Bank and Gaza Strip); Jordan;
Lebanon; Syria
POPULATION: 4.5 million
LANGUAGE: Arabic
RELIGION: Islam; Christianity; Druze

1 ● INTRODUCTION

Palestine is the historical name for the region between the Mediterranean Sea and the Jordan River. The land was first inhabited as long ago as 9000 BC. The Hebrews (ancestors of today's Jews) settled in Palestine in 1900 BC and had formed the kingdom of Israel, ruled by King David, by 1000 BC. Palestine was then taken over by a series of foreign powers. The Arabs took control of the area during the Islamic expansion of the seventh century AD. It is from these Arabs that modern-day Palestinians are descended.

Palestine was under the rule of the Ottoman Empire from AD 1516 until the empire was defeated in World War I (1914–18). During the war period, both Arabs and Jews were made promises by the British concerning the future fate of Palestine. The British controlled Palestine from 1920 to 1948. In 1947, the United Nations (UN) divided Palestine into two states, one Jewish, and the other Arab. When the independent state of Israel was declared on May 15, 1948, the Arab forces of Egypt, Iraq, Lebanon, Saudi Arabia, Syria, and Transjordan advanced into Palestine. After the ensuing war in 1949, the West Bank came under Jordanian rule, the Gaza Strip came under Egyptian rule, and the remainder of Palestine came under Israeli rule. Many, but not all, Palestinian Arabs fled abroad during this time. In 1964, the Palestine Liberation Organization (PLO) was formed in Jerusalem. Yasser Arafat became the head of the PLO in 1969.

In a June 1967 war, Israel captured the West Bank and the Gaza Strip. Also in that year, Israel annexed East Jerusalem. The West Bank and Gaza Strip have since been called the Occupied Territories. Most of the residents there are Palestinian Arabs. December 1987 marked the beginning of the Intifada—an ongoing popular uprising of Palestinians against Israeli occupation of the West Bank and Gaza Strip. The Israeli government and the PLO signed the Declaration of Principles (DOP) in September 1993, resolving that Israeli troops would leave the West Bank and Gaza Strip areas. In 1994, limited Palestinian self-rule was established in Jericho and the Gaza Strip. Fighting continues over the question of a fully independent Palestinian homeland.

2 ● LOCATION

There are more than 4.5 million Palestinians in the world. About 2 million of them live in Israel and the Occupied Territories—the West Bank and Gaza Strip. Most of the rest live in neighboring Arab countries such as Jordan, Lebanon, and Syria. The UN lists 2 million Palestinian refugees. During the war years of 1947–49, between 700,000 and 800,000 Palestinians were driven from their homes. When Israel occupied the West Bank and Gaza Strip in 1967, another 300,000 Palestinians became refugees (and 150,000 who were already refugees were forced to move again).

3 ● LANGUAGE

Palestinians speak Arabic. "Hello" in Arabic is *marhaba* or *ahlan*, to which one replies, *marhabtayn* or *ahlayn*. Other common greetings are *As-salam alaykum* (Peace be with you), with the reply of *wa 'alaykum as salam* (and to you peace). *Ma'assalama* means "goodbye," with the literal translation being "go with peace." "Thank you" is *Shukran*, and "You're welcome" is *'Afwan*. "Yes" is *na'am*, and "no" is *la'a*. The numbers one to ten in Arabic are: *wahad, ithnayn, thalatha, arba'a, khamsa, sita, sab'a, thamanya, tis'a,* and *'ashara*.

Common names for boys are *Ahmad, Shukri, Isma'il,* and *Ibrahim. Muhammad* is a very common Muslim name. *Hanna* is a very common Christian name. *`Isa* (Jesus) is used by both Muslims and Christians. Common names for girls are *Samia, Sawsan, Maysoon, Muna,* and *Fatima*. On rare occasions girls are given politically significant names such as *Al-Quds* (Jerusalem).

4 ● FOLKLORE

Palestinians believe in *jinns*—evil spirits who can take on the shapes of natural forms and cause trouble.

A famous fictional character is Juha. School children read about Juha's exploits in fables that teach lessons. For example, in one story Juha buries a treasure in the ground and tries to remember its whereabouts by remembering the clouds that hover over it. Naturally, he loses his treasure because clouds move about and disappear.

Many Muslim stories cherished by Palestinians are similar to those in the Judeo-

Christian tradition. The stories of Noah and the Ark and Adam and Eve are important to both Muslim and Christian Palestinians. Palestinians take pride in the true story of the capture of Jerusalem by Arab Muslims in the seventh century.

5 ● RELIGION

Most Palestinians—75 percent—are Muslim (followers of Islam), the majority belonging to the Sunni sect. In the seventh century AD, the prophet Muhammad received his revelations from Allah, the one true God (according to Islam). Within just a few years of Muhammad's death in AD 632, Islam had spread through the entire Middle East, gaining converts at a rapid rate.

Mecca is the spiritual center of Islam. All prayers are said facing Mecca. Each Muslim is expected, and greatly desires, to make a pilgrimage *(hajj)* to Mecca at least once in his or her lifetime.

About 17 percent of Palestinians are Christian, and some 8 percent are Druze. Both Christians and Muslims have holy sites in Palestine that are visited by pilgrims from around the world.

6 ● MAJOR HOLIDAYS

Islam uses a lunar calendar, so Muslim holidays occur on a different date of the Gregorian (Western) calendar each year. The major Muslim holidays are *'Eid al-Fitr*, the end of *Ramadan* (a three-day festival); *'Eid al-Adha,* a feast at the end of the *hajj* (the pilgrimage month to Mecca); the *First of Muharram,* the Muslim New Year; and the prophet Muhammad's birthday.

The two major holidays, *'Eid al-Fitr* and *'Eid al-Adha*, are celebrated by visiting close friends and relatives throughout the day. At least one family member, usually the mother, remains home to greet guests, and the rest of the family travels from home to home, delivering holiday greetings. Children are usually showered with money from most of the adults they encounter. At every home, pastries called *Ka`k al-Id* are served. These are made of flour and butter and are stuffed with either walnuts, cinnamon, and sugar, or with dates. After baking, they are sprinkled with powdered sugar. During the three-day 'Eid celebration, everyone eats lots of ka`k.

The Christian holiday of Easter is also moveable, being calculated on a lunar basis.

It always occurs sometime during March or early April. Other Christian holidays are: the Day of the Ascension (May 15); the Feast of the Assumption (August 15); and Christmas and Boxing Day (December 25 and 26). New Year's Day (January 1) is a secular (nonreligious) holiday, not a Christian holiday, and many Muslims also celebrate this day.

In 1977, an International Day of Solidarity with the Palestinian People (November 29) was declared as a political observance. Some politically significant events are observed each year by a general strike and demonstrations. Two examples are November 2, in protest over the 1917 Balfour Declaration (in which the British government promoted the establishment of a Jewish homeland in Palestine); and May 15, in protest over the declaration of the state of Israel.

7 ● RITES OF PASSAGE

Male children are circumcised and the family holds a great feast to celebrate the occasion. Marriage is another important rite of passage. A simple wedding is followed by a huge feast and celebration attended by family and friends who bring gifts. Childbirth is considered an important function of marriage. The Islamic religion favors having children, and, in addition, Palestinians feel that reproduction is an important nationalist (patriotic) duty.

8 ● RELATIONSHIPS

When two Palestinians greet one another they usually shake hands. It is also common for two women to kiss one another on the cheeks in greeting.

© Corel Corporation

A Palestinian shopper in Jerusalem's Muslim Quarter.

Palestinians are known for their hospitality. Neighbors have very friendly relations and look out for one another's interests. Because Palestinians tend to stay in one house or apartment for their entire lives, neighbors establish lifelong relationships.

Palestinian society is very conservative by Western standards. Dating, as it is understood in the West, is not tolerated. If a man and woman are interested in one another, it is customary for the man to first declare his intentions to the woman's family. Dating to socialize or get to know one another is not allowed; the intent must be marriage. However, it is becoming more common for a couple to court before approaching the woman's family.

9 ● LIVING CONDITIONS

Palestinians live in a variety of conditions—from refugee camps to comfortable, middle-class (or even wealthy) homes in modern towns and cities. Traditional villages have one-story houses made of white stone, with a kitchen, a room for bathing, a *liwan* (sitting room) for receiving guests, and a few small rooms for sleeping. Houses are often surrounded by small gardens separated from the street by a high wall (called a *sur*) with a gate. Wealthier families have indoor plumbing and electricity. Other families get their water from local wells and cook on small charcoal stoves.

Refugee camps set up by the UN Relief Workers Agency provide small, cement-block huts with corrugated metal roofs and doors. Some do not have running water or electricity.

10 ● FAMILY LIFE

The family is the central unit of Palestinian society. Traditional village life used to be regulated by the *hamula*—a male-dominated extended family system, or clan-based operation. The hamula is disappearing as ancestral clan-controlled lands are taken away or lost. Nevertheless, families continue to be very important.

Arranged marriages are still the norm in some places. Marriage by individual choice is becoming common in other areas, however. This is the case especially as more males and females meet in universities, which are all coeducational. Child-marriage and polygamy (multiple spouses) still occur, although not in great numbers.

Palestinians have one of the highest birth rates in the world. Children are taught to use good manners and to respect their elders. Women are expected to fulfill the traditional role of homemaker. They are beginning to break out of these roles, however. Under Israeli occupation, many men were arrested by the military government for political activities hostile to the state of Israel. Women were forced to fill in for men held in prison. Women thus assumed jobs and became heads of households. Having attained prominent social and professional roles, many women now insist on equality of the sexes.

11 ● CLOTHING

Palestinians of the older generation still wear traditional clothing. Men wear a long loose robe called a *jallabiyeh* and the common Arab headscarf, or *kaffiyeh*, held in place with a twisted band called an *ogaal*. Women wear a long black peasant dress (known as a *thob*) with an embroidered bodice, and a shawl over the head and shoulders.

Most younger Palestinians wear Western-style clothing, with traditional headscarves covering the hair for young women. Religiosity has increased during the years of the Intifada (or "uprising"), beginning in 1987. This has been reflected in an increase in religious attire, known as *shari`a* clothing or *jilbab,* for young women. This is a long jacketlike dress that covers the entire body. A scarf is worn on the head to cover the hair.

12 ● FOOD

Palestinians eat typical Middle Eastern food, such as *falafel* (deep-fried chickpea balls or patties), *hummus* (ground chickpeas with garlic, lemon juice), *tahini* (a sesame paste), lamb, chicken, rice, nuts, and eggplant. A favorite Palestinian candy is *halvah,* a sweet nougat made of sesame seeds and honey. For eating meals, some rural Palestinians sit on mats or cushions around a cloth laid on the floor and scoop up their food with pieces of pita bread, called *khubz*. They drink lots of strong black Turkish coffee. A recipe for khubz follows.

Recipe

Khubz
(Pita Bread)

Ingredients

2 teaspoons dry yeast
2½ cups warm water
5 to 6 cups whole wheat flour
or 3 cups whole wheat and 2 to 3 cups
    white flour
or 5 to 6 cups white flour
1 tablespoon salt

Directions

Dissolve yeast in half a cup of warm water. Cover and let sit until yeast ferments, about 10 minutes. Stir 3 cups of flour, salt, dissolved yeast, and remaining 2 cups of water in a large bread bowl or mixing bowl. Add remaining 2 to 3 cups of flour in small portions, kneading well with the hands after each addition. Keep adding flour until the dough holds together well and stops sticking to your hands. Knead very well on a lightly floured surface for 8 to 10 minutes. The dough should be smooth and elastic. Return the dough to the mixing bowl and cover with plastic wrap. Wrap the entire bowl, including the bottom, in a blanket or heavy towel, and al-low dough to rise until doubled in size, about 2 to 3 hours.

On a lightly floured surface, cut the dough into 8 balls. Cover the balls and let rest for 30 minutes. Preheat the oven to 400ºF. While the oven is heating, use a rolling pin to flatten each ball of dough into a circle about 1 inch (2.5 centimeters) thick and 8 to 9 inches (20 to 25 centimeters) in diameter.

Beginning with the first loaf you rolled, set each loaf directly on the oven rack. You can bake two loaves at a time, one on each rack. When the loaves begin to brown, turn them so that they brown evenly on both sides (about 3 minutes per side). (If you find it difficult to drop the dough directly onto the oven shelf, use a pizza pan or a pizza stone to put the loaf on.)

As each loaf comes out of the oven, wrap it in a clean cloth or towel to keep it soft until the baking process is complete. After the loaves have cooled, store in plastic bags.

Other Palestinian favorites are zucchini and grape leaves, both stuffed with a rice-and-meat mixture. Palestinians also enjoy olive oil and preserved olives, which are harvested in the summer and are eaten year-round. Almonds, plums, apples, cherries, and lemons are enjoyed in many households fresh off the trees in family gardens. Pork is prohibited in the Muslim religion, as is alcohol. Many Palestinians are Christian, however, so alcoholic beverages are served in some restaurants and sold in some stores, generally in urban centers.

13 ● EDUCATION

Education is highly valued, and families compare the grades of their children. The highest achievers are noted in newspapers. Palestinian children attend schools similar to those in the West. Children begin school in kindergarten and attend elementary, preparatory, and high school. The United Nations Relief and Works Agency (UNRWA) runs schools for refugee children. The majority of Palestinian children attend free public schools. All girls, whether in UNRWA, public, or private schools, wear uniforms. Boys dress as they wish within limits reflecting the social norms. Palestinians have the highest percentage of university graduates in the Arab world.

The average literacy (ability to read and write) rate for Palestinians is 70 percent.

14 ● CULTURAL HERITAGE

Traditional Palestinian dancing is separated by sex. Men dance in a semicircle with their arms around each other or holding hands as they perform the *dabka*. Dancers circle the dance floor following the instructions of a designated leader. Women also perform the *dabka*, and in professional performances men and women do dance the *dabka* together.

Contemporary Palestinian writers include historian and essayist Edward Said, a Palestinian-American. A famous Palestinian poet and short-story writer is Ghassan Kanafani. His poetry and stories, like much Palestinian literature, feature themes of protest against the Israeli occupation and memories of times predating the occupation. Other famous Palestinians include the poet Mahmoud Darwish; Sabri Jiryis, a radio personality and writer; and the painter Jammana al-Husseni.

15 ● EMPLOYMENT

It is difficult for Palestinians in the Occupied Territories to find work. Unemployment is a serious problem among the many refugees. When they do find jobs, they are often paid low wages. Many Palestinians from Gaza, and some from the West Bank, cross over into Israel for employment. In Israel, they hold low-wage jobs as restaurant waiters, street cleaners, construction workers, and dishwashers. Since the signing of the DOP (September 1993), the borders between Israel and the Palestinians have often been closed. This causes extreme hardship for the Palestinians who once relied on Israel for jobs.

Under Israeli Prime Minister Yitzhak Rabin, who was assassinated in 1995, discussions were underway to develop an industrial complex along the borders to solve the unemployment problem. Under the new government led by Benjamin Netanyahu (1996), it is not yet clear if this goal will be pursued.

16 ● SPORTS

Palestinians in the Occupied Territories have little time or space for organized sports activities. However, soccer is popular and is played in schools and during free time in the many fields of the West Bank. There has been little attention given to organized, professional sporting events.

17 ● RECREATION

Informal, streetside games of soccer are popular among Palestinians. They also enjoy listening to poetry and music, and playing the very popular Middle Eastern version of backgammon. Men smoke the

© Corel Corporation

The Dome of the Rock, a mosque in Old Jerusalem. This mosque shelters the rock believed by Muslims to be the place where the Prophet Muhammad ascended for a visit to heaven.

narghila, or water-pipe (like a *hookah*) at corner cafés and coffeehouses. Only men go to coffeehouses, where they socialize, make business deals, and play cards and backgammon.

Children play hopscotch, jump rope, and play marbles on the sidewalks.

Palestinians watch television programs broadcast from Egypt, Israel, Jordan, and sometimes Syria. One of the favorite television characters is Ghawar al-Tosheh, a Syrian comedic character who often criticizes government policies in his storylines. On Fridays, the noon prayer is broadcast on television for Muslims.

18 ● CRAFTS AND HOBBIES

Some Palestinians are skilled in the art of calligraphy (decorative lettering). They sketch verses from the Koran (the sacred text of Islam) in beautiful designs. Other artists draw pictures of political protest, mostly against the occupation. One popular pastime is to memorize and recite verses of the Koran. Children begin this practice at an early age, and it continues through adulthood. Women often sit on their front porches knitting for their families, or cross-stitching or embroidering the bodices for their traditional dresses. They also cross-stitch items for craft shows, such as wall decorations or Koranic verses. Other crafts include making jewelry boxes, crosses, scenes of the Last Supper, camels, mosques, and other items made of olive wood or ivory.

19 ● SOCIAL PROBLEMS

The main social problem for Palestinians is the decades-long war with Israel over rights to the Palestinian homeland. Palestinians are people without a country. At best they live as displaced persons, and at worst as refugees in crowded camps. Younger generations of Palestinians have never known a time when their people were at peace. They grow up with a consciousness shaped by conflict and violence. The PLO (Palestinian Liberation Organization) and the Israeli government signed the Declaration of Principles in 1993, and limited Palestinian self-rule began in 1994. However, the agreement is opposed by extremists on both sides, and

the peace that exists is very shaky. The Palestinian fight for an independent homeland, whose tempo increased with the Intifada begun in December 1987, continues. The casualties are enormous, and the problems—physical, social, psychological, and spiritual—caused by the continual unrest are too numerous to count.

20 ● BIBLIOGRAPHY

Ganeri, Anita. *Why We Left: I Remember Palestine.* Austin, Tex.: Raintree Steck-Vaughn, 1995.

Melrod, George, ed. *Insight Guides: Israel.* Boston: Houghton Mifflin, 1994.

Moss, Joyce, and George Wilson. *Peoples of the World: The Middle East and North Africa,* 1st ed. Detroit: Gale Research, 1992.

Stannard, Dorothy, ed. *Insight Guides: Jordan.* Boston: Houghton Mifflin, 1994.

WEBSITES

ArabNet. Palestine. [Online] Available http://www.arab.net/palestine/palestine_contents.html, 1998.

Embassy of Israel, Washington, D.C. [Online] Available http://www.israelemb.org/, 1998.

World Travel Guide. [Online] Available http://www.wtgonline.com/country/il/gen.html, 1998.

Italy

The people of Italy are called Italians. For centuries, the majority of Italy's people came from similar ethnic backgrounds. Minority groups include the German-speaking people living in the north and the Slavs of the Trieste area.

Italians

LOCATION: Italy

POPULATION: 57 million

LANGUAGE: Italian; French; Slovene; German; Fruilian

RELIGION: Roman Catholicsim; small amounts of Protestantism, Judaism, and Greek Orthodoxy

1 ● INTRODUCTION

The twenty regions that make up Italy were united into a single country in 1870. The country and its people have been a profound political and cultural influence on the world since the days of ancient Rome. Each year millions of tourists visit Italy to see the country's cultural and historical landmarks such as the Colosseum in Rome and the Greek ruins in Sicily. Italy is a modern industrial nation and a leading member of the European Community (EC). In the 1950s economic growth was so fast that its economy was called the "Italian miracle."

2 ● LOCATION

Located in southern Europe, Italy is divided into three major regions: the north Italian Plain and the Italian Alps (continental); the peninsula south of the plain (peninsular); and Sardinia, Sicily, and numerous smaller islands (insular). Italy's only major river, the Po, flows from west to east before it empties into the Adriatic sea. The mainland is a boot-shaped peninsula, with the Mediterranean Sea to the southwest, and the Adriatic to the east and northeast.

There is a sharp division in temperament, traditions, and economic conditions between Italians living in northern and central regions, and those living in the south. The city of Rome marks the boundaries between the two parts of the mainland. The wealthier northern region is considered to be more "European." The poorer, historically neglected south is considered to be more "Mediterranean." There has even been a movement among northerners to create an independent country.

3 ●LANGUAGE

Italian is the official language and is spoken by the vast majority of the population. Other languages spoken in Italy include French, Slovene, German, and Fruilian, which is related to the Romansch language spoken in Switzerland.

NUMBERS

English	Italian
one	uno
two	due
three	tre
four	quattro
five	cinque
six	sei
seven	sette
eight	otto
nine	nove
ten	dieci

DAYS OF THE WEEK

English	Italian
Sunday	Domenica
Monday	Lunedi
Tuesday	Martedi
Wednesday	Mercoledi
Thursday	Giovedi
Friday	Venerdi
Saturday	Sabato

4 ●FOLKLORE

According to myth, the city of Rome was founded by twin brothers, Romulus and Remus, in 753 BC. Their father was Mars, the god of war. They were set adrift in the Tiber River. Instead of drowning as was planned, they floated to the future site of the city of Rome. They were raised by a wolf and later found by a herdsman. After the founding of Rome, Romulus killed Remus and took over his power. After his death, Remus was worshiped as the god Quirinus.

5 ●RELIGION

Italy is an overwhelmingly Catholic country: 99 percent of Italians describe themselves as Roman Catholics. Only about one-third of Italian Catholics, however, attend Mass regularly. Catholicism plays an important role in everyday life, even for those who do not attend church regularly.

Before a 1984 law ended compulsory religious education, priests were the primary teachers in the schools. The Catholic Church's position on abortion and divorce has had a major impact on marriage and family life.

Italy is also the home of the Vatican, a tiny, independent country within Rome. For centuries, the Vatican has been the headquarters of the Catholic Church and is where the Pope lives. For centuries, almost every Pope has been Italian. Becoming Pope in 1978, the Polish-born John Paul II is a notable exception.

There are about 150,000 Protestants living in Italy. Most of them belong to a sect known as Waldensians. Italy is also home to about 35,000 Jews and a small number of members of the Greek Orthodox church.

6 ● MAJOR HOLIDAYS

In additon to the standard holidays of the Christian calendar, legal holidays in Italy are New Year's Day, Liberation Day on April twenty-fifth, and Labor Day on May first. Cities and towns also celebrate the feast days of their individual patron saints. Colorful traditions mark many celebrations of religious holidays.

In Florence, Easter (in March or April) is the occasion for the reenactment of a medieval tradition called *scoppio del carro,* which means "explosion of the cart." It is the eruption of a cartful of fireworks set off by a mechanical dove released from the altar during Mass. On Ascension Day children take part in a "cricket hunt" in the city's largest park.

The annual summer Palio horse race, held in Siena, is a colorful, bareback horse race with racers competing for the banner, the *palio.*

7 ● RITES OF PASSAGE

Italy is a modern, industrialized, Roman Catholic country. Many rites of passage that young people experience are religious sacraments such as baptism, first communion,

and confirmation. In many families, a student's progress through the education system is celebrated with parties.

8 ● RELATIONSHIPS

Italians are characteristically friendly, outgoing, and generous. They love to talk and are easily immersed in conversation. Like people of other Mediterranean nations, they often use body language to illustrate or emphasize what they are saying.

The standard form of greeting among peers is the handshake. Italian people are very affectionate in public. It is common for two grown men to greet by kissing each other on both cheeks, and for either men or women to walk down the street arm in arm. These very informal manners, however, are blended with a deep and traditional respect for the elderly. Young people often stand up when an older relative or friend enters the room.

9 ● LIVING CONDITIONS

Throughout the country there are differences in living conditions between large cities and the smaller towns that dot the Italian landscape. In the cities, people live in apartments and condominiums. In most towns, the average family lives in two-story homes. The standard of living is comparable to industrialized countries such as France, England, and the United States.

Thousands of middle-class Italians who live in large cities also own summer homes in the country, in coastal areas, or in the mountains. They spend weekends there to get away from the hustle and bustle of city life. They also use these retreats during the traditional two weeks of vacation in August called *ferragosto* (August holy days).

10 ● FAMILY LIFE

The family is the backbone of Italian society. Choice of marriage partner, type of employment, business relationships, and often political affiliation are all influenced by family ties. Officially, the father is the authority figure in the family, although mothers have great power. This is especially true in the raising of sons. Italian men are said to have an unusually strong lifetime attachment to their mothers.

Many aspects of Italian family life have been influenced by the Catholic Church, by its own doctrine and the influence it has had on government policy. Until 1971, the sale and purchase of birth control devices were illegal. Abortion was legalized in 1978. Although divorce became legal in 1970, Italy's divorce rate of one in every fifteen new marriages is still much lower than that of other industrialized nations such as France, England, and the United States. Southern Italy has an even lower rate of divorce.

11 ● CLOTHING

Italian fashions are known all over the world. Italy earns more money from selling its clothing, fabrics, and shoes than from any other export. These industries are Italy's largest employers. Designs by such names as Versace, Armani, and Nino Cerruti are among the fashion industry's most expensive and elite. Benetton clothing is marketed throughout the world. Leather goods, from handbags to gloves to jackets, are excellent buys. "Made in Italy" has become synonymous with style, quality, and craftsmanship.

Maintaining a good appearance is very important to Italians. Even their casual clothing is of high quality. Jeans are popular, but not if they are torn. Dress wear includes fashionable silk ties and well-cut suits for men, and elegant dresses and skirts and blouses for women.

12 ● FOOD

Italy's national food is pasta. It is served in many varieties: ravioli in the north of the country, lasagne and tortellini in Bologna, cannelloni in Sicily, spaghetti with tomato or clam sauce in Naples. Northern Italians eat much less pasta. They prefer rice and polenta, a mush made with corn, barley, or chestnut flour. Pasta has been manufactured in the south since the nineteenth century and pasta dishes are often prepared with such vegetables as zucchini and eggplants.

Favorite Italian dishes include *fegato alla veneziana* (liver and onions); *cotoletta alla milanese* (veal cutlets); *bagna cauda* (a garlic-anchovy sauce for dipping vegetables); and *pesto* (a basil-and-garlic sauce now popular in the United States). One regional dish that has become particularly well known is *pizza*, which originated in Naples.

Espresso, a very strong coffee drink, is popular throughout Italy. It can be ordered as *lungo* (diluted), *macchiato* (with milk), or *freddo* (iced). Italy is also the world's largest wine producer, and wine is served with most meals. Tap water is safe in most areas, although most people order bottled *acqua minerale* (mineral water) in restau-

Cory Langley

A mother and her child feed the pigeons in a local square.

rants. A *ristorante* (restaurant) usually posts its menu in the window so one can see what is available before going inside.

13 ● EDUCATION

In 1990 Italy had a literacy rate of about 97 percent. Schools in some rural areas and in the south, however, lag behind those in the rest of the country. Elementary education in Italy is regarded as the most progressive and innovative in the world.

Education is free and required between the ages of six and fourteen. Secondary education is offered in the sciences or humanities, as well as in technical and teacher training schools. A small percentage of students follow their secondary education with study at one of Italy's forty-one state or fifteen private universities and colleges. The oldest is the University of Bologna, founded approximately in A.D. 1060. It is also Europe's first university.

14 ● CULTURAL HERITAGE

Italy's importance in the history of world culture cannot be overstated. Its contributions to culture are as important as any civilization's, including Persian, Chinese and Greek.

In the visual arts, Italy's legacy dates back to the sculpture and architecture of ancient Rome, the city in which Nero fiddled and Mark Antony praised Caesar. The Renaissance, beginning in fifteenth-century Florence, was a movement in art, literature, and philosophy that combined new realism with classical antiquity, especially seen in paintings. It saw the creation of such works as *The Last Supper* and the *Mona Lisa* by Leonardo da Vinci, and Michelangelo's

Cory Langley

Michelangelo's statue of the Biblical figure David is one his most famous pieces of art.

painting of the ceiling of the Sistine Chapel. Other great Italian Renaissance artists included Donatello, Boticelli, Raphael, and Titian.

In music, Italy is known for its glorious operatic tradition, from the early works of Monteverdi, the "father of opera," to the great nineteenth-century achievements of Rossini and Verdi. Verdi is considered the greatest composer of opera. Italy is also known for the music of the composer Vivaldi.

Italy's great masterpieces of literature include the *Aeniad* by the Roman writer Virgil (70 B.C. to A.D. 19). The fourteenth-century works of Dante, Boccaccio, and Petrarch, including Dante's *Divine Comedy,* are considered some of the greatest works in literature. In the twentieth century, six Italians have won the Nobel Prize for literature. The modern Italian writer who is probably best known internationally is Umberto Eco, author of *The Name of the Rose.*

15 ● EMPLOYMENT

In the last half of the twentieth century, employment in Italy's service sector increased rapidly. By 1992, services employed 60 percent of the nation's work force. About 30 percent worked in industry and less than 10 percent in agriculture. Italian industry expanded quickly after World War II (1939–45), especially between the mid-1950s and mid-1960s. The Piedmont region in the north is one of Europe's major auto manufacturing centers.

Southern Italy is less developed economically and has a higher rate of unemployment. Many Sicilians work abroad, and their earnings are important to the island's economy. Labor strikes are common among workers in many areas of the service sector, including the post office, railroads, hospitals, schools, banks, and the media.

16 ● SPORTS

Soccer (called *calcio*) is by far Italy's most popular sport. Nearly all large and medium-size cities have a team in one of the three professional divisions. *Totocalcio* is a very popular betting pool connected with soccer. In addition to its popularity as a spectator sport, soccer is played by most Italians.

Games at the village, city, and district levels are accompanied by intense competition.

Italians also enjoy bicycle and motorcycle racing, basketball, boxing, tennis, and downhill skiing. A type of bowling played on clay court called *bocce* is popular in small towns.

17 ● RECREATION

Like many Europeans, Italians are passionate soccer fans. The fanaticism surrounding this sport has caused major riots in which people have died. Some fans have had heart attacks while watching games at home. Mammoth traffic jams are common on Sunday afternoons, which is when the games are played.

Many Italians like to spend leisure time visiting with friends at cafes. Cafes are also popular spots for solitary pursuits like reading or writing letters. Even daily meals are a form of recreation in Italy: Italians normally spend up to two hours eating their midday meal. Meals are times for families to get together for food, wine, and conversation.

Beaches are popular recreation areas, especially with young people, who also enjoy "hanging out" at the local *piazza*, or town square.

18 ● CRAFTS AND HOBBIES

Italy's handcrafted products include fine laces, linens, glass, pottery, carved marble, leather, and gold and silver work. The sale of these products is important to the Italian economy, and the government subsidizes the artisans who create them.

19 ● SOCIAL PROBLEMS

A problem that has long troubled Italy is organized crime, especially in the southern part of the country. Mafia violence may involve rivalry among competing gangs, kidnapping of wealthy persons or their relatives, and drug-related activities. Italian mob trafficking in drugs has resulted in a drug problem worse than that in most other European countries.

20 ● BIBLIOGRAPHY

Barzini, Luigi. *The Italians: A Full-Length Portrait Featuring Their Manners and Morals.* New York: Atheneum, 1965.

Bell, Brian, ed. *Italy.* Insight Guides. Boston: Houghton Mifflin, 1994.

Gall, Timothy, and Susan Gall, eds. *Junior World-mark Encyclopedia of the Nations.* Detroit: UXL, 1996.

Hofmann, Paul. *That Fine Italian Hand.* New York: Henry Holt, 1990.

Moss, Joyce, and George Wilson. *Peoples of the World: Western Europeans.* Detroit: Gale Research, 1993.

Sproule, Anna. Italy: The Land andIts People. Morristown, N.J.: Silver Burdett Press, 1987.

Travis, David. *The Land and People of Italy.* New York: HarperCollins, 1992.

Winwar, Frances. The Land and People of Italy. Philadelphia: Lippincott, 1972.

WEBSITES

Embassy of Italy, Washington, D.C. [Online] Available http://www.italyemb.nw.dc.us/italy/, 1998.

World Travel Guide. Italy. [Online] Available http://www.wtgonline.com/country/it/gen. html, 1998.

Jamaica

The people of Jamaica are called Jamaicans. About 95 percent of the population is of partial or total African descent. Over 75 percent are black, 15 percent are mulatto (mixed black and white), and 4 percent are of mixed black and Asian Indian or Chinese. Other ethnic groups include Asian Indian (2 percent), Chinese (1 percent), and Europeans (2 percent). Nearly the whole population is native-born Jamaican.

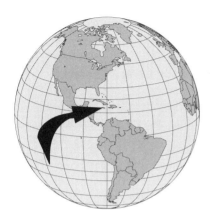

Jamaicans

PRONUNCIATION: juh-MAY-cuns
LOCATION: Jamaica
POPULATION: 2.5 million
LANGUAGE: English; Patois (Creole dialect with West African, Spanish, and French elements)
RELIGION: Christianity (Anglicanism, Protestantism, and Roman Catholicism); Rastafarianism

1 ● INTRODUCTION

The official motto of Jamaica is, "Out of Many People, One People." The motto expresses the fact that Jamaicans include people of African, European, Arabic (Lebanese descendants known as "Syrians"), Chinese, and East Indian descent. If Jamaicans had a second motto, it would be "No problem, Mon." Phrases like this and "No pressure, no problem" reflect the carefree, happy-go-lucky spirit of the Jamaican people.

When Christopher Columbus arrived in Jamaica in 1494 it was inhabited by peaceful Arawak Indians. Under Spanish occupation in the 1500s, the Arawak Indian race died out and African slaves were brought in to work the sugarcane fields. The island remained under Spanish rule until 1655, when it was captured by the British. During the struggle between the Spanish and the British, a number of runaway slaves, known as Maroons, took refuge in the area of the island known as the Cockpit Country. It is still the home of some of their decendants.

Abolition of slavery came in 1833. The decline of the plantations followed, and the former slaves became peasant farmers. After a short period of military rule, Jamaica was organized as a colony with a British-style constitution. On August 6, 1962, Jamaica became an independent member of the Commonwealth (a group of independent countries that were once part of the British Empire).

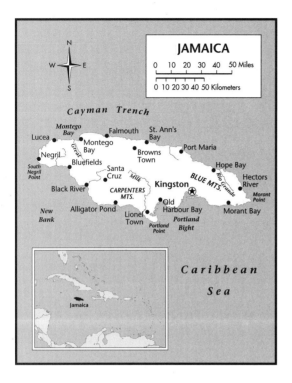

JAMAICA

0 10 20 30 40 50 Miles

0 10 20 30 40 50 Kilometers

Cayman Trench

Lucea
Montego Bay
Montego Bay
Negril
South Negril Point
Bluefields
Falmouth
St. Ann's Bay
Browns Town
Port Maria
Santa Cruz
Black River
CARPENTERS MTS.
Kingston
Hope Bay
BLUE MTS.
Rio Grande
Hectors River
Morant Point
New Bank
Alligator Pond
Lionel Town
Old Harbour Bay
Portland Point
Portland Bight
Morant Bay

Caribbean Sea

Jamaica

Following a brief period in the middle of the twentieth century when Jamaica experimented with socialism, the country is now a relatively stable parliamentary democracy. Percival J. Patterson was elected Prime Minister in 1993 in a landslide victory.

2 ●LOCATION

Jamaica's population of more than 2.5 million is equally divided between urban and rural dwellers. Jamaicans are mostly descendants of Africans. There are also East Indians, Chinese, Europeans, and Arabs.

Located some 90 miles south of Cuba and more than 450 miles west of Hispaniola, Jamaica is the third-largest island in the Caribbean Sea. Since 1870 the capital has been Kingston, now with a population of more than 645,000. It has one of the largest

and best natural harbors in the world. The climate is tropical and tourists flock to Jamaica for its beautiful beaches. Jamaica has been called the Island of Springs, and the luxuriance of the vegetation is striking. The island is susceptible to hurricanes. It suffered serious damage during Hurricane Gilbert in 1988 when nearly 25 percent of the population was left homeless and property damage was more than $300 million.

Another popular tourist attraction are the island's more than 800 caves, many of which were homes for early inhabitants.

3 ●LANGUAGE

Jamaicans speak English, but with a distinct flavor. Elements of Elizabethan English can be heard on the island. A jug, for example, is referred to as a "goblet." Also, the "th" sound is substituted with a "d," so that the word "that" becomes "dat," for example.

Although the official language is English, most Jamaicans who live in the rural areas speak a Creole dialect. Patois, as it is called, is influenced mostly by West African languages. It also contains elements of Spanish and French. Perhaps the most famous of the patois words is *I-rie* (fabulous), which comes from the language of a religious sect called the Rastafarians. Other words, such as *putta-putta* (mud) come from Africa.

4 ●FOLKLORE

Central to Jamaican folklore are the tales of Anansi (or Anancy) the Spider. The tales were brought to the island by the first slaves. They tell of the mythical Anansi, a spider that sometimes takes the form of a man and uses his wits to outsmart his foes.

United Nations

Young Jamaican girl holding baby girl. While women are often held in high regard, men are seen as the heads of households.

Anasi is still the subject of many bedtime stories.

5 ● RELIGION

Religion is an important part of life for Jamaicans. More than 80 percent are Christian. Most practice Anglicanism, Protestantism, and Roman Catholicism. The Jewish, Muslim, Hindu, and Bahai religions are also practiced, as is Rastafarianism.

Nearly one hundred thousand Jamaicans are Rastafarians. Rastafarians are members of a Jamaican messianic (based on the belief in a savior) movement that began in the 1930s. According to Rastafarian belief, the only true God is the late Ethiopian emperor Haile Selassie (originally known as Ras Tafari) and Ethiopia is the true holy land. Rastafarians place great emphasis on spirituality and meditation and the individual. The singular being "I" and the plural being "I and I." They also use *ganja* (marijuana) in their religious rites. Rastafarians are known for wearing their hair in dreadlocks, wearing beards as a sign of a pact with God, and carrying Bibles. Rastafarianism is known outside of Jamaica mainly because its famous believer, the late reggae musician Bob Marley, was an international star.

6 ● MAJOR HOLIDAYS

Jamaicans celebrate their independence on August sixth. For several weeks beforehand, they stage a huge celebration called "Festival!" During this period artists of all types perform, many as part of competitions. School children also are involved in the festivities. This helps foster their sense of national pride and tradition.

Jonkanoo (John Canoe) is a dancing procession held around Christmastime. The origins of this celebration are not clear, but many believe its origins to be in East Africa. Celebrants wearing extravagant costumes dance to the music of drums and cane flutes.

Most other holidays and celebrations are religious ones and include Ash Wednesday (in February), Good Friday, Easter Monday (in March or April), and Christmas (December 25).

7 ● RITES OF PASSAGE

Christian sacraments and traditions define the rites of passage for most Jamaicans and are celebrated much the same way as they are in the United States.

8 ● RELATIONSHIPS

Jamaicans tend to be casual, open, and friendly in their relationships. They have a great deal of national pride and are known for their sense of humor.

9 ● LIVING CONDITIONS

Living conditions vary greatly between rich and poor. Health care is generally considered good, and the average life expectancy is seventy-six years for women and seventy-two years for men. All Jamaicans are accustomed to dealing with interruptions of electricity, mail, water, and telephone services.

10 ● FAMILY LIFE

While women are often highly respected, men are seen as the heads of households. Great importance is placed on a man's virility and a woman's fertility. Men and women tend to marry or start living together at an early age. A couple that does not have children soon after marriage is considered unusual.

11 ● CLOTHING

Everyday wear for Jamaicans is cool and comfortable. Rastafarians have made the colors of the Ethiopian flag—red, green, and gold—popular in clothing. Churchgoers tend to dress very formally on Sundays.

12 ● FOOD

Jamaicans eat foods that are rich in spices. Pimento, or allspice, is native to Jamaica and an important export crop. Other commonly used spices are ginger, nutmeg, and pepper. Cassava (yuca) is a tuber and is widely popular on the island. *Bammy* is a toasted bread-like wafer made from cassava. *Ackee* is the national fruit of Jamaica. If not properly prepared, it can be poisonous. Ackee with saltfish is a popular Jamaican snack or breakfast dish.

"Jerking" is a method of spicing and slowly cooking meat to preserve the juices and produce a unique, spicy flavor. The meat is first marinated in a very spicy mixture and then cooked over an outdoor pit lined with pimento wood.

Many fruits like mangoes, pineapple, papayas, and bananas are eaten fresh or combined in desserts.

For dinner, Jamaicans will typically eat peas and rice accompanied by either chicken or pork. Included in this section is a simple but spicy recipe.

13 ● EDUCATION

About 98 percent of adult Jamaicans are literate (able to read and write). The law requires children to attend school from age seven to age fifteen. There is one university, the University of the West Indies, near Kingston. The Institute of Jamaica, also in Kingston, has a library and museum of Jamaican history, art, and natural history.

14 ● CULTURAL HERITAGE

Jamaica's musical heritage includes Mento, which is a form of music and dance with roots in Africa. Also popular is Ska, a soft-style rhythm-and-blues beat. Reggae, however, is most often associated with Jamaica. Bob Marley was its most famous performer and he spread the music worldwide.

Recipe

Curry Chicken

Ingredients

1 to 3 pounds chicken
2 Tablespoons curry powder
Juice from one lemon or 2 to 3 Tablespoons bottled lemon juice
3 to 4 Tablespoons cooking oil
Dash each of onion powder, thyme, garlic powder, pepper, salt to taste
Cooked white rice, with peas added if desired.

Directions

1. Cut chicken into small pieces, and let sit in lemon juice for at least one hour.
2. Remove chicken and season it with the spices and seasonings. Let rest for several minutes.
3. Heat cooking oil in a skillet. Add chicken and cook until done (about 10 minutes per side).

Serve over white rice (or rice and peas, if preferred).

In 1964, Marley formed his group, the Wailers. Their first hit was "Simmer Down." Three years later, Marley converted to the Rastafarian religion. Rastafarian themes dominated his work. His first international hit was "Stir It Up." In 1973 Bob Marley and the Wailers had their American debut album, *Catch a Fire.* Marley died of cancer in 1981 at the age of thirty-six. He was awarded the Jamaican Order of Merit. His work influenced countless reggae and pop artists all over the world.

Dance-hall music, also known as DJ music, is an offshoot of reggae and is very popular, as is So-Ca, a combination of soul and calypso.

Paintings and sculptures are abundant in Jamaica. One of the most famous painters is John Dunkley. Edna Manley is renowned for her sculptures. Also renowned for sculpting is Mallica "Kapo" Reynolds, whose work is on display at the National Gallery in Kingston. In literature, Jamaican-born poet, critic, and educator Louis Aston Marantz Simpson won the 1964 Pulitzer Prize for poetry for his *At the End of the Open Road.*

15 ● EMPLOYMENT

Approximately 25 percent of Jamaicans work in agriculture. Sugar, tropical fruits, coffee, cacao, and spices are grown for export. Another 25 percent of workers are in finance, real estate, and services. Manufacture and trade each account for a little more than 10 percent. The rest (roughly 30 percent) work in public administration and defense.

Jamaica has recently developed a profitable mining industry. It is among the world's leading producers of bauxite and alumina, which are exported to Canada, Norway, and the United States.

Some Jamaicans make a living as "higglers." These are people who buy inexpensive goods overseas and then sell them for a substantial profit on the sidewalks of Jamaica.

16 ● SPORTS

By far, the most popular sport in Jamaica is cricket. Vaguely resembling baseball, the game of cricket dates back to sixteenth century England. A match can go on for days.

George Headley was a legendary Jamaican cricket player of the 1930s. Children and adults alike play and watch the sport throughout the island.

Jamaicans have also excelled in track and field, boxing, and basketball. Jamaicans also enjoy all types of water sports.

17 ● RECREATION

While Jamaicans are knows for their casual, laid-back attitude, they are passionate about enjoying life. They are not ones to sit and watch television. There are only two television stations on the island. Entertainment and recreation involve listening to live music—usually reggae, getting together with friends, playing sports, or enjoying a day of food and fun at the beach.

18 ● CRAFTS AND HOBBIES

Along the tourist areas, Jamaican artisans display their crafts, which include *bankras* (baskets) and *yabbas* (clay bowls).

19 ● SOCIAL PROBLEMS

Jamaicans have had their share of racial tensions and class struggles that have disrupted an otherwise unified, peaceful existence. Considered sacred by some, *ganja* (marijuana) is illegal. The government's actions against its cultivation and use, however, are often seen as superficial.

20 ● BIBLIOGRAPHY

Bryan, Patrick E. *The Jamaican People, 1880–1902: Race, Class and Social Control.* London: Macmillan Caribbean, 1991.

Hurwitz, Samuel J. and Edith F. *Jamaica: A Historical Portrait.* New York: Praeger, 1971.

Jamaica in Pictures. Minneapolis, Minn.: Lerner Publications Co., 1987.

Jekyl, Walter. *Jamaica Song and Story.* New York: Dover, 1966.

Senior, Olive. *A–Z of Jamaican Heritage.* Kingston: Heineman Educational Books, 1983.

WEBSITES

Embassy of Jamaica, Washington, D.C. [Online] Available http://www.caribbean-online.com/jamaica/embassy/washdc/, 1998.

Interknowledge Corporation, Tourism. [Online] Available http://www.interknowledge.com/jamaica/, 1998.

World Travel Guide, Jamaica. [Online] Available http://www.wtgonline.com/country/jm/gen.html, 1998.

Glossary

aboriginal: The first known inhabitants of a country.

adobe: A brick made from sun-dried heavy clay mixed with straw, used in building houses.

Altaic language family: A family of languages spoken in portions of northern and eastern Europe, and nearly the whole of northern and central Asia, together with some other regions.

Amerindian: A contraction of the two words, American Indian. It describes native peoples of North, South, or Central America.

Anglican: Pertaining to or connected with the Church of England.

animism: The belief that natural objects and phenomena have souls or innate spiritual powers.

apartheid: The past governmental policy in the Republic of South Africa of separating the races in society.

arable land: Land that can be cultivated by plowing and used for growing crops.

archipelago: Any body of water abounding with islands, or the islands themselves collectively.

Austronesian language: A family of languages which includes practically all the languages of the Pacific Islands—Indonesian, Melanesian, Polynesian, and Micronesian sub-families.

average life expectancy: In any given society, the average age attained by persons at the time of death.

Baha'i: The follower of a religious sect founded by Mirza Husayn Ali in Iran in 1863.

Baltic states: The three formerly communist countries of Estonia, Latvia, and Lithuania that border on the Baltic Sea.

Bantu language group: A name applied to the languages spoken in central and south Africa.

Baptist: A member of a Protestant denomination that practices adult baptism by complete immersion in water.

barren land: Unproductive land, partly or entirely treeless.

barter: Trade practice where merchandise is exchanged directly for other merchandise or services without use of money.

Berber: a member of one of the Afroasiatic peoples of northern Africa.

Brahman: A member (by heredity) of the highest caste among the Hindus, usually assigned to the priesthood.

bride wealth (bride price): Fee, in money or goods, paid by a prospective groom (and his family) to the bride's family.

Buddhism: A religious system common in India and eastern Asia. Founded by Siddhartha Gautama (c.563–c.483 BC), Buddhism asserts that suffering is an inescapable part of life. Deliverance can only be achieved through the practice of charity, temperance, justice, honesty, and truth.

Byzantine Empire: An empire centered in the city of Byzantium, now Istanbul in present-day Turkey.

cassava: The name of several species of stout herbs, extensively cultivated for food.

caste system: Heriditary social classes into which the Hindus are rigidly separated according to the religious law of Brahmanism. Privileges and limitations of each caste are passed down from parents to children.

Caucasian: The white race of human beings, as determined by genealogy and physical features.

census: An official counting of the inhabitants of a state or country with details of sex and age, family, occupation, possessions, etc.

Christianity: The religion founded by Jesus Christ, based on the Bible as holy scripture.

Church of England: The national and established church in England.

civil rights: The privileges of all individuals to be treated as equals under the laws of their country; specifically, the rights given by certain amendments to the U.S. Constitution.

coastal plain: A fairly level area of land along the coast of a land mass.

coca: A shrub native to South America, the leaves of which produce organic compounds that are used in the production of cocaine.

colonial period: The period of time when a country forms colonies in and extends control over a foreign area.

colonist: Any member of a colony or one who helps settle a new colony.

colony: A group of people who settle in a new area far from their original country, but still under the jurisdiction of that country. Also refers to the newly settled area itself.

commonwealth: A free association of sovereign independent states that has no charter, treaty, or constitution. The association promotes cooperation, consultation, and mutual assistance among members.

communism: A form of government whose system requires common ownership of property for the use of all citizens. Prices on goods and services are usually set by the government, and all profits are shared equally by everyone. Also, communism refers directly to the official doctrine of the former Soviet Union.

compulsory education: The mandatory requirement for children to attend school until they have reached a certain age or grade level.

Confucianism: The system of ethics and politics taught by the Chinese philosopher Confucius.

constitution: The written laws and basic rights of citizens of a country or members of an organized group.

copra: The dried meat of the coconut.

cordillera: A continuous ridge, range, or chain of mountains.

coup d'ètat (coup): A sudden, violent overthrow of a government or its leader.

cuisine: A particular style of preparing food, especially when referring to the cooking of a particular country or ethnic group.

Cushitic language group: A group of languages that are spoken in Ethiopia and other areas of eastern Africa.

Cyrillic alphabet: An alphabet invented by Cyril and Methodius in the ninth century as an alphabet that was easier for the copyist to write. The Russian alphabet is a slight modification of it.

deity: A being with the attributes, nature, and essence of a god; a divinity.

desegregation: The act of removing restrictions on people of a particular race that keep them socially, economically, and, sometimes, physically, separate from other groups.

desertification: The process of becoming a desert as a result of climatic changes, land mismanagement, or both.

Dewali (Deepavali, Divali): The Hindu Festival of Lights, when Lakshmi, goddess of good fortune, is said to visit the homes of humans. The four- or five-day festival occurs in October or November.

dialect: One of a number of regional or related modes of speech regarded as descending from a common origin.

dowry: The sum of the property or money that a bride brings to her groom at their marriage.

Druze: A member of a Muslim sect based in Syria, living chiefly in the mountain regions of Lebanon.

dynasty: A family line of sovereigns who rule in succession, and the time during which they reign.

Eastern Orthodox: The outgrowth of the original Eastern Church of the Eastern Roman Empire, consisting of eastern Europe, western Asia, and Egypt.

Eid al-Adha: The Muslim holiday that celebrates the end of the special pilgrimage season (hajj) to the city of Mecca in Saudi Arabia.

Eid al-Fitr: The Muslim holiday that begins just after the end of the month of Ramadan and is celebrated with three or four days of feasting.

emigration: Moving from one country or region to another for the purpose of residence.

empire: A group of territories ruled by one sovereign or supreme ruler. Also, the period of time under that rule.

Episcopal: Belonging to or vested in bishops or prelates; characteristic of or pertaining to a bishop or bishops.

exports: Goods sold to foreign buyers.

Finno-Ugric language group: A subfamily of languages spoken in northeastern Europe, including Finnish, Hungarian, Estonian, and Lapp.

fjord: A deep indentation of the land forming a comparatively narrow arm of the sea with more or less steep slopes or cliffs on each side.

folk religion: A religion with origins and traditions among the common people of a nation or region that is relevant to their particular life-style.

Former Soviet Union: Refers to the republics that were once part of a large nation called the Union of Soviet Socialists Republics (USSR). The USSR was commonly called the Soviet Union. It included the 12 republics: Russia, Ukraine, Belarus, Moldova, Armenia, Azerbaijan, Uzbekistan, Turkmenistan, Tajikistan, Kazakhstan, Kyrgizstan, and Georgia. Sometimes the Baltic republics of Estonia, Latvia, and Lithuania are also included.

fundamentalist: A person who holds religious beliefs based on the complete acceptance of the words of holy scriptures as the truth.

Germanic language group: A large branch of the Indo-European family of languages including German itself, the Scandinavian languages, Dutch, Yiddish, Modern English, Modern Scottish, Afrikaans, and others. The group also includes extinct languages such as Gothic, Old High German, Old Saxon, Old English, Middle English, and the like.

Greek Orthodox: The official church of Greece, a self-governing branch of the Orthodox Eastern Church.

guerrilla: A member of a small radical military organization that uses unconventional tactics to take their enemies by surprise.

hajj: A religious journey made by Muslims to the holy city of Mecca in Saudi Arabia.

Holi: A Hindu festival of processions and merriment lasting three to ten days that marks the end of the lunar year in February or March.

Holocaust: The mass slaughter of European civilians, the vast majority of whom were Jews, by the Nazis during World War II.

Holy Roman Empire: A kingdom consisting of a loose union of German and Italian territories that existed from around the ninth century until 1806.

homeland: A region or area set aside to be a state for a people of a particular national, cultural, or racial origin.

homogeneous: Of the same kind or nature, often used in reference to a whole.

Horn of Africa: The Horn of Africa comprises Djibouti, Eritrea, Ethiopia, Somalia, and Sudan.

human rights issues: Any matters involving people's basic rights which are in question or thought to be abused.

immigration: The act or process of passing or entering into another country for the purpose of permanent residence.

imports: Goods purchased from foreign suppliers.

indigenous: Born or originating in a particular place or country; native to a particular region or area.

Indo-Aryan language group: The group that includes the languages of India; also called Indo-European language group.

Indo-European language family: The group that includes the languages of India and much of Europe and southwestern Asia.

Islam: The religious system of Muhammad, practiced by Muslims and based on a belief in Allah as the supreme being and Muhammed as his prophet. Islam also refers to those nations in which it is the primary religion. There are two major sects: Sunni and Shia (or Shiite). The main difference between the two sects is in their belief in who follows Muhammad, founder of Islam, as the religious leader.

Judaism: The religious system of the Jews, based on the Old Testament as revealed to Moses and characterized by a belief in one God and adherence to the laws of scripture and rabbinic traditions.

khan: A sovereign, or ruler, in central Asia.

khanate: A kingdom ruled by a khan, or man of rank.

literacy: The ability to read and write.

Maghreb states: Refers to Algeria, Morocco, and Tunisia; sometimes includes Libya and Mauritania.

maize: Another name (Spanish or British) for corn or the color of ripe corn.

manioc: The cassava plant or its product. Manioc is a very important food-staple in tropical America.

matrilineal (descent): Descending from, or tracing descent through, the maternal, or mother's, family line.

Mayan language family: The languages of the Central American Indians, further divided into two subgroups: the Maya and the Huastek.

mean temperature: The air temperature unit measured by the National Weather Service by adding the maximum and minimum daily temperatures together and diving the sum by 2.

Mecca: A city in Saudi Arabia; a destination of Muslims in the Islamic world.

mestizo: The offspring of a person of mixed blood; especially, a person of mixed Spanish and American Indian parentage.

millet: A cereal grass whose small grain is used for food in Europe and Asia.

monarchy: Government by a sovereign, such as a king or queen.

Mongol: One of an Asiatic race chiefly resident in Mongolia, a region north of China proper and south of Siberia.

Moors: One of the Arab tribes that conquered Spain in the eighth century.

Moslem *see* **Muslim.**

mosque: An Islam place of worship and the organization with which it is connected.

Muhammad (or Muhammed or Mahomet): An Arabian prophet (AD 570–632), known as the "Prophet of Allah" who founded the religion of Islam in 622, and wrote the Koran, (also spelled Quran) the scripture of Islam.

mulatto: One who is the offspring of parents one of whom is white and the other is black.

Muslim: A follower of Muhammad in the religion of Islam.

Muslim New Year: A Muslim holiday also called Nawruz. In some countries Muharram 1, which is the first month of the Islamic year, is observed as a holiday, in other places the new year is observed on Sha'ban, the eighth month of the year. This practice apparently stems from pagan Arab times. Shab-i-Bharat, a national holiday in Bangladesh on this day, is held by many to be the occasion when God ordains all actions in the coming year.

mystic: Person who believes he or she can gain spiritual knowledge through processes like meditation that are not easily explained by reasoning or rational thinking.

nationalism: National spirit or aspirations; desire for national unity, independence, or prosperity.

oasis: Fertile spot in the midst of a desert or wasteland.

official language: The language in which the business of a country and its government is conducted.

Ottoman Empire: A Turkish empire that existed from about 1603 until 1918, and included lands around the Mediterranean, Black, and Caspian seas.

patriarchal system: A social system in which the head of the family or tribe is the father or oldest male. Ancestry is determined and traced through the male members of the tribe.

patrilineal (descent): Descending from, or tracing descent through, the paternal, or father's, family line.

pilgrimage: religious journey, usually to a holy place.

plantain: Tropical plant with fruit that looks like bananas, but that must be cooked before eating.

Protestant: A member of one of the Christian bodies that descended from the Reformation of the sixteenth century.

pulses: Beans, peas, or lentils.

Ramadan: The ninth month of the Muslim calender. The entire month commemorates the period in which the Prophet Muhammad is said to have recieved divine revelation and is observed by a strict fast from sunrise to sundown.

Rastafarian: A member of a Jamaican cult begun in 1930 that is partly religious and partly political.

refugee: Person who, in times of persecution or political commotion, flees to a foreign country for safety.

revolution: A complete change in a government or society, such as in an overthrow of the government by the people.

Roman alphabet: Alphabet of the ancient Romans from which alphabets of most modern European languages, including English, are derived.

Roman Catholic Church: Christian church headed by the pope or Bishop of Rome.

Russian Orthodox: The arm of the Eastern Orthodox Church that was the official church of Russia under the tsars.

Sahelian zone: Eight countries make up this dry desert zone in Africa: Burkina Faso, Chad, Gambia, Mali, Mauritania, Niger, Senegal, and the Cape Verde Islands.

savanna: A treeless or near treeless grassland or plain.

segregation: The enforced separation of a racial or religious group from other groups, compelling them to live and go to school separately from the rest of society.

Seventh-day Adventist: One who believes in the second coming of Christ to establish a personal reign upon the earth.

shamanism: A religion in which shamans (priests or medicine men) are believed to influence spirits.

shantytown: An urban settlement of people in inadequate houses.

Shia Muslim *see* Islam.

Shiites *see* Islam.

Shintoism: The system of nature- and hero-worship that forms the native religion of Japan.

sierra: A chain of hills or mountains.

Sikh: A member of a community of India, founded around 1500 and based on the principles of monotheism (belief in one god) and human brotherhood.

Sino-Tibetan language family: The family of languages spoken in eastern Asia, including China, Thailand, Tibet, and Myanmar.

slash-and-burn agriculture: A hasty and sometimes temporary way of clearing land to make it available for agriculture by cutting down trees and burning them; also known as swidden agriculture.

slave trade: The transportation of black Africans beginning in the 1700s to other countries to be sold as slaves—people owned as property and compelled to work for their owners at no pay.

Slavic languages: A major subgroup of the Indo-European language family. It is further subdivided into West Slavic (including Polish, Czech, Slovak and Serbian), South Slavic (including Bulgarian, Serbo-Croatian, Slovene, and Old Church Slavonic), and East Slavic (including Russian Ukrainian and Byelorussian).

sorghum: Plant grown for its valuable uses, such as for grain, syrup, or fodder.

Southeast Asia: The region in Asia that consists of the Malay Archipelago, the Malay Peninsula, and Indochina.

Soviet Union *see* **Former Soviet Union.**

subcontinent: A large subdivision of a continent.

subsistence farming: Farming that provides only the minimum food goods necessary for the continuation of the farm family.

Sudanic language group: A related group of languages spoken in various areas of northern Africa, including Yoruba, Mandingo, and Tshi.

Sufi: A Muslim mystic who believes that God alone exists, there can be no real difference between good and evil, that the soul exists within the body as in a cage, so death should be the chief object of desire.

sultan: A king of a Muslim state.

Sunni Muslim *see* Islam.

Taoism: The doctrine of Lao-Tzu, an ancient Chinese philosopher (c.500 **BC**) as laid down by him in the *Tao-te-ching.*

Third World: A term used to describe less developed countries; as of the mid-1990s, it is being replaced by the United Nations designation Less Developed Countries, or LDC.

treaty: A negotiated agreement between two governments.

tribal system: A social community in which people are organized into groups or clans descended from common ancestors and sharing customs and languages.

tundra: A nearly level treeless area whose climate and vegetation are characteristically arctic due to its northern position; the subsoil is permanently frozen.

untouchables: In India, members of the lowest caste in the caste system, a hereditary social class system. They were considered unworthy to touch members of higher castes.

Union of the Soviet Socialist Republics *see* Former Soviet Union.

veldt: A grassland in South Africa.

Western nations: General term used to describe democratic, capitalist countries, including the United States, Canada, and western European countries.

Zoroastrianism: The system of religious doctrine taught by Zoroaster and his followers in the Avesta; the religion prevalent in Persia until its overthrow by the Muslims in the seventh century.

Index

All culture groups and countries included in this encyclopedia are included in this index. Selected regions, alternate groups names, and historical country names are cross-referenced. Country chapter titles are in boldface; volume numbers appear in brackets, with page number following.

Junior
Worldmark
Encyclopedia of
World Cultures

Junior Worldmark Encyclopedia of World Cultures

VOLUME 9

Tajikistan to
Zimbabwe

AN IMPRINT OF GALE

DETROIT · LONDON

JUNIOR WORLDMARK ENCYCLOPEDIA OF WORLD CULTURES

U•X•L Staff

Jane Hoehner, *U•X•L Senior Editor*
Carol DeKane Nagel, *U•X•L Managing Editor*
Thomas L. Romig, *U•X•L Publisher*
Mary Beth Trimper, *Production Director*
Evi Seoud, *Assistant Production Manager*
Shanna Heilveil, *Production Associate*
Cynthia Baldwin, *Product Design Manager*
Barbara J. Yarrow, *Graphic Services Supervisor*
Pamela A. E. Galbreath, *Senior Art Director*
Margaret Chamberlain, *Permissions Specialist (Pictures)*

Library of Congress Cataloging-in-Publication Data
Junior worldmark encyclopedia of world cultures / Timothy L. Gall and
Susan Bevan Gall, editors.
    p.   cm.
   Includes bibliographical references and index.
   Summary: Arranges countries around the world alphabetically,
subdivides these countries into 250 culture groups, and provides
information about the ethnology and human geography of each group.
   ISBN 0-7876-1756-X (set : alk. paper)
   1. Ethnology--Encyclopedias, Juvenile. 2. Human geography-
-Encyclopedias, Juvenile. [1. Ethnology--Encyclopedias. 2. Human
geography--Encyclopedias.] I. Gall, Timothy L. II. Gall, Susan B.
GN307.J85 1999
306' .03--dc21   98-13810
                                  CIP
                                  AC

ISBN 0-7876-1756-X (set)
ISBN 0-7876-1757-1 (vol. 1)   ISBN 0-7876-1758-X (vol. 2)   ISBN 0-7876-1759-8 (vol. 3)
ISBN 0-7876-1760-1 (vol. 4)   ISBN 0-7876-1761-X (vol. 5)   ISBN 0-7876-1762-8 (vol. 6)
ISBN 0-7876-1763-6 (vol. 7)   ISBN 0-7876-1764-4 (vol. 8)   ISBN 0-7876-2761-5 (vol. 9)

Printed in the United States of America
10 9 8 7 6 5 4 3 2 1

Contents
Volume 9

Cumulative Contents

CUMULATIVE CONTENTS

CUMULATIVE CONTENTS

CUMULATIVE CONTENTS

Volume 9

Contributors

Editors: Timothy L. Gall and Susan Bevan Gall

Senior Editor: Daniel M. Lucas

Contributing Editors: Himanee Gupta, Jim Henry, Kira Silverbird, Elaine Trapp, Rosalie Wieder

Copy Editors: Deborah Baron, Janet Fenn, Jim Henry, Patricia M. Mote, Deborah Ring, Kathy Soltis

Typesetting and Graphics: Cheryl Montagna, Brian Rajewski

Cover Photographs: Cory Langley

Data Input: Janis K. Long, Cheryl Montagna, Melody Penfound

Proofreaders: Deborah Baron, Janet Fenn

Editorial Assistants: Katie Baron, Jennifer A. Spencer, Daniel K. Updegraft

Editorial Advisors

P. Boone, Sixth Grade Teacher, Oak Crest Middle School, San Antonio, Texas

Jean Campbell, Foothill Farms Middle School, Sacramento, California

Kathy Englehart, Librarian, Hathaway Brown School, Shaker Heights, Ohio

Catherine Harris, Librarian, Oak Crest Middle School, San Antonio, Texas

Karen James, Children's Services, Louisville Free Public Library, Louisville, Kentucky

Contributors to the Gale Edition

The articles presented in this encyclopedia are based on entries in the *Worldmark Encyclopedia of Cultures and Daily Life* published in 1997 by Gale. The following authors and reviewers contributed to the Gale edition.

ANDREW J. ABALAHIN. Doctoral candidate, Department of History, Cornell University.

JAMAL ABDULLAH. Doctoral candidate, Department of City and Regional Planning, Cornell University.

SANA ABED-KOTOB. Book Review Editor, Middle East Journal, Middle East Institute.

MAMOUD ABOUD. Charge d'Affaires, a.i., Embassy of the Federal and Islamic Republic of the Comoros.

JUDY ALLEN. Editor, Choctaw Nation of Oklahoma.

HIS EXCELLENCY DENIS G. ANTOINE. Ambassador to the United States, Embassy of Grenada.

LESLEY ANN ASHBAUGH. Instructor, Sociology, Seattle University.

HASHEM ATALLAH. Translator, Editor, Teacher; Fairfax, Virginia.

HECTOR AZEVES. Cultural Attaché, Embassy of Uruguay.

VICTORIA J. BAKER. Associate Professor of Anthropology, Anthropology (Collegium of Comparative Cultures), Eckerd College.

POLINE BALA. Doctoral candidate, Asian Studies, Cornell University.

MARJORIE MANDELSTAM BALZER. Research Professor; Coordinator, Social, Regional, and Ethnic Studies Sociology, and Center for Eurasian, Russian, and East European Studies.

JOSHUA BARKER. Doctoral candidate, Department of Anthropology, Cornell University.

IGOR BARSEGIAN. Department of Sociology, George Washington University.

IRAJ BASHIRI. Professor of Central Asian Studies, Department of Slavic and Central Asian Languages and Literatures, University of Minnesota.

DAN F. BAUER. Department of Anthropology, Lafayette College.

JOYCE BEAR. Historic Preservation Officer, Muscogee Nation of Oklahoma.

SVETLANA BELAIA. Byelorussian-American Cultural Center, Strongsville, Ohio.

HIS EXCELLENCY DR. COURTNEY BLACKMAN. Ambassador to the United States, Embassy of Barbados.

BETTY BLAIR. Executive Editor, Azerbaijan International.

ARVIDS BLODNIEKS. Director, Latvian Institute, American Latvian Association in the USA.

ARASH BORMANSHINOV. University of Maryland, College Park.

HARRIET I. BRADY. Cultural Anthropologist (Pyramid Lake Paiute Tribe), Native Studies Program, Pyramid Lake High School.

MARTIN BROKENLEG. Professor of Sociology, Department of Sociology, Augustana College.

REV. RAYMOND A. BUCKO, S.J. Assistant Professor of Anthropology, LeMoyne College.

JOHN W. BURTON. Department of Anthropology, Connecticut College.

DINEANE BUTTRAM. University of North Carolina-Chapel Hill.

RICARDO CABALLERO. Counselor, Embassy of Paraguay.

CHRISTINA CARPADIS. Researcher/Writer, Cleveland, Ohio.

SALVADOR GARCIA CASTANEDA. Department of Spanish and Portuguese, The Ohio State University.

SUSANA CAVALLO. Graduate Program Director and Professor of Spanish, Department of Modern Languages and Literatures, Loyola University, Chicago.

BRIAN P. CAZA. Doctoral candidate, Political Science, University of Chicago.

VAN CHRISTO. President and Executive Director, Frosina Foundation, Boston.

YURI A. CHUMAKOV. Graduate Student, Department of Sociology, University of Notre Dame.

J. COLARUSSO. Professor of Anthropology, McMaster University.

FRANCESCA COLECCHIA. Modern Language Department, Duquesne University.

DIANNE K. DAEG DE MOTT. Researcher/Writer, Tucson, Arizona.

MICHAEL DE JONGH. Professor, Department of Anthropology, University of South Africa.

GEORGI DERLUGUIAN. Senior Fellow, Ph.D., U. S. Institute of Peace.

CHRISTINE DRAKE. Department of Political Science and Geography, Old Dominion University.

ARTURO DUARTE. Guatemalan Mission to the OAS.

CALEB DUBE. Department of Anthropology, Northwestern University.

BRIAN DU TOIT. Professor, Department of Anthropology, University of Florida.

LEAH ERMARTH. Worldspace Foundation, Washington, DC.

NANCY J. FAIRLEY. Associate Professor of Anthropology, Department of Anthropology/Sociology, Davidson College.

GREGORY A. FINNEGAN, Ph.D. Tozzer Library, Harvard University.

ALLEN J. FRANK, Ph.D.

DAVID P. GAMBLE. Professor Emeritus, Department of Anthropology, San Francisco State University.

FREDERICK GAMST. Professor, Department of Anthropology, University of Massachusetts, Harbor Campus.

PAULA GARB. Associate Director of Global Peace and Conflict Studies and Adjunct Professor of Social Ecology, University of California, Irvine.

HAROLD GASKI. Associate Professor of Sami Literature, School of Languages and Literature, University of Tromsø.

STEPHEN J. GENDZIER.

FLORENCE GERDEL.

ANTHONY P. GLASCOCK. Professor of Anthropology; Department of Anthropology, Psychology, and Sociology; Drexel University.

LUIS GONZALEZ. Researcher/Writer, River Edge, New Jersey.

JENNIFER GRAHAM. Researcher/Writer, Sydney, Australia.

MARIE-CÉCILE GROELSEMA. Doctoral candidate, Comparative Literature, Indiana University.

ROBERT GROELSEMA. MPIA and doctoral candidate, Political Science, Indiana University.

MARIA GROSZ-NGATÉ. Visiting Assistant Professor, Department of Anthropology, Northwestern University.

ELLEN GRUENBAUM. Professor, School of Social Sciences, California State University, Fresno.

N. THOMAS HAKANSSON. University of Kentucky.

ROBERT HALASZ. Researcher/Writer, New York, New York.

MARC HANREZ. Professor, Department of French and Italian, University of Wisconsin-Madison.

ANWAR UL HAQ. Central Asian Studies Department, Indiana University.

LIAM HARTE. Department of Philosophy, Loyola University, Chicago.

FR. VASILE HATEGAN. Author, *Romanian Culture in America*.

BRUCE HEILMAN. Doctoral candidate, Department of Political Science, Indiana University.

JIM HENRY. Researcher/Writer, Cleveland, Ohio.

BARRY HEWLETT. Department of Anthropology, Washington State University.

SUSAN F. HIRSCH. Department of Anthropology, Wesleyan University.

MARIDA HOLLOS. Department of Anthropology, Brown University.

HALYNA HOLUBEC. Researcher/Writer, Cleveland, Ohio.

YVONNE HOOSAVA. Legal Researcher and Cultural Preservation Officer, Hopi Tribal Council.

HUIQIN HUANG, Ph.D. Center for East Asia Studies, University of Montreal.

ASAFA JALATA. Assistant Professor of Sociology and African and African American Studies, Department of Sociology, The University of Tennessee, Knoxville.

STEPHEN F. JONES. Russian Department, Mount Holyoke College.

THOMAS JOVANOVSKI, Ph.D. Lorain County Community College.

A. KEN JULES. Minister Plenipotentiary and Deputy Head of Mission, Embassy of St. Kitts and Nevis.

GENEROSA KAGARUKI-KAKOTI. Economist, Department of Urban and Rural Planning, College of Lands and Architectural Studies, Dar es Salaam, Tanzania.

EZEKIEL KALIPENI. Department of Geography, University of Illinois at Urbana-Champaign.

CONTRIBUTORS

DON KAVANAUGH. Program Director, Lake of the Woods Ojibwa Cultural Centre.

SUSAN M. KENYON. Associate Professor of Anthropology, Department of History and Anthropology, Butler University.

WELILE KHUZWAYO. Department of Anthropology, University of South Africa.

PHILIP L. KILBRIDE. Professor of Anthropology, Mary Hale Chase Chair in the Social Sciences, Department of Anthropology, Bryn Mawr College.

RICHARD O. KISIARA. Doctoral candidate, Department of Anthropology, Washington University in St. Louis.

KAREN KNOWLES. Permanent Mission of Antigua and Barbuda to the United Nations.

IGOR KRUPNIK. Research Anthropologist, Department of Anthropology, Smithsonian Institution.

LEELO LASS. Secretary, Embassy of Estonia.

ROBERT LAUNAY. Professor, Department of Anthropology, Northwestern University.

CHARLES LEBLANC. Professor and Director, Center for East Asia Studies, University of Montreal.

RONALD LEE. Author, *Goddam Gypsy, An Autobiographical Novel.*

PHILIP E. LEIS. Professor and Chair, Department of Anthropology, Brown University.

MARIA JUKIC LESKUR. Croatian Consulate, Cleveland, Ohio.

RICHARD A. LOBBAN, JR. Professor of Anthropology and African Studies, Department of Anthropology, Rhode Island College.

DERYCK O. LODRICK. Visiting Scholar, Center for South Asian Studies, University of California, Berkeley.

NEIL LURSSEN. Intro Communications Inc.

GREGORIO C. MARTIN. Modern Language Department, Duquesne University.

HOWARD J. MARTIN. Independent scholar.

HEITOR MARTINS. Professor, Department of Spanish and Portuguese, Indiana University.

ADELINE MASQUELIER. Assistant Professor, Department of Anthropology, Tulane University.

DOLINA MILLAR.

EDITH MIRANTE. Project Maje, Portland, Oregon.

ROBERT W. MONTGOMERY, Ph.D. Indiana University.

THOMAS D. MORIN. Associate Professor of Hispanic Studies, Department of Modern and Classical Literatures and Languages, University of Rhode Island.

CHARLES MORRILL. Doctoral candidate, Indiana University.

CAROL A. MORTLAND. Crate's Point, The Dalles, Oregon.

FRANCIS A. MOYER. Director, North Carolina Japan Center, North Carolina State University.

MARIE C. MOYER.

NYAGA MWANIKI. Assistant Professor, Department of Anthropology and Sociology, Western Carolina University.

KENNETH NILSON. Celtic Studies Department, Harvard University.

JANE E. ORMROD. Graduate Student, History, University of Chicago.

JUANITA PAHDOPONY. Carl Perkins Program Director, Comanche Tribe of Oklahoma.

TINO PALOTTA. Syracuse University.

ROHAYATI PASENG.

PATRICIA PITCHON. Researcher/Writer, London, England.

STEPHANIE PLATZ. Program Officer, Program on Peace and International Cooperation, The John D. and Catherine T. MacArthur Foundation.

MIHAELA POIATA. Graduate Student, School of Journalism and Mass Communication, University of North Carolina at Chapel Hill.

LEOPOLDINA PRUT-PREGELJ. Author, *Historical Dictionary of Slovenia.*

J. RACKAUSKAS. Director, Lithuanian Research and Studies Center, Chicago.

J. RAKOVICH. Byelorussian-American Cultural Center, Strongsville, Ohio.

HANTA V. RALAY. Promotions, Inc., Montgomery Village, Maryland.

SUSAN J. RASMUSSEN. Associate Professor, Department of Anthropology, University of Houston.

RONALD REMINICK. Department of Anthropology, Cleveland State University.

BRUCE D. ROBERTS. Assistant Professor of Anthropology, Department of Anthropology and Sociology, University of Southern Mississippi.

LAUREL L. ROSE. Philosophy Department, Carnegie-Mellon University.

ROBERT ROTENBERG. Professor of Anthropology, International Studies Program, DePaul University.

CAROLINE SAHLEY, Ph.D. Researcher/Writer, Cleveland, Ohio.

VERONICA SALLES-REESE. Associate Professor, Department of Spanish and Portuguese, Georgetown University.

MAIRA SARYBAEVA. Kazakh-American Studies Center, University of Kentucky.

DEBRA L. SCHINDLER. Institute of Arctic Studies, Dartmouth College.

KYOKO SELDEN, Ph.D. Researcher/Writer, Ithaca, New York.

ENAYATULLAH SHAHRANI. Central Asian Studies Department, Indiana University.

ROBERT SHANAFELT. Adjunct Lecturer, Department of Anthropology, The Florida State University.

TUULIKKI SINKS. Teaching Specialist for Finnish, Department of German, Scandinavian, and Dutch, University of Minnesota.

JAN SJÅVIK. Associate Professor, Scandinavian Studies, University of Washington.

CONTRIBUTORS

MAGDA SOBALVARRO. Press and Cultural Affairs Director, Embassy of Nicaragua.

MICHAEL STAINTON. Researcher, Joint Center for Asia Pacific Studies, York University.

RIANA STEYN. Department of Anthropology, University of South Africa.

PAUL STOLLER. Professor, Department of Anthropology, West Chester University.

CRAIG STRASHOFER. Researcher/Writer, Cleveland, Ohio.

SANDRA B. STRAUBHAAR. Assistant Professor, Nordic Studies, Department of Germanic and Slavic Languages, Brigham Young University.

VUM SON SUANTAK. Author, *Zo History.*

MURAT TAISHIBAEV. Kazakh-American Studies Center, University of Kentucky.

CHRISTOPHER C. TAYLOR. Associate Professor, Anthropology Department, University of Alabama, Birmingham.

EDDIE TSO. Office of Language and Culture, Navajo Division of Education.

DAVID TYSON. Foreign Broadcast Information Service, Washington, D.C.

NICOLAAS G. W. UNLANDT. Assistant Professor of French, Department of French and Italian, Brigham Young University.

GORDON URQUHART. Professor, Department of Economics and Business, Cornell College.

CHRISTOPHER J. VAN VUUREN. Professor, Department of Anthropology, University of South Africa.

DALIA VENTURA-ALCALAY. Journalist, London, England.

CATHERINE VEREECKE. Assistant Director, Center for African Studies, University of Florida.

GREGORY T. WALKER. Associate Director, Office of International Affairs, Duquesne University.

GERHARD WEISS. Department of German, Scandinavian, and Dutch, University of Minnesota.

PATSY WEST. Director, The Seminole/Miccosukee Photographic Archive.

WALTER WHIPPLE. Associate Professor of Polish, Germanic and Slavic Languages, Brigham Young University.

ROSALIE WIEDER. Researcher/Writer, Cleveland, Ohio.

JEFFREY WILLIAMS. Professor, Department of Anthropology, Cleveland State University.

GUANG-HONG YU. Associate Research Fellow, Institute of Ethnology, Academia Sinica.

RUSSELL ZANCA. Department of Anthropology, College of Liberal Arts and Sciences, University of Illinois at Urbana-Champaign.

Reader's Guide

Junior Worldmark Encyclopedia of World Cultures contains articles exploring the ways of life of over 290 culture groups worldwide. Arranged alphabetically by country in nine volumes, this encyclopedia parallels the organization of its sister set, *Junior Worldmark Encyclopedia of the Nations.* Whereas the primary purpose of *Nations* is to provide information on the world's nations, this encyclopedia focuses on the traditions, living conditions, and personalities of many of the world's culture groups.

Defining groups for inclusion was not an easy task. Cultural identity is shaped by such factors as history, geography, nationality, ethnicity, race, language, and religion. Sometimes the distinctions are subtle, but important. Most chapters in this encyclopedia begin with an article on the people of the country as a nationality group. For example, the chapter on Kenya begins with an article entitled "Kenyans." This article explores the national character shared by all people living in Kenya. However, there are separate articles on the Gikuyu, Kalenjin, Luhya, and Luo—four of the largest ethnic groups living in the country. They are all Kenyans, but each group is distinct. Many profiled groups—like the Kazaks—inhabit lands that cross national boundaries. Although profiled in the chapter on Kazakstan, Kazaks are also important minorities in China, Uzbekistan, and Turkmenistan. In such cases, cross-references direct the student to the chapter where the group is profiled.

The photographs that illustrate the articles show a wonderfully diverse world. From the luxury liners docked in the harbor at Monaco to the dwellings made of grass sheltering the inhabitants of the rain forest, people share the struggles and joys of earning a living, bringing children into the world, teaching them to survive, and initiating them into adulthood. Although language, customs, and dress illustrate our differences, the faces of the people pictured in these volumes reinforce our similarities. Whether on the streets of Tokyo or the mountains of Tibet, a smile on the face of a child transcends the boundaries of nationality and cultural identity to reveal something common in us all. Photographer Cory Langley's images on pages 93 and 147 in Volume 6 serve to illustrate this point.

The picture of the world this encyclopedia paints today will certainly differ from the one painted in future editions. Indigenous people like the Jivaro in Ecuador (Volume 3, page 77) are being assimilated into modern society as forest lands are cleared for development and televisions and VCRs are brought to even the most remote villages. As the global economy expands, traditional diets are supplemented with Coke, Pepsi, and fast food; traditional storytellers are replaced by World Cup soccer matches and American television programs; and cultural heroes are overwhelmed by images of Michael Jordan and Michael Jackson. Photographer Cynthia Bassett was fortunate to be among a small group of travelers to visit a part of China only recently opened to Westerners. Her image of Miao dancers (Volume 2, page 161) shows a people far removed from Western culture . . . until one looks a little closer. Behind the dancers, in the upper corner of the photograph, is a basketball hoop and backboard. It turns out that Miao teenagers love basketball!

ORGANIZATION

Within each volume the chapters are arranged alphabetically by country. A cumulative table of contents for all volumes in the set follows the table of contents to each volume.

Each chapter covers a specific country. The contents of the chapter, listing the culture group articles, follows the chapter title. An overview of the composition of the population of the country appears after the contents list. The individual articles follow, and are organized according to a standard twenty-heading outline explained in more detail below. This structure allows for easy comparison between cultures and enhances the accessibility of the information.

Articles begin with the **pronunciation** of the group's name, a listing of **alternate names** by which the group is known, the group's **location** in the world, its **population**, the **languages** spoken, and the **religions** practiced. Articles are illustrated with maps showing the primary location of the group and photographs of the culture group being profiled. The twenty standard headings by which the articles are organized are presented below.

1 ● INTRODUCTION: A description of the group's historical origins provides a useful background for understanding its contemporary affairs. Information relating to migration helps explain how the group arrived at its present location. Political conditions and governmental structure(s) that affect members of the profiled ethnic group are also discussed.

2 ● LOCATION: The population size of the group is listed. This information may include official census data from various countries and/or estimates. Information on the size of a group's population located outside the traditional homeland may also be included, especially for those groups with large scattered populations. A description of the homeland includes information on location, topography, and climate.

3 ● LANGUAGE: Each article lists the name(s) of the primary language(s) spoken by members. Descriptions of linguistic origins, grammar, and similarities to other languages may also be included. Examples of common words, phrases, and proverbs are listed for many of the profiled groups, and some include examples of common personal names and greetings.

4 ● FOLKLORE: Common themes, settings, and characters in the profiled group's traditional oral and/or literary mythology are highlighted. Many entries include a short excerpt or synopsis of one of the group's noteworthy myths, fables, or legends. Some entries describe the accomplishments of famous heroes and heroines or other prominent historical figures.

5 ● RELIGION: The origins of traditional religious beliefs are profiled. Contemporary religious beliefs, customs, and practices are also discussed. Some groups may be closely associated with one particular faith (especially if religious and ethnic identification are interlinked), while others may have members of diverse faiths.

6 ● MAJOR HOLIDAYS: Celebrations and commemorations typically recognized by the group's members are described. These holidays commonly fall into two categories: secular and religious. Secular holidays often include an independence day and/or other days of observance recognizing important dates in history that affected the group as a whole. Religious holidays are typically the same as those honored by people of the same faith worldwide. Some secular and religious holidays are linked to the lunar cycle or to the change of seasons. Some articles describe customs practiced by members of the group on certain holidays.

7 ● RITES OF PASSAGE: Formal and informal events that mark an individual's procession through the stages of life are profiled. These events typically involve rituals, ceremonies, observances, and procedures associated with birth, childhood, the coming of age, milestones in education or religious training, adulthood, and death.

8 ● RELATIONSHIPS: Information on greetings, body language, gestures, visiting customs, and dating practices is included. The extent of formality to which members of a certain ethnic group treat others is also addressed, as some groups may adhere to customs governing interpersonal relationships more or less strictly than others.

9 ● LIVING CONDITIONS: General health conditions typical of the group's members are cited. Such information includes life expectancy, the prevalence of various diseases, and access to medical care. Information on urbanization, housing, and access to utilities is also included. Transportation methods typically utilized by the group's members are also discussed.

10 ● FAMILY LIFE: The size and composition of the family unit is profiled. Gender roles common to the group are also discussed, including the division of rights and responsibilities relegated to male and female group members. The roles that children, adults, and the elderly have within the group as a whole may also be addressed.

11 ● CLOTHING: Many entries include descriptive information (design, color, fabric, etc.) regarding traditional clothing (or national costume) for men and women, and indicate the frequency of its use in contemporary life. A description of typical clothing worn in modern daily life is also provided, especially if traditional clothing is no longer the usual form of dress. Distinctions between formal and work attire and descriptions of clothing preferences of young people are described for many groups as well.

12 ● FOOD: Descriptions of items commonly consumed by members of the group are listed. The frequency and occasion for meals is also described, as are any unique customs regarding eating and drinking, special utensils and furniture, and the role of food and beverages in ritual ceremonies. Many entries include a recipe for a favorite dish.

13 ● EDUCATION: The structure of formal education in the country or countries of residence is discussed, including information on primary, secondary, and higher education. For some groups, the role of informal education is also highlighted. Some articles include information regarding the relevance and importance of education among the group as a whole, along with parental expectations for children.

14 ● CULTURAL HERITAGE: Since many groups express their sense of identity through art, music, literature, and dance, a description of prominent styles is included. Some articles also cite the contributions of famous individual artists, writers, and musicians.

15 ● EMPLOYMENT: The type of labor that typically engages members of the profiled group is discussed. For some groups, the formal wage economy is the primary source of earnings, but for other groups, informal agriculture or trade may be the usual way to earn a living. Working conditions are also highlighted.

16 ● SPORTS: Popular sports that children and adults play are listed, as are typical spectator sports. Some articles include a description and/or rules to a sport or game.

17 ● RECREATION: Listed activities that people enjoy in their leisure time may include structured pastimes (such as public musical and dance performances) or informal get-togethers (such as meeting for conversation). The role of popular culture, movies, theater, and television in everyday life is also discussed where it applies.

18 ● CRAFTS AND HOBBIES: Entries describe arts and crafts commonly fabricated according to traditional methods, materials, and style. Such objects may often have a functional utility for everyday tasks.

19 ● SOCIAL PROBLEMS: Internal and external issues that confront members of the profiled group are described. Such concerns often deal with fundamental problems like war, famine, disease, and poverty. A lack of human rights, civil rights, and political freedom may also adversely affect a group as a whole. Other problems may include crime, unemployment, substance abuse, and domestic violence.

20 ● BIBLIOGRAPHY: References cited include works used to compile the article, benchmark publications often recognized as authoritative by scholars, and other reference sources accessible to middle school researchers. Website addresses are provided for researchers who wish to access the World Wide Web. The website citation includes the author and title of the website (if applicable). The address begins with characters that follow "http://" in the citation; the address ends with the character preceding the comma and date. For example, the citation for the website of the German embassy appears as follows:

German Embassy, Washington, D.C. [Online] Available http://www.germany-info.org/, 1998.

To access this site, researchers type: www.germany-info.org

A glossary and an index of groups profiled appears at the end of each volume.

ACKNOWLEDGMENTS

The editors express appreciation to the members of the U●X●L staff who were involved in a number of ways at various stages of development of the *Junior Worldmark Encyclopedia of World Cultures.*

SUGGESTIONS ARE WELCOME: We appreciate any suggestions that will enhance future editions. Please send comments to:

Editors
Junior Worldmark Encyclopedia of World Cultures
U●X●L
27500 Drake Road
Farmington Hills, MI 48331-3535
(800) 877-4253

Tajikistan

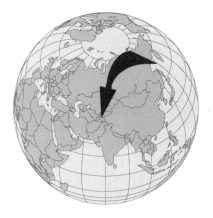

The people of Tajikistan are called Tajiks. People who trace their ancestry to Tajikistan are 62 percent of the population, and include the Pamiri or Mountain Tajiks. Uzbeks live in northwest Tajikistan, and make up almost 25 percent of the total population. Russians comprise over 7 percent, and Tatars, just over 1 percent. To learn more about Uzbeks, see the chapter on Uzbekistan in this volume; about Russians and Tatars, see the chapter on Russia in Volume 7.

Tajiks

PRONUNCIATION: tah-JEEKS
LOCATION: Tajikistan
POPULATION: More than 5 million
LANGUAGES: Tajiki; Russian; Uzbeki
RELIGIONS: Islam; Judaism; Christianity

1 ● INTRODUCTION

The Tajiks are an Indo-European people who settled the upper reaches of the Amu River (territory of present-day Uzbekistan). During the latter part of the nineteenth century, the Tajiks were divided. Most of the population occupied what would become the republic of Tajikistan in the former Soviet Union. The rest became a large minority in Afghanistan.

During the 1992–93 civil war in Tajikistan, thousands lost their lives. More than 10 percent of the population (100,000) fled to Afghanistan. More than 35,000 homes were destroyed, either in battle or as a result of ethnic-cleansing actions. Today, the country is still at war, although it has calmed down considerably.

2 ● LOCATION

Tajikistan is slightly smaller than Illinois. Geographically, it can be divided into two regions, north and south. The Zarafshan mountains and their lush valleys and flat plains form the northern *kulturbund* (boundary of their traditional homeland). Here, Tajik and Uzbek cultures have become fused. The Hissar, Gharategin, and Badakhshan mountains form the southern boundary of their ancestral homeland.

In 1924, the Soviet Union redrew the maps of its Central Asian republics. In doing so, the centers of the old Tajik culture (Samarqand and Bukhara), were given to

TAJIKS

| 0 | 250 | 500 | 750 Miles |
| 0 | 250 | 500 | 750 | 1000 Kilometers |

tus alongside Tajiki. Uzbeki, too, is allowed to flourish in regions predominantly inhabited by Uzbeks.

4 ● FOLKLORE

Tajikistan, Iran, and Afghanistan enjoy a unique cultural heritage. The major contribution to this shared heritage is the magnificent *Shah-nameh (Book of Kings)*, written by the eleventh-century Persian poet Firdawsi. This book is an account of the prehistory of the region. It tells the story of the cosmic battle between Good and Evil, the development of the "divine right of kings," and the history of the Iranian monarchs.

Lesser myths include the story of Nur, a young man who, to attain his beloved, tamed the mighty Vakhsh River by building a dam on it. There is also the story of a sacred sheep that was lowered from heaven to help the Tajiks survive.

5 ● RELIGION

In ancient times, present-day Tajikistan was a part of the empire of the Achaemenian Persians. The religion of that empire was Zoroastrianism. After the Arab conquest in the eighth century, Islam was introduced. It remained unchallenged until the rise of atheism in the early years of the twentieth century. Today atheists, Muslims, Jews, and Christians live together.

6 ● MAJOR HOLIDAYS

Tajiks observe three different types of holidays: Iranian, Muslim, and civil. The most important Iranian holiday is the *Nawruz* (New Year). It begins on March 21 and continues for several days. This holiday dates

Uzbekistan. Restoration of these cities to Tajikistan is one of the goals of the Tajiks.

During the 1980s, the population of Tajikistan grew from 3.8 million to more than 5 million. In addition, many Tajiks live in Uzbekistan, Kyrgyzstan, Afghanistan, and China.

3 ● LANGUAGE

Tajiki is an Indo-European language. It is closely related to Farsi, the language of Iran. In 1989 Tajiki became the sole official language of the country, replacing Russian and Uzbeki. The act boosted Tajik pride, but it failed otherwise. It scared away many foreigners, including Russians, who had helped the country's economy grow. Since 1995, Russian has regained its previous sta-

back to Iranian mythic times. It celebrates the victory of the forces of Good (warmth) over those of Evil (cold). It also marks the beginning of the planting season and commemorates the memory of departed ancestors.

The Islamic holidays are Maulud al-Nabi (the birth of the Prophet Muhammad), Eid al-Adha (celebrating the ancient account of Abraham offering his son for sacrifice), and Eid al-Fitr (celebration of the end of the Ramadan fast). These celebrations had to be observed in secret during the Soviet era. They are now held in the open. Their dates are not fixed due to the rotating nature of the lunar calendar.

Civil holidays with origins in the Soviet era include New Year's Day (January 1), International Women's Day (March 8), Labor Day (May 1), and Victory Day (May 9). Tajik Independence Day is celebrated on September 9.

7 ● RITES OF PASSAGE

There are both traditional and Soviet rites of passage. After marriage, Tajik women traditionally pluck their eyebrows and wear special ornate hats and distinctive clothing. Married men and women both wear their wedding rings on the third finger of the right hand. A ring on the middle finger indicates separation or the death of a spouse.

8 ● RELATIONSHIPS

The Tajiks recognize three privileged groups: children, the elderly, and guests. Children, like adults, participate in most gatherings and contribute to the life of the party. The elderly, often referred to as *muy sapid*, are highly valued. They are consulted and obeyed in important affairs. Guests fall into various categories depending on the nature of relationships.

Family visits and visits by colleagues and friends require the preparation of a *dasturkhan*, a tablecloth spread over the floor or on a low table. On the dasturkhan are placed bread, nuts, fruits, various types of preserves and homemade sweetmeats. The guest of honor is seated at the head of the dasturkhan, farthest from the door.

The Tajiks have many interesting customs and superstitions. For instance, certain items such as keys, needles, and scissors should not be passed from hand to hand. Rather, they are placed on a table for the other person to pick up. It is believed that standing in a doorway will make a person go into debt. Spilling salt in the house will cause a person to get into a fight. A person who whistles in the house is likely to lose something valuable. A person who twirls a key chain on his or her finger becomes a vagabond. If someone sneezes during a departure, he or she should wait a while before leaving. If one returns home for a forgotten item, one should look in a mirror before leaving the house again.

9 ● LIVING CONDITIONS

Living conditions in Tajikistan, especially in Dushanbe, are difficult. Housing in Dushanbe, the largest urban area, consists of many high-rise Soviet-era apartment complexes. In these complexes, which are usually surrounded by large courtyards and common spaces, elevators rarely work and water pressure is weak on the higher floors. There has been no hot water in Dushanbe since 1993 (except for ten days before the presidential elections). Cold water is usually available, but electricity is sporadically shut off. Cooking gas is provided for only four hours in the afternoon.

Telephone service is also deficient. International calls must be made through a centralized office, which requires a two-day notice and advance payment. Express mail reaches Dushanbe in twenty to thirty days. Regular airmail takes three to four months.

10 ● FAMILY LIFE

The Tajiks are family oriented. Families are large but do not necessarily live in the same part of town or even in the same city. In fact, the more widely the family is spread, the more opportunities it has for amassing resources. This allows outsiders to become a part of a family and thus expand it into a clan. There are at least four or five major clans in Tajikistan.

Women's roles vary widely. Soviet-influenced Tajik women participate in all aspects of society and a few are even members of parliament. Muslim wives, on the other hand, stay at home and take care of the children.

Most marriages are arranged. After negotiations, the father of the groom pays most of the expenses for the *tuy* (celebration). Women can initiate divorce procedures and receive half of the family's assets.

11 ● CLOTHING

Men and women, especially in urban centers, wear European clothes. Farmers and herders wear a special heavy boot over their usual shoes. Older Tajik men wear long

AP/Wide World Photos

Tajik refugees. Conflicts caused by ethnic tension and regionalism have made life difficult for many people in Tajikistan.

Islamic cloaks and turbans. They also wear beards.

Students, especially during the Soviet era, wore uniforms with kerchiefs and other distinctive decorations. In recent times, traditional clothing is preferred.

12 ● FOOD

The generic word for food is *avqat*. As is the custom elsewhere in the world, various courses are served. *Pish avqat* (appetizer) includes *sanbuse* (meat, squash, or potatoes with onions and spices wrapped in bread and either deep-fried or baked), *yakhni* (cold meats), and salad.

Recipe

Ash (Stew)

Ingredients

1 small onion, diced
about ½ cup oil
1 pound of beef stew meat, cut into medium pieces
1 pound of carrots, julienned (cut into small, matchstick-sized pieces)
4¼ cups rice, soaked for 40 minutes before adding pinch of cumin seeds

Procedure

1. Heat oil in a large kettle. Add meat and cook until brown.
2. Add onion, lower heat, continue cooking until meat is done (about 15 to 20 minutes).
3. Add enough water to cover the meat. Heat the water to boiling, reduce heat, and simmer (uncovered) until water is gone.
4. Add carrots and cook for 2 or 3 minutes.
5. Drain presoaked rice. Put one cup of water, cumin seeds, and pepper into a kettle. Add the rice. Add lukewarm water to cover the rice by about ½ inch.
6. Add a pinch of salt to taste. Gradually heat the water, and simmer until all water is evaporated.
7. Turn the rice over so that cooked rice comes to the top. Poke 5 or 6 holes into the rice with a chopstick or wooden spoon handle.
8. Cover, lower the heat, and cook for 15 to 20 minutes.

Serve the rice with the carrots and meat.

The avqat is either *suyuq* (broth based) or *quyuq* (dry). Examples of the first include *shurba nakhud* (pea soup), *kham shurba* (vegetable soup), and *qurma shurba* (meat and vegetables sautéed in oil and then simmered in water). The main national dish is *ash,* a mixture of rice, meat, carrots, and onions fried and steamed in a deep pot, preferably over an open fire. *Pilmeni* (meat and onions in pasta and cooked in water or meat stock) and *mantu* (meat and onions in steamed pasta) are examples of dry avqat. Following is a recipe for *ash* (stew).

13 ●EDUCATION

The Soviet education system had both positive and negative effects on the Tajiks. On the positive side, it essentially eliminated illiteracy by 1960 and acquainted the Tajiks with Russian literature. On the negative side, it alienated most Tajiks from their own culture and language.

Today, the English language and American culture are finding their way into Tajikistan. English is stressed in schools because many people, including those who intend to emigrate, want to learn English for its role in international business.

14 ●CULTURAL HERITAGE

Tajik music varies by region. In the north, especially in Samarqand and Bukhara, the *shashmaqam* is recognized as the chief musical system normally played on a *tanbur.* In the south, *falak* and *qurughli* music predominate. The national *hafiz* (singer) is respected by all.

Various regions have reacted to Western culture differently. The Badakhshanis, for instance, have adopted Western musical innovations. The Gharmis have not.

A recurring theme in Tajik literature is the harsh measures of a *bai* (rich man) who "helps" an orphaned boy meet the expenses for his father's funeral. The young man ends up working for the bai for the rest of his life to pay the debt.

15 ● EMPLOYMENT

The makeup and circumstances of the work force in Tajikistan have changed drastically in recent years. Many youth who would traditionally have worked on cotton plantations have migrated to the cities and have become involved in trade. They import goods from Pakistan, Japan, and China and sell them in makeshift shops or in stalls alongside the street.

A large number of Tajiks work in industry. Primary industries include mining, machine-tool factories, canneries, and hydroelectric stations. In general, about 50 percent of the population is under twenty. Over one half of those are not in the labor force. There is a growing population that is neither employed nor in school.

16 ● SPORTS

The national sport of the Tajiks, *gushtigiri* (wrestling), has a colorful tradition. When the towns were divided into *mahallas* (districts), each district had its own *alufta* (tough) who was the best wrestler. The position of the alufta, usually an upright and respected individual, was often challenged by those of lower rank.

Buzkashi (which means, literally, "dragging the goat") is a sport involving strenu-

ous bodily exertion. In this game, the carcass of a goat is dragged by horsemen who grab it from each other. The aim of the riders is to deposit the carcass in a designated circle in front of the guest of honor. Buzkashi is usually performed as part of the Nawruz (New Year's) celebrations.

In recent years, many European sports have also found their way into Tajikistan. Soccer is so popular that many believe it rivals buzkashi.

17 ● RECREATION

During the Soviet period, special attention was paid to the arts. The result was culturally stimulating. The Tajik cinema, for instance, produced a number of worthy films based on Firdawsi's *Shah-nameh*. There were also stunning productions on the lives of other poets, including Rudaki (c. 859–940). With the disintegration of the Soviet Union, the arts lost their primary means of support. Producers, directors, actors, and writers either joined the ranks of the jobless or became involved in business. Many left Tajikistan.

Today, television occupies some of the Tajiks' time. Programs are telecast both from Moscow and locally. *Maria* (a Mexican rags-to-riches soap opera), and the American program *Santa Barbara* are favorites. Local broadcasting is very limited in scope, dealing mostly with regional matters, especially agriculture. Videos allow Tajik youth wider choice of programs.

18 ● CRAFTS AND HOBBIES

Traditional Tajik crafts include the embroidered Bukhara wallhangings and bedcovers popularized in the nineteenth century. The

Tajik style of tapestries typically has floral designs on silk or cotton and is made on a tambour frame. Woodcarving is also an honored Tajik craft.

19 ● SOCIAL PROBLEMS

The social problems of Tajikistan are too numerous to list. Perhaps the most important social problem has to do with authority and control. Since the tenth century, the Tajiks have been ruled by the others, mostly Turks and Russians. Taxes imposed by Russia have driven the Tajiks to revolt a number of times. One such revolt, the Vaase uprising of the 1870s, was put down mercilessly.

The 1992 Tajik attempt at independence was also severely repressed. The civil war that resulted nearly destroyed the country. There is a 25 percent unemployment rate, a high rate of population growth, and a lack of skilled workers. Ethnic tension and regionalism often bring the country to the verge of disintegration.

20 ● BIBLIOGRAPHY

Ahmed, Rashid. *The Resurgence of Central Asia: Islam or Nationalism.* Oxford, England: Oxford University Press, 1994.

Bashiri, Iraj. *Firdowsi's Shahname: 1000 Years After.* Dushanbe, Tajikistan, 1994.

Bennigsen, Alexandre, and S. Enders Wimbush. *The Muslims of the Soviet Empire.* Bloomington: Indiana University Press, 1986.

Soviet Tajik Encyclopedia (Vols. 1-8). Dushanbe, Tajik S.S.R., 1978-88.

Wixman, Ronald. *The Peoples of the USSR: An Ethnographic Handbook.* Armonk, N.Y.: M. E. Sharpe, Inc., 1984.

WEBSITES

World Travel Guide. Tajikistan. [Online] Available http://www.wtgonline.com/country/tj/gen.html, 1998.

Pamiri

PRONUNCIATION: pa-MIR-ee
ALTERNATE NAMES: Mountain Tajiks; Pamirian Tajiks; Pamirtsy
LOCATION: Tajikistan
POPULATION: 120,000
LANGUAGES: East Iranian language variations; Tajik; Russian
RELIGION: Islam (Ismailism and Sunni Muslim)

1 ● INTRODUCTION

The Pamiri people, also called the Pamirian or Mountain Tajiks (*Pamirtsy* in Russian) are made up of seven smaller ethnic groups. They live mostly in Tajikistan.

The Pamiris have never really had their own country. A tiny independent kingdom existed for a short period during the eighth and ninth centuries, however. Pamiri history is marked by conflicts over territory and scarce natural resources. Afghani and Uzbek rulers fought for control over the region where the Pamiris lived throughout the eighteenth and nineteenth centuries. The Russians and the British fought over their lands too. By 1904, Russia had annexed the Pamiri lands from the emir (king) of Bukhara.

After years of war, the Pamiri lands were brought under Soviet rule and in 1925 as part of the province of Tajikistan. Since 1992, independent Tajikistan has been torn by civil war. The Pamiris have played a major role in the fighting.

2 ● LOCATION

Small numbers of Pamiris live in Afghanistan, China, and Pakistan. The vast major-

PAMIRI

0   250   500   750 Miles

0   250 500 750 1000 Kilometers

RUSSIA

KAZAKSTAN

UZBEKISTAN

Zaysan

TURKMENISTAN

Almaty
(Alma-Ata)

Ashkhabad   Tejen   Tashkent   KYRGYSTAN

Dushanbe

IRAN   TAJIKISTAN

AFGHANISTAN   CHINA

Kabul

Zaranj

Saindak   Islamabad

PAKISTAN

Indus

Pasni   New Delhi   NEPAL   BHUTAN

Kathmandu

Arabian   Lakhpat   INDIA
Sea   Dhaka

Surat   BANGLADESH

ity, however, live in a semi-independent area inside Tajikistan. In total, Parmiris number about 120,000. Most live in the high mountain valley of the western Pamirs. These mountains are known as the "Roof of the World" in Persian. They are the second highest in the world after the Himalayas. Several peaks top 20,000 feet (7,000 meters).

Pamiris live close to one another in a small, remote area. On the south side of their territory is the Pyandzh River, separating them from Afghanistan. On the west is Afghanistan, and to the north and east is Tajikistan and Kyrgyzstan. Only two major roads link the Pamiri territory to major centers. They connect Dushanbe and Osh with Afghanistan. Few places in the entire former Soviet Union are as remote as this.

3 ● LANGUAGE

The Pamiris speak East Iranian languages. They are closely related to the modern Persian of Iran, Tajik, and Pashto/Dari (spoken by the majority of Afghanis). Most of these languages are mutually incomprehensible, that is, speakers of one cannot understand speakers of another.

Children are educated in Tajik and Russian. Across international borders, Pamiris communicate in Persian and Dari. Nearly all Parmiris are multilingual.

Some examples of Tajik phrases include: *Turo chi lozim ast?* (What is it that you need?), and *Shumo chi mekhured?* (What would you like to eat?).

4 ● FOLKLORE

Pamiri folklore takes the form of tales, legends, proverbs, and sayings. Heroism relating to bravery in battle and in combatting nature's harsh elements commonly appears in the tales and stories. However, most concrete information about Pamiri folklore generally appears within the context of the greater Tajik folk culture.

5 ● RELIGION

For Pamiris, national pride is strongly based on Islam. They are members of the Ismaili sect, which was spread by the great mystic poet Nasir-i Khoshrow. Ismailism is a secretive branch of Islam. Believers worship Ali, who was the son-in-law of the prophet Muhammad. Although closely related to Shi'ism, Ismailism broke with mainstream Shi'ism in the eighth century AD.

Pamiris do not believe in the need for mosques or clergymen. There are, however, informal houses of prayer and wandering holy men. These people maintain contact with the principal Ismaili center in the world, located in India, whose spiritual leader is the Aga Khan.

Many traditional Pamiri beliefs and rituals relate to agriculture and animal herding. All sorts of beliefs determine when planting and watering may be done. Rituals are connected with the making of bread so that people will be full and satisfied when they eat it. A scarecrow symbolizing an ancient god helps purify the area near piles of wheat. People pour sweets atop the pile and burn sacred grasses around its perimeter. Once the flour is finally made and the first loaf baked, everyone from a given family partakes until they say *bas* (enough). The bread from the first piles of newly threshed grain is known as *basik*.

6 ● MAJOR HOLIDAYS

Pamiris celebrate *Nawruz*. It falls on the vernal equinox (around March 21) and marks the beginning of the Persian new year. Nawruz is celebrated with music, dances, and a great deal of feasting. People generally wear very colorful clothes on this day. They wear new clothes if they have them.

First Furrow marks the beginning of the planting season. People address the saint of farming, known as *Bobo-m-Dekhtona* (Grandpa Farmer). A public feast is held, and people celebrate the origins of irrigation. Another public holiday marks the time in early summer when women take flocks out to be pastured.

7 ● RITES OF PASSAGE

Rites of passage include parties for the circumcision of little boys. Women celebrate a girl's first menstrual period. Other rites include marriages and funerals. Unfortunately, none of these rites are well known. Specific rites of passage for the Pamiris appear to be similar to those of the Tajiks and the people of Afghanistan.

8 ● RELATIONSHIPS

Assalomu alaikum! is the standard way of saying hello. After that, people proceed to ask one another about their families and their work. If told of something unexpected or strange, people are likely to let out a high-pitched "Uhhhhhhhh!" Use of the hands to emphasize and be descriptive is also common. One favorite gesture that all Central Asians use is moving a cupped hand back and forth across the mouth. This signifies going for something to eat.

Spending time with extended family and friends who live nearby is very common. Visiting relatives who have moved away is also routine. Young people do not date. That would be considered immoral. However, young people may meet secretly while out working in the fields or doing chores on behalf of their families. Sex is reserved for marriage.

9 ● LIVING CONDITIONS

As in so many other parts of the former Soviet Union, health standards are declining. This, combined with the Tajik civil war, have made it much harder for people to find food, medicines, and medical treatment. Basic health care is now provided by relief agencies such as the International Red

Cross/Crescent and the France-based *Medecins Sans Frontiers* (Doctors Without Borders).

Most Pamiri villages exist at the triangle of a river delta. Main houses are not arranged on streets. Instead, they stand in fields and orchards. Doors to houses and other farm buildings open inward toward an interior courtyard. Most homes are made of stone with wooden roofs. The roofs are put together with boards and beams.

The standard of living for all Tajiks has decreased markedly since the beginning of the civil war. Conditions for the Pamiris would certainly have been even worse over the past few years had it not been for international aid.

10 ● FAMILY LIFE

Pamiri women traditionally enjoy fewer restrictions than do Tajik women. They participate in public gatherings just like men. They work both outside and inside the home. They were never forced to wear veils, nor were they ever restricted to a particular part of their houses. Still, their work in the household is difficult. Among their specialities are pottery (without potter's wheels) and all aspects of milking and milk product preparation.

In a typical Pamiri household, several extended families live together and cooperate economically. Often all married sons and their families would live in their father's house. Pamiris traditionally married a first or second cousin.

Modern marriages are increasingly based on Koranic law. Members of the groom's family provide all sorts of gifts to ensure an easy start for the newlyweds. Most young women do not marry before the age of eighteen. Weddings are always accompanied by huge parties. According to tradition, the groom goes to the bride's family home to pick her up for the wedding. He is accompanied by a lively band with a flute, clarinet, and drum. The band plays loud music outside the bride's house while they wait for the bride and groom to come out of the bride's home.

Pets are not kept, and even shepherds have no dogs to help them protect their flocks from wolves.

11 ● CLOTHING

Pamiri clothes today are mostly Western. Headwear is important to both men and women. Men wear Central Asian skullcaps (toki). These are often wrapped with thin wool turbans. Women wear either light or heavy woolen kerchiefs and shawls. Summertime kerchiefs are either all white or full of sparkling gold thread. Most clothing is made from cotton or hemp, but Pamiris who can afford to wear white silk.

12 ● FOOD

Until recently, bread was the central food in the Pamiri diet. They ground whatever was available for bread, including peas, millet, and wheat. Pamiris also ate noodle dishes with occasional pieces of mutton, beef, or yak meat. Milk products were common in the form of sour cream and butter from cows and yaks.

For feasts and holidays, the main specialty is boiled meat, which people tend to eat in large quantities because it is so rare. Meat and other dishes are ordinarily consumed with one's fingers. Soups and porridges made from peas or mung beans are eaten with spoons or pieces of bread. A typical breakfast includes bread and butter, and tea, occasionally with honey. Today, Tajik foods are a regular part of the Pamiri diet. Following is a recipe for a typical Tajik dish, "Beef and Peas."

13 ● EDUCATION

Most children finish high school, but very few go on to university or technical schools unless they leave the homeland. Those who do attend university must move to Dushanbe, the Tajik capital. Although parents encourage both boys and girls to finish their required education, they rarely encourage university training. It has little bearing on their lives. Nearly all Pamiris are able to read and write Tajik. A far smaller percentage know Russian. What Russian they do know is from television and radio.

14 ● CULTURAL HERITAGE

Singing accounts for the bulk of Pamiri musical culture. Several types of poetical songs are popular among the Pamiris, including the *lalaik* and *duduvik*. The *zhurni* is a common kind of comic love song.

Pantomime dances accompanied by music, and *bobopirak* satirical dances also take place from time to time. The most common instrument is the guitar-like *rubob*. Literature does not exist, but storytelling is a common pastime.

15 ● EMPLOYMENT

Pamiri work is dominated by collectivized agricultural chores. There are few tasks that are solely the domain of either men or

---

Recipe

Beef and Peas

Ingredients

1½ pounds beef stew meat, cubed
2 onions, chopped
1 pound dried peas, placed in a pot and covered with water to soak overnight
1 bunch green onions, chopped
1 red pepper, chopped
2 cans beef bouillon to serve as accompaniment

Directions

1. Place beef stew meat in a pot. Add water to cover and bring to a boil.
2. Add chopped onion.
3. Drain peas and add to pot.
4. Reduce heat and simmer until meat and peas are tender (approximately one hour).
5. Add salt and pepper and simmer for approximately ten more minutes.
6. During this ten minutes, prepare beef bouillon according to directions to serve with the beef and peas.

Serve, arranging the peas on top of the meat. Garnish with chopped green onions and red pepper. Serve bouillon separately.

---

women. One notable exception is that only women shear sheep and only men shear goats. Women also tend to all of the milking, whereas men act as the shepherds. Women initially take the animals out to pasture.

The few non-agricultural jobs that do exist relate to town life and transportation. Some men and women work in clerical and administrative professions and some as gold miners, power-plant workers, and as long-distance truckers.

The elaborate systems of terraced agriculture practiced in the Pamirs require constant maintenance. The canals must be cleared of rocks and debris, especially after the winter thaw. Farmers must work fast after the snow has melted. People help one another clear the fields of rocks as they dig up and turn the soil over twice.

16 ● SPORTS

Soccer was introduced to the Pamiris relatively recently, along with other sports, such as basketball and volleyball. Traditionally, women play a ball game with a roll of tightly wound wool. Slingshots, tag, bow and arrow competitions, and polo are all favorites. Polo is played by two teams with up to forty people total. Players use long makeshift sticks and a wooden ball.

17 ● RECREATION

A relatively small number of these isolated people own televisions. Those who do are exposed to world culture via Russian television stations. Movie theaters exist in all of the major settlements, including Khorog and Ishkashim. These serve to broaden people's perspective on the world "below them." Much of popular culture today is dominated by grade-B karate movies and violent American films.

18 ● CRAFTS AND HOBBIES

Pamiris historically produced textiles made of wool and imported cotton. Vertical looms were employed for crafting the *palas*—a local rug. Smiths and metalworkers made decorative jewelry. Millstones were another craft item made by the Pamiris for their water-driven grain mills. Pamiris are respected for their wooden containers and pots, particularly for large serving plates. Women make fine pottery from a unique gray clay that they strengthen by tempering with goat hair. Men create textile threads by spinning and weaving yak and goat hair. Women make heavy socks from camel and sheep hair.

19 ● SOCIAL PROBLEMS

The Tajik civil war has destroyed thousands of lives and ruined any chance for national economic growth. Social problems are substantial. The human rights situation of the Pamiris has deteriorated greatly. They are often suspected of being criminals from organized gangs. The Tajik and Russian armies have dealt with many Pamiri communities severely. Civil rights have also become a casualty of war. Social problems involving drugs and alcoholism have become prevalent. The vast majority of the Pamiri population is poor and in desperate need of international food relief, medicine, jobs, and reconstruction. This area was always one of the poorest in the Soviet Union.

20 ● BIBLIOGRAPHY

Friedrich, Paul, and Norma Diamond, ed. *Encyclopedia of World Cultures*. Vol. VI, Russia and Eurasia/China. Boston: G. K. Hall, 1994.

Olson, James S., ed. *An Ethnohistorical Dictionary of the Russian and Soviet Empires*. Westport, Conn.: Greenwood Press, 1994.

WEBSITES

World Travel Guide. Tajikistan. [Online] Available http://www.wtgonline.com/country/tj/gen.html, 1998.

Tanzania

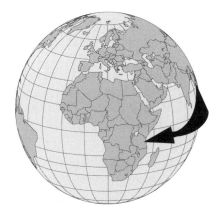

The people of Tanzania are called Tanzanians. Approximately 95 percent of Tanzanians may be roughly classified as Bantu peoples (including the Shambaa). Other major groups include the Nyamwezi, Chagga, Swahili, Maasai, Makonde, and Haya. The inhabitants of Zanzibar and Pemba are mostly descendants of mainland Africans or are of mixed African and Arab ancestry. Among non-Africans, there are about 70,000 Arabs, 40,000 Asians, and 10,000 Europeans in Tanzania.

Tanzanians

PRONUNCIATION: tan-zuh-NEE-uhns
LOCATION: Tanzania
POPULATION: 30.3 million
LANGUAGE: Swahili; English; Arabic; 130 indigenous languages
RELIGION: Islam; Christianity; indigenous beliefs

1 ● INTRODUCTION

The United Republic of Tanzania, or *Jamhuri ya Mwungano wa Tanzania,* includes the mainland of Tanganyika, Zanzibar, and some offshore islands. Zanzibar and the coast have a long history of lucrative trading, which Arabs, Europeans, and Africans each have attempted to control. In 1840, the Sultan of Omani established his capital in Zanzibar. From there the caravan trade brought the Swahili language and Islam into the hinterlands as far as what is now the eastern part of the Democratic Republic of the Congo. In 1885, the Germans gained control of Tanzania. After World War I, Germany ceded control to the British, who ruled until 1946. The United Nations made Tanzania a trust territory under British rule after 1946.

Anti-colonial sentiment grew as the British administration favored white settlers and immigrant farmers. In 1929, Tanzanians formed the Tanganyika African Association. Julius Nyerere transformed it into the Tang-

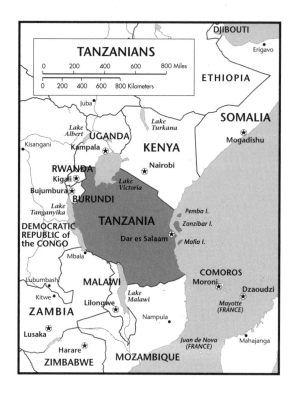

TANZANIANS

| 0 | 200 | 400 | 600 | 800 Miles |
| 0 | 200 | 400 | 600 | 800 Kilometers |

2 ● LOCATION

Tanzania is about twice the size of the state of California. The mainland includes 854 miles (1,374 kilometers) of coastline on the Indian Ocean. Tanzania's climate and topography are varied. The highest point in Africa is at the summit of Mount Kilimanjaro, and the lowest point is at the floor of Lake Tanganyika. Temperatures range from tropical to temperate. Sporadic rainfall makes agricultural and livestock production unpredictable.

Tanzania's physical and climatic variation is rivaled by its ethnic and cultural diversity. Its peoples belong to more than 120 ethnic groups. Tanzania is one of Africa's most populous countries. Most of the population is rural.

3 ● LANGUAGE

Each of the ethnic groups has its own language, giving Tanzania over 130 living languages. Unlike most African countries, Tanzania successfully adopted a single African language for purposes of national unity. Swahili (or KiSwahili) originated on the coast and became the lingua franca (common language) for much of East Africa. It is now the language of instruction in secondary education and in some universities. It is also used in literature, and as a second language by people in rural areas. The media use Swahili in television, radio, and newspapers. English is the official primary language of administration, commerce, and higher education. Arabic is widely spoken on Zanzibar Island.

anyika African National Union in 1954. Nyerere became prime minister in May 1961. On December 9, 1961, Tanzania gained full independence.

After independence, Tanzania embarked on an ambitious, large-scale project of national self-reliance. Led by Nyerere, the government promoted *ujamaa* (family villages), with the goal of bringing scattered families together in cooperatives. Although ujamaa made it easier to organize rural development, it did not achieve the lofty economic goals envisioned. Indeed, the World Bank classifies Tanzania as the second poorest country in the world, after Mozambique.

A newspaper written in Swahili, the common language for most of east Africa.

4 ● FOLKLORE

No one is more highly revered than Tanzania's founder and first president (of independent Tanganyika) Julius Kambarage Nyerere (b.1922). However, ancient heroes were not necessarily chiefs and rulers. The experts in ceremonial rituals in the Maasai tribe, for example, believe themselves to be descended from a boy with magical powers. According to legend, Maasai warriors found the young child naked and seemingly abandoned on a mountaintop, and they decided to adopt him. They observed that he had the power to make springs gush forth, grass grow, and pools of water appear. Even in times of famine, his cattle were always well fed and fat.

In many Tanzanian ethnic groups, heroes are illustrious ancestors who distinguished themselves by their valor, intelligence, or generosity. Younger generations are expected to measure up to these role models.

5 ● RELIGION

Most Tanzanians profess Islam or Christianity. However, indigenous beliefs remain prevalent in custom and culture. The mainland is divided equally between Muslims, Christians, and those professing a form of indigenous belief (which usually includes the Muslim/Christian notion of a high god). Zanzibar is 99 percent Muslim.

6 ● MAJOR HOLIDAYS

Tanzanians remember President Ali Hassan Mwinyi (b.1925) for restoring several holidays in the country. Among the secular (nonreligious) holidays are Labor Day (May 1), Zanzibar Revolution Day (January 12); *Nane Nane* (formerly *Saba Saba*—Farmer's Day, in August); Independence Day (December 9); and Union Day (April 26), which commemorates the unification of Zanzibar and the mainland. Depending on their faith, Tanzanians also celebrate New Year's Day, Christmas, Easter, the prophet Muhammad's birthday, and the beginning and end of Ramadan. As a rule, Christian and Muslim friends invite each other to help celebrate their religious holidays.

7 ● RITES OF PASSAGE

Tanzanians of all ethnic backgrounds participate in rites of passage. The form and content of rites vary according to tribal group and religious faith. For example, to the Maasai, all of life is seen as a conquest. Young boys leave home early to watch the calves, then the cows and other cattle. Their mission is to learn to conquer fear. They soon are left on their own, protecting their herds from lions and other wild beasts.

Circumcision or excision (female circumcision) follows. (Female circumcision is often referred to by outsiders as "female genital mutilation" and has become an international human rights issue.) This most important rite decides the self-control and bravery of the child in becoming an adult. The successful male initiate receives gifts of cattle, and the female feels prepared to undergo whatever pain childbearing entails.

8 ● RELATIONSHIPS

People place much importance on greetings because they denote politeness, respect, and relationship in Tanzania. The type of greeting offered may depend on someone's status. A generic but common Swahili greeting among friends is *Ujambo, habari gani?* (Good morning, what is your news?).

Dating and marriage in Tanzania differ considerably from European and American customs. Western-style dating is uncommon, especially in the rural areas. In the villages, young people choose their spouses, but their families help arrange the marriage.

9 ● LIVING CONDITIONS

Most Tanzanians have little discretionary income after purchasing necessities, and perhaps buying a couple of rounds at the local pub. Living conditions for rural people are rudimentary. Malnutrition and tropical diseases such as malaria, schistosomiasis, and sleeping sickness are widespread. Open sewers, latrines, and uncovered garbage piles breed flies, which carry disease. In the villages, many people draw their water from contaminated streams, lakes, and pools. Electricity and running water exist in towns,

Cory Langley

Children are required to attend primary school for seven years. In order to enter secondary school, students must pass an exam.

but often houses are poorly ventilated and crowded.

10 ● FAMILY LIFE

Tanzanian women enjoy greater social freedom than in Muslim countries to the north. This is a direct result of government policies aimed at improving the status of women. Women vote, and many produce goods for market, engage in trade, and keep some of their earnings. A marriage law in the 1970s superseded customary and Islamic law, and gave women far more latitude in divorce, remarriage, and inheritance matters.

Women represent wealth to their families. In Tanzania the groom's family must reimburse the bride's family for the loss of the young woman. Compensation usually consists of giving gifts or a symbolic sum of money to her parents, grandparents, brothers-in-law, and cousins.

11 ● CLOTHING

In rural regions, Muslim men usually wear a long embroidered cotton gown, called a *kanzu,* with a matching skull cap. Muslim women often wear a *kanga* consisting of brightly colored fabric wrapped around them and covering their head. On the island of Zanzibar and along the mainland coast, Muslim women wear *buibui,* a black veiled shawl, and *chador* (veils), which allow them to go out while avoiding male scrutiny of their physical beauty. Few women wear more jewelry than the Maasai, who adorn themselves with elaborate beaded earrings, necklace bands, rings, and headbands.

In urban areas, Western-style clothing is common. Shorts, miniskirts, and revealing clothing are considered indecent and are avoided.

12 ● FOOD

The most popular rural staple is *ugali,* a stiff dough made of cassava flour, cornmeal, millet, or sorghum. The coastal people prefer rice as a staple, while plantains are consumed daily in the north. Ugali is eaten with a stew of fish, vegetables, or meat from a communal bowl. Tanzanians generally are fond of goat meat, chicken, and lamb. *Pilau* is a delicious dish of rice spiced with curry, cinnamon, cumin, hot peppers, and cloves.

Eating customs vary according to ethnic group and religious beliefs. Some groups have food taboos (prohibitions), while others have taboos regarding who may eat at the same table. The Maasai diet is unique in that it consists of only six foods: meat, milk, blood, animal fat, tree bark, and honey.

13 ● EDUCATION

Tanzanian education received special emphasis under President Nyerere, an educator by profession. Self-reliance and *ujamaa* (family village) programs raised the literacy (ability to read and write) rate to over 80 percent. Literacy programs also aimed to raise consciousness about hygiene, agriculture, crafts, basic math, and personal achievement.

Children are required to attend primary school for seven years. In order to enter secondary school, students are required to pass an exam. In recent years literacy and schooling have suffered from budget cuts.

14 ● CULTURAL HERITAGE

Tanzania has a rich oral and written literature in Swahili. Film is less developed, but filmmaker Flora M'mbugu-Schelling's prize-winning films in Swahili portray significant social issues facing Tanzanian women. Tanzania's major music contribution is its Swahili, Arab-influenced classical music tradition. Many fine composers and musicians produce this unique blend of African-Arab-Indian sound.

In art, Tanzanians produce many fine pieces of jewelry and carved ivory, some to be marketed to tourists. Artists excel most in refined wood sculpture. African art is preoccupied with the human figure and with humanity's moral and spiritual concerns.

15 ● EMPLOYMENT

Most Tanzanians (90 percent) make their living in agriculture, though only 5 percent of the land is arable (farmable). Many people cultivate small field plots with traditional African hoes and without the benefit of irrigation. In some areas, extremely fertile soils produce coffee, tea, and pyrethrum (used in making insecticides). Other cash crops include sisal, cotton, tobacco, cashews, fruits, and cloves. Industry is important, but employs few people. Industry mainly consists of the processing of sugar, beer, cigarettes, sisal twine, and light consumer goods. Some diamond and gold mining exists.

Many Tanzanians look for ways to augment their wages with income in the informal sector. For example, street vendors sell anything from watches to clothing.

16 ● SPORTS

In rural areas, sports may still be regarded as pastimes for foreigners and "lazy" urbanites. Hauling water, tending herds, gathering firewood, cooking meals, caring for children, and mending huts leave little time for leisure. This attitude is changing among young people. In the 1990s, Tanzania produced world-class runners. Soccer and boxing are popular as well. Big-game hunting is almost exclusively a sport for foreign tourists. The locals see it as a business and means of income.

17 ● RECREATION

Tanzanians love music and dancing, storytelling, and socializing at coffee houses and at home. Visiting friends is an important social custom. Young people with spare time enjoy checkers and cards. On the coast, people play *mbao,* a board game that uses small stones. Women dance the *chakacha* at celebrations and marriages. Tanzanians are fond of action-packed martial arts and kung fu films. Movies made in India are also popular.

18 ● CRAFTS AND HOBBIES

Tanzanians produce many arts and crafts of high quality. The Zaramo on the outskirts of Dar es Salaam (in east Tanzania) produce conventional figures of Maasai warriors, elderly men, nude women, and carved walking sticks. They carve these using only hand tools. Meerschaum pipe-carving (pipes with heavily carved bowls) is also one of Tanzania's international trademarks. Besides the tourist market, the Nyamwezi in former times carved thrones for their chiefs. The Maasai make shields with intricate geometric designs. Zanzibar doorways, decorated with geometric patterns, offer a glimpse of the island's Arabic history and tradition.

19 ● SOCIAL PROBLEMS

Tanzania is one of the world's poorest countries. Consequently, people are left to solve their own social problems. In the 1980s and 1990s, government services were cut back, leading to a rise in illiteracy, health risks for rural mothers and children, and neglect of roads. Men now look for work in South Africa, leaving their wives as the sole family provider. Many girls leave school early to find work or help the family. As conditions deteriorate in rural areas, urbanization speeds up. Squatter villages surround Dar es Salaam, adding to water pollution and unsanitary conditions. Large influxes of Mozambican, Rwandan, and Burundian refugees have put added stress on Tanzania's natural and financial resources.

20 ● BIBLIOGRAPHY

Africa on File. New York: Facts on File, 1995.

Africa South of the Sahara. 26th ed. London, England: Europa Publications Limited, 1997.

Heale, Jay. *Tanzania*. Tarrytown, N.Y.: Marshall Cavendish Corp., 1998.

Houston, Dick. *Safari Adventure*. New York: Cobblehill Books, 1991.

Lauri, Jason. *Tanzania*. Chicago: Children's Press, 1994.

Margolies, Barbara A. *Rehema's Journey*. New York: Scholastic, 1990.

McCulla, Patricia E. *Tanzania*. New York: Chelsea House, 1989.

Weber, Valerie, and Tom Pelnar, eds. *Tanzania*. Milwaukee: G. Stevens Children's Books, 1989.

WEBSITES

Africa Online. Tanzania. [Online] Available http://www.africaonline.co.tz/AfricaOnline/aboutz/page4.html, 1997.

Interknowledge Corp. Tanzania. [Online] Available http://www.geographia.com/tanzania/, 1998.

Internet Africa Ltd. Tanzania. [Online] Available http://www.africanet.com/africanet/country/tanzania/, 1998.

Southern African Development Community. [Online] Available http://www.sadc-usa.net/members/tanzania/, 1998.

World Travel Guide. Tanzania. [Online] Available http://www.wtgonline.com/country/tz/gen.html, 1998.

Chagga

PRONUNCIATION: CHAH-guh

ALTERNATE NAMES: Chaga, Waschagga, Jagga, or Dschagga

LOCATION: Kilimanjaro region in northern Tanzania

POPULATION: 832,420

LANGUAGE: Kichagga; Swahili

RELIGION: Christianity; Islam

1 ● INTRODUCTION

On the southern slopes of Mount Kilimanjaro, Africa's highest mountain, live the Chagga people. They are also called Chaga, Waschagga, Jagga, or Dschagga.

Traditionally, the Chagga belonged to different clans (groups of people of common descent) ruled by *mangis* (chiefs). The area was divided into independent chiefdoms. The chiefs sometimes warred with each other. Other times, they formed alliances to try to increase their power. After Tanzania won its independence in 1961, the system of chiefdoms was abolished throughout the country.

2 ● LOCATION

Mount Kilimanjaro has two peaks, Kibo and Mawenzi. Vegetation on the mountain is varied. The lowest plains form the bushland, where maize (corn), thatch grass, and fodder (miscellaneous plants to feed farm animals) are grown. Next lies the coffee and banana belt. Each Chagga family has its own homestead in the middle of a banana grove. This is known as a *kihamba* (the plural of this word is *vihamba*).

The Chagga population rose steadily from 128,000 in the 1920s to over 800,000 in the 1990s. Overpopulation has forced some Chagga people to move to the lowlands and to urban areas.

3 ● LANGUAGE

The main language spoken by the Chagga people is Kichagga. It has various dialects spoken by Chagga in different regions. Despite these differences in dialect, the Chagga people can understand each another.

Almost all Chagga people also speak KiSwahili, the national language in Tanzania. KiSwahili is the language of instruction in primary schools and is used in the workplace. English is the language of instruction in secondary schools and institutions of higher learning.

4 ● FOLKLORE

Chagga legends center on *Ruwa* and his power and assistance. Ruwa is the Chagga name for their god, as well as the Chagga word for "sun." Ruwa is not looked upon as the creator of humankind, but rather as a liberator and provider of sustenance. He is known for his mercy and tolerance when sought by his people. Some Chagga myths concerning Ruwa resemble biblical stories of the Old Testament.

In the past, chiefdoms had chiefs who rose to power through war and trading. Some famous past chiefs include Orombo from Kishigonyi, Sina of Kibosho, and Marealle of Marangu.

5 ● RELIGION

Christianity was introduced to the Chagga people in the middle of the nineteenth century. By the end of the nineteenth century, both Protestants and Catholics had established missions in the region. With the adoption of Western religions, traditional Chagga beliefs and practices have been reduced or adapted to the new Christian beliefs.

Islam was introduced to the Chagga people by early Swahili caravan traders. Islam brought a sense of fellowship not only with the Chagga of different regions, but also with Muslims of other ethnic groups.

6 ● MAJOR HOLIDAYS

The Chagga people celebrate both secular (nonreligious) and religious holidays. The main government holidays are New Year's Day (January 1), Union Day (April 26), Workers' Day (May 1), Peasants' Day (August 8), and Independence Day (December 9). Offices and shops close on these holidays. Government rallies, held around the country, include military parades and speeches.

The major religious holidays of both Christianity and Islam are celebrated. The major Christian holidays are Easter weekend and Christmas. The major Muslim holidays are *Eid al-Fitr* and *Eid al-Adha*. Eid al-Fitr is a three-day celebration that comes after a month of fasting called Ramadan. Eid al-Adha commemorates the willingness of Abraham to obey God's command and sacrifice his son Isaac. After religious ceremonies are over, families gather for celebration and merrymaking.

7 ● RITES OF PASSAGE

A Chagga proverb that translates directly as "He who leaves a child lives eternally" illustrates the Chagga belief that people live through their descendents. Children are taught to do small chores around the homestead as soon as they can walk. Girls' duties include grinding corn and cleaning out cattle stalls. The boys' main duty is to herd cattle. A rite called *Kisusa* is carried out when a child is about twelve years old. This rite is performed to curb unruliness in a child. An elder woman and already initiated youths sing songs about good morals and talk to the initiate about good behavior. This is followed by sacrifice of a goat and, one month later, by a purification ceremony.

In the past, both young men and young women were circumcised. Female circumcision is now discouraged.

Traditionally, before male youth were allowed to marry, the *Ngasi* (male initiation) ceremony, took place. A young man went to live in the forest. He received instruction in manhood, went hunting, and endured various ordeals. The *Shija* (female initiation) ceremony was performed after the young women were circumcised. All initiated young women were instructed in Chagga rituals, sexuality, procreation, and menstruation. Initiation ceremonies were abolished by the Germans, who controlled Tanzania from 1885 to 1946.

8 ● RELATIONSHIPS

Greetings are important in Chagga culture. There are different greetings depending upon the time of day. Younger people are required to show respect to the older generations. It is believed that the more senior a person is, the closer his or her contact with ancestors.

Specific behavioral norms are maintained between various persons in Chagga society. These are based on a show of respect, non-hostility, or distance. A newlywed woman covers her head and squats in the presence of her father-in-law, thereby showing respect to and distance from him. The father-in-law is similarly required to avoid the daughter-in-law. A wife is required to always face her husband on approach lest she be accused of cursing him.

Public show of affection through bodily contact between the sexes is considered highly inappropriate. Traditionally, men and women were socially segregated.

9 ● LIVING CONDITIONS

The traditional Chagga house was cone-shaped, with a roof thatched with dried grass. Another type of dwelling, also commonly built, was a house with a roof thatched with banana leaves. Because these houses tended to be large, they were built with the assistance of other villagers.

By the end of the nineteenth century, Swahili houses were introduced, initially constructed by chiefs. These houses were rectangular, with walls made of wattle (interwoven sticks) and mud, and thatched roofs. Today, these houses are more commonly built with cement walls and corrugated metal roofs.

10 ● FAMILY LIFE

Traditionally, the Chagga marriage ceremony was a long process, starting with betrothal proceedings and continuing long after the couple was married. Bridal payments were made over the wife's lifetime. Today, Christian couples are married in churches. There is much drinking and feasting throughout the marriage negotiations and celebrations.

The groom builds the house where he will live with his wife after marriage. After the birth of the first child, the husband moves into a *tenge* (hut), and the mother lives with her children. Chagga couples have an average of six children. Great importance is placed on having a son to continue the lineage.

11 ● CLOTHING

Traditionally, Chagga clothing was made of cowhide. With contact with the outside world, the Chagga started to wear imported bead ornaments and cloth wraparound garments. These colorful pieces of cloth are called *kangas* and *kitenges*. They may be worn over a dress, or may be used to carry babies on the back or hip.

School-aged boys wear shorts, but adults (both male and female) and young women generally do not wear shorts in public except during sports. *Mitumba* (secondhand clothing from overseas) is sold at the marketplace and is in great demand by low-income people.

12 ● FOOD

The staple food of the Chagga people is bananas. Bananas are also used to make beer, their main beverage. The Chagga plant a variety of food crops, including bananas, millet, maize (corn), beans, and cassava. They also keep cattle, goats, and sheep. Due to limited land holdings and grazing areas, most Chagga people today are forced to purchase meat from butcher shops.

Pregnant women eat a diet of milk, sweet potatoes, fat, yams, and butter; these are considered female foods. Bananas and beer are considered male and are not to be eaten by pregnant women.

13 ● EDUCATION

The initial classroom education available to the Chagga was in the Christian missions. Boys often outnumbered girls in the education facilities because education was not considered as important for girls. After Tanzania's independence, all Chagga people were encouraged to attend at least primary level education. By 1971 primary education was provided free by the government. All children seven years of age and older were required to attend primary level education for at least seven years. Those who passed a qualifying examination went on to secondary education. Private secondary schools, trade schools, and business schools are also available.

14 ● CULTURAL HERITAGE

Traditional Chagga instruments include wooden flutes, bells, and drums. Dancing and singing are part of almost every celebration. With exposure to other ethnic groups and Western culture, the Chagga have shown a liking for various types of music. These include Swahili songs produced by various Tanzanian bands, and West and Central African music and dance forms. Reggae, pop, and rap are popular with the youth.

Cory Langley

Bananas are an important part of the Chagga diet. Here a vendor sells bananas from his bike.

The Chagga have rich oral traditions and have managed to record most of their history. They have many legends and songs. Proverbs are used to guide youth and convey wisdom.

15 ● EMPLOYMENT

Traditionally, Chagga work has been centered on the farm and is divided by gender. Men's work includes feeding goats, building and maintaining canals, preparing fields, slaughtering animals, and building houses. Women's work includes firewood and water collection, fodder cutting, cooking, and cleaning the homestead and stalls.

Women are also in charge of trading in the marketplace.

Many Chagga young people work as clerks, teachers, and administrators, and many engage in small-scale business activities. Women in rural areas are also generating income through activities such as crafts and tailoring. The Chagga are known for their sense of enterprise and strong work ethic.

16 ● SPORTS

Chagga children first encounter sporting events at school. Primary school children are encouraged to participate in interschool competitions that often lead to interregional and national championships. Favorite sports at school are soccer, netball (similar to basketball), and athletics (track and field). At secondary schools, Chagga youth may be exposed to sports such as basketball, table tennis, and volleyball.

Following the national soccer league is a pastime greatly enjoyed by the Chagga. On the weekends, proper and makeshift soccer fields alike are crowded with both spectators and players.

17 ● RECREATION

For many years there were no television stations in Tanzania. Radio broadcasts were a major source of entertainment. Many households have transistor radios, and a favorite pastime is listening to radio plays and sports programs. On occasions of major broadcasts and matches, the Chagga often gather around a radio in a public meeting place, usually with a local brew in hand.

In the past, only the wealthy Chagga could afford television sets. Now many Chagga people own televisions and VCRs. This has led to the opening of many video lending libraries in the town of Moshi.

18 ● CRAFTS AND HOBBIES

Traditionally, the Chagga made their own utensils, mainly from wood. These items included small bowls, huge beer tubs, spoons, and ladles. Iron items included bells, ornaments, hoes, and spears. The Chagga also made their own weapons and animal traps. Chagga musical instruments include wooden flutes, bells, and drums. Basket weaving was also common. This art is now dying out as more items are bought at local stores.

19 ● SOCIAL PROBLEMS

Tanzania has undergone a period of economic hardship, limiting the government's ability to provide adequate social services. Public schools and health facilities are run down. As a result, many private schools and health facilities have opened in the Kilimanjaro region.

Lack of adequate farm land is forcing Chagga youth to seek work away from the *kihamba* (family homestead). This has led to a breakdown in social values and an increase in sexual promiscuity. An increasing number of children are born out of wedlock. The occurrence of sexually transmitted diseases, especially AIDS, has risen. AIDS awareness programs have been initiated to help deal with the problem. Loss of Chagga culture is another consequence of outside contact.

The political scene has changed in Tanzania from a single party in 1965 to multiparty politics in 1992. This has encouraged more Chagga to be politically active. There is an increasing cohesion of the Chagga people along party lines and a renewed sense of cultural identity.

20 ● BIBLIOGRAPHY

Heale, Jay. *Tanzania.* Tarrytown, N.Y.: Marshall Cavendish Corp., 1998.

Houston, Dick. *Safari Adventure.* New York: Cobblehill Books, 1991.

Kaula, Edna Mason. *The Land and People of Tanzania.* Philadelphia: Lippincott, 1972.

Margolies, Barbara A. *Rehema's Journey.* New York: Scholastic, 1990.

McCulla, Patricia E. *Tanzania.* New York: Chelsea House, 1989.

Reader, John. *Kilimanjaro.* New York: Universal Books, 1982.

Weber, Valerie, and Tom Pelnar, eds. *Tanzania.*

Milwaukee: G. Stevens Children's Books, 1989.

WEBSITES

Africa Online. Tanzania. [Online] Available http://www.africaonline.co.tz/AfricaOnline/aboutz/page4.html, 1997.

Interknowledge Corp. Tanzania. [Online] Available httpt://www.geographia.com/tanzania/, 1998.

Internet Africa Ltd. Tanzania. [Online] Available http://www.africanet.com/africanet/country/tanzania/, 1998.

Southern African Development Community. [Online] Available http://www.sadc-usa.net/members/tanzania/, 1998.

World Travel Guide. Tanzania. [Online] Available http://www.wtgonline.com/country/tz/gen.html, 1998.

Maasai

PRONUNCIATION: MAH-sigh
LOCATION: Kenya; Tanzania
POPULATION: Over 150,000
LANGUAGE: Maa (Olmaa)
RELIGION: Traditional beliefs

1 ● INTRODUCTION

The Maasai are thought of as the typical cattle herders of Africa, yet they have not always been herders, nor are they all today. Because of population growth, development strategies, and the resulting shortage of land, cattle raising is in decline. However, cattle still represent "the breath of life" for many Maasai. When given the chance, they choose herding above all other livelihoods. For many Westerners, the Maasai are Hollywood's "noble savage"—fierce, proud, handsome, graceful of bearing, and elegantly tall. Hair smeared red with ochre (a pigment), they either carry spears or stand on one foot tending cattle. These depictions oversimplify Maasai life during the twentieth century. Today, Maasai cattle herders may also be growing maize (corn) or wheat, rearing Guinea fowl, raising ostriches, or may be hired by ecologists to take pictures of the countryside.

Prior to British colonization, Africans, Arabs, and European explorers considered the Maasai formidable warriors for their conquests of neighboring peoples and their resistance to slavery. Caravan traders traveling from the coast to Uganda crossed Maasailand with trepidation. However, in 1880–81, when the British unintentionally introduced rinderpest (a cattle disease), the Maasai lost 80 percent of their stock. The British colonizers further disrupted Maasai life by moving them to a reserve in southern Kenya. While the British encouraged them to adopt European ways, they also advised them to retain their traditions. These contradictions resulted, for the most part, in leaving the Maasai alone and allowed them to develop almost on their own. However, drought, famine, cattle diseases, and intratribal warfare (warfare among themselves) in the nineteenth century greatly weakened the Maasai and nearly destrtoyed certain tribes.

Since Kenyan and Tanzanian independence from Britain in the 1960s, land ownership has changed dramatically. Modern ranching, wheat cultivation techiques, and setting of grazing boundaries in the Maasai district are becoming common. A wage and cash economy is replacing the barter (trade) system. Consequently, the Maasai have begun to integrate themselves into the modern economies and mainstream societies of Kenya and Tanzania, albeit with considerable reluctance.

2 ● LOCATION

The Maasai are thought to have originated in the Upper Nile Valley. Their myths speak about climbing up from a broad and deep crater bounded on all sides by a steep, long cliff. By the 1600s they had begun migrating with their herds into the vast arid, savanna-like (grassland) region of East Africa straddling the Kenya-Tanzania border. Today, their homeland is bounded by Lake Victoria to the west and Mount Kilimanjaro to the east. Maasailand extends some 310 miles (500 kilometers) from north to south and about 186 miles (300 kilometers) at its widest east-west point.

Estimates of the Maasai population include more than 150,000 in Tanzania, and close to 150,000 in Kenya.

3 ● LANGUAGE

The Maasai are speakers of the Maa language, which is also spoken by the Samburu and the Chamus living in central Kenya. The origins of Maa have been traced to the east of present-day Juba in southern Sudan. More than twenty variants of Maa exist. The Maasai refer to their language as Olmaa.

4 ● FOLKLORE

Maasai legends and folktales tell much about the origin of present-day Maasai beliefs. These stories include their ascent from a crater, the emergence of the first Maasai prophet-magician (Laibon), the killing of an evil giant (Oltatuani) who raided Maasai herds, and the deception by Olonana of his father to obtain the blessing reserved for his older brother, Senteu (a legend similar to the Biblical story of Jacob and Esau).

One origin myth reveals much about present-day Maasai relations between the sexes. It holds that the Maasai are descended from two equal and complementary tribes, one consisting strictly of females, and the other of males. The women's tribe, the Moroyok, raised antelopes, including the eland, which the Maasai claim to have been the first species of cattle. Instead of cattle, sheep, and goats, the women had herds of gazelles. Zebras transported their goods during migrations, and elephants were their devoted friends, tearing down branches and bringing them to the women who used them to build homes and corrals. The elephants also swept the antelope corrals clean. However, while the women bickered and quarreled, their herds escaped. Even the elephants left them because they could not satisfy the women with their work.

According to the same myth, the Morwak—the men's tribe—raised cattle, sheep, and goats. The men occasionally met women in the forest. The children from these unions would live with their mothers, but the boys would join their fathers when they grew up. When the women lost their herds, they went to live with the men, and, in doing so, gave up their freedom and their equal status. From that time, they depended on men, had to work for them, and were subject to their authority.

5 ● RELIGION

Unlike the predominantly Christian populations of Kenya and Tanzania that surround them, the Maasai traditionally place themselves at the center of their universe as God's chosen people. Like other African religions, the Maasai believe that one high god (Enkai) created the world, forming three groups of people. The first were the Torrobo (Okiek pygmies), a hunting and gathering people of small stature to whom God gave honey and wild animals as a food source. The second were the neighboring Kikuyu, farmers to whom God gave seed and grain. The third were the Maasai, to whom God gave cattle, which came to earth sliding down a long rope linking heaven and Earth. While the Torrobo were destined to endure bee stings, and the Kikuyu famines and floods, the Maasai received the noble gift of raising cattle. A Torrobo, jealous of the Maasai's gift of cattle, cut the "umbilical cord" between heaven and Earth. For many Maasai, the center of their world remains their cattle, which furnish food, clothing, and shelter.

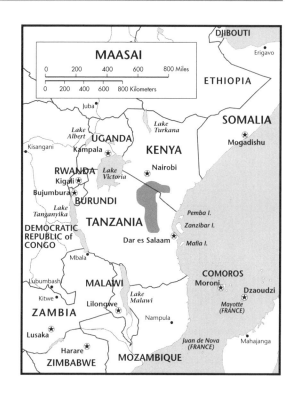

6 ● MAJOR HOLIDAYS

The traditional Maasai calendar has no designated holidays. It is divided into twelve months belonging to three main seasons: *Nkokua* (the long rains), *Oloirurujuruj* (the drizzling season), and *Oltumuret* (the short rains). The names of months are very descriptive. For example, the second month of the drizzling season is *Kujorok*, meaning "The whole countryside is beautifully green, and the pasture lands are likened to a hairy caterpillar."

Maasai ceremonial feasts for circumcision, excision (female circumcision), and marriage offer occasions for festive community celebrations, which may be considered similar to holidays. As the Maasai are integrated into modern Kenyan and Tanzanian life, they also participate in secular (nonreligious) state holidays. In Kenya, these include Labor Day (May 1), Madaraka Day (June 1), and Kenyatta Day (October 20). In Tanzania, these include Labor Day (May 1), Zanzibar Revolution Day (January 12); *Nane Nane* (formerly *Saba Saba*—Farmer's Day, in August); Independence Day (December 9); and Union Day (April 26), which commemorates the unification of Zanzibar and the mainland.

7 ● RITES OF PASSAGE

Life for the Maasai is a series of conquests and tests involving the endurance of pain. For men, there is a progression from childhood to warriorhood to elderhood. At the age of four, a child's lower incisors are taken out with a knife. Young boys test their will by their arms and legs with hot coals. As they grow older, they submit to tattooing on the stomach and the arms, enduring hundreds of small cuts into the skin.

Ear piercing for both boys and girls comes next. The cartilage of the upper ear is pierced with hot iron. When this heals, a hole is cut in the ear lobe and gradually enlarged by inserting rolls of leaves or balls made of wood or mud. Nowadays plastic film canisters may serve this purpose. The bigger the hole, the better. Those earlobes that dangle to the shoulders are considered perfect.

Circumcision (for boys) and excision (for girls) is the next stage, and the most important event in a young Maasai's life. It is a father's ultimate duty to ensure that his children undergo this rite. The family invites relatives and friends to witness the ceremonies, which may be held in special villages called *imanyat*. The imanyat dedicated to circumcision of boys are called *nkang oo ntaritik* (villages of little birds).

Circumcision itself involves great physical pain and tests a youth's courage. If they flinch during the act, boys bring shame and dishonor to themselves and their family. At a minimum, the members of their age group ridicule them and they pay a fine of one head of cattle. However, if a boy shows great bravery, he receives gifts of cattle and sheep.

Girls must endure an even longer and more painful ritual, which is considered preparation for childbearing. (Girls who become pregnant before excision are banished from the village and stigmatized throughout their lives.) After passing this test of courage, women say they are afraid of nothing.

Guests celebrate the successful completion of these rites by drinking great quantities of mead (a fermented beverage containing honey) and dancing. Boys are then ready to become warriors, and girls are then ready to bear a new generation of warriors. In a few months, the young woman's future husband will come to pick her up and take her to live with his family.

After passing the tests of childhood and circumcision, boys must fulfill a civic requirement similar to military service. They live for up to several months in the bush, where they learn to overcome pride, egotism, and selfishness. They share their most prized possessions, their cattle, with other members of the community. However, they must also spend time in the village, where they sacrifice their cattle for ceremonies and offer gifts of cattle to new households. This stage of development matures a warrior and teaches him *nkaniet* (respect for others), and he learns how to contribute to the welfare of his community. The stage of "young warriorhood" ends with the *eunoto* rite, when a man ends his periodic trips into the bush and returns to his village, putting his acquired wisdom to use for the good of the community.

8 ● RELATIONSHIPS

Each child belongs to an "age set" from birth. To control the vices of pride, jealousy, and selfishness, children must obey the rules governing relationships within the age set, between age sets, and between the sexes. Warriors, for example, must share a girlfriend with at least one of their age-group companions. All Maasai of the same sex are considered equal within their age group.

Many tensions exist between children and adults, elders and warriors, and men and women. The Maasai control these with taboos (prohibitions). A daughter, for example, must not be present while her father is eating. Only non-excised girls may accompany warriors into their forest havens, where they eat meat. Although the younger warriors may wish to dominate their communities, they must follow rules and respect their elders' advice.

9 ● LIVING CONDITIONS

By Western standards, Maasai living conditions seem primitive. However, the Maasai are generally proud of their simple lifestyle and do not seek to replace it with a more modern lifestyle. Nevertheless, the old ways are changing. Formerly, cowhides were used to make walls and roofs of temporary homes during migrations. They were also used to sleep on. Permanent and semi-permanent homes resembling igloos were built of sticks and branches plastered with mud, and with cow dung on the roofs. They were windowless and leaked a great deal. Nowadays, tin roofs and other more modern materials are gradually transforming these simple dwellings.

A few paved trunk roads and many passable dirt roads make Maasailand accessible. Much like their fellow Kenyan and Tanzanian citizens, the Maasai travel by bus and bush taxi when they need to cover distances.

10 ● FAMILY LIFE

The Maasai are a patriarchal society; men typically speak for women and make decisions in the family. Male elders decide community matters. Until the age of seven, boys and girls are raised together. Mothers remain close to their children, especially their sons, throughout life. Once circumcised, sons usually move away from their father's village, but they still follow his advice. Girls learn to fear and respect their fathers and must never be near them when they eat.

A person's peers (age-mates) are considered extended family and are obligated to help each other. Age-mates share nearly everything, even their wives. Girls are often promised in marriage long before they are of age. However, even long-term engagements are subject to veto by male family members.

11 ● CLOTHING

Maasai clothing varies by age, sex, and place. Traditionally, shepherds wore capes made from calf hides, and women wore capes of sheepskin. The Maasai decorated these capes with glass beads. In the 1960s, the Maasai began to replace animal-skin with commercial cotton cloth. Women tied lengths of this cloth around their shoulders as capes *(shuka)* or around the waist as a skirt. The Maasai color of preference is red, although black, blue, striped, and checkered cloth are also worn, as are multicolored African designs. Elderly women still prefer red and dye their own cloth with ochre (a natural pigment). Until recently, men and women wore sandals made from cowhides;

© Corel Corporation

Two Maasai women wearing elaborate headwear.

nowadays sandals and shoes are generally made of tire strips or plastic.

Young women and girls, and especially young warriors, spend much time on their appearance. Styles vary by age group. The Maasai excel in designing jewelry. They decorate their bodies with tattooing, head shaving, and hair styling with ochre and sheep's fat, which they also smear on their bodies. A variety of colors are used to create body art. Women and girls wear elaborate bib-like bead necklaces, as well as headbands and earrings, which are colorful and intricate. When ivory was plentiful, warriors wore ivory bands on their upper arms much like the ancient Egyptians. Jewelry plays an important role in courtship.

12 ● FOOD

The Maasai depend on cattle for both food and cooking utensils (as well as for shelter and clothing). Cattle ribs make stirring sticks, spatulas, and spoons. Horns are used as butter dishes and large horns as cups for drinking mead.

The traditional Maasai diet consists of six basic foods: meat, blood, milk, fat, honey, and tree bark. Wild game (except the eland), chicken, fish, and salt are forbidden.

Allowable meats include roasted and boiled beef, goat, and mutton. Both fresh and curdled milk are drunk, and animal blood is drunk at special times—after giving birth, after circumcision and excision, or while recovering from an accident. It may be tapped warm from the throat of a cow, or drunk in coagulated form. It can also be mixed with fresh or soured milk, or drunk with therapeutic bark soups *(motori)*. It is from blood that the Maasai obtain salt, a necessary ingredient in the human diet. People of delicate health and babies eat liquid sheep's fat to gain strength.

Honey is obtained from the Torrobo tribe and is a prime ingredient in mead, a fermented beverage that only elders may drink. In recent times, fermented maize (corn) with millet yeast or a mixture of fermented sugar and baking powder have become the primary ingredients of mead.

The Maasai generally eat two meals a day, in the morning and at night. They have a dietary prohibition against mixing milk and meat. They drink milk for ten days—as much as they want—and then eat meat and bark soup for several days in between. Some exceptions to this regimen exist. Children and old people may eat cornmeal or rice porridge and drink tea with sugar. For warriors, however, the sole source of true nourishment is cattle. They consume meat in their forest hideaways *(olpul)*, usually near a shady stream far from the observation of women. Their preferred meal is a mixture of meat, blood, and fat *(munono)*, which is thought to give great strength.

Many taboos (prohibitions) govern Maasai eating habits. Men must not eat meat that has been in contact with women or that

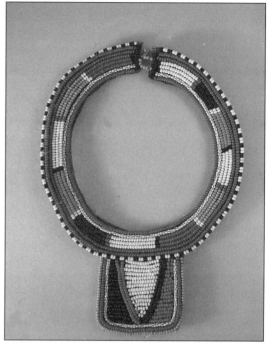

EPD Photos

Maasai women and girls wear bib-like beaded necklaces.

has been handled by an uncircumcised boy after it has been cooked.

13 ● EDUCATION

There is a wide gap between Western schooling and Maasai traditional education, by which children and young adults learned to overcome fear, endure pain, and assume adult tasks. For example, despite the dangers of predators, snakes, and elephants, boys would traditionally herd cattle alone. If they encountered a buffalo or lion, they were supposed to call for help. However, they sometimes reached the pinnacle of honor by killing lions on their own. Following such a display of courage, they became models for other boys, and their heroics were likely to become immortalized in the songs of the women and girls.

Over the years, school participation gradually increased among the Maasai, but there were few practical rewards for formal education and therefore little reason to send a child to school. Formal schooling was primarily of use to those involved in religion, agriculture, or politics. Since independence, as the traditional livelihood of the Maasai has become less secure, school participation rates have climbed dramatically.

14 ● CULTURAL HERITAGE

The Maasai have a rich collection of oral literature that includes myths, legends, folktales, riddles, and proverbs. These are passed down through the generations. The Maasai also compose many songs. Women are seldom at a loss for melodies and words when some heroic action by a warrior inspires praise. They also improvise teasing songs, work songs for milking and for plastering roofs, and songs with which to ask their traditional god (Enkai) for rain and other needs.

15 ● EMPLOYMENT

Labor among traditional herding Maasai is clearly divided. The man's responsibility is his cattle. He must protect them and find them the best possible pasture land and watering holes. Women raise children, maintain the home, cook, and do the milking. They also take care of calves and clean, sterilize, and decorate calabashes (gourds). It is the women's special right to offer milk to the men and to visitors.

Children help parents with their tasks. A boy begins herding at the age of four by

EPD Photos

Maasai produce woodcarvings like the mask pictured here. Such items are popular with tourists and supplement the income of Maasai families.

looking after lambs and young calves, and by the time he is twelve, he may be able to care for cows and bulls as well as move sheep and cattle to new pastures. Girls help their mothers with domestic chores such as drawing water, gathering firewood, and patching roofs.

16 ● SPORTS

While Maasai may take part in soccer, volleyball, and basketball in school or other settings, their own culture has little that resembles Western organized sports. Young children find time to join in games such as playing tag, but adults find little time for sports or play. Activities such as warding off enemies and killing lions are considered sport enough in their own right.

17 ● RECREATION

Ceremonies such as the *eunoto*, when warriors return to their villages as mature men, offer occasions for parties and merriment. Ordinarily, however, recreation is much more subdued. After the men return to their camp from a day's herding, they typically tell stories of their exploits. Young girls sing and dance for the men. In the villages, elders enjoy inviting their age-mates to their houses or to rustic pubs *(muratina manyatta)* for a drink.

18 ● CRAFTS AND HOBBIES

The Maasai make decorative beaded jewelry including necklaces, earrings, headbands, and wrist and ankle bracelets. These are always fashionable, though styles change as age-groups invent new designs. It is possible to identify the year a given piece was made by its age-group design. Maasai also excel in wood carvings, and they increasingly produce art for tourists as a supplemental source of income.

19 ● SOCIAL PROBLEMS

The greatest challenge the Maasai face concerns adaptation to rapid economic and social change. Increasing encroachment on Maasai lands threatens their traditional way of life. In the next decade, Maasai will need to address integration into the mainstream modern economies and political systems of Kenyan and Tanzanian society. The Maasai may fear losing their children to Western schooling, but a modern education has increasingly become a necessity for the Maasai in order to remain competitive with their neighbors and survive.

20 ● BIBLIOGRAPHY

Africa South of the Sahara. 26th ed. London, England: Europa Publications, 1997.

Bentsen, Cheryl. *Maasai Days*. New York: Doubleday, 1989.

Halmi, Robert. *Visit to a Chief's Son: An American Boy's Adventure with an African Tribe*. New York: Holt, 1963.

Spear, Thomas, and Richard Waller. *Being Maasai: Ethnicity and Identity in East Africa*. London, England: James Currey, 1993.

Spencer, Paul. *The Maasai of Matapato: A Study of Rituals of Rebellion*. Bloomington: Indiana University Press, 1988.

WEBSITES

Interknowledge Corp. Tanzania. [Online] Available http://www.geographia.com/tanzania/, 1998.

Interknowledge Corp. Kenya. [Online] Available http://www.geographia.com/kenya/, 1998.

Internet Africa Ltd. Tanzania. [Online] Available http://www.africanet.com/africanet/country/tanzania/, 1998.

Southern African Development Community. [Online] Available http://www.sadc-usa.net/members/tanzania/, 1998.

World Travel Guide. [Online] Available http://www.wtgonline.com/country/ke/gen.html, 1998.

Nyamwezi

PRONUNCIATION: nyahm-WAY-zee
ALTERNATE NAMES: Wanyamwezi
LOCATION: Unyamwezi (Tanzania: Provinces of Tabora and Shinyunga)
POPULATION: 1 million
LANGUAGE: Kinyamwezi; KiSwahili (Tanzania's national language); English; languages of neighboring ethnic groups
RELIGION: Spirituality shaped by traditional beliefs; Islam; Christianity

1 ● INTRODUCTION

The Nyamwezi people, also called the Wanyamwezi, live in the East African country of Tanzania. Their home area is called Unyamwezi, "the place of the Wanyamwezi." Over the years Nyamwezi culture has both influenced and been influenced by the cultures of neighboring African societies as well as the national Tanzanian culture. Islam and Christianity have also had a great impact on modern Nyamwezi customs.

The Nyamwezi are made up of four distinct subgroups, each claiming to descend from its own special ancestor. The first Nyamwezi settlers formed small communities that grew into larger kingdoms ruled by a *mtemi,* or king. The Nyamwezi were well-known traders in the precolonial era.

German and British colonialists created a system in Tanzania where people were separated according to race, similar to apartheid in South Africa. Colonial rule in Tanzania was built upon the notion that Europeans were superior to Africans.

The German colonial occupation of Tanzania was brutal, based on physical violence and a racial hierarchy. During the 1880s and 1890s German military campaigns conducted vicious reprisal raids against African areas that resisted German authority. In 1920, after World War I, Germany ceded control of Tanzania to the British. British administration of the territory was characterized by racial segregation. Africans were denied the right to participate in politics.

In the 1990s, Tanzania changed from a one-party socialist state to a country with multi-party competitive elections and a free-market economy. A number of Nyamwezi emerged as leaders of the opposition parties and played important roles in the ruling party.

2 ● LOCATION

Unyamwezi is located in the western plateau area of the Tanzanian provinces of Tabora and Shinyanga. Much of the land is covered by a dry woodland with strings of ridges and granite outcroppings. Most of Unyamwezi is not considered prime agricultural land. Water is often scarce.

Tanzanians of various ethnic groups live in Unyamwezi. Also present are Arabs as well as Asians whose ancestors came from India and Pakistan. About 30 percent of the Nyamwezi live and work outside Unyamwezi, mainly in Tanzania's commercial and agricultural centers. The Nyamwezi make up about 4 percent of the Tanzanian population and number about 1 million.

3 ● LANGUAGE

Many Nyamwezi can speak at least three languages. Kinyamwezi, which has three dialects, is the mother tongue of most. Most are also fluent in KiSwahili, Tanzania's

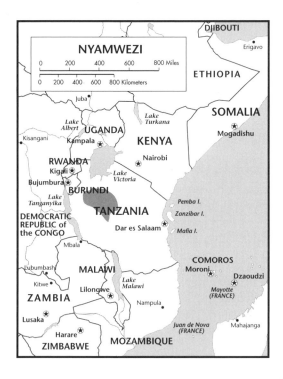

NYAMWEZI

0   200   400   600   800 Miles
0   200   400   600   800 Kilometers

their ancestors. Ancestors are seen as upholding the tradition, law, and values of society.

Relations with the ancestors and respect for Nyamwezi traditions are maintained through ritual activity such as animal sacrifices and other ceremonies. These activities are overseen by diviners, who act as spiritual advisers. They interpret events and determine which spirits are involved and what rituals should be followed to restore balance in people's lives.

6 ● MAJOR HOLIDAYS

The major holidays in Tanzania are Union Day (April 26), which celebrates the creation of the union between mainland Tanzania and the Zanzibar Island; Mayday/Workers Day (May 1); Independence Day (December 9); and New Year's Day (January 1). Major religious holidays for Christians are Christmas, Good Friday, and Easter; and for Muslims, *Eid al-Fitr* (end of Ramadan), *Eid al-Haj* (Festival of Sacrifice), Islamic New Year, and the Prophet Muhammad's Birthday. Religious holidays are usually celebrated by attendance at the church or mosque and visits with family and friends. Secular (nonreligious) holidays such as Independence Day are characterized by military parades and speeches by the country's leaders.

7 ● RITES OF PASSAGE

A series of rituals welcome the birth of a new baby. Many Nyamwezi practices surrounding birth have changed as Western influences have increased.

Marriage is a very important Nyamwezi institution. Courtship typically begins with

national language. Many Nyamwezi also speak English and the languages of neighboring ethnic groups, such as Kisukuma, the language of the Sukuma people.

4 ● FOLKLORE

One of the most important historical figures for the Nyamwezi is the *mtemi* (king) Mirambo. By the time of his death in 1884, he had created a central African empire that incorporated the greater part of Unyamwezi. Mirambo was a brilliant military tactician, known for his fierceness in battle.

5 ● RELIGION

Nyamwezi spirituality has been shaped by traditional beliefs, Islam, and Christianity. Traditional Nyamwezi spirituality centers on the connection between the living and

a young man's search for a suitable young woman to marry. With one or two male friends, he visits her home and discusses the possibility of marriage. If, after consulting with her female elders, the young woman agrees, bride wealth negotiations begin. When the bride wealth is agreed upon, the groom's father holds a large feast. After the bride wealth has been paid, a wedding ceremony is held with much feasting, dancing, and singing.

8 ● RELATIONSHIPS

Greetings are very important in Nyamwezi society. One greets important people by bowing, clapping one's hands, and averting one's gaze before a handshake. A greeting among close friends are less formal and often incorporate some teasing and joking. A greeting is always accompanied by a handshake, as is leave-taking. After the greetings, it is considered impolite to "get straight to the point," and the matter to be discussed is usually approached gradually and in an indirect manner.

Visiting relatives and friends is a favorite activity on the weekends, on holidays, or after work. Hospitality is taken very seriously.

9 ● LIVING CONDITIONS

Tanzania is one of the poorest countries in the world. Within Tanzania the most prosperous area is Dar es Salaam, the capital, while the poorest region is the southern coast. Unyamwezi falls between these two extremes.

Most people in Unyamwezi live in houses made of mud bricks with either thatched grass or corrugated iron roofs and dirt floors. Most houses do not have electricity or indoor plumbing, and most people have few material possessions. Malaria and sleeping sickness are widespread.

10 ● FAMILY LIFE

Most families are made up of a mother, a father, and children. Men have traditionally controlled most of the power within a household. This pattern is changing, as the government has stressed equal rights for women. Within the household, women are responsible for many of the daily chores, such as weeding crops and cooking. Men are responsible for building the house and clearing the fields. Girls help their mothers with household work, while boys help with herding the livestock. It is not unusual for school enrollment rates in rural areas to fall during harvest and planting times as children help their parents with agricultural work.

11 ● CLOTHING

Nyamwezi traditionally wore clothing made of bark cloth. As trade grew in the eighteenth century, imported textiles became popular. Many women wear *khangas,* printed cloth adorned with Swahili sayings and *vitenge,* printed cloth with brightly colored and ornate designs. Dresses based on Arab, European, and Indian styles are also popular. Men wear trousers and shirts. On special occasions Muslim men wear flowing white robes called *kanzus.*

12 ● FOOD

A favorite food is *ugali,* a stiff porridge made from corn, millet, or sorghum meal. It is served with beef, chicken, and vegetables.

Cassava, rice, bread, peanuts, spinach, cassava leaves and other vegetables are also eaten. Snacks often consist of fruits. When available, the meat from wild game is a special treat. A recipe for *mtori,* a common soup made of plantains, follows.

13 ● EDUCATION

Before the European colonial occupation of Unyamwezi, children were educated by their elders. They would learn from their parents how to farm, hunt, cook, herd cattle, and do other work. Stories told by parents or grandparents after the evening meal taught children the ways of Nyamwezi society. Stories typically began with a call and response, in which the storyteller would tease the listeners as follows:

Listeners: Story!

Storyteller: A Story.

Listeners: There once was what?

Storyteller: Someone.

Listeners: Go on!

Storyteller: You know who.

Listeners: Go on!

Many children's stories in the United States are based on African folktales. For example, one Nyamwezi story closely resembles the tale of "Br'er Rabbit." It tells of some farmers who decided to catch a hare that was eating their crops. They used a wood carving covered with glue to try to catch the hare. The rabbit came to the field and tried to talk to the carving. When it did not respond the rabbit resorted to violence, kicking and punching the carving and becoming stuck in its glue. When the farmers returned to kill the rabbit he pleaded

---

Recipe

Mtori
(Cream of Plantain Soup)

Ingredients

1 pound lean beef stew meat
1 can beef broth
5 plantains (green bananas peeled and cut into thin rounds)
1 medium onion, chopped
1 large tomato, chopped
Salt and pepper to taste
1 teaspoon butter or margarine

Directions

1. Put stew meat, canned beef broth, and about 1 cup of water into a large saucepan.
2. Simmer for one-half hour to make a strong stock.
3. Add the plantains, onion, and tomato to the stock. Simmer, covered, over low heat until the ingredients are very soft.
4. Mash the ingredients with a whisk to make a creamy soup. (The soup ingredients may be liquified in a food processor, but great care should be taken when working with the hot mixture.)
5. Reheat the soup but do not allow it to boil. Salt and pepper to taste.

---

with them not to beat him to death on the sand. When the farmers tried to do this, the soft sand broke the rabbit's fall and he was able to run away.

Informal education continues to be important for teaching societal values. At the same time, formal education equips the Nyamwezi with basic skills for life in modern Tanzanian society. After independence (in 1961) the government devoted most of the educational resources to providing free elementary education for all Tanzanian children. Until about 1980, elementary attendance rates improved significantly. However, enrollment rates have dropped in recent years in response to deteriorating economic conditions and the poor quality of some elementary schools.

14 ● CULTURAL HERITAGE

The Nyamwezi have a rich cultural heritage. Perhaps the most important part of their heritage is the emphasis on harmonious and balanced social relations. Nyamwezi society has historically placed a high value on tolerance. This has allowed many people from outside Unyamwezi to live peacefully in the area and has allowed the Nyamwezi to live throughout Tanzania.

For the Nyamwezi, music and dance are an important part of their cultural heritage. Both play an important part in wedding festivities and other ceremonies.

Hunting is also an important part of Nyamwezi culture. Many men belong to secret societies of hunters with special rituals which are considered to help them track various types of animals.

15 ● EMPLOYMENT

Most Nyamwezi are agriculturalists relying on traditional farming techniques. As in the past, most of the farming is done manually, although some tractors and animals are now used. The Nyamwezi live in areas where rainfall is often unreliable. Consequently, they long ago developed techniques, such as ridging their fields, to conserve water. The

major crops are sorghum, millet, maize (corn), rice, sweet potatoes, cassava, peanuts, beans, chickpeas, gourds, sunflowers, pumpkins, cotton, and tobacco.

16 ● SPORTS

By far the most popular sport is soccer. The Tanzanian landscape is dotted with soccer fields, and children and teenagers enjoy playing the game, often in bare feet with homemade soccer balls. On weekends many people enjoy listening to soccer games on the radio. For those who can go to the stadium, Simba and Young Africans of Dar es Salaam are the most popular teams to watch. Many Nyamwezi also support their local team, Milambo, based in the town of Tabora.

17 ● RECREATION

Besides soccer, many people like to play cards or a board game called *bao*. Sometimes called African chess, bao is a very complex game in which good players need to plan many turns in advance to capture their opponents' markers or pieces. More affluent families enjoy watching videos. Perhaps the most important form of relaxation in Unyamwezi, especially in the rural areas, is visiting friends and drinking traditional homemade beer.

18 ● CRAFTS AND HOBBIES

Many children make their own toys. A common toy is a wire car with wheels cut out of old pieces of rubber from tires or flip-flops. Children also make their own soccer balls.

Important crafts in Unyamwezi include ironworking, basket making, and making traditional stools. Some skills are closely guarded secrets passed down within a family or a close-knit secret society.

For adults, beer brewing is an important hobby. After the beer has been prepared, a process that takes several days, the brewer will have a party with much singing and dancing. Traditional beer is used in numerous ceremonies, including weddings, funerals, feasts, and holidays.

19 ● SOCIAL PROBLEMS

The most pressing problem facing the Nyamwezi, as with most Tanzanians, is poverty. Malnutrition, the lack of clean water, and insufficient health care allow diseases to take their toll. As in most countries, poor people are often at a severe disadvantage in protecting their rights and advocating their interests through the official channels of government.

Tanzania was ruled from 1965 to 1992 by a one-party state that tended to restrict political rights and individual liberties. A radical new plan called *ujamaa* (development of family villages based on socialism) was instituted in the 1960s and 1970s. Ujamaa led to numerous economic problems including a shortage of basic goods, corruption, high rates of inflation, declining production, and a deterioration of the nation's physical infrastructure. However, these problems need to be considered within the context of a ruling regime that seemed committed to building a new egalitarian society and promoting a national culture relatively free of ethnic animosity.

20 ● BIBLIOGRAPHY

Abrahams, R. G. *The Nyamwezi Today.* Cambridge, England: Cambridge University Press, 1981.

Abrahams, R. G. *The Political Organization of Unyamwezi.* Cambridge, England: Cambridge University Press, 1967.

Iliffe, J. *A Modern History of Tanzania.* Cambridge, England: Cambridge University Press, 1979.

Unomah, A. C. *Mirambo of Tanzania.* London, England: Heineman Educational Books, 1977.

World Bank. *Tanzania AIDS Assessment and Planning Study.* Washington, D.C.: World Bank, 1992.

WEBSITES

Interknowledge Corp. Tanzania. [Online] Available http://www.geographia.com/tanzania/, 1998.

Internet Africa Ltd. Tanzania. [Online] Available http://www.africanet.com/africanet/country/tanzania/, 1998.

Southern African Development Community. [Online] Available http://www.sadc-usa.net/members/tanzania/, 1998.

World Travel Guide. Tanzania. [Online] Available http://www.wtgonline.com/country/tz/gen.html, 1998.

Shambaa

PRONUNCIATION:: shahm-BAH

ALTERNATE NAMES: Shambala

LOCATION: Shambaai (West Usambara mountain range—northeastern Tanzania)

POPULATION: 445,000

LANGUAGE: Shambala; Swahili

RELIGION: Traditional Shambaa beliefs; *Mufika*; Christianity; Islam

1 ● INTRODUCTION

The Shambaa, also referred to as the Shambala, are a Bantu people found mainly on the west Usambara mountain range in Tanzania. The homeland of the Shambaa is called Shambaai (or Shambalai).

The Shambaa were traditionally ruled by kings. The Shambaa kingdom was made up of several descent groups with a common origin, but the kingdom was governed by a single descent group. The king ruled over several chiefdoms. All the wealth of the land was regarded as the king's. The system of chiefdoms was abolished soon after Tanzanian independence (1961).

2 ● LOCATION

The mountains of the Shambaa are an area of abundant rainfall with thriving banana plants. The Shambaa regard the *nyika* (plains) as a dangerous place of disease and death. Thus, the population density is high in the mountain area. Villages are located near each other with nearly all arable (farmable) land in use. Overpopulation is considered a problem. Some Shambaa people have now moved to the *nyika* and to urban areas such as Dar es Salaam and Tanga. Total Shambaa population is approximately 445,000 people.

3 ● LANGUAGE

Shambala is the main language spoken by the Shambaa. It has three main dialect areas. Despite these differences in dialect, the Shambaa can understand one another's speech. Shambala is used mainly for oral communication; only a few people can write in Shambala at this time.

The Shambaa also speak Swahili, the national language of Tanzania. Young people prefer to speak Swahili, which is taught in primary school. It is used in business and communications (in the media). Instruction in secondary schools and universities is in English.

4 ● FOLKLORE

The story of Mbegha (or Mbega) is the most famous of Shambaa myths. Mbegha was a hunter from Ngulu Hills to the south of Shambaai. He was forced to leave his homeland after a dispute with his kinsmen over his share of an inheritance. Mbegha fled to Kilindi, where he became a blood brother to the chief's son. The chief's son died accidentally while hunting with Mbegha. This caused Mbegha to flee again, into the bush, to escape punishment from the chief. He lived in caves and camps, hunting wild animals. After crossing the Pangani River, Mbegha arrived on the southern escarpment of the Usambaras. The Ziai people saw the smoke of his campfire and approached him. Upon learning that Mbegha was a skilled pig hunter, they asked him to rid their village of pigs. He was invited to live in Bumbuli. There he grew famous as an arbitrator, hunter, and storyteller. The grateful villagers gave Mbegha a wife. Mbegha also helped the people of Vugha and was known as a lion slayer after killing a lion on the way to their village. He was made the chief of Vugha. Mbegha's son Buge grew to be the chief of Bumbuli. When Mbegha died, Buge succeeded him as king of all Shambaai.

5 ● RELIGION

Traditional Shambaa beliefs center on healing the land and the body. Rainmakers were important people in the society. They were believed to have the power to prevent or cause rainfall. *Mufika* (ancestor worship) was important. The Shambaa believed that ignoring one's ancestors, especially one's deceased father, was sure to lead to misfortune.

The Protestant and Catholic faiths are both well established in Shambaai. The Christian influence in Shambaai was spread by missionaries through education and preaching. Islam was spread in Shambaai by the Zigua, mainly in the trading towns.

6 ● MAJOR HOLIDAYS

The Shambaa observe both secular (nonreligious) and religious holidays. The main government holidays now celebrated are New Year's Day, Union Day (April 26), Workers' Day (May 1), Peasants' Day (August 8), and Independence Day (December 9). Government holidays are public rest days when offices and shops are closed. Nationwide public rallies are held in urban areas.

Both Christian and Muslim holidays are celebrated with public observances. The major Christian holidays are Easter weekend and Christmas. The major Muslim holidays are *Eid al-Fitr, Eid al-Hajj,* and *Maulid.* Religious holidays are a very special time for family gatherings.

7 ● RITES OF PASSAGE

Traditionally, the Shambaa held initiation ceremonies for both young men and young women. Initiation for boys began with circumcision at the age of three or four years. At that time a *kungwi* (mentor) was chosen for him. At puberty, the initiate undergoes the *gao* ceremony, in which he is instructed in acceptable behavior.

In modern times, circumcision takes place in health facilities. The initiation ceremony has been shortened but is still required. Young women are not circumcised. However, they also go through a *gao* ceremony of instruction that is required before a young woman can marry or become a mother.

8 ● RELATIONSHIPS

Greetings are important in Shambaa culture. There are particular greetings for different times of the day. Greetings may be prolonged, for it is customary to inquire after a person's family, health, and work. Younger people are expected to show respect and deference to their elders.

Traditionally, men and women were socially segregated, and this has formed the basis for all their relationships. Couples do not eat together at home. Mothers usually eat with their children while the father eats alone. Persons of opposite sexes do not show any affection publicly through bodily contact; this is considered highly inappropriate.

9 ● LIVING CONDITIONS

The Shambaa live in large villages consisting of several lineages (family groups). Villages are usually located on upper hillsides. Banana groves separate the homesteads and provide a source of food, a symbolic and practical insurance against famine. A traditional Shambaa house is round, with thatched roof and sides. There are also rectangular houses in Shambaai, with walls of wattle (interwoven sticks) and mud and thatched roofs. These are modeled on what is called a Swahili design. Now, these houses commonly have cement walls and corrugated metal roofs.

Cory Langley

The photographer (center) poses with a group of Shambaa children in front of a house.

10 ● FAMILY LIFE

Polygyny (having multiple wives) was widely practiced by the Shambaa. A man married as many women as he could support. He also fathered as many children as possible. Under the influence of Christianity, marriages are now often monogamous (having only one spouse).

The wife was responsible for the daily farm work. A husband was responsible for increasing his *mai* (wealth). Wealth was increased mainly through acquisition of goats, cattle, and sheep. A person increased his status and standing in the community by lending out his livestock. This enabled the person to build a network of supporters who could help in times of need.

11 ● CLOTHING

The Shambaa dress code has been greatly influenced by the Tanzanian coastal people who are mainly Muslim. Men wear *kanzus* (long, flowing white robes) and a small cap, or *barghashia,* on their heads. Women use lengths of colorful cloth as wraps for the body; these are called *khangas* and *kitenges.* A wrap may be worn over a dress or used to carry a baby on the back or hip. Married women cover their heads and clothes with two pieces of khanga cloth. Shambaa men often wear shirts and trousers in urban areas. Traditionally, women do not wear shorts in public other than for sporting events or in military camps. Secondhand clothing *(mitumba)* is generally worn by poorer people.

12 ● FOOD

The Shambaa plant many different food crops adapted to the climate of the area, including tubers, medicinal plants, tobacco, beans, and bananas. Banana plants used to be the main food crop of the Shambaa. This has changed with the introduction of maize (corn) and cassava to the area. Cassava, a hardy root vegetable, is drought-resistant, and will survive when other crops fail due to lack of rainfall. Drought-resistant crops like cassava are grown as safeguards against famine.

The Shambaa diet is composed of starchy foods such as rice, maize, and sweet potatoes. These are usually accompanied by beans, meat, and vegetables. Dairy products are available, and sour milk is often drunk for breakfast. Meat consumption is on the increase.

13 ● EDUCATION

Traditionally, Shambaa children have received instruction from their parents. Youths receive further instruction from their elders during the *gao* (adolescent initiation) ceremonies in the form of songs and stories.

The Christian missionaries were the first to offer the Shambaa formal education. Generally young men were sent to these schools while girls were kept at home.

Since 1971, the Tanzanian government has required that all children seven years of age and older attend primary schools for at

least seven years. Primary education was provided free to all Tanzanians, but in the early 1990s the government reinstated school fees. Students who pass qualifying exams advance to four years of secondary education. After another exam, two years of high school follow. Those who wish to continue their education attend university or alternative trade or business schools.

14 ● CULTURAL HERITAGE

The Shambaa have a rich cultural heritage of songs and dances. Songs are used to teach younger people their history and expected behavior for when they are adult members of the tribe. Drums were traditionally used to transmit messages of approaching danger as well as important news such as the death of a king. Storytelling by the elder generation is a popular evening pastime with children. Traditional dances are still popular, especially at wedding celebrations.

A wide variety of African music is popular among the Shambaa. The younger generation prefers to listen and dance to Western music, including reggae, pop, and rap.

15 ● EMPLOYMENT

Traditionally, work centered on the farm and was divided between men and women. Men were responsible for planting and tilling the fields; women were in charge of weeding and harvesting.

Due to diminishing land holdings, declining yields, and soil erosion, Shambaa men are increasingly forced to seek outside employment. Women are usually left in the homestead to tend the farm and children while the husband seeks employment in the urban areas and on plantations.

Educated Shambaa have better chances of finding jobs in the cities as clerks, teachers, and administrators. There is fierce competition for jobs in the private sector.

16 ● SPORTS

Like other Tanzanian children, the Shambaa children first come into contact with sports at school. Primary-school children are encouraged to participate in interschool competitions. These lead to higher-level championships. Popular sports at school are soccer for boys and netball (similar to basketball) for girls. At secondary schools Shambaa youth may also be introduced to basketball, table tennis, and volleyball.

Soccer is the most popular sport in Tanzania. The national soccer league broadcasts games, which are greatly enjoyed by the Shambaa. On weekends, standard and makeshift soccer fields are crowded with spectators and players.

17 ● RECREATION

Radio broadcasts by the state-owned radio station have been the major source of entertainment. Many households have transistor radios, and people enjoy listening to music, radio plays, and sports programs. Shambaa men gather around a radio in public meeting places, usually with a local brew in hand. Recently the government has allowed private TV and radio stations to operate, increasing the choice and quality of programs.

Television ownership has led to the opening of many video lending libraries in Tanga. Action movies are the most popular.

18 ● CRAFTS AND HOBBIES

The Shambaa are mainly agriculturists who prefer tilling the land to craftwork. They have been fortunate to be able to obtain their ornaments and tools through trade. Blacksmiths traditionally forged iron tools and weapons. Toymaking was a favorite pastime for children, who made wooden objects such as small spears and cooking utensils. Children still make their own toys.

19 ● SOCIAL PROBLEMS

The greatest problem facing the Shambaa today is the gradual loss of cultural identity. Young people generally prefer to adopt a national Tanzanian identity instead of a Shambaa identity. The Shambaa are trying to reverse this cultural erosion by recording their cultural values and history. Younger people in urban areas are encouraged to regularly visit Shambaai, where they may learn their traditions and converse in Shambala.

Another serious problem facing the Shambaa is a shortage of land. A population increase has led to a decrease in arable land. Soil depletion has resulted, since the land is never left unplanted to regain its nutrients. The government is trying to introduce more resilant crops and better farming practices into the area.

Like all Tanzanians, the Shambaa face the problem of poverty. The World Bank classifies Tanzania as the second poorest country in the world, after Mozambique.

20 ● BIBLIOGRAPHY

Feierman, Steven. *The Shambaa Kingdom: A History.* Madison: University of Wisconsin Press, 1974.

Feierman, Steven. *Peasant Intellectuals.* Madison: University of Wisconsin Press, 1990.

Pelt, P. *Bantu Customs in Mainland Tanzania.* Tabora, Tanzania: TMP Book Department, 1971.

Winans, Edgar V. *Shambala, the Constitution of a Traditional State.* Berkeley: University of California Press, 1962.

World Bank. *1995 World Development Report.* New York: Oxford University Press, 1995.

WEBSITES

Interknowledge Corp. Tanzania. [Online] Available http://www.geographia.com/tanzania/, 1998.

Internet Africa Ltd. Tanzania. [Online] Available http://www.africanet.com/africanet/country/tanzania/, 1998.

Southern African Development Comm. [Online] Available http://www.sadc-usa.net/members/tanzania/, 1998.

World Travel Guide. Tanzania. [Online] Available http://www.wtgonline.com/country/tz/gen.html, 1998.

Swahili

PRONUNCIATION: swah-HEE-lee
ALTERNATE NAMES: Waswahili
LOCATION: Eastern Africa from southern Somalia to northern Mozambique
POPULATION: About 500,000
LANGUAGE: KiSwahili; English
RELIGION: Islam (Sunni Muslim); spirit cults

1 ● INTRODUCTION

For at least a thousand years, Swahili people, who call themselves Waswahili, have occupied a narrow strip of coastal land extending from the north coast of Kenya to Dar es Salaam (the capital of Tanzania). They also occupy several nearby Indian Ocean islands, including Zanzibar, Lamu, and Pate. Over the past few hundred years, the coastal area has been conquered and colonized several times—by Portuguese in the sixteenth century, by Middle Eastern Arabs who ran a slave trade in the nineteenth century, and by the British in the twentieth century. Thus, Swahili people are accustomed to living with strangers in their midst, and they have frequently acted as middlemen in trade relations. In addition, they have incorporated many people and practices into their vibrant social world.

Swahili are all Muslims. They became Muslim through the influence of people coming from the north and also from across the Indian Ocean. They have forged extensive economic, political, and social ties with Middle Eastern Muslims.

During the colonial period and since independence in the early 1960s, Swahili people have been a minority Muslim population in the secular states of Kenya and Tanzania.

2 ● LOCATION

The deep harbors along the east African coast have long sustained a profitable fishing and shipping economy. The lush coastal plain provides a fertile environment for growing coconut palms, fruit trees, spices, and mangrove in swamp areas. Today, Swahili people live primarily in the urban areas of Lamu, Malindi, Mombasa, Tanga (mainland Tanzania), the island of Zanzibar, and Dar es Salaam.

Hundreds of Swahili people left for the Middle East after the Zanzibar Revolution in 1964. Over the past several decades, thousands have migrated to the Middle East, Europe, and North America largely for economic reasons. The Swahili population is about half a million.

3 ● LANGUAGE

KiSwahili, the Swahili language, is widely spoken across East Africa. For most Kenyans and Tanzanians, KiSwahili is learned as a second language. Swahili people speak KiSwahili as their "mother tongue," and it reflects their mixed origins and complex history. The language includes many words borrowed from Arabic (and other languages), yet its grammar and syntax place it in the Bantu language family, which has roots on the African continent. Like many Kenyans, Swahili people also use English in their daily interactions, particularly in schools, government offices, and the tourist industry.

4 ● FOLKLORE

Myths and heroes are generally from Islamic sources. For example, many people tell short, moralistic tales based on the Prophet Muhammad's life.

5 ● RELIGION

Being Swahili is inextricably connected to being Muslim. Swahili Muslims recognize the five pillars of faith that are basic to Islamic practice worldwide: 1) belief in Allah as the Supreme Being and in Muhammad as the most important prophet; 2) praying five times a day; 3) fasting from dawn to dusk during the month of Ramadan; 4) giving charity; and 5) making a pilgrimage (*hajj*) to the holy city of Mecca, if feasible. For Swahili people, Islam encompasses more than just spiritual beliefs and practices; Islam is a way of life.

6 ● MAJOR HOLIDAYS

Swahili people celebrate the nation's secular (nonreligious) public holidays. These include, in Kenya, Jamhuri Day and Madaraka Day, which mark the steps toward Kenya's Independence in the early 1960s. In Tanzania, secular holidays are Labor Day (May 1), Zanzibar Revolution Day (January 12); *Nane Nane* (formerly *Saba Saba*—Farmer's Day, in August); Independence Day (December 9); and Union Day (April 26), which commemorates the unification of Zanzibar and the mainland.

For Muslims, the most important holidays are religious. *Eid al-Fitr* marks the end of the month of Ramadan. *Eid al-Hajj* celebrates the yearly pilgrimage to Mecca. Each Eid is celebrated by praying, visiting relatives and neighbors, and eating special foods and sweets. During the month of Ramadan, Swahili (along with all other) Muslims fast from sunrise to sunset. *Maulidi,* or the Prophet Muhammad's birthday, is widely celebrated by Muslims.

7 ● RITES OF PASSAGE

There are no specific rites of passage for children or teens. Birthday parties, increasingly popular, include eating cake, disco dancing, and opening presents. Graduation ceremonies mark a young person's educational progress.

Marriage marks the transition to adulthood. Marriages are usually arranged by parents. A young woman cannot get married without her father's permission, but she has the right to refuse someone chosen for her. Weddings can include several days of separate celebrations for men and women. Only men attend the actual marriage vows, which take place in a mosque. A male relative represents the bride.

8 ● RELATIONSHIPS

Swahili people are as likely to greet one another with the Arabic greeting *Asalaam Aleikhum* as they are to say *Jambo*, the common KiSwahili greeting. People who know each other exchange a string of greetings inquiring about the health of family members and the latest news. Children greet an elder with respect by kissing his or her hand.

Swahili people greatly value modest behavior. Men and women are not permitted to mix freely. Dating is generally non-existent. Most people pursue their daily activities with others of the same gender. Women are encouraged to congregate at home, while men spend time in public places.

9 ● LIVING CONDITIONS

Houses vary depending on a family's means and the type of town in which they reside. "Stone towns," like Lamu and Mombasa, are characterized by large stone houses, some divided into apartments. Some Swahili people living in "country towns" still occupy houses made of hardened mud and stones, although these are less common than houses of stone or coral. Most homes have electricity, indoor plumbing, several bedrooms, and a living room furnished with a couch and chairs. Access to water is critical for Muslims who must wash before prayers. In comparison with many people in Kenya, Swahili people enjoy a relatively high standard of living.

10 ● FAMILY LIFE

Under Islam, husbands and fathers have authority in the home. They can make decisions for wives and daughters and compel them to behave properly to preserve the family's honor. But Swahili women also wield considerable power in the daily life of the family.

The average number of children in each family has declined from as many as fourteen children early in the twentieth century to three or four children by the late 1990s. Women who have been educated and/or work outside the home tend to limit births. Residents of an individual household might include many people beyond the immediate family, such as grandparents, nieces and nephews, and in-laws.

11 ● CLOTHING

In the early twentieth century, women generally wore brightly colored cotton cloths (*kanga* or *leso*). These were wrapped around their waists and upper bodies and draped over their shoulders and heads. Men wore a striped cloth (*kikoi*) around the waist that hung to the knees. As a mark of being Muslim some men sported small white caps with elaborate tan embroidery.

Dressing well but modestly is highly valued. Women wear Western-style dresses in many colors, patterns, and fabrics. Outside the house, women wear a black, floor-length cloak with an attached veil, called a *buibui*. Men wear Western-style

Recipe

Sweet Tea with Milk

Ingredients

2 teaspoons loose, black tea
1 cup milk (whole or 2 percent)
1 cup water
2 teaspoons (or more) sugar
Pinch of ground ginger
Pinch of ground cardamon

Directions

1. Combine tea, milk, and water in a saucepan. Heat until the mixture is just beginning to boil. Reduce heat and simmer for about 5 minutes, stirring constantly.
2. Increase the heat and bring the mixture just to the boiling point again. Stir in sugar (at least 2 teaspoons) and the ginger and cardamon.
3. To serve, pour tea through a strainer into cups.

trousers and shirts. On Fridays (the Muslim day of rest), or other religious occasions, they wear long, white caftans. Shorts are worn only by children.

12 ● FOOD

Swahili cuisine, which is highly spiced, has African, Middle Eastern, and Indian influences. Rice, the staple, is cooked with coconut milk and served with tomato-based meat, bean, or vegetable stews. Meals incorporate locally-available vegetables (eggplant, okra, and spinach), fruits (mangoes, coconuts, pineapples), and spices (cloves, cardamon, hot pepper). Fish is also central to the diet. Chicken and goat meat are popular for holiday meals. Sweet tea with milk (see accompanyig recipe) is served several times a day.

Swahili, like all Muslims, are prohibited from eating pork or drinking alcohol. The members of one clan from northern Kenya observe a taboo on eating fish.

13 ● EDUCATION

Through Islam, literacy (the ability to read and write) came to the East African coast much earlier than to most other parts of the continent. Knowing how to read the Koran (Islam's holy book) is important. Some people are literate in Arabic as well as KiSwahili. Those who have been to secular school are literate in English as well.

Young people today tend to finish primary school, and some go on to secondary school. Most parents, particularly in urban areas, recognize the value of education in preparing their children for employment. Families vary as to whether they believe that girls should be educated as extensively as boys.

14 ● CULTURAL HERITAGE

Taarab music, which has distinctly Arabic origins, is performed at weddings and concerts. Band members play keyboards, flutes, brass instruments, and drums to accompany singers. Many KiSwahili lyrics are double entendres (having double meanings) that hint at romantic love.

Several women's dance groups perform at weddings for all-female audiences. They dance *chakacha,* which resembles belly dancing, and also *lelemama,* a very subtle dance with tiny hand movements.

KiSwahili oral literature includes songs, sayings, stories, and riddles. The main written form is poetry. KiSwahili poems include long epics, prayers, and meditations on many subjects.

15 ● EMPLOYMENT

Some Swahili still fish, farm, and trade as they did in previous generations. However, the difficult local economy has meant that many people are unemployed or dependent on the unpredictable tourist industry. Educated men and women enter the civil service (government administration) and work in offices, shops, and schools. Although husbands are obligated to provide for their families, many wives earn money through cooking food, sewing, or trading from their homes.

16 ● SPORTS

Few adults play sports. Many boys join soccer teams and play in hotly contested competitions. Soccer matches involving Kenyan regional teams or local boys' clubs provide rare, exciting entertainment, mostly for men. In school, girls play sports such as netball (similar to basketball) and track. Children are sometimes taken to swim at the ocean.

17 ● RECREATION

Weddings and holiday celebrations are the most important forms of entertainment. Traveling to and from weddings, people sing songs and celebrate with vigor.

Watching videos is a favorite pastime, especially for women and young people. Action films from Japan, romances from India, Islamic epics, and detective stories from the United States are popular. If a video contains love scenes, an adult might fast-forward to protect the modesty of those present. Local and foreign soap operas, news, and sports are popular on television. On the weekends, young people sometimes go to discos, and women enjoy walking on the beach or going for a picnic.

18 ● CRAFTS AND HOBBIES

Artisans on the island of Lamu are famous for their intricately carved wooden furniture and doors. They also construct miniature, painted replicas of the boats (*dhows*) used for fishing. Young boys play with these at the shore. Women use brown colored henna to paint complex flower designs on their hands and feet (up to the knees) as preparation for attending a wedding. The color, which stains the skin and nails, lasts for several weeks.

19 ● SOCIAL PROBLEMS

Swahili view the declining economy and erosion of their culture by tourism as significant social problems. Tourists who walk around in immodest clothing (such as shorts and bikinis), drink alcohol in public, and encourage loose behavior among young people have threatened the proper Islamic life that many Swahili people struggle to maintain.

Swahili face some discrimination by Kenyans who have resented their connection to the slave trade and their ties to Middle Eastern wealth. Their role in

Kenyan politics, though marginal, is increasing as Kenya moves forward in multiparty democracy.

A worrisome problem is the growing prevalence of marijuana use among young men, which is condemned as antisocial. However, chewing *miraa*, a plant grown locally that contains a mild stimulant, is regarded as an acceptable social activity.

20 ● BIBLIOGRAPHY

Allen, James de Vere. *Swahili Origins*. London, England: James Currey, 1993.

Bakari, Mtoro bin Mwinyi. *The Customs of the Swahili People*. Berkeley: University of California Press, 1981.

Caplan, Patricia. *African Voices, African Lives: Personal Narratives From a Swahili Village*. New York: Routledge, 1997.

Kaula, Edna Mason. *The Land and People of Tanzania*. Philadelphia: Lippincott, 1972.

Knappert, Jan. *Four Centuries of Swahili Verse: A Literary History and Anthology*. London, England: Heinemann, 1979.

Margolies, Barbara A. *Rehema's Journey*. New York: Scholastic, 1990.

WEBSITES

Interknowledge Corp. Tanzania. [Online] Available http://www.geographia.com/tanzania/, 1998.

Internet Africa Ltd. Tanzania. [Online] Available http://www.africanet.com/africanet/country/tanzania/, 1998.

Southern African Development Community. [Online] Available http://www.sadc-usa.net/members/tanzania/, 1998.

World Travel Guide. Tanzania. [Online] Available http://www.wtgonline.com/country/tz/gen.html, 1998.

Thailand

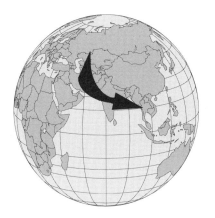

The people of Thailand are called Thai. There are more than 30 ethnic groups, each with its own history, language, religion, appearance, and patterns of livelihood. The Thai, related to the Lao of Laos and the Shan of Myanmar (formerly Burma) make up about 84 percent of the total population of Thailand.

Major ethnic minorities are the Chinese (about 11 percent) and Malays (about 4 percent).

Thai

PRONUNCIATION: TIE
LOCATION: Thailand
POPULATION: Over 61 million
LANGUAGE: Thai
RELIGION: Buddhism; mix of Theravada Buddhism, Hinduism, and animism; Islam

1 ● INTRODUCTION

The forerunners of today's Thais gradually moved from what is now southern China into the area of the Mekong and Chao Phraya river basins. They overcame Mon and Khmer peoples, and later intermingled with them. A Thai kingdom called Siam developed along the lower Chao Phraya River.

Thailand was never directly colonized by the Western colonial powers. It was left as a buffer zone between the British colonial holdings in Burma (modern-day Myanmar) and the French colonies in Indochina (Cambodia, Laos, and Viet Nam). A bloodless coup led by Western-educated Thai elites put an end to Thailand's absolute monarchy in 1932. A constitutional monarchy was established, and early attempts at democracy were made. However, conflicts within the new government led to a successful military coup d'état (overthrow).

Since then, Thailand has alternated between periods of dictatorship and democracy. There were student uprisings in 1973 and 1976. Pro-democracy demonstrations in 1992 tried to stem the power of the military.

King Phumipol Adulyadej, who became king in 1946 and was still on the throne in 1998, is greatly loved and revered. He has been influential in many political crises. (His name, Phumipol, is sometimes spelled Bhumipol when translated into English.)

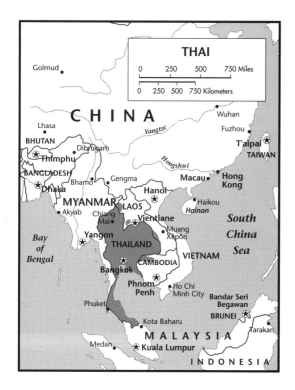

THAI

0   250   500   750 Miles

0   250   500   750 Kilometers

2 ● LOCATION

Thailand is situated in the middle of mainland southeast Asia. The country covers approximately 198,455 square miles (514,000 square kilometers). Thailand has four major regions. The central floodplain is watered by the Chao Phraya River and its tributaries. The mountainous north has forest areas that are rapidly being destroyed. The dry northeast on the Khorat Plateau borders the Mekong River to the east. The long coastlines of the peninsula are bounded by the Andaman Sea and the Gulf of Thailand.

The Thai population is over 61 million. Around 11 million people are living in Bangkok, the capital and the only major city.

3 ● LANGUAGE

Many dialects of the Thai language are spoken throughout the country. Malay is used in the extreme south. The Central Thai dialect, or Standard Thai, is the official language of the schools and of government and business affairs.

Thai is a tonal language, and its alphabet is derived from Mon and Khmer scripts. Last names were just introduced to Thailand in the early twentieth century. (Calling a person by his or her last name is still very unusual.)

Sawaddee is said when greeting someone, regardless of the time of day. *Mai Pen Rai* means "It's O.K., never mind." Women add the polite word *kha* and men the word *khrab* to phrases and sentences when speaking.

4 ● FOLKLORE

The Thais had a traditional creation myth before the arrival of the Buddhist religion. According to this myth, *Than* is the Spirit of the Sky who first created everything. Before this, there was nothing on Earth—no humans, animals, or plants—as well as no Sun or Moon. *Than* brought a bottle gourd (hollow fruit) to Earth, then pierced it until it opened. Five types of human beings came out, and all were brothers and sisters. *Than* instructed them in the ways of life and gave them tools to make a living.

According to legend, the original rice seed was five times the size of a person's fist. But because humans became more and

Cory Langley

A stop sign in downtown Bangkok.

Chinese descent follow Mahayana Buddhism, Confucianism, and ancestor worship.

Animism is common throughout Thailand. Spirits are believed to inhabit almost everything. It is believed that they can help or harm humans. Large, old trees are frequently tied with pieces of colorful cloth and worshiped by local people.

6 ● MAJOR HOLIDAYS

Songkran, the Thai New Year, is the longest official holiday of the year, lasting from April 13 to 15. Traditionally, people visited their home villages to pay their respects to family. Nowadays, the most popular Songkran custom is for people to enthusiastically throw water on each other. Some will add white clay or scent to the water for more lasting effect.

The Chinese New Year in mid-February is not an official holiday. However, for those of Chinese ancestry, it is a big festival. Some Chinese Thai employers give days off and bonuses to their Thai employees. It is a time for family members to reunite, gathering to worship their gods and their ancestors. Children collect gift money in red or pink envelopes.

Thailand's major holidays also include religious and official holidays, as well as the king's and queen's birthdays.

7 ● RITES OF PASSAGE

Thai individual rites, such as birth, ordination into the monkhood, or marriage, are associated with *khwan,* the "body spirit" or "life soul."

more greedy, the rice seed became smaller and smaller.

Mae Phosop is the Spirit of Rice. The old still teach the young, "Don't leave rice in your dish; Mae Phosop will feel sad."

Si Thanonchai is a very popular local trickster hero. Many Thais identify with Si Thanonchai's wit and cunning.

5 ● RELIGION

More than 95 percent of Thais are Buddhist. However, Thai beliefs actually reflect a mix of Theravada Buddhism, Hinduism, and animism (spirit worship). Some southern Thais are Muslim (followers of Islam). Thais of

Cory Langley

Although many people in Bangkok have a standard of living comparable to middle class Americans, the gap between the poor and the rich is very wide and increasing. In the cities, expensive houses may coexist on the same street with slum dwellings.

In the past, most young Thai men spent some period in the monkhood. Many Thai men continue this highly valued tradition. Today, ordination ceremonies involve lavish expenditures.

8 ● RELATIONSHIPS

The head is regarded as the most revered part of the body. Ideally, one should keep one's head lower than the head of a superior, such as a teacher. Improper position or display of the feet is always considered impolite. Gesturing with the feet is terribly rude.

Greeting with kisses is virtually unknown. The most common greeting is the *wai* (made by putting the palms together at chest level and bowing). It is inappropriate for lovers to hug or kiss in public. However, holding hands or hugging by members of the same sex is acceptable and does not have sexual connotations.

Almost all Thais remove their shoes before entering houses and monasteries.

Being late because of a traffic jam is the most popular all-occasion excuse in Bangkok.

9 ● LIVING CONDITIONS

Running water, electricity, and health-care centers have been extended to most rural areas. Wood or thatch houses built on stilts are clustered together in villages or are spread out along the rivers and canals. People often sit under the houses during the heat of the day; there they do minor chores. Some farm animals are also kept there.

In the cities, expensive houses may coexist on the same street with slum dwellings. Most working people live in apartments and condominiums. Living conditions are poor for those in the slums of Bangkok.

Bangkok sometimes has brief periods of water cutoffs and power shortages. Uncollected garbage and sewage back-ups are major problems in Bangkok and Chiang Mai, the second-largest city.

10 ● FAMILY LIFE

Nuclear families are the norm, both in villages and rural areas. Children are taught to respect and obey their elders. Elderly people in the family are usually gladly taken care of by the younger generations. As people's lives are getting more complicated, however, care for the elderly is becoming a problem.

Most young people do not move out of their parents' homes until they marry. Many even continue to live with their parents after marriage.

11 ● CLOTHING

The most common traditional lower garment worn by women in the fields or at the markets is *pha sin* or *pha thung*. The name means "bag cloth." It is a tube of material that looks like a bottomless bag, about one yard (one meter) wide. The length is typically from the waist to the ankle, and one size fits all. *Phakhaoma,* a strip of cloth, usually with a checked design, that hangs to knee length is worn by men in villages. It is sometimes just loosely tied around the waist.

Western-style clothing is preferred by middle- and upper-class people. Jeans and T-shirts can be seen everywhere. Because of the hot and humid weather, many like to wear sandals. Shorts are not generally seen in public, except on young children and as part of boys' school uniforms.

12 ● FOOD

Rice is usually the main course, with side dishes. Glutinous or sticky rice is mostly identified with the north and northeast. Sticky rice and coconut milk are also used in many tasty desserts. A spoon and fork are the most common utensils, but the fingers are usually preferred for eating sticky rice.

The category of *yum* (mixed hot and sour salads) often fills a page or more of a restaurant menu. *Yumwunsen,* for example, is a type of pasta salad. It is usually made with cooked minced pork and a choice of chicken, shrimp, squid, or all of these. The real taste of yum comes from adding fresh celery, mint, and basil leaves.

13 ● EDUCATION

Education is free and required through the sixth grade. The government is considering extending the requirement to grade nine. The standards of schools vary and are much lower in rural areas. In Bangkok, good schools at all levels are highly competitive.

Recipe

Thai Chili Sauce

Ingredients

½ cup rice wine vinegar

1 or 2 hot Thai peppers, seeded and chopped (wear rubber gloves to prepare the peppers)

Directions

1. Combine rice vinegar and chopped peppers. Season with a pinch of salt and set aside at room temperature. Serve with Thai noodles.

Thai Noodles

Ingredients

7 ounces uncooked wide rice noodles

6 Tablespoons soy sauce (low-sodium preferred)

2 Tablespoons sweet soy sauce

¼ cup canned chicken broth

2 Tablespoons sugar

½ teaspoon pepper

3 Tablespoons oil

2 cloves of garlic, minced

2 cups chopped broccoli

2 eggs, lightly beaten

Directions

1. In a small bowl, mix together the soy sauces, chicken stock, sugar, and pepper.

2. Put the rice noodles in a large mixing bowl and cover with water. Set them aside to soak for about 30 minutes.

Drain the noodles in a colander.

3. Heat the oil in a large skillet (or electric wok). Add the garlic and cook until the garlic is light brown.

4. Add the chopped broccoli to the skillet, and cook for about 1 minute.

5. Add the noodles and soy sauce mixture and stir well to mix.

6. Push the noodles and vegetables to one side of the skillet. Pour in the beaten eggs. Wait about 30 seconds before beginning to scramble them.

7. When the eggs are scrambled, stir everything together.

Serve warm with the Thai chili sauce as an accompaniment.

Adapted from "Great Chefs Go to Him to Be Dazzled." *New York Times* (April 29, 1998): p. B12.

Many high school students get extra tutoring to prepare for the entrance examinations for government universities. About 10 percent of examinees get accepted. The rest may go to private colleges and universities, or try again the following year. There are also a number of vocational schools around the country.

14 ● CULTURAL HERITAGE

Masked drama, or *khon,* of the royal court tradition is the most exceptional of the Thai performing arts. Episodes from the Indian epic, the *Ramayana* (*Ramakien* in Thai) are performed. The performance includes masks, dance, and musical accompaniment.

Folk dances vary from region to region. The shadow-puppet theater, *nang talung,* is a popular entertainment in the south.

There are many different types of Thai traditional music. The saw duang is a two-stringed instrument played with a bow that is entwined with its strings. The most important ensemble is *pi phat,* made up of melodic percussion instruments, Thai oboe, and drums. Thai *khuang wong* (gong circles) and *ranat thum* (xylophone-like instrument) are played by ensembles of musicians who sit on the floor. *Khaen,* a mouth organ made of bamboo tubes played in both Thailand and neighboring Laos, has a history going back more than 3,000 years.

The oldest and greatest epic of Thai literature is a poem of about 20,000 lines called *Thao Hung Khun Cheung,* telling the story of a legendary hero. It was probably written during the fifteenth century.

15 ● EMPLOYMENT

Approximately two-thirds of the Thai labor force work in agriculture. However, this is changing rapidly, as Thailand becomes industrialized. Thai farmers are still very poor and suffer from relatively low productivity and low prices for their crops. In some areas, ceremonies accompany agricultural activities, such as plowing of the fields.

The growing economy attracts people to city jobs, although labor is cheap. People with technical skills, such as engineers and computer specialists, are in high demand. Large numbers of people are also involved in the tourism business.

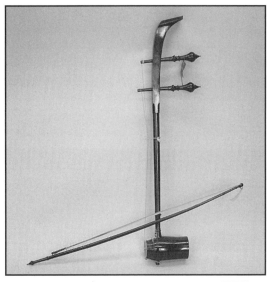

EPD Photos

The saw duang, a two-stringed instrument whose bow is permanently attached. Courtesy of the Center for the Study of World Musics, Kent State University.

EPD Photos

Thai percussion instruments include (clockwise from rear) thon (large drum), krap khu (nutcracker-style clapper), chap lek (cymbals), ching (cymbals), krap phuang (fan), and rammana (small drum). The ching player acts as the conductor of the Thai ensemble, providing the audible beat for the others to follow. Courtesy of Center for the Study of World Musics, Kent State University.

Poor children in urban areas may contribute to family income through various activities such as selling newspapers or small jasmine wreaths on the streets.

16 ● SPORTS

Thai kick-boxing is a very popular spectator sport and is regularly televised. Well-trained boxers can effectively and gracefully attack their opponents with their feet, knees, or elbows.

Many Thais enjoy playing badminton and soccer. Another popular game is called *takraw:* A woven rattan (palm stem) ball is kept in the air using parts of the body other than the hands. There are two main types of takraw: one like volleyball with a net, and one like basketball, with a suspended hoop.

17 ● RECREATION

Televised Thai soap operas and other programs are closely followed and enjoyed by Thais of all ages and occupations, from peasants to prime ministers. Popular Thai singers have a huge following among teenagers as well as adults.

Modern-style entertainment like movies, discos, nightclubs and karaoke bars, attracts the younger generation in the cities. Almost all Thai films are produced just for viewing in Thailand, and standards are low. Hollywood action films are always big hits.

18 ● CRAFTS AND HOBBIES

Thai crafts include handwoven silk and cotton, woodcarvings, silverwork, basketry, and lacquerware. Chiang Mai is the center for crafts. Beautiful handwoven textiles and basketry can also be found in the northeast.

Raising turtledoves and other birds, especially for singing competitions, is a popular hobby in the south.

19 ● SOCIAL PROBLEMS

Thailand is confronting numerous social crises. The gap between the poor and the rich is very wide and increasing. Thailand is notorious for prostitution, especially child prostitutes, and acquired immune deficiency syndrome (AIDS). Bangkok suffers from serious pollution and traffic congestion.

20 ● BIBLIOGRAPHY

Keyes, Charles F. *Thailand: Buddhist Kingdom as Modern Nation-State.* Boulder, Colo.: Westview Press, 1987.

Kulick, Elliott. *Thailand's Turn: Profile of a New Dragon.* New York: St. Martin's, 1992.

LePoer, Barbara Leitch, ed. *Thailand, A Country Study.* 6th ed. Washington, D.C.: Library of Congress, 1989.

McNair, S. *Thailand.* Chicago: Children's Press, 1987.

WEBSITES

Embassy of Thailand, Washington, D.C. [Online] Available http://www.thaiembdc.org/, 1998.

Interknowledge Corp. [Online] Available http://www.interknowledge.com/thailand/, 1998.

World Travel Guide. Thailand. [Online] Available http://www.wtgonline.com/country/th/gen.html, 1998.

Trinidad and Tobago

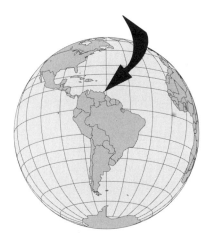

The population of Trinidad is estimated to be 43 percent black, 40 percent Indian, 14 percent of mixed descent, 1 percent European, and 2 percent Chinese and other. Tobago is predominantly black.

Trinidadians and Tobagonians

PRONUNCIATION: tri-nih-DAD-ee-uhns (and) tah-bay-GO-nee-uhns
LOCATION: Trinidad and Tobago (TRI-nih-dad and tah-BAY-go)
POPULATION: 1.3 million
LANGUAGE: English; English-derived Creole with African and other elements; Hindi; Urdu; Spanish
RELIGION: Roman Catholicism; Church of England and Church of Scotland; Methodist, Seventh-Day Adventist, Pentecostal, Baptist, and other Protestant churches; Hinduism; Islam; Christian-African sects

1 ● INTRODUCTION

The nation of Trinidad and Tobago consists of two Caribbean islands that have been united politically since 1962. (The people of both islands are generally referred to today as "Trinidadians.") The islands were originally inhabited by the Arawaks, Caribs, and other Amerindians. In 1498 they were claimed by Christopher Columbus for the Spanish, but Trinidad was ceded to the British by 1802. By 1814, Tobago, which had changed hands several times, was also a British possession. In 1888 Tobago was joined with Trinidad as a colonial territory under the name Trinidad and Tobago.

In the twentieth century, Trinidad's nationalistic hopes were symbolized by one revered leader, Eric Williams. In 1955, Williams founded the People's National Movement (PNM). Trinidad and Tobago became an independent member of the British Commonwealth in 1962 and a republic in 1976.

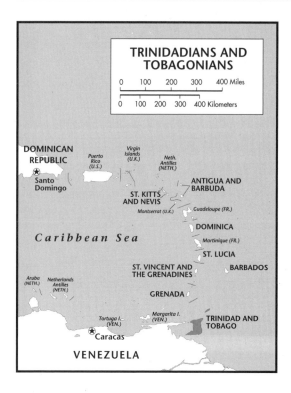

TRINIDADIANS AND TOBAGONIANS

0 100 200 300 400 Miles

0 100 200 300 400 Kilometers

DOMINICAN REPUBLIC

Santo Domingo

Puerto Rico (U.S.)

Virgin Islands (U.K.)

Neth. Antilles (NETH.)

ANTIGUA AND BARBUDA

ST. KITTS AND NEVIS

Montserrat (U.K.)

Guadeloupe (FR.)

Caribbean Sea

DOMINICA

Martinique (FR.)

ST. LUCIA

ST. VINCENT AND THE GRENADINES

BARBADOS

Aruba (NETH.)

Netherlands Antilles (NETH.)

GRENADA

Tortuga I. (VEN.)

Margarita I. (VEN.)

TRINIDAD AND TOBAGO

Caracas

VENEZUELA

Williams remained the head of the government until his death in 1981.

During the worldwide oil crisis of the 1970s, Trinidad and Tobago enjoyed a period of great prosperity and development thanks to offshore oil reserves. However, at the end of the decade, world oil prices declined, and the nation suffered an economic recession. Trinidad and Tobago still faces the challenge of stabilizing its economy and reducing its dependence on world oil prices.

2 ● LOCATION

Trinidad and Tobago are the southernmost islands of the West Indies. With an area of 1,864 square miles (4,828 square kilometers), Trinidad is the largest island of the Lesser Antilles. Three mountain ranges stretch across the country from east to west. Tiny Tobago is only about 26 miles (42 kilometers) long and 7 miles (11 kilometers) wide. It consists of lowlands dominated by a chain of volcanic hills that runs the length of the island.

A little over 40 percent of Trinidad and Tobago's 1.3 million people are black, another 40 percent are of Asian Indian descent, about 15 percent are of mixed descent, and smaller numbers are Chinese or European.

3 ● LANGUAGE

English is the nation's official language. However, the common language of the great majority of residents is an English-derived Creole dialect that contains elements of African and other languages. Hindi and Urdu are spoken by segments of the Indian population. Spanish is spoken in some areas as well.

In Trinidadian Creole, the plural form of "you" is *allyu,* and the French-English *ah wee* means "ours." French expressions such as *il fait chaud* (literally, "it makes hot") and *il y a* (literally, "it there has") are mirrored in the Trinidadian "it making hot" and "it have," which is used for "there is."

Amerindian-derived words include the names of foods—cassava, balata, and roocoo—as well as place names, including Guayaguayare and Carapichaima.

4 ● FOLKLORE

Trinidadian folklore includes devils in disguise, a wolfman named Lagahoo, and a variety of other figures. Folktales are told about Papa Bois, the ruler of the forest, and his son, Callaloo. Other folklore figures include Diablesse, a character comparable to Circe in Greek mythology. She attracts men and then turns them into hogs, after which they fall down a cliff.

5 ● RELIGION

About one-third of Trinidad and Tobago's population are Roman Catholic. Trinidadians of African descent also belong to the Church of England and a variety of other churches. The Baptist religion is especially popular on Tobago. Trinidad's Asian Indian community embraces the Hindu and Muslim religions.

There are also religious sects that combine Christianity with African religious beliefs and practices. The best known of these is Shango. It honors both Shango, the god of thunder and lightning, and Christian saints. Through dance and drumming, its priests, called *mogbas,* summon spirits known as *orishas.*

6 ● MAJOR HOLIDAYS

Due to the nation's religious diversity, Trinidad and Tobago has many public holidays. The major Christian holy days are observed. The Hindu holidays of Divali (pronounced "Duwali") and Ramleema are also recognized. The Muslim festival of Hosay has grown into a four-day festival that includes Trinidadian cultural features such as tassa drumming. Emancipation Day (August 1) and Independence Day (August 31) are secular holidays marking important dates in the nation's history.

Trinidad and Tobago's most important festival is its Carnival. This celebration is recognized as one of the world's most extravagant and colorful pre-Lenten celebrations. The entire nation participates in this 200-year-old tradition, which is held in the final two days preceding Lent (in February). The main activities take place in Port of Spain. Preparations begin months in advance. The participating groups, called "bands," plan their "mas" (short for "masquerade") costumes. Each band chooses a historical, cultural, fantastic, or folkloric theme. Hundreds of coordinated costumes are painstakingly debated, designed, and assembled.

Musical competitions between rival calypso and steel drum groups are held in the period leading up to Carnival. On the Sunday before Ash Wednesday, the King and Queen of Carnival are chosen based on their costumes. The Carnival festivities officially begin at dawn on Monday morning, called *Jour Ouvert,* or *Joovay.* They include massive parades by the organized "bands"—each ranging from 500 to over 2,000 members. The climax of the celebration is the judging of the best costumed band.

7 ● RITES OF PASSAGE

Major life transitions, such as birth, marriage, and death, are marked by religious ceremonies appropriate to each Trinidadian's faith community.

8 ● RELATIONSHIPS

Trinidadians are known for enjoying life, even in the face of hardship. When curfews were imposed in 1970, they held "Curfew fêtes (festivals)." When the country's economy suffered from falling oil prices in the 1980s, people threw "Recession fêtes."

Another aspect of this casual attitude can be seen in the practice called *liming.* (This is the counterpart of "hanging out" in the United States.) Trinidadian men have a long tradition of congregating at street corners, on front stoops, or near movie houses. They chat and pass the time as they take in the passing scene.

Long before it was heard in the United States, the phrase "Yo! Wha' appenin" was a common working-class greeting in Port of Spain, the capital city.

9 ● LIVING CONDITIONS

The traditional Trinidadian house, called an *ajoupa,* was built of thatch and mud. Today, most Trinidadians live in wooden houses with roofs of galvanized metal. The houses generally have three or four rooms. Almost all houses have indoor plumbing, and most have electricity. Several houses often share one yard.

There is a serious housing shortage in Trinidad and Tobago. Many city dwellers live in slums and tenement buildings

10 ● FAMILY LIFE

Women wield considerable authority within African families in Trinidad and Tobago. Many are heads of households. Common-law marriages are widespread within the African community.

Among the Indian population, large extended-family households are common. Even members of smaller households have a strong sense of obligation toward their relatives outside the nuclear family. Arranged

marriages are common, and the man is always considered the head of the household. Divorce and remarriage for widows are discouraged.

11 ● CLOTHING

Most Trinidadians wear modern Western-style clothing. The Caribbean "shirt jac," a belted jacket worn with a scarf and no shirt, is popular among men in Port of Spain. Traditional clothing—including men's turbans and women's saris—is worn by some members of the country's Asian Indian population.

Every year special clubs spend months preparing extravagant costumes for Trinidad and Tobago's famous Carnival celebration. The brightly colored outfits may be made of either cotton or such dressy fabrics as velvet, satin, and lamé. They are often decorated with beads, feathers, sequins, shells, leaves, and straw.

12 ● FOOD

The rich and varied cuisine of Trinidad and Tobago combines African, Asian Indian, Amerindian, Chinese, Middle Eastern, and European influences.

One of the country's most popular foods is *roti.* (A recipe for the bread follows.) Roti is a flat bread, similar to the Indian *naan,* that is filled with curried beef, chicken, lamb, and beef, and cooked vegetables. Curried potatoes and chickpeas are added as well. Another favorite dish is *sans coche,* a pork stew served with dumplings. *Callaloo* is a mixture of okra and puréed dasheen leaves (also called callaloo greens), with either crab or salted pork added for flavor. *Coocoo,* a cake similar to cornbread, is made from corn flour and okra. The national beverage of Trinidad and Tobago is rum.

13 ● EDUCATION

Formal education—which begins at age five—is highly valued in Trinidad and Tobago. The country has a literacy rate of about 96 percent. About 75 percent of high-school-age students are enrolled in school. The University of the West Indies has a campus on Trinidad.

14 ● CULTURAL HERITAGE

Two forms of native Trinidadian music—calypso and steel drum music—have become famous throughout the world. Steel drum music originated when members of traditional African percussion bands began using discarded oil drums. The bottoms are cut off and the tops hammered into a convex shape marked by a pattern of dents that produce different pitches.

Probably the best-known Trinidad-born writer is V. S. Naipaul, author of such books as *Miguel Street* and *A House for Mr. Biswas*. Other well-known writers include Michael Anthony and Samuel Selvon. Derek Walcott, the 1992 Nobel laureate in literature, was born on the Caribbean island of St. Lucia but has spent much of his time in Trinidad.

Peter Minshall, a celebrated designer for Carnival masquerade bands, has also become well-known and well-respected in the international art world.

15 ● EMPLOYMENT

About 34 percent of the labor force in Trinidad and Tobago are employed in service-related jobs; 17 percent in trade; 15 percent in mining and manufacturing; 10 percent in agriculture, forestry, and fishing; and the remainder in other occupations. Agriculture in Trinidad and Tobago is carried out

---

Recipe

Roti

Ingredients
4 cups flour
4 teaspoons baking powder
1 teaspoon salt
1½ cups water
Nonstick cooking spray

Directions

1. Combine flour, baking powder, and salt in a bowl. Add water gradually until a dough is formed.
2. Prepare a clean work surface (cutting board or counter top) by dusting it with flour. Remove the dough from the bowl and knead it on the floured surface.
3. Wet a clean dish towel and wring it out well. Cover the ball of dough with the damp towel and allow it to rest for 30 minutes.
4. Shape the dough into 4 equal-sized balls. Working on the floured surface, form the roti by rolling each ball of dough into a circle about ½ inch thick.
5. Spray a medium skillet with cooking spray. Heat the skillet over medium heat.
6. Cook the roti, one at a time, until brown and puffy. Turn to brown other side.

Serve by wrapping the bread around a filling. Suggestions for fillings include curried chicken salad, or any other sandwich filling or vegetable combination.

Susan D. Rock

Trinidadian steel drum music originated when members of traditional African percussion bands began using discarded oil drums. These objects turn into musical instruments capable of a surprising range of musical nuance and expression in the hands of expert players.

both on large mechanized farms and on small tracts of land worked by peasant farmers without modern farm machinery.

16 ● SPORTS

Sports in Trinidad and Tobago reflect the historical influence of the British. Cricket is extremely popular, as is soccer (called "football"). Horse racing is very popular as well.

17 ● RECREATION

Music plays an important role in everyday life in Trinidad and Tobago. The latest calypso songs can be heard on radios and sound systems throughout the country. SoCa—combining soul ("So-") and calypso ("-Ca")—has been highly popular since the 1980s. Trinidadians also enjoy watching movies and television. American soap operas are especially popular.

18 ● CRAFTS AND HOBBIES

The nation's artisans produce handbeaten copper jewelry, woven straw goods, pottery, woodcarvings, boldly printed fabrics, and other handmade goods.

19 ● SOCIAL PROBLEMS

There is a shortage of housing in the cities, which have difficulties in providing essential public services. High unemployment has led to social unrest, particularly among the country's youth. There has also been an increase in serious crime. Much of it is drug- and gang-related.

20 ● BIBLIOGRAPHY

Bereton, Bridget. *A History of Modern Trinidad.* Portsmouth, N.H.: Heinemann Educational Books, 1982.

Meditz, Sandra W., and Dennis M. Hanratty. *Islands of the Caribbean Commonwealth: A Regional Study.* Washington, D.C.: U.S. Government Printing Office, 1989.

Williams, A. R. "Trinidad and Tobago." *National Geographic* (March 1994), p. 66–89.

Yelvington, Kevin, ed. *Trinidad Ethnicity.* London: MacMillan, 1992.

WEBSITES

Interserv. Discover Trinidad and Tobago. [Online] Available http://discover-tt.net/toc.html, 1997.

World Travel Guide. Trinidad and Tobago. [Online] Available http://www.wtgonline.com/country/tt/gen.html, 1998.

Tunisia

The people of Tunisia are called Tunisians. The population is almost entirely of Arab descent. The small European population consists mostly of French and Italians.

Tunisians

PRONUNCIATION: too-NEE-zhuhns
LOCATION: Western North Africa (the Maghrib)
POPULATION: 8 million
LANGUAGE: Arabic; French
RELIGION: Islam (Sunni Muslim)

1 ● INTRODUCTION

Tunisia is one of the countries forming the Maghrib, the western part of North Africa. Tunisia is the most Westernized state in North Africa. It maintains strong ties with France, the colonizing power from 1881 to 1956.

The various nomadic peoples who first settled the area came to be called Berbers. Roman, Greek, Byzantine, and Arab conquerors all attempted to defeat or assimilate the Berbers into their cultures, with varying degrees of success. In 1574, Muslim troops loyal to the Ottoman Empire (based in present-day Turkey) finally established rule over Tunis, and maintained it for 300 years.

The French seized control of Tunisia in 1881, establishing a protectorate in 1883.

More than 60,000 Tunisians joined the French army to fight in Europe in World War I (1914–18). They also supported France and its allies in World War II (1939–45). Tunisians hoped to be granted independence as a reward but were disappointed. By 1952, Tunisian resistance to French rule turned violent. Many civilians—European and Arab—were killed. By 1956, Tunisia was officially independent. However, France maintained military forces in Tunisia, along with a large civilian presence.

After independence, Tunisia became a one-party socialist state ruled by the Neo-Destour (the New Constitution) Party of Habib Bourguiba. By the 1970s, government oppression and the lack of political freedom led to a series of strikes and demonstrations by students and unions. Throughout the 1980s, the aging Bourguiba became increasingly authoritarian and unreliable in his behavior. In 1987 he was finally deposed by his prime minister, Zine al-

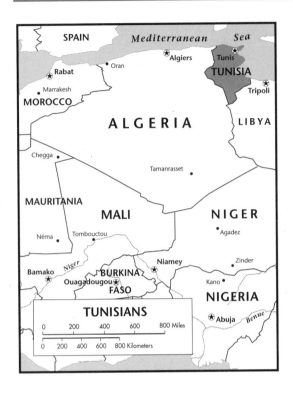

`Abidine Ben `Ali. Ben `Ali was elected president in 1989.

2 ● LOCATION

Tunisia is located on the northern coast of the continent of Africa. It has an area of about 63,320 square miles (164,000 square kilometers). Northern Tunisia is relatively fertile and mountainous. The Dorsale mountain chain extends from the northeast to the southwest. The Mejerda River, which rises in Algeria, drains into the Gulf of Tunis. The far south includes part of the Sahara Desert.

Tunisia has a population of about 8 million people.

3 ● LANGUAGE

Arabic is the national language of Tunisia. Before the Arab conquests, Berber was the chief spoken language. Arabic is a Semitic language related to Hebrew and Aramaic. It is spoken almost universally in Tunisia. After independence, the Tunisian government reintroduced Arabic but maintained the use of French. French is still widely spoken in Tunisia and is used in the sciences, the military, international trade, and foreign diplomacy. Common women's names in Tunisia are *Leila, Hayat, Wasila,* and *Mariam.* Common men's names are *Muhammad, Habib, Moncif,* and `Ali.*

4 ● FOLKLORE

The Maghrib, including Tunisia, has many legends involving Muslim leaders called *marabouts* (holy men). Their burial sites are often sites of pilgrimage. Many people visit their graves to ask for aid.

Some Tunisians believe in evil spirits called *jinn.* These spirits are said to assume the guise of animals. To ward off jinn, Tunisians wear verses from the Koran (the sacred text of Islam) on an amulet, or charm. They also wear the "hand of Fatima," a charm in the shape of the right hand.

Most folklore in Muslim countries tells stories of important figures in religious history. One such story, which is commemorated annually throughout the Islamic world, is that of *al-Isra wa al-Miraj.* According to legend, the Prophet Muhammad traveled at night from Mecca to Jerusalem. From Jerusalem, he rode his wondrous horse, al-Burak, on a nocturnal visit to heaven.

5 ● RELIGION

The overwhelming majority of Tunisians are Muslim. Most Tunisians belong to the Sunni school of Islam.

The Islamic religion has five "pillars," or practices, that must be observed by all Muslims: (1) praying five times a day; (2) giving alms, or *zakat,* to the poor; (3) fasting during the month of Ramadan; (4) making the pilgrimage, or *hajj,* to Mecca; and (5) reciting the *shahada (ashhadu an la illah ila Allah wa ashhadu in Muhammadu rasul 'Allah),* which means "I witness that there is no god but Allah and that Muhammad is the prophet of Allah."

6 ● MAJOR HOLIDAYS

Tunisia commemorates secular and Muslim religious holidays. One major holiday, *Eid al-Fitr,* comes at the end of the fast month of Ramadan. During Ramadan, Muslims refrain from eating, drinking, or sexual relations during the daytime. In Tunisia, however, the practice of fasting is quietly discouraged by the government. However, Eid al-Fitr is still celebrated for three days at the end of the month. The other major Muslim holiday is *Eid al-Adha,* which commemorates the willingness of the prophet Abraham to sacrifice his son to God. Religious holidays are celebrated by going to the mosque for group prayers. Afterwards, worshipers come home to large meals with family and visiting relatives. Part of the feast is normally given to relatives and to the poor.

Secular holidays include the socialist May Day (or Labor Day, May 1); Independence Day (June 1); and Martyrs' Day (April 9), which commemorates a French massacre of Tunisians during the colonial period. There is also a Women's Day (August 13).

7 ● RITES OF PASSAGE

The birth of a child in Tunisia is a much-celebrated event. New mothers are fed a creamy mixture of nuts, sesame seeds, honey, and butter known as *zareer.* On the seventh day after the birth, guests visiting the mother and baby are given the same sweet dessert. On the seventh day, it is also customary to slaughter a lamb and have a dinner party with friends and family.

Under Tunisian law, the minimum marriage age for women is seventeen; men must be at least twenty years old.

Death is considered a natural transition. Mourners are encouraged to bury a loved one as soon as possible after death. Condolences are given for three days after a death. It is understood that the mourning period is over after the third day.

8 ● RELATIONSHIPS

Upon greeting, men shake hands with other men, and with women. Two men who have not seen each other for a long time may kiss on the cheeks. Women either shake hands with other women or kiss each other on the cheeks. Men and women, however, cannot kiss one another in public.

In formal situations, it is common to use titles, mainly French—*Monsieur, Madame, Mademoiselle, Docteur,* and *Professeur.* The

Arabic word for "Mr." is *sayyid*. "Mrs." is *sayyida,* and "Miss" is *anisa.*

Male-female relations are governed by the Islamic code of modesty. Men and women avoid public displays of affection. There is little dating until a man and woman are ready for marriage.

As Muslims, Tunisians eat and shake hands with the right hand. Both men and women smoke, but women hesitate to do so in public.

9 ● LIVING CONDITIONS

Tunisian homes differ from region to region. However, most are built of stone, adobe, or concrete. Most homes have white walls and blue doors. In Tunis, the capital, it is common to find luxury homes and modern apartment buildings. In urban areas, the front doors of houses open directly onto the street. There are no front yards and very few windows. Most single-family homes are small. Many houses are two or three stories high to make up for the small size of the foundation. The flat rooftops are commonly used as outdoor living space.

In rural areas, many families live in *gourbi.* These are permanent tents set up for former herders who are now permanently settled. In southern Tunisia, Berber dwellings are carved out of rocks. In Matmata, homes are built more than 20 feet (6 meters) underground in enormous craters that have a central courtyard. These homes are built out of the mud and stones that are excavated for the construction. They tend to be cool in the summer and warm in the winter.

10 ● FAMILY LIFE

Before the French occupation, Tunisians lived with their extended families in tightly knit communities. Children were raised by the entire extended family. Marriages were conducted by negotiation between the families of the bride and the groom. French occupation and modern industrialization since independence have tended to break down traditional family structures. In the cities as well as rural areas, the nuclear family has begun to be the most common living arrangement.

The role of women has changed noticeably. Women had traditionally been segregated in public life. Their primary responsibilities were raising children and taking care of the home and the husband. Today, women are legally equal to men with regard to inheritance, property ownership, child custody, and divorce. Marriages must have the consent of both parties. Nearly 40 percent of all university students are women. However, traditional expectations of women as keepers of the home and family have continued. This has created unrealistic demands on women and has led to a divorce rate of nearly 50 percent.

11 ● CLOTHING

Many Tunisians dress in Western-style clothing. Traditional dress, however, remains common as well, especially in the villages and among the elderly. Tunisian men often wear a type of fez (headdress) called a *chehia.* It is made of brown or red felt, and is either rounded or flat on top. Traditional male clothing includes a *jalabiyya* (a long dresslike garment) and baggy pants. Women who dress traditionally wear

Cory Langley

Many Tunisians dress in Western-style clothing. Traditional dress, however, remains common as well, especially in the villages.

a *sifsari*. This is a long outer garment with loose folds and a head covering. It is commonly worn over Western-style clothing. Rural women wear a *mellia* (a large, loose head covering) draped across the head and shoulders.

12 ● FOOD

The most popular dish in Tunisia is couscous, which consists of semolina wheat sprinkled with oil and water and rolled into tiny grains. Couscous can be mixed with sauces and used in stews. Lamb cutlets, sea-

food, and shish kebabs are also common foods. *Chakachoukaia* a popular salad made of tomatoes, onions, peppers, and hard-boiled eggs. *Mechouia* (literally, "the grilled") is a main course that combines grilled tomatoes, peppers, and onions with olive oil, tuna fish, sliced hard-boiled eggs, lemon juice, and capers. Tunisians cook a variety of stews called *tajines*. Spinach tajine consists of beans, beef, onions, tomato sauce, pepper, spinach, and egg. Other varieties of tajine make use of everything from chicken to prunes and honey. Tunisians commonly drink strong Turkish coffee and sweet mint tea. Pork and alcohol are forbidden by the Islamic religious code.

13 ● EDUCATION

Tunisia has adopted the French educational system, which has three levels. First, there is a six-year primary-level program that all students must attend. They must pass a major test at the end of their sixth year in order to enter secondary school. After three years of general education, each student specializes during the final four years of high school. Students who do not go to the third level may enroll in three-year vocational programs. All schooling, even at the university level, is free. This includes books, school supplies, uniforms, and meals. Classes are taught in French and Arabic, with an increasing emphasis on Arabic.

14 ● CULTURAL HERITAGE

Malouf, a uniquely Tunisian type of music, is played on lutes, guitars, violins, and drums. Players sing along with the highly rhythmic music. It is thought that malouf originated in North Africa and was exported to Spain in the eighth century. Later it was brought back to Tunisia when Jews and Muslims were expelled from Spain. Today's malouf is sad music. Members of the audience cry as they listen.

15 ● EMPLOYMENT

Almost half of Tunisia's population work in agriculture. Since independence, employment in industrial production has expanded. Many work in oil fields, and in electricity generation, cement production, and mining (especially phosphates). Occupations in the food industry include flour milling, sugar refining, vegetable canning, and water bottling, among others. Tourism is also a major employer. Students attend tourism schools and institutes of hotel management to train for these jobs.

16 ● SPORTS

Tunisia's national sport is soccer (known as "football"). It is a spectator sport and is also played in the streets and open fields. Other popular sports include horseback riding, hunting, and camel racing.

17 ● RECREATION

Tunisians enjoy bathing and socializing in *hammams,* or public bathhouses. There are separate hours for men and women. Cafes are popular hangouts for men in the evenings, where they smoke *chichas* (water pipes) and play cards. Tunisians flock to the beaches that line the coast of the Mediterranean Sea.

Tunisians hold festivals throughout the year. There are camel races at the Sahara festival in January and December, and parades at the Nefta festival in April. A falconry festival is held in the town of el-Hawaria in June.

18 ● CRAFTS AND HOBBIES

Tunisian artisans make goods out of wood, copper, textiles, leather, wrought iron, glass, and ceramics. Rural weavers produce blankets, rugs, and grass mats. Knotted carpets follow traditional decorative designs. Berber rugs *(mergoums)* are brightly colored and have geometric designs.

Jewelry is also handmade in Tunisia. A very popular design is the shape of a hand, known as the *khomsa,* or the "Hand of Fatima." This is made of either gold or silver and is found on earrings and pendants.

19 ● SOCIAL PROBLEMS

Tunisia's greatest problems are economic difficulties and a lack of political freedom. The labor market is tight and it will be increasingly difficult to meet the job demands of the growing work force. In the past, many Tunisians have emigrated to France and Italy in search of work.

20 ● BIBLIOGRAPHY

Brown, Roslind Varghese. *Tunisia,* Cultures of the World. New York: Marshall Cavendish, 1998.
Fox, M. *Tunisia.* Chicago: Children's Press, 1990.
Perkins, Kenneth J. *Historical Dictionary of Tunisia.* Metuchen, N.J.: Scarecrow Press, 1989.
Perkins, Kenneth J. *Tunisia: Crossroads of the Islamic and European Worlds.* Nations of the Contemporary Middle East. Boulder, Colo.: Westview Press, 1986.

WEBSITES
ArabNet. [Online] Available http://www.arab.net/tunisia/tunisia_contents.html, 1998.
World Travel Guide. Tunisia. [Online] Available http://www.wtgonline.com/country/tn/gen.html, 1998.

Turkey

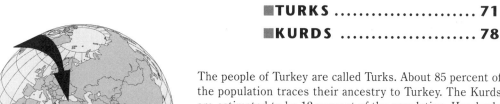

The people of Turkey are called Turks. About 85 percent of the population traces their ancestry to Turkey. The Kurds are estimated to be 12 percent of the population. Hundreds of thousands of Armenians were either killed or forced to flee Turkey during and immediately following World War I; bitterness between Armenians and Turks continues to this day.

Turks

PRONUNCIATION: TUHRKS
LOCATION: Turkey
POPULATION: 61.2 million
LANGUAGE: Turkish
RELIGION: Islam (Sunni Muslim)

1 ● INTRODUCTION

Since the eleventh century, Turks have inhabited the area that is modern Turkey. The ancestors of today's Turks, known as the Seljuk Turks, won control of the region in AD 1071.

By the fifteenth century, Turkish culture and the Turkish language had spread throughout the area. Power peaked under the Ottoman Turks, who overtook the area in 1453. The Ottomans eventually built one of the great empires in world history. It stretched from the Middle East to northern Africa to southern and eastern Europe.

The power of the Ottoman Empire reached its height during the reign of Süleyman the Magnificent in the sixteenth century. During his reign, the Empire took over large parts of southern and eastern Europe. Between the seventeenth and nineteenth centuries, the Ottoman Empire suffered a gradual decline. After World War I (1914–18), the empire was dissolved. The territory of the empire was divided among the United Kingdom, France, Italy, and Greece. The Turks wanted to re-establish their homeland, and were led by Mustafa Kemal (later known as Atatürk) in a successful nationalist uprising. Atatürk helped form a nonreligious, democratic republic in 1923. Over the next fifteen years, until his death in 1938, Atatürk built the modern Turkish nation. Since the end of World War II (1939–45), Turkey has had a series of civilian and military governments. A civilian government has led Turkey uninterrupted since 1984.

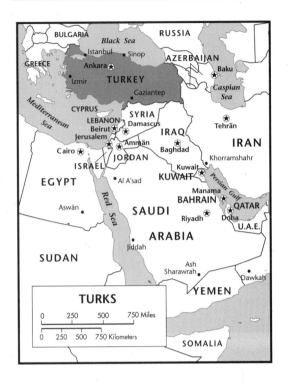

BULGARIA
Black Sea
RUSSIA
Istanbul • Sinop
GREECE
Ankara ☆
AZERBAIJAN
Baku •
İzmir •
TURKEY
Caspian
Sea
Gaziantep
CYPRUS
Mediterranean
Sea
SYRIA
LEBANON • Damascus
Beirut ☆
Jerusalem ☆
IRAQ
Tehrān ☆
IRAN
Cairo ☆ • Ammān
JORDAN
Baghdad •
Khorramshahr
ISRAEL
Kuwait •
EGYPT
• Al A'sad
KUWAIT
Manama
Red Sea
BAHRAIN
QATAR
Aswān •
SAUDI
Riyadh ☆ • Doha
U.A.E.
ARABIA
SUDAN
Jiddah •
Ash
Sharawrah •
• Dawkah
YEMEN

TURKS

0   250   500   750 Miles
0 250 500 750 Kilometers

SOMALIA

Arabs, Greeks, and Armenians. With more than 160 million people worldwide, many of them in Central Asia, the Turks are among the world's largest ethnic groups.

3 ● LANGUAGE

More than 90 percent of Turkey's population speaks Turkish. Words with Arabic and Persian origins are common. In addition, a number of modern words that had no Turkish equivalents were borrowed from European languages. These include words derived from English, such as *otomobil* (automobile), *tren* (train), and *taksi* (taxi).

Turkish words are formed by adding suffixes to a root that does not change. A root and its suffixes can form an entire sentence. The most famous example of this is the following:

Afyonkarahisarlilaturaadiklaimizdanmuymustiniz.

2 ● LOCATION

Turkey lies partly in Europe and partly in Asia. It has historically served as a bridge between the two continents. It is a relatively large country. It is bordered on the west by Greece, Bulgaria, and the Aegean Sea; on the east by Iran, Armenia, and Georgia; on the south by Iraq, Syria, and the Mediterranean Sea; and on the north by the Black Sea. It is slightly larger than the state of Texas but has three times its population.

In 1994, Turkey had an estimated population of 61.2 million (up from 56.5 million in the 1990 census). Between 80 and 90 percent of the population is composed of ethnic Turks. Kurds form the country's largest ethnic minority. Other minorities include

It means:"Weren't you one of the people whom we tried without success to make resemble the citizens of Afyonkarahisar?"

There are two forms of "goodbye." *Allahaismarladik* is said by the person who is leaving. *Güle güle* is said by the person who stays behind. There are also two common words for "no": *hayir*, the more emphatic (and less polite), and *yok*, which literally means "there is none."

4 ● FOLKLORE

The Turks have a rich tradition of folktales. Some folktales can take as long as thirty hours to recite. The most popular involve the legendary Nasreddin Hoca, a comic fig-

Cory Langley

Although many Turks live in modern houses like those above, Turkey faces a housing shortage that is among its most serious social problems.

ure who was a teacher in the thirteenth century. The following are typical Hoca stories:

One day, the Hoca was sitting in his garden under the shade of a walnut tree. Looking around his garden, he wondered why Allah (God) caused large, heavy watermelons to grow on spindly vines while little walnuts grew on tall trees. He mused that, if he had been the creator, he would have done just the reverse. Just then, a walnut fell from the tree, hitting him on the forehead, and the Hoca thanked Allah for arranging the world just as it was, grateful that he hadn't been struck by a watermelon instead.

When the Hoca lost his donkey, he prayed and thanked God. Asked why he was grateful for losing his donkey, he replied, "I'm fortunate that I wasn't riding him when he got lost, or I would be lost as well."

5 ● RELIGION

More than 99 percent of Turks are Muslims (followers of Islam), mostly of the Sunni sect. Shi'ite and Alawite Muslim populations live in the east and southeast of the country. There are a small number of Jews whose ancestors fled the Spanish Inquisition in 1492. There are also small numbers of Armenian, Syrian, and Greek Orthodox Christians.

6 ● MAJOR HOLIDAYS

Turkey observes the following secular (non-religious) holidays: New Year's Day (January 1); Children's Day, also known as National Sovereignty Day (April 23); Atatürk's birthday, also National Youth and Sports Day (May 19); Victory Day (August 30); Republic Day (October 28–29); and the anniversary of Atatürk's death (November 10), a national day of mourning when all forms of entertainment are shut down and the nation observes a moment of silence at 9:05 PM, the time of Atatürk's death.

The Turks also observe a number of Islamic holidays. *Recep Kandili* commemorates the conception of the prophet Muhammad. *Mirac Kandili* marks Muhammad's journey from Mecca to Jerusalem and his ascension to Heaven. *Berat Kandili* is a nighttime holiday similar to All Hallows' Eve in Christianity. *Kadir Gecesi* commemorates the night when the Koran (the sacred text of Islam) was revealed to Muhammad and he received his calling as the Messenger of God.

7 ● RITES OF PASSAGE

A number of popular traditional beliefs and superstitions surround childbirth. Magical formulas are used to ensure the birth of a son. Many people also believe a newborn child is especially vulnerable to evil spirits during the first forty days of life. All male Turkish Muslims are circumcised, either at the age of seven or later as part of an initiation into adulthood.

Wedding ceremonies are performed in the town or city hall. They are followed by private receptions with food, dancing, and music. Dowries (money or material goods paid to the groom's family) are paid by the bride's family in some rural areas.

8 ● RELATIONSHIPS

The Turks are an exceptionally polite people, particularly to visitors. They use many courteous phrases in everyday conversation.

It is considered impolite to hug or kiss members of the opposite sex in public. A handshake that is too firm is also considered a sign of bad manners. On the other hand, it is acceptable and customary for men to publicly display physical affection toward each other. They often embrace and kiss when they greet each other, and walk down the street arm-in-arm or holding hands.

9 ● LIVING CONDITIONS

Turkey faces a housing shortage that is among its most serious social problems. Since the 1950s, people have built temporary shelters called *gecekondus* on the outskirts of major cities. The neighborhoods created by these dwellings have turned into permanent slums. They often lack running water, sewage systems, electricity, and pavement. By the 1980s, it was estimated that more than half the residents of some cities lived in gecekondus.

Between 30 and 40 percent of Turkey's population lives in rural areas, where housing types vary by region. Houses in the rural villages of the Black Sea region are made of wood. On the Anatolian plateau they are generally made of sun-dried brick. Village houses are generally two stories high with

Cory Langley

The quality of education in urban and rural areas varies significantly. Many rural communities do not have high schools making it necessary for children to travel great distances if they want to continue their education.

flat roofs. In the eastern part of the country, many lack running water and some have no electricity.

10 ● FAMILY LIFE

In spite of legal equality, women in Turkey often face discrimination. This is especially true in rural areas. Turkish women are not, however, forced to wear the veil (known as the *chador*) as women are in other Muslim nations.

In urban areas, working women hold positions similar to those of their counterparts in Europe and the United States. The number of professional women has grown significantly in recent years.

In 1993, the American-educated economist Tansu Çiller became the country's first woman prime minister. She served as prime minister until 1995, when her coalition government fell apart.

Traditionally, Turkish marriages were arranged. In rural areas some still are. The extended family is important in rural areas, but less so in cities. In rural areas, women still marry at young ages. Financial arrangements between the two families are important in making marriage decisions.

11 ● CLOTHING

Modern Western-style clothing has been worn in Turkey since the founding of the republic in the 1920s. In urban areas, both adults and teenagers look much the same as those in the cities of the West. In villages and certain tourist areas, one may still see the traditional *salvar,* baggy, loose-fitting trousers that are worn by both men and women.

12 ● FOOD

The most famous dish of Turkish origin is the shish kebab, pieces of lamb grilled on a skewer. Today, the most popular national dish is the *döner kebap*, lamb roasted on a turning vertical spit, from which slices are cut as it cooks.

Turkey is also famous for its appetizers, called *meze,* made from meat, fish, and vegetables. The most popular include *böreks,* rolled dough stuffed with white cheese and parsley; *dolmasi,* various types of vegetables stuffed with rice and meat; and *imam bayildi,* eggplant stuffed with ground lamb, onions, and tomatoes. The name *imam bayildi,* means "the imam swooned," suggesting that the dish was so delicious it made a religious leader (an imam) faint when he tried it.

EPD Photos

The darabuka, *the traditional Turkish drum. Courtesy of the Center for the Study of World Musics, Kent State University.*

13 ● EDUCATION

In 1990, the adult literacy rate (ability to read and write) was 80 percent (90 percent for males aged fifteen and over, compared with only 70 percent for their female counterparts). Primary education has been available to almost all children between the ages of six and ten since the 1980s.

Education is not compulsory past middle school. Even to that level it is estimated that only 60 percent of children attend school. The quality of education in urban and rural areas varies significantly. Many rural communities do not have high schools. This sometimes makes it necessary for children to travel great distances if they want to continue their education.

There are several hundred institutions of higher learning in Turkey. Students are admitted to Turkey's public universities through a central placement system.

14 ● CULTURAL HERITAGE

Whirling dervishes are devotees of a small religious sect who attempt to unite with God by dancing frantically to wild music. Their white-clad, rapidly turning figures in swirling skirts are known the world over. The Turks also have a centuries-old tradition of folk dancing. It varies from one region to the next, each with its own distinctive homemade costumes.

Turkish painting dates back to the court painters of the Ottoman Empire. The contemporary painter Rahmi Pehlivanli is known for his portraits of leading political and diplomatic figures and his landscapes of different regions of the country.

Several of Turkey's leading literary figures in modern times have been involved in political controversies. Many of their works have been censored or banned. Although Turkey's constitution guarantees freedom of expression, the government places restrictions on the media. The writings of Nazim Hikmet, a Marxist poet who died in the former Soviet Union in 1963, were banned for years but are now gaining recognition. The left-wing satirist Aziz Nesin, who published excerpts from Salman Rushdie's controversial *Satanic Verses*, was jailed for much of his life. He died in 1995.

Yasar Kemal, a leading novelist, has been harassed in recent years over the content of a newspaper article he authored. Turkey's most famous filmmaker, Yilmaz Güney, was imprisoned for most of his career, writing screenplays in prison and smuggling them out through friends, along with detailed instructions for their direction.

Traditional Turkish music is rich and complex. Traditional instruments include the *ud* and the *saz* (both of which resemble the lute), the *darabuka* (a drum), and the *ney* (sometimes spelled *nay*—a flute).

15 ● EMPLOYMENT

The services sector, including a growing tourist industry, accounts for more than half of all jobs. Agriculture accounts for most of the rest. In rural areas, all family members participate in agricultural work. Industry employs less than 10 percent of the work force.

16 ● SPORTS

The most popular sport in Turkey is soccer. Matches are played on weekends between September and May. Like their counterparts in Europe and Latin America, Turkey's soccer fans are wildly enthusiastic. Celebrations can sometimes turn into riots.

Wrestling is another favorite sport in Turkey. A unique Turkish variety is greased wrestling, which makes it harder to hold on to one's opponent. Other popular sports include hunting and shooting, skiing (the oldest Turkish ski resort is on Mount Olympus, the legendary home of the Greek gods), and *cirit*, a traditional sport that involves throwing a javelin while mounted on horseback.

17 ● RECREATION

Among the traditional Turkish forms of relaxation, the best known is the steam bath, or *hamam*. Both men and women use the *hamam*, although separately. Wood-burning stoves are used as heat sources, with bathers absorbing heat by lying on raised slabs directly above the stoves.

The time-honored leisure-time haunt of Turkish men is the coffeehouse (*kiraathane*), where backgammon is often played and one can still find customers smoking *hookahs* (water pipes).

18 ● CRAFTS AND HOBBIES

Turkey's most famous handicrafts are its carpets, which sport a dazzling array of designs. Tiles and ceramics have been produced in Turkey since the eleventh century and can still be seen adorning the walls of mosques and other buildings.

Another form of folk art is the traditional shadow-puppet theater called *Karagöz*. It dates back to the 1400s and was sometimes used as a vehicle for political satire. Today *Karagöz* is a dying art due to competition from modern forms of entertainment and a shortage of performers willing to go through the difficult training it requires.

19 ● SOCIAL PROBLEMS

Turkey's most pressing social problem is its very high rate of population growth. Overpopulation strains the country's resources (including its educational resources), results in unemployment, and decreases the amount of agricultural produce available for export. High inflation and widespread tax evasion are other ongoing problems.

20 ● BIBLIOGRAPHY

Ahmad, Feroz. *The Making of Modern Turkey.* New York: Routledge, 1993.
Lye, Keith. *Turkey.* New York: F. Watts, 1987.
Rugman, Jonathan. *Ataturk's Children: Turkey and the Kurds.* New York: Cassell, 1996.

WEBSITES
Embassy of Turkey, Washington, D.C. [Online] Available http://www.turkey.org/turkey/, 1998.
World Travel Guide, Turkey. [Online] Available http://www.wtgonline.com/country/tr/gen.html, 1998.

Kurds

PRONUNCIATION: KURDS
LOCATION: Turkey; Iraq; Syria; Iran; Lebanon; Armenia; Azerbaijan; Germany
POPULATION: 5–22 million
LANGUAGE: Kurdish
RELIGION: Islam

1 ● INTRODUCTION

Kurds have almost never had a country of their own. "Kurdistan" is the mountainous area where the borders of Iraq, Iran, and Turkey meet. The average altitude is 6,000 feet (1,950 meters) and much of the land is inaccessible (difficult to reach). For most of their history Kurds have been a part of the Persian and Ottoman empires. (The Persian Empire became modern Iran. The Ottoman Empire became modern Turkey.)

From 1920 to 1923, an independent Kurdistan existed. In 1923, Kurdistan was divided between the two countries that are Iraq and Turkey today. Since then, the Kurds have been divided between Iran, Iraq, Syria, and Turkey. They have struggled to build an independent nation. Guerrilla fighters called *peshmerga* (one who faces death) fight to win territory for Kurdistan. The long years of war and hostility between Iran and Iraq have put the Kurds in a very difficult position. They have large communities in both countries and are constantly caught in the fighting between the two countries. In Turkey, the Kurdistan Workers Party (PKK) is a radical group that campaigns for Kurdish independence. The PKK is a terrorist organization. Sometimes they resort to killing of civilians to further their cause. Because of this, many Kurds oppose them.

2 ● LOCATION

Population estimates for the Kurds range from 5 million to 22 million. More Kurds live in Turkey than anywhere else. They are the second-largest ethnic group in Turkey, Iraq, and Syria. They are the third-largest group (after Azerbaijanis) in Iran. Kurds also live in Lebanon, Armenia, Azerbaijan, Germany, and other places across Europe, the United States, Canada, and Australia. Although they live among them, Kurds are ethnically unrelated to Turks, Arabs, and Iranians.

3 ● LANGUAGE

The Kurdish language is related to Persian (or Farsi), the language spoken in Iran. Kurdish, like Persian, has also borrowed many words from the Arabic language. Until 1991, it was illegal to speak Kurdish in Turkey except at home. The skillful use of language is highly valued by Kurds. Cleverness and a command of poetry are considered important skills.

COMMON KURDISH WORDS

English	Kurdish	Pronunciation
bread	nan	NAHN
you	tu	TOO
friend	yar	YAHR
child	zar	ZAHR
water	av	AHV

Modern Kurdish names are mostly Arabic or Persian. The mother usually names her child. Kurds did not traditionally use surnames (last names), so most modern surnames are tribal designations or geographic locations.

4 ● FOLKLORE

Modern-day Kurds are descendants of ancient Indo-European peoples known as the Medes. They moved into the Middle East 4,000 years ago. The Muslim hero Saladin (Salah Ad-Din Yusuf Ibn Ayyub, AD 1137–93) was a Kurd, as were many of his soldiers. Saladin became the sultan (king) of Egypt and Syria in 1174.

A well-known folktale, "Kawe the Blacksmith and Zohak," explains the origin of Nawruz, the Persian New Year celebration. According to the story, Zohak was an evil king who enslaved the Kurds. One year, on the first day of spring, Kawe the Blacksmith led the Kurds in a revolt against Zohak. They surrounded Zohak's palace, and Kawe charged past the guards. He grabbed Zohak by the neck with a powerful blacksmith's hand, and struck Zohak on the head with his hammer. The Kurds set bonfires on the mountaintops to announce their freedom from Zohak. The event is said to have taken place around 700 BC.

5 ● RELIGION

The Kurds at first resisted the Islamic invasion during the seventh century AD. They gave in after the Islamic victory near the modern-day Iraqi city of Sulaimaniya in AD 643. Most Kurds are now Sunni Muslims (a branch of Islam). About one-fifth are Shi'ite Muslims, most of whom live in Iran.

Many Kurds belong to Sufi (Islam mystic) brotherhoods. They meet to chant and dance together to worship Allah. The Sufi brotherhoods are very important in Kurdish village life. There are about 1 million Kurdish 'Alawis (a secretive faith based on and distinct from Islam) in Turkey, and 40,000 to 70,000 Yazidis mostly in Armenia and Azerbaijan. Yazidism is a small religion that combines aspects of Islam, Judaism, and Christianity. A very few Kurds are Christian.

6 ● MAJOR HOLIDAYS

The most important Kurdish holiday is the *Nawruz*, or Persian New Year. It is celebrated at the time of the spring equinox, or first day of spring (March 21). There are special foods, fireworks, dancing, singing, and poetry recitations. Spring flowers (such as tulips, hyacinths, and pussy willows) are cut, new clothes are worn, and pottery is smashed for good luck. Families spend the day in the country, enjoying nature and the fresh growth of spring. During the thirteen days after Nawruz, families visit each other and visit the graves of dead relatives. Everyone tries to resolve any conflicts or misunderstandings that may be carried from the year before.

Even though most Kurds are longer nomads, they continue to celebrate important dates associated with that way of life. These include lambing time, celebration before moving the herds to summer pastures, shearing time, and the time of return to the village in the fall. Islamic holidays vary in importance among individual Kurds.

7 ● RITES OF PASSAGE

The greatest occasion for celebration in a Kurd's life is marriage. Kurds marry young, at about seventeen or eighteen. The bride is dressed in gold bracelets, earrings and necklaces, and a new dress and shoes. The highlight of the wedding is the public procession from the home of the bride to the home of the groom.

After they reach the groom's home, the veiled bride enters the house and sits quietly in a corner of the room while the guests feast and dance outside. In some areas, there are horse-riding displays.

Parents and relatives hold a feast for the birth of a child, especially the birth of a first son. Most boys are circumcised during the first week after birth. In some more traditional Kurdish communities, boys are circumcised at age ten, followed by a huge party.

8 ● RELATIONSHIPS

The Kurds are very family oriented. Family lines are patriarhcal—traced along the father's ancestry. Marriage between first cousins is common. A man often marries the daughter of one of his father's brothers. This practice is common among many cultures.

Tribal leadership among the Kurds is inherited. However, local leaders are chosen for their personal qualities, including integrity, generosity, and skill at dealing with government officials.

9 ● LIVING CONDITIONS

Most Kurds live in small villages in remote mountain regions. A typical Kurdish house is made of mud-brick with a wooden roof. In the summer, Kurds sleep on the roof where it is cooler. Some homes have underground rooms to use in the winter to escape the cold. There is rarely indoor plumbing. Water is carried into the house in jars and cans from a central village well. There is no central heating.

The few remaining nomadic Kurds live in tents made of blackened hides. Extended family members cluster their tents together in small communities.

There are only a few Kurdish towns: Diyarbakir (a sort of capital for Kurds) and Van in Turkey; Erbil and Kirkuk in Iraq; and Mahabad in Iran.

10 ● FAMILY LIFE

Few Kurds marry non-Kurds. Couples may live with one or the other's family after marrying, but they have rooms of their own and separate housekeeping arrangements. Men and women both work in the fields, and boys and girls start helping at an early age.

Kurdish women were traditionally not veiled except during parts of the marriage ceremony. They freely associated with men in most gatherings. If there was no qualified male heir, a woman could become a tribal leader. Even today, living in countries with conservative Islamic governments, many Kurdish women fight alongside the men as *peshmerga* (guerilla fighters). More than 1,000 peshmerga are women. The radical Kurdistan Workers Party (PKK) encourages freedom for women.

11 ● CLOTHING

Traditionally, Kurdish women wore colorful skirts and blouses. Men wore baggy, colorful pants with a plain shirt having very full sleeves, which were tied at the elbow.

Bright-colored vests and sashes (often red) were worn over the shirt. A man wore a blue silk turban on his head, and often completed his costume with a dagger worn at the waist. Traditionally, nomadic Kurdish men shaved their heads and wore long moustaches. Women wore bright, colorful, heavily embroidered clothing.

Traditional dress is becoming rare. Kurds generally dress like the people of the countries where they live. In Iran, women must wear a cloth covering their hair and clothes. In Turkey, on the other hand, the government has banned women from covering their hair in universities and public jobs. Women there are required to wear more Western-style clothing. In Iraq, men wear woolen coats and vests, checkered head-scarves, and baggy pants. Women wear the Muslim-style dress, often with baggy trousers underneath. The traditional Kurdish shoe, the *klash,* is a soft crocheted mocassin with a flexible sole.

12 ● FOOD

Bulghur (cracked wheat) used to be the staple food for Kurds. Rice is becoming more popular. The Kurdish diet includes a wide variety of fruits and vegetables. Cucumbers are especially common. In the valleys where grapes are grown, raisins and grape jam are common. Meat is only eaten on special occasions. The usual beverage is tea. Kurdish specialties include a type of wafer bread eaten for breakfast, and any kind of grain cooked in whey.

A recipe for a flatbread appears on the next page.

Recipe

Nane Casoki
(Bulghur Bread)

Ingredients

2 cups bulghur (cracked wheat)
1 teaspoon salt
½ cup onion, finely chopped
2 cups boiling water
2 cups unbleached white flour

Directions

1. Combine the bulghur, salt, and onion.

2. Pour the boiling water over the mixture and let stand for 30 minutes.

3. Put in a food processor and process for about 20 seconds.

4. Add 1 cup of flour and process again until it is a smooth texture.

(You can also work the flour in by hand, if you do not have a food processor.)

5. Turn the mixture out onto a well-floured surface and knead it, adding flour as necessary to keep the dough from sticking, for about 3 to 4 minutes.

6. Cover the dough and let it rest for at least 15 minutes, or up to 3 hours.

7. Place a large baking sheet (or two small ones) on the bottom rack of the oven, leaving an inch of space between the sheet and the walls of the oven. Preheat the oven to 450°F.

8. After the dough has rested, divide it into 8 pieces and flatten each piece on the well-floured surface.

9. With a rolling pin, roll each piece of dough to a very thin round about 8 to 10 inches in diameter.

10. Place the bread on the baking sheet and bake for 1½ to 2 minutes. Turn the bread over and bake for another minute, or until the bread begins to brown around the edges.

Note: For crispier bread, increase baking time until the bread is spotted with brown all over.

Wrap the baked bread in a clean kitchen towel to keep warm while rolling out and baking the rest of the dough. Serve warm or at room temperature. Makes 8 loaves.

Adapted from Alford, Jeffrey, and Naomi Duguid. *Flatbreads & Flavors: A Baker's Atlas*. New York: William Morrow & Co., 1995, p. 175–76.

13 ● EDUCATION

Schools are not widely available. When they are, classes are not taught in Kurdish, and so many children find school too difficult and drop out. The Kurdish literacy (the ability to read and write) rate is very low. Girls often do not attend school at all. Tradition holds that they are needed at home.

14 ● CULTURAL HERITAGE

Kurdish culture has a rich oral tradition. Most popular are epic poems called *lawj*. These often tell of adventure in love or battle.

Kurdish literature first appeared in the seventh century AD. In 1596, Sharaf Khan,

Emir of Bitlis, composed a history of the Kurds in Persian called the *Sharafnama*. Almost one hundred years later, in 1695, a great national epic called the *Memozin* was written in Kurdish by Ahmed Khani.

Traditional music is played on flute, drums, and the *ut-ut* (similar to a guitar). The music of Sivan Perwar, a Kurdish pop music performer, was banned in Turkey and Iraq in the 1980s, so he left the region to live and work in Sweden.

15 ● EMPLOYMENT

Most Kurds are farmers and sheep- and goat-herders. They sell products from their flocks such as leather, goat cheese, and wool. Women make carpets and cloth to sell at market. Some Kurds grow tobacco. Turkish Kurds grow cotton. A few mountain Kurds are still nomadic herders.

In towns, Kurds work as shopkeepers, plumbers, teachers, bankers, and so on. Kurds work as unskilled laborers in large Turkish cities, as well as in Baghdad and Mosul in Iraq, and Tehran in Iran. Some urban Kurds work as bricklayers, butchers, cattle dealers, and small traders. The oil fields in Turkey and Iraq have attracted many Kurdish workers in recent times. Those Kurds who are able to go abroad find a variety of jobs and send the money back home.

16 ● SPORTS

Popular sports include soccer, wrestling, hunting and shooting, and *cirit*, a traditional sport that involves throwing a javelin while mounted on horseback. Camel- and horse-racing are popular in rural areas.

17 ● RECREATION

Only men go out at night. They often sit at tea houses and cafes and play backgammon or dominoes. A favorite pastime is to listen to tapes or live singers at cafes. Singers have only recently been allowed to sing publicly in Kurdish.

18 ● CRAFTS AND HOBBIES

Carpet-weaving is by far the most significant Kurdish folk art. Other crafts are embroidery, leather-working, and metal ornamentation. Kurds are especially known for copper-working.

19 ● SOCIAL PROBLEMS

The greatest problem for the Kurds is the unwillingness of the nations in which they live to give them cultural independence. Kurds do not currently want an independent state. They only wish to be allowed to maintain their own language and culture.

During the Iran–Iraq War (1980–88), the government of Iraq engaged in genocide to stop the Kurds from fighting for Iran. Thousands of villages were destroyed and tens of thousands of Kurds were murdered and buried in mass graves. The Iraqi government also used nerve gas (purchased from European governments) against Kurdish civilians and Iranian troops. These horrible attacks killed thousands of civilians.

One of the worst massacres occurred in the Iraqi Kurd town of Halabja. The entire population of the town was killed. After the Persian Gulf War (1991), thousands more Kurds were forced into refugee camps. Some of these areas are now protected by the United Nations (UN).

Since 1991, the government of Turkey has attacked Kurdish civilian centers inside the UN-protected areas. Many thousands of Kurds have now fled to Iran. The government there is less hostile, but it has trouble supporting millions of refugees. To make matters worse, there is fighting even among Kurds. Two rival Kurdish groups have fought small wars over who truly represents the Kurdish people. Meanwhile, the Kurdish civilians continue to suffer.

20 ● BIBLIOGRAPHY

Alford, Jeffrey, and Naomi Duguid. *Flatbreads & Flavors: A Baker's Atlas*. New York: William Morrow & Co., 1995.

Bulloch, John, and Harvey Morris. *No Friends But the Mountains: The Tragic History of the Kurds*. New York: Viking, 1992.

King, John. *Kurds*. New York: Thomson Learning, 1994.

Moss, Joyce, and George Wilson. *Peoples of the World: The Middle East and North Africa*, 1st ed. Detroit: Gale Research, 1992.

WEBSITES

Embassy of Turkey, Washington, D.C. [Online] Available http://www.turkey.org/turkey/, 1998.

Human Rights. The Kurds. [Online] Available http://www.humanrights.de/~kurdweb/children, 1998.

Kurds. [Online] Available http://www.itlink.se/lasse/Sol/Library/Struggle/kurds.html, 1998.

World Travel Guide, Turkey. [Online] Available http://www.wtgonline.com/country/tr/gen.html, 1998.

Turkmenistan

The people of Turkmenistan are called Turkmens or Turkomans. Over 70 percent of the population are Turkmens. About 10 percent are Russians, 9 percent are Uzbeks, and over 3 percent are Kazaks. For more information on the Russians, see the chapter on Russia in Volume 8; on the Kazaks, see the chapter on Kazakstan in Volume 5; and on the Uzbeks, see the chapter on Uzbekistan in Volume 9.

Turkmens

PRONUNCIATION: TUHRK-mens

LOCATION: Turkmenistan; northern Iran; northwestern Afghanistan

POPULATION: 5 million

LANGUAGES: Turkmen; Russian; Persian

RELIGION: Islam (Sunni Muslim)

1 ● INTRODUCTION

The ethnic origins of the Turkmens are generally traced to the Oghuz, a loose alliance of Turkic tribes in what is now Mongolia in the seventh and eighth centuries AD. By the twelfth century, Turkmen tribes had migrated into what are now Iran, Azerbaijan, Turkey, and other parts of the Middle East. They established dynasties and played an important role in political life. However, in present-day Turkmenistan, they never united into one political force.

In the 1880s, after bitter fighting, Russia conquered the region. In 1924, the Turkmen Soviet Socialist Republic became one of the fifteen republics of the Union of Soviet Socialist Republics (USSR). Under Soviet rule, property was taken over by the government, traditional social structures were attacked, and the traditional nomadic way of life ceased to exist. With the dissolution of the Soviet Union in the early 1990s, Turkmenistan gained its independence. However, since most political, social, and economic institutions are Soviet holdovers, genuine change has been slow.

There are more than two dozen tribal groupings among the Turkmens today, the largest of which are Teke, Yomut, and Ersari.

2 ● LOCATION

Turkmenistan has an area of 188,450 square miles (488,100 square kilometers). Most of Turkmenistan is a vast, arid desert. In fact,

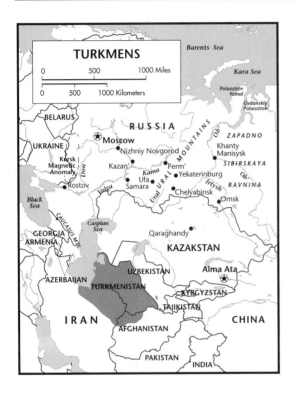

TURKMENS

Central Asia's two largest deserts—the Garagum and the Gyzylgum—make up almost 90 percent of Turkmenistan's territory. To the south are the Balkan and Kopet Dag mountains. Other geographical features are the Caspian Sea in the west, and the Amu Darya River in the east.

An estimated 3 million Turkmens live in Turkmenistan. Some 2 million more live in northern Iran and northwestern Afghanistan.

3 ● LANGUAGE

Turkmen is part of the Oghuz group of Turkic languages. Linguistically, it is close to Azeri (Azerbaijani), Turkish, and Uzbek. It contains many Turkic, Persian, and Ara-bic elements. The Turkmen language used in Turkmenistan borrows many words from Russian.

4 ● FOLKLORE

Like other Central Asian peoples, the Turkmens have a rich folklore tradition of epic stories, tales, and lyric poems. Turkmens maintain a theory of common origin from a mythical ancestor, Oghuz Khan. The original Oghuz tribes—the core of the early Turkmens—are supposed to have descended from this ancestor.

A popular legend says that when Allah (God) made the world, the Turkmens were the first to get a land filled with sunshine, but the last to get any water. The Turkmen folklore tradition also includes various superstitions. Knowledge of and belief in charms, omens, lucky and unlucky days of the week, and the evil eye are common to almost every Turkmen.

Each Turkmen tribe and clan has it own series of legends and tales that define tribal genesis and trace genealogy.

5 ● RELIGION

All Turkmen are Sunni Muslim, and almost every tribe or clan has a legend or account of how it became Muslim. Because they still adhere to some pre-Islamic religious practices, the Turkmens have often been described as "half" Muslims. However, conversion to Islam is often the defining moment in a tribe's or clan's history. Each tribe or clan has its own cemetery and saint's shrine. Members may conduct pilgrimages there when the need arises. At the shrine, a pilgrim may appeal to the saint for good fortune, the safety of a loved one, a cure for an illness, or the birth of a child. Hundreds of such shrines dot the Turkmen landscape.

6 ● MAJOR HOLIDAYS

The most important religious holidays are Islamic holy days celebrated according to the lunar calendar. *Gurban bairamy* commemorates Abraham's willingness to sacrifice his son to God. The *Oraz bairamy* is celebrated at the end of the month of fasting *(Ramadan). Nowruz* (New Year's Day) is an ancient holiday celebrated on March 21. It marks the beginning of spring and the planting season. All of these holidays are marked with family gatherings and feasts. National holidays include Independence Day (October 27) and a series of memorial days. These commemorate Turkmen veterans; victims of the 1948 earthquake in the capital city, Ashgabat; and the end of World War II (1939–45).

7 ● RITES OF PASSAGE

As Muslims, all Turkmen males are circumcised (usually between the ages of three and seven). Through this ceremony they become members of the male community and genuine Muslims. After circumcision, a boy no longer sleeps with his mother, and he spends more time with adult males. Girls make a less dramatic passage into adult womanhood by wearing head scarves, having their ears pierced, and spending more time with women.

Weddings are celebrated with a great deal of festivity and lavish expenditure.

Although funerals are important events, most mourning rituals take place at a later time. On the third, seventh, and fortieth day after a loved one's death, there are large gatherings dedicated to the deceased's memory. These often continue on a yearly basis as well.

8 ● RELATIONSHIPS

Turkmens follow three codes of conduct: *Adat* (Turkmen customary law), *Sherigat* (Islamic law), and *Edep* (rules of proper etiquette and behavior). Much of Turkmen behavior and etiquette come out of these codes. Some aspects of these traditions were lost in the Soviet period (1924–90). However, they still continue to shape social behavior on a daily basis. The essence of these traditions is often referred to as *turkmenchilik,* meaning "Turkmenness." The codes include elaborate and exact modes of greeting based on age and gender, hospitality toward guests, respect toward elders, and a clear sense of tribal identity.

9 ● LIVING CONDITIONS

The traditional Turkmen dwelling is a felt tent called a *gara oy* (black house). It is often called a "yurt" in Western literature. The felt covering is attached to a wooden frame. The tent may be assembled or taken down within an hour. In Turkmenistan it is no longer a primary residence. Instead it is used in summer pasture areas or constructed for recreation or holidays. In rural Turkmenistan, most people live in one-story homes made from clay and straw. Often these homes are located within a walled courtyard which also contains an agricultural plot and livestock. In the cities of Turkmenistan, high-rise apartment dwellings are also common.

The traditional Turkmen dwelling is a felt tent called a gara oy *(black house) or yurt. A felt covering is attached to a wooden frame, and may be assembled or taken down in an hour.*

10 ● FAMILY LIFE

Most Turkmen live in extended families, and elders live with their adult children. Nursing homes are extremely rare. The youngest son bears the primary responsibility for his parents' welfare. Turkmen families are usually large. Families with six or more children are the norm in rural areas. Siblings and close relatives are expected to assist each other in times of need.

Many marriages are arranged, and virtually all must be blessed by the parents. Western-style dating is rare. A suitable match is based on age, social status, education level, tribal affiliation, and other fac-

tors. In most cases, the couple know each other. One common element in the process is the paying of the *galyng* (bride price). This consists of a transfer of either money or goods from the groom's family to the bride's family.

11 ● CLOTHING

The most prominent feature of traditional Turkmen male clothing is the *telpek,* a high sheepskin hat. It may be brown, black, or white and is typically very shaggy. Men who wear the telpek usually wear a skullcap beneath it and shave their heads. Long, deep-red robes with wide sleeves are also common in traditional settings. In the cities, the clothing of the Turkmen male differs little from that of men in the West. A suit jacket (without a tie) and pants are the norm, and no hat is worn.

Turkmen women, both urban and rural, typically wear more traditional clothing than men do. The main features are a long dress, a long head scarf, and a cloak-type red robe called a *kurte*. Western-style clothing is considered too immodest by most Turkmen women. Turkmen women also sew a special type of embroidery called *keshde*, which adorns the collars and fringes of their clothing.

12 ● FOOD

Milk products from camels, cows, goats, and sheep are made into a variety of butters, creams, and yogurts. The meat of these animals is used in the bulk of Turkmen dishes. Most meat dishes are baked (in dough) or boiled. Soups and meat pie-type dishes make up the bulk of the dinner fare.

One favorite Turkmen dish is *dograma,* a thick soup made with diced bread, lamb, onions, tomatoes, and spices. Hot green tea is part of every. meal, even on the hottest days. Round flatbread is a staple throughout Central Asia.

When relatives or guests visit, the food is spread out on plates and dishes on a large cloth on the floor. Guests and family members sit and have their meal around this cloth covered with food (called a *sachak*). A typical Turkmen sachak will include a variety of fruits, vegetables, nuts, sweets, tea and other beverages, and bread, as well as butters and creams—all this before the main meal.

13 ● EDUCATION

All children must attend school and receive at least a high school education. Institutes, trade schools, colleges, and a university train those willing and able to continue their education. The economic crisis since Turkmenistan's independence has led to many problems in education. Low teacher pay, lack of funding, and run-down facilities have resulted in serious problems, especially in rural areas.

14 ● CULTURAL HERITAGE

The most prominent figure in Turkmen cultural history is the eighteenth-century poet, Magtymguly. Virtually all Turkmens know his poetry by heart. The Turkmens also have a unique musical culture that is tied into the oral literary tradition. Turkmen music features the two-stringed *dutar* and the *gyjak* (a violin-like instrument), accompanied by singing.

15 ● EMPLOYMENT

In rural areas of Turkmenistan, virtually all work is centered around agricultural and livestock production. The state owns almost all the land and administers all the farms. *Pagta* (cotton) is Turkmenistan's chief crop. Fruits, vegetables, and grains are also grown throughout the country. Hailed as the "second Kuwait" because of its oil and gas reserves, Turkmenistan has pinned its hopes on oil and gas production and their export to countries outside the former Soviet Union.

16 ● SPORTS

Soccer (called *futbal*) is perhaps the most popular sport among young men. Horse racing has become the most celebrated sport in

Turkmenistan since independence. The horse has long symbolized the Turkmen spirit and occupies the most prominent spot on the state seal.

17 ● RECREATION

Visiting friends and relatives is a favorite pastime among Turkmens. Visits usually involve large meals, some sort of entertainment (such as music), and overnight stays. Many urban Turkmens own summer houses and gardens on the outskirts of town where they spend vacation time. Turkmens also enjoy the theater, movies, musical concerts, and television.

18 ● CRAFTS AND HOBBIES

Turkmen carpets are prized as among the world's best by collectors and experts. Some carpets have up to 37,000 knots per square foot (400,000 knots per square meter). They are often known as Bukharan or "Oriental" carpets. Many Turkmen tribes have a distinct, identifying carpet ornamentation. Almost all of the labor connected with carpet weaving and production is carried out by women. Aside from carpets, women also weave a variety of items connected with the nomadic lifestyle. Adornments for the felt tent, such as storage bags and door coverings, as well as items used for horses and camels, are the most common.

19 ● SOCIAL PROBLEMS

Turkmenistan has experienced severe economic problems since the breakup of the Soviet Union. Poverty, crime, and unemployment have risen sharply. Drug abuse is increasing among young male Turkmens. Turkmenistan's low industrial and manufacturing production has led to a high reliance on imported foodstuffs and consumer goods.

20 ● BIBLIOGRAPHY

Clark, Larry, Mike Thurman, and David Tyson. *Turkmenistan: A Country Study.* Lanham, Md.: Federal Research Division, United States Library of Congress, forthcoming.

Maslow, Jonathan Evan. *Sacred Horses: The Memoirs of a Turkmen Cowboy.* New York: Random House, 1994.

Turkmenistan, Then and Now. Minneapolis, Minn.: Lerner Publications Co., 1993.

WEBSITES

Embassy of Turkmenistan, Washington, D.C. [Online] Available http://www.dc.infi.net/~embassy/, 1998.

World Travel Guide. Turkmenistan. [Online] Available http://twww.wtgonline.com/country/tm/gen.html, 1998.

Uganda

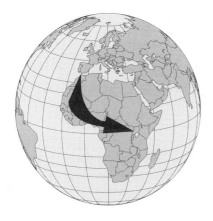

The Baganda, who populate the northern shore of Lake Victoria, constitute the largest single ethnic group in Uganda (about 17 percent of the total population). Ten other main ethnic groups, each accounting for between 3 and 12 percent of Uganda's population, together make up 60 percent of the total. Perhaps 6 percent of the population (not counting refugees) is of Rwandan descent, either Tutsi or Hutu. For more information on the Tutsi, see the chapter on Burundi in Volume 2; on the Hutu, see the chapter on Rwanda in Volume 8.

Ugandans

PRONUNCIATION: yoo-GAN-duhns
LOCATION: Uganda
POPULATION: 20 million
LANGUAGE: English (official); various tribal languages
RELIGION: Christianity; Islam; indigenous beliefs

1 ● INTRODUCTION

Uganda's ethnic history is largely the result of two population movements that occurred between AD 1000 and 1500. Cattle herders, known as Hima, moved into exclusively agricultural areas. They contributed to the development of centralized kingdoms in the west-central portion of the country. Nilotic speakers then moved into the northern and eastern areas. They stimulated the further development of centralized kingdoms to the south by introducing ruling clans (groups of people with common descent). These migrations contributed to political and ethnic divisions that can still be seen today.

The British established Uganda as a protectorate (a territory under British rule) in the latter half of the nineteenth century. Uganda had a promising future at the time of independence (1962). However, ethnic divisions proved insurmountable. In 1967, Prime Minister Milton Obote from the north declared kingdoms illegal. He tried to impose a socialist doctrine on the nation. Sir Edward Mutesa, the Kabaka (King) of Buganda, and the first president of the Republic of Uganda, was overthrown by Obote, who then declared himself the president. In 1971, Obote was overthrown by his army commander, Idi Amin. This led to a repressive reign of terror against all Ugandans. The economy was soon in ruins. Milton Obote returned to power after Amin was

UGANDANS

| 0 | 200 | 400 | 600 | 800 Miles |
| 0 | 200 | 400 | 600 | 800 Kilometers |

driven from the country in 1979. An ensuing guerrilla war ended in 1986, with Yoweri Museveni becoming president. An elected parliament replaced the interim government in 1996. Uganda currently is experiencing a rejuvenated economy and political system. Its present government has maintained an open style of leadership receptive to the participation of all ethnic groups.

2 ● LOCATION

Uganda is located in east Africa astride the equator, and between Kenya and the Democratic Republic of the Congo. Its area is about the size of the state of Oregon. Uganda is landlocked but has several large inland waterways, including Lake Victoria. Its climate is tropical with two rainy seasons; however, the northeast is semi-arid.

The capital city is Kampala. Uganda's population is about 20 million people. About forty ethnic groups are represented, of which the Baganda, the Karamojong, the Iteso, and the Lango are the largest groups. There also are a small number of Europeans, Asians, and Arabs.

3 ● LANGUAGE

The official, national language of Uganda is English. Bantu languages are spoken by the greatest number of speakers in the nation. These are concentrated in the southern and western areas of the country. Nilotic languages predominate in the northern regions.

Ugandans are typically comfortable speaking more than one language. Luganda, English, and Kiswahili, for example, are commonly used in Kampala. In other regions of the country, children learn English in addition to their own ethnic language. Even among the most highly-educated Ugandans, there is a strong preference for the mother tongue at home and in social situations.

4 ● FOLKLORE

All the ethnic groups of Uganda have a rich oral tradition of tales, legends, stories, proverbs, and riddles. Folk heroes include those thought responsible for introducing kingship into society. Morality tales were common throughout Uganda. The Ankole peoples' tales include one about a wise woman and her selfish husband, which teaches faithfulness to one's wives during hard times; one about a pig and a hyena, which preaches against self-indulgence; and the wisdom of the hare, which demonstrates the advantages of being quick-witted and friendly.

Proverbs and riddles are perhaps the most significant mechanisms for teaching values to the young. They also provide entertainment. The importance of parenting, for instance, can be seen in the following proverbs from the Baganda:

I will never move from this village, but for the sake of children he does.

He who does a good service to one's child, does better than one who merely says he loves you.

An only child is like a drop of rain in the dry season.

My luck is in that child of mine if the child is rich.

A skillful hunting dog may nevertheless produce weaklings.

A chicken's feet do not kill its young.

That which becomes bad at the outset of its growth is almost impossible to straighten at a later stage.

Collective games of riddle-making are a popular evening entertainment in rural villages. Among the Baganda, these games involve men and women of all ages. A person who solves a riddle is given a village to rule as its "chief." Some examples of riddles are:

Pass one side, and I also pass the other side, so that we meet in the middle? (a belt)

He built a house with only one pole standing? (a mushroom)

He goes on dancing as he walks? (a caterpillar)

He built a house with two entrances? (a nose)

He has three legs? (an old man walking with his stick)

5 ● RELIGION

About two-thirds of Ugandans are Christian, evenly divided between Protestants and Roman Catholics. The remaining third are about evenly divided between Muslims and those practicing indigenous (native) African religions.

Indigenous supernatural ideas such as belief in witchcraft, the evil eye, and night dancers are still widespread. A widely-feared person throughout Uganda is the night dancer. He is a community member by day; by night he is thought to roam about eating dead bodies while floating along the ground with fire between his hands. People generally avoid traveling alone at night for fear of these night dancers *(Basezi)*. Ancestors are highly respected and feared. They communicate with the living through dreams to warn them of impending dangers and to advise them on family matters.

6 ● MAJOR HOLIDAYS

There is a single national holiday, celebrated on October 9. It commemorates the day in 1962 when Uganda achieved its independence from the United Kingdom.

7 ● RITES OF PASSAGE

Infancy is considered an important period in a child's development. Ceremonies during the first year of life celebrate milestones such as sitting up alone and obtaining one's clan name.

Childhood varies depending on whether the child comes from a wealthy or a poor family, or lives in the city of Kampala or in a rural village. Due to the cost of schooling, family members often need to pool their resources in order to send children (or, in some cases, only the most promising child). This child, if successful, is expected to help other family members in turn. Boys and girls generally have household tasks. Girls seven to nine years old care for younger siblings. In rural areas, young boys typically are expected to tend the livestock. Children from wealthy parents have fewer work responsibilities and more leisure time.

The teenage years are devoted to education, work, and courtship. Pubescent girls were traditionally secluded and formally instructed by elder women (such as one's *Ssenga*, or father's sister). Boys were initiated into an age-set, a generational hierarchy. Women from western Uganda traditionally went into seclusion prior to marriage. They spent an extended period of time drinking milk in order to gain weight. Plumpness is still considered desirable today.

8 ● RELATIONSHIPS

Ugandans on the whole are extremely involved in the social life of their communities. Social activities may center around villages, schools, neighborhoods, clubs, churches, mosques, age-sets, clans, homesteads, or extended families.

Sociability is best symbolized through a pattern of ritualized greetings. These vary according to time of day, a person's age, social status, and length of time since an encounter. Not to greet someone is considered to be a serious impropriety. The following is an example of a Kiganda greeting:

Mawulire ki? (What is the news?)

Tetugalaba. (We have none.)

Mmm or *Eee.* (OK.)

Mpoza mmwe? (Perhaps you have?)

Naffe tetugalaba or *Nedda.* (We have none either.)

Mmm or *Eee.* (OK.)

Dating occurs prior to marriage in a variety of social contexts. Young people meet at funerals, weddings, churches, and school socials. Nightclubs are popular for dancing with friends or with "dates." Love songs are popular with people of all ages.

9 ● LIVING CONDITIONS

Homes in rural areas are frequently made of wattle and daub (woven rods and twigs plastered with clay and mud) and have thatched or corrugated-iron roofs. Affluent residents of rural areas may have elaborate homes. Urban homes are typically of concrete with corrugated-iron or tile roofs, and have glass windows. In the suburbs of Kampala, multi-level and ranch homes are very plush, with servant quarters, swimming pools, and elaborate gardens. Urban gardens where vegetables and flowers are grown are also common.

10 ● FAMILY LIFE

Marriage and family life are primary pursuits of most Ugandans, whatever their ethnic group or religion. The extended family continues to be important to Ugandans. However, individualism and the nuclear family are increasing due to European and

Jason Laure

A Ugandan man. Most Ugandans wear Western-style clothing.

Christian influences. Monogamy (having only one spouse) is now the national ideal, even though polygyny (a husband with several wives) is sometimes encountered.

Ugandans typically pay some form of marriage fee, maintain allegiances to their extended families and clans, and generally marry outside of these clans (a custom known as exogamy). Traditional marriage ceremonies, rituals, and practices prevail. Most women, regardless of their educational level, desire children.

11 ● CLOTHING

Most Ugandans wear Western-style clothing. Young people are especially attracted to American clothing styles such as jeans and slacks. The most prominent indigenous (native) clothing is found in southern Uganda among the Baganda. The woman typically wears a *busuuti* (a floor-length, brightly colored cloth dress with short puffed sleeves, a square neckline fastened by two buttons, and a sash placed just below the waist). Baganda men frequently wear a *kanzu* (long white robe). For special occasions, a western-style suit jacket is worn over the kanzu. In western Uganda, Bahima women wear full, broad cotton dresses and a floor-length shawl. Northern societies such as the Karamojong wear cowskins. They signify social status (such as warrior, married person, or elder) by items of adornment such as feather plumes and large coiled, copper necklaces and armlets.

12 ● FOOD

Each region of Uganda has its own foods and traditions. Among pastoral groups such as the Karamojong, there is a strong emphasis on cattle. They provide meat, milk, clothing, blankets, horns and hoofs for containers, and other resources. Millet and sorghum are common grains available throughout northern regions. Root crops (cassava, manioc, and sweet potatoes) and plantains are staples in southern and eastern Uganda where rain is plentiful year-round. *Matooke* (plantains, a fruit of the banana family) is the staple of the Baganda, the largest ethnic group in Uganda. Matooke is served with various sauces made of peanuts, green leaves, mushrooms, tomatoes, meat, fish, white ants, and/or grasshoppers.

13 ● EDUCATION

During the administrations of Milton Obote and Idi Amin, the educational standard of the country deteriorated. The present government is in the process of rebuilding the nation's school system. About half the total population age fifteen and over are illiterate (unable to read or write). Literacy is higher among males than females. This imbalance is due in part to a policy of favoritism shown by the British for the education of boys. In addition, there is a high rate of pregnancy among schoolgirls, usually requiring that they leave school. Poverty is another factor contributing to illiteracy, given that schooling can be expensive.

Parents have high expectations for the education of their children. Success in school is seen as the means to a better livelihood for the individual who is, in turn, expected to help his or her extended family. For this reason, Ugandan students are typically very hardworking and achievement-oriented.

14 ● CULTURAL HERITAGE

Music and dance are a significant part of Uganda's cultural heritage. Dance forms vary somewhat by ethnic group. People of all ages participate in dance and song in the course of routine rituals, family celebrations, and community events. Among the Karamojong and their neighbors, dance is especially significant during times of courtship.

Many Baganda households contain at least a small cowhide drum for regular use in singing and dancing. Baganda dancers are skilled in their ability to swiftly move their hips to the alternating beats of drums playing simultaneously. Among the Banyankole, pots filled with various levels of water are used as percussion instruments.

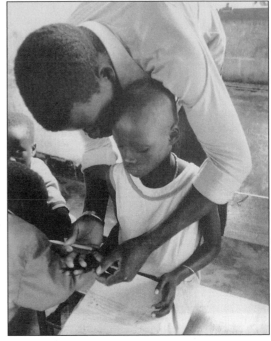

AP/Wide World Photos

A teacher leans over his student. Parents have high expectations for the education of their children and Ugandan students are typically very hardworking and achievement-oriented.

Men and women accompany the rhythms by singing, dancing, and beating their hands on their bodies.

Modern nightclub and disco dancing are also part of the teenage scene, particularly in urban areas.

Before the devastation of Uganda's economic and intellectual life, Uganda was in the process of developing an extremely rich literary tradition in English. The Baganda people also had developed a robust vernacular literature in the Luganda language, including novels, short stories, essays, historical writings, songs, plays, and poems. Perhaps the most famous Ugandan writer from the pre-Amin years was Okot p'Bitek. He was an essayist, poet, and social critic. Although he died in 1982, his work is still read throughout east Africa, as well as internationally.

15 ● EMPLOYMENT

During the Amin years, the economy in Uganda lost virtually all its foreign population. Most had been involved in banking, commercial activities, and industry. Nevertheless, Uganda has maintained a strong subsistence agricultural base (growing crops for food as opposed to profit). Important subsistence crops include millet, corn, cassava, and plantains. Beef, poultry, and milk are also significant, especially among pastoral populations.

Small-scale businesses employ numerous Ugandans in Kampala and throughout the country's smaller towns and villages. Such work includes tailoring, shopkeeping, hair care, various kinds of repair work, carpentry, and the marketing of food and other household necessities. The professions, including teaching, law, and medicine, are growing and employ support staffs that include secretaries, receptionists, and computer personnel.

Comparatively poor people operate small all-purpose stands, selling items such as cigarettes, matches, candy, soft drinks, biscuits, cookies, and bread.

The leisure-time industry is quite lively, encompassing restaurants, bars, and nightclubs. Tourism, involving safaris to game parks, is once again on the upswing as well.

16 ● SPORTS

Soccer is the most popular sport, with a national league and hotly contested play-offs. Cricket, rugby, and boxing are also enjoyed by many spectators. Uganda sends competitors abroad to international events such as the Olympics. In the past it has won medals for excellence in track and field.

17 ● RECREATION

Most Ugandans own radios and enjoy listening to a variety of educational programs, plays, stories, news, and music. Stations broadcast in English and the major ethnic languages. There is a national television station that includes local programs as well as those from the United States and England. Television is available in most affluent homes and in hotels.

Individuals and families enjoy visiting restaurants and clubs where they can watch traditional dancing. Popular theater is also a significant source of entertainment in Uganda. Plays center on themes of broad public appeal such as politics, social change, and health and family matters. Recently, plays have been used throughout the country to promote health education, especially about HIV/AIDS awareness and prevention. The significance of public plays for educational purposes cannot be underestimated in a country where about half the population is illiterate.

18 ● CRAFTS AND HOBBIES

Much of Ugandans' artistic endeavors involve everyday objects. These include colorful straw mats, tightly woven coiled baskets, wooden milk pots and bowls, and smoking pipes. Basketry is a highly developed art form in Uganda. Common fibers are banana palm, raffia, papyrus, and sisal. Weaving is used for house walls, fences, roofs, baskets, mats, traps, table mats, cushions, and receptacles for drink and food. Bark-cloth was once a widespread craft used for many purposes, including clothing. Today, bark-cloth is used as decoration on place mats and greeting cards, as well as in the making of blankets and shrouds. Another art form is batik, a type of cloth painting that can be hung on walls for decoration. The current revival of the tourist industry is likely to stimulate the production of arts and crafts for foreign consumption.

19 ● SOCIAL PROBLEMS

Uganda suffers from one of the highest HIV/AIDS infection rates in the world. However, it has one of the best public awareness programs associated with HIV/AIDS anywhere. Many families have experienced the loss of loved ones to this disease, resulting in a large number of orphans. Another problem is the flow of refugees coming to Uganda from neighboring nations suffering from political turmoil. Hundreds of thousands of southern Sudanese have fled to Uganda in recent years, due to religious conflict in the Sudan. Rwandan refugees fleeing from ethnic conflict enter Uganda from the west.

Idi Amin's brutal rule was one of the most highly publicized terrorist regimes in modern times. However, Uganda is now well on the way to democracy, although it is still under one-party rule. Ugandans, on the whole, are optimistic about their future.

20 ● BIBLIOGRAPHY

Curley, Richard T. *Elders, Shades, and Women*. Berkeley: University of California Press, 1973.

Hansen, Holger Bernt, and Michael Twaddle, ed. *Uganda Now: Between Decay and Development*. London, England: James Currey, Ltd., 1988.

Kilbride, Philip L., and Janet C. Kilbride. *Changing Family Life in East Africa: Women and Children at Risk*. University Park: The Pennsylvania State University Press, 1990.

Mair, Lucy. *African Societies*. London, England: Cambridge University Press, 1974.

Roscoe, John. *The Banyankole*. London, England: Cambridge University Press, 1923.

WEBSITES

Embassy of Uganda, Washington, D.C. [Online] Available http://www.ugandaweb.com/ugaembassy/, 1998.

Government of Uganda. Uganda Home Page. [Online] Available http://www.uganda.co.ug/, 1998.

World Travel Guide. Uganda. [Online] Available http://www.wtgonline.com/country/ug/gen.html, 1998.

Baganda

PRONUNCIATION: bah-GAHN-dah
ALTERNATE NAMES: The King's Men
LOCATION: Uganda
POPULATION: About 3 million
LANGUAGE: Luganda
RELIGION: Christianity (Protestantism and Roman Catholicism); Islam

1 ● INTRODUCTION

The Baganda people of Uganda are sometimes referred to as The King's Men because of the significance of the role of their king—the *Kabaka* in their political, social, and cultural institutions. Until 1967, the Baganda were organized into a tightly centralized, bureaucratized kingdom. Between 1967 and 1993, the Ugandan national government abolished all kingdoms. In 1993, the national government reinstated the Kabakaship (kingship) by permitting the coronation of Ronald Muwenda Mutebi II as the thirty-sixth king of the Baganda.

Traditionally, the Kabaka ruled over a hierarchy of chiefs who collected taxes in the form of food and livestock. Portions were distributed through the hierarchy, eventually reaching the Kabaka's palace in the form of tribute (taxes). The Kabaka made direct political appointment of all chiefs so as to maintain control over their loyalty to him. Many rituals surrounded the person of the king. Commoners had to lie face down on the ground in his presence.

Today, the Kabaka has only ritual functions and no political power. He was removed of his power so that tribal differences would not interfere with the formation of a nation state. All Baganda participate in the Ugandan government system. Nevertheless, the kingdom and associated institutions remain strong forces in the cultural practices and values of the Baganda.

2 ● LOCATION

The *Baganda* are located along the northern and western shores of Lake Victoria in the east African nation of Uganda. They number about 3 million people. The former Kingdom of Buganda, which today is the area occupied by the Baganda, is bounded on the north by the former Kingdom of Bunyoro and on the east by the Nile River. To the south of Buganda is the present country of Tanzania. The Baganda are the largest tribe in Uganda, and the Kingdom of Buganda was the largest of the former kingdoms. It comprises slightly more than one-fourth of Uganda's total land mass. Kampala, Uganda's largest city and capital, is in Buganda.

3 ● LANGUAGE

The Baganda speak a Bantu language called Luganda. It is a member of the Niger-Congo family of languages. In the Luganda language, the singular form of Baganda is *Muganda*. Like many other African languages, Luganda is tonal, meaning that some words are differentiated by pitch. Words that are spelled the same may carry different meanings according to their pitch. Luganda is rich in metaphor and in proverbs and folktales.

Children learn speech skills that prepare them for adult life in a verbally rich culture. A clever child can masterfully engage his or her peers in a game of *ludikya* or "talking backward." For example, *omusajja* ("man") becomes *jja-sa-mu-o*. Another version of this game involves inserting the letter *z* after each syllable containing a vowel, followed by the vowel in that syllable. In this version, *omusajja* would become *o-zo-mu-zu-sa-za-jja-za*. Both boys and girls play *ludikya*, which they claim is frequently done to conceal secrets from adults. In the evening many families play collective riddling games *(okukokkya),* which involve men and women of all ages. Some examples of common riddles are:

I have a wife who looks where she is coming from and where she is going at

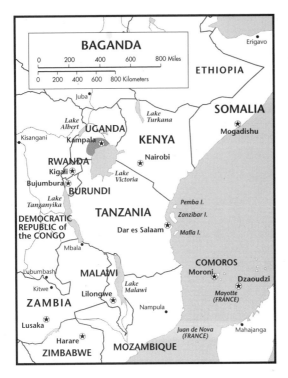

the same time (a bundle of firewood, since the two ends are similar).

I have a razor blade which I use to shave hills (fire that is used to burn the grass for planting).

When my friend went to get food for his children, he never came back (water in a river).

My man is always surrounded by spears (the tongue, surrounded by teeth).

4 ● FOLKLORE

Riddles, myths, legends, and proverbs tell the origin and history of the Baganda, as well as the workings of the everyday world. The most significant legend involves Kintu, the first Kabaka (king). He is believed to have married a woman called Nambi. First Nambi had to return to heaven. Gulu, her father, objected to her marriage because Kintu did not know how to farm but only how to obtain food from cattle. Nambi's relatives tested Kintu in order to determine his suitability as a spouse. In one test Kintu was asked to identify his own cow in a herd, a difficult task since there were many cows like his own. By chance, a bee told Kintu to choose the cow on whose horns he would alight. After several large herds were brought to him, Kintu reported that his cow was not among them. (He was continuing to watch the bee who remained on the tree.) Eventually, Kintu, with the help of the bee, identified his cow, along with several calves that had been born to his cow. The amazed father eagerly gave his daughter's hand in marriage. He prodded them to hurry to leave for Kintu's home before *Walumbe* (Death) came and wanted to go with them. Gulu warned that they should not come back even if they forgot something, for fear that Death would follow them. They left carrying with them cows, a goat, fowl, sheep, and a plantain tree. Unfortunately, over the protests of Kintu, Nambi went back to obtain grain that had been forgotten. Although she tried to run away from Death, she was unsuccessful. After many years of happiness on earth, Walumbe (Death) began to bring illness and death to children and then adults. Up to the present day, Death has lived upon the earth with no one knowing when or whom he will strike.

5 ● RELIGION

The majority of present-day Baganda are Christian, about evenly divided between Catholic and Protestant. Approximately 15 percent are Muslim (followers of Islam). In the latter half of the nineteenth century, most Baganda were practicing an indigenous (native) religion known as the *Balubaale* cult. This cult consisted of gods who had temples identified with them. These gods were each concerned with specific problems. For example, there was a god of fertility, a god of warfare, and a god of the lake.

The Baganda also believed in spiritual forces, particularly the action of witches, which were thought to cause illness and other misfortune. People often wore amulets (charms) to ward off their evil powers. The most significant spirits were the *Muzimu* or ancestors who visited the living in dreams and sometimes warned of impending dangers. The Balubaale cult no longer exists. However, belief in ancestors and the power of witches is still quite common.

Contemporary Baganda are extremely religious, whatever their faith.

6 ● MAJOR HOLIDAYS

Important religious holidays include Christmas (December 25) for Christians and Ramadan (varying according to the lunar calendar) for Muslims. Funerals are major ceremonial and social events. People travel from all parts of the nation to attend funerals, which last many days.

7 ● RITES OF PASSAGE

A Muganda (Baganda individual) passes through the stages of *omwana* (child), *omuvubuka* (youth), and *omusajja* or *omukazi* (man, woman). At death one becomes an *omuzima* (spirit) and a candidate for reincarnation.

At birth the umbilical cord is retained for later use in a ceremony called *Kwalula Abaana*. During this ceremony the child gathers with other members of the father's clan to receive their clan names.

Boys and girls are expected to conform in their behavior to what the Baganda refer to as *mpisa* (manners). This includes being obedient to adults, greeting visitors properly, and sitting correctly (for girls). Sex education for females is more systematic than it is for males. The father's sister (*Ssenga*) is the most significant moral authority for girls. Grandmothers instruct girls soon after their menstruation, during a period of seclusion, about sexual matters and future domestic responsibilities. Marriage and the birth of children are prerequisites for adult status.

8 ● RELATIONSHIPS

The Baganda place paramount emphasis on being sociable. Cleverness and assertiveness are valued as ways to achieve upward mobility. Elaborate greeting rituals best symbolize the importance attached to being sociable. Propriety requires that neighbors exchange lengthy greetings when meeting along the road. Greetings vary according to the time of day, age of participants, and length of time since previous encounter. In Kampala, greetings are far less frequent and shorter in duration than in rural areas. Also, women in Kampala are much less likely to kneel while greeting men or other social superiors, a custom still prevalent in rural areas.

Dating and courtship are significant in the lives of most younger Baganda. Men are expected to develop the art of flattery.

Women do not flatter, but they are expected to deceive a man into thinking that he is her only suitor. Affection between the sexes is not shown in public.

9 ● LIVING CONDITIONS

Rural homes are usually made of wattle and daub (woven rods and twigs plastered with clay and mud). Homes generally have thatched or corrugated iron roofs. More affluent farmers live in homes constructed of cement, with tile roofs. Some homes have electricity and running water. However, for many Baganda, water must be fetched from a well or collected when it rains. Cooking is commonly done in a separate cooking house over an open wood fire. Urban homes, by contrast, are typically of concrete with corrugated iron or tile roofs and glass windows. Indoor plumbing, indoor kitchens, electricity, and toilet facilities are common in the city.

All Baganda have daily access to a plentiful food supply, given their year-round growing season. However, Baganda suffer from malaria, and children are frequently afflicted with *kwashiorkor*, a form of protein-calorie malnutrition.

10 ● FAMILY LIFE

The traditional term for marriage was *jangu enfumbire* (come cook for me). This symbolized the prevailing authority patterns in the typical household. The husband and father was supreme. Children and women knelt to the husband in deference to his authority, and he was served his food first. Today, Baganda children frequently describe feelings of fear and respect for

their fathers and warm attachment to their mothers.

After marriage a new household is established, usually in the village of the husband. Most marriages are monogamous (having one spouse), although polygamy (more than one spouse) was not uncommon in the past.

11 ● CLOTHING

The rural Muganda (Baganda individual) woman typically wears a *busuuti*. This is a floor-length, brightly colored cloth dress with a square neckline and short, puffed sleeves. The garment is fastened with a sash placed just below the waist over the hips, and by two buttons on the left side of the neckline. Traditionally, the busuuti was strapless and made from bark-cloth. The busuuti is worn on all festive and ceremonial occasions. The indigenous dress of the Baganda man is a *kanzu*, a long, white cotton robe. On special occasions, it is worn over trousers with a Western-style suit jacket over it. Younger people wear Western-style clothing. Slacks, jeans, skirts, suits, and ties are also worn.

12 ● FOOD

The staple food of the Baganda is *matooke,* a plantain (a tropical fruit in the banana family). It is steamed or boiled and commonly served with groundnut (peanut) sauce or meat soups. Sources of protein include eggs, fish, beans, groundnuts, beef, chicken, and goats, as well as termites and grasshoppers in season. Common vegetables are cabbage, beans, mushrooms, carrots, cassava, sweet potatoes, onions, and various types of greens. Fruits include sweet bananas, pineapples, passion fruit, and papaya. Drinks include indigenous fermented beverages made from bananas *(mwenge),* pineapples *(munanansi),* and maize *(musoli).* Although Baganda have cutlery, most prefer to eat with their hands, especially when at home.

13 ● EDUCATION

Missionaries introduced literacy (reading and writing) and formal education to Uganda in the nineteenth century. The Baganda value modern education and will often sacrifice a great deal to obtain schooling for their children. Members of a family will combine resources to support a particularly promising student. Upon the completion of education the family member is expected to help his or her relatives.

14 ● CULTURAL HERITAGE

Baganda number among the best songwriters, playwrights, poets, novelists, artists, and musicians in Uganda. Performing arts, especially music and dance, have enjoyed a longstanding tradition. The Kabaka's Palace was a special place where royal dancers and drummers regularly performed. Most Baganda households contained at least a small drum for regular use in family singing and dancing. Other musical instruments included stringed instruments such as fiddles and harps, and woodwind instruments such as flutes and fifes.

Dancing is frequently practiced by all Baganda, beginning in early childhood. Today, Uganda dancers and musicians are frequently seen performing abroad.

Basketry is still a widespread art, especially mat-making by women. These mats are colorful and intricately designed. In addition to creating useful household containers, woven and coiled basketry serve as the foundation for stockades, enclosure fences, and houses.

15 ● EMPLOYMENT

Most Baganda are peasant farmers who live in rural villages. Rich red clay on hillsides, a moderate temperature, and plentiful rainfall combine to provide a good environment for the year-round availability of plantain, the staple crop, as well as the seasonal production of coffee, cotton, and tea as cash crops.

Some Baganda reside in towns and in Kampala, working in a variety of professional and nonprofessional occupations. They may also practice "urban agriculture" by growing crops in small available spaces and by keeping goats, chickens, and, occasionally, cows. Some Baganda in rural areas fish, or work as carpenters, mechanics, or convey produce to market via bicycles, which is more common than the automobile.

16 ● SPORTS

Football (soccer), rugby, and track and field are popular sports in Uganda. Baganda boys participate in all these sports, while girls participate in track and field. Traditionally, the Baganda were renowned for their skills in wrestling. Males of all ages participated in this sport. Wrestling events were accompanied by beer-drinking, singing, and drumming. It was, however, considered inappropriate to defeat the Kabaka. Other traditional outdoor games for boys include the competitive throwing of sticks and a kicking game in which boys stand side by side and attempt to knock over the other boy.

17 ● RECREATION

Children play games involving a chief for boys or a mother role for girls. *Okwesa* is a game of strategy involving a wooden board and stones or beans that are placed in pockets in the board. Verbal games such as riddling are played frequently, especially at night and in the company of grandparents.

18 ● CRAFTS AND HOBBIES

In addition to basketry and musical instruments, the manufacture of products from bark-cloth was and continues to be significant. The bark from a species of fig tree called *mutuba* is soaked in water, then beaten with a wooden mallet. This yields a soft material that is decorated with paint and then cut into strips of various sizes. Larger strips traditionally were used for partitions in homes. Smaller pieces were decorated with black dye and worn as clothing by women of royalty. Later, bark-cloth dress became the national dress. Today, one rarely sees bark-cloth dresses. They have been replaced by the cotton cloth Busuuti. Bark-cloth is found today as decorative placemats, coasters, and designs on cards of various sorts.

19 ● SOCIAL PROBLEMS

The Baganda have had problems integrating their political culture into the nation state of Uganda. The first president of independent Uganda (1962) was Sir Edward Mutesa, who was also King of Buganda. The first prime minister was Milton Obote. Within four years, Obote had abolished the king-

doms, and Mutesa fled Uganda. In 1971, Obote was overthrown by dictator Idi Amin. Under Amin all Ugandans suffered greatly from political and social oppression, death, and the loss of personal property. Currently, the Baganda are recovering from the havoc and dissension of the Obote and Amin years.

Since the mid-1980s, AIDS has resulted in many Baganda deaths. Caring for the children of parents who have died of AIDS is an especially serious problem. The disease has been the subject of a broad public educational effort aimed at prevention.

20 ● BIBLIOGRAPHY

Fallers, L. A., ed. *The King's Men: Leadership and Status in Buganda on the Eve of Independence.* New York: Oxford University Press, 1964.

Kavulu, David. *The Uganda Martyrs.* Kampala, Uganda: Longmans of Uganda, Ltd., 1969.

Kilbride, Philip, and Janet Kilbride. *Changing Family Life in East Africa: Women and Children at Risk.* University Park: Pennsylvania University Press, 1990.

Lugira, A. M. *Ganda Art.* Kampala, Uganda: OSASA Publications, 1970.

Roscoe, Rev. John. *The Baganda: An Account of Their Native Customs and Beliefs.* London, England: Macmillan and Co., 1911.

Southwold, Martin. "The Ganda of Uganda." In *Peoples of Africa,* edited by James L. Gibbs, Jr. New York: Holt, Rinehart and Winston, 1965.

WEBSITES

Embassy of Uganda, Washington, D.C. [Online] Available http://www.ugandaweb.com/ugaembassy/, 1998.

Government of Uganda. Uganda Home Page. [Online] Available http://www.uganda.co.ug/, 1998.

World Travel Guide. Uganda. [Online] Available http://www.wtgonline.com/country/ug/gen.html, 1998.

Banyankole

PRONUNCIATION: bahn-yahn-KOH-lay

LOCATION: Ankole in southwestern Uganda

POPULATION: Unknown

LANGUAGE: Runyankole; English; KiSwahili

RELIGION: Christianity (Roman Catholicism, Church of Uganda—Anglican, and Fundamental Christianity); indigenous Kinyankole religion

1 ● INTRODUCTION

The Banyankole are located in southwestern Uganda. At the turn of the nineteenth century they numbered about 400,000 people. This former kingdom is well known for its long-horned cattle, which were objects of economic significance as well as prestige. The *Mugabe* (King) was an absolute ruler. He claimed all the cattle throughout the country as his own. Chiefs were ranked not by the land that they owned but by the number of cattle that they possessed. Banyankole society is divided into a high-ranked caste (social class) of pastoralists (nomadic herders) and a lower-ranked caste of farmers. The Bahima are cattle herders and the Bairu are farmers who also care for goats and sheep.

In 1967, the government of Milton Obote, prime minister of Uganda, abolished kingdoms in Uganda, including the Kingdom of Ankole. This policy was intended to promote individualism and socialism in opposition to traditional social classes. Nevertheless, cattle are still highly valued among the Banyankole, and the Bahima are still held in high regard.

2 ● LOCATION

Ankole lies to the southwest of Lake Victoria in southwestern Uganda. Sometime during or before the seventeenth century, cattle-keeping people migrated from the north into central and western Uganda and mingled with indigenous farming peoples. They adopted the language of the farmers but maintained their separate identity and authority, most notably in the Kingdom of Ankole. The country was well suited for pastoralism (nomadic herding). Its rolling plains were covered with abundant grass. Today, ideal grazing land is diminishing due to a high rate of population growth.

3 ● LANGUAGE

The Banyankole speak a Bantu language called Runyankole. It is a member of the Niger-Kordofanian group of language families. In many of these languages, nouns are composed of modifiers known as prefixes, infixes, and suffixes. Word stems alone have no grammatical meaning. For example, the prefix *ba-* signifies plurality; thus, the ethnic group carries the name *Ba*nyankole. An individual person is a *Mu*nyankole, with the prefix *mu-* carrying the idea of singularity. Things pertaining to or belonging to the Banyankole are referred to as *Ki*nyankole, taking the prefix *ki-*. The pastoral Banyankole are known as *Ba*hima; an individual of this group is referred to as a *Mu*hima. The agricultural Banyankole are known as *Ba*iru; the individual is a *Mu*iru.

4 ● FOLKLORE

Legends and tales teach proper moral behavior to the young. Storytelling is a common means of entertainment. Both men

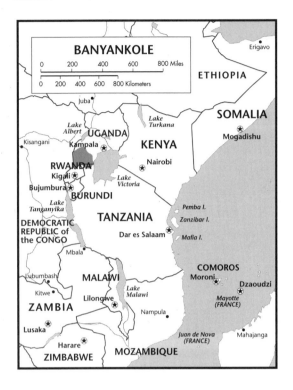

BANYANKOLE

0 200 400 600 800 Miles
0 200 400 600 800 Kilometers

ETHIOPIA

SOMALIA

Mogadishu

UGANDA

Lake
Albert

Kisangani

Kampala

Juba

Lake
Turkana

KENYA

Nairobi

RWANDA

Kigali

Bujumbura

BURUNDI

Lake
Victoria

Lake
Tanganyika

DEMOCRATIC
REPUBLIC of
the CONGO

TANZANIA

Dar es Salaam

Pemba I.

Zanzibar I.

Mafia I.

Mbala

Lubumbashi

Kitwe

MALAWI

Lake
Malawi

Lilongwe

COMOROS

Moroni

Dzaoudzi

Mayotte
(FRANCE)

Nampula

ZAMBIA

Lusaka

Harare

Juan de Nova
(FRANCE)

Mahajanga

ZIMBABWE

MOZAMBIQUE

Erigavo

and women excel in this verbal art form. Riddles and proverbs are also emphasized. Of special significance are legends surrounding the institution of the kingship, which provide a historical framework for the Banyankole.

Folktales draw on themes such as royalty, cattle, hunting, and other central concerns of the Banyankole. Animals figure prominently in the tales. One well-known tale concerns the Hare and the Leopard. The Hare and the Leopard were once great friends. When the Hare went to his garden for farming, he rubbed his legs with soil and then went home without doing any work, even though he told Leopard that he was always tired from digging. Hare also stole beans from Leopard's plot and said that they were his own. Eventually, Leopard realized that his crops were being stolen, and he set a trap in which Hare was caught in the act of stealing. While stuck in the trap, Hare called to Fox, who came and set him free. Conniving Hare told Fox to put his own leg into the trap to see how it functioned. Hare then called Leopard, who came and killed Fox, the assumed thief, without asking any questions. The Banyankole recite this story to illustrate that one should not trust easily, as Leopard trusted Hare. One should also not act too quickly, as Leopard did in killing the innocent Fox.

5 ● RELIGION

The majority of Banyankole today are Christians. They belong to major world denominations, including the Roman Catholic Church, or the Church of Uganda, which is Anglican. Fundamental Christianity, such as Evangelicalism, is also common. Public confessions of such sins as adultery and drunkenness are common, as well as rejection of many traditional secular and religious practices.

The element of indigenous Kinyankole religion that survives most directly today is the belief in ancestor spirits. It is still believed that many illnesses result from neglect of a dead relative, especially a paternal relative. Through divination it is determined which ancestor has been neglected. Presents of meat or milk and/or changes in behavior can appease the ancestor's spirit.

6 ● MAJOR HOLIDAYS

The majority of Banyankole celebrate Christian holidays, including Christmas

(December 25) and Easter (in March or April).

7 ● RITES OF PASSAGE

Traditionally, in early childhood, children began to learn the colors of cows and how to differentiate their families' cows from those of other homesteads. Boys were taught how to make water buckets and knives. Girls were taught how to make milk-pot covers and small clay pots. By seven or eight years of age, boys were taught how to water cattle and calves. Girls helped by carrying and feeding babies. They were also expected to wash milk-pots and churn butter.

Among the Bahima (the herders), girls began to prepare for marriage as early as eight years of age. They were kept at home and given large quantities of milk in order to grow fat. Today, heaviness is still valued. Among the Banyankole, the father's sister was (and still is) responsible for the sexual morality of the adolescent girl. Nowadays schools, peer groups, popular magazines, and other mass media are rapidly replacing family members as sources of moral education for teenagers.

Traditionally, adulthood was recognized through the establishment of a family by marriage. The acquisition of large herds of cows for Bahima and of abundant crops for Bairu (farmers) were other markers of adulthood. Full adult status was achieved through the rearing of a large family.

8 ● RELATIONSHIPS

Social relations among the Banyankole cannot be understood apart from rank. In the wider society, the Mugabe (king) and chiefs had authority over herders (Bahima). The Bahima had authority over the Bairu (farmers). Within the family, husbands had authority over wives, and older children had authority over younger ones. Inheritance typically involved the eldest son of a man's first wife, who succeeded to his office and property. Relations between fathers and sons and between brothers were formal and often strained. Mothers and their children, and brothers and their sisters, were often close.

Social relations in the community centered around exchanges of wealth, such as cows and agricultural produce. The most significant way that community solidarity was and still is expressed is through the elaborate exchange of formalized greetings. Greetings vary by the age of the participants, the time of day, the relative rank of the participants, and many other factors. Anyone meeting an elder has to wait until the elder acknowledges that person first.

9 ● LIVING CONDITIONS

The Mugabe's (king's) homestead was usually constructed on a hill. It was surrounded by a large fence made from basketry. A large space inside the compound was set aside for cattle. Special places were set aside for the houses of the king's wives, and for his numerous palace officials. There was a main gate through which visitors could enter, with several smaller gates for the entrance of family members.

Traditionally, Bahima (herders) maintained homes modeled after the king's but much smaller. The Bairu (farmers) traditionally built homes in the shape of a beehive. Poles of timber were covered with a framework of woven straw. A thick layer of grass frequently covered the entire structure.

Today, housing makes use of indigenous materials such as papyrus, grass, and wood. Homes are primarily rectangular. They are usually made from wattle and daub (woven rods and twigs plastered with clay and mud) with thatched roofs. Cement, brick, and corrugated iron are used by those who can afford them.

10 ● FAMILY LIFE

Among the Bahima, a young girl was prepared for marriage beginning at about age ten, though sometimes as early as eight. Marriages often occurred before a girl was sexually mature, or soon after her initial menstruation. For this reason, teenage pregnancies before marriage were uncommon. Polygyny (multiple wives) was associated with rank and wealth. Bahima herders who were chiefs typically had more than one wife, and the Mugabe (king) sometimes had over one hundred. Marriages were alliances between clans and large extended families. Among both the Bahima and the Bairu, premarital virginity was valued.

Today, Christian marriages are common. The value attached to extended families and the importance of having children have persisted as measures of a successful marriage. Monogamy is now the norm. Marriages occur at a later age than in the past, due to the attendance at school of both girls and boys. As a consequence, teenage pregnancies out of wedlock have risen. Girls who become pregnant are severely punished by being dismissed from school or disciplined by parents. For this reason, infanticide is now more common than in the past, given that abortion is not legal in Uganda.

11 ● CLOTHING

Dress differentiates Banyankole by rank and gender. Chiefs traditionally wore long robes of cowskins. Ordinary citizens commonly were attired in a small portion of cowskin over their shoulders. Women of all classes wore cowskins wrapped around their bodies. They also covered their faces in public. In modern times, cotton cloth has come to replace cowskins as a means of draping the body. For special occasions, a man might wear a long, white cotton robe with a Western-style sports coat over it. A hat resembling a fez may also be worn. Today, Banyankole wear Western-style clothing. Dress suitable for agriculture such as overalls, shirts, and boots is popular. Teenagers are attracted to international fashions popular in the capital city of Kampala.

12 ● FOOD

Bahima herders consume milk and butter and drink fresh blood from their cattle. The staple food of a herder is milk. Beef is also very important. When milk or meat are scarce, millet porridge is made from grains obtained from the Bairu. Buttermilk is drunk by women and children only. When used as a sauce, butter is mixed with salt, and meat or millet porridge is dipped into it. Children can eat rabbit, but men can eat only the meat of the cow or the buffalo. Herders never eat chicken or eggs. Women consume mainly milk, preferring it to all other foods. Cereals domesticated in Africa—millet, sorghum, and eleusine—dominate the agricultural Bairu sector. The Bairu keep sheep and goats. Unlike the herders, the farmers do consume chickens and eggs.

13 ● EDUCATION

In the past, girls and boys learned cultural values, household duties, agricultural and herding skills, and crafts through observation and participation. Instruction was given where necessary by parents; fathers instructed sons, and mothers instructed daughters. Elders, by means of recitation of stories, tales, and legends, were also significant teachers.

Formal education was introduced in Uganda in the latter part of the nineteenth century. Today, Ankole has many primary and secondary schools maintained by missionaries or the government. In Uganda, among those aged fifteen years and over, about 50 percent are illiterate (unable to read or write). Illiteracy is noticeably higher among girls than among boys. Teenage pregnancy often forces girls to end their formal education. Schools in Ankole teach the values and skills needed for life in modern-day Uganda. At the same time, schools seek to preserve indigenous (native) Ankole cultural values. The Runyankole language is taught in primary schools.

14 ● CULTURAL HERITAGE

All schools have regular performances and competitions. They involve dances, music, and plays. Where appropriate, instruction also makes use of Ankole folklore and artistic expression.

15 ● EMPLOYMENT

Among the Bahima, the major occupation was tending cattle. Every day the herder traveled great distances in search of pasture. Young boys were responsible for watering the herd. Teenage boys were expected to milk the cows before they were taken to pasture. Women cooked food, predominantly meat, to be taken daily to their husbands. Girls helped by gathering firewood, caring for babies, and doing household work. Men were responsible for building homes for their families and pens for their cattle.

Among the Bairu, both men and women were involved in agricultural labor, although men cleared the land. Millet was the main food crop. Secondary crops were plantains, sweet potatoes, beans, and groundnuts (peanuts). Maize (corn) was considered a treat by the children. Children participated in agriculture by chasing birds away from the fields.

16 ● SPORTS

Sports, such as track and field and soccer, are very popular in primary and secondary schools. Children play an assortment of games including hide-and-seek, house, farming, wrestling, and ball games such as soccer. Ugandan national sporting events are followed with great interest in the Ankole region, as are international sporting events.

17 ● RECREATION

Radio and television are important means of entertainment in Ankole. Most homes contain radios that have broadcasts in English, KiSwahili (the two national languages), and Runyankole. Books, newspapers, and magazines also are popular.

Social events such as weddings, funerals, and birthday parties typically involve music and dance. This form of entertainment includes not only modern music, but also traditional forms of songs, dances, and instruments. The drinking of alcoholic and nonalcoholic bottled beverages is common at festivities. In the past, the brewing of beer was a major home industry in Ankole.

18 ● CRAFTS AND HOBBIES

Carpenters, ironworkers, potters, musicians, and others were once permanent features of the Mugabe's (king's) homestead or were in constant contact with it. Carpenters fashioned stools, milk-pots, meat-dishes, water-pots, and troughs for fermenting beer. Iron-smiths manufactured spears, knives, and hammers. Every family had a member who specialized in pottery. Pipes for smoking displayed the finest artistic creativity. Small colored beads were used to decorate clay pipes, which came in various shapes and sizes, and walking sticks.

Traditional industries are not nearly as significant as in the past. Nevertheless, one can still observe the use of traditional pipes, water-pots for music, decorated walking sticks exchanged at marriage, and the use of gourds and pottery.

19 ● SOCIAL PROBLEMS

Milton Obote ruled Uganda from 1962 until 1971, when he was overthrown by Idi Amin. Obote prohibited the formation of ethnic kingdoms within Uganda. During Idi Amin's dictatorship in the 1970s, all Ugandans suffered from political oppression and the loss of life and property. Obote once again took over in 1980 after the overthrow of Amin and ruled oppressively. Resistance to Amin and Obote resulted in the destruction of towns and villages. Uganda is currently working toward economic recovery and democratic reform.

Since the mid-1980s, AIDS has been a serious problem. As adult Ugandans die of AIDS, many children become orphans. There has been a strong national effort to educate the public through mass media about AIDS prevention.

A growing population, in spite of AIDS, remains a threat to a pastoral way of life. Warfare in neighboring countries such as Rwanda has contributed to population growth, as refugees have regularly come into the region.

20 ● BIBLIOGRAPHY

Bahemuka, Judith Mbula. *Our Religious Heritage*. Nairobi, Kenya: Thomas Nelson and Sons, Ltd., 1984.

Hansen, Holger Bernt, and Michael Twaddle, ed. *Uganda Now: Between Decay and Development*. London, England: James Currey, Ltd., 1988.

Kiwanuka, M. S. M. *The Empire of Bunyoro Kitara: Myth or Reality*. Kampala, Uganda: Longmans of Uganda, Ltd., 1968.

Mushanga, Musa T. *Folk Tales from Ankole*. Kampala, Uganda: Uganda Press Trust, Ltd., n. d.

WEBSITES

Embassy of Uganda, Washington, D.C. [Online] Available http://www.ugandaweb.com/ugaembassy/, 1998.

Government of Uganda. Uganda Home Page. [Online] Available http://www.uganda.co.ug/, 1998.

World Travel Guide. Uganda. [Online] Available http://www.wtgonline.com/country/ug/gen.html, 1998.

Ukraine

The people of Ukraine are called Ukrainians. About 75 percent of the population traces their origins to the Ukraine. Other groups include Russians (about 22 percent), mainly in eastern Ukraine, in an area known as the Crimean Peninsula. Crimean Tatars, also concentrated on the Crimean Peninsula, represent a small percentage of the total population. For more information on the Russians and Tatars, see the chapter on Russia in Volume 7.

Ukrainians

PRONUNCIATION: yoo-KRAY-nee-uhns
LOCATION: Ukraine
POPULATION: Over 50 million (total population of country; 75 percent, or 37.5 million, are ethnic Ukrainians)
LANGUAGE: Ukrainian
RELIGION: Christianity

1 ● INTRODUCTION

Ukraine has had three periods of national statehood. The first period was that of Kievan Rus, with its capital in Kiev, which existed from the ninth to fourteenth centuries AD. The second was the Cossack period, lasting from the middle of the seventeenth century to the end of the eighteenth century. The third period began with the fall of tsarist (royal) Russia in 1918. A sovereign Ukrainian state, the Ukrainian National Republic, was established on January 22, 1918. However, it lasted only a few years. Ukraine was then divided among Russia, Poland, Czechoslovakia, Hungary, and Romania. After World War II (1939–45), all Ukrainian territories were integrated into the Soviet Union as the Ukrainian Soviet Socialist Republic.

With the dissolution of the Soviet Union in 1991, Ukraine gained its independence. Leonid Kravchuk was elected president. The government began implementing democratic, free-enterprise policies. On June 29, 1996, the Ukrainian Parliament approved the first Constitution of Ukraine, just a few weeks before the fifth anniversary of its independence.

2 ● LOCATION

Ukraine is the second-largest country in Europe, after France. It covers about 233,000 square miles (604,000 square kilometers) of land in Eastern Europe. Thanks to its wheat production, Ukraine is commonly referred to as the "breadbasket of Europe." Approximately 65 percent of its soil is fertile "black earth" (chornozem). It

UKRAINIANS

0   500   1000 Miles

0   500   1000 Kilometers

is also rich in mineral resources. Ukraine has a population of over 50 million people; 37.5 million of which are ethnic Ukrainians.

3 ● LANGUAGE

Ukrainian is the native language of over 40 million people. It is now the official language of Ukraine. It is spoken widely in central and western Ukraine. In cities where there are large concentrations of ethnic Russians, the Ukrainian and Russian languages are both commonly used. In eastern Ukraine near the border with Russia, the Russian language, spoken with a Ukrainian accent, dominates.

The Ukrainian alphabet resembles Russian, with a few subtle differences.

Examples of everyday Ukrainian words include *dobryj den* (hello), *tak* (yes), *nee*

(no), *bood laska* (please), *dyakooyoo* (thank you), and *do pobachenya* (goodbye).

4 ● FOLKLORE

Ukrainian legends include tales of the founding of the city of Kiev by the three brothers Kyi, Scheck, and Khoryv, and their sister Lybed. Other legends tell of the magical weed of the steppes region called *yevshan zillia*. It had the power of bringing lost souls back to their homeland. There is also the tale of Oleksa Dovbush, a Ukrainian Robin Hood who lived in the Carpathian Mountains. He stole from the rich to give to the poor. A number of different sites in the Carpathians are named after him.

5 ● RELIGION

In 1988 Ukrainians celebrated the 1,000-year anniversary of Christianity in Ukraine. About 75 percent of Ukrainians belong to the Eastern Orthodox faith.

Under the communist regime (1920–91), the Ukrainian Orthodox Church was forcibly incorporated into the Russian Orthodox Church. The Ukrainian Catholic Church met a similar fate soon after its abolition by the Soviet government in 1946.

6 ● MAJOR HOLIDAYS

The most important holiday in the Ukrainian church is Easter. Ukrainians are known throughout the world for their *pysanky* (pie-SANK-ee), decorating of eggs at Easter. Acrylic or oil paint is applied to hollow eggshells in bold, geometric patterns. Families save their finest examples, passing the decorated eggshells down as treasured family heirlooms.

Both Christmas and Easter are celebrated according to the Julian calendar. (The Julian calendar was established during the rule of Julius Caesar in 46 BC. It was modified by Pope Gregory in AD 1582. The modified calendar, called the Gregorian calendar, is used by most countries of the world. Some religions, including Eastern Orthodoxy, use the Julian calendar, which is thirteen days behind the Gregorian. Thus Christmas Day is celebrated on January 7 rather than December 25.) New Year's is celebrated with special carols called *shchedrivky*.

7 ● RITES OF PASSAGE

The majority of Ukrainians mark the major events of the life cycle within the traditions of the Orthodox church.

The Ivan Kupalo festival has remained a popular custom among Ukrainian youth. Kupalo was believed to be the god of love and fertility. In his honor, young men and women gather around streams and ponds, where they build fires and sing songs. Some youths even practice jumping over the fire. They may braid field flowers into wreaths that are sent floating on the water. If the wreath floats, they will be lucky in love; if it sinks, they will be unhappy.

8 ● RELATIONSHIPS

Ukrainians are very warm and hospitable. They greet visitors with the standard *Dobry-iden* (Good day), and very often with three kisses on the cheek. Hugging is another way Ukrainians greet one another, followed by a hearty handshake. During the early 1990s, a popular greeting among Ukrainians was *Slava Ukraini* (Glory to Ukraine). The toast is also a popular custom among Ukrainians.

Susan D. Rock

A couple strolls in the park. Approximately two-thirds of Ukraine's population live in cities.

Often one person in a group will announce a toast, followed by the words *na zdorovia* (to your health), or *day Bozhe* (glory to God).

9 ● LIVING CONDITIONS

Approximately two-thirds of Ukraine's population live in cities. High-rise apartments built during the Soviet era (1920–91) are the most common dwellings there. Living quarters are often poorly constructed, overcrowded, and small by Western standards.

About one-third of Ukraine's population live in rural areas. In the small villages and homesteads, farming is the most common occupation. The standard of living in rural areas is lower than in cities. Recently, many rural dwellers have migrated to the cities to find more profitable work.

10 ● FAMILY LIFE

Family size has decreased rapidly in Ukraine. Many families have only one child because they cannot afford to have any more. Marriage is a festive affair, involving many old customs and traditions. In recent years, the divorce rate has been rising.

Women in Ukraine have been, and remain, economically dependent on men. The Ukrainian parliament is nearly all male, with only a few female deputies out of over four hundred parliament members.

11 ● CLOTHING

Ukrainians generally wear Western-style clothing. Young Ukrainians enjoy following Western trends and fashions. They especially like popular brand-name or designer clothes. Different regions of Ukraine have their own traditional costumes. These are worn on holidays or other special occasions. The costumes are decorated with beautiful, colorful embroidery unique to each region.

12 ● FOOD

Ukrainian cuisine plays a role in customs and rituals. There are ritual breads for Christmas, Easter, weddings, and funerals. These include Easter *paska* bread, and wedding *korovai* and *dyven*. Other traditional foods are *pyrohy* (baked pies with fillings), *varenyky* (filled, cooked dumplings), and *holubtsi* (stuffed cabbage rolls). *Borshch* (red beet soup) is served with dinner. Pork and pork products, such as ham, sausage *(kovbasa),* and blood sausage *(kyshka),* are the most popular meats. Ukrainians also eat large amounts of potatoes, cooked buckwheat *(kasha),* and different types of rye bread. Some popular drinks include tea, coffee, honey liqueur, *kvas (*an alcoholic beverage make from fermented bread and water, and sold from barrels by street vendors),

kompot (homemade fruit drink), and vodka *(horilka* in Ukrainian).

Recipe

Borshch Ukrainsky

Ingredients

2 cans of sliced beets (12 ounces each)
2 cans of beef broth
4 hard-boiled eggs, shelled and cut in half lengthwise
½ cup sour cream (plain yogurt may be substituted)

Directions

1. Combine beets and beef broth in pan.
2. Heat slowly, stirring occasionally, for about 10 minutes.
3. Ladle into bowls.
4. Float a hard-boiled egg half, cut side up, in each bowl, and top with a spoonful of sour cream or yogurt.

Note: This may be served hot or cold.

Adapted from Webb, Lois Sinaiko. *Holidays of the World Cookbook for Students.* Phoenix, Ariz.: Oryx Press, 1995.

13 ● EDUCATION

Ukrainian children are required to attend school for eleven years, from about the age of seven to the age of eighteen. After grade nine, students have two choices: they can continue in a general academic program or enroll in technical or trade school. There are about 150 schools of higher education in Ukraine, including 9 universities. The largest and most popular universities are the Kiev State University, Lviv State University, and Kharkiv State University.

EPD Photos/Taras Mahlay

Ukrainian bandura player, wearing shirt with vyshyvannia (embroidery), loose-fitting red trousers, and matching red leather shoes.

14 ● CULTURAL HERITAGE

The music of Ukraine is firmly rooted in its folklore. The *bandura,* Ukraine's national instrument, may have from twenty to sixty-five strings and is similar to a lute. The bandura is most often played to accompany dancers and singers. In the late 1800s, Ukrainian musicians known as *kobzari* (kawb-ZAHR-ee) developed epic songs called *duma* (DOO-mah), depicting heroic efforts of Ukrainians to win freedom and peace. The compositions of Mykola Lysenko (1842–1912) are infused with Ukrainian folk themes and motifs. Borys Lyatoshynsky (1895–1968) is considered the father of modern Ukrainian music. Leading contemporary composers include Volodymyr Huba, Ivan Karabyts, and Oleh Kyva. To date, the most important Ukrainian pop composer is Volodymyr Ivasiuk (1949–79). The most original of the newer songwriters is Taras Petrynenko.

The "father" of modern Ukrainian literature was Ivan Kotliarevsky, author of the *Eneida* (1798), which transformed the heroes of Virgil's *Aeneid* into Ukrainian Cossacks. The most outstanding poet of the nineteenth century was Taras Shevchenko (1814–61). The greatest realist of the late 1800s was Ivan Franko, whose novels told of life in contemporary Galicia (a western region of Ukraine, later ceded to Poland).

During much of the communist era (1920–91) in Ukraine, literature was strictly censored by the government. Certain literary styles, such as Socialist Realism, were promoted by the Communist Party during this time.

15 ● EMPLOYMENT

Ukraine is now in the process of moving into a market economy, which has been socially and politically difficult because of inflation, unemployment, and general economic uncertainty. Most of Ukraine's population is employed in agriculture or in the metalworking, construction, chemical, or food industries.

16 ● SPORTS

Ukrainians engage in soccer, volleyball, track and field, basketball, hockey, skating, and swimming. Soccer is definitely the biggest sport, and the favorite team is Kiev Dynamo. With the success of Olympic medal-winners Oksana Baiul and Victor Petrenko, ice skating has also become very popular. Ukrainian gymnasts won twenty-two medals in the Summer 1996 Olympics in Atlanta, Georgia. Skiing, mostly in the Carpathian mountains, is also a sport enjoyed by many.

17 ● RECREATION

Ukraine's new democratic government lacks funds to support the arts. However, one can still find numerous art exhibits, concerts, literary evenings, and plays in most cities. The Shevchenko National Opera Company, Ivan Franko National Theater, and State Operetta are home to opera and ballet performances, as well as other cultural events.

Folk dancing is done on special occasions, such as weddings and festivals. In a popular folk dance called the *hopak,* male dancers compete against each other, performing acrobatic leaps.

18 ● CRAFTS AND HOBBIES

Embroidery *(vyshyvannia)* is the most popular Ukrainian folk art and hobby. It is known for its varied colors, complex stitches, and intricate designs. The Ukrainian *vyshyvka* (embroidered design) is applied to many everyday items, including pillows, aprons, towels, and other household articles.

19 ● SOCIAL PROBLEMS

As a newly independent country, Ukraine faces a number of social problems similar to those in the West. Alcoholism, unemployment, organized crime, drugs, prostitution, and the AIDS epidemic are the main areas of concern. The crime rate has also risen, especially in the cities.

20 ● BIBLIOGRAPHY

Kardash, Peter. *Ukraine and Ukrainians.* Australia: Fortuna Co., 1991.

Kubijovyc, Volodymyr, and Danylo Husar Struk, ed. *Encyclopedia of Ukraine.* Toronto, Canada: University of Toronto Press, Inc., 1993.

Subtelny, Orest. *Ukraine: A History.* Toronto, Canada: University of Toronto Press in association with the Canadian Institute of Ukrainian Studies, 1988

WEBSITES

World Travel Guide. [Online] Available http://www.wtgonline.com/country/ua/gen.html, 1998..

United Arab Emirates

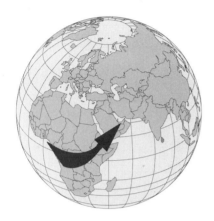

South Asians (Asian Indians, Pakistanis, Bangladeshis, and Sri Lankans) account for about 45 percent of the population of the UAE, followed by Arabs (about 33 percent), and Iranians (17 percent). Westerners (Americans and Western Europeans) account for about 5 percent. Jordanians, Palestinians, Egyptians, Iraqis, and Bahrainis are employed throughout the government bureaucracy.

Emirians

PRONUNCIATION: em-EE-ree-uhns
LOCATION: United Arab Emirates (UAE)
POPULATION: 460,000
LANGUAGE: Arabic
RELIGION: Islam (Sunni Muslim majority)

1 ● INTRODUCTION

The United Arab Emirates (UAE) is a confederation of seven sheikdoms (regions headed by a sheik or emir), or emirates, located on the shore of the Persian Gulf. Its Bedu (Bedouin) tribes were converted to Islam during the seventh century AD. The following centuries were marked by continual wars and violence between rival dynasties.

After signing two peace treaties with Britain (1820 and 1853), the emirates became known as the Trucial States. The formal relationship established between Britain and the kingdoms of the southern Gulf lasted until 1971. At that time, Bahrain and Qatar became independent states. On December 2, 1971, the emirates of Abu Dhabi, Dubai, Sharjah, Ajman, Umm al-Qaiwain, and Fujairah formed the UAE. In February 1972, the emirate of Ras al-Khaimah united with them as well. Because Abu Dhabi is the largest and most powerful of the seven emirates, its emir is designated the president of the UAE.

The discovery and production of oil in 1962 brought new wealth into the area. Emirians, who had been among the poorest people in the world, soon became some of the wealthiest. Proven oil reserves in Abu Dhabi are estimated to last for another 200 years at the current rate of production.

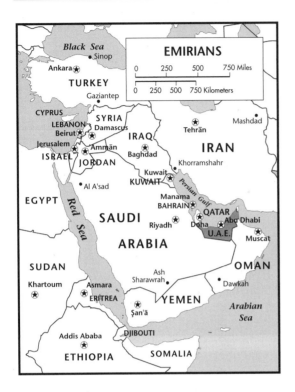

2 ● LOCATION

The UAE is located on the southern coast of the Persian Gulf, and the northwestern coast of the Gulf of Oman. The total area of the UAE is 30,000 square miles (82,880 square kilometers), which is about the size of the state of Maine. Abu Dhabi is by far the largest emirate, and Dubai is the second-largest. The land is mostly desert, with a mountain range in the north and oases scattered across the sands. The emirate of Ras al-Khaimah is called the "garden spot" of the UAE because its land is very fertile.

The population of the UAE is estimated at 2.3 million people. Only about 20 percent (460,000 people) of these are UAE citizens. The rest are foreign workers.

3 ● LANGUAGE

The official language, and the native language of UAE citizens, is Arabic. Languages spoken by foreign workers include English, Hindi, Urdu, Persian, and Tagalog.

"Hello" in Arabic is *marhaba* or *ahlan*. Other common greetings are *As-salam `alaykum,* "Peace be with you," with the reply of *Wa `alaykum as-salam,* "And to you peace." *Ma'assalama* means "Goodbye." "Thank you" is *Shukran,* and "You're welcome" is *`Afwan;* "yes" is *na'am* and "no" is *la'a.* The numbers one to ten in Arabic are: *wahad, ithnayn, thalatha, arba'a, khamsa, sitta, saba'a, thamanya, tisa'a,* and *`ashara.*

4 ● FOLKLORE

Pearl divers in Abu Dhabi traditionally left their homes during the entire four-month pearling season. The following folk song depicts the hope and patience of an Emirian woman awaiting the safe return of her loved one:

Neighbor of mine, my adventurous sailor shall return.

Neighbor of mine, he shall return from the world of dangers.

With perfumes, precious stones, rosewater, and incense he shall return.

He shall return, and to see him again will be like seeing the Moon.

5 ● RELIGION

Native-born Emirians are all Muslims (followers of Islam). Most of the foreign workers are also Muslims, although there are also Hindus and Christians. The majority of

Emirians are Sunni Muslim, with a small Shi'ah minority.

The Islamic religion has five "pillars," or practices, that must be observed by all Muslims: (1) praying five times a day; (2) giving alms, or *zakat,* to the poor; (3) fasting during the month of Ramadan; (4) making the pilgrimage, or *hajj,* to Mecca; and (5) reciting the *shahada (ashhadu an la illah ila Allah wa ashhadu in Muhammadu rasul Allah*), which means "I witness that there is no god but Allah and that Muhammad is the prophet of Allah."

6 ● MAJOR HOLIDAYS

Secular national holidays include National Day (December 2), and New Year's Day (January 1). The emirates also celebrate their own holidays. For example, in Abu Dhabi August 6 is a holiday marking the accession of Shaykh Zayed. Other official holidays are Muslim ones. There are two main Muslim holidays: *Eid Al-Fitr* is a three-day festival at the end of the holy month of fasting, Ramadan. *Eid Al-Adha* is a three-day feast of sacrifice at the end of the month of pilgrimage *(hajj)* to Mecca. Families who can afford it slaughter a lamb and share the meat with poorer Muslims. Other holidays are the First of *Muharram,* or the Muslim New Year; *al-Mawlid An-Nabi,* the Prophet Muhammad's birthday; and *Eid al-Isra wa al-Miraj,* a feast celebrating Muhammad's nocturnal visit to heaven. Friday is the Islamic day of rest, so most businesses and services are closed. All government offices, private businesses, and schools are also closed during Eid al-Fitr and Eid al-Adha.

7 ● RITES OF PASSAGE

The first word spoken to a baby is *Allah* (God). After birth, the next important event in a boy's life is circumcision. It is performed at the age of seven and formally makes him a member of the religious community.

Traditional arranged marriages still take place today. The groom pays the bride a dowry, or *mahr.* This becomes her property, no matter what happens. The mahr has two parts. The *muqaddam* is a dowry given before the wedding; this allows the bride to buy things for herself and her new home. The second part, the *muta'akhir,* is a form of insurance for the woman in the event of divorce. The groom pledges in a contract that he will pay the bride an agreed-upon amount if he should divorce her.

8 ● RELATIONSHIPS

Emirians talk a great deal. They speak loudly, repeat themselves often, and interrupt each other constantly. Conversations are highly emotional and full of gestures. When talking, Emirians make physical contact much more often than Westerners do. They also stand much closer together. People of the same sex often hold hands while talking or walking. In former days, members of the opposite sex (even married couples) never touched in public.

9 ● LIVING CONDITIONS

Before the discovery and production of oil, conditions in the UAE were very primitive. Emirians had no electricity, running water, or sewage disposal system. There were no paved roads or telephones. Housing consisted of the bare minimum needs for shelter. Since oil production began in 1962, conditions have rapidly improved. Today almost all Emirians live in thoroughly modern homes in modern cities. Medical care is still not up to Western standards, but it is improving.

10 ● FAMILY LIFE

Marriages are traditionally arranged by parents. First cousins are the preferred match. Polygamy (more than one spouse) is legal but rarely practiced. In theory (and according to Islamic law), a man may have up to four wives. Divorce is fairly simple but also rare. In a divorce, the father is given custody of all children over the age of five. The mother takes the younger ones with her to her parents' house, where she will live until she remarries.

Women are much less restricted in the UAE than in other Arab countries. At least 98 percent of the female population of school age is attending primary or intermediate school. Women account for 70 percent of the students at the Higher Colleges of Technology and over 60 percent at the UAE University. Emirian women have also joined the armed forces and the police force.

11 ● CLOTHING

Emirians wear traditional Arab clothing. For men, this consists of an ankle-length robe called a *dishdasha* or *kandura.* A large piece of cloth, called a *ghutra,* is worn on the head. It is held in place with an `aqal, a thick, black band made of twisted wool. With the new flow of wealth, some women import the latest fashions from the West. A traditional UAE woman's attire, however, is the `*abaya.* This black garment covers her

© Robert Azzi/Woodfin Camp & Assoc.
Traditional woman's attire when going out is public is the `abaya, *a black garment that covers her from head to toe.*

from head to toe when she is in a public place.

12 ● FOOD

Rice, meat, and fish are the Emirians' staple foods. Among the most commonly used spices are coriander, cardamom, saffron, and turmeric. Islam prohibits the consumption of pork or alcohol.

A favorite dish in the UAE is *machbous,* rice and meat seasoned with spices, onions, tomatoes, and dried lemon. During Ramadan, the month of daytime fasting, *harees* is usually served at night. For this dish, small pieces of shredded meat are mixed with wheat and water that have been beaten to the consistency of porridge. Favorite desserts include *al-halwa,* made from sugar, eggs, starch, water, and oil; and *Kul Wiskut,* a mixture of peanuts and sugar.

Coffee and tea are the most popular beverages and are often mixed with spices (cardamom for coffee, and saffron or mint for tea).

13 ● EDUCATION

Public schooling was almost nonexistent before the late 1950s. Today enrollment at public primary schools is almost 100 percent. Education is required from age six to age twelve, and it is free through the university level. The government also provides full scholarships for study abroad. The United Arab Emirates University opened in Al Ain in 1977.

14 ● CULTURAL HERITAGE

The only native Emirian artistic traditions are those passed down from the Bedu (or Bedouin) nomads. These include traditional Arab music and dances, and a strong passion for poetry. Traditional Emirian music has a strong drumbeat accompanied by various percussion and stringed instruments. The *oud* is an ancient stringed instrument that is the ancestor of the European lute. Wind instruments include the Arabian flute or *nai.*

The *ayyala* is a traditional men's dance frequently performed in the UAE.

15 ● EMPLOYMENT

About 90 percent of the work force in the UAE are foreign workers. In 1995, the UAE launched a nationwide campaign aimed at bringing more Emirians into the work force. Most of the UAE's income is from the oil industry. The oil wealth comes mainly from the emirate of Abu Dhabi. In the smaller emirates, sheep and goat herding, fishing, and farming are the main occupations. Business and industrial workers in the cities often take a two- to three-hour lunch break. They then stay at work until 7:00 PM or later.

16 ● SPORTS

The traditional sports of camel and horse racing attract great crowds. Owners and fans often speed alongside the race course in four-wheel-drive vehicles, shouting instructions and cheering. The annual Dubai Desert Classic Golf Tournament draws top international golfers. Water sports are also popular throughout the UAE.

17 ● RECREATION

Movies are very popular with Emirians. Theaters show movies in Hindi, Urdu, Persian, Arabic, and English. Videos can be rented, but they are censored.

There are radio and television broadcasts in Arabic and other languages. Broadcasts from other countries are also picked up via satellite dishes on apartment buildings and private homes.

18 ● CRAFTS AND HOBBIES

Most of the folk art sold in UAE markets is imported. The UAE's Women's Association runs a Handicrafts Center in Abu Dhabi that produces some local basketry and weaving. Baskets are made of palm tree fronds, called *al Khoos*. Wool from sheep is woven into colorful fabrics that are then used for pillowcases, covers, blankets, carpets, and bags.

19 ● SOCIAL PROBLEMS

The emirates have a long history of intertribal wars and violence. Although they are now united, old conflicts continually erupt. Abu Dhabi has the greatest authority because of its size and its wealth (due to oil reserves). This creates resentment among the smaller emirates. Dubai is the only emirate large and wealthy enough to challenge Abu Dhabi's decisions. Dubai occasionally acts independently of decisions handed down by the Abu Dhabi leaders.

20 ● BIBLIOGRAPHY

Crocetti, Gina L. *Culture Shock! United Arab Emirates.* Portland, Ore.: Graphic Arts Center Publishing Co., 1996.

Higgins, Kevin. *The Emirates: Abu Dhabi, Dubai, Sharjah, Ras Al Khaimah, Fujairah, Umm Al Qaiwain, Ajman.* Reading, Pa.: Garnet Publishing, 1995.

Peck, Malcolm C. *The United Arab Emirates: A Venture in Unity.* Boulder, Colo.: Westview Press, 1986.

WEBSITES

ArabNet. [Online] Available http://www.arab.net/uae/uae_contents.html, 1998.

Emirates Center for Strategic and Research Homepage. [Online] Available http://www.ecssr.ac.ae, 1998.

World Travel Guide. United Arab Emirates. [Online] Available http://www.wtgonline.com/country/ae/gen.html, 1998.

United Kingdom

The people of the United Kingdom are called British or English, Welsh, Scots, and Irish. Over 90 percent of United Kingdom residents are native-born. The ethnic minorities include West Indian or Guyanese (499,000), Indian (840,000), Pakistani (475,000), or Bengali (160,000). There are also sizable numbers of Africans, Americans, Australians, Chinese, Greek and Turkish Cypriots, Italians, Spaniards, and Southeast Asians.

English

PRONUNCIATION: ING-lish
LOCATION: United Kingdom (England)
POPULATION: Over 48 million
LANGUAGE: English
RELIGION: Church of England; Protestantism; Judaism; Sikhism; Hinduism; Islam

1 ● INTRODUCTION

England is unique among European countries. As an island, it has been protected by surrounding waters that form a natural barrier. No country has successfully invaded England for the last 1,000 years.

The area now called England was occupied by many European cultures and tribes. In 1066 AD the Normans, from France, invaded and became the new rulers of England. London was established as the country's capital. Soon after, England began expanding into its neighboring countries—Wales, Ireland, and Scotland. England's history has been continuously linked with these three nations through to present times.

In the seventeenth century, the first English colonies in America were established. England continued to expand its colonies and became an empire (a government with many territories under its rule) that covered one-quarter of the world.

England suffered enormous losses during World War I (1914–18). After the war, England began to lose authority over its colonies. Ireland was the first to become independent. World War II (1939–45) was also devastating to England. In the twenty-five years that followed, the British Empire granted independence to the majority of its other colonies. Most of the former colonies

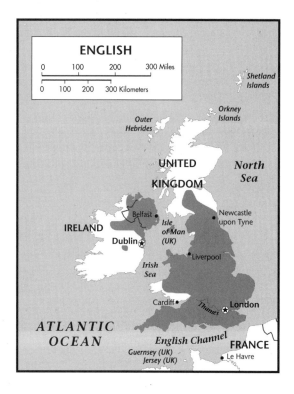

ENGLISH

0   100   200   300 Miles

0   100   200   300 Kilometers

Shetland Islands

Orkney Islands

Outer Hebrides

UNITED KINGDOM

North Sea

IRELAND

Belfast

Isle of Man (UK)

Newcastle upon Tyne

Dublin

Liverpool

Irish Sea

Cardiff

Thames

London

ATLANTIC OCEAN

English Channel

Guernsey (UK)
Jersey (UK)

FRANCE

Le Havre

still retain economic and political ties to Britain. The British economy and society still have a strong influence in world affairs today. The British royal family, which no longer has any political power, is often the focus of international publicity.

2 ● LOCATION

England is the largest of the four countries that make up the United Kingdom. Two others—Scotland and Wales—share the same island (Britain) with England, and the three countries are collectively known as Great Britain. The fourth, Northern Ireland, is a close neighbor. England is roughly triangular in shape, with a long, irregular coastline. Its countryside includes many types of terrain, including mountains, plains, lowlands and low hills, and moors (marshy, open areas). London is the capital city.

England has a high population density (many people living close together). Most of England's inhabitants live in cities. Ethnically, they come from a mixture of European groups. Many people have moved from Scotland, Wales, and Ireland to live in England. Immigrants have also come from former British colonies in South Asia and the Caribbean.

3 ● LANGUAGE

English is the most widely spoken language in the world. It is spoken throughout the United Kingdom and by close to 450 million people around the globe. Many varieties of English are spoken worldwide, and many dialects and regional accents exist within England. Although Americans speak English, they may have difficulty understanding the speech of the English people. In addition to differences in pronunciation, people in the two countries often use different words for the same thing. Examples include:

U. S. ENGLISH	BRITISH ENGLISH
ballpoint pen	biro
car hood	bonnet
car trunk	boot
phone booth	call box
elevator	lift
truck	lorry
diaper	nappy
gasoline	petrol
stroller (for baby)	pushchair
baby buggy	pram
flashlight	torch

4 ● FOLKLORE

The most famous folklore of England is about King Arthur and the Knights of the

Round Table. If there was a real King Arthur, he most probably lived in the sixth century AD. King Arthur is believed to have ruled justly, which was uncommon for rulers of that era. Famous characters from that folklore include Queen Guinevere and Sir Lancelot. Many books and movies tell these stories, including T. H. White's *The Once and Future King* and the movies *Camelot* and *Excalibur.*

Also famous are the English legends about Robin Hood and his Merry Men. These noble outlaws lived in Sherwood Forest near the city of Nottingham in the twelfth century AD. They were famous for stealing from the rich and giving to the poor.

5 ● RELIGION

Church and state are closely intertwined in England, unlike in the United States. About 60 percent of England's population are members of the Church of England (also called the Anglican Church). Other Protestant sects are also active in England, as is the Roman Catholic Church. England has one of Europe's largest Jewish populations. In addition, many cities have recently become home to large immigrant populations of Sikhs (followers of a Hindu-Islamic religion), Hindus, and Muslims (followers of Islam).

6 ● MAJOR HOLIDAYS

Most of England's holidays are those celebrated by the Christian religion. Other holidays include New Year's Day (January 1), May Day (May 1), and the August bank holiday.

There is also a great deal of celebration related to the government and the monarchy. Much ceremony surrounds the State Opening of Parliament (the governing council) each year. Traditions also surround anniversaries of many historical events. Among them is Remembrance Sunday, which commemorates the armistice (military truce) that ended World War I (1914–18).

7 ● RITES OF PASSAGE

England is a modern, industrialized country. Therefore, many of the rites of passage that young people undergo are connected with their progress through the educational system. Other rites of passage include getting a first job, being promoted, getting married, having children, and retiring in one's sixties. These are the main markers of significant life changes.

8 ● RELATIONSHIPS

English people are known for their politeness and their respect for law and order. They wait patiently in lines (which they call "queues") at stores, bus stops, and movie theaters. It is uncommon for people to try to push ahead of each other. Those living in the south are usually more reserved than northerners, and are less likely to greet strangers. The English are also known for their acceptance of other people's views and eccentricities (peculiar behaviors).

Social class is an important feature of English society. In earlier times, people from wealthy families enjoyed great privileges not available to working-class and poor people. After World War II (1939–45), working-class people gained access to better education and therefore to better jobs.

Cory Langley

The Royal Guard at Buckingham Palace in London.

As a result, many barriers between classes weakened. However, class identity is still inferred from such things as patterns of speech, which school one attended, and one's parents' occupations.

9 ● LIVING CONDITIONS

Even though England has a high population density, there is less overcrowding than in most European countries. About half the population now live in dwellings constructed after World War II (1939–45). These are usually two-story houses with gardens. More than 80 percent of England's population live in houses, while the rest occupy apartments (called "flats.") There is a shortage of low-income rental housing.

This has contributed to a growing homeless population in London and England's other major cities.

10 ● FAMILY LIFE

England's families have gotten smaller over the years. Grandparents are more likely to live alone or in retirement homes rather than with their families. More young couples are living together without marrying. Those who marry do so at a later age than in previous times. They often establish themselves in their occupations before starting a family. Gender roles of men and women are changing, both at home and in the workplace.

Women are moving toward greater equality in relationships and responsibility. A 1975 law established equal pay for men and women performing the same work.

11 ● CLOTHING

There is no unique national costume for England. For the most part, the English wear modern-style clothing similar to that worn in the United States and other industrialized countries. Blue jeans and T-shirts are very popular. The cold, damp winters require heavy coats, mackintoshes (raincoats), and warm woolen clothes.

The most famous traditional costumes in England are the red uniforms and high black hats worn by the royal guard at Buckingham Palace. Ceremonial dress is worn by government troops and the royal family on official occasions. In rural areas, traditional folk costumes are worn for festivals such as May Day (May 1, a celebration of spring).

12 ● FOOD

English cuisine can seem bland and unimaginative to people from other countries. It usually does not include many herbs or spices, or fancy presentations. This may be why food from other countries, especially India and China, is popular in England.

The traditional English breakfast is quite substantial. It includes bacon, eggs, sausages, mushrooms, grilled tomatoes, fried bread, and kipper (a type of smoked fish). Modern English people rarely take the time to prepare such an elaborate breakfast before going off to work or school. They usually eat a lighter meal, often cereal and toast with marmalade.

Recipe

Bubble and Squeak

Ingredients

2½ cups shredded cabbage
½ pound roast beef (corned beef may be used), cut into bite-sized pieces
3 Tablespoons unsalted butter
¼ cup sliced onions
½ cup mashed potatoes
Pepper

Directions

1. Fill a pot large enough to hold the shredded cabbage with water. Heat until the water is boiling.

2. Add the cabbage, reduce heat, and simmer for 5 minutes. Remove the cabbage, and drain in a colander. Press on the cabbage to squeeze out most of the water.

3. Melt the butter in a large skillet. Add the onions and cook them over low heat, stirring constantly, until the onions are softened (about 2 minutes).

4. Add the cabbage to the skillet and stir to combine with the cooked onions.

5. Add the mashed potatoes and mix. Cook the mixture for about 3 minutes.

6. Add the meat to the mixture.

7. Cook until the meat is heated through (about five minutes), stirring occasionally.

Adapted from Howard Hillman, *Great Peasant Dishes of the World.* Boston: Houghton Mifflin, 1983.

The main meal of the day may be eaten either at midday or in the evening. It usually consists of a meat dish, vegetables, and a dessert. Sunday lunch is the most important meal of the week.

Tea is the national beverage. The English are known for their custom of afternoon tea, accompanied by cakes and sandwiches. The custom originated with the wealthier classes who were able to eat at 4:00 PM when most people were at work. Nowadays, afternoon tea is mostly a weekend event.

Bubble and Squeak is a dish with a funny name that was invented to make use of leftovers from a roast beef dinner. The "bubble and squeak" refers to the dish as it cooks. A recipe for Bubble and Squeak is on the previous page.

13 ● EDUCATION

Education is required for all children between the ages of five and sixteen. Nearly all English people are literate (able to read and write). Most students attend state-run schools. Primary education lasts until the age of eleven, followed by secondary education. At the age of sixteen, pupils sit for exams in several subjects to get the General Certificate of Secondary Education (GCSE). After that, they may either leave school to find a job, or continue secondary education until the age of eighteen. At that age, they may take more advanced exams (A-Level). These are usually taken in preparation for attending a university.

14 ● CULTURAL HERITAGE

England has a distinguished cultural heritage, including one of the greatest writers ever, the sixteenth-century playwright William Shakespeare. Other great writers include the poets William Wordsworth and John Keats; novelists Jane Austen, Charles Dickens, the Brontë sisters (Charlotte, Emily, and Anne), George Eliot, and Thomas Hardy; and modern writers D. H. Lawrence, Virginia Woolf, W. H. Auden, George Orwell, and T. S. Eliot.

Great English painters include Joseph Turner and John Constable (nineteenth century), and Francis Bacon, David Hockney, and Graham Sutherland (twentieth century). Henry Moore was a famous twentieth-century sculptor. English composers include John Dowland, William Byrd, and Henry Purcell (1500s and 1600s); Gilbert and Sullivan (nineteenth-century light operas); and Ralph Vaughan Williams and Benjamin Britten in modern times. In the 1960s, England became a trendsetter in popular music as the home of The Beatles and The Rolling Stones.

15 ● EMPLOYMENT

The average English workweek is five days and thirty-five to forty hours long. This is about half of the workweek of a century ago. Approximately half of England's workers are employed in service sector jobs (jobs that directly serve the public). A third work in manufacturing and engineering. The rest work in agriculture, construction, mining, and energy production.

16 ● SPORTS

The most popular sport in England, both for watching and playing, is soccer (called "football"). It is played in professional and amateur leagues as well as in schools, colleges, and small towns. Other favorite sports include cricket and rugby. These three games all originated in England and spread throughout the world due to the influence of the British Empire. Other popular sports include horse racing, hockey, cross-country running, tennis, swimming, and other water sports. Gambling on sports—which is legal in England—is popular.

17 ● RECREATION

Many people in England spend their leisure time relaxing at home watching television or videos. Most are regular newspaper readers, and nearly half read books regularly. The English also enjoy going to a local pub (bar) for good traditional food as well as alcoholic beverages.

Angling (fishing with a hook and line) is the most popular pastime in the country. The English are also very fond of games, including snooker (a billiards game) and darts. Older people often enjoy bingo and cribbage (a card game). The English are known for their love of gardening. Even apartment dwellers cultivate window boxes full of flowers, or rent a piece of land on which to garden. Fishing, hiking, and horseback riding are also popular, as are raising pets and taking a variety of evening classes.

18 ● CRAFTS AND HOBBIES

England has a history of fine furniture-making. This dates back to the eighteenth-century work of Thomas Chippendale and George Hepplewhite. The ceramics of Josiah Wedgwood and Josiah Spode also date back to that time. England still exports blue-and-white Wedgwood jasperware. The most famous English folk dance is the Morris dance, still seen at local festivals. Male dancers stomp and leap while waving pieces of cloth and jingling bells.

19 ● SOCIAL PROBLEMS

The most serious social problems in modern-day England are class divisions and economic inequality. Over 20 percent of the nation's wealth is owned by 1 percent of the people. Unemployment hit 10 percent in 1993.

Many immigrants from the West Indies, India, Pakistan, Hong Kong, and other countries have settled in England's urban areas. They often suffer the effects of discrimination and have high rates of unemployment. Racial tension between the white English community and nonwhite immigrants has erupted into riots in several major cities.

20 ● BIBLIOGRAPHY

England in Pictures. Minneapolis, Minn.: Lerner Publications Co., 1990.

Fuller, Barbara. *Britain: Cultures of the World.* London, England: Marshall Cavendish, 1994.

Gall, Timothy, and Susan Gall, eds. *Junior Worldmark Encyclopedia of the Nations.* Detroit: UXL, 1996.

Greene, Carol. *England. Enchantment of the World Series.* Chicago: Children's Press, 1994.

Helweg, Arthur W. "English." In *Encyclopedia of World Cultures (Europe).* Boston: G. K. Hall, 1992.

Langley, Andrew. *Passport to England.* New York: Franklin Watts, 1994.

WEBSITES

British Council. [Online] Available http://www.britcoun.org/usa/, 1998.

British Information Service. United Kingdom. [Online] Available http://www.britain-info.org, 1998.

British Tourist Authority. [Online] Available http://www.visitbritain.com, 1998.

Scots

PRONUNCIATION: SCAHTS
LOCATION: United Kingdom (Scotland)
POPULATION: Over 5 million
LANGUAGE: Scottish dialect of English (also called Scots); Gaelic
RELIGION: Church of Scotland, a Presbyterian sect; Roman Catholic; small numbers of Baptists, Anglicans, and Methodists

1 ● INTRODUCTION

Scotland is one of four countries that make up the United Kingdom. (The other three are England, Wales, and Northern Ireland.) Scotland covers the northern part of the island of Great Britain, which it shares with England and Wales.

For centuries, social and political life in the northern (Highland) area of Scotland was organized around clans (communities of people with strong family ties). Chieftains protected clan members from invasion in exchange for their loyalty. (The cultural tradition of clans still exists today at ceremonial gatherings such as weddings.) The southern areas of Scotland were more influenced by English patterns of organization.

Repeated disputes with England sometimes led to war. Before the early fourteenth century, the Scottish were ruled by English monarchs. In 1707 the Act of Union made Scotland, England, and Wales all part of the United Kingdom.

Scotland has seen difficult times in the twentieth century. Extensive unemployment began in the 1930s, forcing thousands to emigrate in search of a better life. Oil was discovered off the North Sea coast in the 1960s. Many new jobs were created as a result, and emigration slowed. Since the 1980s national feeling in favor of separation from England has strengthened. In 1997, Scotland voted to establish its own parliament (government council) by 1999. This change will increase Scotland's independence from England.

2 ● LOCATION

Scotland is located in the northern part of the island of Great Britain. The country can be divided into three main areas. The Southern Uplands are a hilly region noted for sheep-raising. The more densely populated Central Lowlands have flatter and more fertile land. The Highlands, the northern two-thirds of the country, include lochs (lakes), glens (valleys), mountains, and numerous small islands.

Over three-fourths of Scotland's population live in the Central Lowland area. Two hundred years ago, almost half of all Scottish people lived in the Highlands. Most Scots are descended from Celtic tribes who were the original inhabitants of their land. The bloodlines of Viking, Norman, and English invaders are mixed in as well. The Highland and Lowland Scots are considered two different groups, as are mainland and island dwellers.

3 ● LANGUAGE

Scotland's official language is English. It is spoken with a unique Scottish accent, or "burr," that is especially prominent in words containing "r" sounds. Scottish English (also called Scots) contains words borrowed from Gaelic (a Scottish dialect), French, Dutch, and Scandinavian languages. Its grammar sometimes differs from standard English, as in expressions like "Are you no going?" and "I'm away to bed." Gaelic is spoken as a second language by less than 2 percent of the population, mostly in the Highlands and Hebridean islands.

COMMONLY USED SCOTS TERMS

U. S. English	Scots
don't, can't, won't	dinnae, canae, willnae
small	wee
yes	aye
know	ken
weep	greet
church	kirk
pants	breeks
girl	lassie
child	bairn
pretty	bonny
stay	bide

TYPICAL SCOTS PHRASES

Scots	U. S. English
I'm exhausted.	Ah'm fair farfochen.
The child's a little tired.	The bairn's a wee bit wabbit.

4 ● FOLKLORE

The oldest Gaelic songs tell stories of warriors battling Norsemen, magic rowan (mountain ash) trees, and monstrous old women living in the sea. There is also a rich folk tradition of belief in fairies and other supernatural forces. The most famous character in Scottish folklore is the Loch Ness monster. "Nessie" is said to be a dinosaur-like creature living in a large lake. Although it has supposedly been sighted by hundreds of people, its existence has never been scientifically proven.

A popular Scottish legend tells the tale of the "wall flower." In a castle near the river Tweed, a fair maiden was held prisoner because she had promised her love to a

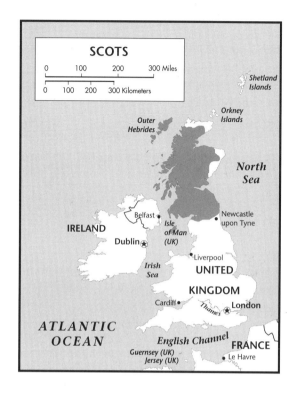

member of a neighboring enemy clan. Her lover tried various tactics to rescue her. He finally was able to get inside the castle by pretending to be a troubadour (wandering musician). Once inside, he found the maiden and the two made a plan for her escape. She climbed out the window, and planned to climb down the wall of the castle using a silk rope. While her lover waited below to rescue her, something went wrong, as this poem relates:

Up she got upon a wall
Attempted down to slide withal;
But the silken twist untied,
She fell, and bruised, she died,
And her loving, luckless speed,
Twined her to the plant we call
Now the "Flower of the Wall."

5 ● RELIGION

The country's dominant religion is the Church of Scotland, a Presbyterian sect. It is commonly known as "the Kirk," and has been Scotland's official religion since 1690. Other religions in Scotland include Catholic, Baptist, Anglican, and Methodist, as well as more modern evangelical sects. Church attendance in Scotland is very low.

6 ● MAJOR HOLIDAYS

Scots celebrate the major holidays of the Christian calendar. In addition, they honor Saint Andrew, patron saint of Scotland, on November 30, and the Scottish poet Robert Burns on Burns Night, January 25.

Another unique celebration is the Hogmanay (New Year's Eve, December 31) celebration. Until the 1960s, this holiday held more importance than Christmas (December 25). It involved the ceremony of "first footing," the custom of visiting friends, neighbors, and even strangers, in the "wee sma' hours" (early) of New Year's Day. Christmas was formerly frowned upon by the Scottish Church. It only became a public holiday in 1967. Christmas in Scotland now resembles celebrations in England and the United States, with fir trees, carols, and gift-giving.

Halloween, October 31, is also an important celebration. Like "trick-or-treaters" in the United States, Scottish "guisers" go from door to door in costumes asking for candy or money. Unlike in the United States, the guisers must perform a song or poem to earn their treat. Halloween decorations include the Scottish version of the jack-o'-lantern: a scooped-out rutabaga called a "neep lantern" ("neep" is short for turnip).

7 ● RITES OF PASSAGE

Scotland is a modern, industrialized, Christian country. Many of the rites of passage that young people undergo are religious rituals. These include baptism, first communion, confirmation, and marriage. In addition, a student's progress through the educational system is often marked with graduation parties.

8 ● RELATIONSHIPS

The Scottish are known for their silent and reserved manner. It is unusual for Scots to be seen holding hands, kissing, or touching in public. They tend to minimize direct expressions of enthusiasm. The handshake is less common than in other parts of Britain. It is considered unacceptable to criticize others in public, or to discuss personal problems with anyone other than a close associate. Within the household, however, family members maintain close relationships that include many "inside jokes." Scottish humor tends toward the deadpan (said with an expressionless face) and ironic (meaning the opposite of what is expressed).

9 ● LIVING CONDITIONS

Most Scottish houses have a small garden. Many houses are built in rows called terraces. Homes built before World War I (1914–18) were generally made of stone. Single-story stone cottages can still be found in the Highlands as well as in some urban areas. Most newer dwellings are built of brick or concrete blocks. Slate roofs are

© Corel Corporation

Pitlochry, Scotland, the home of the Highland Games.

common, and many houses are covered by a painted coating of cement. Over half of all Scots live in "council houses," low-cost housing built by local authorities. These are generally high-rise apartment complexes.

10 ● FAMILY LIFE

Women have worked as laborers in the textile, jute, and fish processing industries since as far back as the nineteenth century. This work has given them both economic independence and more authority within the family. Women are increasingly entering the professions. There are nearly as many women as men in attendance at Scotland's colleges and universities. Traditionally male

skilled trades such as steelmaking and mining still do not hire female employees.

Scots are legally allowed to marry by the age of sixteen. Many marry as teenagers, although marrying in the early twenties is most common. The divorce rate in Scotland, which has risen in recent years, is still low when compared with the American divorce rate.

11 ● CLOTHING

People throughout the world generally picture the Scots in their famous traditional costume, the kilt. However, this skirtlike garment is generally worn only for ceremonial and formal occasions. Otherwise, most

Scots wear standard Western-style clothing. Because of the cold, damp climate, Scottish clothing is usually made of heavy fabrics such as wool, including the native tweed. Each of Scotland's clans has its own tartan (or plaid), developed over the centuries. There are over 300 designs in all. Women's ceremonial costumes include tartan skirts and white blouses worn under snug, black, vestlike bodices.

12 ● FOOD

The Scottish national dish is *haggis.* This is a sausage-like food made from chopped organ meat of a sheep or calf mixed with oatmeal and spices. It is traditionally boiled in the casing of a sheep's stomach, although today a plastic bag is often used. Scottish dietary staples include oats and potatoes (tatties). The main meal of the day is tea, served at dinnertime. However, in rural areas, the midday meal is still the main one. Typical Scottish desserts include oatcakes, shortbread, a rich fruitcake called "Dundee cake," and a New Year's specialty called "black bun."

13 ● EDUCATION

The Scots are a well-educated people. Universal education has existed in their country for centuries. Scots read more newspapers than any other European people. About 95 percent of adult Scots are literate (able to read and write). The educational system in Scotland is operated separately from that in England. After seven years of primary school, Scottish children attend secondary school for six years. After that, students can attend one of Scotland's eight universities, or go on to vocational school. Great value is placed on higher education.

14 ● CULTURAL HERITAGE

The Scots have a particularly distinguished tradition in the realm of literature, especially poetry and novels. Scotland's most famous poet, Robert Burns, lived and wrote in the late eighteenth century. Lord Byron (1788–1824), another Scottish poet, was born and educated in Aberdeen. Other famous writers include Sir Walter Scott (1771–1832) and Robert Louis Stevenson (1850–94), both writers of adventure novels. Arthur Conan Doyle (1859–1930), another Scot, created the famous fictional detective Sherlock Holmes. Doyle's countryman J. M. Barrie (1860–1937) wrote the famous play *Peter Pan,* which has delighted audiences throughout the twentieth century.

15 ● EMPLOYMENT

An estimated 60 percent of Scotland's labor force is employed in service industries. Manufacturing employs 25 percent, and agriculture, forestry, and fishing each employ about 2 percent. Most manufacturing is concentrated in the Central Lowlands. Important industries include textiles, chemicals, steel, electronics, whiskey, and petroleum products. Scotland has a unique agricultural tradition, primarily in the Highlands, called *crofting.* Farmers live on crofts, a term that refers both to their land and their family home. They raise grains or vegetables on their own land, and raise animals communally on a larger grazing area. Today, crofting provides supplemental income but is rarely a primary source of income or food.

16 ● SPORTS

The Scottish national sport is soccer (called "football"). It is associated with fierce rivalries between Catholic and Protestant teams that sometimes erupt in violence. The nation's second-most-popular sport is golf, which Scotland claims to have invented. Present-day Scotland boasts over 400 golf courses. Rugby, similar to American football, is the country's third-favorite sport. Other popular sports include tennis, lawn bowling, skiing, and curling.

17 ● RECREATION

Many Scots relax after work by watching the BBC (Great Britain's government-owned television broadcasting service). Others visit local bars called "pubs" (short for "public houses"), where they eat, drink, and socialize with friends. Popular outdoor recreation includes fishing, hunting, hiking, and mountain climbing. Scottish teenagers share many interests with teenagers in other Western countries. These include popular music, clothes, and dating (according to local customs). The influence of U.S. television shows and movies is narrowing the gap between Scottish teenagers and their American peers.

18 ● CRAFTS AND HOBBIES

Scottish crafts such as pottery, hand-knitting, jewelry-making, and weaving are widely practiced. Harris tweed, a densely woven wool fabric, originated on the Isle of Harris in the Outer Hebrides and is still made there.

Scotland has two main folk-song traditions: bardic compositions and work songs. Traditionally, each clan had a bard (a sort of poet/composer). The bard sang the praises of the clan and preserved its musical traditions. Bards commonly memorized as many as 350 different stories and poems. The tradition of Gaelic work songs developed as rhythmic accompaniment to such tasks as milking, harvesting, spinning, and weaving. The most famous feature of Scotland's traditional music is its national instrument, the bagpipe. It is played at weddings and other celebrations, in military marching bands, and as a hobby.

19 ● SOCIAL PROBLEMS

Scotland has a high rate of alcoholism, particularly on the islands of Lewis and Harris in the Outer Hebrides. Scots also have the United Kingdom's highest rate of hospitalization for depression. Another problem is Scotland's dwindling population as people emigrate to England and other countries in search of better jobs. Scottish government and industry are working to create new industries to provide jobs and hopefully stem the tide of emigration.

20 ● BIBLIOGRAPHY

Meek, James. *The Land and People of Scotland.* New York: Lippincott, 1990.

Moss, Joyce, and George Wilson. *Peoples of the World: Western Europeans.* Gale Research, 1993.

Scotland in Pictures. Minneapolis, Minn.: Lerner Publications Co., 1991.

WEBSITES

British Council. [Online] Available http://www.britcoun.org/usa/, 1998.

British Information Service. United Kingdom. [Online] Available http://www.britain-info.org, 1998.

British Tourist Authority. [Online] Available http://www.visitbritain.com, 1998.

Welsh

PRONUNCIATION: WEHLSH
LOCATION: United Kingdom (Wales)
POPULATION: 2.8 million
LANGUAGE: English; Welsh
RELIGION: Methodism; Anglicanism;
Presbyterianism; Roman Catholicism; small
numbers of Jews, Muslims, Hindus, and Sikhs

1 ● INTRODUCTION

Wales is one of the four countries of the United Kingdom. (The others are England, Scotland, and Northern Ireland.) The Welsh people are Celtic (central and western European) in origin and have their own language and cultural heritage. The southern part of Wales was colonized by Normans during the eleventh century AD. The last independent principality—Gwynedd, made up of most of North and Central Wales—was conquered by Edward I of England in 1284. Edward's oldest son was given the title Prince of Wales. That title has been held by the oldest son of England's reigning monarch ever since. Wales was officially joined with England in 1707 by the Act of Union, which established the United Kingdom.

South Wales became heavily industrialized in the eighteenth and nineteenth centuries with the development of coal and iron mining. In the twentieth century, much of the Welsh population has emigrated to England and other countries in search of better job opportunities. In recent decades there has been a renewal of Welsh nationalism (patriotism). Political and cultural groups have worked to strengthen a unique Welsh identity separate from a British identity.

2 ● LOCATION

Wales occupies the western part of the island of Great Britain. It is slightly smaller in size than the state of Massachusetts. It has such beautiful farmland, mountains, valleys, and rivers that one-fifth of the country is designated as national parkland. The country's vegetation is mostly grasslands and forests. The rugged Cambrian mountains dominate the northern two-thirds of the country. The central and southern parts of the country are made up of plateaus and valleys. Roughly 80 percent of the Welsh population live in cities. The most populous area is the south, an industrial region containing the cities of Swansea, Cardiff, and Newport.

3 ● LANGUAGE

Both English and Welsh are the official languages of Wales. The use of Welsh has declined gradually since the late eighteenth century. Almost all Welsh people speak English. Welsh is a Celtic language, closest to the Breton language spoken in a part of France. Welsh was recognized as an official language in 1966. Since the 1960s there has been a movement to increase the use and recognition of Welsh. It is now taught in schools, and there are Welsh radio and television broadcasting facilities.

Welsh is known for its long words, double consonants, and scarce vowels. English-speakers find the language quite difficult to pronounce. The Welsh language contains what is probably the longest place name in the world: Llanfairpwllgwyngyllgogerychwyrndrobwllllantysiliogogogoch, a town name that means "Church of St. Mary in the

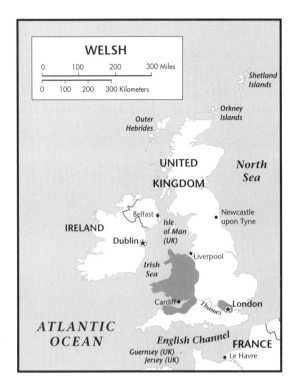

mountain, river, and lake, as well as many farms and villages, are associated with some legend of *tylwyth teg* (fairies), magical properties, or fearful beasts. The Welsh claim that the legendary British hero King Arthur, as well as his magician-counselor Merlin, were from Wales. Another popular subject of Welsh legend is the prince Madog ab Owain. He is said to have discovered America in the twelfth century AD.

5 ● RELIGION

Most of the Christian population of Wales is Methodist (also called Nonconformist). Wales also has an Anglican Church, a Presbyterian Church, and one Catholic province. The Welsh are generally quite strict about religious observance. Wales also has small numbers of Jews, Muslims (followers of Islam), Hindus, Sikhs (followers of a Hindu-Islam religion), and other religious minorities. These are concentrated mainly in the large cities of South Wales.

6 ● MAJOR HOLIDAYS

Legal holidays in Wales include New Year's Day (January 1), St. David's Day (March 1), Good Friday (March or April), Easter Monday (March or April), spring and summer bank holidays, Christmas (December 25), and Boxing Day (December 26). St. David's Day commemorates Wales' patron saint. On this day, daffodils are sold everywhere and are either worn on lapels or taken home to adorn houses. Every January, the Festival of St. Dwyhwon, the Welsh patron saint of lovers, takes place. However, it is gradually being replaced by St. Valentine's Day (February).

Hollow by the White Aspen near the Rapid Whirlpool and Church of St. Tysilio by the Red Cave." (It is usually referred to as Llanfair.)

EXAMPLES OF WELSH WORDS

English	Welsh
church	llan
small	fach
big	fawr
head	blaen
rock	craig
valley	cwm
lake	llyn
mountain	mynydd
little (one)	bach

4 ● FOLKLORE

Welsh culture is full of myths and legends. Even the country's national symbol—the dragon—is a mythical beast. Almost every

© Corel Corporation

A harbor on the Welsh coast.

7 ● RITES OF PASSAGE

The Welsh live in a modern, industrialized, Christian country. Many of the rites of passage that young people undergo are religious rituals. These include baptism, first communion, confirmation, and marriage. In addition, a student's progress through the educational system is often marked with graduation parties.

8 ● RELATIONSHIPS

The Welsh are known for their warmth and hospitality. People are friendly with their neighbors. Acquaintances always stop to chat when they encounter each other. Invitations to tea are readily offered and accepted.

9 ● LIVING CONDITIONS

Rural dwellers have traditionally lived in whitewashed stone cottages and farmhouses. In the past, many cottages consisted of only one or two rooms, plus a sleeping loft. Another type of traditional dwelling was the long-house, a single-story structure that housed the family at one end and livestock at the other. Housing in the coal-mining areas generally consists of row houses built in the nineteenth century. They have slate roofs, stone walls, and outside bathrooms. Much of the older housing lacks the modern amenities (such as central heating) that people in the United States take for granted. As recently as the 1970s, it was common for people living in older housing to use coal-fired stoves for heat. Fireplaces or electric heaters were used to heat rooms other than the kitchen.

10 ● FAMILY LIFE

Family and kinship are extremely important in Wales. The Welsh dote on their children. Special occasions are spent with members of one's extended family. When Welsh people first meet, they often ask each other questions to find out if they have relatives in common. The Welsh traditionally married late and had lengthy courtships. In farming communities, adult sons generally remain at home working on their parents' farms until they marry, and a younger son usually inherits the farm.

Most families today have between one and three children. Welsh families spend a lot of time at home. Life in rural areas tends to be very secluded, and a 20-mile (32-kilometer) trip to a neighboring village is considered a major undertaking. On Sunday, many attend church, which is followed by Sunday dinner, the most important meal of the week. After dinner, men often meet their friends at a pub (bar). In traditional working-class families, few women have traditionally been employed outside the home.

11 ● CLOTHING

The Welsh wear typical Western-style clothing for ordinary casual and formal occasions. However, at festivals one can still see women wearing their traditional national costumes. These consist of long dresses, checkered aprons, white collars, and tall black hats (something like a witch's hat but less pointy and with a wider brim) worn over white kerchiefs. On such occasions, men may wear striped vests over white shirts and knee-length breeches with high white socks.

12 ● FOOD

Traditional Welsh cuisine is simple, down-to-earth farmhouse cooking. Soups and stews are popular dishes, and the Welsh are known for the excellent quality of their lamb, fish, and seafood. The well-known Welsh Rarebit is a genuine Welsh dish. It consists of toast coated with a mixture of milk, eggs, cheese, and Worcestershire sauce—the original toasted cheese sandwich. One dish that some visitors prefer to avoid is *laverbread,* a type of seaweed traditionally prepared with oatmeal and bacon. The Welsh bake a variety of hearty desserts including *bara brith,* a popular bread made with raisins and currants that have been soaked in tea overnight, and Welsh gingerbread—made without ginger!

13 ● EDUCATION

Welsh education follows the same pattern as that in England, with schooling required between the ages of five and sixteen. Students take an exam at age eleven. After that, they attend either middle schools that prepare them for college, comprehensive schools that provide a general education, or technical schools for vocational training.

14 ● CULTURAL HERITAGE

Welsh-language literature is among the oldest continuous literary traditions in Europe, with some of its earliest masterpieces dating

Rugby is the most popular Welsh sport.

from the sixth century AD. Welsh poets have gained recognition in the English-speaking world since the seventeenth century. Wales' most illustrious modern poet was Dylan Thomas (1914–53), author of the beloved *A Child's Christmas in Wales,* the radio play *Under Milk Wood,* and many well-known poems.

The Welsh are a very musical people. Their choral tradition includes celebrated male choirs, a variety of soloists, and pop singers including Tom Jones. Rock bands like the Alarm and the Manic Street Preachers also come from Wales. Several famous actors are Welsh, the best-known being

Anthony Hopkins and the late Richard Burton.

15 ● EMPLOYMENT

Between the mid-1800s and the mid-1900s, coal mining and iron and steel production flourished in Wales. However, workers suffered deprivation and harsh working conditions, as much of the wealth went to industrialists based outside the country. Other major Welsh industries included textiles and slate quarrying. Many Welsh emigrated to England in the early 1930s due to mass unemployment as a result of the Great Depression. Since World War II (1939–45), traditional Welsh industries have been replaced by light industry, plastics, chemicals, and electronics. Many people are employed in service industries including construction and power production. Dairy, cattle, and sheep farming still thrive, and the Welsh still fish in their traditional boats—called *coracles*—constructed from willow and hazel branches covered with hide. Workers in Wales' industries have a high level of unionization. Wales has recently experienced a significant increase in foreign investment. However, it remains economically behind the more prosperous regions of England.

16 ● SPORTS

Rugby is the most popular Welsh sport. It was introduced to Wales about a century ago from England, where it originated. International matches, especially those against England, generate great national spirit. They are accorded the same status as are the World Series or the Super Bowl in the United States. Soccer (called "football") and cricket are also widely played, and dog racing and pony racing are popular as well.

17 ● RECREATION

In their spare time, Welsh people enjoy movies and television. Many people participate in some type of music-making. Choral singing is especially popular. Men commonly spend many of their leisure hours socializing in neighborhood pubs (bars). Women's circles with weekly meetings are widespread in rural Wales, as are young farmers' clubs. In Welsh-speaking areas, the youth organization *Urdd gobaith Cymru* (The Order of Hope of Wales) organizes summer camps, recreational outings, and musical and dramatic productions, and car-

ries a message of peace to world youth. Popular outdoor activities include hunting, fishing, mountain climbing, pony trekking, (horseback riding) golf, swimming, rock climbing, and hang-gliding.

18 ● CRAFTS AND HOBBIES

Such traditional crafts as blacksmithing, tanning, clog-making, and copperworking had virtually disappeared by the 1950s. Woodwork, metalwork and pottery remain strong, however. The use of ancient Celtic designs is popular with many artisans.

The Welsh have a great tradition of choral singing. Their musical and poetic traditions are preserved through a series of competitive folk festivals throughout the nation. The culmination is the Royal National Eisteddfod, an annual contest for poets and musicians attended by tens of thousands of people every August. The festival includes folk dancing and all types of music, from brass bands to Welsh rock groups. Competitions also take place in the fields of poetry, literature, drama, theater, and the visual arts. Events are conducted in Welsh with instantaneous English translation. The festival functions as a major force for the preservation of Welsh cultural identity. The International Eisteddfod at Llangollen, held every July, invites competitors from all over the world to compete for prizes in traditional singing and dancing. The event attracts a wide variety of participants. Another competition is the Cardiff Singer of the Year, which attracts some of the brightest young talent in the opera world. Its prestige has launched a number of highly successful careers.

19 ● SOCIAL PROBLEMS

Unemployment, especially in rural areas, is a serious problem in Wales. Like Scotland, Wales has had a high level of emigration by people seeking better employment opportunities abroad. Concern exists on many fronts about the preservation of Welsh culture. Many are worried that English values and culture will increasingly dominate, and that indigenous values and traditions will be lost. Even with the success of the movement to promote the use of the Welsh language, there is still concern about the survival of rural communities in which the language thrives. Conflicts of interest between monolingual English-speakers and bilingual Welsh-speakers are becoming important issues in many areas.

20 ● BIBLIOGRAPHY

Fuller, Barbara. *Britain. Cultures of the World.* London, England: Marshall Cavendish, 1994.

Illustrated Encyclopedia of Mankind. London: Marshall Cavendish, 1978.

Moss, Joyce, and George Wilson. *Peoples of the World: Western Europeans.* Gale Research, 1993.

Sutherland, Dorothy. *Wales. Enchantment of the World Series.* Chicago: Children's Press, 1994.

Theodoratus, Robert B. "Welsh." *Encyclopedia of World Cultures (Europe).* Boston: G. K. Hall, 1992.

Thomas, Ruth. *South Wales.* New York: Arco Publishing, 1977.

WEBSITES
British Council. [Online] Available http://www.britcoun.org/usa/, 1998.

British Information Service. United Kingdom. [Online] Available http://www.britain-info.org, 1998.

British Tourist Authority. [Online] Available http://www.visitbritain.com, 1998.

Uruguay

The inhabitants of Uruguay are primarily (about 88 percent) white and of European origin, mostly Spanish and Italian; a small percentage is descended from Portuguese, English, and other Europeans. Mestizos (mixed white and Amerindian lineage) represent 8 percent of the population, and blacks and mulattoes (mixed black and white) about 4 percent.

Uruguayans

PRONUNCIATION: yoor-uh-GWAY-ens
LOCATION: Uruguay
POPULATION: Over 3 million
LANGUAGE: Spanish; Portuñol dialect
RELIGION: Roman Catholicism; some Judaism; Afro-Brazilian churches; evangelical Protestantism

1 ● INTRODUCTION

The Portuguese, based in Brazil, migrated south into Uruguay in 1680 where they founded a colony called Colonial de Sacramento. In 1726, Spain established a fort in nearby Montevideo (mohn-teh-vih-DAY-oh), the present-day capital of Uruguay. After a struggle between the two colonial powers, Uruguay fell under Portuguese control. It later became a province of Brazil. Uruguay was granted full independence in 1828, through an agreement between Argentina and Brazil. After independence, power alternated between two major political parties. They were called the *Colorados* (Reds) and the *Blancos* (Whites). A violent civil war lasted from the mid-1830s to 1851.

In the late 1960s, economic difficulties and the activities of a terrorist group known as the *Tupamaros* led to political instability. In 1973, a military dictatorship assumed control of the government. Democracy was restored in 1985.

2 ● LOCATION

Uruguay is located between Brazil and Argentina on the Atlantic coast of South America. Its terrain is characterized by gently rolling hills and natural grasslands. A high proportion of Uruguay's territory is suitable for agriculture. Most of Uruguay's grasslands are currently used for grazing.

The total population of Uruguay is over 3 million people. Uruguay does not have a native population. Since 1830 the Uruguayans have been ethnically European, descended mainly from Italians or Spaniards.

3 ● LANGUAGE

The official language of Uruguay is Spanish. In regions close to the Brazilian border, a Spanish-Portuguese dialect called Portuñol (or Portuniol) is spoken.

4 ● FOLKLORE

There are conflicting legends explaining the name given to Uruguay's capital, Montevideo. Both originate in Ferdinand Magellan's visit to the region in 1520. According to one legend, a sailor on Magellan's ship saw land and shouted, *"Monte vide eu"*—"I see a hill." The other version is based on a Spanish phrase found on early maps: *"Monte VI de E.O.,"* or "The sixth hill from east to west."

5 ● RELIGION

Most Uruguayans are Roman Catholic. There is a sharp separation between church and state. Many religious holidays have even been given secular names. Christmas, for instance, is widely referred to as Family Day. Similarly, Easter Week is known as Criollo Week.

6 ● MAJOR HOLIDAYS

Perhaps the most celebrated holiday in Uruguay is Carnival. This is a week-long celebration that marks the beginning of Lent (in February). There is a series of street parades, as well as drinking, feasting, and dancing.

Many of Uruguay's festivals celebrate its cattle-raising heritage. During Easter Week (in March or April), a Cowboy Festival *(Fiesta Gaucha)* is held in Montevideo. Rodeo competitions are the main event.

7 ● RITES OF PASSAGE

Major life transitions, such as birth, puberty, and death, are marked by rituals appropriate to each Uruguayan's religion.

8 ● RELATIONSHIPS

To say goodbye, most Uruguayans have adopted the Italian *ciao* or *addio* in place of the Spanish *adios*. It is proper to kiss someone both when saying hello and upon departing.

When invited to an Uruguayan home, one may be offered *mate,* an herbal tea. Traditionally, *mate* is drunk through a silver straw, called a *bombilla,* from a carved gourd (hollow fruit).

9 ● LIVING CONDITIONS

Montevideo is a modern city, with high-rise apartments and office buildings. Many of the poorer residents, however, live in small homes or shacks on the outskirts of the city. In rural areas, Uruguayan cowboys, called *gauchos,* live in simple communal housing on farms where they work. Other rural dwellers live in adobe homes.

10 ● FAMILY LIFE

Marriage in Uruguay can be formalized through a civil ceremony. Families in Uruguay are relatively small compared with other countries in the region. Most urban families choose to limit the size of their families. In rural areas, however, there is less access to birth control, and women typically have more children.

11 ● CLOTHING

Urban Uruguayans wear modern Western dress. Today's youths favor jeans and T-shirts. Suits and ties are appropriate attire for businessmen. Uruguay's *gauchos* (cowboys) proudly wear the distinctive clothing of their ancestors. They sport baggy pants called *bombachas.* Wide-brimmed black hats offer protection from the midday sun. Woolen ponchos are used for warmth in the evenings.

12 ● FOOD

Not surprisingly for a cattle-ranching country, beef figures prominently in Uruguayan cuisine. *Churrasco,* or grilled steak, can be said to be the national dish. Also very popular are *chivitos:* hot steak sandwiches, topped with bacon, eggs, cheese, lettuce, and tomatoes.

Recipe

Puchero
(Uruguayan meat stew)

Ingredients

water
4 pounds osso buco (veal shanks), cut into six pieces
6 carrots, peeled
1 onion
1 pound green beans
6 ears of sweet corn, husked
1 squash (medium size), cut into 6 pieces, unpeeled
1 cup chopped celery
6 white potatoes, peeled
6 zucchini
1 bunch parsley
4 teaspoons salt

Directions

1. Fill a large saucepan with water and bring it to a boil.
2. Add all ingredients to boiling water in the following order: the meat, then carrots, onion, green beans, corn, squash, and celery. Then add potatoes, zucchini, and corn. Add parsley and salt to season the stew.
3. Cover and simmer for 30 minutes, or until potatoes are tender.
4. Drain off most of the liquid.

Serve the meat and vegetable in bowls with a little of the broth. Mustard, mayonnaise, tomato, onion, or pepper sauce may be served as accompaniments.

Recipe courtesy of the Embassy of Uruguay.

The Uruguayans have also adapted traditional Spanish dishes. A Uruguayan version of *puchero,* Spanish meat stew, is sometimes cooked with blood sausage.

13 ● EDUCATION

Uruguayans have a literacy rate (percentage of the population who can read and write) of over 97 percent. Children receive six required years of elementary education. These are followed by six years of secondary schooling, divided into two three-year stages.

14 ● CULTURAL HERITAGE

Perhaps the most celebrated Uruguayan poet was Juan Zorrilla de San Martín (1855–1931). A more recent writer of international acclaim is Juan Carlos Onetti, a contemporary novelist. Uruguay's musical tradition reflects a historical Spanish influence. As in Argentina, the tango is a popular dance form. *Candombe,* an Afro-Brazilian music and dance form, is also popular.

15 ● EMPLOYMENT

Agriculture is the driving force behind the Uruguayan economy. Sheep and cattle ranching are the most important agricultural activities. Many urban dwellers find work in industries related to the processing of agricultural products. These including canning, brewing, and the leather industry. Montevideo businesses offer jobs as waiters, taxi drivers, and shopkeepers. Unemployment, however, is a major problem. Many Uruguayans resort to such jobs as street vending and tailoring.

16 ● SPORTS

Uruguayans love soccer *(futbol),* both as spectators and participants. They are equally passionate about horses. Rodeos are always well attended. Horse racing is also very popular. Like Argentina, Uruguay also has a passion for polo.

17 ● RECREATION

Many Uruguayan families flock to the beaches on weekends for rest and recreation. The coastal forests provide numerous sites for camping and fishing. Montevideo has a varied night life. Restaurants, cinemas, and musical shows are widely attended on weekends.

18 ● CRAFTS AND HOBBIES

Uruguayans excel in producing handcrafted leather goods auch as belts, hats, boots, and purses. Montevideo has a well-known handicraft cooperative called *Manos de Uruguay* (Hands of Uruguay). Members of the cooperative spin and dye wool, knit sweaters, and also make ceramic crafts.

19 ● SOCIAL PROBLEMS

Unemployment is high, typically ranging from 10 to 15 percent. There is also a serious lack of housing.

20 ● BIBLIOGRAPHY

Finch, Martin. *Uruguay.* Santa Barbara, Calif.: Clio, 1989.

Haverstock, Nathan A. *Uruguay in Pictures.* Minneapolis, Minn.: Lerner Publications Co., 1987.

Morrison, Marion. *Uruguay.* Enchantment of the World Series. Chicago: Children's Press, 1992.

WEBSITES

Embassy of Uruguay, Washington, D.C. [Online] Available http://www.embassy.org/uruguay/, 1998.

World Travel Guide. Uruguay. [Online] Available http://www.wtgonline.com/country/uy/gen.html, 1998.

Uzbekistan

It is estimated that about 70 percent of the population is Uzbek. Russians constitute 8 percent; Tajiks, 5 percent; Kazaks, 4 percent; Tatars, 3 percent; and Karakalpaks, 2 percent. To learn more about the Russians and the Tatars see the chapter on the Russia in Volume 7; for the Tajiks see Tajikistan in this volume; and for the Kazaks see Kazakstan in Volume 5.

Uzbeks

PRONUNCIATION: OOZ-beks
LOCATION: Uzbekistan; Afghanistan; China
POPULATION: Over 16.7 million
LANGUAGE: Uzbek
RELIGION: Islam (Sunni Muslim)

1 ● INTRODUCTION

The Uzbeks were the third largest ethnic group of the former Soviet Union when it collapsed in 1991. Although they were originally nomads, most Uzbeks have been settled for more than three hundred years.

The Uzbek homeland is situated on the site of the ancient Bactrian and Sogdian civilizations. Ancient invaders who laid claim to the territory included the Persian Empire of Darius the Great and the Greek Empire of Alexander the Great. The region was invaded by Arabs in the eighth century AD and Islam was introduced. In the thirteenth century, the Mongol Empire controlled the area. It was followed, in the fourteenth century, by the empire of the Mongol chieftain Tamerlane (Timur).

Around the fifteenth century, the Uzbeks began to emerge as an organized group of tribes. Their region was eventually divided into three separate *khanates* (territories ruled by a khan, or chieftain). Uzbeks made up more than 50 percent of the people of the Khiva khanate and almost 35 percent of the Bukhara khanate.

All three khanates fell to the Russians between 1865 and 1873. The Imperial Russian government renamed the annexed area Russian Turkistan. Uzbekistan was formed as a separate Soviet Socialist Republic in 1925. The Soviet era brought tremendous cultural changes to Uzbek society. Informal herding and subsistence (basic-level) agriculture gave way to enormous state-operated farms.

UZBEK

0   500   1000 Miles

0   500   1000 Kilometers

Since it gained independence in 1991, the government of Uzbekistan has been slow to make democratic or free-market (economic) reforms. However, business development has grown since the mid-1990s.

2 ● LOCATION

Much of Uzbekistan's landscape consists of deserts, dry steppes (plains), and fertile oases near rivers. The Aral Sea, which once was larger than Lake Michigan, used to be an important water resource. In the last thirty to forty years, however, the sea has lost about 60 percent of its water due to irrigation methods.

The Uzbeks are the world's second-largest group of Turkic people (after the Turks of Turkey). They number almost 17 million. Eight-five percent (or 14.5 million) live in what is now Uzbekistan.

The capital of Uzbekistan is Tashkent.

3 ● LANGUAGE

The Uzbek language belongs to the Turkic family of languages. It is related to Kazakh and Karakalpak. The Uzbek language borrowed many words of Russian or European origin during the early Soviet years. However, it has borrowed more heavily from Turkic and Arabic since the 1960s.

Everyday terms in the Uzbek language include *salaam aleikhem* (hello), *shundei* (yes), *yok* (no), *markhamat* (please), and *rakhmat* (thank you). Examples of Uzbek sayings include *Äytkän gäp atqan oq* (A word said is a shot fired); *Kob oylä, az soylä* (Think much, say little); and *Yamandän yäkhshilik kutmä* (Don't expect good from evil).

4 ● FOLKLORE

Two ancient heroes play an important role in Uzbek folklore. One is Tamerlane (1336–1405), a Mongol who conquered parts of present-day India, Syria, and southern Russia. His grandson, Ulughbek (1394–1449), has become another legendary, almost sacred personality. He made great contributions to the sciences, especially astronomy.

5 ● RELIGION

Religion has an important place in traditional Uzbek culture. Most Uzbeks are Sunni Muslims of the Hanafi sect. During the Soviet era (1918–91), the government discouraged religious practices. The Muslim clergy was persecuted. Since the end of Soviet rule, many new mosques have been built. Tashkent is one of central Asia's leading Islamic spiritual centers. Sufism (another branch of Islam) is also practiced by some Uzbeks.

6 ● MAJOR HOLIDAYS

No holiday is enjoyed by Uzbeks more than *Novruz* (the traditional Persian new year). It is rapidly replacing New Year's Eve as the number-one holiday. It coincides with the first day of spring (March 21 or 22). At this time, there are speeches, skits in the schools, and celebrations in the town squares. At home, people prepare *sumalak*, a sweet pudding. People cook young wheat plants in huge cauldrons overnight to prepare the dish. The Islamic month of fasting (Ramadan) and various forms of *Haiit* (days to remember relatives who have died) are now officially recognized.

Uzbekistani Independence Day is September 1. On Victory Day (May 9), Uzbekistani citizens mark the Soviet defeat of Nazi Germany in 1945. This holiday has both solemn and joyous aspects.

7 ● RITES OF PASSAGE

Birth, male circumcision, a girl's first menstrual period, marriage, and death are the primary events around which Uzbeki rites of passage occur. The *sunnat toi* (circumcision party) and the *kelin toi* (wedding) are events for which people spend the most money and celebrate the most enthusiastically.

8 ● RELATIONSHIPS

Uzbeks practice elaborate greetings. Simply saying, "Hi," or "What's up?" as one passes by is not acceptable. First, Uzbeks approach each other and shake hands. Then they rapidly fire off a number of questions about each other's health, family situation, and work. Uzbeks love to invite strangers into their homes. They will signal a passerby in with gestures indicating the offer of a cup of tea or something to eat.

The Uzbeks have a strong sense of duty to the elderly and to the community. Children are typically taught that it is wrong to openly confront an adult.

9 ● LIVING CONDITIONS

Woven rugs often cover the floors of Uzbek houses. Traditional folk art is a common wall decoration. It often includes subjects from the natural world, such as mountains, deer, or peacocks. Most homes have two or three rooms. Men and women have separate quarters. Outside the home stands a large platform known as the *sura*. It is used for eating and resting. A great deal of time is spent there during hot weather. In most homes, the kitchen is in a separate building.

10 ● FAMILY LIFE

The average Uzbek family has five children. Households may include two, three, or four generations. The *kelin toi*, or wedding, is the most important and joyous celebration in Uzbek social life. A new Uzbek wife usually moves in with her husband's family. She will do most of the housework until she has a few children and the next son is ready to marry. It is customary for the youngest

Charlotte Kahler

Group of citizens in Samarqand, Uzbekistan. Uzbeks maintain a strong sense of duty to the elderly and to the community. Children are typically taught that openly confronting adults is wrong, and that they should be quiet and composed even if they are upset or angry with their elders.

son and his wife to live permanently in his father's home.

The Soviet era (1918–91) introduced women to the work force, but their responsibilities at home never lessened.

11 ● CLOTHING

Traditional national costumes are still often worn by the Uzbeks. Men wear the *doppilar,* a small, square black skullcap. Doppilar are embroidered with elaborate patterns. These indicate the wearer's family ties, place of birth, or other personal information. Many men wear Western-style clothes or outfits that combine Western and traditional Uzbek styles. These are often brightly colored. Some men wear the traditional *chopan*, a long quilted robe originally used by shepherds.

Many women wear Western clothes. However, some still wear traditional tie-dyed brightly-colored dresses. In summer, women wear white head coverings or brightly colored kerchiefs. During winter, they wear large woolen shawls.

12 ● FOOD

Uzbek cuisine makes frequent use of Eastern spices such as cumin, coriander, and dried hot red pepper. The all-time favorite

EPD Photos

The doppilar, *a small, square black skullcap, is a popular hat worn by men.*

Uzbek dish is *plov*. It consists of rice with beef (or mutton or chicken), cottonseed oil or *dumba* (sheep tail fat), vegetables, spices, garlic, and quinces. Other traditional Uzbek dishes include *lagman* (homemade noodles with mutton, garlic, and vegetables), *d'igh-man* (meat with pastry in a rich broth), and *dymlama* (a layered vegetable and beef stew). Breakfast consists of bread, some fruits or nuts, and tea, sometimes with a serving of *qattiq* (yogurt).

13 ● EDUCATION

Education in Uzbekistan is universal (provided for all) and mandatory (required) until the age of sixteen. City schools are often much better than rural ones. Turkish *lycees* (European-style high schools) and *medresses* (Muslim schools) have opened in all the major cities. Almost all Uzbek parents want an advanced education for their children. Many hope their children will be accepted to Tashkent State University or be able to study outside Uzbekistan.

14 ● CULTURAL HERITAGE

Classical Uzbek singing is plaintive (sounding sad) and drawn out—a kind of wailing. The hand-held *doira* is a tambourine-drum with a deep sound. It adds rich beats and rhythms to the songs. Some folksinging is accompanied only by the *doira*. Popular Uzbek music is a mixture of traditional styles with rock and pop.

A famous example of classic Uzbek literature is *Baburname (The Memoirs of Babur)*. It tells the story of the sixteenth-century military leader who founded the Mogul Empire and became its first emperor. There is a puppet theater in Tashkent that was founded in 1939. Puppet shows using glove and hand puppets, shadow puppets, and marionettes are performed there, depicting stories from Uzbek history.

Famous Uzbek plays of the 1960s express protest against Soviet policies. They include Izzat Sultan's *Iman (Faith*, 1960) and Rahmatullah A. Uyghun's *Dostlär (Friends*, 1961).

15 ● EMPLOYMENT

Over 60 percent of the Uzbek population is rural, and most work is agricultural. Uzbeks grow wheat, cotton, and fruits. Many also raise silkworms. Some labor on small household garden plots, raising fruits and vegetables. Spring, summer, and fall are periods of hard work. Winter is a time to rest and relax.

Industrial work ranges from aircraft manufacturing to gold mining and oil drilling. Today, retail business is growing, in the form of an increasing number of privately owned shops.

16 ● SPORTS

Soccer is the number-one team and spectator sport. Table tennis first became popular during the Soviet era (1918–91). Since the mid-1980s, softball has been a popular women's sport. Basketball and volleyball are favorites in the schools.

Kurash is a unique form of wrestling enjoyed by Uzbek men and boys.

The martial arts have become especially popular in recent years. Many children train in local clubs.

Another sport is a form of polo in which hundreds, or even thousands, of horsemen participate. The two huge teams attempt to capture the carcass of a goat or sheep and get it to the opponents' goal.

17 ● RECREATION

An ancient form of entertainment still enjoyed by the Uzbeks is *payr*, an unrehearsed public debate. Two competitors exchange witty comments about each other related to a specific topic chosen ahead of time. The first competitor who fails to respond quickly enough is the loser. The crowd decides the outcome. Sometimes a good payr match will draw thousands of spectators.

Bakka (tightrope walking) draws large crowds during celebrations or parties. It is one of the most popular forms of entertainment.

Children love to play games such as *top tosh* and *askiia*. Top tosh is like jacks, except that Uzbek children play it with rocks or pebbles. Askiia is a riddle game. One player makes up questions about a given thing. The other's answers must show that he or she knows what the object is.

Movies and television are very popular. Favorite programs include martial arts and other action movies, comedies, and films from India, also known as "Bombay cinema."

Gap is a time-honored Uzbek custom that continues today. Men get together with friends and former classmates. They eat, play games of cards or bingo, and discuss social and intellectual issues. They also discuss their personal problems.

18 ● CRAFTS AND HOBBIES

Pottery is the oldest craft practiced among the Uzbeks. Other crafts include silk weaving, quilt making, and *suzama* (embroidery). *Hunarmandlik* (craftsmanship) shines through in Uzbek *naqsh* (wood carving) and mosaic tile work. Intricate carving can be seen on the doors of family homes and on the columns that support buildings. Ceramics include fine porcelain tea sets. Metalworking (especially urns and pitchers) and bootmaking are other traditional crafts.

Stamp collecting and writing to pen pals are favorite hobbies for young people.

19 ● SOCIAL PROBLEMS

The Uzbeks' two greatest problems are a troubled economy and environmental problems. The water needed for irrigation to grow cotton in Uzbekistan diverted most of the water from the two main rivers that feed the Aral Sea. The sea has decreased in area since 1960. Much of the soil around it is now too salty for growing crops. Pesticides, herbicides, and chemical fertilizers have also polluted much of the remaining water supply.

Growing poverty since the late 1980s has contributed to increased alcoholism, drug addiction, and violent crime in present-day Uzbekistan.

20 ● BIBLIOGRAPHY

Allworth, Edward A. *The Modern Uzbeks: From the Fourteenth Century to the Present*. Stanford, Calif.: Hoover Institution Press, 1990.

Critchlow, James. *Nationalism in Uzbekistan: A Soviet Republic's Road to Sovereignty*. Boulder, Colo.: Westview Press, 1991.

Gippenreiter, Vadim Evgenevich. *Fabled Cities of Central Asia: Samarkand, Bukhara, Khiva*. New York: Abbeville Press, 1989.

Nazarov, Bakhtiyar A., and Denis Sinor, eds. *Essays on Uzbek History, Culture, and Language*. Bloomington, Ind.: Indiana University, Research Institute for Inner Asian Studies, 1993.

Uzbekistan. Minneapolis, Minn.: Lerner Publications Co., 1993.

WEBSITES

World Travel Guide, Uzbekistan. [Online] Available http://www.wtgonline.com/country/uz/gen.html, 1998.

Karakalpaks

PRONUNCIATION: kar-uh-kuhl-PAKS
ALTERNATE NAMES: Qoraqolpoqlar
LOCATION: Uzbekistan (territory of Karakalpakistan); Kazakstan; Russia; Turkmenistan
POPULATION: 350,000
LANGUAGES: Karakalpak; Russian
RELIGION: Islam (Sunni Muslim)

1 ● INTRODUCTION

The Karakalpaks (who call themselves *Qoraqolpoqlar*) are a people of Central Asia. They lived within the Uzbek Soviet Socialist Republic of the Soviet Union until it was dissolved in 1991. Today their territory is within independent Uzbekistan.

The Karakalpaks' ancestors originally came from the Irtysh River areas in southern Siberia. They settled in their current homeland in the tenth and eleventh centuries AD. The Qipchoq people they encountered referred to the newcomers as "Karakalpaks" (black hats) supposedly because they wore black wool or felt hats. The Karakalpaks' culture has been influenced by their harsh desert and steppe existence. It has also been affected by invaders such as the Mongols, Timurids, Kalmyks, Khorezmian Uzbeks, and Russians. The Russians colonized the Karakalpaks during the second half of the nineteenth century.

2 ● LOCATION

The Karakalpak homeland, Karakalpakistan *(Qoraqolpoqiston),* lies in the northwestern part of Uzbekistan. It occupies nearly 40 percent of Uzbekistan's total territory. Until recently, the major feature of its landscape was the Aral Sea. Today, however, the sea is drying up at a rapid rate due to irrigation methods.

About 2.3 million people live in the Karakalpakistan region. Of these, approximately 350,000 are Karakalpaks. Other Karakalpak people live in the surrounding countries of Uzbekistan, Kazakstan, Russia, and Turkmenistan.

3 ● LANGUAGE

The Karakalpak language is part of the Turkic language family. It is related to such languages as Turkish, Kazak, Kyrgyz, Turkmen, and Uzbek. There was no written form

KARAKALPAKS

0   250   500   750 Miles

0   250 500 750 1000 Kilometers

RUSSIA

KAZAKSTAN

Zaysan

UZBEKISTAN

Almaty
(Alma-Ata)

TURKMENISTAN   Tashkent

Ashkhabad   Tejen   ☆ KYRGYSTAN

Dushanbe ☆ TAJIKISTAN

IRAN

AFGHANISTAN   CHINA

Kabul ☆

Zaranj

Saindak   Islāmābād

PAKISTAN

Indus

Pasni

New Delhi ☆ NEPAL

Gulf of Oman

BHUTAN

Ganges Kāthmāndu

Arabian
Sea

Lakhpat   INDIA

Surat   BANGLADESH   Dhaka

of the Karakalpak language until the 1920s. Today it is written in a modified Cyrillic alphabet (the alphabet used by Russians, Serbs, and Bulgarians). Newspapers, magazines, and books are printed in the Karakalpak language.

Russian remains an important second language for educated Karakalpaks.

4 ● FOLKLORE

Folklore is divided into lyrical tales and epic poems (*zhyr* and *dostan*). There are tales about boys, such as Tarzshi and Aldarkose, whom everybody tries to outsmart. But the boys always manage to come out on top. There are also tales about animals, such as the cunning fox who can trick just about anyone and anything. Other tales involve wolves, tigers, and, occasionally, even God himself.

The epics are almost always about historical events and heroic figures. Epic heroes often turn out to be women. In *Kyrk Qiz (The Forty Maidens)*, the heroine Gulaim defends her homeland from invading Kalmyks. *Maspatsha* is the story of Aiparshir, a woman of great beauty and tremendous courage.

5 ● RELIGION

The Karakalpaks are Sunni Muslims. In addition, they have long been influenced by Sufism, the mystical sect of Islam. Until the collapse of the Soviet Union in 1991, religious practice and teaching played a minor role in the lives of most Karakalpaks. More recently, however, faith in Soviet communist ideals has given way to faith in the doctrines of the Muslim religion.

Many Karakalpaks have also held onto some religious beliefs that are not formally included in the Muslim religion. These often are about the natural world. They relate to saints or patrons (guardians) who watch out for herds, fishermen, farmers, and so forth. Many people believe that each type of herd or flock has its own patron.

6 ● MAJOR HOLIDAYS

Four major secular (nonreligious) holidays are celebrated by the Karakalpaks, together with their fellow Uzbeks. *Novruz* (New Day) marks the beginning of spring, on March 20 or 21. The holiday is celebrated with festivals, contests, game playing, and especially feasting. Schoolchildren celebrate with their teachers and put on skits. The favorite food for this holiday is *sumalak*, made from young wheat plants. It takes about twenty-four hours to prepare this sweet, tasty pudding. Sumalak parties are always part of the *Novruz* festivities.

Victory Day celebrations, commemorating the end of World War II (1939–45), take place on May 9. There are military parades that include veterans of World War II. Uzbekistan Independence Day, September 1, has been celebrated since 1991. This day is marked by parades, speeches, and festive events throughout Uzbekistan. Constitution Day, December 8, is another new holiday. It marks the creation of the Uzbekistan constitution in 1992. Businesses and other workplaces are closed on that day. Most people simply stay home and relax.

7 ● RITES OF PASSAGE

Parents with a newborn baby visit relatives constantly for the first few months to introduce their infant into the family. Boys undergo circumcision at approximately age five. It is marked by a big celebration known as the *sunnat toi.*

The major rite of passage in adulthood is marriage. The wedding ceremony, called the *kelin toi,* symbolizes the joining of families and the continuation of family lines. The *kelin toi* is marked by feasts, dances, music, and speeches that continue for days. The festivities take place at various locations belonging to both of the families.

Death is marked by ritual outpourings of grief at the home of the person who has died. Mourners come to share their sympathy with the bereaved family. A clergyman (*mullah)* leads a procession of mourners to the cemetery. The closest relatives perform the burial after prayers are said.

8 ● RELATIONSHIPS

When one person approaches another, the one who is approaching offers the first greeting. (This custom is typical of many Central Asian peoples.) Usually, the greeting is *Assalomu alaikum!* ("Peace be with you!" in a dialect of Arabic). The person being greeted responds, *Valaikum assalom!* (And may peace be with you, too!). Then men shake hands. They use either one or two hands, depending on their degree of closeness. Women typically hug one another. A rapid series of questions about one another's health and family usually follows.

Respect for older people is taken very seriously in Central Asia. This is true even between people who differ in age by only a few years. A younger person usually bows slightly. One may also cover the lower part of one's chest with one's right hand as a sign of respect.

When visiting, Karakalpaks always bring presents or food. Neighbors constantly visit with one another to chat and snack.

Dating is rare among the Karakalpaks, except for those living in large cities such as Nukus. Marriages are often arranged.

9 ● LIVING CONDITIONS

Since the breakup of the Soviet Union, economic conditions have deteriorated for most Karakalpaks. Few people are able to buy more than basic necessities.

The traditional Karakalpak dwelling is a dome-shaped tent known as a *yurt.* A yurt has a wooden frame; huge pieces of felt cloth are thrown over the frame and then carefully arranged.

Some European-style furniture is found in Karakalpak homes. However, most people relax and sleep on thick, dense quilts called *kurpas*. Kurpas are often placed on raised platforms that are built into the room. The family sits on these platforms for meals and recreation, such as watching television. Kurpas are easily moved and stored. Large wooden cabinets known as *sandals* are used for storage.

10 ● FAMILY LIFE

Karakalpak families are usually large, with four to ten children. Most women prefer to have four or five. Households of extended families (parents and children plus other relatives) are common. A family of four generations may live in a single home. A group of families descended from a common male ancestor is called a *koshe*. Several koshe make up an *uru*, a kind of clan.

Girls marry early, usually as young as sixteen years of age. Marriages are arranged through consenting sets of parents. A woman is given a dowry (gifts and money for her new married life) by her parents. She is also presented with bride gifts by the groom's parents. The new wife moves in with her husband's family.

Women do most of the cooking, cleaning, and child care. Men are usually responsible for buying groceries, preparing certain feast dishes, and doing home repairs, especially electrical work or carpentry.

Polygyny (marrying more than one woman) is illegal, but some men do it secretly. On the whole, though, it is rare; it is very expensive to have more than one family.

11 ● CLOTHING

Karakalpaks often wear a mix of traditional and Western-style clothing. Women wear the *kiimeshek*, a long capelike dress with a head covering. Older women wear white, and younger women wear red. Tunic-like shirts and baggy trousers are also worn.

A man's typical summer outfit consists of loose trousers and a *koilek*. This is a long, loose white shirt with an open collar and no buttons.

Some type of hat or head covering is almost always worn because of the extreme temperatures and strong sunlight. Men wear silk or cotton embroidered skullcaps (*duppi*). They also wear the thick wool hats (*qoraqolpoq*), from which the Karakalpak got their name. Women wear long cotton or woolen scarves (*rumol*) that cover their heads, ears, backs, and shoulders.

12 ● FOOD

Grain is a staple food of the Karakalpak diet, especially rice, sorghum, barley, and millet. From these grains, tasty breads, noodles, and dumplings are made.

Fruits and vegetables include onions, carrots, plums, pears, grapes, apricots, and all kinds of melons and squashes. Pumpkin is often used in turnovers known as *samsa*. Milk products include yogurt, butter, cream, and cheeses.

Boiled beef, mutton, and smoked horsemeat are among the favorite meats. Beef and mutton are ingredients in *palov*, a Central

Asian favorite. *Palov* recipes use rice, meat, carrots, garlic, steamed quinces (a kind of fruit), and mutton tail fat (*dumba*).

As Muslims, Karakalpaks do not drink alcohol or eat certain foods, especially pork.

13 ● EDUCATION

The Soviet educational system is still in place. Almost all children receive a high-school education. Some then go on to technical and university training. Karakalpakistan has only one university, located in Nukus. Recently, *medresses,* schools for higher religious education, have opened in the region.

14 ● CULTURAL HERITAGE

In the past, Karakalpak bards (performing poets) roamed from village to village, reciting stories and verses. They were accompanied on instruments such as the two-stringed *dutar,* and the *qobyz* and *ghypzhek*, which were played with bows.

Two Karakalpak poets of the nineteenth century—Azhiniaz Kosybai uly and Berdakh Kargabai uly—are among Central Asia's greatest writers. Modern Karakalpak writers have adopted Western literary forms such as novels, short stories, and plays.

15 ● EMPLOYMENT

Most of the work in Karakalpakistan is agricultural. Almost 70 percent of the population is rural. The only real manufacturing jobs are centered around the cotton industry. These jobs include ginning and baling cotton, and pressing cotton seeds for their oil.

Silk manufacture is also a significant part of the agricultural economy. Farmers feed silkworms mulberry leaves from nearby trees. The worms produce cocoons, which people bring to regional collection centers. Profits depend on the quality of the cocoons.

Farm workers work twelve to fifteen hours a day at harvest time.

16 ● SPORTS

Volleyball and soccer are popular at school. Boys also engage in a type of wrestling known as *Qurash*. It involves grabbing one another on the back of the neck and the thigh. The object is to force the opponent to lose his grip, and thus lose his balance.

Women and girls are rarely, if ever, encouraged to participate in sports.

17 ● RECREATION

Movies and television programs are imported from the West, especially action movies and Latin American soap operas. Plays in the theaters, on humorous or historical themes, are popular.

Pop music is important to Karakalpak young people. Iulduz Usmanova is one of the most popular young singers.

Adults entertain themselves by getting together with friends at conversation sessions known as *gap,* which means "talk." Men and women meet in separate groups, perhaps twice a month. They eat, play games, sing songs, catch up on news, and offer each other advice.

Children enjoy an elaborate game of riddles called *askiia*. Two children try to outsmart one another with a series of questions about a particular thing. One child starts with a description. The other must ask questions about what is being described.

18 ● CRAFTS AND HOBBIES

Karakalpak rugs are narrow and not usually used as floor coverings. They are hung as doorway coverings at the entrance to a *yurt* (tent). They are also used as wall coverings or saddlebags. Bright blues, yellows, and greens are the main colors.

Jewelry is mostly silver. Blue stones, such as lapis lazuli, and red stones are often added. Necklaces, earrings, and bracelets are the most common kinds of jewelry.

Men specialize as woodworkers (especially carvers) and shoemakers. Some of the most skilled craftsmanship goes into carving house doors and support beams for buildings. Central Asian woodcarving has unique floral (flower) and geometric patterns.

Hobbies among Karakalpak young people include collecting stamps, coins, photos of pop-music stars, records, and tapes. Some young people have pen pals.

19 ● SOCIAL PROBLEMS

The rapid development of agriculture and fisheries in Karakalpakistan during the Soviet period harmed the environment. The water needed for irrigation to grow cotton in Uzbekistan diverted most of the water from the two main rivers that feed the Aral Sea. The sea has decreased in area since 1960. Much of the soil around it is now too salty for growing any crops. In addition, agricultural chemicals have washed into irrigation canals and have been deposited in the sea. Now the region suffers from health problems and economic decline. Statistics show that more than 70 percent of Karakalpaks are in poor health.

Few people have safe drinking water, and not enough food is being produced. Loss of the fisheries industry has led to rising unemployment. Alcoholism and drug addiction (mainly to heroin) are growing problems for the young and middle-aged. Crime has greatly increased since the breakup of the Soviet Union. It ranges from petty theft to organized drug smuggling and Mafia-style murders.

20 ● BIBLIOGRAPHY

Akiner, Shirin. *Islamic Peoples of the Soviet Union*. London, England: Kegan Paul International, 1983.

Critchlow, James. *Nationalism in Uzbekistan: A Soviet Republic's Road to Sovereignty*. Boulder, Colo.: Westview Press, 1991.

Thomas, Paul. *The Central Asian States: Tajikstan, Uzbekistan, Kyrgyzstan, Turkmenistan*. Brookfield, Conn.: Millbrook Press, 1992.

WEBSITES

World Travel Guide. Uzbekistan. [Online] Available http://www.wtgonline.com/country/uz/gen.html, 1998.

Vanuatu

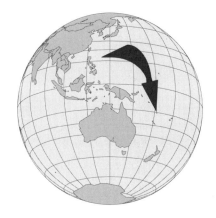

Nearly 95 percent of the total population of Vanuatu is of Melanesian origin. Minority groups include Europeans (mostly French) and other Pacific Islanders.

Ni-Vanuatu

PRONUNCIATION: nee-vahn-uh-WAH-too

LOCATION: Vanuatu

POPULATION: 170,000

LANGUAGE: English; French; Bislama

RELIGION: Christianity; traditional native religions

1 ● INTRODUCTION

The Ni-Vanuatu are the Melanesian people that make up the population of the Republic of Vanuatu. This Y-shaped chain of islands in the Pacific Ocean was previously called the New Hebrides. It gained independence from Britain and France in 1980. Vanuatu is probably best known to Americans as the setting for James Michener's novel *Tales of the South Pacific*. The book was made into a popular musical movie, *South Pacific*.

2 ● LOCATION

A total of eighty-three islands in the southwest Pacific Ocean make up the Republic of Vanuatu. Twelve of the islands are considered the main islands of the group. Some of the islands were formed by volcanoes, and others by the buildup of coral. Thus there is a wide range of landscape features within the country.

The capital city of Vanuatu is Port Vila, located on Efate. The total population of Vanuatu is approximately 170,000.

3 ● LANGUAGE

Over one hundred distinct languages are spoken in the Republic of Vanuatu. There are three official languages: English, French, and Bislama. Bislama developed from South Pacific English, a simplified language that spread throughout the region during the nineteenth century. Traders and other foreigners used it to communicate with speakers of the many local languages.

4 ● FOLKLORE

Yams are the Ni-Vanuatu's main source of food after the taro root. They are important in the group's mythology. On South Pentecost Island, the following myth recounts the origin of yams:

> In the beginning, there was no food. There was an old man who stayed alone in his hut, lying down and never going out. One day, he was cutting his fingernails and toenails. He threw the pieces out the door. The nails sprouted a plant that grew out of the ground. He tried the plant and it tasted good.

5 ● RELIGION

The main religion of the Ni-Vanuatu is Christianity. However, many Ni-Vanuatu still practice traditional native religions. These include cargo cults, which believe that wealth can be obtained through religious ceremonies. Best known among these is the John Frum movement. This group holds on to some traditional practices that are considered pagan by church authorities. These include ritual dancing and the drinking of *kava*. Kava is a drink made from a plant that contains a mildly intoxicating drug.

6 ● MAJOR HOLIDAYS

The major national holiday in Vanuatu is Independence Day, celebrated on July 30, marks the day in 1980 when the islands achieved autonomy from England and France.

In a community on the island of Tanna, John Frum Day is celebrated in February.

7 ● RITES OF PASSAGE

Some Ni-Vanuatu practice male initiation, which usually involves circumcision. A boy who refuses to undergo circumcision may not be considered an adult man. Following the ritual, a young man wears a cover of braided fibers over his genitals.

People of the northern islands of Vanuatu pass through a series of status levels during adulthood. A person gains entry to each stage by purchasing the symbols associated with it and by making a large sacrifice of animals, usually pigs. Men mainly pass through the status levels, but women may also participate.

8 ● RELATIONSHIPS

Family ties traditionally rule interpersonal relations among the Ni-Vanuatu. For example, in some communities, there is a strict rule that brothers and sisters must avoid each other. After reaching adolescence, they are not permitted to speak to each other, or even to be in the same place. In these communities, brothers and sisters must communicate through a young girl who acts as a go-between.

9 ● LIVING CONDITIONS

Housing styles vary by region. In the cities, Ni-Vanuatu live in buildings like those found in industrialized nations. Modern houses, apartments, and condominiums are found in the cities. On their outskirts, however, houses are built from scrap materials.

Rural housing includes both traditional houses and those of mixed construction, which combines traditional elements, such as woven bamboo walls and dirt floors, with roofs of galvanized sheet metal.

10 ● FAMILY LIFE

The role of women varies among the Ni-Vanuatu. In some areas, men are in charge. In others, especially parts of Espiritu Santo and Efate, women have more power. In these societies, descent is traced through the female side of the family.

For the rural Ni-Vanuatu, the choice of a marriage partner is determined by family and descent. The marriage itself is usually accompanied by an exchange of gifts, including woven mats and pigs.

11 ● CLOTHING

A wide range of clothing is found among the Ni-Vanuatu. In the cities, Ni-Vanuatu wear modern, Western-style clothing. Those living in villages often combine Western clothes with local forms of dress. Women often wear fiber skirts without a blouse or top. Men may wear a traditional loincloth or a pair of shorts and a T-shirt.

12 ● FOOD

Traditional food crops include taro root and yams. Food is prepared in rural areas without the use of electricity or gas. City dwellers have a wide selection of food. Shops sell imported food products. A large market in Port Vila brings in traditional produce from rural areas.

13 ● EDUCATION

Many Ni-Vanuatans do not have an opportunity to participate in any form of public, institutionalized education. Education has often been provided by mission schools run by various Christian groups.

14 ● CULTURAL HERITAGE

Dancing is an important part of Ni-Vanuatan culture. Many villages have family dancing grounds called *nasara*. The slit gong is a musical instrument made from a hollowed-out tree trunk. It is used to represent the voices of the spirits.

15 ● EMPLOYMENT

In Port Vila, there are office jobs in the government and in international development agencies.

Traditional forms of work have been different for men and for women. Women are often the main food producers.

16 ● SPORTS

People living in the cities play tennis and golf.

17 ● RECREATION

Adult Ni-Vanuatu men drink an intoxicating beverage called *kava*. Typically, adult men drink kava at night. The drinking session is a quiet occasion that usually lasts a couple of hours.

Commercial kava bars have sprung up in villages, towns, and cities. These local gathering places are called *nakamals*. Departing from traditional patterns of kava drinking, nakamals permit women to drink. However, a woman must not be from the same village as the owner of the bar.

A lack of electricity has limited the availability of television for most Ni-Vanuatu.

18 ● CRAFTS AND HOBBIES

Tapa cloth was a traditional product of many groups in Vanuatu. It is now produced for sale to tourists and collectors.

19 ● SOCIAL PROBLEMS

One of the greatest problems facing the Ni-Vanuatu is maintaining their traditional culture in the face of Western influences.

The economy is not thoroughly developed and stable. Unlike other South Pacific nations, Vanuatu receives only a small number of tourists, about 35,000 per year.

20 ● BIBLIOGRAPHY

Aldrich, Robert. *France and the South Pacific Since 1940.* Honolulu: University of Hawaii Press, 1993.

Allen, Michael, ed. *Vanuatu: Politics, Economics and Ritual in Island Melanesia.* New York: Academic Press, 1981.

Bonnemaison, Jokl, ed. *Arts of Vanuatu.* Honolulu:University of Hawaii Press, 1996.

Douglas, Norman. *Vanuatu: A Guide.* Sydney, Australia: Pacific Publications, 1987.

Lini, Walter. *Beyond Pandemonium: From the New Hebrides to Vanuatu.* Wellington, New Zealand: Asia Pacific Books, 1981.

MacClancy, Jeremy. *To Kill a Bird with Two Stones: A Short History of Vanuatu.* Port-Vila, Vanuatu: Vanuatu Cultural Center, 1981.

WEBSITES

Vanuatu Online. [Online] Available http://www.vanuatu.net.vu/, 1998.

World Travel Guide. Vanuatu. [Online] Available http ://www.wtgonline.com/country/vu/gen.html, 1998.

Venezuela

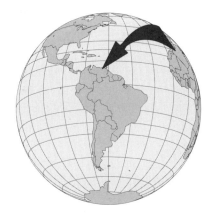

The original inhabitants of Venezuela were Amerindians, mainly Caribs and Arawaks. The bulk (about 68 percent) of the present population is mestizo (mixed race); an estimated 21 percent is unmixed white, 8–10 percent is black, and 2 percent is Amerindian. Among the Amerindian groups living in Venezuela are the Guajiros and the Pemon, both of which are profiled in this chapter.

Venezuelans

PRONUNCIATION: ve-neh-zoo-AY-lens

LOCATION: Venezuela

POPULATION: 21 million

LANGUAGE: Spanish; Amerindian languages

RELIGION: Roman Catholicism; some Protestantism, Judaism, and native Amerindian religions

1 ● INTRODUCTION

Venezuela was colonized by Spain in the sixteenth century. The Spanish conquerors at first explored its long Caribbean coastline. They fought with a variety of American Indian peoples and later brought slaves from Africa. Venezuelans today are descended from all three groups—Spanish, Indian, and African. There are still about twenty groups of American Indian tribes in the country.

Venezuela holds an honored place in Latin American history because its capital, Caracas, is the birthplace of the great liberator Simón Bolívar (1783–1830). He freed Venezuela, along with Colombia, Peru, Ecuador, and Bolivia, from Spanish rule. Thanks to his efforts, Venezuela became an independent nation.

Venezuela suffered under various dictatorships during the twentieth century. But since 1958, there have been free elections and democratically elected presidents. Because it has large oil reserves, Venezuela has made rapid economic progress. The wealth produced by the petroleum industry may be the reason Venezuela has avoided the violence that has arisen in some neighboring countries, including Colombia and Peru.

2 ● LOCATION

Venezuela is the size of the states of Texas and Oklahoma combined. It shares a border

VENEZUELANS

0   250   500   750 Miles

0   250   500   750 Kilometers

3 ● LANGUAGE

The official language of Venezuela is Spanish. Many of the surviving American Indian peoples continue to speak their own languages.

4 ● FOLKLORE

Folklore in Venezuela has evolved from the blending of Spanish, African, and American Indian customs. Several colorful festivals are the result of this blending of cultures. *Carnaval* is a yearly nationwide event that lasts for several days and begins just before Ash Wednesday (usually in February). On the holiday of Corpus Christi (in May or June), there is a dramatic "Dance of the Devils" in the town of San Francisco de Yare. People parade and dance in the streets in costumes and masks in the streets. Black African music influences the Fiesta de San Juan, held in the state of Miranda in June.

5 ● RELIGION

Most Venezuelans are Roman Catholic. There are also some Protestants and a Jewish community in Caracas. Some Venezuelan American Indians have also adopted Roman Catholicism.

with Colombia to the west, with Brazil to the south, and with Guyana to the east. To the north, its Caribbean coastline is about 1,865 miles (3,000 kilometers) long. Most of the country has a warm climate.

While most of the population is descended from the Spanish or is of mixed Spanish and American Indian or Spanish-African descent, there are still about twenty pure American Indian groups. They usually speak their own languages. They number about 200,000 out of a total population of 21 million.

During the twentieth century, immigrants have arrived in Venezuela from Italy, Spain, and Portugal, as well as from neighboring Colombia.

One of Venezuela's important religious events takes place in the town of Guanare. It is a yearly feast day honoring the Virgin Mary, who is known in Venezuela as *Nuestra Señora de Comoroto*, Venezuela's patron saint. It commemorates the day in 1652 when the Virgin is said to have appeared to an American Indian chief on the shores of the Guanaguare River. She encouraged him to accept Christian baptism and left him a tiny image of herself. The chief was frightened and ran away. He later died of a snake-

High-rise buildings in Caracas.

Mary A. Dempsey

bite. Just before his death, however, he asked to be baptized and advised his people to do the same.

6 ● MAJOR HOLIDAYS

Aside from religious festivals and the national *Carnaval,* the major holiday in Venezuela is Independence Day. It is celebrated on April 19. Other public holidays also mark important historical events. They include Simón Bolívar's birthday on July 24, the victory over the Spanish in the Battle of Carabobo on July 5, and the arrival of Columbus in the Americas on October 12. Labor Day, May 1, is also a public holiday.

7 ● RITES OF PASSAGE

Since most of Venezuela is Roman Catholic, baptism and first communion are important occasions. Most children have the name of a saint as part of their name, so many celebrate their saint's day as well as their actual birthday.

When a person dies, prayers are held at the person's home for nine days. Relatives and close friends usually attend.

8 ● RELATIONSHIPS

Venezuelans are considered outgoing and friendly. The spirit of fun is evident in their love of social gatherings and parties.

Anne Kalosh

Residential houses in Tacacas, Venezuela. The expansion of education has contributed to the development of a growing middle class. This is reflected in the building of more middle-class houses.

Like many other Latin Americans, Venezuelans have an easygoing attitude toward time. They are tolerant of late arrivals to meetings and social gatherings. Even business lunches can be lengthy, lasting two or three hours.

9 ● LIVING CONDITIONS

Even in the prosperous 1960s and 1970s, when the oil boom changed Caracas from a relatively quiet town to a busy modern city, the contrast between wealthy and poor housing was very clear. Lavish hotels and apartment blocks were only a few blocks away from shantytowns. Some of this hill-side housing was so poorly built that it would slide down the mountain after heavy rains.

This contrast also existed, but to a lesser extent, in other less-populated towns. More recently, the expansion of education and the newer universities have contributed to the development of a growing middle class. This is seen in the building of more middle-class houses.

10 ● FAMILY LIFE

Venezuelans value family ties. The bonds between the extended family—which includes grandparents, aunts, uncles, and cousins—are very important. Occasions for large family gatherings include birthdays, baptisms, first communions, weddings, and major holidays. Extended families also gather on weekends or on short holiday visits to beaches and parks. In smaller towns, the extended family gathers often for family meals and celebrations. The family offers a secure network for support. This is important because there is a lack or shortage of some government services and benefits.

Women have made good progress in entering the traditionally male professions, including medicine, dentistry, economics, and law. In middle-class households, the working woman relies on servants to help in the home. In poorer households, older relatives or older children provide help wherever possible.

11 ● CLOTHING

In cities, men wear lightweight suits or shirts and trousers that suit Venezuela's climate. Women are usually very fashion-conscious and dress in popular Western styles.

12 ● FOOD

A typical Venezuelan dish is *carne mechada,* shredded beef. It comes from the cattle-ranching areas of Los Llanos. It is served with fried plantains, black beans, cornmeal pancakes called *arepas,* rice, and, sometimes, white cheese.

Another type of cornmeal pancake, called a *cachapa,* is often served for breakfast with jam. A staple, tasty snack is the *empanada,* a fried cornmeal turnover sometimes stuffed with cheese, meat, or chicken.

In many low-income households, tropical fruits such as coconuts, mangoes, watermelons, pineapples, and papayas provide variety to the basic diet of beans, rice, and plantains. In coastal areas, the diet includes fish. It is often served fried or in a stew with vegetables, which is called *sancocho.*

13 ● EDUCATION

Formal schooling begins in Venezuela at the age of six and is compulsory (required) for the first six years. The four-year high school program leads to a one-year preparation for college. College usually takes four years, but university training in medicine or engineering, for example, takes more time. Many poorer households cannot afford schooling. Young people who have to go to work to add to the family income are unable to complete high school.

Greater numbers of Venezuelans are finding their way to universities and colleges. A few of these have completely free tuition. There are about thirty universities. The largest is Universidad Central in Caracas, with about 70,000 students. Another well-known university, Universidad de los Andes, in the Andean town of Mérida, has 30,000 thousand students.

Women have made great progress in university education, and about half the students at the university level are now women.

14 ● CULTURAL HERITAGE

Venezuela has produced fine writers, painters, poets, musicians, and, more recently, playwrights. The work of Expressionist painter Armando Reverón is admired throughout the continent. One of Venezuela's first poets was Andrés Rello, who

The *joropo* is Venezuela's national dance. The music for it is played on a small harp and a four-string guitar called the *cuatro,* with rattles for keeping the rhythm.

15 ● EMPLOYMENT

The prosperity (increase in wealth) of the 1960s and 1970s, based on the oil boom, was followed by a worldwide drop in oil prices. Job opportunities declined for many Venezuelans. A recent period of difficult economic adjustment has been a burden to poor people in particular, but it has also affected the middle class in Venezuela. Traditionally, the poor relied on government support to pay for basic food and transportation. When this support was withdrawn and prices rose, many people suffered.

Farming and cattle ranching are major sources of work in rural areas. In cities, people work in businesses or factories. For university graduates, the possibilities vary depending on the field. Mining is an important activity, and mining engineers usually find jobs; so do oil engineers. Economists find work in business or banking. Doctors and lawyers are in demand. There are new career possibilities in the field of communications, and television is a growth industry in Venezuela.

16 ● SPORTS

Soccer is a national passion in Venezuela. In coastal areas, water sports such as swimming, boating, and fishing are very popular.

Inland, in the grassy plains known as Los Llanos, horseback riding is popular. Fine equestrians take part in colorful rodeos known as *toros colcados,* in which they

Mary A. Dempsey

Harvesting coffee.

knew Simón Bolívar. Venezuela's best-known poet is Andrés Eloy Blanco, who died in 1955.

Venezuela's most famous novelist is Rómulo Gallegos. In one of his novels, *Doña Bárbara,* he created a strong-willed, unforgettable character. His novel *Canaima* is a dramatic account of the struggle of humans to survive, psychologically and physically, in the jungle. Another writer of the same generation was Miguel Otero Silva, who died in 1985. His novel, *Casas Muertas,* is widely admired.

compete to bring a bull down by grabbing its tail while riding a horse at top speed.

17 ● RECREATION

Venezuelans enjoy visiting their beautiful national parks. They are also fond of traveling to take part in a variety of festivals around the country. In the major cities, there are nightclubs and discos. Venezuelans also enjoy eating in restaurants.

Television is popular. Venezuela produces a variety of soap operas, which are called *telenovelas*.

Going to bullfights is also a popular pastime.

18 ● CRAFTS AND HOBBIES

Anthropologists and local historians have played an important part in making Venezuelans aware of the arts and crafts of the various American Indian peoples. Much of their handiwork is now more easily available. It includes pottery, baskets, hammocks, and rugs.

19 ● SOCIAL PROBLEMS

Venezuela has undergone a period of economic and political uncertainty that has affected job opportunities. There has also been an increase in crime. Over half of the population is under eighteen years of age. In this uneasy social and economic situation, groups within the military have tried to take power by force at two different times. Both of these attempts failed, and Venezuela has remained a democratic country. But the social ease and confidence of the more economically successful years (of the 1960s and 1970s) have not yet returned.

20 ● BIBLIOGRAPHY

Fox, Geoffrey. *The Land and People of Venezuela.* New York: HarperCollins, 1991.

Galeano, Eduardo. *Faces and Masks.* London, England: Mandarin, 1989.

George, Uwe. "Venezuela's Islands in Time." *National Geographic* (May 1989), p. 526–562.

Haggerty, Richard A., ed. *Venezuela: A Country Study.* 4th ed. Washington, D.C.: Library of Congress, 1993.

Morrison, M. *Venezuela.* Chicago: Children's Press, 1989.

Nagel, Rob, and Anne Commire, ed. "Simon Bolivar." In *World Leaders, People Who Shaped the World.* Volume III: North and South America. Detroit: UXL, 1994.

Venezuela in Pictures. Minneapolis, Minn.: Lerner Publications Co., 1987.

Waddell, D. A. G. *Venezuela.* Oxford, England, and Santa Barbara, Calif.: Clio Press, 1990.

WEBSITES

Embassy of Venezuela, Washington, DC. [Online] Available http://venezuela.mit.edu/embassy/, 1998.

Ruiz-Garcia, Pedro (The Latino Connection). [Online] Available http://www.ascinsa.com/LATINOCONNECTION/venezuel.html, 1998.

World Travel Guide, Venezuela. [Online] Available http://www.wtgonline.com/country/ve/gen.html, 1998.

Guajiros

PRONUNCIATION: gwah-HEE-rose
LOCATION: Venezuela and Colombia
POPULATION: Unknown
LANGUAGE: Guajiro
RELIGION: Mixture of Roman Catholicism and indigenous religious traditions

1 ● INTRODUCTION

The Guajiros are a people of northeastern Colombia and northwestern Venezuela. They have been seminomadic (not keeping permanent homes) for hundreds of years. They existed before the arrival of the Spanish conquerors, although their precise origins are uncertain. The Guajiro people is divided into clans. Each clan is made up of several family groups, with leaders who are recognized as princes.

2 ● LOCATION

The Guajiros live in the dry lands and coastal areas of the Guajira peninsula. This area borders the Caribbean Sea to the north and east, and Venezuela and the Gulf of Maracaibo to the west. The Guajiros have traditionally ignored the border that divides Venezuela and Colombia. They roam freely into and out of both countries. Their nomadic habits have been recognized and respected by both countries. They have been given citizenship by both. They have never had to follow the rules and formalities normally required of border crossers.

Reluctance to recognize national borders continues to this day. Members of the same extended families and clans may live either in remote desert areas or in cities such as Riohacha, the capital of the Guajira department (state). They may live in a neighborhood of the Venezuelan city of Maracaibo, where some have migrated to find work, or in smaller settlements such as Puerto López at the mouth of the oil-rich Gulf of Maracaibo. Many move from one location to another, freely crossing borders.

3 ● LANGUAGE

Although many Guajiros have had contact with Spanish-speaking people for many years, they continue to speak their own language. They often have three names each: a Guajiro name, a Catholic name given to them at birth, and another Spanish name that they usually use with white people. The Guajiro name is often kept secret. It is used only by close members of the family on the mother's side.

The story of Guajiro lives, their work, their loves and sorrows, and the landscape of sand and boat and sea is often recorded in poetic songs. These are often very sad. For example, in a song about a boat and an anchor, the following line is repeated in a lengthy, sad tone, like the repetitive call of a bird: "Eeeeeeeeee guarapáin tanai, eeeeeeeee guarapáin tanai." Then this sad lament changes into a joyful song.

4 ● FOLKLORE

Although the Guajiro Indians were gradually converted to Catholicism, some beliefs and practices from earlier times persist. Each clan has a symbol, usually drawn from the animal world. It stands for certain virtues and traits with which the clan identifies. This symbol is usually understood by outsiders as a *totem*. This means that the

GUAJIROS

0   250   500   750 Miles

0 250 500 750 Kilometers

Caribbean Sea

Barranquilla
Maracaibo
Panama
★Caracas   Ciudad
        Orinoco ⋅Guayana
PANAMA
San Cristóbal
        VENEZUELA
            GUYANA
⋅Medellín
★Bogotá
Cali   COLOMBIA
        Mitú⋅
            Negro
                Manaus
★Quito   *Amazon*
ECUADOR
Guayaquil
    Iquitos⋅
        BRAZIL
PERU
Marañón *Ucayali*
        ⋅Pôrto Velho
Trujillo⋅   Rio Branco⋅

power, hopes, and virtues that the clan considers valuable are expressed by their choice of symbol. Sometimes this symbol is tattooed on a person's arm.

5 ● RELIGION

Religious life for the Guajiros is a mixture of Catholicism and traditional beliefs. These include a different view of the afterlife. The cape at the head of the Guajira peninsula, called the Cabo de la Vela (the Cape of the Sail), is called *Jepira* by the Guajiros. They consider it a sacred place because they believe that Guajiros who have passed away still wander there.

The Wayúu clan records its origin with this poetic myth: "We were born of the Wind of the Northeast and the Goddess of the Rains." Winter itself is thought of as the brother of the Goddess of the Rains, and the winter is appreciated by all the Guajiro Indians because it brings life-giving rains.

6 ● MAJOR HOLIDAYS

Guajiros who have migrated to the towns have become more involved in the celebrations and religious festivals of Catholicism. The Guajiros also mark special events in their lives according to their own traditions, especially the Guajiro ceremonial dance known as the *Chichimaya*. This is a fertility dance; it is often performed when a young girl reaches adolescence and is considered able to marry.

The Festival of Uribia mixes dances, songs, and music of African, Spanish colonial, and Guajiro Indian origins.

7 ● RITES OF PASSAGE

Many Guajiro infants are not only baptized into the Catholic Church, but also given a private Guajiro naming ceremony. The Guajiro name is part of the special relationships among family members. Clan identity comes to the infant through its mother. Similarly, the Guajiro name is usually spoken only by close family members on the mother's side. Maternal uncles have special authority and importance.

When Guajiros become teenagers, they are separated for a time. When they reach adolescence, girls are kept apart from other people and cared for by their maternal aunts. This is to help girls prepare for married life. For months, the girls have to drink specially brewed herbal teas. It is believed that the tea helps them get rid of childish attitudes and become more mature.

They also improve their skill in crafts such as weaving. This time apart is seen as a rebirth, and each girl is given a new name. After this, they are ready to go out into the world again, to meet the boys who will eventually become their husbands.

At this stage the girls have a coming-out party, and the *Chichimaya,* the Guajiro ritual fertility dance, is performed. During the dance, which takes place at dusk, a boy takes off his hat and waves it, dancing backward in a circle, daring a girl to catch him. The girl has to dance and chase him, trying to step on his feet so that he will lose his balance and fall.

8 ● RELATIONSHIPS

Greetings can be very friendly and enthusiastic. When guests arrive, hosts hang up extra hammocks so that the visitors will be able to spend time with them—and spend the night if necessary. Then the hosts will ask the visitor, "What news do you bring, *waré?*" The *waré* (friend) is expected to provide news about relatives and friends.

9 ● LIVING CONDITIONS

The health of the Guajiros depends on where they live. The Guajiros as a whole are in a period of change. Some have migrated to the towns. In larger cities, such as Maracaibo in Venezuela, there is a Guajiro district.

Even those who do not live permanently in towns are going more often to medical doctors in the cities and towns.

Guajiros who have not migrated to the towns still live in simple circular huts. Traditional house building is done by the community. The whole family lives under one roof, often in small groupings of huts with other members of their clan.

10 ● FAMILY LIFE

The role of the woman is very important among the Guajiros. The society is matrilineal. This means that the family name is passed on from the mother to children. The mother's relatives are very important. Most important are the maternal uncle and the maternal aunt.

If a boy wants to marry, his family has to offer a generous bride price. This may include thirty more goats. The Guajiros regard goats as extremely valuable assets.

Guajiros usually look for wives from a different clan. If a wife is unfaithful, the husband can return her to her family and her family must return the gifts they had received. If a husband has been unfaithful, he has to pay her family with a gift that equals the original bride price.

When a woman is expecting a child, her husband is required to protect her in specific ways. For instance, he has to ride ahead of her to search out dangerous snakes that might harm her or the unborn child.

11 ● CLOTHING

Traditional clothes are striking and distinctive. Women wear long, flowing, flowery dresses down to the ankles. They fit loosely and therefore are cool in the hot climate. They also protect the skin from the sun.

Men are often tall and thin, with strong limbs. Their traditional loincloths are sometimes decorated with bright tassels and pompoms. They also wear pompoms on their sandals as a sign that may indicate their rank as a prince. When they go to town, they wear simple cotton shirts and trousers, as do other town dwellers in the hot climates of South America.

12 ● FOOD

Corn and products made from corn meal are part of the basic diet. Protein is obtained from fish caught in the coastal waters of the peninsula. Turtles sometimes provide a source of protein and are considered a delicacy. On festive occasions, meat (usually goat meat) is grilled on simple open fires. Some Guajiros also keep pigs and hens.

13 ● EDUCATION

The first efforts to provide schooling for the Guajiros were begun by missionaries. Literacy (ability to read and write) has been low. But in the last few decades this has been changing, as more Guajiros have migrated to towns, where education is more widely available.

Many young Guajiros do not go beyond primary school. Others may have just a few years in primary school without completing it. Those who have moved into towns are able to complete high school.

Parents who stay in isolated villages feel it is important for young people to survive in that environment. For them, education does not mean going to school but rather learning to herd, hunt, or fish; to build simple shelters; and to weave.

14 ● CULTURAL HERITAGE

The Guajiros have preserved important parts of their own culture as they have absorbed belief systems and attitudes from the surrounding culture. The ritual *Chichimaya* is a ceremonial dance that has been preserved. Traditional instruments, such as flutes, rattles, and drums, are still in use.

Their myths, which often deal with their origins as a people, are preserved in storytelling and song.

15 ● EMPLOYMENT

For centuries, the Guajiros have dived for pearls around the Cabo de la Vela. They have also mined salt on land that traditionally belongs to them. Much of this land was taken over by the Colombian government, which then hired the Guajiros as paid labor. Guajiros do not usually like long, regimented working hours. They are used to working in a freer pattern, and working just enough for their basic needs. Relatives often share the same shift on a single job.

Some Guajiros have found work in coal mines, since Colombia has rich coal deposits in the region. Others work in the oil-rich area of Maracaibo in Venezuela.

16 ● SPORTS

Children who are adapting to town life are also beginning to enjoy Western-style sports.

In the traditional way of life, spectator sports do not exist. Elements of sports and athletics are included in dances and rituals during festivals, or in the tasks of daily life.

17 ● RECREATION

Town dwellers enjoy local radio and television programs and go to movie theaters. But the aspect of popular culture that people living along the Caribbean enjoy most is the carnival. Guajiros enjoy *fiestas* and carnivals as much as everyone else. The best-known fiesta in Guajira is the yearly event in Uribia. The Guajiros come in all their finery. Women wear jewelry and colorful flowered dresses, their faces dramatically made up with ceremonial paint. In Uribia, they mingle with other (non-Guajiro) peoples living along the coast, enjoy the dancing, and admire the ceremonial elegance of the Guajiros.

18 ● CRAFTS AND HOBBIES

Weaving, jewelry making, and crafting musical instruments such as flutes and drums form part of Guajiro life. Their hammocks are well-known and are now sold in coastal towns. The women make their own dresses. Their specific cut and choice of flowery prints are much admired. Guajiros also make dugout canoes and basic fishing equipment such as nets, rods, and spears.

19 ● SOCIAL PROBLEMS

In the early 1990s, constitutional reform in Colombia allowed representatives of indigenous (native) peoples to serve in Congress. This is an important step forward. But it is still too early to know what effect this will have on the Guajiros and their problems. These mainly have to do with changing lifestyles and the growing differences between the people who live in towns and the rural people who continue to live in poverty.

20 ● BIBLIOGRAPHY

De Friedemann, Nina S. *Fiestas*. Hogta: Villegas Editores, 1995.

Los Pueblos Nómadas, National Geographical Society. Mexico: Ediciones Diana, S. A., 1978.

Zalamea Borda, Eduardo. *Cuatro arìos a bordo de mi mismo*. Bogota, Colombia: Compañia Gran Colombiana de Ediciones S. A., 1959.

Pemon

PRONUNCIATION: PAY-mahn
ALTERNATE NAMES: Arecuna; Kamarakoto; Taurepan
LOCATION: Venezuela
POPULATION: Unknown
LANGUAGE: Pemon
RELIGION: Indigenous beliefs mingled with Christian elements

1 ● INTRODUCTION

The Pemon-Caribs of Venezuela used to be called *Arecuna, Kamarakoto,* and *Taurepan.* But they call themselves *Pemon.* There are no historical records of their lives from the time before 1750. At the end of the nineteenth century, English Protestant missionaries started to Christianize the Pemon. In 1931, the first Capuchin (a Catholic religious order) mission post in the Pemon area was established. Gold and diamond rushes began in the area in 1936. During the 1960s, the area was connected with other parts of Venezuela by airplane and by new roads.

Diamond mining has not been a major activity in recent years. This, together with the poor quality of Pemon agricultural land and the late opening of the area, has spared the Pemon from major land invasions from the outside world. Many of their traditions and their original methods of communication—their language, smoke signals, and messages carried by people on foot—have survived.

2 ● LOCATION

The Pemon territory covers the coastal area of the Atlantic Ocean in Venezuela, the inland mountain savanna (plains) area, and the Amazon River area.

The region is unique for its *tepuis,* the remains of mighty sandstone plateaus that once stretched across the entire area. In the course of time, the plateaus were worn down by erosion. This left only the tepuis as giant monuments to their existence. There are more than one hundred of them. Fewer than half have been thoroughly explored. Many of them are so tall that they are hidden by dense cloud cover for days at a time. Much of the plant and animal life atop the tepuis is unique—found nowhere else.

In the area south of the Orinoco River, the country is mainly lowlands. Farther south, toward the Amazon region, the landscape turns mountainous.

3 ● LANGUAGE

Father Cesareo de Armellada was the author of the first dictionary of the Pemon language (published in 1943). At the time it was called *Taurepan.* Many words in this language show interesting patterns of formation. For example, the word for "sugarcane" is *kaiwara-kún-imá,* which means "pineapple with a very long leg." The word for "pineapple" itself, *kaiwara,* means "a sweet with wrinkles." The Pemon word for "dew" is *chirké-yetakú,* which means "star's saliva." *Yetakú* is "saliva" or, more precisely, "juice of the teeth."

There is no word for "year" in the Pemon language. The day is divided into "dawning," "morning," "noontime," "afternoon,"

and then just "dark" or "nighttime." Most time words only cover "yesterday," "today," "tomorrow," and "time past" *(pena).*

The Pemon speak their own language among themselves, and Spanish or a simplified form of Spanish with outsiders. In the mission villages and mining areas of the state of Bolívar, more and more young people also use Spanish among themselves. Most Pemon people now have Christian (Spanish) names. They often have two American Indian names as well. One of these is a sacred and secret name.

4 ● FOLKLORE

The Pemon have traditionally believed that each person has five souls, which look like the shadows of a human being. The fifth soul is the one that talks and that leaves the body to travel around when the person is dreaming. This is the only one that goes away—to the Milky Way—after death. Before arriving there, it meets the Father of the Dogs. If the person has mistreated his or her dogs, the dogs' souls will recognize the person and kill him or her.

One of the other four souls lives in the knee and stays put for a while after death; later, it turns into a bad spirit. The other three souls turn into birds of prey after death. All animals and plants are believed to have souls. Stones do not have souls, but they house bad spirits.

The *Makunaima* is a series of creation stories of the Pemon land, crops, techniques, and social practices. It starts with the creation of a wife for the first Pemon— the Sun—by a water nymph. At that time, the Sun was a person. One day he went to the stream and saw a small woman with long hair. He managed to grasp her hair, but she told him, "Not me! I will send you a woman to be your companion and your wife."

Her name was *Tuenkaron*, and the next day she sent the Sun a white woman. He fed her, and she lit a fire. But when the Sun sent her to the stream, she collapsed into a little heap of clay. The woman was made of white earth, or clay. The next day Tuenkaron sent him a black woman. She was able to bring water, but when she tried to light a fire, she melted. The woman was made of wax. The third woman was red, a rock-colored woman. The sun tested her and she did not melt or collapse. She was strong and able to help run the household. The woman and the Sun had several children, and these are the Pemon.

5 ● RELIGION

Most American Indian belief systems have been mixed to some degree with Christian elements. In spite of the strength of Catholicism, the Pemon still believe in *Kanaima*— the spirit of evil. Also, some social traditions, such as the marriage of cousins, that are opposed by the church are practiced by many Pemon. The Pemon have also mixed traditional cult saints with Catholic saints.

6 ● MAJOR HOLIDAYS

As most Pemon have been Christianized, their major holidays are the same as those celebrated by Catholics. Holy Week and Christmas are the most important.

7 ● RITES OF PASSAGE

Traditional rites of passage were associated with the life cycle (birth, adolescence, and death), but most are no longer celebrated. Baptism in a Catholic mission is now the only important rite of passage.

Often a father gives a child a secret name in the Pemon language. It is forbidden to use a secret name when speaking to any person, male or female. This is not the case with Spanish names, and the Pemon are eager to baptize their children with Spanish names. Women usually do not have last names. Men sometimes adopt the last name of their boss in the diamond mines. Brothers sometimes end up with different last names for this reason.

Traditionally, a boy's passage into adolescence was marked with a special ceremony. A Pemon religious leader lashed a boy's body, made incisions in his skin, and applied what were believed to be magic substances to the wounds. For one year after the ceremony, certain foods could not be eaten.

A girl's passage into adolescence was marked by a haircut before the first menstruation. In addition, the edges of a girl's mouth was tattooed in a traditional design. At the first sign of menstruation, the girl retired to her hammock and was considered impure. Her grandmother would then paint her whole body in a special way.

8 ● RELATIONSHIPS

Marriage is the key to the social organization of the Pemon people. It determines the pattern of visits between villages, which is at the heart of their social life. Visits for beer parties and meetings with relatives tie neighborhoods and regions together. The respect that a village or neighborhood receives is often gauged by the quality and quantity of *manioc* (cassava) beer offered by the hosts.

Conversation is lively when the family gathers for a meal. If guests are present, the men eat first.

Open conflict, anger, and fighting are strongly discouraged. The basic response to conflict is to withdraw. Often this means a person will leave home and make an extended visit to relatives somewhere else, waiting for things to calm down. Since the Pemon do not approve of anger or displays of hostility, physical punishment of children is very rare. If an adult hits a child at all, it is done so mildly that it is just a reminder. Pemon children learn by example and are given much freedom.

9 ● LIVING CONDITIONS

In the old days, when somebody became ill, the local shaman or *paisan* connected the cause of the illness with one of the many mythical spirits. For healing, the shaman uses his *taren* recipes. These are a mixture of medicinal plants and charms. The taren is believed to be a magic spell that can aid in the birth of a child, counter the bite of various snakes, heal headaches and stomach pains, and so forth. The taren can only be taught to one person at a time, and it is performed in the presence of as few people as possible.

The Pemon's traditional housing consists of huts whose walls are made of clay or bark, with roofs made of palm leaves. Hammocks are hung from the beams of the roof, and a fire is kept at one or two corners of the house. Arrows, knives, axes, and fishing rods are piled up in one corner. Baskets, carrying sacks, and pumpkins hang on the walls.

10 ● FAMILY LIFE

Marriage is the basis of the main social and economic unit. The relationship between the father-in-law and the son-in-law is most important. For the father-in-law, his son-in-law is the substitute for his own son. Therefore, after the marriage, the son-in-law detaches himself from his own father and takes care of his father-in-law. In the Pemon society, there is no wedding ceremony. The new husband simply moves his hammock to his father-in-law's house and starts working with him.

According to traditional beliefs, the solid parts of babies—the bones—come from the father, and the blood comes from the mother. The mother gives birth behind a partition installed in the hut. She is helped by her mother or mother-in-law. For ten days after the birth, the parents stay behind the partition with their newborn child.

The Pemon love their children. Their attitude toward them is lenient. Parents do not constantly remind their children about their behavior. Children learn by following the parents' example, and they very seldom need to be disciplined or punished.

11 ● CLOTHING

In the past, the Pemon went naked or used only loincloths. The traditional clothing of a Pemon woman was an apron made of cotton or beads. In the twentieth century, the men's loincloths were made of a bright red cloth obtained from the criollos (Venezuelans of mixed descent).

By 1945, the Pemon had started wearing Western cotton clothing. The men tend to wear khaki, while the women make their dresses using cotton fabrics printed with patterns. At the beginning of the twentieth century, the women wore metal earrings known as "butterfly" earrings, which they bought. It was also common for them to have facial tattoos and to wear bands of cotton cloth or glass beads around their arms and legs.

12 ● FOOD

Yucca, manioc root, or cassava is an important ingredient of the Pemon diet. The women peel, wash, and grate this root. They then squeeze out the acid and make it into a dough. With this, they prepare their flat bread or fermented drinks. One of these beverages, the *cachiri,* is made with bitter yucca paste, which is grated and chewed and mixed with a red root, *cachiriyek,* that has also been grated. The mixture is then boiled for a whole day. This brew is mildly intoxicating.

Also part of the Pemon diet is *aurosa,* a spinachlike vegetable. The Pemon also eat peppers, potatoes, pineapple, plantain, sugarcane, and more than ten varieties of bananas. Women gather peppers and *aurosa* daily for the pepper pot, a soup that forms part of every meal.

Fishing provides an important source of animal protein in the Pemon diet. In the past, hunting was not very effective, even though the men put a great deal of time into it. The situation changed, however, with the arrival of firearms in the 1940s. Birds and mammals, such as deer and vampire bats, then became an important part of the diet.

During the rainy season, the Pemon capture flying ants. Throughout the year, they gather the insect larvae found in the *moriche* palm.

13 ● EDUCATION

One of the tools of the Pemon for educating their young is oral tradition. Their many stories are used by the elders to teach their sense of morality and concept of the world. The storyteller's closing words are usually *A-pantoní-pe nichii* (May you take advantage of this story).

Since 1979, bilingual (two-language) education at American Indian primary schools has been compulsory (required). Most of the main languages in American Indian territory have at least one schoolbook. Although the teachers' organizations and the government have proved their good will in the recent past, there are many difficulties in keeping up this system. Some Pemon children spend time in mission boarding schools or day schools through the primary-school years and sometimes longer.

14 ● CULTURAL HERITAGE

Music and dance are important components of Pemon culture. They accompany all sorts of public festivals and rituals. *Mari'* or *Mari'k,* for example, is the Pemon word for the dance and music that used to be performed in public by the *paisan* (shaman) and his assistants.

Nowadays there are no paisans left in the Christianized Pemon villages. Some Pemon even seem to be ashamed of tokens from the past, such as old musical instruments. Still, on occasions when *cachiri* drinking makes them receptive to tradition, spontaneously an old dance starts. With sticks and empty cans and tins for instruments, they sing songs full of endlessly repeated short phrases, varied by made-up phrases, jokes, and bits of the old shaman songs.

15 ● EMPLOYMENT

For the Pemon, work is a basic part of life. There is no word for "working" other than *senneka,* which means "being active" more than "laboring." Only when the Pemon started working with the missionaries or miners did they adopt the Spanish word *trabajo* (work), which turned into *trabasoman* to describe work done in the European way.

The Pemon's means of subsistence (getting enough food to live on) are based on slash-and-burn farming, fishing, hunting, and collecting wild fruits and insects. There is now more flexibility in the division of work among the Pemon people. Traditionally, for example, men were responsible for preparing the soil for planting, while women were in charge of weeding, harvesting, and transporting the crops.

16 ● SPORTS

Spectator sports have never been common among aboriginal peoples. Most of the talents valued by these societies are part of their day-to-day life—essential survival skills. Fishing, hunting, and merely getting from one place to another require the ability to run fast, jump high and far, use the bow and arrow, swim, and so forth.

Pemon Indians who are in close contact with whites do pay some attention to spectator sports.

17 ● RECREATION

The Pemon culture is rich in oral literature: tales and legends that the American Indians call *pantón.* There is no specific time dedicated to telling stories, but the favorite moment is just before going to sleep. The morning is the time for telling and interpreting dreams, and storytelling might happen again after meals. Stories and legends are considered luxuries. People take special trips to visit other groups in order to collect them. The possessor of stories is called *sak.* A guest who tells stories or brings news or new songs is always welcome.

18 ● CRAFTS AND HOBBIES

The Pemon value the abilities of their artisans. Outstanding persons are recognized for their individual skills. Some women are famous for the quality of their clay bowls.

Basketry is another major art form. Men make all of the baskets and fiber articles, including the eating mats and strainers used in everyday household work and cooking. But everyday basketry is different from the more complicated forms, which can be used in trade. As in the case of pottery, only certain men are skilled at making complex baskets.

The Pemon also make wooden dugout and bark canoes, paddles, and bows, and they weave hammocks and baby carriers.

19 ● SOCIAL PROBLEMS

Authorities and international support organizations identified land rights as the most pressing issue facing the Pemon in the 1990s. Venezuela recognizes land rights for its American Indian population. But in many cases it provides only provisional titles to land, which can be ignored easily. Gold, diamonds, and timber are once again attracting outsiders. Their arrival often leads to violation of Indian rights. The tourist industry is also threatening the region. What has been a controlled, eco-friendly enterprise could turn into an invasion if plans to build big hotels are approved.

20 ● BIBLIOGRAPHY

Brill, E. J. *Continuity & Identity in Native America.* New York: E. J. Brill, 1988.

Cuentos y no cuentos. Fray Cesareo de Armellada. Caracas, Venezuela: Instituto Venezolano de Lenguas Indigenas, 1988.

George, Uwe. "Venezuela's Islands in Time." *National Geographic* (May 1989).

Vietnam

About 87 percent of the population of Vietnam is composed of ethnic Vietnamese. In addition to the ethnic Vietnamese, there are fifty-three other ethnic groups living in Vietnam. Many are nomadic tribal peoples living in mountainous areas. The Cham and the Khmer are remnants of past civilizations that controlled the southern parts of the country. For more information on the Khmer, see the chapter on Cambodia in Volume 2.

Vietnamese

PRONUNCIATION: vee-et-nuh-MEEZ
LOCATION: Vietnam
POPULATION: 70–80 million
LANGUAGE: Vietnamese
RELIGION: Confucianism; Taoism; Buddhism, Roman Catholicism; Cao Daism

1 ●INTRODUCTION

The Socialist Republic of Vietnam, commonly known as Vietnam, is located in Southeast Asia. The country's history has been shaped by its location between China and India. Straddling lines of trade between north and south, east and west, Vietnam has been a center of human trade, interaction, and conflict for centuries.

Archaeological excavations reveal that the the Dong-son peole lived in Vietnam around 800 BC. The Dong-son built dikes and canals to control the rivers and irrigate their rice fields, and crafted bronze drums, tools, and weapons.

Aroung 200 BC, a Chinese military commander demanded that the people in Vietnam join China. At that time, Vietnam was called Nam Viet—Nam meaning "south" and Viet referring to the people living along China's southern border.

Nam Viet was ruled by China until AD 900. China's influence on Vietnam could still be seen in 1990s, in ways including ideas about government, philosophy, script, education, religion, crafts, and literature.

In the 1500s and 1600s, Portuguese and French traders came to Vietnam. Some Roman Catholic missionaries converted Vietnamese to Christianity. In the 1800s, the French returned to Vietnam to explore eco-

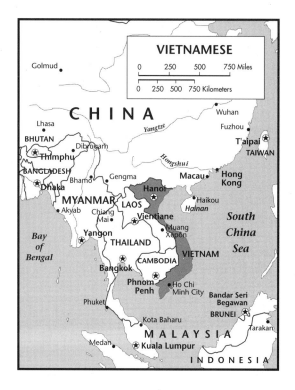

VIETNAMESE

0   250   500   750 Miles

0   250   500   750 Kilometers

Vietnam conquered South Vietnam and reunited the country. Almost a million Vietnamese escaped their homeland and were resettled in Western countries. Another million fled Vietnam by sea in 1978. Vietnamese continued to flee their country until the early 1990s.

By the late 1990s, there was an increase in international investment and trade in Vietnam. The government was run by the Communist Party of Vietnam (the country's only political party), and its general secretary, Do Muoi, was the political leader of the country.

2 ● LOCATION

Vietnam has between 70 and 80 million people, making it one of the most populous countries in the world. Most Vietnamese live in the Red and Mekong River deltas.

Vietnam is long and slender, stretching in an S-shape more than 1,000 miles (1,600 kilometers) from China in the north to Cambodia in the south. It is only 50 miles (80 kilometers) wide at its narrowest point. River deltas sit at each end of the country, yielding enormous quantities of rice.

Located just north of the equator, Vietnam has a tropical monsoon climate. In northern Vietnam, the rainy season extends from April to October. In the southern part of Vietnam, the rainy season extends from May to November. Humidity is high throughout the year. Summers are generally hot and wet and winters are mild and dry. The typhoon season extends from July through November, often causing serious damage to crops and people especially along the central coast area.

nomic and trade opportunities. For the next eighty years, France drained resources from Vietnam, and taxed the people. In the mid-1950s the Vietminh, nationalist communists led by Ho Chi Minh (1890–1969), gained power and forced the French to leave.

In 1955, Vietnam was divided into two countries. The area north of the seventeenth parallel became North Vietnam, led by Ho Chi Minh and the communists; south of the line lay South Vietnam, run by a pro-Western prime minister, Ngo Dinh Diem. The United States sent advisors and soldiers to help South Vietnam fight communism. This led to years of devastating war.

The war continued until 1973, when the United States Congress ceased military funding for South Vietnam. In 1975, North

Cory Langley

A billboard written in Vietnamese featuring the communist symbols of the hammer and sickle.

3 ● LANGUAGE

The Vietnamese language has been influenced by Chinese more than any other language. Chinese was the language used by government officials, scholars, and artists during the thousand years that China ruled Vietnam, but Vietnamese remained the popular language.

In the seventeenth century, missionaries transcribed the Vietnamese language into Roman letters (the letters used to write English and other languages). By the end of the nineteenth century, this system, called *quoc ngu*, had replaced the Chinese system of writing. Quoc ngu uses diacritical marks above or below letters to indicate pronunciation and tone.

Vietnamese is a tonal language, so that a change in tone alone can change the meaning of a word. To Vietnamese, their language has the sound of poetry, but it is very difficult for English-speakers to learn to pronounce.

Vietnamese use their father's family name, but unlike Americans, they use the family name first to reinforce the importance of family over the individual. The family name comes first and the individual's name second. For example, if Mr. Nguyen names his son Tai, then the boy will be known as Nguyen Tai. If Mr. Nguyen also gives his son the middle name, Thanh, his son will be called Nguyen Tai Thanh (family name, first name, and finally middle name).

4 ● FOLKLORE

In AD 40–43, the Trung sisters (Trung Trac and Trung Nhi) led a revolt against China. They failed, but are remembered as great Vietnamese heroines.

A Vietnamese patriot who also sought independence for his country in the 1400s was Le Loi. After leading an elephant-mounted army against Chinese invaders in the 1420s, Le Loi became King of Vietnam. He is remembered as a benevolent ruler who increased agricultural production and built dams, dikes, and bridges for the Vietnamese people.

Ho Chi Minh (1880–1969), the first president of North Vietnam, is a national hero. Ho Chi Minh traveled extensively, becoming committed to the goal of freeing his country from French colonialism. He is revered as a communist patriot.

5 ● RELIGION

The Vietnamese sometimes practice several religions at the same time. Confucianism, which came from China over 2,000 years ago, emphasizes good behavior, education, and respect for hierarchy and has been very influential in Vietnam.

Another religion inherited from China is Taoism, which emphasizes beliefs in the spirit world and ancestor worship. Most homes have an altar to the ancestors holding a small vase of flowers, some incense, a plate or two of food, and candles. Taoism also includes belief in geomancy, which focuses on the importance of aligning human objects and activities with the landscape. Thus, a father's grave must face the proper direction or his son will suffer.

In addition, most Vietnamese call themselves Buddhists. Vietnamese Buddhists believe in reincarnation and karmic destiny (the belief that people get what they deserve). If a man is good in this life, he will have a better life the next time round. If he is bad, however, the opposite will happen.

There are also several million Catholics, mostly in urban areas in the south, where the French missionaries had the greatest influence.

Cao Dai, a small but important religion, is followed by more than 1 million people. It combines elements from Buddhism, Christianity, and history. Its saints include Jesus Christ, the Buddha, Joan of Arc, and Charlie Chaplin. Cao Dai maintains a standing army, which was involved in the Vietnam War. Cao Dai adherents believe they are combining the best beliefs of all the world's religions.

6 ● MAJOR HOLIDAYS

The most important Vietnamese holiday is Tet (New Year), a celebration that falls in late January or early February. Tet is celebrated over three days. Vietnamese try to return to the home of their parents to unite with family and friends. People repay their debts and ask for forgiveness from all those whom they have wronged during the year. They put on new clothes, pray for blessings,

Cory Langley

In rural areas, boys help their fathers with farm work. In cities, boys are more likely to go to school, help their mothers with house chores or errands, or take part-time jobs on their own.

exchange gifts, and give thanks for being together.

Tet decorations include peach tree branches and red and gold paper, the colors of happiness. They light firecrackers at night and spare no expense in preparing the feast.

Other holidays include January 27, the anniversary of the peace agreement that resulted in America's withdrawal of troops from Vietnam; March 29, the actual withdrawal of American troops; and September 2, the establishment of the Democratic Republic of Vietnam.

7 ● RITES OF PASSAGE

The birth of a child is a welcome occasion, especially if the child is a boy. A couple without children is pitied, while a family with several offspring is considered fortunate. Children are cared for by an extended family of grandparents and aunts and uncles, especially on the father's side.

On all important family occasions, such as the birth of a child, engagements, marriages, funerals, and the anniversaries of ancestors' deaths, families hold celebrations and notify gods and ancestors of family events by special offerings.

8 ● RELATIONSHIPS

Vietnamese have great respect for hierarchy and take care to demonstrate respect to all they consider their superiors and demand respect from those they consider their inferiors. Older people are generally considered superior to younger people, men to women, the wealthy to the poor, and those of higher occupation or status to those of lower.

Vietnamese may greet one another with a slight bow and always with a broad smile. Civility is greatly valued, and one's true feelings are concealed beneath smiles and friendliness. Vietnamese also honor reserve and modesty, attributing loudness and brashness to immaturity and vulgarity.

Dating is virtually unknown in the countryside, where young people are closely supervised by their elders until marriage. There is little touching in public even by married couples, although young people of the same sex often hold hands as a sign of friendship.

9 ● LIVING CONDITIONS

The health of the Vietnamese people has suffered from decades of war, upheaval, and population increase. While the infant mortality rate is lower and life expectancy at birth is higher than the average for Southeast Asia, the Vietnamese continue to be plagued by numerous health problems. Malaria and tuberculosis are widespread, and cholera and bubonic plague continue to threaten many Vietnamese. Malnutrition also affects many in the country. An additional legacy of the Vietnam War is a high percentage of birth defects which are linked to chemicals sprayed on Vietnam's forests. Bombs and shells left over from the war continue to cause injury, especially to children, soldiers, and farmers.

Since the end of the Vietnam War, Vietnam's economy has frustrated many Vietnamese in their desire for consumer goods. When the Americans left and Vietnam was shut off from trade with many Western nations, goods stopped flowing into the country. Many Vietnamese have compensated by purchasing goods on the black market (the informal, unregulated, and illegal economy). Access to consumer goods is increasing as the country's economy has become incorporated into the global economy.

Close to 80 percent of the Vietnamese population lives in rural areas, primarily in small villages. The housing of northern and southern Vietnam differs due to climatic differences. In the cooler north, most rural people live in houses made of wood or bamboo with tile roofs. In the south, which is warmer, most country folk live in houses made of straw, thatch, or palm leaves. Many families now use sheets of metal or plastic to roof their houses.

The majority of urban dwellers live in small apartments. Most dwellings are small and cramped, crowding numerous family members into a few small rooms. Building materials are predominately wood, brick, and tile.

Few homes have electricity or running water, and families carry water to their homes from nearby streams and ponds. Furniture is rare, seldom more than beds on the floor and a low table around which family members gather to eat while sitting on the floor.

American bombing during the Vietnam War destroyed many roads, bridges, rails, and ports, and the country continues to struggle with modern transportation. The poor condition of the railroads, ports, and roads continue to hamper Vietnam's ability to increase industrial productivity. However, the number of cars, buses, and trucks is increasing in Vietnam, so much so that the country's roads can scarcely handle them.

Motorbikes are a popular means of transportation for successful Vietnamese. Most families make do with bicycles, and travel any distance at all by bus, ferry, or boat.

10 ● FAMILY LIFE

Vietnamese are likely to marry young and have four or five children, although many continue to have as many as possible either out of desire or the inaccessibility of birth control. Children are highly valued, not least for their potential in helping with family chores and supporting their parents in their older years.

Cory Langley

Obligations of children to their parents, wives to husbands, and younger people to their elders are constantly emphasized in Vietnamese families. Individual interests are less important than family interests.

Marriage is viewed as a social contract between two people and their families. It is arranged by intermediaries and approved by parents who may or may not allow their children some choice in their spouse.

Vietnamese say that family is the most important element of their lives, and the obligations of children to their parents, wives to husbands, and younger people to their elders are constantly emphasized. Individual interests are less important than family interests, and each individual is seen as one in a long family line that includes ancestors already dead and current and future family members.

Vietnamese families are patriarchal (headed by the father). Families generally live in nuclear family groups, although grandparents sometimes share the home with a grown child and family. Families also socialize together, gathering with other extended family members for festivals, marriages, funerals, and other important occasions.

Individuals are identified primarily by their patrilineal ties, and larger kin groups are defined through men rather than women. Women join their husbands' families, children belong to their father's family, and male children are preferred over female children. Although the government has attempted to equalize relationships between men and women, most Vietnamese continue to hold traditional views of family, marriage, and childrearing.

Children assist in the support of their family. In rural areas, boys help their fathers with farm work. In cities, boys are more likely to go to school, help their mothers with house chores or errands, or take part-time jobs on their own.

Girls assist their mothers with housework, caring for younger siblings, and helping with work outside the home. For children in rural areas, that includes farming, gardening, and caring for animals. For urban children, it includes helping their mothers in the shop or preparing food to sell.

Animals are primarily for eating, selling, or working. Dogs are used for guarding the home, hunting, and as food. Cats are kept to keep down rats and mice. Animals kept strictly as pets are a luxury most families cannot afford.

11 ● CLOTHING

A special type of Vietnamese women's gown is the *ao dai*. This garment is a dress or long blouse worn over trousers. Usually made of light material, the gown flutters at the slightest movement, being both modest and sensuous at the same time.

For everyday wear, most urban Vietnamese wear Western clothes. Men wear short- or long-sleeved and collared shirts, tucked in for business and hanging out for informal activity. Businessmen and students usually wear long trousers, while children and physical laborers often prefer shorts. Shirts are usually light colored, while trousers tend toward dark colors. Because of the heat and humidity of Vietnam, shirts and trousers are made of light material.

In the countryside, farmers often wear baggy pajama-like shirts and pants made of black cotton. Both men and women usually wear sandals. Many Vietnamese, especially in the countryside, wear straw hats as protection from the sun.

12 ● FOOD

Rice is served at virtually every meal, including breakfast. Fish is almost as important, since Vietnam is a country that has abundant water with vast resources of fish. Fish and other fresh and salt water life is eaten fresh, but is also frequently dried.

Fowl, such as chicken, ducks, and geese, along with eels and eggs, provide additional protein. Beef and pork are enjoyed only by the wealthy or on special occasions such as at weddings or festivals.

A common traditional food of Vietnam is *nuoc mam*, a liquid sauce made from fermented fish. Characterized by an extremely strong smell, nuoc mam is frequently used in Vietnamese dishes.

The typical Vietnamese meal consists of a bowl of rice and vegetables cooked in fermented sauce. Vegetables are mainly grown at home and include bamboo shoots, soybeans, sweet potatoes, corn, greens of various kinds, onions, and other root crops. Fruit includes bananas, coconuts, mangos, mangosteens, and pineapple. Noodle dishes are also popular. A distinctive Vietnamese dish is *pho*, a hot soup containing any variety of noodles in sauce with vegetables, onions, and meat or fish.

Many Vietnamese drink tea at every meal and other times throughout the day and evening. On special occasions or when guests are visiting, the Vietnamese serve rice wine, beer, soft drinks, or coffee.

Breakfast is usually eaten shortly after awakening. The large meal of the day is eaten around noon, after the morning's work, before the lighter work of the late afternoon, and during the hottest portion of the day. A lighter meal follows the day's work.

The Vietnamese eat with chopsticks, and typically dine while sitting on a mat on the floor. Vietnamese eat loudly, slurping, sucking, chomping. Such table noises are not considered bad manners; they are considered evidence that people are enjoying their food.

Cory Langley

Motorbikes are a popular means of transportation for successful Vietnamese. Most families make do with bicycles, and travel longer distances by bus, ferry, or boat.

13 ● EDUCATION

Most Vietnamese are literate (able to read and write). Children begin school at age five and usually complete at least the first five years of schooling. Children in cities continue their education more often than children in the country. If children are able to pass the examinations given at the end of an additional four years of secondary school, they can go to three years of high school or a vocational school. Those who cannot pass go into the military or try to find a job. High school graduates are considered fortunate, for they receive better jobs, higher pay, and more respect.

Vietnamese have traditionally valued education and their children to receive as much schooling as possible. The government offers twelve years of schooling for free, but many parents cannot afford the cost of school books and the loss of earning power that occurs when a child is in the classroom.

14 ● CULTURAL HERITAGE

Vietnamese music is very different from Western music in rhythm, sound, and even scale. Classical music is played on instruments that include a two-stringed mandolin, a sixteen-string zither, a long-necked guitar, a three-stringed guitar, and a four-stringed guitar. Traditional bands include instruments that most closely resemble Western flutes, oboes, xylophones, and drums.

Many traditional tunes are sung without accompaniment, with each region having its own folk melodies. Western love songs, especially slow, sad songs recorded by Asian artists, are also much loved by the Vietnamese. Popular theater combines singing with instruments and has dance, mime, and poetry. Classical theater or opera which came from China in the thirteenth century is popular, as are puppet shows. A unique Vietnamese form is water puppetry, with the controlling rods and strings handled beneath water so that the puppets appear to be dancing on the water.

Poems relate love stories, epic tales from long ago, or discuss love of country. One famous poem, *Kim Van Kieu (The Tale of Kieu)*, tells how a young girl struggles to preserve her family's honor. Many Vietnamese know the entire epic by heart.

15 ● EMPLOYMENT

In the cities, men work at construction, in government offices, and as teachers, drivers, retailers, and mechanics. Women are primarily tradespeople or street vendors, selling clothing and a myriad of other items in the marketplace or cooked food on the streets. Women also work in clinics, as teachers, and as factory workers.

In the rural areas, most men are rice farmers. Men's work also includes caring for draft animals (such as water buffaloes, which are used for pulling carts and plows), fishing, repairing equipment, and helping clear gardens. Other men are full-time fishermen, merchants, traders, drivers, monks, or officials.

16 ● SPORTS

Vietnamese children play a variety of games, but the most popular sport is soccer. Because most Vietnamese families continue to struggle to make a living, children spend most of their time assisting their parents or going to school.

17 ● RECREATION

Vietnam is blanketed by a loudspeaker system and music and programs are offered regularly. Many people now own radios, and most of the country also receives television broadcasts, although many Vietnamese do not own a television set. Watching videos or television or hanging around and chatting with their friends are especially valued leisure activities for most Vietnamese youth.

18 ● CRAFTS AND HOBBIES

Since the 1400s, Vietnamese artisans have been making lacquerware. Wooden objects are painted and decorated with pearl, gold, silver, shell, and other objects. The objects are then coated repeatedly with a lacquer made from the tree sap.

Another popular craft is to make block prints on which scenes have been carved, inked, and then pressed onto paper. The Vietnamese also make porcelain and other ceramics, which they learned from the Chinese many centuries ago.

19 ● SOCIAL PROBLEMS

Reports of arbitrary arrest, detention, and surveillance continue. Freedom of speech and movement are limited. However, there is an increasingly tolerant attitude toward literary and artistic expression. A number of political prisoners have been released since the late 1980s.

In the 1980s, the government admitted that alcoholism was a problem in the cities.

20 ● BIBLIOGRAPHY

Crawford, Ann Caddell. *Customs and Culture of Vietnam.* Rutland, Vt.: Charles E. Tuttle, 1966.

Hall, D.G. E. *A History of South-East Asia.* New York: St. Martin's Press, 1968.

Osborne, Milton E. *The French Presence in Cochinchina and Cambodia.* Ithaca, N.Y.: Cornell University Press, 1969.

Thayer, Thomas C. *War Without Fronts: The American Experience in Vietnam.* Boulder, Colo.: Westview Press, 1985.

WEBSITES

Embassy of Vietnam, Washington, D.C. [Online] Available http://www.vietnamembassy-usa.org/, 1998.

Interknowledge Corp. [Online] Available http://www.interknowledge.com/vietnam/, 1998.

World Travel Guide. Vietnam. [Online] Available http://www.wtgonline.com/country/vn/gen.html, 1998.

Cham

PRONUNCIATION: CHAHM
LOCATION: Cambodia; Vietnam
POPULATION: About 400,000–1 million
LANGUAGE: Cham; Cambodian
RELIGION: Islam; orthodox Cham; Hinduism

1 ● INTRODUCTION

The Cham live in Vietnam and Cambodia. They are descendants of refugees from the ancient kingdom of Champa who fled central Vietnam 500 years ago.

The ancient Cham were heavily influenced by India, as can be seen in their religion and art. Cham were fishermen, rice cultivators, and masters at temple construction. The remains of their religious monuments dot the landscape of Vietnam and Cambodia today.

From the sixteenth century on, the great Champa kingdom was gone. The Cham people were being persecuted and murdered by the Vietnamese. Numerous Cham fled central Vietnam for Cambodia, including a number of nobles and other dignitaries. Sometime in the seventeenth century the Cham were converted to Islam. The last royal Cham descendent died in the early 1900s.

In the twentieth century, the Cham were again the victims of massacre by the majority population, this time in Cambodia. From 1975 to 1979, Cambodia was ruled by the Khmer Rouge, communist extremists determined to erase all non-Khmer characteristics from the population. The Cham are believed to have been special targets of the Khmer Rouge.

The Cham were forced to adopt Cambodian language and customs and to abandon their own. Fishermen were forced to grow rice and dig canals, and religious leaders were stripped of their authority. Many were killed. In just two districts in Cambodia where Cham lived, over 40,000 Cham were killed by Khmer Rouge soldiers in the late 1970s. The Cham claim that over one hundred of their mosques were destroyed during the Khmer Rouge period.

In Vietnam, the Cham have fared better, but have also been subject to discrimination and ridicule, and to pressure to assimilate to Vietnamese society.

2 ● LOCATION

By the late 1800s, there were only small numbers of Cham—maybe as few as 15,000—living in both Vietnam and Cambodia. Their numbers increased rapidly, however. By 1975 there were between 150,000 and 200,000 Cham in Cambodia the about 150,000 in Vietnam. Currently there are between 400,000 and 1 million Cham in both countries.

In Vietnam, most Cham continue to live in the south central area of the country. In Cambodia, the Cham have settled along the Tonle Sap and Mekong Rivers and in western, southern, and central Cambodia.

Cham villages are usually comprised of only Cham. Most are small, with between 200 and 300 people, and are located near a river or lake.

3 ● LANGUAGE

Cham is related to languages spread over much of Asia and the Pacific. Most Cham in Cambodia are bilingual, speaking both Cham and Cambodian. Cambodian Cham speak a dialect called Western Cham. Cham in coastal central Vietnam speak Eastern Cham. Words in the Cham language contain up to three syllables.

The Cham language has its own writing system. Western Cham speakers use Arabic script rather than the traditional Cham script. Eastern Cham speakers in Vietnam use the traditional Cham script.

4 ● FOLKLORE

Many ancient Cham are remembered as great men. A king named Che Bong Nga ascended the Cham throne of central Vietnam in 1360. He led his armies against the Vietnamese and reoccupied Cham land to the north. His victories were temporary because the Vietnamese soon conquered the Cham empire, but Che Bong Nga's triumphs are remembered and retold.

The most renowned king of all, Po Rome, ruled Champa from 1627 to 1651. His rule is remembered as glorious by present-day Cham. When Po Rome was killed by his Vietnamese enemies, his Vietnamese wife threw herself on his burning funeral pyre in grief.

5 ● RELIGION

The Cham who fled the Champa kingdom of central Vietnam in the fifteenth century converted to Islam sometime before the seventeenth century. Cambodian Cham are Muslims (adherents of Islam). Cham decidation to their religion has helped them survive as an ethnic group.

The Cham worship in their own mosques. Their holy book is called the *Quran* (also spelled Koran). Each Cham community has a leader called the *hakem*. The *bilal* calls the faithful to prayer, and the *imam* leads them in prayer.

The spiritual center for Cham within Cambodia is Chrouy Changvar Peninsula, near Phnom Penh. Cham travel there to consult the high Muslim officials and to celebrate special occasions. Young Cham men may travel to Malaysia or Mecca (the holy city in Saudia Arabia) to study the Quran.

Like Muslims worldwide, every Cambodian Cham hopes to make a pilgrimage (religious journey) to Mecca.

Most Cham in Vietnam are Hindus. Important Hindu officials are priests who are chosen for life. Some of these priests learned religious rituals when they were only ten or eleven years old.

6 ● MAJOR HOLIDAYS

Both Hindu and Muslim Cham observe a number of religious and magic ceremonies. Most religious and magical ceremonies contain rituals that originate in Islam, Hinduism, and traditional religions of the area.

The two most important festivals of the Hindu Cham, both honoring spirits of the dead, are the Bon Kate and Bon Cabur. (Both Hindu and Muslim holidays are set by the lunar calenday, so they fall on different days in the Western calendar each year.) Bon Kate is celebrated over five days in late September or early October. Hindu Cham make religious offerings to the statue of their god. These offerings include a goat, two cups and one box of cooked rice, a tray of ground rice cakes, five cups of sticky rice, lemon juice, and ten pieces of betel (a pepper plant).

Bon Cabur is held over five days during late January or early February. Cham gather to share celebrations and an elaborate feast.

7 ● RITES OF PASSAGE

The birth of a Cham child is greeted by the family and community with great joy. Babies are nursed by their mothers until two to four years of age. At age four, children are expected to feed, bathe, and control themselves, and shortly thereafter, to care for their younger siblings.

Most parents exercise almost complete control over their children until they are married. Even after marriage, the influence of parents is strong. Children are expected to show respect to their parents and elders, and are severely punished for any lapse. Cham express pride in the fact that their children have been less rebellious and their families have had less conflict than many other Cambodian families.

The Cham keep all a deceased person's rings before holding the funeral and burial. In the year following the funeral, several more ceremonies are held to honor the deceased person. At the end of the year, the bones of the deceased are exhumed (dug up). The bones are carried to the final permanent cemetery and are buried, with the person's rings, in one final ceremony.

8 ● RELATIONSHIPS

The Cham often exchange the traditional Muslim greeting. One person begins by saying "Salamu alaikum," to which another responds "Alaikum salam."

Cham in Cambodia also greet each other with the *sampeah* (traditional Khmer greeting). The sampeah involves joining the palms together, with fingers pointing up or slightly tilted toward the other person, then bringing their hands up to their chest or forehead.

The Cham place great importance on hierarchy and proper behavior. Women must respect men, children must respect their elders. Everyone must respect their superiors, which includes anyone with higher status, greater wealth, or a more important job. Inferiors greet their superiors with a deeper bow. All visitors are treated to the best the household has to offer.

Few young people date, and virginity remains highly valued for brides. Girls and boys have the opportunity to talk and flirt only on special occasions, surrounded by relatives and neighbors.

Most men marry between nineteen and twenty-five years of age; women are slightly younger, usually between sixteen and twenty-two. It is common for a young man to ask his parents' permission and assistance in finding a wife than to do so on his own. His parents or a matchmaker approach the young woman's family to see if they are interested in a match. If the response is positive, the families negotiate the terms and time of the marriage.

After an exchange of gifts, the young couple marries. It is still common for many young couples to spend the first year of marriage in the home of the woman's parents. After the parents are assured of their son-in-law's stability, or after the birth of the first child, the young couple moves into a new house built for them by their families.

9 ● LIVING CONDITIONS

Cham homes are made of split bamboo and thatch. Most houses are built on stilts 4 to 12 feet (1.3 to 4 meters) off the ground to protect them from seasonal flooding. Chickens, ducks, and oxen are kept in the area beneath the house. Family members often gather beneath the house during the heat of the day to do chores, look after the children at play, and visit with neighbors and passersby. In the evening, most Cham retreat upstairs to their homes, where they eat, chat, and rest.

The upstairs portion of the house may be an open room or may be divided into several rooms: a private room for keeping possessions and a public room for entertaining guests, eating, and visiting. A lean-to kitchen may be attached to the house, also on stilts.

Cham do not have electricity, running water, sewage systems, or appliances. Houses usually contain little furniture, decoration, or utensils. A few books, a pad of paper, and a pencil or two may be wrapped in plastic and placed in the rafters for safekeeping. People sleep on mats, which are rolled up and leaned against the wall or stored overhead during the day. Some Cham, especially in Cambodia, have low platform beds.

Cham cook over an earthenware stand placed over a fire. Because most Cham do not have refrigeration, they use preserved, salted, or fresh food. Kitchen utensils include pots, bowls, cooking ladles, and spoons made of coconut shells.

10 ● FAMILY LIFE

Cham observe a fairly strict division of labor, with women caring for children and the household. Men are responsible for rice cultivation and the chores of construction, tool craft, and repair.

Women do most of the textile manufacture, such as carding, spinning, and weaving cotton. They are also responsible for the family vegetable and fruit gardens and for threshing, husking, and milling the grain.

Women carry the family's water from the nearest lake, river, or pond.

The vast majority of Cham marry within their group and religion. When a girl and her parents (or a boy and his parents) agree on a selection, the parents approach the other's parents.

Cham marriages are simple, involving little expense or ceremony. In the presence of an *imam* (spiritual leader) who acts as the witness, the parents of the young woman ask the groom if he will accept their daughter as his bride. After he agrees, the marriage is concluded and is then celebrated with a feast. Polygynous marriages are allowed (up to four wives), although the first wife must approve the selection of any subsequent wives. Divorce is also permitted. Most polygamy and divorce occurs in families with more resources.

Cham trace their descent and pass inheritance through the maternal line. Residence is also matrilocal, so that young couples go to live with the wife's family.

11 ● CLOTHING

The Cham wear distinctive clothing. Both men and women wear a *batik,* a garment much like a sarong, which is worn knotted around the waist. Men wear a shirt over their batik, while women wear close-fitting blouses with tight sleeves over theirs. Men and women usually cover their heads with turbans or scarves.

On religious days, leaders dress completely in white and shave their heads and beards. Children usually wear shorts and go barefoot or wear rubber thongs.

12 ● FOOD

Cham of Cambodia and Vietnam eat much as their fellow countrymen. Rice is eaten at almost every meal. Fish is almost as important and is eaten fresh, dried, and salted.

A traditional meal is a bowl of steamed rice eaten with a sauce containing bits of fish, fowl, or meat, eggs, vegetables, and spices such as onions, chilies, garlic, mint, ginger, or lemon grass. Pork and alcohol, consumed by many Cambodians, are forbidden to Muslim Cham.

Cham usually eat an early meal of leftover rice, cakes, or fruit either at home or in the field. The big meal of the day is lunch around midday, followed by supper at twilight.

Cham men usually eat together, women and children later. Each has a bowl of rice, and all take bites of food from several dishes sitting in the middle of the group. Cham may eat sitting in a squatting position, with their feet flat on the ground and their knees bent sharply. In Vietnam, most Cham use chopsticks to eat, while in Cambodia, most use spoons.

13 ● EDUCATION

Literacy (the ability to read and write) is greatly valued and parents and religious leaders go to great lengths to teach reading and writing to their children. Cham children attend their own schools, where they learn Cham language and writing, Cham history and traditions, and receive religious instruction. Some children also attend Cambodian or Vietnamese public schools.

14 ● CULTURAL HERITAGE

Literature and religion are both important to the Cham. They highly value their books and religious texts.

15 ● EMPLOYMENT

Most Cham are involved in subsistence agriculture (growing enough to meet the family's needs, with little left over). Some are engaged in raising livestock (such as buffalo, goats, dogs, and fowl), hunting, and fishing. Hunting is done with guns, nets, dogs, and traps. Fishing is done with nets. They use animals not only for food but for making tools and in religious ceremonies.

Cham grow rice, maize (corn), manioc, peanuts, ferns, and vegetables. Nonfood plants grown by the Cham include cotton, tobacco, and plants that yield castor oil. Women may make extra money by weaving.

16 ● SPORTS

Most Cham do not engage in organized sports. Children do not have free time, since they must help their families make a living. Even the smallest children help their parents fish, cook, gather firewood, and do a variety of chores. Children are often responsible for caring for the animals. Boys herd the water buffalo and oxen when they are not being used for plowing, and girls feed the pigs and chickens. Boys climb up sugar palm or coconut trees seeking syrup or coconuts.

Children find time during their daily activities for play. A popular game is played with rubber thongs. The boys draw a line in the dirt, then stand back and throw their sandals at the line. The boy who gets the closest is the winner. Girls and smaller children play a similar game with rubber bands, and the winner wears his captured bands around his wrist. Girls also play hopscotch.

17 ● RECREATION

In Cham villages, local festivals remain the most common and popular leisure activity. Visiting and gossiping are everyday pleasures. Modern leisure activities, such as television, movies, and videos, are rare in Cham villages and homes.

18 ● CRAFTS AND HOBBIES

Cham enjoy music, and use musical instruments that are similar to those in Cambodia and Vietnam. They range from guitars to gongs, drums, and xylophones.

19 ● SOCIAL PROBLEMS

The Cham are proud of never having completely assimilated to either Cambodian or Vietnamese culture. Some Cham hope that Champa, their ancient nation, will be reestablished. But most Cham are content to raise their families and practice their religion. Most of all the Cham hope for peace.

20 ● BIBLIOGRAPHY

Hickey, Gerald C. "Cham" In *Ethnic Groups of Mainland Southeast Asia,* Frank M. LeBar, G. Hickey, and J. K. Musgrave, eds. New Haven, Conn.: Human Relations Area Files Press, 1964.

WEBSITES

Embassy of Vietnam, Washington, D.C. [Online] Available http://www.vietnamembassy-usa.org/, 1998.

Interknowledge Corp. [Online] Available http://www.interknowledge.com/vietnam/, 1998.

World Travel Guide. Vietnam. [Online] Available http:/www.wtgonline.com/country/vn/gen.html, 1998.

Western Samoa

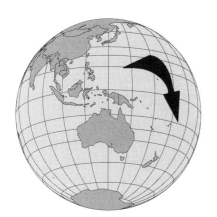

Samoans comprise almost 93 percent of the total population of Western Samoa. Samoans also account for 89 percent of the population of neighboring American Samoa, a territory of the United States. The Samoans are the second-largest branch of the Polynesians, a people occupying the scattered islands of the Pacific from Hawaii to New Zealand and from eastern Fiji to Easter Island. Most of the remaining Western Samoans are of mixed Samoan and European or Asian descent.

Samoans

PRONUNCIATION: suh-MOH-uhns
LOCATION: Polynesian archipelago comprising Western Samoa and American Samoa; west coast of the United States (including Hawaii)
POPULATION: Over 330,000
LANGUAGE: Samoan; English
RELIGION: Christianity (Methodist, Seventh Day Adventist, Catholic, Mormon)

1 ● INTRODUCTION

Samoans are the residents of a chain of islands, or archipelago, in the Polynesian culture area of the south Pacific Ocean. The Samoan archipelago is politically divided into the independent nation of Western Samoa and the United States territory of American Samoa. Western Samoa was owned by Germany, England, and New Zealand before gaining independence in 1962. It has many cultural and historical ties with neighboring Tonga, the Cook Islands, and Tahiti.

The population of Western Samoa is estimated at around 214,000. That of American Samoa is about 59,000. Many people (an estimated 65,000) have left American Samoa and moved to the west coast of the United States. Another 20,000 now live in Hawaii. This section focuses on the Samoan way of life, or, as it is called by Western Samoans, *fa'a Samoa*.

2 ● LOCATION

Western Samoa is located about 2,300 miles (3,700 kilometers) southwest of Hawaii in the Pacific Ocean. Western Samoa is made up of two main islands, Upolo and Savai'i, and a few smaller ones. The two main islands are of volcanic origin. They are mountainous with rocky soil and lush vegetation, thanks to the tropical climate and plentiful rainfall. The average humidity is 80 percent. Of the two main islands of

Western Samoa, Savai'i is more rural and has a much smaller population. The only city in Western Samoa, Apia, is located on Upolo.

3 ● LANGUAGE

The official language of Western Samoa is Samoan. It is closely related to the other languages of Polynesia including Tahitian, Tonga, Maori, and Rarotongan. Although English is spoken by educated Samoans in the city of Apia, it is rarely used by rural Samoans.

4 ● FOLKLORE

Samoans have a creation myth very similar to the creation story in the Bible. The Samoan creator God is Tagaloa. Many of the traditional myths have been forgotten because many Samoans have been converted to Christianity.

5 ● RELIGION

Ninety-eight percent of Samoans are Christians. They are extremely proud of their devotion. Several Christian denominations, including Methodists, Seventh Day Adventists, Catholics, and Mormons, have built churches in Samoan villages. In traditional Samoan belief systems, at the time of death the body separates from the soul. The soul is believed to live on as an "ancestor spirit" called *aitu*. Rituals devoted to the aitu were an important part of religious life in pre-contact Samoa (before the arrival of Europeans).

6 ● MAJOR HOLIDAYS

Samoans celebrate the holidays in the Christian calendar as well as some secular holidays. Samoan Mother's Day is celebrated on May 15 and is a public holiday. There are elaborate song and dance performances by the Women's Committees throughout the country. They celebrate the contributions that mothers have made to Samoan society. Samoan national independence celebrations last for the first three workdays of June.

7 ● RITES OF PASSAGE

From the time they are toddlers, children are expected to obey their elders without question or hesitation. There is no tolerance for misbehavior or disobedience. Older children are expected to take care of their younger brothers and sisters. Adulthood in traditional Samoan society is marked by receiving a tattoo.

8 ● RELATIONSHIPS

Status (position or rank) in society governs every interaction in Samoan society. Greetings are determined by status. A very informal greeting in Western Samoa is *talofa*. For more formal greetings at home, neither person speaks until the visitor is seated. Then the host will begin a formal greeting and introduction with, *"Susu maia lau susuga,"* which translates roughly as "Welcome, sir."

Unmarried women are almost always chaperoned in Samoan society. Premarital sex is discouraged and rare.

9 ● LIVING CONDITIONS

Huge amounts of foreign aid have come to Western Samoa since independence in 1962. It has been used to modernize even the most isolated parts of rural Savai'i. Today there are many European-style houses with wooden frames, iron roofs, and glass windows.

Traditional Samoan-style houses can still be found in Western Samoa. These houses are rectangular and built on black, volcanic boulder foundations. Traditional roofs are high-peaked and covered with thatch. There are no walls, but shutters or blinds of braided coconut leaves can be lowered to keep out the blowing rain.

The Western Samoan standard of living is hard to describe. On one hand, food is plentiful and the pace of life is relaxed. On the other hand, people are always striving to find ways to make money. The economy is very limited. Most money comes from foreign aid.

10 ● FAMILY LIFE

In traditional Samoan society, households were centered on the extended family (parents and children, plus other relatives). The nuclear family (just parents and children living together) has now become the most common family unit. Nuclear families can be very large by American standards. Many women have as many as a dozen children.

Names for relatives in the Samoan language are different from those in Western cultures. There is a single term for the mother, mother's sisters, and father's sisters, and a single term for the father, father's brothers, and mother's brothers. This pattern continues through each generation, so that female cousins (in the American sense) are called "sisters" and male cousins are called "brothers."

11 ● CLOTHING

Traditional Samoan clothing has been adapted to modern life in Western Samoa. The wraparound skirt, called *lavalava,* is worn by men and children. Even important village leaders who work in the city may choose to wear a formal lavalava, a sport shirt, and a wide leather belt around the waist. Women wear dresses or matching long blouses and skirts called *puletasi.* Civil servants (government workers), both male and female, often wear uniforms in dark colors.

Tattooing is a very important form of adornment. Western Samoa is one of the areas of Polynesia that has seen a rebirth of the tradition of tattooing. Young men, more than young women, have returned to the custom of tattooing.

12 ● FOOD

Traditional Samoan foods included taro root, yams, bananas, coconuts, breadfruit, fish, turtle, and chicken. Even though pigs are raised, pork is reserved for ceremonial occasions. Samoan meals are always accompanied by a salted coconut cream condiment called *pe'epe'e.* It is poured over boiled taro root and heated before serving. For many rural Samoans, this is a staple food and is served at the two daily meals.

Coconut is not eaten in Western Samoa as it is in other areas. For a Samoan, eating coconut is a sign of poverty. The favorite Samoan beverage is *koko Samoa,* which is made from fermented cacao beans (the source of chocolate and cocoa), water, and brown Fijian sugar. It is an essential part of the village meal in Western Samoa.

13 ● EDUCATION

The literacy rate (proportion of the people who are able to read and write) in Western Samoa is about 90 percent. Parents see education as absolutely necessary for their children's future. Even in the most isolated villages, parents send at least some of their children to school.

14 ● CULTURAL HERITAGE

In Western Samoa, as opposed to American Samoa, traditional Samoan songs are the favorites of young and old alike. In American Samoa, American popular music is preferred by the young people. Polynesian dancing is still practiced in Western Samoa.

Making persuasive speeches is considered an art among all Samoans. Village leaders participate in political debates to show off their skill in public speaking.

15 ● EMPLOYMENT

The city of Apia provides Samoans with work opportunities in many fields, including jobs as government workers, teachers, nurses, clerks, business entrepreneurs, and secretaries. Men hold approximately 60 percent of the wage-earning jobs.

16 ● SPORTS

Cricket is an important game, and there is a cricket pitch in the middle of every village green. Rugby is also a very big spectator and participant sport. Boxing, wrestling, and American football are favorite sports in both parts of Samoa. A number of professional football players in the United States are of Samoan descent.

17 ● RECREATION

For Samoans who live in or near Apia, most of the usual forms of entertainment found in any modern city are available. Longboat races, called *fautasi,* are held at important festivals and public celebrations. Dominoes are a favorite pastime of Samoan men in both rural areas and towns.

18 ● CRAFTS AND HOBBIES

The traditional art of barkcloth (*siapo*) manufacturing has been all but lost in Samoan culture today. In traditional Samoan society, artists who specialized in house construction, canoe building, and tattooing were organized into guilds, groups somewhat like modern unions. These artists worked for families of high status who could afford to pay them well.

19 ● SOCIAL PROBLEMS

Migration out of the area is a major problem for both Western Samoa and American Samoa. Over 60 percent of the American Samoan population has moved to the U.S. mainland and Hawaii.

20 ● BIBLIOGRAPHY

Lockwood, Victoria S., Thomas G. Harding, and Ben J. Wallace, ed. *Contemporary Pacific Societies: Studies in Development and Change.* Englewood Cliffs, N.J.: Prentice Hall, 1993.

Mead, Margaret. *Coming of Age in Samoa.* London, England: Penguin, 1961 (orig. 1928).

O'Meara, Tim. *Samoan Planters: Tradition and Economic Development in Polynesia.* Chicago: Holt, Rinehart & Winston, 1990.

WEBSITES

Western Samoan Visitors Bureau. [Online] Available http://public-www.pi.se/~orbit/samoa/welcome.html, 1998.

Yemen

Since independence, the population has been almost entirely Arab. Many ethnologists contend that the purest "Arab" stock is to be found in Yemen. There is a small minority of Akhdam.

Yemenis

PRONUNCIATION: YEM-uh-neez

LOCATION: Republic of Yemen

POPULATION: 15.8 million

LANGUAGE: Arabic

RELIGION: Islam; Judaism

1 ● INTRODUCTION

Ancient Yemen was known as "Happy (or Fortunate) Arabia" because of its great wealth. Its riches were the result of both its location on the most important trade routes of the time—over land and sea—and its profitable trade in frankincense and myrrh. Frankincense and myrrh are made from resins from trees growing only in that area. They are used to make perfumes and incense used for religious purposes. They were rare and hard to obtain, and much sought after in the ancient world. Today,

however, Yemen is one of the poorest countries in the world.

Yemen has seen many rulers come and go. The earliest-known advanced civilization in the region was that of the Sabeans, who called their land *Saba* (or *Sheba*). They occupied the land around 1000 BC. The famed Queen of Sheba was a legendary Sabean ruler.

In modern times, Yemen has been ruled by Ottoman Turks and by Britain. These two powers drew a border between the north and south regions in 1905. The land remained divided into North Yemen and South Yemen throughout most of the twentieth century. After decades of wars and attempts at unification, North Yemen and South Yemen were united on May 22, 1990, becoming the Republic of Yemen. The main reason for unification was the discovery of oil along their common border in 1988. Rather than fight for rights to the oil, or split the badly

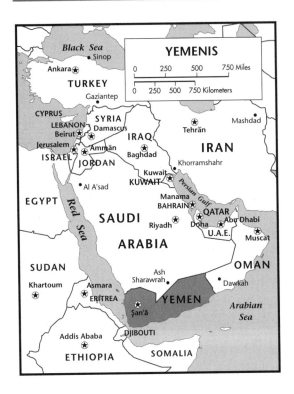

The population of Yemen is increasing rapidly; it is expected to double within twenty years. More than half (52 percent) of the population is under the age of fifteen.

3 ● LANGUAGE

The official language of Yemen is Arabic. "Hello" in Arabic is *marhaba* or *ahlan*, to which one replies, *marhabtayn* or *ahlayn*. Other common greetings are *As-salam alaykum* (Peace be with you) with the reply of *Walaykum as-salam* (And to you peace). *Ma'assalama* means "Goodbye." "Thank you" is *Shukran*, and "You're welcome" is *Afwan*. "Yes" is *na'am* and "no" is *la'a*.

The numbers one to ten in Arabic are *wahad, itnin, talata, arba'a, khamsa, sitta, saba'a, tamania, tisa'a,* and *ashara*.

4 ● FOLKLORE

Yemeni tradition says that Shem, the son of the biblical figure Noah, founded the city of Sana.

Another legendary figure is the Sabean queen Bilqis, better known as the Queen of Sheba. Legend says that she visited King Solomon of Israel (who ruled from 965 to 925 BC) to establish friendly relations, since she and Solomon controlled the two ends of an important trade route. Her visit with Solomon is mentioned in both the Hebrew and Christian Bibles (the Old Testament and New Testament), as well as the Koran (the sacred text of Islam).

The Ethiopians believe that they are descended from a child born to King Solomon and Queen Bilqis. No one knows whether the Queen of Sheba actually

needed income, the two countries decide to join and cooperate.

2 ● LOCATION

Yemen is located in southwestern Asia, on the southern tip of the Arabian Peninsula. It is bordered by Oman to the northeast and Saudi Arabia to the north. The Gulf of Aden (part of the Indian Ocean) lies to the south of Yemen, and the Red Sea lies to the west.

Yemen's landscape is made up of mountains and highlands, deserts, and plains. Yemen is cut off from the northern countries of the Arabian Peninsula by vast stretches of desert, called the Empty Quarter. The 1994 census counted 15.8 million people. Less than 25 percent of the population lives in cities and towns.

© Corel Corporation

Men shop for used clothes at the entrance to a market.

existed. Queens did rule in Arabia at that time, so it is possible that she existed.

5 ● RELIGION

The ancient Yemenis were polytheistic—they worshiped many different goddesses and gods. In the seventh century AD, the Islamic revolution swept through the Middle East. The Persian ruler of Yemen at that time converted to Islam while the Prophet Muhammad (570–632) was still alive. Most Yemenis followed him and converted, too.

About 50 percent of the people of Yemen now belong to the Shafai sect of Sunni

Islam. Some 33 percent belong to the Zaydi sect of Shi'ah Islam.

6 ● MAJOR HOLIDAYS

Muslim holidays follow the lunar calendar, moving back by eleven days each year, so their dates are not fixed. The main Muslim holidays are Ramadan, the month of complete fasting from dawn until dusk; *Eid al-Fitr*, a three-day festival at the end of *Ramadan; Eid al-Adha*, a three-day feast of sacrifice at the end of the month of pilgrimage to Mecca (known as the *hajj*); the First of *Muharram*, or the Muslim New Year; *Mawoulid An-Nabawi*, the Prophet Muhammad's birthday; and *Eid al-Isra wa Al-*

Miraj, a feast celebrating Muhammad's nighttime visit to heaven.

Friday is the Islamic day of rest, so all government offices are closed on that day. In Yemen, unlike in some of the neighboring Islamic countries, many shops stay open on Fridays.

Secular holidays in Yemen include January 1, New Year's Day; May 1, Labor Day; May 22, National Unity Day; September 26, Revolution Day; October 14, National Day; and November 30, Independence Day.

7 ● RITES OF PASSAGE

Weddings are occasions for much celebrating. First, there is the betrothal (engagement) feast, usually held on a Thursday or Friday. This is when the future groom and his father visit the bride's father to settle on a wedding date and bride-price. The wedding itself lasts for three days, usually from Wednesday through Friday.

The most public part takes place on Friday and is called the *laylat az-Zaffa*. Men have a *qat* party in the afternoon. They sit together and chew qat leaves (a mild narcotic) and smoke the *narghile,* or waterpipe. Women help to prepare the food.

In the evening, the men go to the mosque (the building in which Muslims worship). They return dancing and singing around the groom, who carries a golden sword. Then they feast on the wedding food, chew more qat, and smoke the narghile once again. Incense is passed around with blessings, poems are recited, a lute is played, and songs are sung.

Some of the women go to the bride's home to help her dress. A special make-up artist paints delicate designs on her hands and feet. Eventually, the men line up outside the groom's house. He walks with them toward the door, leaping over the threshold.

The men sing the whole time. The women climb up on the roof and begin making a high-pitched sound, called the *zaghrada*. The bride arrives at the groom's house later. The guests may or may not wait for her to arrive. Once the bride enters the groom's house, she becomes part of his family.

8 ● RELATIONSHIPS

Arab hospitality reigns in Yemen. As they talk to each other, Arabs touch each other much more often, and stand much closer together, than Westerners do. Arabs talk a long time, talk loudly, repeat themselves often, and interrupt each other constantly.

The Arab sense of time is also quite different from that of the West. Schedules are loose and flexible, with the day divided not into hours and minutes but into "morning," "lunchtime," and "evening." There are no clocks in public places.

9 ● LIVING CONDITIONS

Yemen has been trying to improve living conditions for its people. In rural areas, where 75 percent of the population live, running water has been made available in most villages. Sewer systems have yet to be installed, however. The water is often polluted, and diseases such as dysentery are common.

© Corel Corporation

An old house that has been updated with modern windows.

Medical care is limited, if it is available at all. The government has begun to establish some rural medical clinics. Few children are vaccinated, so diseases such as measles and tuberculosis spread quickly. Malnutrition is widespread.

Buses and cars have only recently replaced camels and donkeys for transportation in the country. Although life in the cities and larger towns is better, conditions are still far below modern Western standards.

10 ● FAMILY LIFE

The nuclear family (parents and children), called *'ayla* in Arabic, is the basic social unit of Yemeni society. Most families are large, with eight to ten members. Several generations of an extended family may live together in one home.

Men and women are separated in public. Women keep themselves veiled and fully covered when anyone but family is present. Most Yemeni women will not eat in public restaurants. More women are going to school and getting jobs outside the home today. However, the Islamic tradition of separating men and women makes this difficult.

The average age for marriage is twenty-two for men and eighteen for women. Sometimes girls marry as early as fourteen years of age. Parents usually arrange marriages for their children.

Divorce is fairly simple for both men and women. It carries no sense of shame, and it happens relatively often. Some 15 to 20 percent of Yemeni women have been divorced and remarried at least once in their lifes.

In rural areas, only one girl attends school for every ten boys. Yemeni universities now accept women as students, but men are still chosen first for admission.

11 ● CLOTHING

Clothing styles in Yemen vary by region. In hot coastal regions, men wear a lightweight shirt with an embroidered skirt called a *futa* and a straw hat or other head covering. In the cooler highlands, they wear a calf-length shirt called a *zanna* with a jacket. Many men wear a belt with a *jambiyya,* or ceremonial dagger, tucked in at the waist. A man's *jambiyya* identifies his clan and is a symbol of manhood. Boys start wearing it at about the age of fourteen.

Women's styles are much harder to classify. Yemeni women like bright colors and lots of jewelry, especially silver. In Sana, many women wrap themselves in brilliant cloth imported from India, called *sitaras*. In the highlands, they wear baggy embroidered trousers called *sirwals* under their dresses. In eastern Yemen, women wear black robes and pointed straw hats to work in the fields.

Many Yemeni women throughout the country wear the traditional Islamic covering, the *abaya*—a loose black robe that covers the woman from head to toe—when they go out in public. The *sharshaf*—a black

Recipe

Shourba Bilsen (Thick Lentil Soup)

Ingredients

1 pound soup bones (beef or lamb)
8 cups water
2 cups brown lentils
2 onions, finely chopped
3 cloves garlic, finely chopped
2 cups stewed tomatoes
¼ cup finely chopped fresh cilantro (the green leaves of an herb also known as *coriander*), **OR** 3 tablespoons dried cilantro
salt and pepper to taste

Directions

Rinse soup bones and put into a large saucepan with water. Bring to a boil over high heat, then reduce heat to a simmer. Add lentils, onions, garlic, tomatoes, cilantro, and salt and pepper to taste. Cover and cook for 1½ hours, stirring every few minutes to prevent sticking. Makes 6 servings.

Adapted from Albyn, Carole Lisa, and Lois Sinaiko Webb. *The Multicultural Cookbook for Students.* Phoenix, Ariz.: Oryx Press, 1993, p. 72.

skirt, cape, veil, and head covering—is also worn by women throughout Yemen.

12 ● FOOD

The Yemeni diet is quite simple. Staples are rice, bread, vegetables, and lamb, with fish in the coastal regions. Breakfast is a light meal consisting of scrambled eggs with tomatoes, or a bean dish called *ful,* served with flat bread. Supper in the evening is similar.

Lunch is the largest meal. It generally consists of chicken, lamb, or beef, with cooked vegetables, and rice mixed with raisins and almonds. Flat bread soaked in buttermilk and covered with tomatoes, onions, and spices is served at almost every meal, as well as a spicy green stew called *salta.* Salta probably can be called the national dish of Yemen. It is made with meat broth, onions, tomatoes, mince meat, eggs, and *hulba*—a mixture of fenugreek (an herb) and grated leeks (which look like large scallions, or green onions). Sweet custards are usually served for dessert, with either tea or coffee.

Coffee originated in Mocha, a port town on the Red Sea in Yemen. It made its way to Europe on trading ships during the sixteenth and seventeenth centuries. In Yemen, both the husks and the beans are used to make beverages.

Yemenis make a drink called *qishr* by steeping coffee husks in hot water, then adding ginger, cinnamon, and cardamom for flavor. Qishr is milder than bean coffee and is actually preferred in Yemen.

A soup that is popular in Yemen is *shourba bilsen,* made with lentils.

13 ● EDUCATION

For much of Yemen's history, education was available only to the wealthy. The new constitution guarantees the right of all citizens to an education. The government has opened a number of public schools in large cities and towns. Rural areas still have only Muslim religious schools.

The literacy rate (proportion of the population that can read and write) continues to be very low. In the early 1990s, under 27 percent of Yemenis were literate. That average breaks down to about 46 percent of men and 7 percent of women.

14 ● CULTURAL HERITAGE

Arab music can be rich, repetitive, and dramatic. The *oud,* or *kabanj,* is a popular traditional instrument. It is an ancient stringed instrument that is the ancestor of the European lute. Another traditional instrument is the *rebaba,* which has only one string.

A traditional Arab dance is the *ardha,* or men's sword dance. Men carrying swords stand shoulder-to-shoulder and dance. Within the group, a poet sings verses and drummers play the rhythm.

Islam forbids making pictures of the human form, so Arab art concentrates on geometric and abstract shapes. Yemen is famous for its silver jewelry. Stained glass and pottery are also important art forms. Calligraphy (ornamental writing) is a sacred art; texts from the Koran are the main subject matter.

15 ● EMPLOYMENT

More than half of all Yemenis are small farmers. In cities and towns, there is a very high unemployment rate. This was made worse in 1990, when Saudi Arabia threw out all of its Yemeni workers. Over 700,000 people lost their jobs and returned home. In 1992, thousands of refugees from Somalia arrived in Yemen, also looking for work.

Rural women have very heavy workloads. They do as much as three-quarters of the work in the fields. They are also responsible for fetching all the wood and water—which means carrying loads weighing forty-four to fifty-five pounds (twenty to twenty-five kilograms) on their heads for long distances, often uphill. They also must cut alfalfa to feed the cow (it takes six to eight hours of work per day to care for one cow), do all the cooking and housework, and care for the children.

16 ● SPORTS

Soccer is the national pastime of Yemenis. Organized sports are rare, and Yemen has few athletes with enough skill to compete at an international level. Yemen has sent athletes to recent Olympic Games, but as of 1998 they had yet to win a medal. The Yemeni Cricket League finished its first season in 1995.

17 ● RECREATION

The favorite form of entertainment in Yemen is chewing *qat* leaves, a mild narcotic. Men gather every afternoon for qat parties that last until sunset. Women chew qat as well, but not nearly so much as men.

Women's afternoon gatherings are known as *tafritas*. At these, marriages are arranged, goods are sold, and information and experiences are shared.

18 ● CRAFTS AND HOBBIES

Silver jewelry is one of the most important forms of art in Yemen. Other crafts include textiles, leatherwork, basketry, and stained glass.

19 ● SOCIAL PROBLEMS

The use of the narcotic *qat* is a problem in Yemen, although most Yemenis would dis-

agree. Farmers are growing qat on land where they used to grow food because qat brings a much higher price. Once cultivated, qat leaves only retain their narcotic quality for a couple days. In addition, men spend so much time chewing qat that the women are left to do most of the work to provide for their families. Qat is legal in Yemen. However, it is considered an illegal drug in international markets, so it can not be sold outside the country.

The extremely high rate of unemployment is a tremendous problem. The economy is improving only very slowly, so it does not appear that there will be any significant growth in jobs in the near future.

20 ● BIBLIOGRAPHY

Albyn, Carole Lisa, and Lois Sinaiko Webb. *The Multicultural Cookbook for Students*. Phoenix, Ariz.: Oryx Press, 1993.

Chwaszcza, Joachim, ed. *Insight Guides: Yemen*. Singapore: APA Publications (HK) Ltd., 1992.

Crouch, Michael. *An Element of Luck: To South Arabia and Beyond*. New York: Radcliffe Press, 1993.

Dresch, Paul. *Tribes, Government, and History in Yemen*. New York: Oxford University Press, 1989.

Hämäläinen, Pertii. *Yemen: A Lonely Planet Travel Survival Kit*. Hawthorn, Australia: Lonely Planet Publications, 1996.

Wenner, Manfred W. *The Yemen Arab Republic: Development and Change in an Ancient Land*. Boulder, Colo.: Westview Press, 1991.

WEBSITES

ArabNet. [Online] Available http://www.arab.net/ yemen/yemen_contents.html, 1998.

World Travel Guide, Yemen. [Online] Available http://travelguide.attistel.co.uk/country/ye/ gen.html, 1998.

Zambia

The people of Zambia are called Zambians. Seventy ethnic groups live in Zambia, including the Bemba (37 percent) and Tonga (19 percent). Also living in Zambia are a small number of Asians, mainly migrants from the Indian subcontinent, people of mixed race, and Europeans, mainly of English descent.

Zambians

PRONUNCIATION: ZAM-bee-uhns
LOCATION: Zambia
POPULATION: 8.5 million
LANGUAGE: English; Bemba; Nyanja
RELIGION: Christianity; Christianity with traditional African beliefs; Hinduism; Islam; traditional African beliefs

1 ● INTRODUCTION

Zambia is a landlocked country in southern Africa. Its political boundaries were drawn by the European colonizers. The separate groups living within the artificial boundaries were first referred to as Northern Rhodesians under British rule. They became Zambians after gaining independence.

The first Europeans in the area were the Portuguese in the sixteenth century. Britain became interested in the area in the 1850s.

In 1889, the British South Africa Company (BSAC) received permits to trade and set up a government in what would become Northern Rhodesia. The BSAC had economic and political control of the region until 1924. Then British government took over administration of the country. Between 1929 and 1939, four large copper mines were opened in the north-central part of the country. Northern Rhodesia became a supplier of copper to the world.

Along with many other African countries, Zambia won its independence in 1964. It had several political parties until 1973, when it became a "one-party participatory democracy." The freedom-fighter leader Kenneth Kaunda was president of Zambia from 1964 to 1991. President Kaunda's greatest strength as a leader was his ability to unite the various ethnic groups of Zambia. The first decade after independence was

ZAMBIANS

the decade of prosperity. Copper prices were high and so were people's spirits.

Economic growth throughout Africa has slowed since the mid-1970s. Throughout the continent, economic troubles have increased. A decrease in agricultural production and the continued growth of cities are among the causes. Zambia's problems were worsened in the mid-1970s by the sudden drop in the price of copper on the world market. In the face of economic problems, President Kaunda's government tried several economic reforms, all of which failed. Throughout the 1980s, support for the government continued to erode. In 1991, for the first time in many years, Zambia held elections with more than one political party. President Kaunda was voted out of power in

October 1991, and President Frederick Chiluba was voted in.

2 ● LOCATION

Zambia has a tropical savanna (grassland) climate. Most of the country has a single rainy season. Zambia has four great rivers that are a valuable potential resource in the form of hydroelectric power. Zambia has a wealth of minerals, including copper, lead, zinc, and coal. The soil is characterized as red and powdery and not very fertile. The country was very rich in game before widespread hunting began. Now many species are endangered.

Half of Zambia's 8.5 million people live in cities and towns, although movement back to the countryside is increasing.

Most of the people are of Bantu origin (including the Bemba, Tonga, Malawi, Lozi, and Lunda). Some 98 percent of the population is African. Less than 2 percent are European and Asian. Seventy recognized ethnic groups live in Zambia.

3 ● LANGUAGE

The national language of Zambia is English, which also serves as the *lingua franca* (common language). There are several other major language groups. Bemba is spoken in the Copperbelt, where most of the labor force is Bemba. Nyanja is another common language, spoken by the Chewa and Nsenga people of Malawi, and from people of the eastern province of Zambia.

4 ● FOLKLORE

Zambians have an active tradition of oral history. Proverbs, fables, riddles, and cre-

Cory Langley

In Zambia there has been tremendous growth in the second-hand clothing industry, or salaula. *The term salaula means "to rummage through a pile." In this case, the term refers to the used clothing that arrives from industrialized nations, including Canada, Denmark, and Britain.*

ation myths have been passed down through many generations.

5 ● RELIGION

Some 72 percent of Zambia's population is Christian or combines Christianity with traditional African religions. The remainder practice traditional African beliefs, or are Hindu or Muslim.

6 ● MAJOR HOLIDAYS

Official holidays include New Year's Day (January 1), Easter weekend (late March or early April), Labor Day (May 1), Youth Day (March 19), African Freedom Day (May 25), Heroes Day and Unity Day (the first Monday and Tuesday in July), Farmer's Day (the first Monday in August), Independence Day (October 24), and Christmas (December 25).

7 ● RITES OF PASSAGE

A number of Zambia's tribal groups conduct initiation ceremonies for boys. These rituals involve circumcision, as well as instruction in hunting and in the group's culture and folklore. At adolescence, girls are also

Cory Langley

Men are wage-earners and homeowners more often than are women, and they have greater access to money and property than women do.

taught about the ways of their culture and receive instruction in sex, marriage, and child rearing.

Both traditional arranged marriages and modern marriages involve the *lobola,* or bride-price. This is a payment by the man to his fiancians have church weddings.

The funeral of a relative, even a distant relative, is considered an event of great importance. People feel they must attend to show respect for the dead.

8 ● RELATIONSHIPS

In formal situations, Zambians call each other by their last names, preceded by the term for Mr., Mrs., or Miss in their local languages. Different greetings are used in different parts of the country. *Mulibwanji* (How are you?) is common in the Lusaka area. *Mwapoleni* (Welcome) is generally used in the Copperbelt region. *Mwabonwa* (Welcome) is a standard greeting in the southern part of the country.

In most parts of Zambia, people usually greet each other with a handshake, using the left hand to support the right—a gesture traditionally considered a sign of respect. People in the Luapula, Western, and Northwestern provinces frequently use a greeting that involves clapping hands and squeezing thumbs.

People often kneel in the presence of their elders or those who are higher in social status. Like many other Africans, Zambians often avoid eye contact out of politeness. It is considered unacceptable for men and women to touch when greeting each other.

9 ● LIVING CONDITIONS

Zambia's towns are bustling centers with a host of problems that are common to cities in general. Most of Zambia's city residents live in poverty in low-cost, crowded housing. They live out of sight of the small upper class that lives in the few low-density, previously European-occupied sections of town. In the decade following independence, the population of Zambia's cities doubled in size. In those years (the mid-1960s to mid-1970s) the city represented opportunity and privilege. There was food on the table, transportation in the streets, and goods in the shops. Economic decline began in Zambia in the mid-1970s. As a result, many Zambians are moving back to rural settings and trying to make a living growing food.

10 ● FAMILY LIFE

Relationships between men and women in Zambia are difficult and not always strong. As heads of households, men have authority within the home. The culture's double standards accept polygyny (having more than one wife) and men's love affairs. But women must be completely faithful. This causes tension in many households. Men are not obliged to share their wealth with the rest of the family even though it is easier for men to earn a living. Cultural norms and assumptions support men's authority and power. A woman very often cannot make a living without the help of a man (usually her father, husband, uncle, or brother). And when a man dies, his property goes to his children, not to his wife. Women's access to and rights over property are still much more limited than men's.

11 ● CLOTHING

In Zambia, there has been tremendous growth in the second-hand clothing industry, or *salaula*. The term salaula means "to rummage through a pile." In this case, the term refers to the bundled used clothing that arrives from industrialized nations, including Canada, Denmark, and Britain.

During colonial times, and in the decade after independence, Zambians could afford to produce their own cloth and wear tailor-made clothing. Since the decline in the economy in the mid-1970s, they have been forced to buy used clothing from local traders. They buy large bundles and sell pieces individually. Zambians still have a keen sense of style.

12 ● FOOD

The most important dietary staple is a dough or porridge called *nsima*. It is made from cornmeal, cassava, or millet, and is typically eaten with meat stew, vegetables, or a topping made from fish. Sweet potatoes and peanuts are commonly eaten in rural areas. Families that can afford to eat hot meals at both lunch and dinner, and a breakfast of nsima or bread and tea. Beer is a popular beverage.

13 ● EDUCATION

In 1976, the government of Zambia made education tuition-free (although there are still fees and other expenses parents must pay). The result has been a great increase in literacy (ability to read and write). Some parents, especially in the cities, place high value on education. In rural areas, however, children's labor is viewed as more important to daily living.

Education in Zambia is modeled on the British system. Children begin in kindergarten and progress through the grades to high school. Eight years of school are mandatory. In high school, fees and uniforms are more expensive than the average Zambian can afford. As a result, only a small percentage of students go on to high school. Only 20 percent of Zambians have a high school education, and only 2 percent are college graduates.

14 ● CULTURAL HERITAGE

Dance, accompanied by the drum, xylophone, or thumb piano *(mbira)*, plays an important cultural role in Zambia. Most dances are done in two lines, with men in one and women in the other. Tradition associates dances with the casting out of evil spirits. Dances are performed to celebrate personal milestones (such as initiation) as well as major community and group events. In addition to their own traditional forms of music, Zambians enjoy modern music and music from nearby African countries.

15 ● EMPLOYMENT

When the British arrived, the people in Zambia were farmers and/or cattle herders. The people (mainly men) were recruited by the British to work for cash, either in the copper mines or as house servants in the cities. For rural businessmen and farmers, finding workers is sometimes a problem,

EPD Photos

The thumb piano, mbira, *is used to accompany dances. Most dances are done in two lines, with men in one and women in the other. Tradition associates dances with the casting out of evil spirits. Dances are performed to celebrate personal milestones as well as major community and group events.*

and women have more trouble finding jobs than men do. Men are wage-earners and homeowners more often than are women, and they have greater access to money and property than women do. The census defines the working population as those engaged in agriculture, forestry, hunting, fishing, or production and other related occupations. Subsistence farming, which is not included under the category of "work," is done mostly by women.

16 ● SPORTS

Soccer is the leading sport in Zambia. Zambia entered a soccer team in the 1988 Summer Olympic Games held in South Korea. Also popular are baseball, rugby, badminton, and squash. Golf is considered a game of the upper class. The most popular sport among young women is a version of basketball called netball.

17 ● RECREATION

In the rural areas of Zambia, the main forms of recreation are drinking and traditional dancing. City-dwellers participate in social clubs, church activities, and volunteer groups. Other leisure-time activities include dancing at discos, amateur drama *(ifisela),* and a variety of sports. Television is available to people living in the cities and larger towns.

18 ● CRAFTS AND HOBBIES

The people of the Northwestern province of Zambia are known for their masks, which are made of bark and mud. Fierce faces are painted on the masks in red, black, and white.

A traditional art among Zambian men is the carving of wood sculptures, which are sometimes decorated with costumes made of beads. Woven craft items include baskets and also *chitenges,* the national costume. It consists of a brightly dyed cloth that is wrapped around the body.

Some of the designs on Zambian pottery are thousands of years old.

19 ● SOCIAL PROBLEMS

Poverty, crime, unemployment, rapid inflation, lack of health and education opportunities, and housing shortages are causing growing discontent among residents of Zambia's cities and towns. Destruction of the land by soil erosion and the clearing of forests is causing environmental deterioration. Estimates indicate that of the over 59 million acres (24 million hectares) of arable (farmable) land in the country, only 6 percent is farmed. The present government must distribute land in the future so as to encourage investment and economic development.

20 ● BIBLIOGRAPHY

Burdette, M. *Zambia: Between Two Worlds.* Boulder, Colo.: Westview Press, 1988.

Holmes, Timothy. *Zambia.* New York: Benchmark Books, 1998.

Lauré, Jason. *Zambia.* Chicago: Childrens Press, 1994.

Karpfinger, Beth. *Zambia Is My Home.* Milwaukee: Gareth Stevens, 1993.

Rogers, Barbara Radcliffe. *Zambia.* Milwaukee: Gareth Stevens, 1991.

WEBSITES

Southern African Development Community. Zambia. [Online] Available http://www.sadc-usa.net/members/zambia/, 1998.

World Travel Guide. Zambia. [Online] Available http://www.wtgonline.com/country/zm/gen.html, 1998.

Zambian National Tourist Board. Zambia. [Online] Available http://www.zamnet.zm, 1998.

Bemba

PRONUNCIATION: BEM-bah
LOCATION: Northeastern Zambia
POPULATION: 3.1 million Bemba (or Bemba-speaking)
LANGUAGE: Bemba; English
RELIGION: Protestantism; traditional beliefs; Roman Catholicism; African Christianity; Islam

1 ● INTRODUCTION

The Bemba occupy the northeastern part of Zambia. They are a matrilineal group (tracing descent through the mother's line). The Bemba belong to a larger ethnic group usually referred to as the Central Bantu. The

Bemba came to their present location during the great Bantu migrations of the sixteenth and seventeenth centuries. They organized themselves into a loosely united government. At its head was a paramount chief, known as Chitimukulu (the Great Tree), and he was served by subchiefs belonging to the royal Crocodile clan. The Bemba were seen as a warlike and fearsome people by early European travelers and explorers.

Zambia was colonized (occupied and ruled) by the British in the early 1890s. They named it Northern Rhodesia.

Zambia obtained independence in 1964 under the leadership of President Kenneth Kaunda. He ruled as president for twenty-seven years of one-party government.

After unrest in 1990, elections were opened to other political parties. President Kaunda lost the presidential election held in 1991 to Frederick Chiluba, who had been a trade-union activist.

2 ● LOCATION

The Bemba and related groups live in the northeastern high plateau of Zambia. Although the area is well watered, the soil is mostly poor and covered by bush, scrub, and low trees typical of an African savannah (plain with few trees). Lakes Mweru and Bangweulu are major geographical features on the plateau. Because of the dense scrub, the Bemba have been described as a forest people.

It is estimated that of the eight and one half million people in Zambia, 36 percent (or 3.1 million) are Bemba or speak the Bemba language.

3 ● LANGUAGE

In Zambia, as in many southern and central African countries, people speak a variety of languages. Most of the languages belong to the Bantu language family. They share a similar vocabulary, but for the most part they are not mutually comprehensible (a speaker of one cannot understand another). Therefore, many modern-day Zambians are multilingual. They speak a maternal, or first, language as well as several other languages.

English is the national language of Zambia. Education in high school and universities is also in English.

4 ● FOLKLORE

The Bemba have a myth about the origins of their group. It is sometimes called the Bemba Charter Myth. Long ago in the land of Kola, there lived White and Black people. After a quarrel, the White people sailed away to get rich in Europe. The Black people remained under their chief Mukulumpe Mubemba. The name *Bemba* comes directly from this chief's last name.

The chief had sons with Mumbi Mukasa Liulu, a queen of heaven who had fallen from the sky. She belonged to the "Crocodile clan," *Ng'andu.*

Because of quarrels within the royal family, the sons fled with a group of loyal followers. After much traveling and many conquests, the sons and followers who had survived settled in the area where the Bemba live to this day. They set up a central government with a paramount chief, named *Chitimukulu,* "The Great Tree." By making war on other peoples, they increased Bemba control over more and more land. The Crocodile clan stayed in power over the other clans.

The full telling of the myth brings out the richness of its poetic, political, religious, and ceremonial aspects. The Bemba use folklore, myths, and the oral tradition to pass on needed information about beliefs, customs, and culture from one generation to the next.

5 ● RELIGION

The Bemba traditionally believe in the existence of a single high god, Leza. He does not deal with the problems of everyday life, and he lives in the sky. He is all-powerful and controls things such as thunder and fertility (the ability to have children). He is also the source of magic power.

Christian missionaries came to Zambia during colonization in the late nineteenth century. They converted many of the peoples of Zambia, including the Bemba, to Christianity. But few Zambians have totally given up their traditional beliefs. Most of them do not see any conflicts between the two and tend to practice both religions together.

6 ● MAJOR HOLIDAYS

The major national holiday in Zambia is Independence Day on October 24. Zambia obtained its independence from Great Britain on that day in 1964. On this day every year, celebrations are arranged in major cities and throughout the country. There is much drinking, dancing, and singing. In the afternoon, people go to stadiums to watch soccer games between major leagues or between the national team and the team of a nearby country such as Malawi.

7 ● RITES OF PASSAGE

There is no initiation ceremony for Bemba boys. Girls go through an initiation ceremony called *Chisungu.* This rite of adolescence is intended to teach girls the traditional roles women. A girl whose breasts have started to develop lives away from the group for six weeks to three months. Rites representing the duties of the girl as cook, gardener, hostess, and mother are carried out. During the ceremony there is much drumming, dancing, singing, and drama.

Although it is still practiced in both rural areas and cities, the Chisungu ceremony is slowly disappearing. Most girls grow up in Christian families and attend modern schools, which has become a new rite of passage. In school, subjects such as biology present information different from the teachings of Chisungu. The older rite keeps men in control and women in a lesser role, and these roles are slowly changing in some African societies. But many Bemba still believe that initiation ceremonies have a place in their cultural and moral heritage and believe that the tradition should continue.

8 ● RELATIONSHIPS

Older persons are given greater respect in Bemba society, where a person's age has much to do with how others treat him or her. Shaking hands is the normal way of greeting, especially among members of the same age group.

There are also special relationships between members of different clans. Clans are descent groups, each tracing its descent from a common female ancestor. The Bemba have about forty clans. Most clans have a partner clan whose members they can marry. (Marriage of persons in the same clan is usually not allowed.) Most clans are named after living things such as plants and animals. For example, the Crocodile clan is the partner of the Fish clan. Members of these two clans can marry each other. There is also a custom of making jokes with the partner clan. For example, a member of the Crocodile clan can tease a member of the Fish clan by saying, "You are my meal today." A member of the Fish clan can

answer back that without the Fish, the Crocodile would have starved to death.

9 ● LIVING CONDITIONS

The Bemba live in rural villages organized around a number of extended families (in families, inheritance is through the mother's side). Villages generally have between thirty to fifty huts. Huts are made of wattle and daub (woven rods and twigs plastered with clay and mud) and have thatched roofs. The village is also the basic political unit. It is run by a headman to whom most of the villagers are related.

The main occupation of the Bemba is subsistence farming (growing their own food with little or none left to sell) in the form of shifting cultivation. *Chitemene* (shifting cultivation) is a system in which crops are grown in the ash produced by burning wood from a cleared forest area. Due to the poor condition of the soil, a field is abandoned after a few years and a new one is prepared. The village may be relocated as a result of the practice of shifting cultivation. This lifestyle requires a simple building style, and people have very few material possessions.

Disease is a major problem for Bemba society. Malnutrition is common, making it possible for tropical diseases such as malaria and bilharzia to spread.

10 ● FAMILY LIFE

Family among the Bemba refers to the extended family that includes several generations, much like a clan. The extended family is a cooperative work group that shares food, gifts, money, and other material items. Within the extended family system, a person usually has several "mothers," several "fathers," and many "sons" and "daughters."

Polygamy (having more than one spouse) was once quite common among the Bemba. The coming of Christianity and modernization have weakened this practice.

Since the Bemba are a matrilineal society (with descent through the mother), large payments in money or goods by the bride's family are not required at the time of marriage. (This practice, called bride wealth, is commonly done in patrilineal societies, where descent is through the father.) In order to become engaged to a girl, a young man is expected to offer a small present to the parents of the girl. When they have married, the young son-in-law moves to the wife's village and works for her parents.

In the past, girls were often engaged before adolescence. Younger boys and girls are encouraged to play together before adolescence and can indulge in "puppy love." But as soon as girls begin maturing, sexual contact with men is prohibited until marriage. These days, young people find their own partners and then inform their parents of their choice.

11 ● CLOTHING

Before the arrival of Europeans, the most common type of cloth was made from bark. Women wore it around the waist as a loincloth. Today most Zambians, including the Bemba, wear modern clothes. Men wear Western clothing (shorts, pants, and shirts). However, the designs and fashions in women's dresses are usually of Zambian or African origin.

12 ● FOOD

The staple food for the Bemba is millet, which is ground into flour. A thick porridge is made from the flour and is eaten with a side dish of vegetables or meat. Two other important staple crops are cassava and maize. Other crops include peanuts, beans, squash, pumpkins, cucumbers, sweet potatoes, bananas, and cowpeas.

Because of the presence of the tsetse fly, large animals such as cattle and goats are not kept. But the Bemba vary their diet by hunting small game, fishing, and gathering wild fruits. Honey, insects such as caterpillars and grasshoppers, fruits, and wild plants are collected throughout the year. Dogs are usually kept for hunting small game such as bush pig and *duiker* (a small antelope).

13 ● EDUCATION

At the time of independence in 1964, education was underdeveloped in many parts of Zambia. The colonists had neglected the education of the Africans. Very few people were literate (able to read and write) prior to 1964. Since independence, the government of Zambia has spent much money to develop the educational system. It is similar to the British system: students spend eight years in primary school, four years in high school, and another four years in college. The University of Zambia has a capacity of about 4,000 students, and admission into the university is highly competitive.

14 ● CULTURAL HERITAGE

Like many peoples of Africa, the Bemba have a rich cultural heritage that is transmitted by word of mouth from one generation to the next. Very little Bemba folklore has been written down. Traditional music is part of daily life, from initiation rites and marriage ceremonies to hunting parties.

15 ● EMPLOYMENT

In traditional Bemba society, men spend their time on political affairs and business. Farming is left to the women, who are responsible for most of the food. But men are involved in clearing new fields.

With the introduction of the modern economy during colonization, men began to move away from home for job opportunities. They worked in the copper mines of Zambia as well as South Africa. Because so many young men have left for the mines, the rural areas contain a large proportion of women. Farming is not progressing because of the lack of men to clear trees. The absence of men in rural areas has caused problems in food production, the economic standing of women and children, marriage, and family life. In most cases, women have become poorer.

16 ● SPORTS

Throughout Zambia, the most popular sport played by children and young men is soccer. The national team of Zambia has included some acclaimed Bemba soccer players.

17 ● RECREATION

In trading centers throughout the Bemba region, beer pubs are a common part of the landscape. People gather to drink both traditional and bottled beer.

Television broadcasts are available for viewing in Zambia, but few people in rural areas can afford to buy a television set.

18 ● CRAFTS AND HOBBIES

The Bemba people are not generally known for a complex folk art culture. The making of iron tools was practiced until the 1940s. A Bemba man has four basic implements: an ax for clearing the bush and cutting wood; a hoe for farming; a spear for hunting; and, in the past, a bow (also for hunting).

Woodcarving is less developed among the Bemba compared with other peoples in the region, and weaving is unknown among the Bemba. The chief Bemba crafts are pottery and baskets.

19 ● SOCIAL PROBLEMS

Zambia has been relatively stable since independence (1964). Fighting between ethnic groups has not been a major problem. However, because of economic problems in the 1970s and 1980s, people became angry with the government. Unemployment in the cities and poverty in rural areas caused discontent among the government leaders, political party members, businesspeople, and university students. The result was an early 1990s change to a democracy including other political parties. President Kenneth Kaunda was peacefully removed from power in 1991. Apart from the economic misery found in rural areas, most Bemba were not directly involved in these political conflicts.

20 ● BIBLIOGRAPHY

Burdette, M. *Zambia: Between Two Worlds*. Boul-

der, Colo.: Westview Press, 1988.

Holmes, Timothy. *Zambia.* New York: Benchmark Books, 1998.

Karpfinger, Beth. *Zambia Is My Home.* Milwaukee: Gareth Stevens, 1993.

Lauré, Jason. *Zambia.* Chicago: Children's Press, 1994.

Maxwell, Kevin B. *Bemba: Myth and Ritual: The Impact of Literacy on an Oral Culture.* New York: Peter Lang, 1983.

Roberts, Andrew. *A History of the Bemba.* Madison: University of Wisconsin Press, 1973.

Rogers, Barbara Radcliffe. *Zambia.* Milwaukee: Gareth Stevens, 1991.

WEBSITES

Southern African Development Community. Zambia. [Online] Available http://www.sadc-usa.net/members/zambia/, 1998.

World Travel Guide. Zambia. [Online] Available http://www.wtgonline.com/country/zm/gen.html, 1998.

Zambian National Tourist Board. Zambia. [Online] Available http://www.zamnet.zm, 1998.

Tonga

PRONUNCIATION: TAWNG-guh
LOCATION: Southern Zambia
POPULATION: 1.3 million
LANGUAGE: Chitonga
RELIGION: Christianity combined with indigenous religious beliefs

1 ● INTRODUCTION

The Tonga live in southern Zambia along the Zambezi River. The name *Tonga* is apparently from a word in the Shona language that means "independent."

Many other ethnic groups in southern Africa traditionally had centralized forms of government, but the Tonga recognized no chiefs. There were, however, certain people within Tonga society who had authority. The *Sikatongo* was a priest who made sure that the spirits would take care of the people and make the crops grow. In every neighborhood (a grouping of several villages), there was also a man called the *Ulanyika,* the owner of the land. The Ulanyika was usually the first settler in the neighborhood. He had some influence in his neighborhood, and hunters gave him part of every animal they killed there.

Like all the peoples of Zambia, the Tonga came under British rule at the end of the nineteenth century. Zambia gained independence in 1979 under the leadership of Dr. Kenneth Kaunda. He ruled until 1991, when he lost the presidential election to Frederick Chiluba, a trade-union activist.

2 ● LOCATION

The Tonga belong to the Bantu group of peoples. They are concentrated in southern Zambia along the Kafue River and Zambezi River. Most of the Tonga area has poor soil and irregular rainfall, which makes farming difficult. For the most part, the area is thinly populated.

The Tonga make up 15 percent (or 1.3 million) of Zambia's total population, which is currently estimated at 8.5 million people.

3 ● LANGUAGE

The Tonga belong to the Bantu language family. Their language is known as *Chitonga.* It contains many words that are similar to those in other Bantu languages such as *Bemba, Chichewa,* and *Luyana.* For example, "to write" in all three languages is *kulemba.* A chicken is known as *a'nkoko* in

Bemba, *nkuku* in Luyana, *nkhuku* in Chichewa, and *inkuku* in Tonga. In all four languages, a traditional doctor is called *ng'anga*.

4 ● FOLKLORE

The Tonga have no written history from the time before British explorer David Livingstone arrived in the early 1850s. But like many other peoples in Africa, they have a rich tradition of oral history and folklore. In almost all the villages, elders are the keepers of mythical stories. The stories, usually with animal characters, are told around a fire at night. They convey traditional principles, values, and customs, as well as the origins of the Tonga people.

One of the stories deals with the beginning of Tonga society. A local tradition suggests that before the arrival of the British there was a powerful chief in the town of Monze. According to oral tradition, the first Monze chief descended from heaven. He called the Tonga people to join him and settle in his chiefdom. Most people liked the chief because he had the power to heal, to cause rain, and to keep the peace. He did that by frustrating enemies through his communication with the spirits of the ancestors.

5 ● RELIGION

In traditional Tonga society, there is a well-developed cult of the "shades," or *muzimu*. It is believed that at death each person leaves a shade or spirit, a muzimu. The muzimu commutes between the spirit world and the world of humans. Witchcraft and sorcery are also part of traditional beliefs.

Many Tonga have been converted to Christianity because of missionary work by

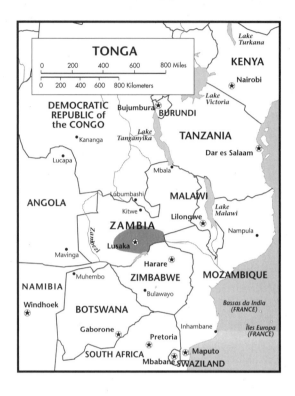

Europeans. Missionaries demanded that the Tonga and other people give up traditional beliefs and practices such as polygamy (having more than one spouse), ancestor worship, and witchcraft. At first, there were only a few converts. In modern times, many Tonga practice both Christianity and traditional religious beliefs.

6 ● MAJOR HOLIDAYS

The major national holiday in Zambia is Independence Day on October 24. Zambia obtained its independence from Great Britain on that day in 1964. During this day every year, celebrations are arranged in major cities and throughout the countryside. There is much drinking, dancing, and singing. In the afternoon, people gather in stadiums to watch soccer matches.

7 ● RITES OF PASSAGE

In the past, most Zambian peoples had special initiation ceremonies and education for children as they reached adolescence. The Tonga did also, but their initiation ceremony was simpler than most. A girl trained for her future role as a man's wife. Usually, there was a period of living away from the village, and a short ceremony marked the girl's maturity. She was given a new name to signify her adult status.

A prospective husband had to pay bride-wealth to the family of his bride-to-be, usually in the form of cattle. After marriage, a couple lived in the husband's village. Polygamy (having more than one spouse) was traditionally encouraged, but this practice is dying out.

Among the Tonga, there is a strong belief that children must be taught and trained for adult life. Children are taught proper manners by older people. During their teenage years, boys and girls are encouraged to do their separate chores according to their sex. Girls' chores are to draw water from wells and fetch firewood, while boys hunt small game and fish. But there are times when boys do girls' chores, and vice versa.

8 ● RELATIONSHIPS

Girls and boys who have not reached adolescence are encouraged to play together. People talk freely in the presence of children about matters such as menstruation, pregnancy, and childbirth. Most parents feel that sexual play between children of the same age is not a matter for concern. However, an older man or woman is not permitted to have a sexual relationship with a girl or boy.

When a boy who has reached adolescence decides to marry, he can find his own bride. However, he must tell his parents and uncles so that they can negotiate with the parents of the girl, since bride-wealth must be paid.

Married women are expected to respect and cook for their husbands, and men are expected to take care of their wives. In the presence of men, a woman is expected to observe traditional female etiquette such as looking downward and behaving humbly. Women are also expected to dress modestly, especially keeping their knees and thighs covered. However, in the cities many women have tried to maintain independence and resist men's control. Many stay single and earn their own living at a regular job or by doing some type of home-based work.

9 ● LIVING CONDITIONS

In colonial times, the Tonga participated fully in agriculture as a business. Early on, they were one of the few peoples to accept agricultural improvements such as ox-drawn plows and the use of fertilizer. Thus a relatively wealthy group of Tonga commercial farmers developed. There also developed a series of smaller cities along the railroad line, which helped create a rich class in the cities as well. Today, these Tonga have modern homes and, occasionally, cars.

In rural areas, people live in isolated homesteads or villages consisting of a few huts. In most cases, houses, granaries, and cattle *kraals* (corrals) are temporary structures that can be easily left behind when new fields must be cleared. With the coming of commercial farming and a cash economy, some modern, durable houses have been built. Their roofs are corrugated iron sheets.

As in other parts of Zambia, tropical diseases such as malaria, bilharzia, and intestinal worms are quite common among the Tonga.

10 ● FAMILY LIFE

Similar to many African societies, family among the Tonga extends to the wider extended unit rather than the nuclear family of wife, husband, and children. The extended family, much like a clan, shares many tasks, including farming and the provision of food. In times of trouble, such as famine and drought, the extended family serves as a safety net.

Bearing as many children as possible is important in a Tonga marriage. Children are valued for their labor and as "social security" for parents in old age. There is a feeling nowadays that modern city life has made families less stable and that the divorce rate is much higher than it used to be. Many women are staying single and breaking away from the traditional rules that kept women in a lower position.

11 ● CLOTHING

Clothing among the Tonga is used to differentiate the sexes. As soon as children begin to run about, girls are given a dress or a skirt, while boys are given a shirt and a pair of shorts. Children are taught that boys and girls wear different types of clothes; thus,

dress marks the beginning of sex identification. Some women in the cities do wear pants and shirts, but most women still prefer traditional women's clothing.

12 ● FOOD

Most of the area in which the Tonga live is rural. Most people follow a subsistence way of life, growing food mainly for their own needs with little left over. Maize is the main staple; others include millet and sorghum. The diet consists of *inshima* (thick porridge), eaten with either meat and gravy or vegetables such as beans and pumpkin leaves. A group of relatives eat from the same dish. With their fingers, they break off a piece of inshima and dip it in gravy before eating it.

13 ● EDUCATION

Most parents send their children to a nearby primary school. At school they learn a few basic subjects such as English, biology, and arithmetic. After eight years of primary school, some students are selected to attend high school, which is modeled on the British system of education. Subjects may include mathematics, chemistry, physics, and biology. The few lucky students who do extremely well in government examinations are selected to attend the university or different types of colleges.

In 1976, the government of Zambia made education free in the hope that more people would take advantage of this opportunity. The result has been a great increase in literacy (ability to read and write). Some parents, especially in the cities, value education highly and have great hopes for their children. In rural areas, however, children's labor is viewed as more important to daily living.

14 ● CULTURAL HERITAGE

Music, dance, and literature are part of Tonga daily life. Grandparents tell stories around the evening fire passing on knowledge and principles to the children. Each story can have several different lessons for both the young and the old. The lessons may be as varied as how to act clever, how to be imaginative, how to be smart and get a beautiful girl's attention, how to be successful by working hard, and how to behave in certain situations.

15 ● EMPLOYMENT

Most of the Tonga people are subsistence farmers, with only a little surplus food to sell for money. They also raise cattle and goats. Livestock add to the diet but are mainly a source of wealth. Cattle are also important in paying bride-wealth for marriage.

Some local farmers who have adopted Western farming techniques have become relatively wealthy and are in a special class of their own.

Many educated city people find jobs in the government. Others find jobs as teachers, nurses, or office workers, Some work on the railway. Others sell fish, salt, sugar, and other basic products in open markets.

16 ● SPORTS

Even in the most remote parts of Tongaland, soccer (locally called "football") is the favored sport for boys and young men. There is usually a makeshift soccer field in each village. Whenever a ball is available, boys play soccer until they are exhausted. Schoolgirls like to play netball, a game somewhat like basketball. In well-equipped high schools, boys and girls participate in sports familiar to students in the West, such as tennis, badminton, and gymnastics. In rural areas, boys and girls make up games and play together when they have free time from household chores.

17 ● RECREATION

The most popular game among boys and girls who have not reached adolescence is playing house. Children build playhouses at the edge of the village and pretend they are adults. Girls take on the roles of women, and boys the roles of men. Girls do the cooking and boys come to eat the food.

Although game is rare, men still like to go out hunting and fishing in the nearby woodlands and rivers.

Drumming, singing, and dancing at beer parties, funerals, and naming ceremonies are frequent activities among the Tonga. At beer parties, men and women dance together.

18 ● CRAFTS AND HOBBIES

Pottery, carvings, baskets, and mats are crafted by older men and women for use in their daily lives. Pots are made in various sizes for drawing water, cooking, brewing beer, and storing grain and other foods.

19 ● SOCIAL PROBLEMS

At the time when Zambians were demanding independence from British rule, one of the most famous politicians in Zambia was

Harry Nkumbula, a school teacher from Tongaland. Alongside Bemba-speaking leaders such as Simon Kapwepwe and Kenneth Kaunda, he opposed colonial rule. In time, Nkumbula lost the support of Kaunda and Kapwepwe. He was pushed aside in the new, independent Zambia. Naturally, the Tonga were not pleased. Nkumbula continued to draw support from his ethnic group. It became a political force against President Kaunda. Although the government of Kaunda did not punish the Tonga openly, few Tonga were invited to join in national politics. Despite the ethnic hostility between the Tonga and the government leadership, however, human rights in Zambia have generally been better than in other African dictatorships.

20 ● BIBLIOGRAPHY

Aldridge, Sally. *The Peoples of Zambia.* London, England: Heinemann Educational Books, 1978.

Burdette, M. *Zambia: Between Two Worlds.* Boulder, Colo.: Westview Press, 1988.

Holmes, Timothy. *Zambia.* New York: Benchmark Books, 1998.

Kaplan, Irving. *Zambia: A Country Study.* Washington, D.C.: The American University, 1984.

Karpfinger, Beth. *Zambia Is My Home.* Milwaukee: Gareth Stevens, 1993.

Lauré, Jason. *Zambia.* Chicago: Childrens Press, 1994.

Saha, Santosh C. *History of the Tonga Chiefs and Their People in the Monze District of Zambia.* New York: P. Lang, 1994.

Vickery, Kenneth Powers. *Black and White in Southern Zambia: the Tonga Plateau Economy and British Imperialism, 1890–1939.* New York: Greenwood Press, 1986.

WEBSITES

Southern African Development Community. Zambia. [Online] Available http://www.sadc-usa.net/members/zambia/, 1998.

World Travel Guide. Zambia. [Online] Available http://www.wtgonline.com/country/zm/gen.html, 1998.

Zambian National Tourist Board. Zambia. [Online] Available http://www.zamnet.zm, 1998.

Zimbabwe

Zimbabweans are mainly related to the two major Bantu-speaking groups, the Shona (about 77 percent of the population) and the Ndebele (about 18 percent). Europeans in Zimbabwe are almost entirely either immigrants from the United Kingdom or South Africa or their descendants.

Zimbabweans

PRONUNCIATION: zim-BAHB-wee-uhns
ALTERNATE NAMES: (Formerly) Rhodesians
LOCATION: Zimbabwe
POPULATION: 10.4 million
LANGUAGE: ChiShona; isiNdebele; English
RELIGION: Indigenous beliefs; Christianity; Islam

1 ● INTRODUCTION

Zimbabwe is known for its rich tradition of stone sculpture and for its natural tourist attractions such as the Great Zimbabwe Falls and Victoria Falls. It was a British colony known as Rhodesia from 1896 until 1980. Before the British arrived, the country was made up of a number of separate kingdoms. The earliest people to inhabit the country were the San, sometimes called the Qoisan or Khoisan. They are also sometimes called "Bushmen," but this is an insulting name that was given to them by outsiders.

After the San, the Shona arrived. They built stone walls in the region around 1200 AD. The best-known of these walls survive today as the remains of two cities, Great Zimbabwe and Khami. The city of Great Zimbabwe prospered until the fifteenth century, and gave modern Zimbabwe its name.

2 ● LOCATION

Zimbabwe is in southern Africa. In 1992, the country's population was 10.4 million. Of these, 98 percent were African, and about 2 percent were European, Asian, and mixed-race. People of mixed race are sometimes called "colored persons."

Most of the good farm land is owned by the former European colonists (whites). Africans (blacks) cultivate poorer, overcrowded land. The industries in cities and towns are also mostly controlled by Europeans, Asians, and people of mixed race. Among Africans, those who live and work in the city are better off economically than those who live in the countryside.

3 ● LANGUAGE

The African population of Zimbabwe is made up of at least ten ethnic groups, each speaking a different language. The two largest are the Shona and Ndebele. The Shona people make up about 60 percent of the population. They are well known for their skill in working with iron, gold, and copper. The Ndebele people, recognized for their skill as military strategists before the arrival of the British, make up about 20 percent of the population. Most people speak at least two languages, including one of the three official languages: chiShona, isiNdebele, and English.

Even though there are many different groups, certain cultural practices or customs

unite all Zimbabweans. One of the greatest experiences shared by all these groups was the war for independence. In 1980, the nation of Zimbabwe was born when the people won independence from the British.

4 ● FOLKLORE

Each ethnic group has its own heroes and heroines, legends, and myths. These stories record a group's origins, traditions, and history. Some of the ethnic heroes, such as Mbuya Nehanda, Kaguvi, and Lobengula, have become national symbols.

5 ● RELIGION

History has altered traditional African life. Because of colonization, most Zimbabwean families live in two worlds: the African and the European (or Western). However, in their daily lives, Zimbabweans blend these two. So, while ancestor worship is the most common religious practice, Christianity and Islam are also observed. In fact, about 75 percent of the population observes either Christianity or Islam.

6 ● MAJOR HOLIDAYS

A dozen public holidays are observed nationally. The most important national holidays are Independence Day (April 18), Heroes' Day (August 11), Workers' Day (May 1), Defense Forces' Day (August 12), and Africa Day (May 25). There are others that are observed by religious groups such as Muslims (followers of Islam) and Christians. There are no indigenous African holidays, but families may have special days in the year on which they remember their relatives who have died.

7 ● RITES OF PASSAGE

Most of the traditional rites of passage are being replaced with Western ones, such as Christian baptism and birthday parties. The old celebrations of birth and entry into adolescence have almost ended. A few groups still observe them, however; one such group is the amaFengu. They practice adolescent male circumcision in public to announce boys' graduation to manhood.

Marriage and burial are still conducted traditionally in many areas. Marriage is still a symbol of graduation into adulthood. Death and burial mark a person's passage into the world of the "living dead," that is, ancestors.

8 ● RELATIONSHIPS

Each Zimbabwean ethnic group has its own greetings and visiting customs. In some groups elders begin greetings, while in others someone younger does. Some groups shake hands and some do not. Bowing one's head, and bending one's knees in a bow are followed by some groups but not others. Whenever a person visits another's home, the visitor has to humble himself or herself before the hostess or host. Gestures, including facial expressions, are also an important aspect of greetings.

Dating has been affected by European contact. Traditionally, most people will not date a stranger. To do so is thought to bring bad luck to a relationship. Another explanation is that people who do not know each other's family histories risk being involved in a relationship with a relative. However, these beliefs are changing today. Most young people meet and date in schools, colleges, and universities without meeting each other's family.

9 ● LIVING CONDITIONS

Not all Zimbabweans enjoy the same living conditions. Most rural families do not have tap water. Most of the roads in the rural areas are not well paved. Some rural areas are not served by any modern form of transportation. This situation worsens during the rainy season.

The whole country has inadequate health care, but the rural population is hardest hit. Some communities do not regularly have the services of a fully trained nurse, let alone a doctor. Medicines are always in short supply. Some of the most common diseases are malaria, bilharzia, sexually transmitted diseases, tetanus, cholera, polio, and typhoid.

In both the city and the country, there are local differences in the standard of living. In the city, the differences are based on a person's race, gender, and social and economic class. People of European origin, Asians, and people of mixed race enjoy the best standard of living. They are followed by upper class blacks, including business owners and intellectuals.

In cities, women are in the worst situation. They face employment discrimination and other sexist practices. In the country, some families are wealthier than others because of support from their children who work in the city. Others earn money from jobs such as teaching.

10 ● FAMILY LIFE

The family is the foundation of Zimbabwean society. Marriage is an important rite of passage and a sacred practice. Through marriages the living are connected with their ancestors. Gender roles are defined within the family.

Most ethnic groups have patriarchal (male-headed) families. In these, women play a subordinate role. They are expected to serve their husbands, work for them, and bear them children. However, women do have certain rights.

A typical family today is made up of a husband and wife and at least two children. Traditional families are big, including five or more children, plus grandparents and the children of relatives. Some men have more than one wife. It is not unusual to find a man with ten wives.

Zimbabwean families, especially in the rural parts of the country, keep animals. Most animals are not just pets but serve other purposes. For instance, cats are kept to kill pests such as mice and rats. Dogs are used for protection and for hunting.

11 ● CLOTHING

Modern, Western-style clothing is the usual outfit in Zimbabwe. There are very few people who wear traditional clothes on a regular basis. Traditional dress include a headdress, a wraparound cloth, and ornaments such as earrings, necklaces, and bracelets. This is usually seen on ceremonial and state occasions such as Independence Day and Heroes' Day.

Recipe

Sadze (Dumpling)

Ingredients

2 pound of white corn meal or millet flour
Water

Directions

1. Boil 4½ cups of water in a heavy saucepan.
2. Mix half the flour with enough water to form a paste.
3. Add this paste to the boiling water. Stir vigorously with a wooden spoon to break up the lumps.
4. Heat the mixture until it boils. Simmer, stirring constantly, for about 5 minutes.
5. Slowly stir in the remaining flour, stirring constantly. It will become difficult to stir, but it is important to stir constantly.
6. Reduce the heat and continue cooking for about 5 more minutes.

To serve, wet a small bowl with cold water. Spoon some sadza into the bowl and roll it around until it forms a ball.

12 ● FOOD

Zimbabwe's staple, or basic, food is called *sadza*. It is made of cornmeal and eaten with vegetables or meat (particularly beef and chicken). A recipe for sadza follows. Other traditional foods are milk, wild fruits, rice, green maize (corn on the cob), cucumbers, peanuts, beans, and home-brewed beer.

Since colonization, Zimbabweans have adopted some foods introduced by Europeans, especially sugar, bread, and tea. Most families usually have at least three meals: breakfast, lunch, and dinner. For breakfast people may eat porridge made of cornmeal or oatmeal, cereal, or bread and tea.

For lunch, people usually have *sadza*. A similar meal might be eaten for dinner. However, foreign foods such as macaroni and cheese and mashed potatoes are now part of the staple diet. In cities, workers get lunch and sometimes dinner from restaurants or take-out food stores.

There are taboos (restrictions) associated with certain types of foods. In some cultures, certain foods are eaten only when they are in season. For instance, the amaNdebele discourage the eating of corn on the cob outside its season. Most ethnic groups also discourage people from eating animal, plant, or other form of food that has their family name. For instance, if one's family name is Nkomo (meaning "cattle," "cows," or "oxen"), one is not supposed to eat beef. Young children are discouraged from eating eggs. When a woman is menstruating, she is not supposed to drink milk because it is believed that doing so might harm cows and calves.

13 ● EDUCATION

Zimbabwe is one of the very fortunate countries in southern Africa to have basic education, especially for young people. While there are still some people who cannot read or write, most people have at least three years of elementary education. Education is seen as valuable since it can be the way to a good job. Parents are usually willing to spend money on the education of their children as an investment in the future. Children

are a form of social security system; they are expected to look after their parents in old age.

The national adult literacy rate (the percentage of adults that can read and write) has been increasing since the early 1980s. Over three-fourths of all Zimbabweans are literate. The rate is higher—over 90 percent—in cities and towns. In rural areas, only about 70 percent of all people are literate. Everywhere, more men than women can read and write, and more men than women complete higher education levels.

University or college education brings pride to a family. Most Africans in the country believe in educating sons rather than daughters; when daughters marry, they take their family's resources to another family.

14 ● CULTURAL HERITAGE

Zimbabwe has a very rich artistic tradition, including music, dance, fine arts and crafts, and literature. Traditionally, Africans passed on knowledge through music and dance. Music and dance were part of ceremonies and rites of passage; in many places, they still are. Culture is still passed on through praise songs (equivalent to poems), stories, and proverbs.

15 ● EMPLOYMENT

Traditionally, work is divided along gender lines. Most domestic work, such as cooking, brewing, and housekeeping, is performed by women. Men work outside the home tending cattle, hunting, and cultivating land. However, women also participate in farming. They usually do jobs that are consid-

Jason Lauré

Education is regarded as an asset in a family since it is perceived as a passport to a good job. Zimbabwean parents are willing to spend money to educate their children as an investment, because children are supposed to look after their elderly parents.

ered "light," such as planting and cultivation.

These roles are changing, however. Men help with some of the roles that were once set aside for women, and women and girls now herd and milk cattle. The colonial government did not allow women, especially black women, to work outside the home. Despite these constraints, women found their way into cities to seek work. The independent government abolished labor discrimination against women. As a result, the number of women working in factories, corporate offices, and government positions increased. There is still much to be done, however, for women—as well as the disabled—to improve their situation.

16 ● SPORTS

The country's national sport is soccer. The Zimbabwe national soccer team is one of the rising soccer powerhouses in Africa. The team plays in the African Cup and World Cup competitions. There are even some Zimbabweans who play on European soccer teams, especially in Great Britain, Germany, and Belgium.

Other sports are track and field, golf, cricket, rugby, wrestling, boxing, netball (women's), tennis, and horse racing. Sports in Zimbabwe are organized and supported along racial lines. Soccer, boxing, wrestling, and track and field are popular among Africans. Europeans prefer golf, cricket, rugby, tennis, and horse racing. But people from either group can cross over to other sports that are not common in their community.

Before colonization, people played traditional games such as hide-and-seek. While herding cattle, boys often ran races or climbed upon and rode small bulls. They also played a type of stone game called *intsoro* or *tsoro*. Girls also had their own games such as *nhoda,* also a stone game.

17 ● RECREATION

Traditional forms of entertainment such as drinking, singing, and dancing have continued into modern society. Traditional ceremonies, state events, and rites of passage also serve as entertainment.

Children have their own forms of entertainment and hobbies. They watch television and listen to "top forty" radio. Most of the television programs, videotapes, and films come from Great Britain and the United States. As a result, young people dress like musicians and actors from these two countries and try to imitate their lifestyles. They also listen to local and regional pop artists, especially those from South Africa and the Democratic Republic of the Congo. Some of the local well-known musicians are Dorothy Masuka, Thomas Mapfumo, Lovemore Majaivana, the Bhundu Boys, and Andy Brown and Storm.

Two films known all over the world have come from Zimbabwe. One is *Neria,* a story about a woman whose property is about to be taken away from her by the relatives of her dead husband. The other is *Jit,* a romantic comedy about a young man who is torn between Western life and his ancestors.

18 ● CRAFTS AND HOBBIES

Zimbabwe is well known for its folk arts, particularly stone sculpture and wood carving. Stone sculpture is a tradition of the Shona people. Mat making and related arts and crafts are popular among the Ndebele, Kalanga, and Nambya people.

Before British colonization, Zimbabweans made weapons, hoes, and other tools for their own use. Wild cotton and wild bark were used to weave mats, dresses, beehives, food containers, and water coolers. Baskets, storage containers, chairs, fish traps, carpets, and sleeping mats are still made from cane, reed, grass, sisal, and similar materials. They are made both for personal use and for sale.

19 ● SOCIAL PROBLEMS

In spite of the gains that Zimbabwe has made building a democratic society, much remains to be done. Soon after independence in the early 1980s, there was political instability in the southwestern part of the country. The government claimed it was caused by some political rebels. Government troops killed many civilians and violated other people's human rights in the region while trying to deal with the situation. This continued until 1988. It is estimated that more than 5,000 people were killed.

Another area of concern is the treatment of women. The present government has treated women improperly and arrested some women that it claimed were prostitutes. It has also taken away some of the gains that women had made since independence. Some of the laws that helped women gain some power and confidence are likely to be repealed, or taken away. One such law, the Legal Age of Majority Act, gave women the right to marry whomever they wanted, with or without their parents' approval.

20 ● BIBLIOGRAPHY

Barnes-Svarney, Patricia L. *Zimbabwe.* Philadelphia, Penn.: Chelsea House, 1997.

Cheney, Patricia. *The Land and People of Zimbabwe.* New York: Lippincott, 1990.

Jacobsen, Karen. Zimbabwe. Chicago: Children's Press, 1990.

Lye, Keith. *Take a Trip to Zimbabwe.* New York: F. Watts, 1987.

McCrea, Barbara, and Tony Pinchuck. *Zimbabwe and Botswana: The Rough Guide.* Kent, England: Harrap Columbus, 1990.

Nkomo, Joshua. *The Story of My Life.* London, England: Mowbrays, 1984.

O'Toole, Thomas. *Zimbabwe in Pictures.* Minneapolis, Min.: Lerner Publications Co., 1988.

Sheehan, Sean. *Zimbabwe.* New York: Marshall Cavendish, 1993.

Spectrum Guide to Zimbabwe. Derbyshire, England: Moorland Publishing Co., Ltd, 1991.

WEBSITES

ZimWeb. Embassy of Zimbabwe, Washington, DC. [Online] Available http://www.zimweb.com/Embassy/Zimbabwe/, June 6, 1997.

Interknowledge Corporation. [Online] Available http://www.geographia.com/zimbabwe/, 1997.

Southern African Development Community. [Online] Available http://www.sadc-usa.net/members/zimbabwe/, 1998.

Glossary

aboriginal: The first known inhabitants of a country.

adobe: A brick made from sun-dried heavy clay mixed with straw, used in building houses.

Altaic language family: A family of languages spoken in portions of northern and eastern Europe, and nearly the whole of northern and central Asia, together with some other regions.

Amerindian: A contraction of the two words, American Indian. It describes native peoples of North, South, or Central America.

Anglican: Pertaining to or connected with the Church of England.

animism: The belief that natural objects and phenomena have souls or innate spiritual powers.

apartheid: The past governmental policy in the Republic of South Africa of separating the races in society.

arable land: Land that can be cultivated by plowing and used for growing crops.

archipelago: Any body of water abounding with islands, or the islands themselves collectively.

Austronesian language: A family of languages which includes practically all the languages of the Pacific Islands—Indonesian, Melanesian, Polynesian, and Micronesian sub-families.

average life expectancy: In any given society, the average age attained by persons at the time of death.

Baha'i: The follower of a religious sect founded by Mirza Husayn Ali in Iran in 1863.

Baltic states: The three formerly communist countries of Estonia, Latvia, and Lithuania that border on the Baltic Sea.

Bantu language group: A name applied to the languages spoken in central and south Africa.

Baptist: A member of a Protestant denomination that practices adult baptism by complete immersion in water.

barren land: Unproductive land, partly or entirely treeless.

barter: Trade practice where merchandise is exchanged directly for other merchandise or services without use of money.

Berber: a member of one of the Afroasiatic peoples of northern Africa.

Brahman: A member (by heredity) of the highest caste among the Hindus, usually assigned to the priesthood.

bride wealth (bride price): Fee, in money or goods, paid by a prospective groom (and his family) to the bride's family.

Buddhism: A religious system common in India and eastern Asia. Founded by Siddhartha Gautama (c.563–c.483 BC), Buddhism asserts that suffering is an inescapable part of life. Deliverance can only be achieved through the practice of charity, temperance, justice, honesty, and truth.

Byzantine Empire: An empire centered in the city of Byzantium, now Istanbul in present-day Turkey.

cassava: The name of several species of stout herbs, extensively cultivated for food.

caste system: Heriditary social classes into which the Hindus are rigidly separated according to the religious law of Brahmanism. Privileges and limitations of each caste are passed down from parents to children.

Caucasian: The white race of human beings, as determined by genealogy and physical features.

census: An official counting of the inhabitants of a state or country with details of sex and age, family, occupation, possessions, etc.

Christianity: The religion founded by Jesus Christ, based on the Bible as holy scripture.

Church of England: The national and established church in England.

civil rights: The privileges of all individuals to be treated as equals under the laws of their country; specifically, the rights given by certain amendments to the U.S. Constitution.

coastal plain: A fairly level area of land along the coast of a land mass.

coca: A shrub native to South America, the leaves of which produce organic compounds that are used in the production of cocaine.

colonial period: The period of time when a country forms colonies in and extends control over a foreign area.

colonist: Any member of a colony or one who helps settle a new colony.

colony: A group of people who settle in a new area far from their original country, but still under the jurisdiction of that country. Also refers to the newly settled area itself.

commonwealth: A free association of sovereign independent states that has no charter, treaty, or constitution. The association promotes cooperation, consultation, and mutual assistance among members.

communism: A form of government whose system requires common ownership of property for the use of all citizens. Prices on goods and services are usually set by the government, and all profits are shared equally by everyone. Also, communism refers directly to the official doctrine of the former Soviet Union.

compulsory education: The mandatory requirement for children to attend school until they have reached a certain age or grade level.

Confucianism: The system of ethics and politics taught by the Chinese philosopher Confucius.

constitution: The written laws and basic rights of citizens of a country or members of an organized group.

copra: The dried meat of the coconut.

cordillera: A continuous ridge, range, or chain of mountains.

coup d'ètat (coup): A sudden, violent overthrow of a government or its leader.

cuisine: A particular style of preparing food, especially when referring to the cooking of a particular country or ethnic group.

Cushitic language group: A group of languages that are spoken in Ethiopia and other areas of eastern Africa.

Cyrillic alphabet: An alphabet invented by Cyril and Methodius in the ninth century as an alphabet that was easier for the copyist to write. The Russian alphabet is a slight modification of it.

deity: A being with the attributes, nature, and essence of a god; a divinity.

desegregation: The act of removing restrictions on people of a particular race that keep them socially, economically, and, sometimes, physically, separate from other groups.

desertification: The process of becoming a desert as a result of climatic changes, land mismanagement, or both.

Dewali (Deepavali, Divali): The Hindu Festival of Lights, when Lakshmi, goddess of good fortune, is said to visit the homes of humans. The four- or five-day festival occurs in October or November.

dialect: One of a number of regional or related modes of speech regarded as descending from a common origin.

dowry: The sum of the property or money that a bride brings to her groom at their marriage.

Druze: A member of a Muslim sect based in Syria, living chiefly in the mountain regions of Lebanon.

dynasty: A family line of sovereigns who rule in succession, and the time during which they reign.

Eastern Orthodox: The outgrowth of the original Eastern Church of the Eastern Roman Empire, consisting of eastern Europe, western Asia, and Egypt.

Eid al-Adha: The Muslim holiday that celebrates the end of the special pilgrimage season (hajj) to the city of Mecca in Saudi Arabia.

Eid al-Fitr: The Muslim holiday that begins just after the end of the month of Ramadan and is celebrated with three or four days of feasting.

emigration: Moving from one country or region to another for the purpose of residence.

empire: A group of territories ruled by one sovereign or supreme ruler. Also, the period of time under that rule.

Episcopal: Belonging to or vested in bishops or prelates; characteristic of or pertaining to a bishop or bishops.

exports: Goods sold to foreign buyers.

Finno-Ugric language group: A subfamily of languages spoken in northeastern Europe, including Finnish, Hungarian, Estonian, and Lapp.

fjord: A deep indentation of the land forming a comparatively narrow arm of the sea with more or less steep slopes or cliffs on each side.

folk religion: A religion with origins and traditions among the common people of a nation or region that is relevant to their particular life-style.

Former Soviet Union: Refers to the republics that were once part of a large nation called the Union of Soviet Socialists Republics (USSR). The USSR was commonly called the Soviet Union. It included the 12 republics: Russia, Ukraine, Belarus, Moldova, Armenia, Azerbaijan, Uzbekistan, Turkmenistan, Tajikistan, Kazakhstan, Kyrgizstan, and Georgia. Sometimes the Baltic republics of Estonia, Latvia, and Lithuania are also included.

fundamentalist: A person who holds religious beliefs based on the complete acceptance of the words of holy scriptures as the truth.

Germanic language group: A large branch of the Indo-European family of languages including German itself, the Scandinavian languages, Dutch, Yiddish, Modern English, Modern Scottish, Afrikaans, and others. The group also includes extinct languages such as Gothic, Old High German, Old Saxon, Old English, Middle English, and the like.

Greek Orthodox: The official church of Greece, a self-governing branch of the Orthodox Eastern Church.

guerrilla: A member of a small radical military organization that uses unconventional tactics to take their enemies by surprise.

hajj: A religious journey made by Muslims to the holy city of Mecca in Saudi Arabia.

Holi: A Hindu festival of processions and merriment lasting three to ten days that marks the end of the lunar year in February or March.

Holocaust: The mass slaughter of European civilians, the vast majority of whom were Jews, by the Nazis during World War II.

Holy Roman Empire: A kingdom consisting of a loose union of German and Italian territories that existed from around the ninth century until 1806.

homeland: A region or area set aside to be a state for a people of a particular national, cultural, or racial origin.

homogeneous: Of the same kind or nature, often used in reference to a whole.

Horn of Africa: The Horn of Africa comprises Djibouti, Eritrea, Ethiopia, Somalia, and Sudan.

human rights issues: Any matters involving people's basic rights which are in question or thought to be abused.

immigration: The act or process of passing or entering into another country for the purpose of permanent residence.

imports: Goods purchased from foreign suppliers.

indigenous: Born or originating in a particular place or country; native to a particular region or area.

Indo-Aryan language group: The group that includes the languages of India; also called Indo-European language group.

Indo-European language family: The group that includes the languages of India and much of Europe and southwestern Asia.

Islam: The religious system of Muhammad, practiced by Muslims and based on a belief in Allah as the supreme being and Muhammed as his prophet. Islam also refers to those nations in which it is the primary religion. There are two major sects: Sunni and Shia (or Shiite). The main difference between the two sects is in their belief in who follows Muhammad, founder of Islam, as the religious leader.

Judaism: The religious system of the Jews, based on the Old Testament as revealed to Moses and characterized by a belief in one God and adherence to the laws of scripture and rabbinic traditions.

khan: A sovereign, or ruler, in central Asia.

khanate: A kingdom ruled by a khan, or man of rank.

literacy: The ability to read and write.

Maghreb states: Refers to Algeria, Morocco, and Tunisia; sometimes includes Libya and Mauritania.

maize: Another name (Spanish or British) for corn or the color of ripe corn.

manioc: The cassava plant or its product. Manioc is a very important food-staple in tropical America.

matrilineal (descent): Descending from, or tracing descent through, the maternal, or mother's, family line.

Mayan language family: The languages of the Central American Indians, further divided into two subgroups: the Maya and the Huastek.

mean temperature: The air temperature unit measured by the National Weather Service by adding the maximum and minimum daily temperatures together and diving the sum by 2.

Mecca: A city in Saudi Arabia; a destination of Muslims in the Islamic world.

mestizo: The offspring of a person of mixed blood; especially, a person of mixed Spanish and American Indian parentage.

millet: A cereal grass whose small grain is used for food in Europe and Asia.

monarchy: Government by a sovereign, such as a king or queen.

Mongol: One of an Asiatic race chiefly resident in Mongolia, a region north of China proper and south of Siberia.

Moors: One of the Arab tribes that conquered Spain in the eighth century.

Moslem *see* **Muslim.**

mosque: An Islam place of worship and the organization with which it is connected.

Muhammad (or Muhammed or Mahomet): An Arabian prophet (AD 570–632), known as the "Prophet of Allah" who founded the religion of Islam in 622, and wrote the Koran, (also spelled Quran) the scripture of Islam.

mulatto: One who is the offspring of parents one of whom is white and the other is black.

Muslim: A follower of Muhammad in the religion of Islam.

Muslim New Year: A Muslim holiday also called Nawruz. In some countries Muharram 1, which is the first month of the Islamic year, is observed as a holiday, in other places the new year is observed on Sha'ban, the eighth month of the year. This practice apparently stems from pagan Arab times. Shab-i-Bharat, a national holiday in Bangladesh on this day, is held by many to be the occasion when God ordains all actions in the coming year.

mystic: Person who believes he or she can gain spiritual knowledge through processes like meditation that are not easily explained by reasoning or rational thinking.

nationalism: National spirit or aspirations; desire for national unity, independence, or prosperity.

oasis: Fertile spot in the midst of a desert or wasteland.

official language: The language in which the business of a country and its government is conducted.

Ottoman Empire: A Turkish empire that existed from about 1603 until 1918, and included lands around the Mediterranean, Black, and Caspian seas.

patriarchal system: A social system in which the head of the family or tribe is the father or oldest male. Ancestry is determined and traced through the male members of the tribe.

patrilineal (descent): Descending from, or tracing descent through, the paternal, or father's, family line.

pilgrimage: religious journey, usually to a holy place.

plantain: Tropical plant with fruit that looks like bananas, but that must be cooked before eating.

Protestant: A member of one of the Christian bodies that descended from the Reformation of the sixteenth century.

pulses: Beans, peas, or lentils.

Ramadan: The ninth month of the Muslim calender. The entire month commemorates the period in which the Prophet Muhammad is said to have recieved divine revelation and is observed by a strict fast from sunrise to sundown.

Rastafarian: A member of a Jamaican cult begun in 1930 that is partly religious and partly political.

refugee: Person who, in times of persecution or political commotion, flees to a foreign country for safety.

revolution: A complete change in a government or society, such as in an overthrow of the government by the people.

Roman alphabet: Alphabet of the ancient Romans from which alphabets of most modern European languages, including English, are derived.

Roman Catholic Church: Christian church headed by the pope or Bishop of Rome.

Russian Orthodox: The arm of the Eastern Orthodox Church that was the official church of Russia under the tsars.

Sahelian zone: Eight countries make up this dry desert zone in Africa: Burkina Faso, Chad, Gambia, Mali, Mauritania, Niger, Senegal, and the Cape Verde Islands.

savanna: A treeless or near treeless grassland or plain.

segregation: The enforced separation of a racial or religious group from other groups, compelling them to live and go to school separately from the rest of society.

Seventh-day Adventist: One who believes in the second coming of Christ to establish a personal reign upon the earth.

shamanism: A religion in which shamans (priests or medicine men) are believed to influence spirits.

shantytown: An urban settlement of people in inadequate houses.

Shia Muslim *see* Islam.

Shiites *see* Islam.

Shintoism: The system of nature- and hero-worship that forms the native religion of Japan.

sierra: A chain of hills or mountains.

Sikh: A member of a community of India, founded around 1500 and based on the principles of monotheism (belief in one god) and human brotherhood.

Sino-Tibetan language family: The family of languages spoken in eastern Asia, including China, Thailand, Tibet, and Myanmar.

slash-and-burn agriculture: A hasty and sometimes temporary way of clearing land to make it available for agriculture by cutting down trees and burning them; also known as swidden agriculture.

slave trade: The transportation of black Africans beginning in the 1700s to other countries to be sold as slaves—people owned as property and compelled to work for their owners at no pay.

Slavic languages: A major subgroup of the Indo-European language family. It is further subdivided into West Slavic (including Polish, Czech, Slovak and Serbian), South Slavic (including Bulgarian, Serbo-Croatian, Slovene, and Old Church Slavonic), and East Slavic (including Russian Ukrainian and Byelorussian).

sorghum: Plant grown for its valuable uses, such as for grain, syrup, or fodder.

Southeast Asia: The region in Asia that consists of the Malay Archipelago, the Malay Peninsula, and Indochina.

Soviet Union *see* Former Soviet Union.

subcontinent: A large subdivision of a continent.

subsistence farming: Farming that provides only the minimum food goods necessary for the continuation of the farm family.

Sudanic language group: A related group of languages spoken in various areas of northern Africa, including Yoruba, Mandingo, and Tshi.

Sufi: A Muslim mystic who believes that God alone exists, there can be no real difference between good and evil, that the soul exists within the body as in a cage, so death should be the chief object of desire.

sultan: A king of a Muslim state.

Sunni Muslim *see* Islam.

Taoism: The doctrine of Lao-Tzu, an ancient Chinese philosopher (c.500 BC) as laid down by him in the *Tao-te-ching*.

Third World: A term used to describe less developed countries; as of the mid-1990s, it is being replaced by the United Nations designation Less Developed Countries, or LDC.

treaty: A negotiated agreement between two governments.

tribal system: A social community in which people are organized into groups or clans descended from common ancestors and sharing customs and languages.

tundra: A nearly level treeless area whose climate and vegetation are characteristically arctic due to its northern position; the subsoil is permanently frozen.

untouchables: In India, members of the lowest caste in the caste system, a hereditary social class system. They were considered unworthy to touch members of higher castes.

Union of the Soviet Socialist Republics *see* Former Soviet Union.

veldt: A grassland in South Africa.

Western nations: General term used to describe democratic, capitalist countries, including the United States, Canada, and western European countries.

Zoroastrianism: The system of religious doctrine taught by Zoroaster and his followers in the Avesta; the religion prevalent in Persia until its overthrow by the Muslims in the seventh century.

Index

All culture groups and countries included in this encyclopedia are included in this index. Selected regions, alternate groups names, and historical country names are cross-referenced. Country chapter titles are in boldface; volume numbers appear in brackets, with page number following.